Holocaust Cinema Complete

Holocaust Cinema Complete

A History and Analysis
of 400 Films, with a Teaching Guide

RICH BROWNSTEIN

Forewords by
TIM BLAKE NELSON,
WALTER REICH,
MICHAEL BERENBAUM and EDWARD JACOBS,
and DAVID ZUCKER

McFarland & Company, Inc., Publishers
Jefferson, North Carolina

LIBRARY OF CONGRESS CATALOGUING-IN-PUBLICATION DATA

Names: Brownstein, Rich, 1962– author. | Nelson, Tim Blake,
writer of foreword. | Berenbaum, Michael, 1945– writer of foreword. |
Jacobs, Edward (Designer), writer of foreword. | Reich, Walter, 1943–
writer of foreword. | Zucker, David (Filmmaker), writer of foreword.
Title: Holocaust cinema complete : a history and analysis of 300 films,
with a teaching guide / Rich Brownstein ; forewords by Tim Blake Nelson,
Michael Berenbaum and Edward Jacobs, Walter Reich, and David Zucker.
Description: Jefferson, North Carolina : McFarland & Company, Inc., Publishers, 2021 |
Includes bibliographical references and index.
Identifiers: LCCN 2020056684 | ISBN 9781476684161 (paperback : acid free paper) ∞
ISBN 9781476641928 (ebook)
Subjects: LCSH: Holocaust, Jewish (1939-1945), in motion pictures.
Classification: LCC PN1995.9.H53 B76 2021 | DDC 791.43/658405318—dc23
LC record available at https://lccn.loc.gov/2020056684

BRITISH LIBRARY CATALOGUING DATA ARE AVAILABLE

ISBN (print) 978-1-4766-8416-1
ISBN (ebook) 978-1-4766-4192-8

Front cover image © 2021 Shutterstock/Sandra Matic

Printed in the United States of America

*McFarland & Company, Inc., Publishers
Box 611, Jefferson, North Carolina 28640
www.mcfarlandpub.com*

Acknowledgments

I start by thanking Barbara Schwartz, who hired me when I was in college in 1983 to teach Sunday school to sixth-graders at Congregation Shaarie Torah in Portland, Oregon, where I first taught Holocaust studies. And I thank Sylvia Frankel and the late Shirley Tanzer who invited me a few years later onto the Board of the Oregon Holocaust Resource Center (now the Oregon Jewish Museum and Center for Holocaust Education).

I thank my dear friend and thesis advisor at Reed College, the late Richard Katzev (and his wife, Aphra), who empowered me throughout my undergraduate studies. Similarly, I thank Elizabeth Loftus for taking me into her Ph.D. program at the University of Washington, and for maintaining our friendship all these years, even though I ditched the program after a semester to move to Los Angeles.

I thank Rich Markey, David Zucker, Randy Tat, Mike Watkiss, Theresa Mckeown and Deborah Kent-Clark for my Hollywood education. I am also grateful to my hundreds of wonderful former staff and clients at the company I founded in 1989 and sold in 2003, The Transcription Company of Burbank. I am especially grateful to Michele Bartmon, my former company president, along with Kevin Kuzma, Tenille Turek, Samantha Somers, Cameron Meyer, Gena Pavey, Linda O'Brien, Tricia Fellenz, Kate Ricci, Hawthorne Flaherty and the late David Pierce.

I am grateful to my childhood friend Rabbi Robert Kahn and the staff at Young Judaea Year Course in Jerusalem where I taught for ten years, developing my theories about Jewish and Holocaust film and about pedagogy. I am thankful for my many hundreds of college students there, including those whose research contributed to this book: Leor Rosen, Sydney Goldman and Marissa Kashkett.

I cannot thank enough Ephraim Kaye, from Yad Vashem's International School for Holocaust Studies, who hired me years ago to teach the proper use of Holocaust films in the classroom to various groups of Holocaust educators and experts from around the world. For me, it was like a JCC league player being called up to the NBA. I also thank Yad Vashem's Rabbi Moshe Cohn, who has greatly helped refine my lessons and Mr. Israel de Vries, at Yad Vashem's Visual Center, who has been welcoming and helpful to this "outsider." Thanks, too, to Nohar Cohen in the Yad Vashem Pedagogical Center. And to the "Radar O'Reilly" of Yad Vashem's International School, the indefatigable Dorit Raviv, who has helped me many times with logistics and with "*chizuk*." And I thank Stephanie McMahon-Kaye, whose introductions of me to my classes have been impossibly generous. Extra special thanks to Lori Gerson, also at Yad Vashem, who was gracious enough to have read this very young manuscript and to have given feedback and encouragement. I thank you all at Yad Vashem for putting me on the team and giving me the honor of my life of teaching with you.

I also thank producer Peggy Gormley who connected me with Barry Langford, Head of the Media Department at Royal Holloway in London, who suggested that I contact McFarland in Jefferson, North Carolina, about publishing my manuscript. Overall, McFarland's midwifery of this huge project has been exemplary, from start to finish, especially Charles "Charlie" Perdue, Dylan Lightfoot and Steve Wilson.

I also express enormous gratitude to Professor Michael Berenbaum and Eddie Jacobs, who helped shepherd this manuscript along to a publishable set of ideas and for their fulsome foreword. I am humbled by the other gracious and exceedingly generous forewords by Tim Blake Nelson, Professor Walter Reich and David Zucker, as well as by the dozen kind souls who wrote blurbs: Tom Brink, Hannah Brown, Professor David A. Frank, Professor Marat Grinberg, Phyllis Greenberg Heideman, Ephraim Kaye, Professor Holli Levitsky, Professor Caroline Joan "Kay" S. Picart, Professor Michael Polgar, Professor Karen Shawn, Professor Gil Troy and Professor Froma I. Zeitlin.

I am grateful to Lawrence "Big Yehuda" Davidson for his copious notes, down to the dots, and for pointing out many embarrassing errors, including the difference between a "navel invasion" and a "naval invasion." And I cannot heap enough thanks upon my dear cousin, Professor Karen Askarinam, who has spent hundreds of hours editing, chiding and encouraging me with this book. Karen refused to let even the slightest participle dangle or verb disagree. I am grateful, too, to Bill Dickerman, who went through the manuscript with his fine-tooth comb, and among other important corrections, pointed out each Oxford-comma, each non–Oxford-comma, and so on.

The lists of films in the appendices were prepared with the dogged assistance of Holocaust film scholar, Professor Lawrence Baron, author of 2005's *Projecting the Holocaust into the Present: The Changing Focus of Contemporary Holocaust Cinema*, as well as with the help of Professor Caroline Picart's expansive *The Holocaust Film Sourcebook, Volumes I and II* (2004).

I thank my loving late parents, who always encouraged me to overcome myself; specifically, my mother, Elisabeth Baer Brownstein (1930–1973), who worked tirelessly to help me overcome dyslexia, and my father, Richard J. Brownstein (1930–2011), who let me draft my high school writings on his law firm's word processing machines (before there were PCs) and who then edited each sentence for me. So too, I am grateful to my siblings, Jeb and Jois, who have been encouraging me from the beginning.

My two remarkable children, Batya and Yehuda, have each elucidated many ideas for me about the Holocaust and film. Batya started reading my college students' assignments before she was even in high school, and was astute enough to find plagiarism committed by two of those students. Yehuda, while in high school and the IDF, has given me great insight into many films, and substantial feedback while attending my lectures at Yad Vashem.

Finally, I dedicate this book to my love, Tamara Mendelson, who has read or been read every iteration of the book and who encouraged me to write this book long before I ever contemplated such an endeavor. This book would not have happened without Tamara, who has helped and reassured me every step of the way, and who has been my soulmate since we met at camp in third grade (which is how I choose to remember it).

Table of Contents

Foreword

by Tim Blake Nelson

New York City—June 2020

Whether narrative "Holocaust films" should even exist, let alone constitute a genre, is itself a matter of dispute. One of the greatest documentarians on the subject of the Shoah, Claude Lanzmann, who made the astonishingly comprehensive and equally impactful work of the same title, would have it that any attempt to depict the atrocities in filmed narrative is itself harmful, simply because with such work inheres the claim that the horrors can be represented artistically at all, thereby trivializing them. Leaving aside Mr. Lanzmann's having arrogated to his chosen category of filmmaking (interview-based documentary) exclusive rights to addressing the subject on film, I've always admired the rhetorical simplicity of his argument. Better, like the Protestants of the great schism who would denounce the depiction of Jesus and God as somehow to corrupt the purity of the divine, to look at the Holocaust as too catastrophically tragic even to try and show, other than with witness interviews and perhaps archival footage.

And yet I look at art at its most impactful as striving to get us closer to truths rather than distancing us from them. With this in mind, I've watched most Holocaust films that have been made, and I endeavored to make one of my own. In doing the work, however, I always imagined Claude Lanzmann in my ear, demanding that at least if we were going to violate his principles, we do our best to get our depiction right. Each of us, from the cast, to the designers—and in particular our director of photography Russell Lee Fine, and our production designer Maria Djurkovic—set ourselves to this with a commitment and rigor that never relented, and the result was the film *The Grey Zone* generously lauded in this book. Our film has its own issues associated with being an American film. It's in English, with characters not speaking in accents, except for the Germans. I have a recurring dream in which I'm directing the same script with the same crew on the same sets in Hungarian, Polish, Yiddish and German. But that's not a film I could have made back then, nor would it have put American audiences in the predicament of seeing themselves on the screen in the impossible predicament faced by the Sonderkommandos. With all art, and obviously Claude Lanzmann would agree, comes compromises.

In this book, Rich Brownstein has done something astonishing. Clearly, intelligently, sensitively and comprehensively, he has applied a unique insider's perspective to an unwieldy genre of films all of us at some level wish didn't exist. With a scholar's exhaustive care, and a clear style that's the opposite of pretentious, he leads us through the history of these movies in a way that's frank, perspicuously clear, and never precious. The

1

sheer organizing rigor of it would alone suffice, but he's also furnished the gift of incisive thought backed up by keen viewing, and a knowledge so comprehensive it almost intimidates. Perhaps just as importantly, everywhere within is found a stout resistance to theoretical exclusivity. This is a book for anyone interested in the subject, no matter his or her purpose or training. It also dares to contextualize and critique, but without ever seeming animated by a personal or political agenda, other than to adhere to Mr. Brownstein's own kind of Claude Lanzmann–like admonition: that the filmmakers, no matter the specific narrative and aesthetic terms set by each work, apply a discipline, seriousness of purpose and care that addressing one of the most horrific passages in human history demands.

It's important finally to remember that so-called "Holocaust films" will always involve failure, because ultimately Mr. Lanzmann was right: One cannot adequately depict what went on. Ever. I'd even go so far as to say we cannot even *imagine* the reality; that only those there to have experienced it can lay any claim to its *real* truth. That, in and of itself, makes Mr. Brownstein's book and the films described within something of a paradox. Because in our ideal world the Holocaust wouldn't have happened and yet we're drawn to the movies that depict it, the genre can easily encompass a kind of queer fetishizing of the indescribably horrific. That said, if movies—the medium that presently most pervades our culture—cannot fathom an avowed attempt to erase an entire people from existence, then what should movies explore? And so a book such as what follows, hopefully to be appended as other filmmakers apply their efforts to a genre that shouldn't be but hopefully will never abate, must be approached with respect, profound regret and immense gratitude.

Tim Blake Nelson is an actor, with more than 70 feature film credits, including in the Coen Brothers' O Brother, Where Art Thou? *(2000) and* The Ballad of Buster Scruggs *(2018) and Steven Spielberg's* Lincoln *(2012) and* Minority Report *(2002). He has directed five feature films, including* The Grey Zone *(2001). Nelson is a graduate of Brown University, where he was a Classics major as well as Senior Orator for his class of 1986. He is a member of the Phi Beta Kappa Society. Nelson won the Workman/Driskoll award for excellence in Classical Studies. He graduated from Juilliard in 1990, a member of Group 19.*

Foreword

by Walter Reich

Washington, D.C.—June 2020

As the Holocaust recedes in time, fewer and fewer people around the world know much about the Holocaust, and most of us who know something about it only know what we *think* we know. And what we think we know is drawn from whatever it is to which we're exposed.

Most of that exposure is to film. Few of us read history books or the diaries of victims who lived in ghettos or memoirs, and few of us are exposed to Holocaust survivors or watch testimonies of their experiences—documents that actually convey what the Holocaust was. So it's films that inform what we *think* we know.

By now many films have been made. Very few, with the exception of movies such as Tim Blake Nelson's *The Grey Zone*, have been brutally honest—really, works that stretch the boundaries of the bearable. Other films, such as *Life Is Beautiful*, have been, to use the term of one critic of that film, sentimental lies. Most of us have preferred sentimental lies. Most of us have sought uplifting, feel-good tales. And no wonder. Films are made to be commercial successes, and they fail commercially if they don't draw crowds. And crowds don't watch films that don't entertain. To be sure, some will go to films that will at least leave them feeling elevated or morally improved—but not at the price of being immersed too much in the pain of what actually happened. As a result, what they think they know about the Holocaust is, to one degree or another, usually distorted—indeed, even false.

In this extraordinary book, Rich Brownstein, in a way that has never been done before, systematically catalogs and explores the world of Holocaust films, and examines the ways in which they have conveyed the sense of what the Holocaust was. He does so with intelligence, rigor, incisiveness, decency and honesty—and, surprisingly, with a light touch, unlike many academic treatises on the subject. Anyone who cares about Holocaust memory—a memory that's vital in a world that's experiencing resurgent and in many ways annihilationist antisemitism—should read this book, consult it, and begin to know what he or she *should* know.

And, by the way: Brownstein's definition of the Holocaust—that it was an event aimed at the elimination of Jews, "an exclusively Jewish catastrophe"—is correct. He doesn't broaden his definition in order to be generously, but falsely, inclusive.

Read this book. And learn about the main, but often distorted, source of what we *think* we know about the Holocaust.

Walter Reich is the Yitzhak Rabin Memorial Professor of International Affairs, Ethics and Human Behavior, and Professor of Psychiatry and Behavioral Sciences, at The George Washington University, and former Director of the United States Holocaust Memorial Museum. He is also a Non-Resident Senior Fellow at the Brookings Institution and a Global Fellow at the Woodrow Wilson International Center for Scholars.

Foreword

by Michael Berenbaum and Edward Jacobs

April 2020

Rich Brownstein's *Holocaust Cinema Complete* is as audacious as it is ambitious. In this work of encyclopedic scope, Brownstein analyzes over 400 Holocaust films and made-for-television movies, identifying the greatness and the flaws, with equal vigor. With a deep love of filmmaking, Brownstein has depicted and detailed, evaluated and critiqued, contextualized and compared all narrative Holocaust filmmaking since 1945, even those films released within months of the publication of this book. He has scrutinized each available film, pinpointed their broader implications, and evaluated their value generally, as well as specifically as Holocaust films. He has also contrasted them with other films of their genre and era.

No stranger to the inner workings of the film industry, Brownstein analyzes these films from the different perspectives of directors, writers and producers. He also includes insightful analogies and disparities within the corpus of their other works. His unique classification of Holocaust films into "4+1" logical genres facilitates this deep analysis. He has the rare ability to consider films as both a filmmaker and a Holocaust educator.

Blessed with a sense of humor and irony, Brownstein's scholarly material is very readable and entertaining, exploring the landmarks and landmines that have emerged in 75 years of Holocaust filmmaking, finding gems that have been buried in this emotionally challenging film genre. Films are evaluated contextually, taking into consideration the specific cultural and historic periods of their production. Almost without the reader sensing it, great swaths of basic Holocaust education are delivered.

Further broadening the scope of this book, Brownstein not only examines American-produced Holocaust films, but also the 70 percent of all Holocaust films made in other countries, never allowing an American-centric sentiment to influence the discussion. For example, he examines the vast contribution to the genre made behind the Iron Curtain, where artistic freedom was limited and the very act of gaining permission to produce a film was often perilous, a place where censors acted as executive editors, thwarting both historical accuracy and creative freedom, forcing creators to adopt cunning modalities and tropes of expression. These particular films demand greater sensitivity and discernment in interpretive analysis, which Brownstein ably provides.

Brownstein is also willing to express controversial opinions, which he brings with biting humor and a large dollop of *chutzpah*. Even when his tastes and standards can be in conflict with prevailing popular opinion—and sometimes even with professional movie critics and distinguished Holocaust scholars—Brownstein consistently defends his sometimes unorthodox positions with facts and class. We value his opinions and employ them to sharpen our own dissent. Brownstein is inviting us *not* to agree, but to learn, to think, and then think again. Brownstein challenges us, as our best educators are wont to do.

Although Brownstein regularly slaughters many sacred cows, his analysis is respectful and balanced. Even the high priests of cinema are not immune. For example, Brownstein's discussion of *Schindler's List* will certainly be an eye-opener for the film's aficionados and advocates. Brownstein's critical examination of the MPAA (Motion Picture Association of America) ratings system, as well as the Production Code which preceded it, is insightful and useful. Even Elie Wiesel's attacks against Holocaust films are thoughtfully addressed and then rebutted. Brownstein does not back down, and we are edified that he does not.

While the book is not strictly a pedagogical roadmap, Brownstein does devote one chapter to the proper use of Holocaust films in the classroom, as is his specialty as a lecturer for Yad Vashem's International School for Holocaust Studies in Jerusalem, Israel. He has done an enormous service to teachers advising them of the best films to be used in educational settings, as well as those less suited to the classroom owing to contextual pitfalls such as the prevalence of violence and nudity, length and other problematic content. He even apprises the reader of their availability. For teachers, this authoritative work empowers, enlightens and informs, allowing them to use his accessible analyses to sensibly and sensitively shape their students' classroom experience. Parents may similarly gain a greater understanding of the most appropriate films to see with their children, as well as how to frame critically important follow-up discussions.

Brownstein has focused on narrative Holocaust films, as opposed to Holocaust survivor testimonials and Holocaust documentaries. He makes a substantial and credible case that, in reality, the well-made narrative film brings viewers closest to understanding the events being depicted. Brownstein emphasizes and substantiates the importance of narrative film in the transmission of Holocaust knowledge to general audiences. It is not only what is said that has impact, but what is seen. Exceptional films recreate scenes that take us into the inner chambers of the unique hell of the death camps. And since narrative films command the majority of the public's attention and viewership, a critical analysis of this range and scope has long been needed.

This is Brownstein's ambitious and audacious achievement.

Michael Berenbaum, Los Angeles, California, is an American scholar, professor, rabbi, writer, and filmmaker, who specializes in the study of the Holocaust. He served as Deputy Director of the President's Commission on the Holocaust (1979–1980), Project Director of the United States Holocaust Memorial Museum (USHMM) (1988–1993), and Director of the USHMM's Holocaust Research Institute (1993–1997). Berenbaum is currently the Director of the Sigi Ziering Institute: Exploring the Ethical and Religious Implications of the Holocaust, at the American Jewish University in Los Angeles, California. Berenbaum co-produced One Survivor Remembers *(1995), winner of an Academy Award, an Emmy Award and the Cable Ace Award. Among his many other film credits, Berenbaum was executive producer of* Swimming in Auschwitz *(2007) and was a consultant for* Defiance *(2008) and* Uprising *(TV 2001). Berenbaum is the author and editor of eighteen books, including* After Tragedy and Triumph, *a study of the state of American Jewry in the early 1990s, as well as* The World Must Know: Anatomy of the Auschwitz Death Camp. *Berenbaum is the Executive Editor of the* New Encyclopedia Judaica,

2nd ed., that includes 22 volumes, six million words, and 25,000 individual contributions to Jewish knowledge, published in December 2006, which won the Dartmouth Medal of the American Library Association for the outstanding reference work of 2006.

Edward Jacobs, Efrat, Israel, is Principal and co-founder of Berenbaum Jacobs Associates, whose portfolio includes designing the Dallas Holocaust & Human Rights Museum, the Cincinnati Holocaust and Humanity Center, and Holocaust Memorial Museum of Macedonia.

Foreword

by David Zucker

September 2020

Rich Brownstein's *Holocaust Cinema Complete* is a startling triumph! If that sounds like I've gone overboard, how about: Rich Brownstein's *Holocaust Cinema Complete* is an enjoyable Holocaust and film book from beginning to end.

First, the book's hybrid writing approach—blended academic and commercial prose—is highly readable and equally entertaining, which was great for me, since generally, my lips move as I read. The book is also impeccably organized, framing 75 years of filmmaking with remarkable clarity. In fact, it was understandable, even to me. And finally, unlike me, the book is humble, never betraying the solemn historical topic, while, at the same time, never making assumptions regarding readers' knowledge of the Holocaust or of film.

Brownstein also refuses to rubber stamp the otherwise lionized giants of Holocaust cinema, including Oscar winners *Schindler's List* (1993), *Life Is Beautiful* (1997) and *Jojo Rabbit* (2019), two of which I genuinely loved. Sometimes with only a few words and other times in complete chapters, Brownstein deconstructs countless film icons—filmmakers and their films—not for sport, but in search of truth. Conversely, with a passion evocative of the late Roger Ebert (who, by the way, loved *Airplane!*, the *Naked Guns*, and even *Top Secret!*) Brownstein discusses countless worthy films that have either been ignored, unappreciated or forgotten.

Yet, perhaps Mr. Brownstein's greatest accomplishment is his underlying principle: by watching Holocaust films, the public longs to make sense of the incomprehensible. Here, we're not being sent back to textbooks, testimonies or documentaries. Instead, he seems to understand inherently that, for better or worse, we have chosen cinema as our Holocaust source material. We have chosen an art form that is inherently derivative of reality and that tells an imperfect story. And because we prefer cinema, Brownstein fashions the tools we need to find deeper meaning in narrative Holocaust film. This was my great surprise and joy. And I'm left longing for a sequel to this work, perhaps a *Spoof Cinema Complete*—but one can only dream.

David Zucker is an American film director, producer, and screenwriter. Associated mostly with parody comedies, Zucker directed and wrote the critically successful 1980 film Airplane! *as well as created* The Naked Gun *franchise and directed* Ruthless People *(1986).*

Author's Preface
and Introduction

During one of my many lectures to visiting American educators at Yad Vashem in Jerusalem, I was asked to support my assertion that Tim Blake Nelson's *The Grey Zone* (2001) is, by far, the greatest narrative Holocaust film ever made. After composing the first few thousand words over the ensuing weeks, I realized that a complete discussion of *The Grey Zone* is impossible without a comprehensive exploration of all Holocaust films through many divergent lenses, including historically, chronologically, thematically, sociologically, geographically and individually. These analyses ultimately became Chapters 1 through 5 of this book, building to my discussion about *The Grey Zone* in Chapter 6: The Greatest Narrative Holocaust Film Ever Made, followed by Chapter 7: Roman Polanski and *The Pianist* (2002) and then Chapter 8: Holocaust Film Curriculum Planning—The "SOFTA" System, a pedagogical roadmap for Holocaust films. The last half of this book consists of Chapter 9: Recommended Holocaust Films, complete with Holocaust-specific reviews of each of my 52 Holocaust film recommendations, together with two large appendices. The first lists all Holocaust films I have identified, indicating the genre and subgenre of each, pointing where possible to a source where the film may be found, and providing information about its plot, director, cast, awards, country of origin, language, running time, date, rating on IMDb, and MPAA or equivalent rating. The second appendix lists works that do not qualify as Holocaust films but are often miscategorized as such; each entry includes a concise summary and reason for disqualification.

For better or worse, narrative films have become the tip of the spear of today's Holocaust knowledge. Many adults can rattle off a half dozen Holocaust film titles, adding where, when and with whom they watched their favorites. And many young adults today regard Quentin Tarantino's decidedly ahistorical *Inglourious Basterds* (2009) as the quintessential Holocaust film. This is not a criticism of Quentin Tarantino's work, which is delightfully twisted, but a statement of fact. Indeed, because of *Inglourious Basterds*, an entire generation believes that Adolf Hitler was killed in a movie theater by "Ryan the Temp" from *The Office*.

Elie Wiesel (1928–2016)—the revered Holocaust survivor, author and scholar—famously lamented that narrative Holocaust films and television have supplanted scholarly sources as the primary mode of Holocaust education.[1] In that regard, I agree with Wiesel; narrative Holocaust films are no substitute for foundational Holocaust education. While narrative Holocaust films are diverse in story, and while they span a wide spectrum of intended audiences, Holocaust films do not "teach the Holocaust," but instead expound upon a few themes and lives that were caught up in the Holocaust. And

Holocaust films cannot be treated like *Sesame Street*, plopping someone down in front of a TV and hoping that knowledge will be passively imparted. Most Holocaust films need context and forethought. For example, of the dozens of Anne Frank films that are purportedly recommended for children, many portray menarche (first menstruation) and even masturbation, which is certainly not the focus of Holocaust study.

Likewise, Oskar Schindler was not Mr. Rogers, despite Schindler's ultimate cinematographic veneration, which literally includes Schindler's grave in Jerusalem having been elevated to a de facto place of worship for tourists. *Schindler's List* (1993)—which is impulsively peddled in Holocaust education—depicts rape, sexual nudity and graphic violence. As noted in *Common Sense Media* about *Schindler's List*, "There are arbitrary murders and mass killings, Nazi commanders compare Jews to rats, children are killed, and there are scenes of shocking, grisly violence."[2] The ongoing need for forethought about Holocaust films is highlighted by an incident chronicled in *The Los Angeles Times*:

> When a group of Oakland [California] high school students went on a Martin Luther King Jr. holiday field trip to see Steven Spielberg's *Schindler's List*, their teachers hoped they'd learn about hatred and compassion. Instead, the 69 students were evicted from the theater because some of them laughed and talked while Holocaust horrors were on screen.[3]

Misinterpretation of storytelling, however, is not confined to youth. Many adults have been misled about the nature of evil by such unscrupulous films as *The Reader* (2008) and *The Boy in the Striped Pyjamas* (2008), both of which shamelessly humanized barbarians. As mocked by Steven Alan Carr in *Film Criticism*, "The 2008 Disney film [*The Boy in the Striped Pyjamas*] tastefully retells the story of how two boys, one the son of a concentration camp commandant and the other a Jewish inmate, befriend each other across curiously non-electrified barbed wire."[4] Without external context, Holocaust films like these can perpetuate a corrupt agenda that suggests an equivalence between victims and perpetrators. And without such analysis, the objectionable aspects of films such as *The Reader* and *The Boy in the Striped Pyjamas* can go unnoticed.

But critiquing film is tricky because, as the Kinks sang in their 1972 *Celluloid Heroes*, "everybody's in movies, it doesn't matter who you are." Because we internalize the films we have championed, we are uncomfortable when opinions are challenged about "our" films. Yet, our opinions are often impacted by random reviews, as well as by box office and Oscar gold. For instance, many people infer the quality of a film from its box office success and awards. But, concretely, no one could suggest with a straight face that *Minions* (2015) is a better film than *Annie Hall* (1977), *Eternal Sunshine of the Spotless Mind* (2004) or *Whiplash* (2014), even though *Minions* grossed a billion dollars more than those three films combined.[5] Similarly, *The Artist* (2011)—winner of five Oscars and nominee for five more—should be proof enough that awards can be perfunctory, especially for mediocre films that win during weak production years.

Beyond our sensitivity to the Holocaust's underlying sanctity in portrayals, Holocaust films have additional hurdles that can skew their evaluation. For example, Holocaust films generally lack commercial success. Indeed, approximately 440 features have grossed more than *Schindler's List* and *Inglourious Basterds* (2009), the highest-grossing Holocaust films in history; in contrast, *Crocodile Dundee* (1986) and *The SpongeBob Movie: Sponge Out of Water* (2015) have outgrossed those Holocaust film icons. *The Pianist* (2002) does not even approach the all-time top thousand grossing films. Conversely, of the 77 American-produced or co-produced Holocaust-related feature films, 21 have won or been nominated for at least one Oscar, with a grand total of 109 wins or nominations. This disproportionate 27 percent nomination rate—an average of 1.4 Oscar nominations per every American Holocaust film—when compared to the *de minimis* percentage of Oscars awarded to the other hundreds of thousands of American non–Holocaust films, twists any reasonable relationship between Holocaust film quality and industry recognition (unless one mistakenly believes that Holocaust films are endemically superior to all other film genres). Thus, given the dichotomy between sales and trophies, neither measure can be conclusive when evaluating Holocaust films.

Critical analysis about Holocaust films—which is the heart of this book—can be jarring. Like any umpire, I strive to be fair when calling balls and strikes about films, despite my profound desire to see all Holocaust films succeed. Further, like many others working professionally with tragedy, we Holocaust educators often shield ourselves emotionally from the horrifying information that must be processed. While we are certainly disturbed by the Holocaust in general and specific individual stories, we must maintain a clinical approach, unbiased by the inherent emotions of the subject matter. I offer a few brief examples of these sentiments through my reactions to three recently screened films.

First is *A Bag of Marbles—Un Sac De Billes* (2017), a remake of Jacques Doillon's undistinguished *A Bag of Marbles—Un sac de billes* (1975), which portrays a French Jewish family in hiding during German occupation. While watching the 2017 version—which was co-produced by French, Canadian and Czech companies—I acknowledged the good intentions of the director, Christian Duguay. And I was also mindful that *A Bag of Marbles* was based on a true story about real people who survived hell. Nevertheless, I concluded that *A Bag of Marbles* was superfluous, needlessly sappy, with regressive dialogue and a plot that added nothing to the pantheon of Holocaust film. Objectively, much better films have been made about Jewish families in hiding, about French Jews during World War II, about resilient children, about fealty and filial love, about patriotism, Judaism, charity, conduct, purity and fraternity, about repression and oppressors, about suffering and loss, about tenacity and luck, about the Holocaust. *A Bag of Marbles* was not a bad film; *A Bag of Marbles* was an unnecessary film. It failed to build on decades of Holocaust filmmaking and was not even a significant improvement over the 1975 version.

The second film is *The Resistance* (also known as *The Invisibles—Die Unsichtbaren*) (2017), which is about Jews who hid in Berlin during the War (World War II). *The Resistance*, too, is well-intentioned, albeit a textbook example of German filmmakers minimizing German brutality while disproportionately emphasizing German righteousness in helping Jews. These German filmmakers assuredly felt they were telling important stories and making great art by intersplicing interviews with the real survivors portrayed in the film, Jews who dodged death uniquely, like many others. But it is fanciful to believe that, simply by subject matter, a film about Jews who outlived the Holocaust is necessarily laudable. There are many reasons *The Pianist* (2002)—also a story about surviving the Holocaust—is rated 38th on IMDb's list of best films and won three major Oscars, while nobody saw *The Resistance*. But the most likely reason for the obscurity of *The Resistance* is the clunky stylistic premise coupled with the anomaly of sympathetic locals. The difference between *The Pianist* and *The Resistance* is the essence of all things great.

And the third recently screened film is the newest cupcake of Holocaust films: Taika Waititi's *Jojo Rabbit* (2019), which made a big splash upon its American release, drabbled with big named stars Sam Rockwell and Scarlett Johansson, and blended up with saccharine performances from adorable children, all cooked up in an Easy-Bake Oven using rudimentary ingredients that offer bite-sized kitsch when a real meal is expected. This righteous Gentile film set in 1944 Germany was a puerile attempt at comedy and is the essence of overt Holocaust commercialization, complete with horrible accents, inappropriate costuming, inane dialogue and anachronistic music starting with the Beatles' German version of "I Want to Hold Your Hand" from their 1964 album *Something New*. While more than a dozen Holocaust comedies have been made—some superb, including *Harold and Maude* (1971) and *Inglourious Basterds*—*Jojo Rabbit* is a sloppy confection of *Benny Hill* slathered over Jewish suffering which epitomizes the danger of letting any yahoo whip up a Holocaust soufflé. Some have enjoyed the flat concoction of empty calories, but it cannot be mistaken for anything of value. And, as a rule of thumb: if the most vicious German in a Holocaust film (in this case, Sam Rockwell's character) turns out to be a pussycat, it is a bad Holocaust film.

I must confess that I, personally, do not want to know anything about films before watching them. I want films to speak for themselves, flowing and unfolding at the filmmaker's pace, their timing and reveals. For example, *Fight Club* (1999), *A Beautiful Mind* (2001), *Black Swan* (2010) and *Shutter Island* (2010) are each ruined for first-time viewers with the same single word: schizophrenia; to know that word concerning those films before watching them is to cheat oneself of the experience intended by their filmmakers. So, if you prefer to see a film without foreknowledge, watch the 400 films listed in Appendix I and then continue reading. That is my global "spoiler alert." That being said, viewing *The Grey Zone* and *Schindler's List* before continuing is highly encouraged.

Finally, for decades internecine disagreements have raged in Holocaust studies. Although not exhaustive, these issues have included:

- The appropriate name for the destruction of European Jewry: "Holocaust" vs. "Shoah" (Hebrew);
- The spelling of anti–Semitism (anti–Semite) vs. antisemitism (antisemite)[6];
- And there has even been a debate concerning whether the "Holocaust" should exclusively be defined as Jewish suffering, or if other victims of World War II should also be included as Holocaust victims.[7]

For the purposes of this book, for simplicity and for clarity of scope, the following conventions regarding those disputes will be incorporated herein:

- Instead of the Hebrew word "Shoah," I will use the universalized word "Holocaust," as defined by the United States Holocaust Memorial Museum as "…the systematic, bureaucratic, state-sponsored persecution and murder of six million *Jews* by the Nazi regime and its collaborators [emphasis added]."[8]
- I will adhere to Yad Vashem's preference for the non-hyphenated spelling of "antisemitism," even though that was not the normative spelling throughout my professional life, and without regard to the many (unaltered) outside citations below that use the traditional spelling of "anti–Semitism."[9]
- And finally, notwithstanding or minimizing the suffering of any other victims at the hands of Germany's Nazi regime—including, but not limited to, political prisoners, mentally and physically disabled, partisans, Jehovah's Witnesses, Freemasons, homosexuals, Slavs, Romani (Gypsies), the non–Jewish clergy, prisoners of war, Communists and bystanders—in this book, the Holocaust is assumed to be an exclusively Jewish catastrophe.

1

Narrative Holocaust Film Basics

Defining Narrative Film

Despite their inherent truth-stretching, narrative films are much more popular and emotionally accessible than are documentaries. To be perfectly mawkish, for all ages, a spoonful of narrative helps the medicine go down. Of course, the downside to this approach is that narrative films can be historically tone-deaf and quite easily misinterpreted. While documentaries do not shy away from exhaustive exposition, good narrative films tend to be more subtle than documentaries when disclosing facts, which is often a problem when seeking historical knowledge from narrative films. Also, the narrative genre—as opposed to documentaries—uses actors to recreate stories; documentaries do not act out stories and are assumed to be documenting the truth. In fact, all narrative films are either fictitious or fictionalized regardless of any claims otherwise, even when based on verifiable stories, including every biopic and historical reenactment, such as *Amistad* (1997), *Catch Me If You Can* (2002), *Munich* (2005), *Bridge of Spies* (2015) and *The Post* (2017). For example, *Argo* (2012)—Oscar winner for Best Picture, Writer and Editor for a film about a group of American hostages during the Iranian Revolution—was so loosely fictionalized that the New Zealand Parliament unanimously condemned the film, stating "its regret that the director of the movie *Argo* saw fit to mislead the world about what actually happened during that crisis..."[1]

Famously, the Coen Brothers' preamble to their 100 percent fictitious film *Fargo* (1996) begins with an explicit lie: "This is a true story. The events depicted in this film took place in Minnesota in 1987. At the request of the survivors, the names have been changed. Out of respect for the dead, the rest has been told exactly as it occurred." When pressed on the falseness of his opening card, *Fargo* co-director/co-writer Ethan Coen clarified, "We wanted to make a movie just in the genre of a true story movie. You don't have to have a true story to make a true story movie."[2] In other words, claiming that *Fargo* was non-fiction is a cinematic device intended to put viewers in a specific frame of mind; films that are thought to be true are perceived differently from films known to be fictitious.

This was the same brain-twisting technique used a quarter-century earlier with the opening card of Wes Craven's first film, the very fictional *The Last House on the Left* (1972): "The events you are about to witness are true. Names and locations have been changed to protect those individuals still living."* None of *The Last House on the Left*

---

* *The Last House on the Left* was a remake of Ingmar Bergman's Best Foreign Language Oscar winner *The Virgin Spring* (1960), which was based on the fictional 13th-century Swedish tale "Töres döttrar i Wänge." Interestingly, the remake *The Last House on the Left* (2009), produced by Craven, did not employ the "True Story" schtick.

was true, with or without a card. Contrast those statements with the opening card in the Holocaust film *Never Forget* (TV 1991), produced by and starring Leonard Nimoy, who portrayed a Holocaust survivor litigating against a Holocaust denier:

> This film is based on events culminating in the lawsuit entitled *Mel Mermelstein v. Institute for Historical Review, et al.*, Los Angeles Superior Court case no. C356 542. While certain scenes are adapted from incidents in the lives of the Mermelstein family and other individuals, all legal proceedings portrayed are based on actual transcripts and documents.

The filmmakers of *Never Forget* are tacitly acknowledging that, even when parts of a film are based on verifiable dialogue, the story is still fictionalized, which should have been obvious with *Never Forget*'s opening scene depicting 1944 Hungary, not a California courtroom. In fact, *Never Forget*'s first verbatim court proceeding does not start until 68 minutes into the 93-minute made-for-television film. With all of that in mind, consider Abraham Lincoln's following speech in Best Picture nominee *Lincoln* (2012):

> I can't listen to this anymore. I can't accomplish a goddamn thing of any human meaning or worth until we cure ourselves of slavery and end this pestilential war, and whether any of you or anyone else knows it, I know I need this! This amendment is that cure! We're stepped out upon the world stage now, now, with the fate of human dignity in our hands. Blood's been spilled to afford us this moment! Now! Now! Now! And you grouse so and heckle and dodge about like pettifogging Tammany Hall hucksters!

This passage from *Lincoln* was never spoken by the 16th American President, perhaps nary a pretentious sentence. These Oscar-nominated words were written nearly 150 years after Abraham Lincoln's death by screenwriter Tony Kushner, Best Writing Oscar nominee for *Lincoln*, interpreted by actor Daniel Day-Lewis, for which he won his third Best Actor Oscar, as directed by *Lincoln* nominee Steven Spielberg, in a setting created by Best Cinematographer *Lincoln* nominee Janusz Kaminski and production design Oscar winner for *Lincoln* Rick Carter, edited by *Lincoln* nominee Michael Kahn, with the support of nearly one thousand other cast and crew members. To believe anything in the melodramatic passage above from *Lincoln*, including that the speech was even in the spirit of Abraham Lincoln, is like believing that Dorothy left Kansas, let alone that she ever lived there or anywhere. Yet, Kushner's imaginary speech, in time, might well become Abraham Lincoln's second most remembered oration, after the Gettysburg Address.

The narrative theatrical format is so hypnotic that viewers often confuse actors with the characters they portray. Consider the iconic opening line from a 1984 commercial for Vicks Formula 44 Cough Syrup: "I'm not a doctor, but I play one on TV," uttered soap opera actor Chris Robinson from *General Hospital* (TV 1963–).[3] The irony, of course, is that the commercial was effective because consumers conflated the actor with his character. More troubling, Actress Dame Helen Mirren testified before the United States Senate Judiciary Committee in 2016 as a Holocaust art restitution expert. Mirren, who is neither a Holocaust survivor nor a restitution expert nor even Jewish, was asked to testify simply because she was once hired to portray the Holocaust survivor Maria Altmann in *Woman in Gold* (2015), one of over 130 of her acting credits listed on IMDb. Indeed, 54 years after Canadian philosopher Marshall McLuhan warned that "The medium is the message,"[4] Mirren's Congressional testimony began:

> My name is Helen Mirren. I am an actor who portrayed the role of Maria Altman in the 2015 film *Woman in Gold*. In the film, I portrayed Maria Altmann. The film is the remarkable true story of a woman who overcame great odds and righted a wrong that had stood for decades. Sixty years after fleeing Vienna, during World War II, Altmann, an elderly Jewish woman....[5]

Helen Mirren's preposterous Congressional appearance as a Holocaust restitution expert is analogous to suggesting that Mirren was also an expert regarding Queen Elizabeth II because Mirren won the Best Actress Oscar for portraying Her Majesty in *The Queen* (2006), or that O.J. Simpson should have testified to the "9/11 National Commission on Terrorist Attacks Upon the United States," because O.J. Simpson appeared in *The Towering Inferno* (1974), or that Matt Damon could have helped with NASA's InSight Mars Lander because Damon starred in *The Martian* (2015). Yet Helen Mirren, who was merely paid to act out a script, was elevated to Holocaust despoilment expert status simply for her rendition of Maria Altmann, just one of hundreds of other gigs throughout Mirren's distinguished, half-century acting career.*

Or consider Texas Tech University Associate Professor of Educational Leadership Joseph G. Claudet, Ph.D., who wrote of the above-quoted *Lincoln* speech as if it were real. Claudet wrote the following in his 19,000-word paper, "Deconstructing the Breakthrough Leadership Thinking of Visionary Social Change Agents—Insights and Strategies for Leading Transformative Change from Four Case Studies":

> Another subsequent scene in the *Lincoln* (2012) movie showcases vividly the manner in which Lincoln was able to leverage his remarkable moral leadership thinking and decision-making clarity in combination with his strong, action-oriented leadership temperament to challenge his executive cabinet "team of rivals" to move past their endless, discordant debate and resulting hesitancy toward political action and see more clearly the compelling moral leadership choice that is presently before them and regarding which there is only limited time to act.[6]

The notion that a Texas Tech Ph.D. and members of the U.S. Senate's Judiciary Committee confuse performances with reality is shameful. But characters on the silver screen bend our perception of history. Who does not believe that the Nazi Oskar Schindler was a demigod? Regardless of the facts, Schindler's depiction in Spielberg's film has become Schindler's permanent legacy. Welcome to narrative film.

Defining Holocaust Film

In this book, "Holocaust films" include narrative feature films, home video, and non-episodic made-for-television and streaming Holocaust content. And, notwithstanding Charlie Chaplin's *The Great Dictator* (1940) and Ernst Lubitsch's *To Be or Not to Be* (1942), the working definition of Holocaust film here only includes films made after World War II. Although *The Great Dictator* and *To Be or Not to Be* are essential for film literacy, these films are not responses to the Holocaust, but to Adolf Hitler.

With that narrowing of the field, thousands of productions may still be miscategorized as "Holocaust films." Consider *The Producers* (1967), *To Be or Not to Be* (1983) and *The Producers* (2005). Many viewers are convinced that those classics, along with *The Sound of Music* (1965), should be considered Holocaust films merely because Nazis are portrayed in all of them. But merely touching on the Holocaust does not impart Holocaust status upon films. What of the Spanish film *The Photographer of Mauthausen—El fotógrafo de Mauthausen* (2018), which takes place in a concentration camp with neither Jewish characters nor Jewish content? This non–Holocaust film is instead about Spanish

---

* Decades earlier, in 1994, Steven Spielberg also testified to the U.S. Senate's Judiciary Committee—as a hate crimes expert—based solely on having directed *Schindler's List*.

Communists sent by Spain to a German labor camp. Except in the very broadest sense, *The Photographer of Mauthausen* cannot be considered a Holocaust film.

And then there is Alan J. Pakula's *Sophie's Choice* (1982), starring Meryl Streep, for which she won her first Best Actress Oscar. In the film and in William Styron's 1979 novel of the same name, Zofia "Sophie" Zawistowski (Streep) was sent to Auschwitz because of her association with the Polish resistance. Sophie, who was famously forced to choose between her two children at the gates of Auschwitz, was definitely not Jewish; Sophie and her kids never claimed to have Jewish blood or relatives; Sophie was undeniably Catholic before, during and after the War, and was explicitly recognized as Catholic in the titular scene. So, if the Holocaust is defined exclusively as Jewish suffering resulting from German persecution during Nazi rule, then, strictly speaking, *Sophie's Choice* cannot be a Holocaust film. Instead, *Sophie's Choice* is about a Polish woman suffering during World War II, akin to those portrayed in Andrzej Wajda's Polish film *Katyń* (2007), a Best Foreign Language Film Oscar nominee, which depicts the slaughter of 22,000 Polish POWs at the hands of the Soviets during World War II. Neither film, *Sophie's Choice* nor *Katyń*, attempts to see the War from a Jewish perspective. Yet, few consider *Katyń* to be a Holocaust film, while *Sophie's Choice* is universally acclaimed as one of the greatest Holocaust films ever made. The difference is that *Sophie's Choice* also depicts Jewish suffering at Auschwitz/Birkenau.

So, for the purposes of this book, the working definition of Holocaust film is: narrative feature films or made-for-television films that significantly depict:

1. Jews who suffered at the hands of the Germans (or German proxies) during World War II; or
2. Those who either helped or hurt Jews during the Holocaust.

Creating a Definitive Holocaust Film List

Film lists are everywhere, especially since the advent of the Internet. For example, *Ranker.com* published a list of 54 Holocaust films, some of which were never even released to the public.[7] Similarly, Amazon's International Movie Database (IMDb) lists more than one thousand titles with the keyword "Holocaust,"[8] including several definitively non–Holocaust films that were made before the Holocaust, like *Love and Sacrifice* (1936), described as "The tale of a middle-class matron who shoots the man who compromises her."[9] Hundreds of other IMDb "Holocaust" films are either documentaries, Holocaust-unrelated, still in production or uncertainly awaiting release. Surprisingly, the most reliable publicly available list is on Wikipedia, which separates Holocaust narrative and documentary films, and which yields approximately 200 narrative titles, with only about 10 percent incorrectly categorized as Holocaust films.[10]

The biggest of all Holocaust film lists, predictably, is the Yad Vashem Visual Center—Online Film Database, with approximately 10,000 titles, including 150,000 pieces of publicly available data.[11] The database includes narrative feature films, documentaries, television episodes, testimonials, ceremonies and commemorations. What's more, anyone over 15 years old can simply walk into the actual Yad Vashem Visual Center in Jerusalem during business hours and screen many of the database's titles on any of the 35 workstations in a viewing room that also contains the donated Best Picture Oscar for *Schindler's List*.

According to Yad Vashem, "The Visual Center is a digital film library and comprehensive database of *Holocaust-related* cinema information and reference material [emphasis added]."[12] But Yad Vashem's list is extremely broad. For example, the earliest entry is a silent film from 1914, *Lost and Found*, a film that was made long before the Holocaust, the same year that Adolf Hitler enlisted as an Austrian soldier in World War I. Further, searching only for feature films in the database still yields almost 1,400 titles. Narrowing the list down just to post–War features that are at least 70 minutes and were either American-produced or co-produced still yields 188 titles, including, as just a small example, the following decidedly non–Holocaust films: *Gentleman's Agreement* (1947), *Stalag 17* (1953), *The Guns of Navarone* (1961), *The Sound of Music* (1965), *The Dirty Dozen* (1967), *Kelly's Heroes* (1970), *Fiddler on the Roof* (1971), *21 Hours at Munich* (TV 1976), *Raiders of the Lost Ark* (1981), *Empire of the Sun* (1987), *Barton Fink* (1991), *School Ties* (1992), *Hotel Rwanda* (2004) and *The Monuments Men* (2014).

Conversely, the obvious Holocaust-related film *Murderers Among Us: The Simon Wiesenthal Story* (TV 1989), starring Ben Kingsley, is not listed on any of these sites as a Holocaust film. And none of those three websites lists Bryan Singer's *X-Men* (2000) as a Holocaust film, even though the entire franchise is framed by its three-minute opening scene at the Auschwitz gate, which young "Magneto" destroys. Yad Vashem, however, does list the DVD, *X-Men 1.5* (2000). Wikipedia alone lists the first *X-Men* sequel, Singer's *X2* (2003), which has no Holocaust connection. And, most tellingly, neither Yad Vashem, IMDb nor Wikipedia lists Matthew Vaughn's *X-Men: First Class* (2011), which spends its first nine minutes in Auschwitz, capped by a liberated "Magneto" (Michael Fassbender) in a hotel room displaying his Auschwitz tattoo. Although the entire film builds toward "Magneto" avenging his Auschwitz commandant (Kevin Bacon), as of this writing, *X-Men: First Class* has not been included on any of those three important lists of Holocaust films.

Further, many lists are bloated by ancillary World War II films. Yad Vashem lists several films about Operation Valkyrie, which have nothing to do with the Holocaust. Yad Vashem also lists a staggering 101 titles with the "D-Day" keyword, almost none of which are Holocaust-related. The irony is found in George Seaton's very engaging *36 Hours* (1965), starring James Garner, which is about the Germans trying to discover information about D-Day. *36 Hours* is not listed by Yad Vashem or as a Holocaust film by Wikipedia or IMDb, even though Eva Marie Saint co-starred in *36 Hours* as an authentically tattooed Auschwitz survivor.

Availability also plays a role in making lists. How should we account for films that were completed, but never released, or were released decades ago, but cannot be obtained today? In this age of video-on-demand, it is assumed by many that all films are available, online in one way or another. However, to be online means that a film has been converted from a physical analog celluloid film or from an analog video format to a digital format and then uploaded for wider use. But many films that were distributed in theaters decades ago have never been rendered onto video or been digitized. For example, gone is *Charlie Grant's War* (TV 1984), which is summarized on IMDb as "A Canadian artist turned diamond merchant in Vienna, Austria risks his life to smuggle Jews out of the Third Reich."[13] Other films are difficult to find even after having been Oscar-nominated for Best Foreign Language Film, like *Jacob the Liar—Jakob, der Lugner* (1974), *The Revolt of Job—Jób lázadása* (1983) and *Angry Harvest—Bittere Ernte* (1985). So, too, even recent films like *Quezon's Game* (2018), about Philippine President Manuel L. Quezon saving Jewish refugees, is currently unavailable. And *The Last Suit—El último traje* (2017) is a good Argentinian film about a Holocaust survivor. Unfortunately, although *The Last Suit* played the international film festival circuit just after being made, the film is now almost impossible to find.

Other Holocaust films may have never made their way to the larger world. It has been reported that at least one Soviet Holocaust film was actually washed right off of its filmstock.[14] And a handful of other Soviet Holocaust films have effectively disappeared.[15] Indeed, it is a miracle that any Soviet Holocaust films have survived, let alone the three listed, which include one of the first Holocaust films: *The Taras' Family—The Unvanquished—Nepokoryonnye* (1945). Some films, too, are still being released, including *The Painted Bird* (2019), based on Jerzy Kosinski's controversial autobiographical novel and starring Holocaust film veteran actors Stellan Skarsgård and Harvey Keitel, which has also only been shown at festivals. Its release is uncertain, especially after an article about it in *The Daily Beast* entitled "The Child-Rape Holocaust Movie That's Causing Festival Walkouts."[16]

Further, some Holocaust films on all major lists were never released by their producers such as the late Jerry Lewis' *The Day the Clown Cried* (1972), of which Lewis said, "I was embarrassed. I was ashamed of the work. And I was grateful that I have the power to contain it all and never let anyone see it. It was bad, bad, bad."[17] Notably for gluttons of misguided cinema, in 2014 Jerry Lewis (né Joseph Levitch) (1926–2017) donated *The Day the Clown Cried* to the Library of Congress with the caveat that it could not be screened for ten years, which will be June of 2024.[18] Regardless, as of today, *The Day the Clown Cried* and other unviewable productions may be listed aspirationally as Holocaust films, yet they cannot exist on any practical list, except when explicitly acknowledged as unavailable.

Some other films are also genuine head-scratchers for inclusion on any list, such as the 62-minute Polish film *Passenger—Pasazerka* (TV 1963), which was mostly made by director Andrzej Munk, who died during *Passenger*'s production. *Passenger* was finished by director Witold Lesiewicz, who speculated about Munk's intent, shot missing scenes and used documentary footage from the production to fill in the blanks. A case could easily be made that *Passenger* is just a documentary about an unfinished film. Another case could be made that *Passenger* is simply an unfinished film and should not be listed altogether. In this case, enough of *Passenger* exists as a narrative Holocaust film to have included it here as a Holocaust film.

Other issues, too, must be considered while culling the vast lists of purported Holocaust films. For example, non–Holocaust films include "Nazisploitation," Holocaust pornography that has neither historical mooring nor educational intent.[19] *Ilsa: She Wolf of the SS* (1975) is classic Nazisploitation:

> Ilsa is Kommandant of a Nazi prison camp, who conducts sadistic scientific experiments designed to demonstrate that women are more capable of enduring pain than men are, and therefore should be allowed to fight in the German armed forces (it is late in the war and the Nazi military is in dire need of reinforcements). Ilsa is also portrayed as a buxom woman with a voracious sexual appetite for men. Every night, she chooses another of her male prisoners and rapes him. However, owing to her hypersexuality, she is disappointed when her current victim eventually ejaculates, and promptly has him castrated and put to death. Only one American prisoner, who can avoid ejaculating, manages to use her weakness to his favor. He hopes that the Allies will arrive soon, but a faction of the SS wants to eliminate all evidence and witnesses.[20]

Some lists are so indiscriminate that they include other Holocaust porn.[21] Although Yad Vashem does not list *Ilsa*, it does include the equally tasteless *SS Experiment Love Camp—Lager SSadis Kastrat Kommandantur* (1976), *Beast in Heat—Horrifying Experiments of the S.S. Last Days—La bestia in calore* (1977), and *Helga, She Wolf of*

Stilberg—Helga, la louve de Stilberg (1978), which is not described in the database, but is summarized on IMDb as:

> Vicious warden Helga runs the castle penitentiary Stilberg for female political prisoners with an iron fist. Stubborn and recalcitrant new inmate Elisabeth Vogel, who's the daughter of a rebel leader, runs afoul of Helga after she finds herself incarcerated in Stilberg. Elisabeth eventually plots to escape from Stilberg in the wake of becoming fed up with being on the receiving end of Helga's endless cruelty and perverse sexual desires.[22]

Regardless of crassness or debauchery, these films also generally do not significantly involve Jewish characters. Nazi porn has as much to do with the Holocaust as does *The Sound of Music*. So, too, while *The German Doctor—Wakolda* (2013) meaningfully portrays Dr. Josef Mengele on the run in South America, the Holocaust porn version of Mengele, *Commando Mengele* (1987), cannot be taken seriously as a Holocaust film: "A Jewish commando unit hunting Nazi war criminals tracks down the infamous Dr. Mengele in the jungle, and find [*sic*] that he is torturing nubile young virgins and performing horrible medical experiments on the locals."[23] So the red line is clear: no Ilsa, Helga, Commando Mengele or Maria von Trapp.

For decades, from the above-listed sources, together with video catalogs, recommendations, feedback and other sources, I have curated 443 titles that I consider to be Holocaust films. (See Appendix I: List of Holocaust Films.) Additionally, listed in Appendix II: Non-Holocaust Films Often Miscategorized as Holocaust Films are approximately 130 other titles that have been classified by others as Holocaust films, but are not considered here as having sufficient Holocaust content to be classified as Holocaust films. Best efforts notwithstanding, however, to suggest that every Holocaust film ever made can be found would be both presumptuous and foolhardy. Whether due to political barriers, classifications, disappearances or errors, some Holocaust films may still have slipped through the cracks.*

Finally, only 76 (17 percent) of the listed films are impractical to obtain, whether sought by individuals, theaters, television stations or educational institutions. On the other hand, more than 275 of these Holocaust films (62 percent) can be streamed, many for free on YouTube.com, Ok.Ru, DailyMotion.com and CDA.Pl. Paid streaming services—such as Apple TV, Netflix and Amazon Prime—are also reliable sources. So too, the majority of Holocaust films can be purchased as DVDs or VHS on Amazon or eBay.com (as can be DVD and VHS players). And believe it or not, many public libraries have impressive catalogs of Holocaust films. WorldCat.org, with its phenomenal search engine, identifies libraries within specified radii where most films can be found. Listed in Appendix I is one source for each accessible film, the result of a cursory search just before publication.

Grouping Holocaust Films: The "4+1 Genre" System

The grouping of Holocaust films into meaningful categories is essential for analysis. Holocaust film experts have organized Holocaust film books by geography, production date, fiction versus nonfiction, societal importance, intended media delivery (theatrical

---

* As this book nears publication, additional Holocaust films are still being released, including *Anne Frank Video Diary: After the Arrest* (2021), *The Auschwitz Report* (2020), *Dara of Jasenovac—Dara iz Jasenovca* (2020), *The Life Ahead—La vita davanti a sé* (2020), *Persian Lessons* (2020), *Pieces of a Woman* (2020), *Resistance* (2020), *Where Is Anne Frank* (2021), some of which are listed in Appendix I, but are not part of the 443 or statistics because they are beyond the first 75 years of Holocaust film production.

or television), intended audience and film style. Grouping films in these ways can reveal valuable trends and ideas. Yet, these methods still can lead to comparing apples to oranges.

For example, analyzing films by date, while ignoring the type of core depiction, can be misleading, as with *Schindler's List* (1993) and *Life Is Beautiful—La Vita è bella* (1997), the two most successful core Holocaust feature films in history. They were released within four years of each other and they both depict Auschwitz. But *Schindler's List* is about a Nazi saving more than a thousand Jews, while *Life Is Beautiful* depicts a Jewish father saving his son. *Schindler's List* uses gravitas to pursue a happy ending, while *Life Is Beautiful* is a comedic tragedy. *Schindler's List* is based on a true story, while *Life Is Beautiful* is sheer fantasy. *Schindler's List* is American-made, while *Life Is Beautiful* is Italian. Both were made for theatrical release. Both grossed hundreds of millions of dollars. And both were highly decorated. But, like comparing late-1970s classic comedies *Annie Hall* (1977) and *Animal House* (1978), only in the broadest sense can *Schindler's List* and *Life Is Beautiful* be lumped together.

Or consider the following ten Western-produced (or co-produced) Holocaust films: *The Stranger* (1946), *The Search* (1948), *The Juggler* (1953), *Singing in the Dark* (1956), *The Young Lions* (1958), *Me and the Colonel* (1958), *The Diary of Anne Frank* (1959), *Conspiracy of Hearts* (1960), *Exodus* (1960) and *Kapò* (1960). Each of these theatrical films is notable. Most either won or were nominated for Academy Awards. Many were cast with prominent stars, including Marlon Brando, Montgomery Clift, Paul Newman, Orson Welles, Susan Strasberg, Eva Marie Saint, Danny Kaye (né David Daniel Kaminsky), Kirk Douglas (né Issur Danielovitch Demsky), Edward G. Robinson (né Emanuel Goldenberg) and Shelley Winters (née Shirley Schrift). Some of these films were directed by Hollywood's greatest filmmakers, including Orson Welles, Fred Zinnemann, Edward Dmytryk, Otto Preminger and George Stevens. Some of these films were box office successes. Some are cultural icons to this day. Others are simply remembered; and others, still, have been completely forgotten. These films range in length from 84 to 208 minutes. Although features had been released on color film since before World War II, only the longest of these films (*Exodus*) was shot in color. Some depicted graphic violence and sex, while others were self-consciously anodyne. Some were Western European productions, while others were produced by Hollywood.

Thematically, too, those Holocaust films had little in common. Some were set during the Holocaust, while others were primarily set after. Some simply alluded to the Holocaust, while others depicted roundups and camps. Some plots revolved around individual Holocaust victims, like Anne Frank and her family, while others featured Gentiles who saved many Jews during the Holocaust, like *Conspiracy of Hearts*. Some depicted the challenges after surviving the Holocaust, like *The Juggler*, while others concentrated on hidden perpetrators post–War, like *The Stranger*. One film, *Exodus*, which was chiefly about the founding of the State of Israel, only dealt tangentially with the Holocaust, portraying survivors as subordinate characters. So, why compare *Exodus* to *Anne Frank*? Why compare *Conspiracy of Hearts'* nuns saving Jewish children with *The Juggler's* traumatized survivor? In 1960, grouping these films in any way other than post–War Holocaust films would have been difficult.

And finally, the Western jingoistic twist here is that the above-listed ten films account for approximately a quarter of Holocaust films made from 1945 through 1960.

Surprisingly, half of the first Holocaust films came from behind the "Iron Curtain" and from the nascent State of Israel. (See Table 1.)*

TABLE 1: THE FIRST 36 HOLOCAUST FILMS (1945–1960)

Title	Country
The Last Chance—Die letzte Chance (1945)	Switzerland
The Taras' Family—The Unvanquished—Nepokoryonnye (1945)	USSR
Murderers Among Us—Die Mörder sind unter uns (1946)	East Germany
The Stranger (1946)	U.S.
The Great Promise—Dim'at Ha'Nehamah Ha'Gedolah (1947)	Israel
The Illegals—Lo Tafhidenu (1947)	Israel
Marriage in the Shadows—Ehe im Schatten (1947)	East Germany
My Father's House—Beit Avi (1947)	Israel
Seven Journeys—In Those Days—In jenen Tagen (1947)	Germany
Tomorrow's a Wonderful Day—Adamah (1947)	Israel
Border Street—Ulica Graniczna (1948)	Poland
The Last Stage—The Last Stop—Ostatni etap (1948)	Poland
Morituri (1948)	West Germany
The Search (1948)	U.S.—Switzerland
The Wandering Jew—L'ebreo errante (1948)	Italy
The Earth Cries Out—Il grido della terra (1949)	Italy
Long Is the Road—Lang ist der Weg (1949)	West Germany
Monastero di Santa Chiara (1949)	Italy
Distant Journey—Dalek cesta (1950)	Czechoslovakia
Out of Evil—Mi Klalah L'Brahah (1950)	Israel
It Will Never Happen Again—Unzere Kinder (1951)	Poland
Skipper Next to God—Maître après Dieu (1951)	France
The Juggler (1953)	U.S.
I Know Why I Live—Ich weiß, wofür ich lebe (1955)	West Germany
Springtime in Budapest—Budapesti tavasz (1955)	Hungary
Singing in the Dark (1956)	U.S.
The Diary of Anne Frank—Das Tagebuch Der Anne Frank (TV 1958)	East Germany
Me and the Colonel (1958)	U.S.
The Diary of Anne Frank—Dnevnik Ane Frank (TV 1959)	Yugoslavia
The Diary of Anne Frank (1959)	U.S.
Stars—Sterne (1959)	East Germany—Bulgaria
Conspiracy of Hearts (1960)	U.K.
Exodus (1960)	U.S.
Kapò (1960)	Italy—France—Yugoslavia
The Ninth Circle—Deveti krug (1960)	Yugoslavia
Romeo, Juliet and Darkness—Romeo, Julie a tma (1960)	Czechoslovakia

Without knowing that these Eastern European films were, in many cases, filmed at or near the actual locations depicted—including at Auschwitz/Birkenau and Babi Yar—the analysis of post–War Holocaust film is hollow, stilted and insulting to those films

---

* West Germany and East Germany were not officially established until 1949 (and were reunified in 1990). Many Eastern European sovereignties and Israel/British Palestine were also transitioning just after the War. Thus, some films were retroactively assigned to their de facto producing countries.

from Communist countries that dared depict Jewish suffering. These Eastern European films concentrated on the victims more than the survivors and, for the most part, Eastern European Holocaust films pulled fewer punches and created fewer plastic heroes. But the ultimate comparisons can only be made when comparing films with similar themes.

Holocaust historians such as Raul Hilberg (1926–2007) have classified the citizenry of the Holocaust into three groups of either: perpetrators, victims or bystanders.[24] Subsequent scholars added the category of "upstanders," a group that was mostly sheared-off from the bystander group. This four-category framework—perpetrators, victims, bystanders and upstanders—defines Holocaust-contemporaneous populations, but it lacks the dimension of time. Specifically, a Holocaust "victim" who outlived the Third Reich is generally regarded as a Holocaust "survivor," the difference between a diary and a memoir. Further, stories told in cinema about Holocaust perpetrators during the Holocaust are vastly different from plotlines about old Nazis in hiding long after the War. Factually, both characters are or were Nazi perpetrators. But both are starkly different over time, from seemingly omnipotent in 1944, rendered practically powerless by 1954.

So, today, with cinematic history populated by hundreds of Holocaust films, four simple thematic categories have become visible to me: "Victim," "Survivor," "Gentile" and "Perpetrator," as explained below. Each of these four categories is identified by answering the following two binary questions about the protagonists and when the film was set:

1. Who was the protagonist: (A) Jew(s) who suffered during the Holocaust or (B) Gentile(s) who either helped or harmed Jew(s) during the Holocaust?
2. When was the story primarily set: (A) during the Holocaust or (B) after the Holocaust?

There is, however, the "plus 1" additional "Tangential" genre, which fills in the gap caused by Holocaust films such as *Sophie's Choice* and *Inglourious Basterds*, which are not primarily about Jews or the strict definition of the Holocaust, but still, undeniably have

TABLE 2: HOLOCAUST FILM 4+1 GENRES WITH THE TOTAL NUMBER PRODUCED

		WHEN	
		During the Holocaust	After the Holocaust
WHO	Jewish Protagonists	"Victim" 156	"Survivor" 86
	Gentile Protagonists	"Gentile" 86	"Perpetrator" 47
		"Tangential" 68	

significant Holocaust content. Table 2 illustrates the 4+1 genre system and the number of Holocaust films in each category.

Victim Holocaust Films

The heart of Holocaust films is the depiction of Holocaust victims. While victims are also depicted in Gentile films and also often in Survivor films through flashbacks, Victim Holocaust films are distinguished by having Jewish protagonists suffering during the Holocaust (or mostly during the Holocaust). Seeing the Holocaust through the eyes of Jews should be a primary objective when trying to understand the Holocaust. Thus, the most important Holocaust films are generally Victim Holocaust films, both historically and pedagogically. To date, 156 Victim Holocaust films have been made, of which a whopping 22 are recommended in Chapter 9: Recommended Holocaust Films.

Gentile Holocaust Films

In the parlance of Yad Vashem, a righteous Gentile is regarded as "Righteous Among the Nations," as defined:

1. Active involvement of the rescuer in saving one or several Jews from the threat of death or deportation to death camps;
2. Risk to the rescuer's life, liberty or position;
3. The initial motivation being the intention to help persecuted Jews: i.e., not for payment or any other reward such as religious conversion of the saved person, adoption of a child, etc.;
4. The existence of testimony of those who were helped or at least unequivocal documentation establishing the nature of the rescue and its circumstances.[25]

There are two sub-categories of Gentile films, which are the rough equivalent to "upstanders" and Hilberg's Holocaust-contemporaneous "perpetrators" during the War. To date, 86 Gentile Holocaust films have been made, of which 80 percent (68) have portrayed righteous Gentiles or "upstanders," while the remaining quarter, 18 films, have been stories about antisemitic Gentiles during or immediately after the War, people who would be defined as wartime "perpetrators" by Hilberg.

First, righteous Gentile films generally depict a fiction that the German-occupied landscape was filled by bystander and upstander Gentiles, very few of whom agreed with German policies. These sad stories with mostly happy endings are perfectly suited for telling and retelling. Most of us are eager to hear stories about selflessness and helping the oppressed. After the love story, people saving people is our favorite storyline; stories about personal redemption, like *Schindler's List* (1993), are also in the sweet spot of general film production. Yet few righteous Gentile films ever imply that the chances of finding even one righteous Gentile, as defined by Yad Vashem, in occupied Europe was infinitesimal: roughly one righteous Gentile for every 18,000 non-righteous Gentiles in German lands, European Axis Powers, and German-occupied territories (almost a half a billion divided by 27,362[26] certified righteous Gentiles, as of this writing). To put that in perspective for those making movies, the one-off chance of a Jew finding a righteous Gentile during the Holocaust is half as great as the chance of winning any Oscar when working in the film industry, which is 1 in 11,500.[27] In other words, as *The Jerusalem Post*'s Hannah Brown wrote of *The*

Round Up—La rafle (2010), "A viewer who knew nothing of the true events of World War II would think there was a guardian angel that looked out for sweet young children."[28]

But, more fundamentally, as discussed in Chapter 4 regarding *Schindler's List*, why do we need righteous Gentile films at all, when many films about Jews trying to save Jews were made, Victim films such as: *For Those I Loved—Au nom de tous les miens* (1983), *Hanna's War* (1988), *Korczak* (1990), *Haven* (TV 2001), *Uprising* (TV 2001), *Defiance* (2008) and *Süskind* (2012)? Certainly, righteous Gentiles are praiseworthy and admirable, but chiefly because of their rarity. The incredible bravery of righteous Gentiles was so uncommon that it easily distracts from the constant mortal danger of those they saved, as in the righteous Gentile films *The Only Way* (1970), *The Hiding Place* (1975), *The Scarlet and the Black* (TV 1983), *The Assisi Underground* (1985) and *Schindler's List*.

Righteous Gentile films teach us that some Gentiles saved Jews, which is a hopeful theme, but these films tend to humanize the saviors more than the Jewish victims who are usually one-dimensional cutouts. Disregarding their filmmakers' good intentions, these films usually depict more courage mustered by their righteous Gentiles saving the condemned Jews than is depicted about the courage of the condemned, themselves. Although not the only criterion for recommending righteous Gentile films, only those films that struck the right balance between victim and hero make the cut here.

Second are the 18 antisemitic Gentile films, which need fewer contortions to make their point, expressing the more common local activities that were prevalent during German occupation when faced with the Final Solution: to participate and/or ignore the genocide and/or profit from the Holocaust. Most of these antisemitic Gentile films tell the stories of people who enabled the Final Solution—macro and micro. In some cases, like *Conspiracy* (TV 2001), the entire hierarchical organization of the Holocaust is established, while in *1945* (2017), just one rural community of antisemites is portrayed. In these antisemitic Gentile films, no one is rehabilitated or pampered; antisemitic Gentile films mostly expose perpetrators and collaborators in the act. Finally, while 13 of the 68 righteous Gentile films are American productions or co-productions, exactly none of the antisemitic Gentile films are solo American productions, a clear window into Hollywood's storytelling preferences.

Survivor Holocaust Films

The 86 Holocaust Survivor films depict post–War Holocaust victims who are usually peculiar, shattered human shells. This may seem like an obvious representation of Holocaust survivors, but, in fact, it has always been difficult to find Holocaust survivors who share those aberrant characteristics. On the contrary, Holocaust survivors are resilient, generally vibrant, well-adjusted, normal, fully-functioning members of society. True, they always carry the weight of the Holocaust and are certainly not dismissive of their experiences, but Holocaust survivors are not incapacitated or cartoonish, as grossly exaggerated in films. Another misleading characteristic of Holocaust survivors in film is their reticence to discuss their suffering. While many real Holocaust survivors, in fact, did not speak freely about their experiences for a decade or two, survivors were not paralyzed by their experiences, as implied in most Holocaust films.

The children and grandchildren of Holocaust survivors are the protagonists of ten Survivor Holocaust films. While the progeny of Holocaust survivors in films are universally portrayed as running toward the Holocaust, trying to understand their dead or dying ancestors through the Holocaust, the actual survivors are depicted as running from the Holocaust, hiding it in their minds and discussions. Regardless, almost all protagonists in Holocaust Survivor films are acutely unstable and eccentric.

Little can be learned from most Survivor Holocaust films, with the notable exception of *The Birch-Tree Meadow—La petite prairie aux bouleaux* (2003). Most other films in this genre use flashbacks, which are much less effective for Holocaust education than are Holocaust Victim films. On the other hand, several Survivor Holocaust films are far more entertaining than most Holocaust Victim films, including *Harold and Maude* (1971), *Everything Is Illuminated* (2005), *This Must Be the Place* (2011) and *Phoenix* (2014), all of which are recommended. Many other Survivor films, however, are depressing and unsatisfying.

Perpetrator Holocaust Films

Few Perpetrator Holocaust films are actually about the Holocaust, and all Perpetrator films are set after the Holocaust. The 47 Perpetrator films usually use the Holocaust as a prop, simply a convenient opportunity to create and then destroy evil incarnate. Although Holocaust references and flashbacks occasionally are included in Perpetrator films, like diet cola, these entertaining films impart nothing of substance, instead delivering a little fizz and the sweetness of a vanquished foe.

Except for the twenty Mengele and Eichmann films, Perpetrator films are mostly imaginary, with an amazingly consistent formula. Typically, these fictional Perpetrator stories focus on a cunning Nazi who escaped apprehension after the War and has been hiding, often in South America. The Nazi is somehow exposed and flees or is careless near the end of his life, and then the Nazi dies or is killed or, as in *Music Box* (1989), is apprehended. In many of these films, the Nazi kills himself either inadvertently or to otherwise escape justice, including in *Genghis Cohn* (1993), *Apt Pupil* (1998), *Made in Israel* (2001), *The Debt—Ha-Hov* (2007) and its remake *The Debt* (2010), and *Remember* (2015).

For example, at the end of Orson Welles' *The Stranger* (1946), the Nazi, played by Welles, leaps to his death from a tower rather than being captured. In Perpetrator films, the Nazi is never killed directly by the hand of a Jew, let alone a Holocaust survivor, even if a Jew is present during the Nazi's death. Indeed, even if a Jew has the chance to kill the Nazi, either someone or something else, instead, kills the Nazi.

The most fascinating examples of this come from two Perpetrator films made within a few years of each other that both starred Laurence Olivier: *Marathon Man* (1976), in which Olivier plays the Nazi, and *The Boys from Brazil* (1978), in which Olivier plays the Nazi hunter. At the end of Franklin J. Schaffner's *The Boys from Brazil*, Olivier's character is on the verge of shooting Josef Mengele (Gregory Peck), when a pack of dogs runs in and kills Mengele for him. More interestingly, in John Schlesinger's *Marathon Man*, William Goldman's script calls for the young, Jewish graduate student, played by Dustin Hoffman, to kill the Nazi (Laurence Olivier). As explained by Dustin Hoffman in a 2006 article in *The Jewish Chronicle*, the *Marathon Man* script was changed because Dustin Hoffman refused to play a Jewish character who kills the Nazi:

> "The big sticking point in *Marathon Man* was the ending," he explains. "I was called on, as the character, to fire point-blank at the Laurence Olivier character, Dr Szell [a Nazi dentist], and kill him in that last scene. And I said that I couldn't do it. The screenwriter, William Goldman, was quite upset about it, because first of all, how dare I? He wrote the book. 'Your job isn't to rewrite—your job is to play it as written.' I think we had an outdoor meeting in LA at the home of the director, John Schlesinger. There

was me, Goldman, and Schlesinger around the table—and it got nasty. I said: 'Go hire someone else'—
[Al] Pacino wanted the part—'Go get Al.' I remember [Jewish] Goldman saying: 'Why can't you do this?
Are you such a Jew?' I said, 'No, but I won't play a Jew who cold-bloodedly kills another human being.
I won't become a Nazi to kill a Nazi. I won't demean myself. I don't give a f*** what he did. Even though
he tortured me, I won't do it.'"[29]

And so it has been remarkably consistent, before and after Hoffman's objection; even
if Hoffman did not make the rule, Hoffman accurately articulated the cinematic tradition of clean-handed Jewish characters. Regardless, Perpetrator Holocaust films cannot
be taken seriously as tools for Holocaust understanding, but can be considered as surrep-
titious retribution.

A common question arises: what is the difference between antisemitic Gentile Holocaust films and Perpetrator Holocaust films. In both cases, Germans or German sympathizers are exposed. Yet, while antisemitic Gentile Holocaust films take place during or
just after the War, Perpetrator films are set long after the rubble has been cleared. Further, Perpetrator films are usually purely fictitious (unless based on Adolf Eichmann's
capture or Josef Mengele) and concentrate on one particular Nazi who escaped justice.
Antisemitic Gentile films, on the other hand, are usually based on true events and portray a group or community of people who are not hunted during the film, but, rather, are
exposed for their complicity, whether explicit involvement as in *Conspiracy* (TV 2001)
and *Labyrinth of Lies—Im Labyrinth Des Schweigens* (2014), or tacit communal involvement in genocide, as in *The Shop on Main Street—Obchod na korze* (1965), *Three Days in
April—Drei Tage im April* (TV 1995) and *1945* (2017).

Of note, too, the Amazon Prime series *Hunters* (TV 2020–)—starring Al Pacino—
has turned the Perpetrator genre on its ear, seeming more like *Jojo Rabbit* (2019) than
Marathon Man. Both *Hunters* and *Jojo Rabbit* make a mockery of the Holocaust with
plot-turns that abuse the facts. As Stephan Smith, executive director of the USC Shoah
Foundation, wrote in an op-ed, "I believe it's [*Hunters* is] the most egregious distortion
of Holocaust history in my lifetime.... I fear its pernicious blend of fact and fiction risks
being weaponized by Holocaust deniers."[30] As binge content, some moments in *Hunters*
are entertaining. But it is so convoluted that its many historical tidbits disappear in a tor-
rent of bad writing and pretzel logic. *Hunters* is especially disappointing for those who
appreciate the accomplishments of its great actors who have been particularly compromised in the series, especially Lena Olin (*Enemies, A Love Story* [1989]), Saul Rubinek
(*The Quarrel* [1991]) and Carol Kane (*Hester Street* [1975]).

Tangential Holocaust Films

The "plus one" genre, Tangential Holocaust films, exists because 68 films have
enough Holocaust relevance that they cannot be dismissed as non–Holocaust films, yet,
by definition, they also cannot be classified in the main four Holocaust film genres: Victim, Gentile, Survivor and Perpetrator. Most of the 52 Tangential Holocaust films are
either not primarily about the Jewish experience during the Holocaust, are not primarily
Holocaust depictions, or are simply about the rise of Nazism in pre–War Germany.

Notwithstanding this added category, Tangential Holocaust film, there is also a minimum threshold of Holocaust content that films must have even to be regarded as Tangential
Holocaust films. Many of the non–Holocaust films that failed to contain enough Holocaust
content are listed in Appendix II, including *Tin Drum—Die Blechtrommel* (1979), *Come and*

See—Idi i smotri (1985), *Shining Through* (1992), *The Ring* (TV 1996), *I'm Alive and I Love You—Je suis vivante et je vous aime* (1998), *Taking Sides* (2001) and *The Book Thief* (2013).

Many Tangential films are important culturally or cinematically, including *Exodus* (1960), *Cabaret* (1972), *The Last Metro—Le dernier métro* (1980), *The Wave* (TV 1981), *Sophie's Choice* and *Inglourious Basterds. Bent* (1997), too, has had some cultural importance, especially in the LGBTQ community. Nonetheless, if the protagonist is not Jewish or if the protagonist is not persecuted for being Jewish—as in *Bent*, where the Jewish protagonist is persecuted for being a homosexual—then it is not a Victim Holocaust film, but Tangential. For the most part, Tangential Holocaust films teach something about the Holocaust and cannot be disregarded out of hand as non–Holocaust films. Some Israeli films, too, have characters who are Holocaust survivors, yet the stories are principally about non–Holocaust characters, and thus are not listed here as Holocaust films. These titles include the very interesting *The Matchmaker—Once I Was* (2010), *Berlin-Jerusalem—Berlin-Yerushalaim* (1989) and *Blind Man's Bluff—Dummy in a Circle—Golem Ba'Maagal* (1993).

A few films can be difficult to place into just one genre. For example, Anna Justice's *Remembrance* (2011) jumps equally between a victim and her lover during the Holocaust and then the same people as survivors in 1976. Is *Remembrance* a Victim or Survivor film? Ultimately, it is categorized here as a Victim film based on the more extensive (and excellent) depictions of concentration camp life and hiding during the War.

The other film that straddles categories was Liliana Cavani's troubling and controversial *The Night Porter—Il portiere di notte* (1974), which has been wrongly accused of being Nazisploitation. This Italian-made film stars Oscar nominee Charlotte Rampling as a deranged Holocaust survivor who is still enraptured by the same SS officer who enslaved her at a concentration camp. Both characters die at the end of the film, which is equally about each of them. *The Night Porter*, however, is a Survivor film, because, while Holocaust survivors in films are expected to be unhinged, the perpetrators in Holocaust films are generally neither self-destructive nor irrational. Since both characters are unhinged, *The Night Porter* must be a Survivor film.

As the final example of a genre quandary, consider two films based on Hubert Monteilhet's 1961 novel *Le Retour des cendres* ("*The Return of the Ashes*"): the Tangential film *Return from the Ashes* (1965) and the Survivor film *Phoenix* (2014). Both films are about the estate of a woman presumed to have died during the Holocaust. In each case, the woman returns to her home city while healing after being disfigured. In both films she finds her husband, who assumes she is dead and does not recognize her. So how could films with essentially the same plot be categorized in two different Holocaust film genres? In the 1965 version, the woman purportedly returns from Dachau (although with a tattoo, which is suspect, since tattoos were only applied in Auschwitz/Birkenau). After the woman's return, nothing more is made of her wartime experience. In other words, she could have returned from a hurricane or a harrowing car accident just as easily as Dachau. But in the 2014 *Phoenix* version (and the novel), the woman's wartime betrayal by her husband to the Nazis is revealed. While the surviving women in both films are uncharacteristically lucid, which is contrary to the general formula for the Survivor genre, *Phoenix* is undeniably a Survivor story, while *Return from the Ashes* treats the Holocaust as an afterthought and is, therefore, a Tangential Holocaust film.

Overall, though many other groupings will be used in this book to understand the history of Holocaust films, the 4+1 Genre system, which I created to simplify Holocaust film analysis, is the overarching lens through which all Holocaust films are viewed here. And finally, throughout this book the word "core" or phrases such as "core Holocaust films" are occasionally used, which is simply shorthand for Victim and Gentile films, all of which are defined above as having been set primarily during the Holocaust. As such, the moniker "core Holocaust films" is not a term of merit or excellence, but is just a broader term referring to Victim and Gentile films.

Non-Holocaust Films: Shorts, Television Episodes, Documentaries and Miniseries

The following are also not included as narrative Holocaust films here: Holocaust documentaries, short films, television episodes, theater, miniseries and episodic streaming content. Nonetheless, these formats have had a vast cultural impact. The exception is Holocaust short films, which are difficult to find and mostly unimpressive. Of the dozen Holocaust shorts listed in Appendix II, only *Torte Bluma* (2005), starring Stellan Skarsgård, and the simple Argentinian *Numbers of Life—Jai vida* (2005), directed by Ariel Zylbersztejn can be recommended. *Numbers of Life* depicts the reaction of grandchildren to their grandparents' Auschwitz tattoo. On the other hand, Oscar winner for Best Short Film, Live Action, *Toyland—Spielzeugland* (2007) and *Porcelain Unicorn* (2010) are manipulative propaganda shorts, disingenuously suggesting that the Holocaust was not implemented by Germans, but by Nazis, and all the other Germans either disagreed or were ignorant of Hitler's stated genocidal goal.[31]

Holocaust television episodes are not listed in Appendix II, but do have a rich history. Many television episodes have veered into Holocaust territory and have been cultural landmarks, especially in America, including: a 1953 episode of the NBC weekly program *This Is Your Life* (TV 1952–1987) featuring Hanna Bloch Kohner, an Auschwitz survivor; a 1961 episode of *The Twilight Zone* (TV 1959–1964) "Deaths-Head Revisited," which was an astonishingly brave Perpetrator story; a 1969 episode of *Night Gallery* (TV 1969–1973) "The Escape Route," a Perpetrator plot evocative of Edgar Allan Poe's writings; and the 2001 episode "Why We Fight" from the miniseries *Band of Brothers* (Miniseries 2001), featuring the liberation of a concentration camp.[32] As noted above, the Holocaust has also appeared on Broadway, sometimes with great success, including: *The Diary of Anne Frank* (Broadway 1955–1957), *Cabaret* (Broadway 1966–1969) and *The Producers* (Broadway 2001–2007).

Holocaust documentaries are neither included here as Holocaust films, nor are listed in Appendix II. The Yad Vashem—Online Film Database lists more than 900 documentaries that have a running time of at least 75 minutes made since 1945. Documentaries have served a vital role in explaining the Holocaust, even though, generally, documentaries are pedagogically less effective than are narrative films. Many Holocaust documentaries are excellent sources of history, but are prohibitively long, especially for classroom use, including: *Shoah* (1985) (566 minutes); *The Sorrow and the Pity* (1969) (251 minutes); *The Last of the Unjust* (2013) (220 minutes); and *Auschwitz: The Nazis and the "Final Solution"* (2005) (285 minutes). By contrast, the longest core narrative Holocaust feature film is *Schindler's List*, clocking in at 195 minutes, which is still quite a chunk of film time.

In fairness, too, hundreds of great Holocaust documentaries have reasonable running times, including Best Documentary Oscar winners *Genocide* (1982) and *The Long*

Way Home (1997), and nominee *Against the Tide* (2009), three of ten Holocaust documentaries produced by Rabbi Marvin Hier, dean and founder of the Simon Wiesenthal Center. Also of interest is Oscar Winner for Short Documentary, *The Lady in Number 6: Music Saved My Life* (2013). Two extraordinary Holocaust documentaries were also made relatively recently, both shorter than 90 minutes: Yael Hersonski's *A Film Unfinished* (2010) and André Singer's *Night Will Fall* (2014). Each film is based on heretofore publicly unseen Holocaust footage. In both cases, the underlying stories are about how and why the footage was shot and by whom. Each is fascinating. Also worth watching are James Moll's *Inheritance* (2006) and Ashton Gleckman's *We Shall Not Die Now* (2019).

Most importantly, aside from running time or merit, many Holocaust documentaries also include real Holocaust images. While Claude Lanzmann's documentary-style specifically avoided Holocaust footage in favor of interviews, the sidestepping of graphic footage in Holocaust documentaries is rare. Conversely, narrative filmmakers control the images to keep our attention, but not to scald us. Even at Holocaust museums, graphic footage is brief and visitors can walk away when overwhelmed, which is less of an option when planted in front of a feature-length film. Documentaries such as *A Film Unfinished* and *Night Will Fall* include footage of the dead and dying, images which, by definition, cannot be subconsciously passed off as actors and special effects. Viewers are profoundly disturbed when looking at suffering in documentaries, when watching real dead, dying and decaying bodies in piles or pits or withering in streets. But in narrative films, even in the most gruesome scenes, we have a cognitive buffer; we are reassured by the little mantra in the back of our heads when watching actors: "this is not real, this is not real, this is not real…." Narrative films versus documentaries is the difference between fireworks and artillery.

Next, made-for-television Holocaust miniseries are not considered here as Holocaust films, except for sub-200 minute two-parters, such as *Wallenberg—A Hero's Story* (TV 1985), *Murderers Among Us: The Simon Wiesenthal Story* (TV 1989), *Twist of Fate—Pursuit* (TV 1989), *Nuremberg* (TV 2000), *Uprising* (TV 2001), *Anne Frank: The Whole Story* (TV 2001) and *Perlasca. The Courage of a Just Man—Perlasca. Un eroe italiano* (TV 2002). Long-form Holocaust miniseries, however, are the extinct dinosaurs of Holocaust film, having blotted out almost everything in their paths for the decade and a half they roamed the airwaves. (See Table 3.)

TABLE 3: AMERICAN HOLOCAUST TELEVISION MINISERIES

Year	Title	Network	IMDb Description	Length
1974	*QB VII*	ABC (U.S.)	A physician sues a novelist for publishing statements implicating the doctor in Nazi war crimes.	390 Minutes 2 Episodes
1978	*Holocaust*	NBC (U.S.)	The saga of a Jewish family's struggle to survive the horror of Nazi Germany's systematic marginalization and extermination of their community.	475 Minutes 4 Episodes
1988	*War and Remembrance*	ABC (U.S.)	The trials of the Henry and the Jastrow families amidst the events after the U.S.'s entry into World War II.	1,620 Minutes 12 Episodes

Historically, these overtly commercial ventures liberated conversations about the Holocaust from whispers to mandatory education. These broadcast behemoths gave some Holocaust survivors enough courage to start documenting their stories. American Holocaust miniseries started a chain reaction that has been transformed into part of the

American soul. At the same time, Holocaust miniseries were so badly produced and so misguided that they also created a roadmap of how not to portray the Holocaust. Indeed, none of these Holocaust miniseries would be considered watchable by today's standards. Their depictions of generic Jews are laughable, verging on insulting. Today, those miniseries are merely a glimpse at a time-gone-by when nonspecific characters passed as Jews, a time when commercials ruled the airwaves, and a time when the Holocaust was taught as a parable, not as history. Yet, ironically, these three American Holocaust miniseries have been much more culturally impactful than all feature Holocaust films combined.

The early TV miniseries format included the enormously successful (all non–Holocaust) *Rich Man, Poor Man* (Miniseries 1976), *Roots* (Miniseries 1977) and *Shōgun* (Miniseries 1980). However, *QB VII* (Miniseries 1974) was the first. Based on Leon Uris' 1970 hit novel of the same name, *QB VII* was the first miniseries and, obviously by extension, the first Holocaust miniseries. *QB VII* was also the first American Holocaust television production of any kind (save a lost 1967 television production of Anne Frank).* The 6½ hour *QB VII* starred Ben Gazzara and Anthony Hopkins, 17 years before Hopkins' immortal role as "Dr. Hannibal Lecter" in *The Silence of the Lambs* (1991). In *QB VII*, Hopkins starkly portrayed a German doctor who was revealed as having conducted medical experiments on Jews during the War. But watching *QB VII* today, the first miniseries, is like looking at an old car that was purportedly hot in its day, but is no longer either roadworthy or glamorous.

Four years after *QB VII*, NBC's *Holocaust* (Miniseries 1978) became the most influential Holocaust production in history, with one out of every two Americans and one in three West Germans tuning in.[33] After the airing of the four-part *Holocaust* miniseries, Holocaust survivors felt empowered to tell their stories, which opened the floodgates for Holocaust oral histories.[34] Tom Shales wrote in *The Washington Post* of *Holocaust* that it was "The most powerful drama ever seen on TV."[35] Notwithstanding Shales' review and the commercial and cultural significance of *Holocaust*, by today's standards *Holocaust* is an inartistic train wreck. Its eight-hour running time is six hours longer than necessary, with or without its somewhat happy ending. Moreover, the commercial success of the miniseries set an unimaginably low bar for Holocaust television production.

Even so, attacking the first major Holocaust television productions today is akin to ridiculing the laughable special effects in *Star Wars* (1977). In fact, the earliest film recommended in this book that portrays the full scope of the Holocaust—from Nazification through liberation—is *For Those I Loved—Au nom de tous les miens* (1983), which was more than 140 films deep chronologically into Holocaust film production. So, to be fair, by 1978 the production standards of *Holocaust* were simply middling. Indeed, there was nothing nefarious about *Holocaust*. As was pointed out in a retrospective 35 years later, "*Holocaust* informed a rather uninformed public about the central events of the Holocaust and established it as a discrete and Jewish event."[36] †

Ten years after *Holocaust*, *War and Remembrance* (Miniseries 1988) was aired on

---

* Certainly, had the miniseries format been available, Leon Uris' other, more famous book, 1959's *Exodus*, would have been a miniseries instead of Otto Preminger's 3½ hour movie marathon. Ironically, the third of Uris' Holocaust-related books, 1961's *Mila 18*, was slated for production by Harvey Weinstein just a month before his #MeToo demise (Spiro, Amy, August 9, 2017, "Harvey Weinstein to Adapt 'Mila 18' as Film: Hollywood producer has long dreamed of tackling tale [*sic*] of Warsaw Ghetto uprising." *The Jerusalem Post*. https://www.jpost.com/Diaspora/Harvey-Weinstein-to-adapt-Mila-18-as-film-501992).

† For more about the making of *Holocaust* (Miniseries 1978) and its impact, especially in Germany, see Alice Agneskirchner's *How the Holocaust came on TV—Wie Holocaust ins Fernsehen kam* (2019).

ABC, and was anything but "mini." *War and Remembrance* was *Holocaust* on steroids. I have a pedagogical card trick where I ask a child to pick a card and I ask if the child thinks I can figure out what card they are holding. I proceed to make four piles of cards— ace through king by suit. Within about 10 seconds, the child will catch on that I am simply eliminating 51 cards. Dan Curtis' 12-part, 27-hour miniseries *War and Remembrance* was like that card trick; in 27 hours, it is no great feat to portray anything. So, artistically and educationally, economically presenting a three-hour story in 27 hours is less of an accomplishment than a fiasco. As Hedmar Stefan noted in the article "*War and Remembrance*: The Last of the Elephants" in *ThrillMeSoftly.com*, "Watching *War and Remembrance* now is an almost curious experience; made on a budget exceeding $100 million, you can virtually see where all the money went, as we're swiftly taken from battles in the Pacific to swank locations in Europe to concentration camps in Poland."[37] Nonetheless, few portrayals of the War and the entire killing process are more detailed than in *War and Remembrance*. It was one of the harshest Holocaust depictions. Yet, while there is no question that many aspects of Auschwitz had never been reproduced before *War and Remembrance*, it hardly matters if no one will ever binge-watch it because *War and Remembrance* feels as long as the War itself.

Another miniseries, as noted above, is the 10-part *Band of Brothers* (Miniseries 2001), which was executive-produced by Steven Spielberg and Tom Hanks, and is rated by IMDb users as the second greatest television show ever produced.* *Band of Brothers* is exemplary of the categorizing dilemma for Holocaust film and television. While this ten-hour miniseries alludes to the Holocaust with its Jewish characters, *Band of Brothers* dedicates only 20 minutes of its ten hours of screen time specifically to the Holocaust, when American soldiers liberate a Dachau sub-camp (Kaufering IV), this in the ninth episode, "Why We Fight." Granted, those 20 minutes are much better produced than anything in the previously discussed three miniseries. Yet, those looking to *Band of Brothers* as a Holocaust film must wade through most of World War II to find it. On the other hand, when teaching the Holocaust using clips or portions of productions, *Band of Brothers* "Why We Fight" is a viable candidate.

Overall, like dinosaurs, Holocaust miniseries collapsed under their own weight. While the miniseries genre continues to be a mainstay of today's television production, Holocaust miniseries ended in 1988 concurrently with the outcry engendered by ABC's brutal *War and Remembrance*.

---

* The top 25 rated television programs in *IMDb* are: 1. *Planet Earth II* (TV 2016); 2. *Band of Brothers* (TV 2001); 3. *Game of Thrones* (TV 2011); 4. *Planet Earth* (TV 2006); 5. *Breaking Bad* (TV 2008); 6. *The Wire* (TV 2002); 7. *Cosmos* (TV 2014); 8. *Blue Planet II* (TV 2017); 9. *Rick and Morty* (TV 2013); 10. *Cosmos* (TV 1980); 11. *The Sopranos* (TV 1999); 12. *The World at War* (TV 1973); 13. *Avatar: The Last Airbender* (TV 2003); 14. *Life* (TV 2009); 15. *Sherlock* (TV 2010); 16. *The Vietnam War* (TV 2017); 17. *The Twilight Zone* (TV 1959); 18. *Human Planet* (TV 2011); 19. *Dekalog* (TV 1989); 20. *The American Civil War* (TV 1990); 21. *Firefly* (TV 2002); 22. *Fullmetal Alchemist: Brotherhood* (TV 2009); 23. *True Detective* (TV 2014); 24. *Fargo* (TV 2014); 25. *Batman: The Animated Series* (TV 1992). https://www.*IMDb*.com/chart/toptv?ref_=tt_awd

2

Stats and Eras

Holocaust Film Stats

In the 75 years from 1945 through 2019, approximately 443 Holocaust films have been produced worldwide for theatrical, video and televised release. (See Graph 1.)

On average, since 1945 one Holocaust film has been released every two months, or six per year. No Holocaust films were released in 1952, 1954 and 1957. Roughly 82 percent of Holocaust films (361) were intended for theatrical release; 82 (18 percent) were made-for-television. (See Graph 2.)

Because Holocaust films are often conflated with World War II films, it is natural to assume that Holocaust and World War II film production have been related. More than one thousand post–War titles are listed on IMDb when searching with the "World War II" keyword. Interestingly, over half of these films were made within 25 years of the War, through 1969. (See Graph 3.)

Although the reasons for reduced World War II film production at the end of the 1960s are beyond the scope of this book, it appears that the World War II film production dive coincided with the anti–Vietnam War movement, and production only started to rise again with the upsurge of American patriotism after 9/11. On the other hand, while most World War II films were made before the 1970s, Holocaust film production spiked during the late 1990s when Holocaust film production started to rival World War II film production. So, while the natural assumption is that these two categories of film are linked, at the very least, there is no positive correlation between them and, more importantly, Holocaust film production and World War II film production should not be confused.

By running time, a positive correlation of 0.19 exists between the length of Holocaust films and their IMDb rating. In simpler terms, without positing causation, longer Holocaust films are more highly rated than shorter Holocaust films. By genre, as seen in Table 4, Survivor films are the shortest, the running time outlier.

TABLE 4: AVERAGE LENGTH OF HOLOCAUST FEATURE FILMS BY GENRE

Genre	Average Length (Minutes)
Victim	108
Gentile	110
Survivor	100
Perpetrator	110
Tangential	109

Holocaust Productions: Annual Worldwide Total
The First 75 Years (1945 through 2019)

— 5 per. Mov. Avg. (Total)

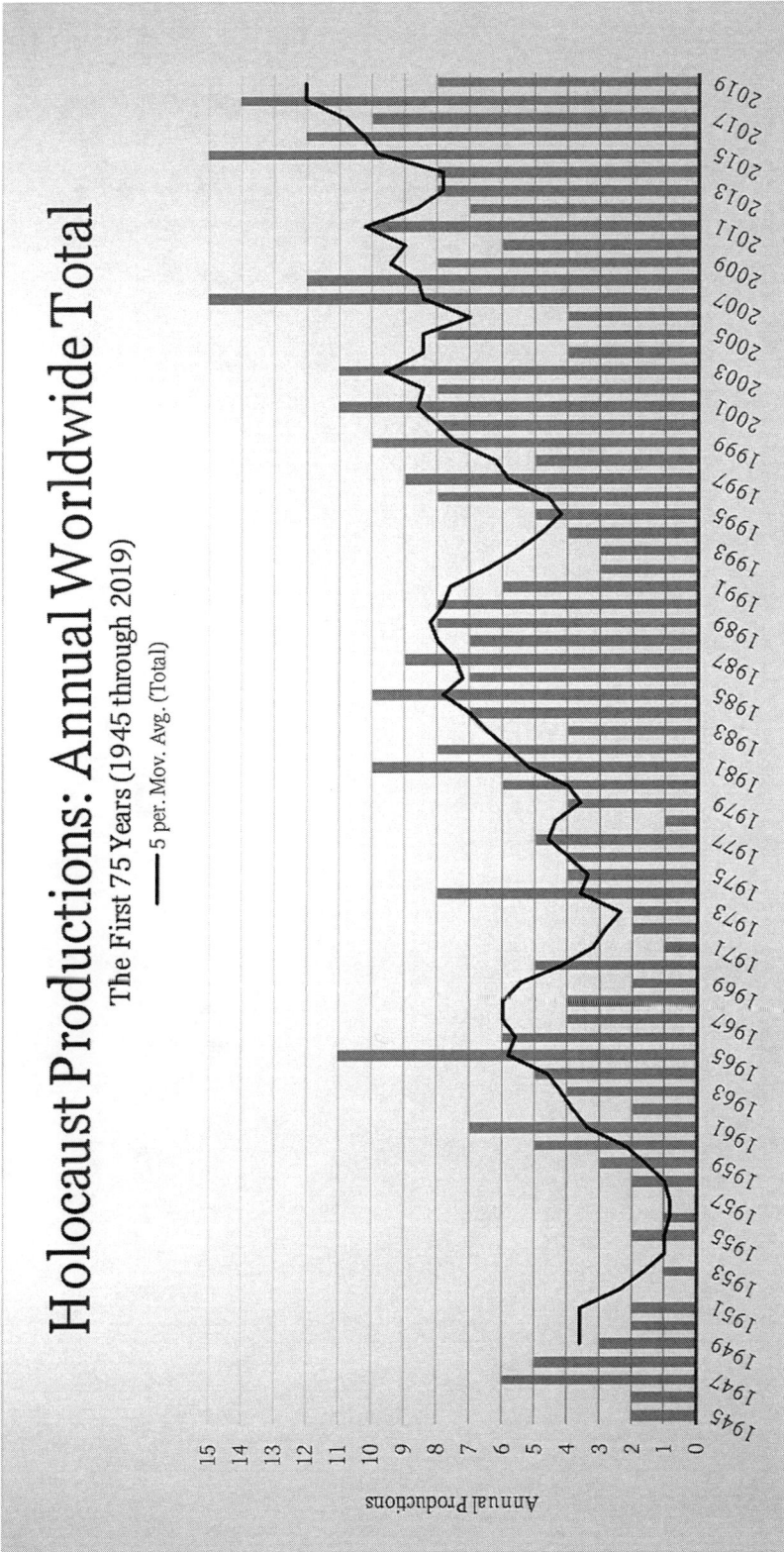

Graph 1: Holocaust Film and Television Productions by Year

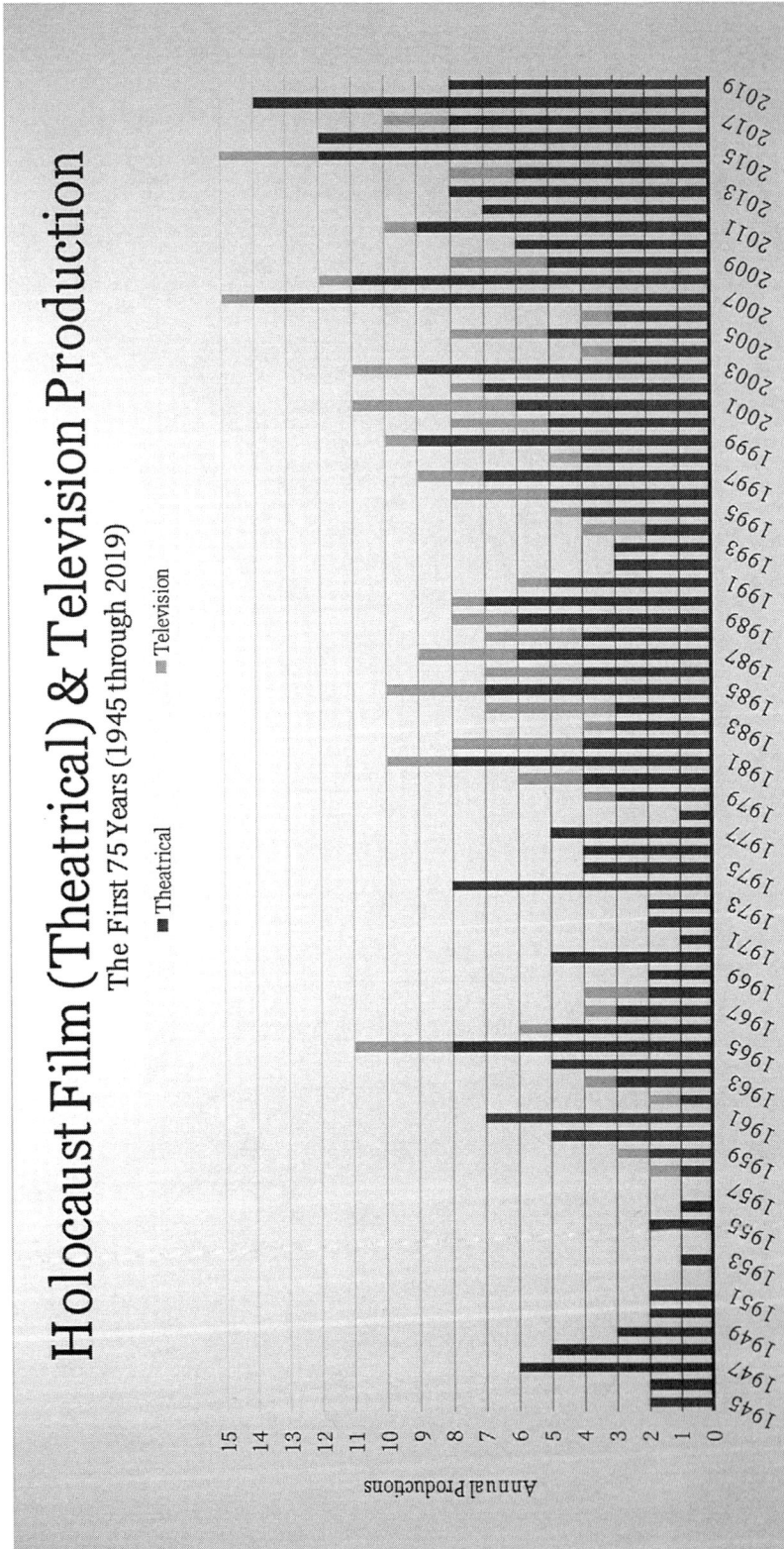

Graph 2: Theatrical vs. Television Holocaust Film Productions by Year

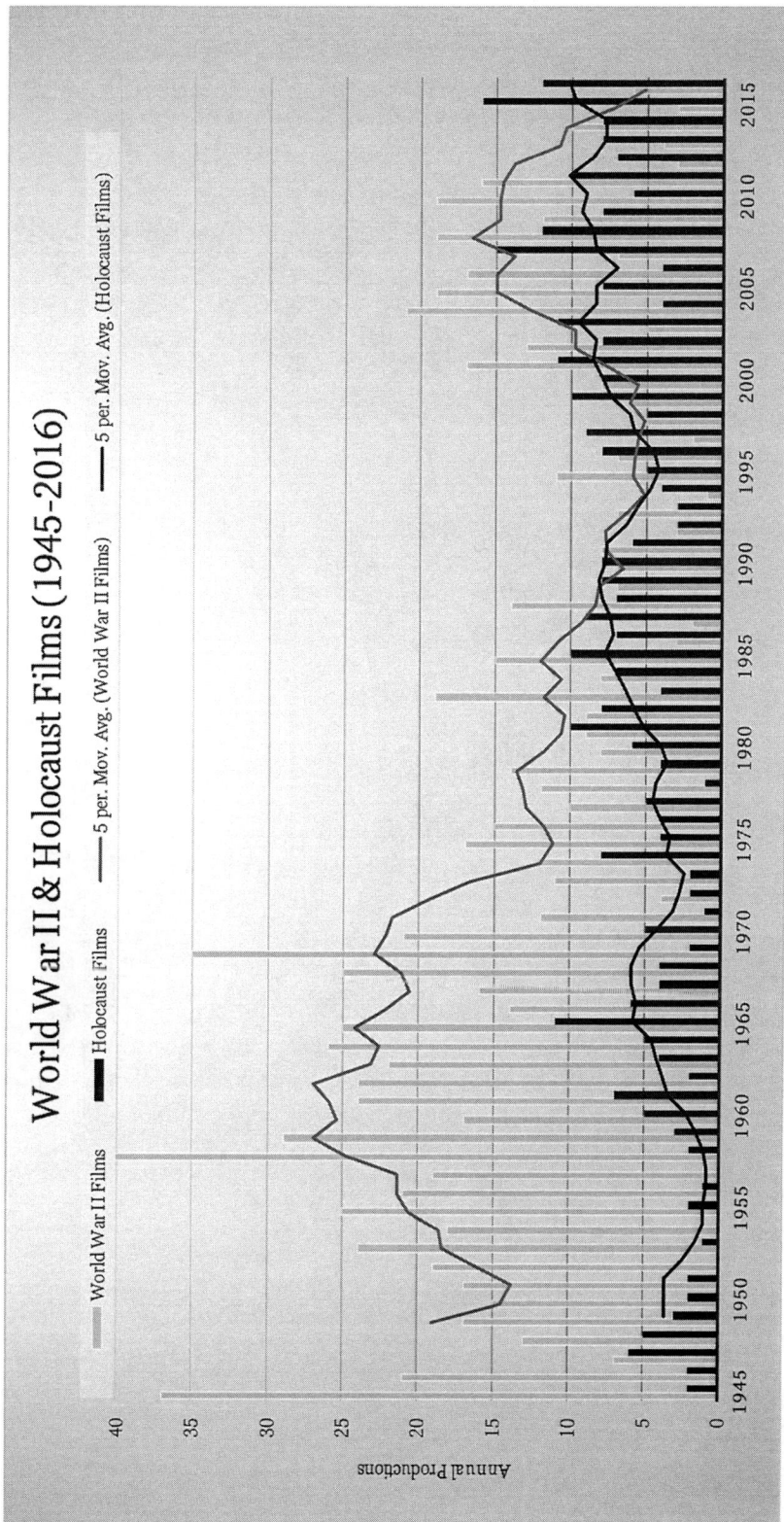

Graph 3: Narrative World War II and Narrative Holocaust Films

Oscar nominations for American-produced Holocaust films also positively correlate with running time, 0.42. In fact, the nine longest of 75 American-produced Holocaust feature films account for 59 of 109 total Holocaust film Oscar nominations. (See Table 5.) Of those, only Billy Graham's attempt to co-opt the Holocaust for evangelical purposes, *The Hiding Place* (1975), failed to draw Oscar's attention.

TABLE 5: THE NINE LONGEST AMERICAN-PRODUCED HOLOCAUST FEATURE FILMS
Recommended in **Bold** (3 of 52). "One of the Best" in **Bold and Underlined** (2 of 15).

Title	Genre	Length	Oscar Winner	Oscar Nomination
Exodus (1960)	Tangential	208	Music (Adaptation Score)	Supporting Actor
Schindler's List (1993)	Gentile	195	Picture, Directing, Writer, Cinematography, Art Direction, Editing, Music (Adaptation Score)	Actor, Supporting Actor, Costume Design, Makeup, Sound
Judgment at Nuremberg (1961)	Perpetrator	179	Writer	Picture, Directing, Actor, Supporting Actor, Supporting Actress, Cinematography, Art Direction, Costume Design, Editing
The Diary of Anne Frank (1959)	Victim	170	Supporting Actress, Cinematography, Art Direction	Picture, Directing, Supporting Actor, Costume Design, Music (Adaptation Score)
Inglourious Basterds (2009)	Tangential	153	Supporting Actor	Picture, Directing, Writer, Cinematography, Editing, Sound
Sophie's Choice (1982)	Tangential	151	Actress	Writer, Cinematography, Costume Design, Music (Adaptation Score)
The Hiding Place (1975)	Gentile	150		
The Pianist (2002)	Victim	150	Directing, Actor, Writer	Picture, Cinematography, Costume Design, Editing
Ship of Fools (1965)	Tangential	149	Cinematography, Art Direction	Picture, Actor, Supporting Actor, Actress, Writer, Costume Design

IMDb attention is also a measure of success. Table 6 is a list of the 25 Holocaust feature films with the most IMDb user votes. As will be discussed in greater detail in subsequent chapters, a few of these films are, indeed, exceptional, while several are among the most objectionable of all Holocaust films, in premise and production. It should be noted, too, that the quantity of user votes is not necessarily interchangeable with user ratings. This is obvious when comparing the atrocious Tangential film *The Unborn* (2009), which received 45,763 votes and a rating of 4.8, with the superb *Sophie's Choice* (1982), which received 34,643 votes and a rating of 7.6.

TABLE 6: 25 HOLOCAUST FEATURE FILMS WITH THE MOST IMDb VOTES
Recommended in **Bold** (10 of 52). "One of the Best" in **Bold and Underlined** (4 of 15).

Title	Genre	Country	IMDb Rating	IMDb Votes
Inglourious Basterds (2009)	Tangential	U.S.	8.3	1,061,435
Schindler's List (1993)	Gentile	U.S.	8.9	1,026,681
The Pianist (2002)	Victim	U.S.	8.5	603,378
X-Men: First Class (2011)	Survivor	U.S.	7.7	586,020

Title	Genre	Country	IMDb Rating	IMDb Votes
Life Is Beautiful—La Vita è bella (1997)	Victim	Italy	8.6	518,795
X-Men (2000)	Survivor	U.S.	7.4	515,161
Jojo Rabbit (2019)	Gentile	U.S.	7.9	284,013
The Reader (2008)	Perpetrator	U.S.	7.6	211,305
The Boy in the Striped Pyjamas (2008)	Victim	U.S.—U.K.	7.8	160,268
Defiance (2008)	Victim	U.S.	7.3	127,214
Black Book—Zwartboek (2006)	Victim	U.K.—ND—GRM—BE—Myanmar	7.8	66,373
Freedom Writers (2007)	Tangential	U.S.	7.5	59,783
The Debt (2010)	Perpetrator	U.S.—U.K.	6.9	59,630
Judgment at Nuremberg (1961)	Perpetrator	U.S.	8.2	58,028
Everything Is Illuminated (2005)	Survivor	U.S.	7.5	54,110
Marathon Man (1976)	Perpetrator	U.S.	7.5	50,533
Shine (1996)	Survivor	Australia	7.7	47,314
Woman in Gold (2015)	Survivor	U.S.—U.K.	7.3	45,904
The Unborn (2009)	Tangential	U.S.	4.8	45,763
Ida (2013)	Survivor	Poland	7.4	43,090
Cabaret (1972)	Tangential	U.S.	7.8	41,673
The Counterfeiters—Die Fälscher (2007)	Victim	Austria—Germany	7.6	40,087
Son of Saul (2015)	Victim	Hungary	7.5	36,269
Harold and Maude (1971)	Survivor	U.S.	8.0	36,209
Sophie's Choice (1982)	Tangential	U.S.	7.6	34,643

But IMDb user ratings do provide a few tiles in the mosaic of understanding films. (Those who wished to rate a film on IMDb are already a statistically skewed population; their willingness to rate films, at the very least, is a meaningful subgroup of film watchers, which may imply other confounding variables.) Nonetheless, within that group, the ratings by IMDb users indicates a fairly large drop over time in average user ratings of Holocaust films. (See Graph 4.)

In other words, counterintuitively, older Holocaust films have better ratings than newer Holocaust films. *The Singing Forest* (2003), with an IMDb user rating of 1.8, and *Auschwitz* (2011), rated 3.2, are not the only stinkers on the chart, but are part of the trend. At least by this measure, it could be argued that the quality of Holocaust feature films has deteriorated. This surprising trend also flies in the face of those who believe that IMDb users are biased toward films made in their lifetimes and prefer more recent films.

Filmmakers relentlessly feed off successes. So it is not surprising that 52 Holocaust films depict just four Holocaust personalities: Anne Frank, Adolf Eichmann, Janusz Korczak and Josef Mengele. In fact, approximately one-third of Holocaust television productions portray these four people.* (See Table 7.)

---

* The remarkable history of Eichmann films is wonderfully detailed in Professor Martin Kramer's "The Truth of the Capture of Adolf Eichmann: Sixty years ago, the infamous Nazi official was abducted in Argentina and brought to Israel. What really happened, what did Hollywood make up, and why?" published in *Mosaic Magazine* (June 1, 2020). The resplendent rejoinder, also in *Mosaic*, is entitled "The Vital Task of Holocaust Memory: The need is great for accurate cinematic portrayals of not only Eichmann, his capture and his trial, but of the Holocaust itself," by Professor Walter Reich.

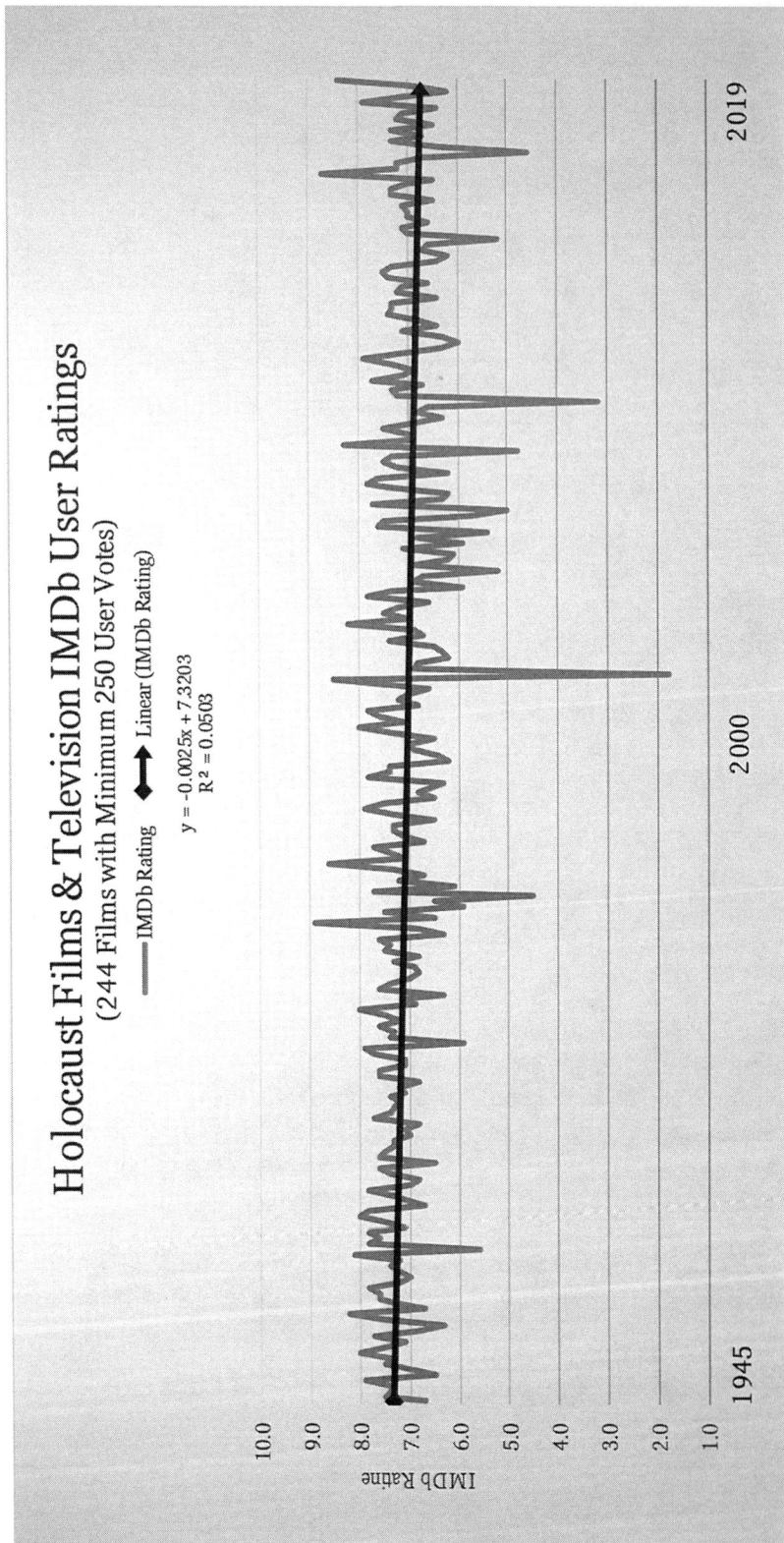

Holocaust Films & Television IMDb User Ratings
(244 Films with Minimum 250 User Votes)

— IMDb Rating   ◆ Linear (IMDb Rating)

$y = -0.0025x + 7.3203$
$R^2 = 0.0503$

Graph 4: Holocaust Film User Ratings by Year (206 Films with Minimum 250 Votes)

TABLE 7: RECURRING HOLOCAUST FILM CHARACTERS

Recommended in **Bold** (9 of 52). "One of the Best" in **Bold and Underlined** (3 of 15).
Unavailable in ~~Strikeout~~ (9).

Adolf Eichmann **(15)**	1961	*Operation Eichmann* (1961)
	1975	***The Man in the Glass Booth*** **(1975)**
	1977	*Death Is My Trade—Aus einem deutschen Leben* (1977)
	1979	*The House on Garibaldi Street* (TV 1979)
	1984	*The Final Solution: The Wannsee Conference—Die Wannseekonferenz* (TV 1984)
	1985	~~*Wallenberg—A Hero's Story* (TV 1985)~~
	1989	~~*Murderers Among Us: The Simon Wiesenthal Story* (TV 1989)~~
	1996	*The Man Who Captured Eichmann* (TV 1996)
	2001	***Conspiracy*** **(TV 2001)**
	2002	*Perlasca. The Courage of a Just Man—Perlasca. Un eroe italiano* (TV 2002)
	2004	*The Aryan Couple* (2004)
	2007	*Adolf Eichmann* (2007)
	2015	*The Eichmann Show* (TV 2015)
	2015	***The People vs. Fritz Bauer—Der Staat gegen Fritz Bauer*** **(2015)**
	2018	*Operation Finale* (2018)
Anne Frank **(19)**	1958	~~*The Diary of Anne Frank—Das Tagebuch Der Anne Frank* (TV 1958)~~
	1959	~~*The Diary of Anne Frank—Dnevnik Ane Frank* (TV 1959)~~
	1959	*The Diary of Anne Frank* (1959)
	1962	~~*The Diary of Anne Frank—Dagboek van Anne Frank* (TV 1962)~~
	1967	~~*The Diary of Anne Frank* (TV 1967)~~
	1980	*The Diary of Anne Frank* (TV 1980)
	1985	*The Diary of Anne Frank—Het dagboek van Anne Frank* (TV 1985)
	1987	~~*The Diary of Anne Frank* (TV 1987)~~
	1988	*The Attic: The Hiding of Anne Frank* (TV 1988)
	1995	*The Diary of Anne Frank—Anne no nikki* (1995)
	1996	~~*The Diary of Anne Frank—El diari d'Anna Frank* (TV 1996)~~
	1996	*Forget Me Not: The Anne Frank Story* (TV 1996)
	1999	*The Diary of Anne Frank—Le Journal d'Anne Frank* (1999)
	2001	***Anne Frank: The Whole Story*** **(TV 2001)**
	2007	*Freedom Writers* (2007)
	2009	*Memories of Anne Frank—Mi ricordo Anna Frank* (TV 2009)
	2009	*The Diary of Anne Frank—The Diary of Anne Frank* (TV 2009)
	2015	***My Daughter Anne Frank—Meine Tochter Anne Frank*** **(TV 2015)**
	2016	***The Diary of Anne Frank—Das Tagebuch Der Anne Frank*** **(2016)**
Janusz Korczak **(7)**	1974	~~*The Martyr—Dr. Korczak and His Children—Sie sind frei, Doktor Korczak* (1975)~~
	1982	*L'adieu aux enfants* **(TV 1982)**
	1983	***For Those I Loved—Au nom de tous les miens*** **(1983)**
	1990	***Korczak*** **(1990)**
	2001	*Uprising* (TV 2001)
	2009	*The Courageous Heart of Irena Sendler* (TV 2009)
	2017	*The Zookeeper's Wife* (2017)

	1974	*Remember Your Name—Pomni imya svoye* (1974)
	1978	*The Boys from Brazil* (1978)
	1980	*Playing for Time* (TV 1980)
	1999	*After the Truth—Nichts als die Wahrheit* (1999)
Josef Mengele	2001	***The Grey Zone* (2001)**
(11)	2002	*Gebürtig* (2002)
	2003	*Out of the Ashes* (TV 2003)
	2003	*Rua Alguem 5555: My Father* (2003)
	2009	*The Unborn* (2009)
	2013	*The German Doctor—Wakolda* (2013)
	2019	*The Angel of Auschwitz* (2019)

Final bits of statistical trivia concerns the actors and directors of Holocaust films. Over the past 75 years, the following actors have been among the top billed in at least two of the 443 Holocaust films:*

Jacqueline Bisset
Tatjana Blacher
Kenneth Branagh
Alex Brendemühl
Patrick Bruel
Daniel Brühl
Gedeon Burkhard
Montgomery Clift
Kaipu Cohen
Daniel Craig
Blythe Danner
Bruce Davison
Julie Delpy
Gérard Depardieu
August Diehl
Nina Dobrev
Kirk Douglas
Kirsten Dunst
Shimen Dzigan
Mia Farrow
Alexander Fehling
Tovah Feldshuh
Louise Fletcher
Brigitte Fossey
Bruno Ganz
Ben Gazzara
Erwin Geschonneck
John Gielgud
Hannah Taylor Gordon
Antonina Gordon-Górecka

Helmut Griem
Agnieszka Grochowska
Sylvester Groth
Ryszarda Hanin
Rosemary Harris
Rutger Hauer
William Hurt
Robert Joy
Danny Kaye
Marthe Keller
Sebastian Koch
Juliane Köhler
Jeroen Krabbé
Alice Krige
Mélanie Laurent
Michael Lonsdale
Elina Löwensohn
Mark Margolis
Karl Markovics
Erika Marozsán
James Mason
Ian McKellen
Helen Mirren
Jeanne Moreau
Ulrich Mühe
Marcell Nagy
Liam Neeson
Laurence Olivier
Sarah Jessica Parker
Gregory Peck

Wojciech Pszoniak
Charlotte Rampling
Lynn Redgrave
Vanessa Redgrave
Isabella Rossellini
Geoffrey Rush
Eva Marie Saint
Susan Sarandon
Roy Scheider
Maria Schrader
Liev Schreiber
David Schwimmer
Hanna Schygulla
Rade Serbedzija
Simone Signoret
Leelee Sobieski
Rod Steiger
Loretta Swit
Max von Sydow
Ysrael Szumacher
Noah Taylor
R.H. Thomson
Chaim Topol
Jon Voight
Christoph Waltz
Rachel Weisz
Orson Welles
Tom Wilkinson
Michael York
Ronald Zehrfeld

Several other actors have been among the top-billed in at least three Holocaust films: Willem Dafoe, Ralph Fiennes, Lukas Haas, Joachim Król, Martin Landau, Sophia Loren, Antony Sher, Stellan Skarsgård and Ulrich Tukur. The following actors have

---

* The list is not exhaustive. Although most names were caught, the core of this list is based on top-billed actors. Thus, others who were farther down the list have fallen through the cracks.

appeared in at least four Holocaust films: Alan Arkin, Martin Brandt, Allan Corduner, Evgenia Dodina, Harvey Keitel, Ben Kingsley, Thomas Kretschmann, Christopher Plummer and Rade Serbedzija. Gila Almagor, "the queen of Israeli cinema," has also acted in at least six Holocaust films as well as written two, which were both autobiographical. And then there are the Michael Jordan and Lebron James of Holocaust films: Armin Mueller-Stahl (8) and Maximilian Schell (9). Mueller-Stahl was Oscar-nominated for his role in *Shine* (1996), while Schell won the Best Actor Oscar for *Judgment at Nuremberg* (1961) and was nominated for *The Man in the Glass Booth* (1975) and *Julia* (1977). Twenty-four directors have made two Holocaust films. Six directors have made three Holocaust films. Polish director Andrzej Wajda has directed four Holocaust films, but is known for his Best Foreign Language nominee *Katyń* (2007), about the Soviet slaughter of Polish POWs. (Wajda was also awarded an Honorary Oscar in 2000 "For five decades of extraordinary film direction."[1]) Together, these directors account for 70 Holocaust films, or 16 percent of all Holocaust films. (See Table 8.)

TABLE 8: DIRECTORS OF MULTIPLE HOLOCAUST FILMS
Recommended in **Bold** (6 of 52). "One of the Best" in **Bold and Underlined** (1 of 15).

Andrzej Wajda (4) (1926–2016)	*Holy Week—Wielki tydzien* (1995)
	Korczak **(1990)**
	Landscape After Battle—Krajobraz po bitwie (1970)
	Samson (1961)
Eli Cohen (3) (born 1940)	**The Quarrel (1991)**
	The Summer of Aviya—Ha-Kayitz Shel Aviya (1988)
	Under the Domim Tree—Etz Hadomim Tafus (1994)
Axel Corti (3) (1933–1993)	*A Woman's Pale Blue Handwriting—Eine blaßblaue Frauenschrift* (TV 1984)
	Where to and Back—Part 1: God Doesn't Believe in Us—Ferry or How It Was—Wohin und zurück—Teil 1: An uns glaubt Gott nicht mehr—Ferry oder Wie es war (TV 1982)
	Wohin und zurück—Santa Fe (1986)
Agnieszka Holland (3) (born 1948)	*Angry Harvest—Bittere Ernte* (1985)
	Europa Europa (1990)
	In Darkness (2011)
Wanda Jakubowska (3) (1907–1998)	*Invitation—Zaproszenie* (1986)
	The End of Our World—Koniec naszego swiata (1964)
	The Last Stage—The Last Stop—Ostatni etap (1948)
Moshé Mizrahi (3) (1931–2018)	*The Customer of the Off Season—Ore'ach B'Onah Metah* (1970)
	A Life Ahead—Madam Rose—Madame Rosa—La Vie devant soi (1977)
	War and Love (1985)
Michael Verhoeven (3) (born 1938)	*My Mother's Courage—Mutters Courage* (1995)
	The Nasty Girl—Das schreckliche Mädchen (1990)
	Let's Go! (TV 2014)
Uri Barbash (2) (born 1946)	*Kapo in Jerusalem—Kapo be'Yerushalaim* (2015)
	Spring 1941 (2007)
Frank Beyer (2) (1932–2006)	*Jacob the Liar—Jakob, der Lügner* (1974)
	Naked Among Wolves—Nackt unter Wölfen (1963)
Milan Cieslar (2) (born 1960)	*Colette* (2013)
	Spring of Life—Pramen zivota (TV 2000)

Terry Lee Coker (2) (Unknown)	*The Guard of Auschwitz* (2018)
	The Angel of Auschwitz (2019)
Costa-Gavras (2) (born 1933)	*Amen.* (2002)
	Music Box (1989)
Natan Gross (2) (1919–2005)	*It Will Never Happen Again—Unzere Kinder* (1951)
	The Cellar—Ha-Martef (1963)
Vittorio De Sica (2) (1901–1974))	*The Condemned of Altona—I sequestrati di Altona* (1962)
	The Garden of the Finzi-Continis—Il Giardino dei Finzi-Contini (1970)
Zoltán Fábri (2) (1917–1994)	*Darkness in Daytime—Nappali sötétség* (1963)
	Late Season—Utószezon (1967)
Karel Kachyna (2) (1924–2004)	*Forbidden Dreams—Death of the Beautiful Robucks—Smrt krásných srncu* (1987)
	The Last Butterfly—Poslední motýl (1991)
Aleksander Ford (2) (1908–1980)	*Border Street—Ulica Graniczna* (1948)
	The Martyr—Dr. Korczak and His Children—Sie sind frei, Doktor Korczak (1975)
Roberta Grossman (2) (born 1959)	*Blessed Is the Match: The Life and Death of Hannah Senesh* (2008)
	Who Will Write Our History (2018)
András Kovács (2) (1925–2017)	*Cold Days—Hideg napok* (1966)
	Temporary Paradise—Ideiglenes paradicsom (1981)
Jeroen Krabbé (2) (born 1944)	*Het dagboek van Anne Frank* (TV 1985) (Co-Directed)
	Left Luggage (1998)
Stanley Kramer (2) (1913–2001)	*Judgment at Nuremberg* (1961)
	Ship of Fools (1965)
Joseph Lejtes (1901–1983)	*My Father's House—Beit Avi* (1947) (Co-Directed)
	The Great Promise—Dim'at Ha'Nehamah Ha'Gedolah (1947)
Claude Lelouch (2) (born 1937)	*Bolero Dance of Life—Les uns et les autres* (1981)
	Les Misérables (1995)
Caroline Link (2) (born 1964)	*Nowhere in Africa—Nirgendwo in Afrika* (2001)
	When Hitler Stole Pink Rabbit—Als Hitler das rosa Kaninchen stahl (2019)
Louis Malle (2) (1932–1995)	***Au Revoir les Enfants (1987)***
	Lacombe, Lucien (1974)
Daniel Mann (2) (1912–1991)	*Judith* (1966)
	Playing for Time (TV 1980)
Alberto Negrin (2) (born 1940)	*Memories of Anne Frank—Mi ricordo Anna Frank* (TV 2009)
	Perlasca. The Courage of a Just Man—Perlasca. Un eroe italiano (TV 2002)
Joseph Sargent (2) (1925–2014)	*Never Forget* (TV 1991)
	Out of the Ashes (TV 2003)
Bryan Singer (2) (born 1965)	*Apt Pupil* (1998)
	X-Men (2000)
Konrad Wolf (2) (1925–1982)	*Stars—Sterne* (1959)
	Professor Mamlock (1961)
Fred Zinnemann (2) (1907–1997)	*Julia* (1977)
	The Search (1948)

Of note, Liev Schreiber, television's "Ray Donovan," has acted in two Holocaust films, as well as having written and directed (but not appearing in) the fine Survivor film *Everything Is Illuminated* (2005). Jeroen Krabbé, who co-directed *The Diary of*

Anne Frank—Het dagboek van Anne Frank (TV 1985) and directed *Left Luggage* (1998), co-starred in both. Polish director Agnieszka Holland, who directed three Holocaust feature films, also wrote the recommended *Korczak* (1990). Israeli Eli Cohen is the only director to have made a pair of recommended Holocaust films: *The Quarrel* (1991) and *Under the Domim Tree—Etz Hadomim Tafus* (1994). Cohen also acted in several, even some that he did not direct. Three Holocaust films were based on the novels of Romain Gary (né Roman Kacew) (1914–1980). Abby Mann (né Abraham Goodman) (1927–2008) wrote four Holocaust films, including Stanley Kramer's Oscar-winning *Judgment at Nuremberg* (1961) and Best Picture nominee *Ship of Fools* (1965), as well as the rightfully obscure *War and Love* (1985) and *Murderers Among Us: The Simon Wiesenthal Story* (TV 1989).

And then there is Holocaust film producer Artur "Atze" Brauner (1918–2019) a.k.a. Art Bernd (né Abraham Brauner). Brauner was born in Łódź, Poland, but fled with his family to the USSR where they survived the War. The Yad Vashem Visual Center lists 29 films either produced by or about Brauner. IMDb lists Brauner as the producer of an astounding 316 films, from 1946 through 2018, in addition to his 34 writing credits. Thirteen Holocaust films listed in this book were produced or co-produced and/or written by Brauner, including (co-)producing the Best Foreign Language Oscar winner *The Garden of the Finzi-Continis—Il Giardino dei Finzi-Contini* (1970).

Four Eras of Holocaust Film

Although the Holocaust film 4+1 genre system is the underpinning of Holocaust film analysis here, chronology is also a significant lens. And classifying art forms by periods has been a mainstay of art analysis. For example, general film historians have attempted to classify film production into eras, with some connoisseurs suggesting that the "Golden Age" of film was the first 20 years after sound was introduced, roughly 1927 to 1947. Other historians bypass such arbitrary labels as mere Hollywood marketing tools, in lieu of descriptive titles for the various periods, such as "silent," "sound," "color," "television" and "blockbuster." One expert suggests that film production breaks down into the following eras:

- 1895 to 1910—The Pioneer Era
- 1911 to 1926—The Silent Era
- 1927 to 1940—Talkies and the rise of the Hollywood studios
- 1941 to 1954—Golden Era of Film and restructuring of Hollywood
- 1955 to 1976—Changes
- 1977 to late 1990s—Dawn of modern film industry and appearance of Blockbusters
- 2000 to present—New millennium—Modern film industry[2]

Although outside the purview here, even a cursory review of total film production from 1941 to 1954, including total annual box office—adjusted or otherwise—indicates that the only thing golden about the "Golden Age" of cinema was Hollywood's studio heads' hegemony over labor, film production and international distribution. Creatively and monetarily, the late 1960s through the early 1980s was vastly more golden than was film production during World War II through the mid–1950s. Assigning a subjective term such as "Golden" to an amorphous set of years does little to further the understanding of cinematic history.

The distillation of Holocaust films into eras is more straightforward and less American-centric than traditional film histories. Holocaust films break into four eras based on Holocaust documentation, production density and intended media. The labels used here for Holocaust film production eras are somewhat nuanced, not simply labeled by the years they represent. The eras and their names, as laid out below, also imply the development of the art form: Post-War, Commercial, Mature and Consolidated. (See Table 9.)

TABLE 9: HOLOCAUST FILM ERA CUMULATIVE PRODUCTION

Era	Period	Number of Years	Holocaust Films	Films per Year
Post-War Era	1945–1973	28	91	3.3
Commercial Era	1974–1996	23	138	6.0
Mature Era	1997–2013	17	145	8.5
Consolidated Era	2014–2019	6	69	11.3

The Post-War Era (91 Films)

The first 28 years of Holocaust film production, 1945–1973, were the "Post-War Era," accounting for the first 91 Holocaust films, or approximately 3.3 films annually. These productions coincided with the first attempts at scholarly documentation of the Holocaust. During the Post-War Era, four countries produced made-for-television Anne Frank attic films, all based on the standard Goodrich and Hackett script (which was also used for the 1959 American feature film): East Germany in 1958, Yugoslavia in 1959, Netherlands in 1962 and the U.S. in 1967. Features accounted for 47 Post-War Era Holocaust films, which earned an aggregate of 52 Oscar nominations resulting in 19 Oscars.

Several Post-War Era Holocaust films were shot in post–War German ruins, including *Murderers Among Us—Die Mörder sind unter uns* (1946), *The Stranger* (1946) and *Judgment at Nuremberg* (1961). Four Polish films were shot partially at Auschwitz/Birkenau: *The Last Stage—The Last Stop—Ostatni etap* (1948), *Passenger—Pasazerka* (TV 1963), *The End of Our World—Koniec naszego swiata* (1964), as well as the non–Holocaust *A Trip to the Unknown—Wycieczka w nieznane* (1968). Over 40 percent of the Post-War Era Holocaust Films (38) were produced by Soviet or Eastern Bloc countries.

At least ten other films were produced that touched on the Holocaust or Auschwitz/Birkenau, but lacked enough Holocaust content to be considered Holocaust films. The aforementioned Polish film *A Trip to the Unknown—Wycieczka w nieznane* (1968) is a prime example. It portrayed a non–Jewish, Polish writer who goes to Auschwitz/Birkenau to find himself emotionally. While there, while on the Auschwitz museum tour, the protagonist actually, unabashedly and repeatedly tries to pick up a nubile tourist. The best that can be said of *A Trip to the Unknown* is that it was never reprised.

Three Post-War Era films were big stories featuring considerable Hollywood firepower, including Marlon Brando, Dean Martin, Spencer Tracy, Burt Lancaster, Richard Widmark, Marlene Dietrich, Maximilian Schell (twice), Judy Garland, Montgomery Clift (twice), William Shatner, Werner Klemperer, Paul Newman, Eva Marie Saint, Peter Lawford and Lee J. Cobb. None of the Western Post-War Era Holocaust films tried to depict the full scope of a German camp, although Sidney Lumet's *The Pawnbroker* (1964) is peppered with passing repressed memories (flashbacks) from a nondescript camp.

From the Post-War Era came the prototypical Perpetrator film formula, which

Holocaust Film Production: Post-War Era

1945 through 1973

■ Theatrical ■ TV

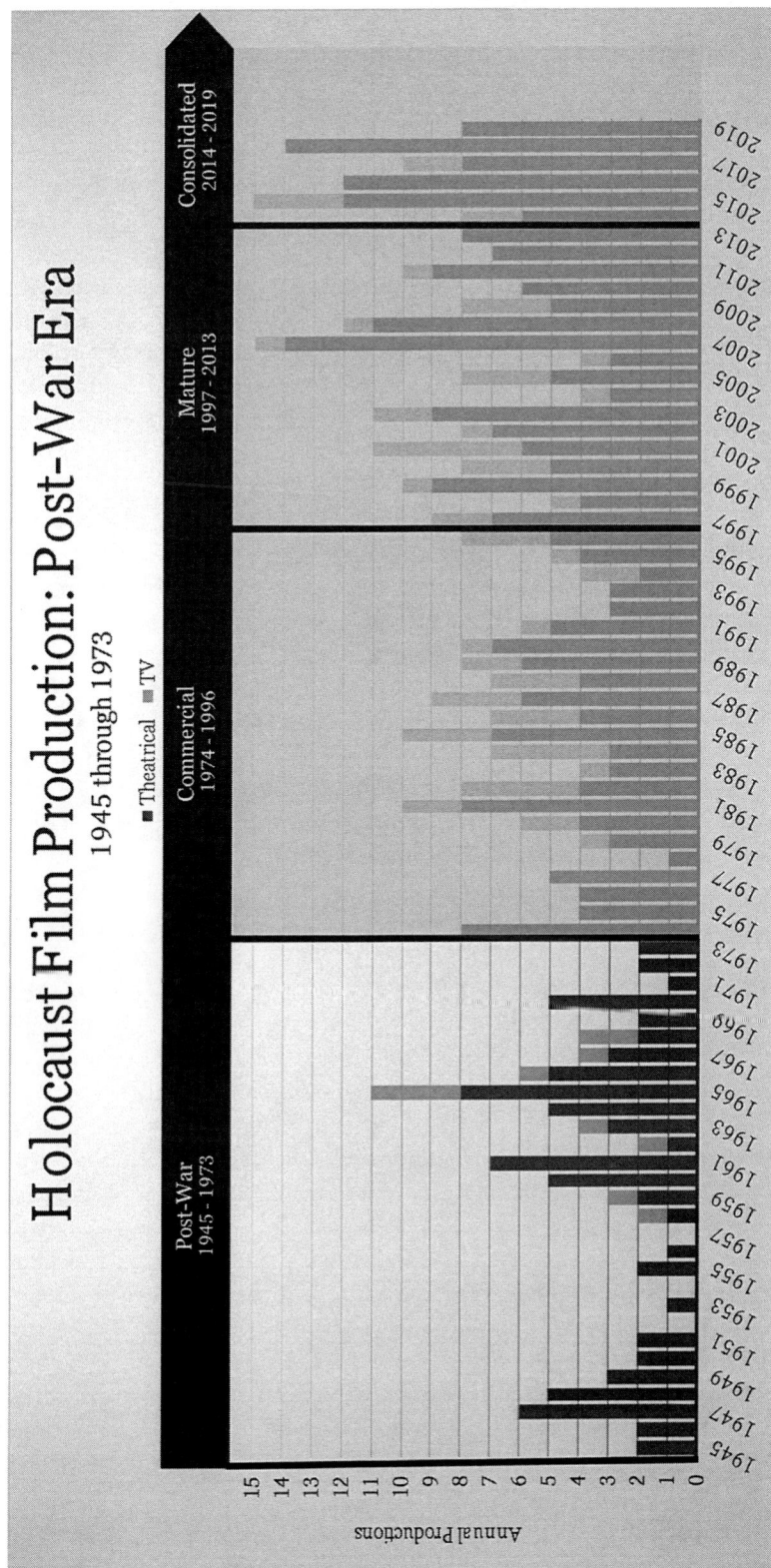

Graph 5: Holocaust Film Production Eras (The Post-War Era: 1945–1973)

has not changed since Orson Welles' *The Stranger* (1946). Fred Zinnemann's *The Search* (1948) was the first Survivor film, and Ralph Thomas' *Conspiracy of Hearts* (1960) was the first righteous Gentile film. At the end of the Post-War Era came one of the greatest films of any kind ever made, Hal Ashby's *Harold and Maude* (1971), the subtlest of all Survivor films. And in 1965 Stanley Kramer made the sardonic *Ship of Fools*, a Tangential Holocaust film that mocked the pre–War German Jewish community's suicidal patriotism toward the Fatherland. The great *Ship of Fools* was nominated for the Best Picture Oscar, but lost to Robert Wise's perpetually overrated non–Holocaust *The Sound of Music*.

Three of the greatest European Holocaust films were consecutively released during the Post-War Era in the mid–1960s: Czechoslovakian *The Shop on Main Street—Obchod na korze* (1965), French *The Two of Us—Le vieil homme et l'enfant* (1967) and Italian *The Garden of the Finzi-Continis—Il Giardino dei Finzi-Contini* (1970). The final film of the Post-War Era starred Judy Garland's daughter, Best Actress winner Liza Minnelli in Bob Fosse's Tangential Holocaust film *Cabaret* (1972) winner of more Oscars (8) than any other Holocaust film ever made, and was nominated for two others.

And of course, smack dab in the middle of the Post-War Era was the most important Holocaust film of its generation, George Stevens' three-hour *The Diary of Anne Frank* (1959), winner of three Oscars and nominated for five others. With that reverence in mind, it also must be noted that the 1959 version of Anne Frank was inferior artistically to almost every other feature in the Post-War Era and, indeed, inferior to most later cinematic versions of Anne Frank. Regardless, the three-hour 1959 version was the first Western Victim film and stood alone for a generation as the benchmark of Holocaust filmmaking.

As expected, the Post-War Era was about baby-steps, especially in the West, which was still relatively clueless about the Holocaust. Films like *Judgment at Nuremberg* and *The Pawnbroker* established an invaluable footing for the Western Holocaust depictions of the next period: the "Commercial Era."

The Commercial Era (138 Films)

Holocaust television production marked the beginning of the "Commercial Era" of Holocaust film, which spanned 1974 through 1996 with 138 films. Annual Holocaust film production during The Commercial Era's 23 years increased to 6.0 releases per year. The Commercial Era saw the most experimentation and greatest variety of Holocaust films, including a few of the best and many of the worst Holocaust productions, practically bookended by the two most successful and influential Holocaust productions: *Holocaust* (Miniseries 1978) and *Schindler's List* (1993). A more accurate classification for most of the Commercial Era would be "adolescent," sometimes finding its voice and other times landing with the thud of a watermelon on pavement,* especially with American-produced or co-produced films, which accounted for a third of the Commercial Era Holocaust productions.

The Commercial Era also straddled the dissolution of the Soviet Union and the fall of Communism in most Soviet satellite countries. For example, during the Commercial Era, 22 Holocaust films were produced by West Germany, three by East Germany, and nine by post-unification (1990) Germany. *The Last Butterfly—Poslední motýl* (1991) which

---

* This phrase is attributable to Los Angeles Laker Kareem Abdul-Jabbar when recalling the sound when his teammate, Kermit Washington, punched the face of an opposing player, Rudy Tomjanovich, in a game time brawl, as quoted in David Halberstam's *The Breaks of the Game*, 1981, Knopf.

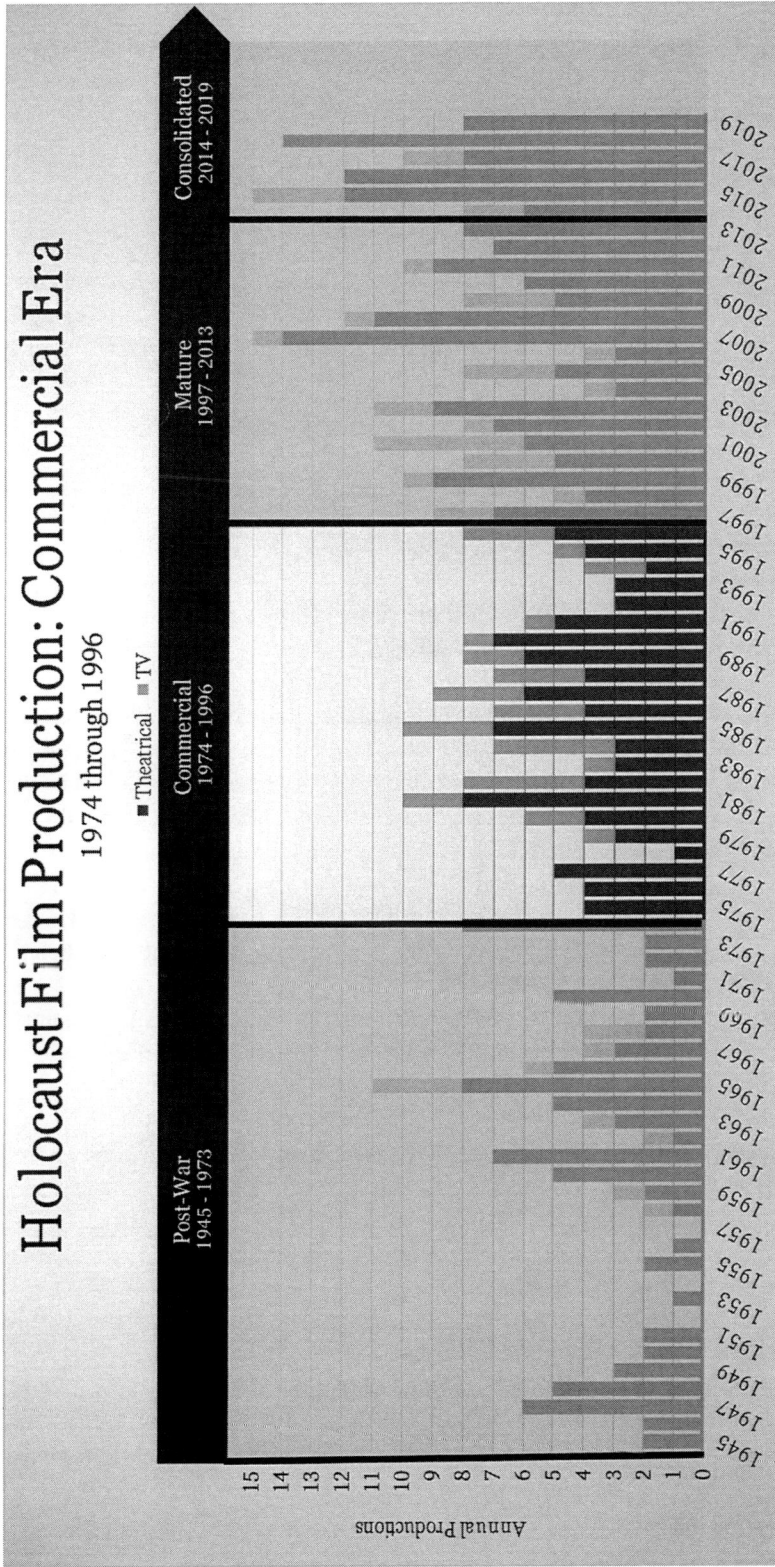

Graph 6: Holocaust Film Production by Year (The Commercial Era: 1974–1996)

was jointly produced by Czechoslovakia, France and the U.K., was released during the year of the Czechoslovakian "Velvet Revolution," but two years before Czechoslovakia split into the Czech Republic and Slovakia. So, too, the two Yugoslavian Holocaust films during this period were produced before Yugoslavia's breakup into the separate countries of Serbia, Montenegro, Kosovo, Slovenia, Bosnia & Herzegovina and (North) Macedonia, some of which subsequently produced Holocaust films.

The Commercial Era was marked by the first American Holocaust miniseries and made-for-television films, which, without exception, do not hold up by today's standards; 35 of the 138 Holocaust films made during the Commercial Era were made for television, plus three American miniseries. Five of these made-for-television films were about Anne Frank. Except for the outstanding German *Three Days in April—Drei Tage im April* (TV 1995), none of the first television efforts are anything other than examples of an obsolete form of production. More generally, to say that television production was playing catch-up with theatrical Holocaust films while trying to find their footing is a massive understatement. Yet, with few exceptions, most of these made-for-television Holocaust films included television commercials, which were inherently disruptive and certainly exacerbated the claim that the Holocaust was being commercialized.

On the other hand, the 103 Holocaust feature films produced were certainly an incremental improvement from the standards of the Post-War Era of Holocaust films, but did not keep pace with the startling improvement in general film production during the 1970s and 1980s. Seventy-eight feature films were made by non–American and non–British production companies, of which eight are recommended. Conspicuous exceptions included the Japanese animated *The Diary of Anne Frank—Anne no nikki* (1995) and the French *Bolero Dance of Life—Les uns et les autres* (1981). The British, too, were responsible for the ostentatiously cast and painfully produced *Voyage of the Damned* (1976). The German film about Rudolf Höss, *Death Is My Trade—Aus einem deutschen Leben* (1977), which shot a few scenes at Auschwitz was an improvement. But the Commercial Era's cheesy death camp representations started in earnest with *Holocaust* (Miniseries 1978).

Nineteen Commercial Era films were righteous Gentile, while six were antisemitic Gentile films. Twenty-six Survivor films were produced, mostly an upgrade over the Post-War Era's Survivor films. And Perpetrator films, too, came into their own, with 15 productions, including John Schlesinger's *Marathon Man* (1976).

But it was the 54 Victim films that were the most uneven, which included the time-travel film *Forget Me Not: The Anne Frank Story* (TV 1996), about a neo–Nazi who visits the Simon Wiesenthal Center Museum of Tolerance in Los Angeles with a spray-paint can and loads of malice. The young man was intent on vandalizing the exhibits, but, instead, was sent back in time by a curator to Anne Frank's attic to be saved by Anne Frank and her family. *Forget Me Not: The Anne Frank Story* necessitates bathing after watching.

Three of the most thoughtful and genuine Survivor films were released during the Commercial Era, all made by Israeli director Eli Cohen: *The Summer of Aviya—Ha-Kayitz Shel Aviya* (1988), *The Quarrel* (1991) and *Under the Domim Tree—Etz Hadomim Tafus* (1994). Also worthwhile was Paul Mazursky's Survivor film *Enemies: A Love Story* (1989), based on an Isaac Bashevis Singer novel. Less interesting, but more celebrated was Scott Hicks' Oscar-decorated *Shine* (1996), starring Best Actor Geoffrey Rush. Liliana Cavani's

Survivor film *The Night Porter—Il portiere di notte* (1974) and Arthur Hiller's *The Man in the Glass Booth* (1975) were crazy films about crazy survivors, which provided fodder for generations of aspiring critics. And Jack Smight's well-meaning Survivor film *Remembrance of Love* (TV 1982)—starring Kirk Douglas, *Hogan's Heroes'* Robert Clary and *Mork & Mindy* (TV 1978–1982) co-star Pam Dawber—was an utter catastrophe, in theme and production; Spartacus, LeBeau and Mindy looked more like Moe, Larry and Curly in this clumsy, unfortunate made-for-television production.

During the Commercial Era, 46 Oscar nominations were earned by Holocaust feature films, with 13 winners, including 11 nominations for Fred Zinnemann's *Julia* (1977), five nominations for Alan J. Pakula's *Sophie's Choice*, six nominations for Scott Hicks' *Shine* and 12 nominations for Steven Spielberg's *Schindler's List*. Eighty-three Emmy nominations were split between 29 American made-for-television films and three miniseries. That programming accounted for 5,600 minutes of airtime, or approximately one Emmy nomination for every 67 minutes of Holocaust programming.

Because of the influx of made-for-television Holocaust films, the Commercial Era was much more lucrative than was the Post-War Era. Between the most popular films (*Schindler's List* & *Sophie's Choice*) and the gargantuan miniseries (*QB VII, Holocaust* and *War and Remembrance*), the Commercial Era from 1974 through 1996 was also the most financially successful of all Holocaust film eras.

The Mature Era (145 Films)

When compared with the previous 50 years, annual Holocaust film production from 1997 through 2013, the Mature Era of Holocaust film production increased dramatically, from 4.5 to 8.6 Holocaust films per year. During the 17-year Mature Era, 145 Holocaust films were produced by 34 countries—including 41 co-productions—with one new Holocaust film released, on average, every six weeks. American and German companies produced or co-produced nearly half (74) of these films.

Holocaust film production during the Mature Era was driven partially by market demands and profit incentives, not primarily as altruistic attempts to add to Holocaust education or understanding. The multi-year film production pipeline together with *Schindler's List*'s success in 1993 might be linked to the massive annual production increase during the Mature Era, starting in 1997, the same year that *Life Is Beautiful* was released, pumping even more into the Holocaust film pipeline.

During the Mature Era, too, many of the most shamelessly horrible Holocaust films were made. Indeed, of the 145 films made from 1997 through 2013, approximately one quarter were distasteful, exploitative, or simply disgusting. These failures are epitomized by the following five films, with end-products that film schools could use to teach shoddy filmmaking. (See Table 10.)

TABLE 10: THE WORST HOLOCAUST FILMS OF THE MATURE ERA

Title	Genre	Country	Length	Director	Language	IMDb Rating
The Singing Forest (2003)	Tangential	U.S.	72	Jorge Ameer	English	1.8
Auschwitz (2011)	Victim	Germany	73	Uwe Boll	German	3.2
The Unborn (2009)	Tangential	U.S.	87	David S. Goyer	English	4.8
Death in Love (2008)	Survivor	U.S.	100	Boaz Yakin	English	5.0
The Poet—Hearts of War (2007)	Gentile	Canada	100	Damian Lee	English	5.2

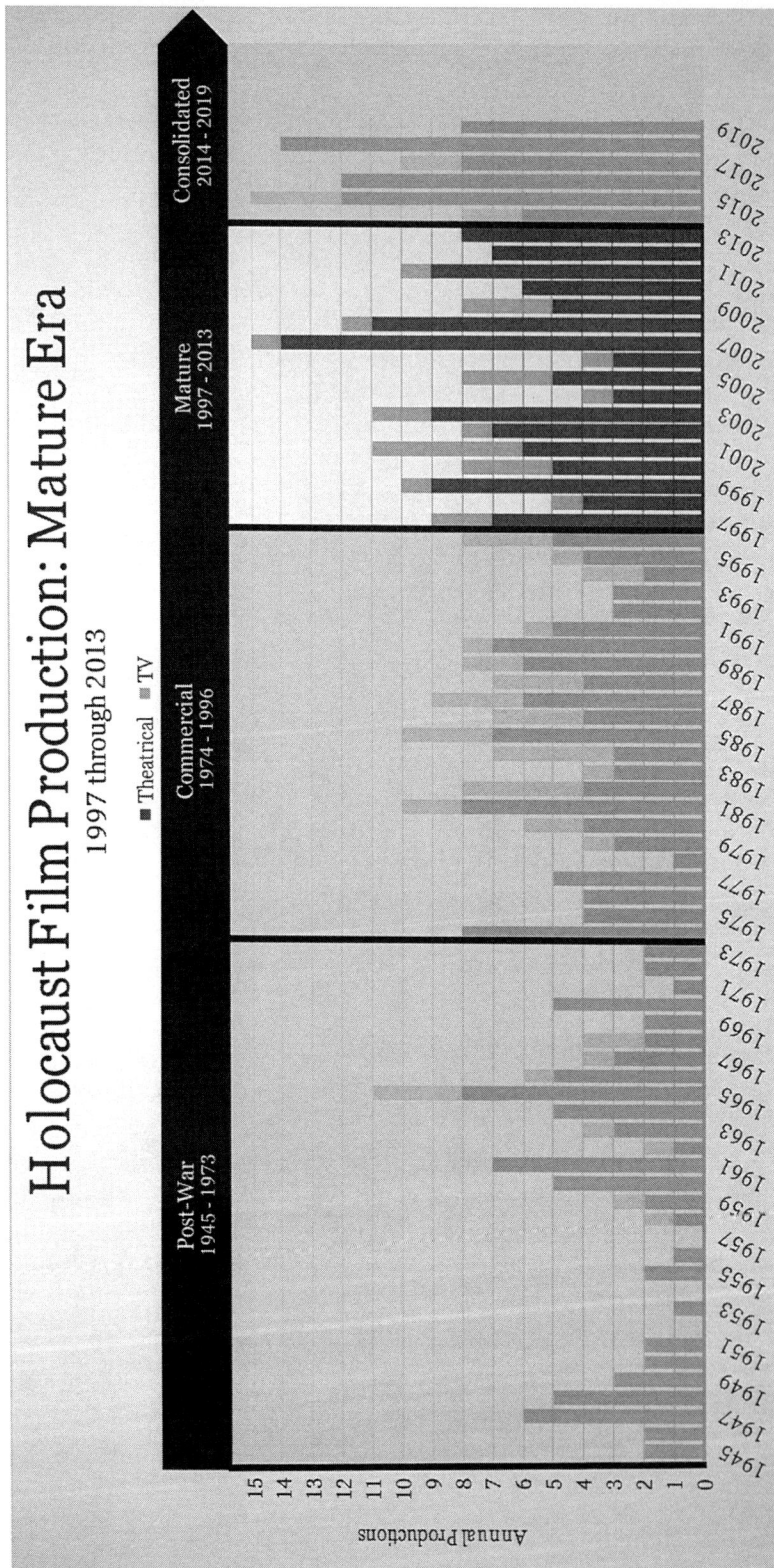

Graph 7: Holocaust Film Production by Year (The Mature Era: 1997–2013)

On the other end of the spectrum, 23 of the 52 best Holocaust films ever made came during the Mature Era, with 16 of these recommended films produced by non–American companies. Six of the best were made-for-television, considerably upgrading Holocaust television quality.

While normal distribution might account for the disparity between atrocious and extraordinary Holocaust films during those 17 years, it might be more accurate to suggest that the appalling films were simply trying to cash in on an ostensibly lucrative subject, while the great films from that period had learned the lessons of proper Holocaust portrayal over the previous 50 to 65 years. During this period, in the wake of *Schindler's List*, the three most realistic and sensitive death camp depictions were produced: *The Grey Zone* (2001), *Fateless—Sorstalanság* (2005) and *The Counterfeiters—Die Fälscher* (2007). Arguably, *Schindler's List* raised the bar for many filmmakers in terms of authenticity.

The 118 feature films produced during the Mature Era received 11 Oscars and 22 other Oscar nominations. Of those nominated films, 28 Oscars and nominations were lavished onto two regrettable films, *Life Is Beautiful—La Vita è bella* (1997) (7) and *The Reader* (2008) (5), and on two great films, *The Pianist* (2002) (7) and *Inglourious Basterds* (2009) (7). The rapid-fire release of Holocaust films during the Mature Era was extremely complicated, like the finale of an amateur fireworks show, with considerable anticipation, excitement and flashes, coupled with more than a few thuds and duds.

The Consolidated Era (69 Films)

The latest period of Holocaust film production, 2014 through 2019, is the "Consolidated Era." Holocaust releases have increased markedly to 69 during the full six years, to 11.3 films per year, with only eight made-for-television, none of which were made for American television.

During the Consolidated Era, 22 Holocaust films were German productions or co-productions, while only 11 were American-made. Few of the Consolidated Era films were poorly produced, although several were superfluous and had questionable stories. While four of the Consolidated Era films depict life in a German camp, for the most part, the other films of the period told smaller, more personal stories, as opposed to epic death camp spectacles. The exceptions were the Russian remake *Sobibor* (2018) and László Nemes' Birkenau portrayal *Son of Saul*, which was also only one of two Oscar winners (or nominees) in the Consolidated Era, winning the Best Foreign Language Film trophy. The other Oscar Winner of the Era, for Best Screenplay, was *Jojo Rabbit* (2019), having been nominated for five other Oscars. In fact, during the first three Eras, 1945 through 2013, one out of every seven Holocaust feature films made worldwide was nominated for at least one Oscar; during the Consolidated Era, only one in 30 Holocaust features were nominated. That includes 20 Best Foreign Language Film winners and nominees over 75 years of Holocaust film production. Further, during the first three Eras, one of every three American Holocaust feature films was nominated for at least one Oscar; during the Consolidated Era, only one of 13 American Holocaust features was nominated.

Seven of the Consolidated Era films are recommended. Nonetheless, in 2015, Steven Alan Carr, Purdue University's Director of the Institute for Holocaust and Genocide Studies, wrote in *Film Criticism*, "The Holocaust film is dead. *Son of Saul* has temporarily

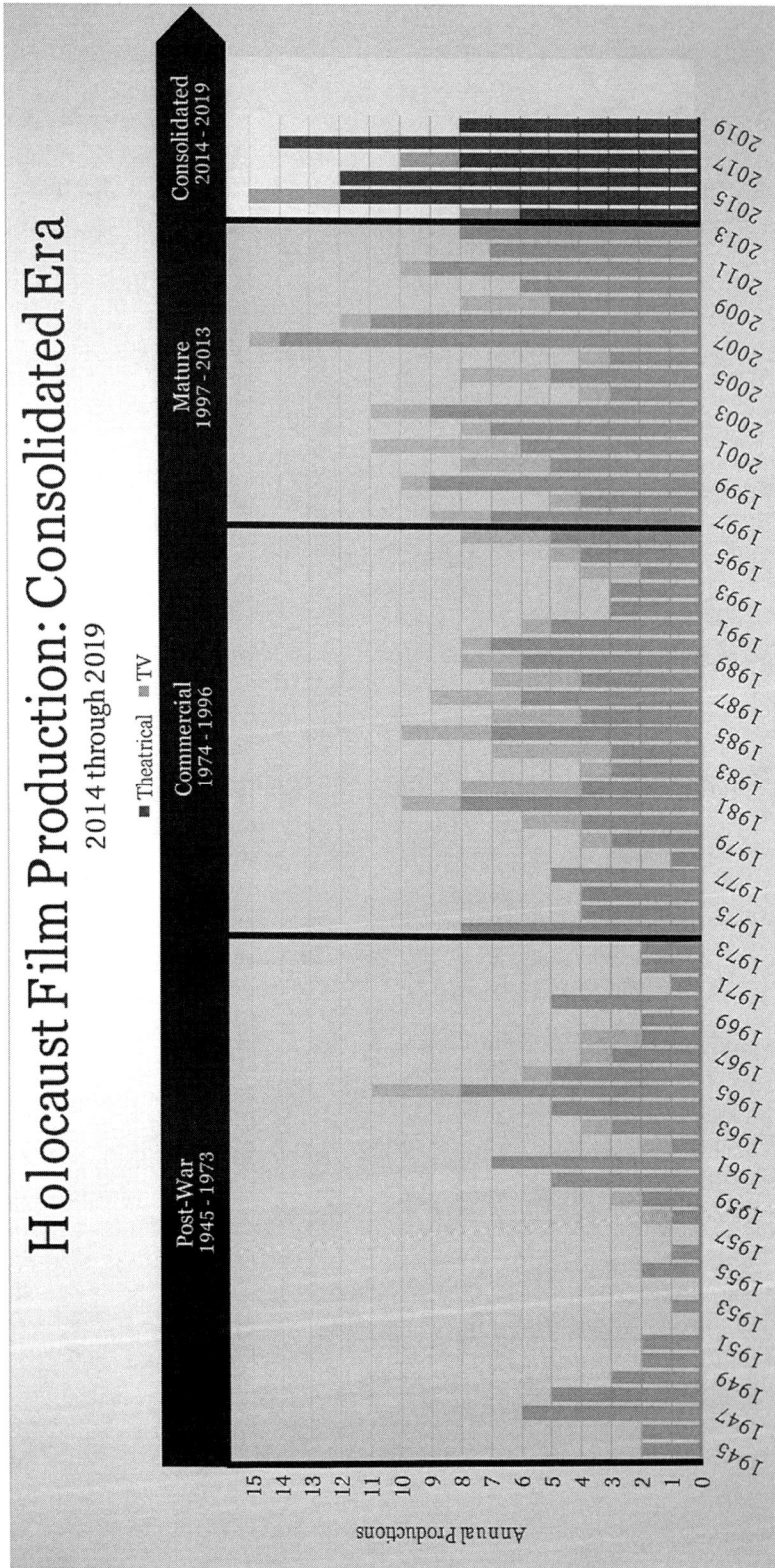

Graph 8: Holocaust Film Production by Year (The Consolidated Era 2014–Present)

found a way to turn its style and form inside out. Long live the Holocaust film...."[3] Although slightly hyperbolic, Carr's suggestion has some merit: we are in a new era of Holocaust film production that is largely derivative. Tellingly, many of the Consolidated Era films are remakes of other Holocaust films or stories.* (See Table 11.)

TABLE 11: THE CONSOLIDATED ERA REMAKES

Remade Version	Original Film
A Bag of Marbles—Un Sac De Billes (2017)	*A Bag of Marbles—Un sac de billes* (1975)
My Daughter Anne Frank—Meine Tochter Anne Frank (TV 2015)	Many Previous Anne Frank Films
Naked Among Wolves—Nackt unter Wölfen (TV 2015)	*Naked Among Wolves—Nackt unter Wölfen* (1963)
Operation Finale (2018)	Many Previous Eichmann Capture or Trial Films
Persona Non Grata—Sugihara Chiune (2015)	*Nippon no Shindorâ: Sugihara Chiune monogatari* (TV 2005)
Phoenix (2014)	*Return from the Ashes* (1965)
Sobibor (2018)	*Escape from Sobibor* (TV 1987)
Son of Saul (2015)	*The Grey Zone* (2001)
The Diary of Anne Frank—Das Tagebuch Der Anne Frank (2016)	Many Previous Anne Frank Films
The Eichmann Show (TV 2015)	Many Previous Eichmann Capture or Trial Films
The People vs. Fritz Bauer—Der Staat gegen Fritz Bauer (2015)	Many Previous Eichmann Capture or Trial Films
The General Case—Die Akte General (TV 2016)	*The People vs. Fritz Bauer—Der Staat gegen Fritz Bauer* (2015)

While the *Son of Saul* remake of Tim Blake Nelson's *The Grey Zone* (2001) is discussed at length in Chapter 6: The Greatest Narrative Holocaust Film Ever Made and Chapter 9: Recommended Holocaust Films, most of these other remakes were better than the originals. In particular, of the Anne-Frank-in-hiding films, *The Diary of Anne Frank—Das Tagebuch Der Anne Frank* (2016) is the highest quality produced to date. And *Phoenix* (2014) is a far better film than the original, *Return from the Ashes* (1965).

The obvious question of "The Consolidated Era" is: have most of the good stories been told? Most likely, the big gold nuggets have been extracted, leaving filmmakers very few remnants in a once-rich stream, essentially reducing Holocaust film production to the rehashing of previously produced films and hackneyed stories, such as *Jojo Rabbit* (2019), which is nothing new in tone or substance. Looking into the future, an IMDb "Holocaust" keyword search yields a dozen Holocaust feature films "in production" or awaiting release. Like the completed *The Painted Bird* (2019), which stars veteran Holocaust actors Harvey Keitel and Stellan Skarsgård, many may struggle to be released.

The last six years of Holocaust film production, the Consolidated Era, suggests that

---

* Hollywood loves remakes. During the writing of this book, the latest version of *A Star Is Born* was born, *A Star Is Born* (2018), starring Lady Gaga and Bradley Cooper, directed by Bradley Cooper, which followed *A Star Is Born* (1976 film), starring Barbra Streisand and Kris Kristofferson, directed by Frank Pierson, which followed *A Star Is Born* (1954 film), starring Judy Garland and James Mason, directed by George Cukor, who had directed Garland in *The Wizard of Oz* (1939). And that version followed the original *A Star Is Born* (1937 film), starring Janet Gaynor and Fredric March, directed by William A. Wellman. At the same time, *Halloween* (2018), starring Jamie Lee Curtis, was released 40 years after Jamie Lee Curtis's *Halloween* (1978).

very few new Holocaust stories will be produced. This is not an elegy of Holocaust film production, but a recognition of the scarcity of stories that could shine new light on this heretofore thoroughly examined subject. *My Daughter Anne Frank—Meine Tochter Anne Frank* (TV 2015) and *1945* (2017) are hopeful signs that Steven Alan Carr's proclamation, "The Holocaust film is dead,"[4] is overstated.

3

Surprising Holocaust Film Traits

The four topics in this chapter are critical to establishing a broader aperture for viewing Holocaust films: (1) Fiction vs. Non-Fiction; (2) Non-American Holocaust Film Production; (3) American Guilt; and (4) God, the Holocaust and Holocaust Exploitation.

Fiction vs. Non-Fiction

Fiction has played an essential role in Holocaust films. Many of the most decorated early Holocaust films were untrue stories in the spirit of tales that were filtering through the emerging field of Holocaust documentation. Yet, today, the notion of using a fictional story in Victim or righteous Gentile Holocaust films seems almost absurd. Table 12 is a rough list of the 50 most prominent Holocaust productions, sorted by 4+1 Genre. Table 12, however, does not even remotely correlate with the list in Chapter 9: Recommended Holocaust Films, the 52 Holocaust films that are recommended in this book. Instead, Table 12 is based on awards, box office, social impact and notoriety.

TABLE 12: MOST IMPORTANT HOLOCAUST FILMS BY 4+1 GENRE
Recommended in **Bold** (17 of 52). "One of the Best" in **Bold and Underlined** (6 of 15).

Film	Year	Fictional/ Non-Fiction	Genre	Oscar/ Emmy Nom.
The Diary of Anne Frank	1959	Non-Fiction	Victim	Yes
Kapò	1960	Fiction	Victim	Yes
The Garden of the Finzi-Continis	1970	Non-Fiction	Victim	Yes
Holocaust (Miniseries TV)	1978	Fiction	Victim	Yes
Escape from Sobibor (TV)	1987	Non-Fiction	Victim	Yes
The Attic: The Hiding of Anne Frank (TV)	1988	Non-Fiction	Victim	Yes
War and Remembrance (Miniseries TV)	1988	Fiction	Victim	Yes
Europa Europa	1990	Non-Fiction	Victim	Yes
Life Is Beautiful—La Vita è bella	1997	Fiction	Victim	Yes
The Truce—La tregua	1997	Non-Fiction	Victim	
Gloomy Sunday—Ein Lied von Liebe und Tod	1999	Fiction	Victim	
Jakob the Liar	1999	Non-Fiction	Victim	
The Devil's Arithmetic (TV)	1999	Fiction	Victim	Yes
The Grey Zone	2001	Non-Fiction	Victim	
Uprising (TV)	2001	Non-Fiction	Victim	Yes

Film	Year	Fictional/ Non-Fiction	Genre	Oscar/ Emmy Nom.
The Pianist	2002	Non-Fiction	Victim	Yes
Out of the Ashes (TV)	2003	Non-Fiction	Victim	Yes
Fateless—Sorstalanság	2005	Non-Fiction	Victim	
The Counterfeiters—Die Fälscher	2007	Non-Fiction	Victim	Yes
Defiance	2008	Non-Fiction	Victim	Yes
God on Trial (TV)	2008	Non-Fiction	Victim	Yes
The Boy in the Striped Pyjamas	2008	Fiction	Victim	
La Rafle	2010	Non-Fiction	Victim	
Son of Saul	2015	Non-Fiction	Victim	Yes
Wallenberg: A Hero's Story (TV)	1985	Non-Fiction	Gentile	Yes
Au Revoir les Enfants	1987	Non-Fiction	Gentile	Yes
Schindler's List	1993	Non-Fiction	Gentile	Yes
Conspiracy (TV)	2001	Non-Fiction	Gentile	Yes
Amen.	2002	Non-Fiction	Gentile	
The Relief of Belsen (TV)	2007	Non-Fiction	Gentile	Yes
The Courageous Heart of Irena Sendler (TV)	2009	Non-Fiction	Gentile	
Aftermath—Poklosie	2011	Fiction	Gentile	
In Darkness	2011	Non-Fiction	Gentile	Yes
The Zookeeper's Wife	2017	Non-Fiction	Gentile	
The Pawnbroker	1964	Fiction	Survivor	Yes
The Man in the Glass Booth	1975	Fiction	Survivor	Yes
Enemies: A Love Story	1989	Fiction	Survivor	Yes
Everything Is Illuminated	2005	Fiction	Survivor	
Ida	2013	Fiction	Survivor	Yes
Woman in Gold	2015	Non-Fiction	Survivor	
QB VII (Miniseries TV)	1974	Fiction	Perpetrator	Yes
Marathon Man	1976	Fiction	Perpetrator	Yes
Music Box	1989	Fiction	Perpetrator	Yes
Apt Pupil	1998	Fiction	Perpetrator	
Adolf Eichmann	2007	Non-Fiction	Perpetrator	
The Reader	2008	Fiction	Perpetrator	Yes
Remember	2015	Fiction	Perpetrator	
Sophie's Choice	1982	Fiction	Tangential	Yes
Bent	1997	Fiction	Tangential	
Inglourious Basterds	2009	Fiction	Tangential	Yes

Of the Gentile films, the only fictional story is the solid Polish "antisemitic Gentile" *Aftermath—Poklosie* (2012). The other films about righteous Gentiles were based on true stories, with the glaring exception of Taika Waititi's intensely fictional *Jojo Rabbit* (2019), which is not listed above and which failed as a Holocaust film partly because it was so obviously fictional. Conversely, almost all Perpetrator and Survivor films are fictional. The Victim films, however, are mixed until 2000, after which only one major film, the pitiful *The Boy in the Striped Pyjamas,* was based on a fictional story.

Many of the early Auschwitz productions relied on completely fictional plots, which is unthinkable today for Victim films. It is safe to say that Roberto Benigni's

Holocaust fairytale *Life Is Beautiful—La Vita è bella* (1997) killed off most subsequent fictional Victim genre Holocaust films. Although *Life Is Beautiful* is rated by IMDb users as one of the 30 best films of all time, and although *Life Is Beautiful* won three Oscars (Best Actor, Foreign-Language Film, and Music) and was nominated for four others (Best Picture, Director, Writing, and Film Editing), and although *Life Is Beautiful* grossed a quarter of a billion dollars and is the third-highest grossing foreign-language film in U.S. history,* *Life Is Beautiful* ruined any remaining appetite for fictional depictions of death camps. Even though no specific death camp is mentioned in *Life Is Beautiful*, since one character is tattooed and another gassed, Auschwitz is uniquely implied. Yet, aside from its undressing room, the depiction of Auschwitz is generic, at best. As one reviewer understated *Life Is Beautiful*'s premise, "Had the film attempted to capture that historical accuracy, it's likely its uplifting story wouldn't have been possible."[1] *Life Is Beautiful* crassly implies that Auschwitz could have been turned into a playground where a father and his five-year-old son could have pranced around like Andy and Opie in Mayberry.

Of the fictional Victim films in Table 12, only two are excellent: *The Garden of the Finzi-Continis* (1970) and *Gloomy Sunday—Ein Lied von Liebe und Tod* (1999). Nonetheless, *The Finzi-Continis* was very loosely biographical and the antagonist in *Gloomy Sunday* is based on the very real Kurt Andreas Becher, also exposed in Wolfgang Luderer's *Living Goods—Lebende Ware* (1969). Yet, those two films never leave their home cities, Ferrara, Italy and Budapest, Hungary, respectively. Those two Victim films are tasteful. They do not overreach. They do not belittle the gravity of the Holocaust through fanciful plots that rely on historically irresponsible storylines. *The Garden of the Finzi-Continis* and *Gloomy Sunday* succeed because they are uncomplicated, smart stories about life under German occupation and moored in historical events.

It is easy to speculate as to the factors responsible for mostly non-fictional Victim films being produced since the turn of the millennium. Some have speculated that *Schindler's List*'s success in the early 1990s encouraged the production of non-fictional Holocaust films. Others suggest that *Schindler's List* and its stepchild, the USC Shoah Foundation, the leading American repository for Holocaust survivor testimonies, helped make new stories available. The survivor testimony theory spuriously suggests that a finite number of films could have been made and the non-fictional films left no room for the fictional stories. That theory also ignores the massive number of stories that started to come out in 1978 after *Holocaust* the miniseries. Further, while hundreds of thousands of testimonies were suddenly made public, only a few dozen extra Holocaust films were produced. In fact, enough survivor stories existed before 1993 and, for that matter, before 1978 to have filled theaters for generations.

The simplest answer to the question of why fictional Victim Holocaust films have gone out of style is the market. The public does not want to see contrived Victim stories anymore because basic Holocaust history is no longer such a mystery. In other words, the public is no longer so uneducated that fairy tales are necessary; enough has been taught about the Holocaust that the public wants to see real stories. As noted in *The Forward*:

* The highest grossing foreign-language film in U.S. history is *Crouching Tiger, Hidden Dragon* (2000), which worldwide has grossed $128 million, $100 million less than *Life Is Beautiful* worldwide. http://www.boxofficemojo.com/genres/chart/?id=foreign.htm. The second highest is *Parasite* (2019), which surpassed *Life Is Beautiful* after winning four Oscars at the 2020 Academy Awards, including Best Picture.

Exactly how popular culture has grappled with Nazism over the past 60-odd years forms a peculiar sort of curve. In films, the trajectory began with stock-villain propaganda and then evolved (in the 1950s and '60s) toward a defensive, Jewish-comic sardonicism, which found itself capable of using the German fascism as farce. This abated in the '80s, when it became impossible to joke about so many things, and then the impulse emerged, oddly, after the feel-good trauma of *Schindler's List*, as comedy again, in the '90s (*Life Is Beautiful*, etc.). By now, of course, only toll-taking documentaries and occasional sojourns into history, like *The Pianist*, can be tolerated.[2]

But the same trend is largely true of non–Holocaust World War II films, generally. Where once there was a big market for fictional War films like *Casablanca* (1942), *The Dirty Dozen* (1967) and *Kelly's Heroes* (1970), War biopics, for the most part, are now in fashion, such as *Saving Private Ryan* (1998), *Letters from Iwo Jima* (2006), *Valkyrie* (2008), *Hacksaw Ridge* (2016) and *Dunkirk* (2017). So, the tendency toward non-fiction is not limited to Holocaust films.

Some Holocaust films, too, are historical reenactments, which have less historical leeway than other Holocaust films. Faithful historical reenactments are bound by true events, which are inflexible. Historically reenacted Holocaust films regularly break with their established 4+1 Genre formula. Typically, these films have one source—a diary or transcript—and the producers stick to it. Consider, for example, *Woman in Gold*'s "Maria Altmann" (Helen Mirren), who is a somewhat rational Holocaust survivor. Of the 56 Survivor Holocaust films, almost every protagonist except the historically reenacted Altmann is mentally unbalanced, disturbed or irreparably damaged. For example, *The Pawnbroker*'s "Sol Nazerman" (Rod Steiger), *X-Men*'s "Magneto" (Ian McKellen) and *Harold and Maude*'s "Maude" (Ruth Gordon) are caricatures when compared to Maria Altmann. Because *Woman in Gold* is the real story of Maria Altmann's quest to gain ownership of her family's art that was looted by the Germans, there was little room for fictional, formulaic crazy. These plot inflexibilities must also be considered when judging the greatness of strict historical reenactments. *Woman in Gold* and *Denial* (2016) are not great films, but rather, both are small stories about contemporary women, plots that could not veer into Christopher Nolan-territory.

A hybrid form of Holocaust film has also been created. These films use interviews of victims and eyewitnesses mixed with reenactments of their stories by actors. Often, too, wartime documentary footage is interspliced. Since 2005, several historically reenacted Holocaust films have tried this hybrid style to straddle narrative and documentary filmmaking. These films have had mixed results, including: *Auschwitz the Nazis and the "Final Solution"* (2005), *Nina's Journey—La Maison De Nina* (2005), *Nuremberg: Goering's Last Stand* (TV 2006), *Blessed Is the Match: The Life and Death of Hannah Senesh* (2008), *My Daughter Anne Frank—Meine Tochter Anne Frank* (TV 2015), *Auschwitz* (2011), *The Resistance—The Invisibles—Die Unsichtbaren* (2017) and *Who Will Write Our History* (2018). Of these, only the recommended *My Daughter Anne Frank—Meine Tochter Anne Frank* was able to mix genres effectively, largely because it was able to introduce new information to the best known Holocaust story ever told, while also featuring thoughtful interviews with Otto Frank and some of Anne Frank's surviving friends. As a cinematic technique, mixing documentary footage into a narrative film is generally a sign of weakness, indicative of either the writers' inability to convey the needed exposition through a narrative format or as a sign of budgetary constraints caused by overreaching productions.

And then there is Holocaust comedy, which seems oxymoronic. Yet, in 2015 Yad Vashem published Chaya Ostrower's *It Kept Us Alive: Humor in the Holocaust*. Amazingly, at least 20 Holocaust feature films have a comedic tone or are outright farcical. (See Table 13.)

TABLE 13: SOME HOLOCAUST COMEDIES (20 FILMS)

Recommended in **Bold** (5 of 52). "One of the Best" in **Bold and Underlined** (2 of 15).
Unavailable films in S̶t̶r̶i̶k̶e̶o̶u̶t̶ (1).

Film	*Genre*
Harold and Maude (1971)	Survivor
Enemies: A Love Story (1989)	Survivor
The Nasty Girl—Das schreckliche Mädchen (1990)	Gentile
Genghis Cohn (1993)	Perpetrator
My Mother's Courage—Mutters Courage (1995)	Victim
Life Is Beautiful—La Vita è bella (1997)	Victim
Mendel (1997)	Survivor
The Truce—La tregua (1997)	Survivor
Train of Life—Train de vie (1998)	Victim
Jakob the Liar (1999)	Victim
Invincible (2001)	Tangential
Unfair Competition—Concorrenza sleale (2001)	Victim
Monsieur Batignole (2002)	Gentile
Everything Is Illuminated (2005)	Survivor
My Führer—Mein Führer—Die wirklich wahrste Wahrheit über Adolf Hitler (2007)	Victim
Inglourious Basterds (2009)	Tangential
Protector—Protektor (2009)	Gentile
Simon Konianski (2009)	Survivor
~~*The Last Suit—El último traje (2017)*~~	Survivor
Jojo Rabbit (2019)	Gentile

Most of these films succeed, both comedically and thematically. To be fair, all Holocaust comedies include or imply the death of Jews and/or their protectors. None of these films are rollicking laugh-fests from start to finish, like *The Producers* (1967), which is not considered here as a Holocaust film. Holocaust comedies are, instead, deemed comedies because of tone and spirit. Yet, they universally have tragic moments, usually near the end.

Many Holocaust comedies are admirable, including *The Nasty Girl—Das schreckliche Mädchen* (1990), the recommended *My Führer—Mein Führer—Die wirklich wahrste Wahrheit über Adolf Hitler* (2007) and *The Truce—La tregua* (1997), starring John Turturro as Primo Levi. *Everything Is Illuminated* (2005), adapted from Jonathan Safran Foer's novel and directed by Liev Schreiber and starring Elijah Wood, is also recommended and beautifully made. *Genghis Cohn* (1993), too, starring Antony Sher, is surprisingly effective, as are *Protector—Protektor* (2009), *Mendel* (1997) and *Train of Life—Train de vie* (1998). Paul Mazursky's *Enemies: A Love Story* (1989), starring Ron Silver and based on an Isaac Bashevis Singer novel, also makes its comedic and apostatic points effectively, with Oscar nominations earned by Anjelica Huston and Lena Olin. And *Harold and Maude* (1971) is first-class, as is *Inglourious Basterds* (2009).

In fact, the only comedic Holocaust films on the list that fail are *Unfair Competition—Concorrenza sleale* (2001), *Life Is Beautiful—La Vita è bella* (1997), *Jakob the Liar* (1999) and *Jojo Rabbit* (2019). Further, none of those films is particularly sophisticated or funny beyond a gag or two. Notwithstanding box office success, their humor is misguided, and their messages got lost in meandering plots used to justify laughs. Still, that many Holocaust features attempt humor and that most succeed suggests that skilled film-makers can transcend any genre.*

Non-American Holocaust Film Production

What is meant by "the producing country" in film? In most Communist countries, the film business (and every other business) was effectively owned by the state, by definition, despite artifice. In such cases, "the producing country" is essentially literal. But in most other countries, films are financed by companies and investors, notwithstanding public film grants, tax subsidies and other financial incentives. In these cases, for the most part, "the producing country" is the country of the production company (business entity) responsible for financing and producing a film. More than one company can be involved in financing and producing a film, and those co-producing companies might be in different countries. Thus, a film can have more than one producing country.

One-quarter of all 443 Holocaust films—109—were co-produced, produced by more than one country. On average, those co-produced films were each made by three producing countries. The record is held by *Witnesses—Svideteli* (2018), which is a trilogy of vignettes co-produced by seven countries: Russia, Belarus, Ukraine, Poland, France, Czech Republic and Israel. Second place, with five producing countries, is shared by three films: *Train of Life—Train de vie* (1998), in French, produced by France, Belgium, Netherlands, Israel and Romania; *Black Book—Zwartboek* (2006), in Dutch, produced by U.K., Netherlands, Germany, Belgium and Myanmar; and *I Do Not Care If We Go Down in History as Barbarians—Îmi este indiferent daca în istorie vom intra ca barbari* (2018), in Romanian, produced by Romania, Czech Republic, Germany, Bulgaria and France.

When considering countries that have united or divided since the dissolution of Eastern European Communism, 45 national entities have participated in Holocaust film production. For example, German Holocaust films were made by three national entities: East Germany, West Germany, and reunified Germany. Further, every country that had been occupied by Germany during World War II (with a population greater than three million) and every Axis-aligned country has produced or co-produced at least one Holocaust film. Thirty-seven countries have produced 443 Holocaust films. (See Table 14.)

TABLE 14: HOLOCAUST FILMS BY COUNTRIES (JOINT PRODUCTION INCLUDED)

Production Company Home Country	Films	%
U.S.	107	24.2%
Germany	106	23.9%
East Germany	(11)	
Germany	(64)	
West Germany	(31)	
France	64	14.4%
U.K.	49	11.1%
Israel	37	8.4%
Poland	34	7.7%

---

* For more about Holocaust comedies, see Ferne Pearlstein's delightful documentary *The Last Laugh* (2016), which includes interviews with Mel Brooks, Robert Clary, Harry Shearer and many others.

Production Company Home Country	Films	%
Italy	30	6.8%
Czechoslovakia	(28)	6.3%
Czech Republic	(13)	
Czechoslovakia	(11)	
Slovakia	(4)	
Hungary	24	5.4%
Canada	20	4.5%
Austria	19	4.3%
Yugoslavia	13	2.9%
Macedonia	(1)	
Serbia	(1)	
Slovenia	(1)	
Yugoslavia	(10)	
Netherlands	11	2.5%
Belgium	9	2.0%
Switzerland	9	2.0%
Russia	6	1.4%
Russia	(2)	
USSR	(4)	
Ireland	4	0.9%
Japan	4	0.9%
Romania	4	0.9%
Spain	4	0.9%
Sweden	4	0.9%
Australia	3	0.7%
Belarus	3	0.7%
Bulgaria	3	0.7%
Denmark	3	0.7%
Greece	3	0.7%
Luxembourg	3	0.7%
Argentina	2	0.5%
Norway	2	0.5%
Ukraine	2	0.5%
Brazil	1	0.2%
China	1	0.2%
Latvia	1	0.2%
Lithuania	1	0.2%
Myanmar	1	0.2%
Philippines	1	0.2%
Portugal	1	0.2%

Many of these countries weighed in long after the War to provide national viewpoints about their Holocaust history, including: *Mendel* (1997) (Norway), *Fugitive Pieces* (2007) (Greece), *A Jewish Girl in Shanghai* (2010) (China), *The Third Half—Treto poluvreme* (2012) (Macedonia), *When Day Breaks—Kad svane dan* (2012) and *Dara of Jasenovac—Dara iz Jasenovca* (2020) (Serbia), *Akte Grüninger* (TV 2014) (Switzerland),

Persona Non Grata—Sugihara Chiune (2015) (Japan), *The Photographer of Mauthausen—El fotógrafo de Mauthausen* (2018) (Spain) and *Quezon's Game* (2018) (Philippines). Some of these films are more nationalistic than others.

Despite this breadth, there is still a tendency, perhaps because of Hollywood and the Oscars, to assume that American production companies have made a preponderance of Holocaust films. Of 361 Holocaust feature films, roughly a fifth were American produced or co-produced (75 or 20.8 percent), with just 54 (15 percent) being solo American productions. In fact, excluding television, a paltry 18 of the 189 core Holocaust films (Victim or Gentile) features have been produced solely by American companies (or just under ten percent). (See Table 15.) Some Victim and Righteous Gentile features have been jointly produced with American companies: *War and Love* (1985), *Edges of the Lord* (2001), *The Aryan Couple* (2004), *The Boy in the Striped Pyjamas* (2008) and *The Zookeeper's Wife* (2017).

TABLE 15: HOLOCAUST VICTIM AND RIGHTEOUS GENTILE FEATURE
FILMS SOLELY MADE BY AMERICAN PRODUCTION COMPANIES
Recommended in **Bold** (3 of 52). "One of the Best" in **Bold and Underlined** (1 of 15).
Unavailable films in ~~Strikeout~~ (3).

Title	Genre	Oscar Winners	Total Oscar Nominations
The Diary of Anne Frank (1959)	Gentile	3	5
~~*The Song and the Silence* (1968)~~	Victim		
The Only Way (1970)	Gentile		
The Hiding Place (1975)	Gentile		
The Assisi Underground (1985)	Gentile		
Hanna's War (1988)	Victim		
Triumph of the Spirit (1989)	Victim		
Schindler's List (1993)	Gentile	7	12
Jakob the Liar (1999)	Victim		
The Grey Zone (2001)	Victim		
The Pianist (2002)	Victim	3	7
~~*House of the Generals* (2003)~~	Victim		
Defiance (2008)	Victim		1
Walking with the Enemy (2013)	Victim		
~~*A Rose in Winter* (2018)~~	Victim		
Who Will Write Our History (2018)	Victim		
Jojo Rabbit (2019)	Gentile	1	6

Television is a different matter, where half of televised Holocaust content has been produced by Americans. While American companies have produced or co-produced 32 made-for-television Holocaust films, solely Non-American producers have made 50 television Holocaust films. Most of these non–American productions have thoughtfully introduced important content into the pantheon of Holocaust film.

Overall, comparing American and non–American Holocaust film production is not simply a matter of national pride or having a good spreadsheet. In Holocaust education, it is understood that Europeans and Americans have vastly different perceptions of the Holocaust vis-à-vis their respective national experiences, which also shines through in their respective War films. World War II demarcates the unshakable apex of American jingoism, the belief that Uncle Sam saved the world twice from itself during World War I and then World War II, as if John Wayne and Brad Pitt took time from their busy schedules to hop the pond and vanquish the Jerrys. And then, in American eyes, after the U.S. ended a set of European wars that had been raging for a millennium, Americans ultimately had to adjudicate the war crimes and foot-the-bill to fix Europe's interminable mess. In fact, without becoming political, this chauvinism has been the prevailing American mindset for over a hundred years, since World War I, irrespective of the actual history, regardless of the White House's occupant.

Conversely, for Europeans World War II is more personal, even for post–War generations, who live in the shadow of guilt or memories of occupation. Except for Denmark, no European-combatant country lost a smaller percentage of its population during World War II than did the United States (0.32 percent), including Australia (0.58 percent) and Canada (0.38 percent). On the other hand, many European countries lost more than 5 percent of their respective populations in the War, including Poland where 17 percent of Poles vanished. And the round figure estimated for the Soviet Union is 20 million dead, although a more recent Russian study suggests that 26.6 million Soviets died as a result of the War.[3] Again, without becoming political, the inexorable Russian creed is that, while the West may have paid for the defeat of the Axis powers in gold, the Soviets paid in blood.

European Holocaust films have plots that directly expose their local populations' complacency toward or collaboration with the Germans. Many of these films are an expression of national guilt, seeking atonement through expository art. European Holocaust films are generally more clever, less inhibited and less contrived than American Holocaust films. The remainder of this section will break down Holocaust film production from the nine European countries responsible for the majority of Holocaust films.

Germany—East, West, and Reunified (106 Films)

German Holocaust films started being produced just after the War with the Communist East German *Murderers Among Us—Die Mörder sind unter uns* (1946). East Germany made 11 Holocaust films; West Germany produced or co-produced 31 Holocaust films; their remaining 64 Holocaust films were completely or partially produced by reunified Germany, post–1990.

Since 2007, six of the ten solo German productions have been remarkable and are recommended. Germany has produced two of the three best Anne Frank films, *My Daughter Anne Frank—Meine Tochter Anne Frank* (TV 2015) and *The Diary of Anne Frank—Das Tagebuch Der Anne Frank* (2016). Two fine German films expose the systematic West German insinuation of Nazis into post–War West German bureaucracy, *Labyrinth of Lies—Im Labyrinth Des Schweigens* (2014) and *The People vs. Fritz Bauer—Der Staat gegen Fritz Bauer* (2015). Germany also produced the insanely satirical *My Führer—Mein Führer—Die wirklich wahrste Wahrheit über Adolf Hitler* (2007), which is everything *Jojo Rabbit* (2019) wanted to be. And Germany produced the thoughtful *Phoenix* (2014), a remake of the British film *Return from the Ashes* (1965). *Run Boy Run—Lauf Junge lauf* (2013), too, a co-production with France and Poland, is an unflinchingly honest biopic. Post-War German films are a shining rebuke of any assertion that the German film community has shirked German responsibility for the Holocaust. Many German films deal with national guilt, while other films are more traditional. Overall, German filmmakers have been courageous and honest about the Nazi regime.

That being said, it also must be noted that some German films have pushed the fallacy that the Holocaust was not perpetrated by Germans, but by Nazis, which is a self-serving distinction without a functional difference. The tendency in late twentieth-century German education to shift blame from the German state to the Nazi party is explored in Barbara Wenzeler's 2003 book, "The Presentation of the Holocaust in German and English School History Textbooks—A Comparative Study."[4] In film, the best and most recent examples of this post hoc illusion are *The Resistance—The Invisibles—Die Unsichtbaren* (2017) as well as in the shorts *Porcelain Unicorn* (2010) and *Toyland—Spielzeugland* (2007), which won the 2009 Oscar for Best Short Live Action. The ahistorical commonality of these films is that most Germans were willing to help Jews when given a chance, especially in Berlin. Of course, not all Germans were Nazis, and some Germans (and even Nazis) helped Jews, but highlighting this extreme anomaly masks the overwhelming German complicity in the formulation and execution of the Holocaust. For more about German Holocaust films, see Thomas Elsaesser's *German Cinema: Terror and Trauma: Cultural Memory Since 1945* (New York: Routledge, 2014).

France (64 Films)

The French started making Holocaust films in 1960. Many of their productions have tried to make peace with French collaboration under German occupation. The willingness of the French to give up their Jews has been overshadowed by Germany's more overt war crimes. But French collaboration has been the subject of many smaller, yet wonderfully rich French films, including *The Two of Us—Le vieil homme et l'enfant* (1967), *Mr. Klein—Monsieur Klein* (1976) and *Au Revoir les Enfants* (1987). Several of France's joint productions are also set apart among the best in their genres, including the most genuine Survivor film ever made, *The Birch-Tree Meadow—La petite prairie aux bouleaux* (2003), a co-production with Germany and Poland, and the very entertaining *This Must Be the Place* (2011), a co-production with Italy and Ireland, starring Sean Penn. For more about early French Holocaust films, see André Pierre Colombat's *The Holocaust in French Film* (Metuchen, NJ: Scarecrow, 1993).

United Kingdom (49 Films)

The British Holocaust films have been mostly impactful with their television productions, all of which since 2001 have been as good or better than most other made-for-television Holocaust films. These winners include: *Conspiracy* (TV 2001), *Varian's War: The Forgotten Hero* (TV 2001), *Primo* (TV 2005), *The Relief of Belsen* (TV 2007), *God on Trial* (TV 2008), *The Diary of Anne Frank* (TV 2009) and *The Eichmann Show* (TV 2015). Not all are great, but all are worth watching. Of the 22 Holocaust features produced by the UK, only two have been solo productions, *Prague* (1992) and *Adolf Eichmann* (2007). Instead of being demeaned for this paucity of solo efforts, the Brits should be celebrated for their involvement in the co-production of many other features, including three of the best films in their genres: *The Last Butterfly—Poslední motýl* (1991) (Tangential), *Genghis Cohn* (1993) (Perpetrator) and *Fateless—Sorstalanság* (2005) (Victim).

Israel (37 Films)

Israeli Holocaust films concentrate on smaller Survivor and Perpetrator stories. None of the Israeli solo productions will be mistaken for grand Hollywood epics.

Nonetheless, perhaps because these Israeli films do not overreach, together they are the most consistently good and emotionally honest of all Holocaust films by nationality. Israeli national guilt for having denigrated Holocaust survivors—guilt for implying that the survivors were weak for purportedly allowing the destruction of European Jewry—is the undercurrent of these films. Eli Cohen's *Under the Domim Tree—Etz Hadomim Tafus* (1994) and Hanan Peled's *Dear Mr. Waldman—Michtavim Le America* (2006) pull hard and effectively at these national scabs. However, the most entertaining Israeli Holocaust film is Ari Folman's sublime *Made in Israel* (2001), which imagines the last Nazi being transported to Jerusalem for trial. In every respect, from attitude to production style to plot, *Made in Israel* is, indeed, made in Israel. For more about Israeli Holocaust films, see Nurith Gertz's *Holocaust Survivors, Aliens, and Others in Israeli Cinema and Literature* (Tel Aviv: Am Oved, 2004).

Poland (34 Films)

The common theme in Poland's 34 Holocaust films, and especially their solo productions, is pain. From the Communist era *Border Street—Ulica Graniczna* (1948) through *Aftermath—Poklosie* (2012) and Best Foreign Language Film Oscar winner *Ida* (2013), independent Polish Holocaust films have left no room for pouting or denial. Their co-productions have largely surrendered ground, with the exceptions of *Korczak* (1990), *The Birch-Tree Meadow* and *Run Boy Run*. Without taking sides regarding the controversy concerning the phrase "Polish Death Camps" and the implicit rebuke of Poland—and the implication that Poland is unwilling to accept any culpability for the Holocaust—most Polish Holocaust films do not sugarcoat in any way Polish attitudes and actions toward the Jews during the Holocaust. For more information about Polish Holocaust films, see, Marek Haltof's *Polish Film and the Holocaust: Politics and Memory*, (New York: Berghahn, 2012).

Italy (30 Films)

Italy's Holocaust films are headlined by the fabulously successful *Life Is Beautiful—La Vita è bella* (1997). Italy has also made some great Holocaust films, not least of which was *The Garden of the Finzi-Continis—Il Giardino dei Finzi-Contini* (1970) winner of the Best Foreign Language Film Oscar. *The Truce—La tregua* (1997), too, starring John Turturro as Primo Levi, is a sturdy watch. And *Perlasca. The Courage of a Just Man—Perlasca. Un eroe italiano* (TV 2002) is a particularly good righteous Gentile film about a man who saved thousands of Jews, without much fanfare. The controversial *The Night Porter—Il portiere di notte* (1974), however, is more of a watch-through-your-fingers film, as is *Rua Alguem 5555: My Father* (2003), starring the dreadfully miscast Charlton Heston as Josef Mengele. For more information about Italian Holocaust films, see Millicent Marcus' *Italian Film in the Shadow of Auschwitz* (Toronto and London: University of Toronto Press, 2009).

Czechoslovakia (and the Czech Republic and Slovakia) (28 Films)

Holocaust films from Czechoslovakia (and the Czech Republic) are a good bet, usually well made. Czech solo productions worth watching include *Diamonds of the*

Night—Démanty noci (1964), the Oscar-winning *The Shop on Main Street—Obchod na korze* (1965) and the Oscar-nominated *Divided We Fall—Musíme si pomáhat* (2000). *Protector—Protektor* (2009), too, has some fine moments and terrific editing. And the Czech co-production with France and the U.K., *The Last Butterfly—Poslední motýl* (1991) is an outstanding look into the Theresienstadt Concentration Camp. For more information about Czech Holocaust films, see Stuart Liebman and Leonard Quart's *Czech Films of the Holocaust* (Cinéaste 22.1 1996).

Hungary (24 Films)

The Hungarian productions or co-productions from 1983 through 2017 have been very unflattering toward wartime Hungary, as with *1945* (2017) which credibly describes how one rural Hungarian community discouraged their already-despoiled Jews from returning after the War. This type of self-examination is standard for Hungarian Holocaust films, which are more focused on Victims than are Holocaust films produced by most other countries. Hungarian Holocaust films are beautifully made and highly effective. *Gloomy Sunday—Ein Lied von Liebe und Tod* (1999) is an insightful look into the downward spiral of Budapest during German occupation. Best Foreign Language Film Oscar-winner *Son of Saul* (2015) is an uncompromising depiction of Auschwitz/Birkenau. And Lajos Koltai's *Fateless—Sorstalanság* (2005) is one of the greatest Holocaust films of any genre. For more information about Hungarian Holocaust films, see Catherine Portuges' *Traumatic Memory, Jewish Identities: Remapping the Past in Hungarian Cinema In East European Cinemas* (New York: Routledge, 2005).

Canada (20 Films)

Of the 20 Canadian Holocaust films, only five have been solo. Aside from *The Quarrel* (1991), which was directed by Israeli Eli Cohen, Canadian produced or co-produced Holocaust films have easily been the worst Holocaust films made by nationality, films that include: *The Lucky Star* (1980), starring Rod Steiger and Louise Fletcher; *Max* (2002), starring John Cusack and Noah Taylor; Norman Jewison's *The Statement* (2003), starring Michael Caine, Tilda Swinton and Charlotte Rampling; *Autumn Hearts: A New Beginning—Emotional Arithmetic* (2007), starring Susan Sarandon, Christopher Plummer and Gabriel Byrne; *Fugitive Pieces* (2007); and the almost incomparably incompetent *The Poet—Hearts of War* (2007), with a cast that included Nina Dobrev, Roy Scheider and Daryl Hannah. In fact, uniquely along with Yugoslavia, among the major solo Holocaust feature producing countries, no books have been written about Canadian Holocaust film production.

Yugoslavia (11)—Serbia (1)—Macedonia (1)—Slovenia (1)

Five of the 8 Yugoslavian Holocaust films are unavailable. One of the remaining three was a solo production, *The Ninth Circle—Deveti krug* (1960), which is not recommended. The Serbian film *When Day Breaks—Kad svane dan* (2012) adds some color to the local reaction to the Holocaust, but is trite and meandering. The same is true of Macedonia's *The Third Half—Treto poluvreme* (2012), which is only slightly more entertaining.

Winners and Losers

After these summaries by national origin, a niggling question might pop up concerning the efficacy of co-productions vs. solo productions. Do films improve when adding more national viewpoints to the pot? The answer is: probably. The number of international co-productions has risen substantially since 1990, from 18 percent of all Holocaust films made before 1990 to 31 percent after. Certainly, with the fall of Soviet Communism around 1990, a prima facie case could be made to account for the increase in joint productions. So the niggle, too, seems to be correct: for whatever reasons, Holocaust films seem to be better when more perspectives are heard. Producers have been seeking more diverse input over the past 30 years. The more substantial question of national success also is in play here. Of the 52 films recommended in this book, more than half were produced or co-produced by Americans and/or Germans. (See Table 16.)

TABLE 16: RECOMMENDED HOLOCAUST FILMS
BY PRODUCTION AND CO-PRODUCTION COUNTRY

Producing Country	*Recommended Films*	%
U.S.	14	28%
Germany (& East & West)	14	28%
France	9	18%
U.K.	7	14%
Czechoslovakia (& Czech Republic & Slovakia)	4	8%
Hungary	4	8%
Israel	3	6%
Italy	3	6%
Poland	3	6%
Austria	2	4%
Canada	2	4%
Denmark	1	2%
Ireland	1	2%
Netherlands	1	2%
Sweden	1	2%
Switzerland	1	2%

It should not be surprising that the countries making the most Holocaust films have also made the highest number of good Holocaust films. That being said, Nolan Ryan struck out the most batters in MLB history (5,714), but also allowed the most walks (2,795).[5] And Kobe Bryant scored the seventh most field goals in NBA history (11,719), yet Bryant also missed more shots than anyone else in the history of American professional basketball (14,481).[6] So, simply taking shots is not the same as making shots.

What country (of major producers) has the highest percentage of good Holocaust films? Hungary, a relative newcomer, holds the title, having made most of their Holocaust films in the last 20 years (14 of 24), which are honest and compelling. This skewing variable is completely prejudicial against those nations who blazed the trail for the first 55 years, pioneers whose early efforts advised recent filmmakers. Yet, for those keeping score, Table 17 is the leaderboard and should disabuse anyone who maintains that Hollywood is the Holocaust film gold standard. America has, of course, produced some great

Holocaust films, artistically and financially, but Holocaust films are now and have always been an international art form, best appreciated with an open mind.

TABLE 17: RECOMMENDED HOLOCAUST FILMS PERCENTAGE SUCCESS
BY PRODUCTION AND CO-PRODUCTION COUNTRY

Country	Films	%	Recommended	%
Hungary	24	5.4%	4	17%
France	64	14.5%	9	14%
U.K.	49	11.1%	7	14%
Czechoslovakia	28	6.3%	4	14%
U.S.	107	24.2%	14	13%
Germany	106	24.0%	14	13%
Austria	19	4.3%	2	11%
Switzerland	9	2.0%	1	11%
Italy	31	7.0%	3	10%
Canada	20	4.5%	2	10%
Poland	34	7.7%	3	9%
Netherlands	11	2.5%	1	9%
Israel	37	8.4%	3	8%

Non-Native Language and Accents

Overall, 35 Holocaust films used more than one language. Further, 32 languages are used in Holocaust film, of which English is spoken in 170 films (38 percent), followed by German in 106, French in 52, Polish in 35 and Hebrew in 25. Yiddish is only spoken in 12 Holocaust films (and Ladino in two). The utilized-language champ is *Son of Saul* (2015), Oscar Winner for Best Foreign Language Film, using eight languages in the film: German, Hungarian, Polish, Yiddish, Russian, Slovak, Czech and Greek. Seventy years earlier, *The Last Chance—Die letzte Chance* (1945) used seven languages: German, Italian, English, French, Yiddish, Dutch and Polish.

More broadly, from any rational perspective, when hearing languages, voices and accents that are plainly inauthentic, there is an immediate suspension of disbelief that is required by the viewer. Since the dawn of theater, spoken languages have often not matched their settings. For example, more than two-thirds of William Shakespeare's plays were set in non–English-speaking countries, yet Shakespeare obviously wrote in English. Elie Wiesel did not write in the languages of Auschwitz—primarily German, Polish and Yiddish—but mostly wrote in French. Indeed, the fattest target for criticism about Holocaust representations in film is native language, which rarely has been a consideration for filmmakers. A generation before viewers noticed that James Woods' dialect was inauthentic in the *Holocaust* miniseries, neither Shelley Winters nor Millie Perkins, Danny Kaye nor Marlon Brando, Kirk Douglas nor Susan Strasberg were using the native language of their characters in Holocaust-related films.

But this has never been solely an American quandary. For example, *Babi Yar: The Forgotten Crime—Babij Jar* (2003) is a German film that portrays the destruction of Kyiv's Jews in Soviet Ukraine in 1941. It is one thing for the primary dialect to be German in an area that was known to have been in historically contested cities, such as the Polish city of Gdańsk/Danzig or Strasbourg or the Sudetenland, but the local Ukrainian population never used German as a natural dialect. Yet German, not Yiddish, Russian or Ukrainian was the language spoken in *Babi Yar*, which is a seemingly odd choice. The same issue arises in the otherwise distinguished *For Those I Loved—Au nom de tous les miens* (1983), which surprisingly relies exclusively on French in the Warsaw Ghetto. These choices—along with English in most American productions—must be addressed to understand Holocaust films.

Accents, too, are landmines. "Hank Azaria and especially David Schwimmer," wrote reviewer Reinier Verhoef of *Uprising* (TV 2001), "have accents so stupid I almost laughed during the cruelties."[7] Unintentional tension is added in *Uprising* simply by trying to decipher David Schwimmer's tortured, generic European accent. The same is true of Liam Neeson's nondescript accent in *Schindler's List*.[8] All of these attempts at accents are devoid of any hint of intended nationality or even finesse. American producers have been struggling with this dilemma since the beginning of Holocaust film production. There is no easy answer, especially when casting stars who only speak English; not everyone is Meryl Streep, who learned some German and Polish for her starring role in *Sophie's Choice*.[9]

The language choice quandary, however, has an answer: in most cases, the language of the film is the language of the primary production company. This explains why Japanese is spoken in the Japanese-produced *The Diary of Anne Frank—Anne no nikki* (1995), and French is spoken in the French-produced release of the identical animation, *The Diary of Anne Frank—Le Journal d'Anne Frank* (1999). It should also be noted that non–English-speaking countries have also produced a few English language Holocaust films, including *The Island on Bird Street* (1997), *The Truce—La tregua* (1997), *Left Luggage* (1998), *Amen.* (2002), *Spring 1941* (2007) and *Colette* (2013). That notwithstanding, overall, the dialect of most films—Holocaust or otherwise—is usually that of the producing country, which is almost always the home of the target audience.

Non-native language films present additional challenges, not just because of the external distraction of having to monitor subtitles, but also because subtitles alter timing. To enjoy a story, we must accept its internal logic and situational consistency. Dr. Emmett Brown's DeLorean is a time travel device only because director Robert Zemeckis spent the first ten minutes of *Back to the Future* (1985) establishing Brown's credentials. Dozens of small and medium planks made from dialogue and exposition are required before that internal logic is accepted by the audience. The best directors, however, pace their logical foundation with an archer's precision. Subtitles, which cause cognitive delay, run the risk of diminished language nuance and timing. In short, subtitles disrupt the process just enough for viewers to check out. For example, the protagonist in the French Survivor film *One Day You'll Understand—Plus tard* (2008) is an executive who ends up in a room with a woman his age, who happens to be his sister, which is obvious only from the nuance of the spoken language, French. Those relying on bad subtitles could easily conclude that the woman is his paramour, which would destroy the film's internal logic.

So, most Holocaust films intended for an English-speaking audience must either build the internal logic slower to compensate for the subtitles or use accented English dialogue that also can interfere with timing. Either way, viewers must be patient with films that were not intended for the viewers' native language.* Having laughably nonspecific accents just complicates the equation.

---

* Ironically, this calculus places inordinate importance onto film translator/subtitlers, who can liberate or destroy any non-native film during post-production.

American Guilt

Partly because of Holocaust films, the Holocaust has become woven in the American fabric. From museums to local memorials to theaters and books, the Holocaust has become the embodiment for Americans of global injustice. But why the Holocaust? Other twentieth-century genocides—such as the ineffable slaughters of Armenians, Cambodians, Rwandans, Russians under Stalin, and victims in Maoist China—do not resonate in America as do victims of the Holocaust, notwithstanding the great Oscar-recognized films *The Killing Fields* (1984) (Cambodia) and *Hotel Rwanda* (2004).

Perhaps Americans relate to the Holocaust because Holocaust survivors (witnesses) came to America during and after the War. Americans in major cities also associated with more Jews than with victims of other genocides, so Holocaust victims were not completely "other": Americans could relate to these suffering Europeans. Americans also knew about the evil Adolf Hitler and Nazi Germany, against whom America had embarked upon the greatest military investment in modern world history. And then there was the U.S. Army's liberation of several concentration camps, including Buchenwald and Dachau, documented by Hollywood's finest filmmakers, who were commissioned as officers and sent to make a record for posterity. And perhaps the conflation of the Holocaust with the 1948 birth of the State of Israel also represented those scrappy Jews. All of these slices are part of the American identification with the Holocaust.

But, perhaps the most compelling reason for post–War American outrage about the Holocaust was that when America was in Europe during the latter part of World War II, the American government knew about the slaughter of Jews, yet the official U.S. policy was: "the best way to save the Jews of Europe was to defeat the Nazis as quickly as possible."[10] Worse yet, Hitler told us what he was going to do in *Mein Kampf* in 1925 and he repeated his intentions to rid Germany of its "Jewish Problem"—and he did it—ultimately in full view of the world. And we were there but did nothing, is the logical conclusion for many Americans.

It is helpful, here, to pause and underscore the difference between various German camps: slave, concentration and death camps. Most numerous were slave labor camps—of which tens of thousands were operated throughout occupied Europe—and the many fewer "concentration camps" (some of which are listed in Table 18), which were originally intended as political prisons, especially for dissidents, communists, socialists, Jehovah's Witnesses, homosexuals and Roma (Gypsies).

Beyond those concentration camps, the Germans built six camps specifically for slaughter, interchangeably known as "death camps," "extermination camps" or "killing centers." All six of these death camps were in occupied Poland: Chelmno, Belzec, Sobibor, Treblinka, Majdanek, and the camp system of Auschwitz/Birkenau. While some concentration camps had small gas chambers—Dachau, Stutthof, Mauthausen, Sachsenhausen, and Ravensbrück[11]—extermination was the main business of the six death camps, even if labor sub-camps were part of a specific camp's system, like at Auschwitz/Birkenau. Most death camps used carbon monoxide gas generated by diesel engines to kill Jews. Some camps used specially designed trucks with the exhaust pumped into the rear cabin, while other camps pumped the exhaust into gassing rooms. At Auschwitz, however, and to a lesser extent Majdanek, the Germans used a pesticide called Zyklon B made by IG Farben (better known as the Bayer company,

TABLE 18: GERMAN CONCENTRATION CAMPS (NOT GERMAN DEATH CAMPS),
NON-EXHAUSTIVE

Country and Concentration Camps	Country and Concentration Camps	Country and Concentration Camps
Germany	**Austria**	**Netherlands**
Bergen-Belsen	Mauthausen-Gusen	Herzogenbusch
Buchenwald	**Czechoslovakia**	Westerbork
Dachau	Theresienstadt	**Norway**
Flossenbürg	**France**	Bardufoss
Kaufering/Landsberg	Natzweiler-Struthof	Bredtvet
Kemna	**Estonia**	**Poland**
Malchow	Vaivara	Fort VII (Posen)
Mittelbau-Dora	**Hungary**	Stutthof
Neuengamme	Kistarcsa	Warsaw
Niederhagen	**Latvia**	**Serbia**
Oberer Kuhberg	Kaiserwald	Banjica
Oranienburg	Salaspils (Kirchholm)	Crveni Krst
Ravensbrück		**Romania**
Sachsenhausen		Bogdanovka

as in aspirin) to kill millions. It has been estimated that from 1933 through 1945 in all German camps—concentration, labor and death—between 15 and 20 million people were killed or imprisoned.[12]

In the spring of 1944, there were two unquestionable salient facts about the American government vis-à-vis the biggest of these camps: first, the Roosevelt administration was fully aware of the genocidal purpose of Auschwitz/Birkenau; and second, Americans had the ability to strike Oswiecim, Poland, the home of Auschwitz/Birkenau, using B-17 Flying Fortress bombers. The question, of course, is: why didn't America target Auschwitz/Birkenau? That question assumes that bombing a death camp was the right thing to do, or even that bombing was desired by the afflicted party. Instead, Chairman of the Jewish Agency David Ben-Gurion wrote on June 11, 1944, "The view of the board is that we should not ask the Allies to bomb places where there are Jews."[13] Although Ben-Gurion soon after reversed his opinion, bombing Auschwitz was not even advocated by Jewish leadership until after more than 5.5 million Jews had already been slaughtered in ghettos, killing fields, scores of concentration camps, and five other death camps. Instead, Jewish focus had been on Jewish emigration out of Europe.

It should also be remembered that concurrent with David Ben-Gurion's letter of June 1944, the Allies were otherwise busy with the largest naval invasion in world history, D-Day. This was fully sixteen months after Germany's devastating defeat by the Soviets in the Battle of Stalingrad, starting the inexorable Soviet drive to Berlin. The Majdanek death camp in Lublin, Poland, was liberated by the Soviets on July 22, 1944, just a month after the Jewish Agency's official opinion might have changed. By then, the Soviets had pushed the Axis armies out of all Soviet Russia, had vanquished the Germans in Vilnius and Minsk (the respective largest cities of Lithuania and Belarus). By August of 1944, the Soviets were already in Romania and deeper into Poland. So, by the summer of 1944, the question was not if Auschwitz would be neutralized, but when.

Another flawed assumption is that American bombers could have destroyed the

Auschwitz/Birkenau infrastructure. But, according to the United States Strategic Bombing Survey, by 1944 only 7 percent of all bombs dropped by the Eighth Air Force hit within 300 meters of their aim point.[14] To be clear, that means only 1 in 14 bombs landed as close as three football fields to its target. Indeed, it would have required 108 B-17 bombers (18 squadrons), crewed by 1,080 airmen, dropping 648 bombs for just two of them to have hit within a 150-square meter area, with an effective blast radius of a thousand-pound bomb on a railway target of approximately 10 meters. Conversely, the majority of the other 646 bombs would have landed on the 100,000 Jewish laborers barracked within a few hundred meters of tracks at Birkenau, some of whom ultimately survived to liberation.

Yet, even if the American bombers had hit all their targets, there was still the question of efficacy. It is assumed that 80 percent of the infrastructure required for a railway is in the foundation; it was understood by the Allies that a German rail track that was bombed on Friday would be rebuilt by Monday. Further, even though Jewish prisoners destroyed two of five Birkenau crematoria in October of 1944, the Germans continued killing Jews and then burning some in overflow pyres. Even if the tracks and gas chambers had been destroyed, the Germans would simply have reverted to bullets or gas vans for the remaining Hungarian Jews, who were the last to be deported.

While Auschwitz/Birkenau was the most efficient killing machine, killing over a million people, the Einsatzgruppen (mobile German killing squads), for example, were responsible for even more deaths: "At least 1.5 million and possibly more than two million Holocaust victims died in mass shootings or gas vans in Soviet territory."[15] This period—sometimes referred to as "Holocaust by bullets"—was certainly messier and less efficient than the subsequent German methods, but just as lethal. So, to suggest that the Germans had only one remaining killing method after the construction or destruction of Auschwitz/Birkenau is farfetched. In context, the Hutu-led government in Rwanda murdered at least 750,000 Rwandan Tutsis in 14 weeks in 1994, largely with machetes. Thus, while the jewel of the German killing machine was Auschwitz/Birkenau, even if it had been destroyed, most of the remaining half-million Hungarian Jews would have been shot or simply starved to death, from Budapest to Oswiecim.

There is also a longstanding accusation that, because of antisemites in the Roosevelt Administration, America did little to help the Jews during the Holocaust. For example, it is now well-documented that Breckinridge Long, Assistant Secretary of State from 1940 to 1944, directly thwarted the legal immigration of Jewish refugees to America. Long's subterfuge—aided by like-minded antisemites on both sides of the Atlantic—was ultimately revealed in 1944 to President Roosevelt by Secretary of the Treasury Henry Morgenthau, Jr., who was known as "Roosevelt's Jew." Breckinridge Long was soon after dismissed in disgrace, and the War Refugee Board was created, which was responsible for settling 200,000 Jews in America. But Breckinridge Long was not solely responsible for inhibiting Jewish immigration; he was merely one of the many bureaucrats who impeded refugee entry.

The more complicated answer as to why America did so little to help the Jews of Europe was pervasive American racism. Indeed, within the lifetime of many who were elders in American government during the early rise of Nazism, America had enslaved and then segregated Blacks, slaughtered and despoiled Native Americans, enacted the Chinese Exclusion Act of 1882, and criminalized free speech via the Sedition Act of 1918. From 1934 to 1945, approximately 350,000 Americans were sterilized due to eugenics laws. Homosexuality and miscegenation were punishable in America until well after

World War II. And, of course, Japanese Americans were put in internment camps after Pearl Harbor, branded as enemies of the State, just as Jews were classified by Nazi Germany. Indeed, from that perspective, the totality of American history concerning non–Europeans appeared to be no different in law or practice from the stated Nazi policies. And frankly, why would anyone have expected the racially segregated U.S. military to have fought the racism of other nations?

Further, Jews and many other American minorities were systematically barred from certain housing, black-balled in private clubs, faced quotas in education, and were hindered in prominent professions. From General Ulysses S. Grant's order to expel Jews from the southern territories he controlled during the Civil War to Henry Ford's distribution of a half million copies of *The Protocols of the Elders of Zion* in the 1920s, discrimination against Jews in America was much greater than was discrimination against the Jews in Germany, at least until the early 1930s. So when it came time to call out German racism, despoilment and "resettlement," men like Breckinridge Long and Henry Ford found nothing either new or objectionable about German policies.

While many lessons can be learned from history, truth must be the starting point. First, just as America had no desire to help Europe before Japan's attack on Pearl Harbor (December 7, 1941), the American public was generally uninterested in helping Europe's Jews because America was a racist country that only started to shed its xenophobia in the 1950s, and only then because Hitler had given racism such a bad name.[16] And second, the bombing of Auschwitz has become a retroactive panacea—a catchphrase—that falsely implies a military solution to the German killing machine.

Certainly, the U.S. government lied about its inability to conduct air raids over Auschwitz. And certainly, in a post–*Inglourious Basterds* world, it is optimistic to have thought that Uncle Sam could have done more. But, the U.S. did accept more refugees than any other country, and approximately one-quarter of German Jews found refuge in America. As professor Michael Berenbaum argues, the bombing of Auschwitz was less of a military question than "a moral question emblematic of the Allied response to the plight of the Jews during the Holocaust."[17] True enough; the moral rot was deep, many thousands survived Auschwitz/Birkenau to liberation, partly due to one correct decision, which is something.

The majority of Holocaust films have been made by the European countries whose Jews were murdered, despoiled and ruined in the Holocaust. But many Holocaust films have been produced by Americans whose Jews were safe from Hitler's ghettos, killing fields and gas chambers. Reasonable responses to Professor Berenbaum's "moral question" have been memorials, museums and Holocaust education. But the earliest and most consistent American response to the Holocaust has been feature films and television productions. In the aggregate, American Holocaust cinema can be seen as the broader memorial.*

God, the Holocaust and Holocaust Exploitation

For those seeking to understand *how* the Holocaust occurred, many Holocaust films can elucidate; for those seeking to understand *why* the Holocaust occurred, Holocaust

---

* A portion of this section was first published in the *Jerusalem Post* on February 3, 2020, in an article by this author entitled "Why wasn't Auschwitz bombed, really?"

films are illusory. In *The Truce—La tregua* (1997), Primo Levi states with great certainty, "God cannot exist if Auschwitz exists." From the writings of Elie Wiesel (1928–2016) through Viktor Frankl (1905–1997) and beyond, the obvious Holocaust questions will always be: how and why did the God of the Jews allow His "chosen people" to suffer the fate of the Holocaust?

These questions have been ignored in all but a few Holocaust films. But one film willing to ask many theological questions of the Holocaust was the British television production *God on Trial* (TV 2008), which spent an hour and a half grappling with difficult issues. Based on the 1979 Elie Wiesel play *The Trial of God*,* God is not spared in *God on Trial*. Many of the same questions about God's place in the Holocaust are asked in *The Quarrel* (1991), directed by Eli Cohen, screenplay by David Brandes. In *The Quarrel*, three years after the War, two survivors/former best friends bump into each other in a Montreal park on Rosh Hashanah. One friend is secular while the other is the head of a yeshiva (seminary). While neither man's respective beliefs about the existence of God had been formed during the Holocaust, their positions were certainly hardened by it.

The theological questions are addressed much more subtly in Paul Mazursky's *Enemies: A Love Story* (1989), based on Isaac Bashevis Singer's 1966 novel *Enemies, A Love Story*. In the film version, one survivor (Ron Silver) uses his simultaneous marriage to three female survivors as an expression of his post–War agnosticism and nihilism. *Enemies, A Love Story* is a tender Survivor film that remembers not to be preachy. Other films that speak to retaining faith after the Holocaust include *The Pawnbroker* (1964), *The Revolt of Job—Jób lázadása* (1983) and *Korczak* (1990).

From Wiesel to Frankl to Singer, there is an almost implicit understanding that Jews, between themselves, can criticize God, but external suggestions of the proper Jewish responses to the Holocaust are completely different. And few topics are more explosive than using the Holocaust to advance non–Jewish goals. The Jewish community instinctively defends the Holocaust from being co-opted, which is vastly different from fighting Holocaust denial, which is more like arson than shoplifting. The notion that someone is "using" the Holocaust for non–Jewish purposes is fundamentally provocative. Even Jews who had no family in the Holocaust are proprietary toward the Holocaust. Of course, every ethnicity has their own version of "allow us our suffering." But the Holocaust, through film, has provided long coattails which some have ridden relentlessly, regardless of religion.

Mel Brooks brilliantly banked on that exact premise in *The Producers* (1967). His protagonists believed that the idea of nakedly exploiting the Holocaust, in a Broadway musical no less, was the ultimate taboo in Jewish New York. The joke, of course, was the ease with which the general public accepted Holocaust exploitation in *The Producers*, as long as it was entertaining. Brooks foresaw—a decade before *Ilsa: She Wolf of the SS* (1975)—that Holocaust exploitation was quite possible, both from a creative and a consumer standpoint.

The first major Holocaust commercialization was in a 1953 episode of the NBC weekly program *This Is Your Life*. Just eight years after the end of the War, Hanna Bloch Kohner, a survivor of Theresienstadt, Auschwitz and Mauthausen, was featured on a *This Is Your Life* episode. The show's host, Ralph Edwards, narrated for Mrs. Kohner an

---

* "The Trial of God (as it was held on February 25, 1649, in Shamgorod)" (Le procès de Shamgorod tel qu'il se déroula le 25 février 1649, first published in English in 1979 by Random House). "1649" is not a typo.

account of her life in a death camp, as if he were talking about any other personal tragedy. As recounted long after in the *New York Times*:

> Sitting in the "chair of honor," Mrs. Kohner watches in wonder as people from her past materialize to recall her childhood in Czechoslovakia, her deportation in a cattle car to Theresienstadt, her survival at Auschwitz and liberation at Mauthausen. A studio band plays Beethoven's Fifth Symphony, "The Horst Wessel Song" and the Kol Nidre prayer from Yom Kippur in the background.[18]

The episode was no less crass than *The Producers*, except *This Is Your Life* was no joke. This episode should have been the starting point for Elie Wiesel's tirade against Holocaust exploitation. Yet, a different type of Holocaust exploitation has also emerged. To understand non–Jewish exploitation of the Holocaust, "the Holocaust" must be defined. In the simplest terms, the Holocaust consisted of actions taken against the Jews by the Germans and their allies. Yad Vashem has a more specific definition:

> The Holocaust ... is defined as the sum total of all anti–Jewish actions carried out by the Nazi regime between 1933 and 1945: from stripping the German Jews of their legal and economic status in the 1930's; segregating and starvation in the various occupied countries; the murder of close to six million Jews in Europe. The Holocaust is part of a broader aggregate of acts of oppression and murder of various ethnic and political groups in Europe by the Nazis.[19]

In other words, a tire is part of a car, but a tire is a tire; German persecution of the Jews is the Holocaust, which is part of all suffering during World War II, but not all suffering during World War II was the Holocaust. Asians and Pacific Islanders were victims of Japanese war crimes. Interned Japanese Americans suffered during World War II at the direction and/or with the explicit consent of all three branches of the American government. The Germans directly or indirectly murdered approximately 200,000 handicapped Germans; between 1.8 and 2.8 million non–Jewish Poles; 15,000 German and Austrian homosexuals; 500,000 other Slavs; perhaps that many Romani (Gypsies), but at least 90,000; the clergy; POWs; political prisoners; Communists and bystanders. Many other non–Jews were murdered or damaged during World War II by scores of sovereignties and countless individuals. They all can make claims about suffering, recognition, memorials, reparations, empathy and names for their respective suffering. Nevertheless, the "Holocaust" (or "Shoah" in Hebrew) was—by definition—the uniquely Jewish experience of the persecution, despoilment, displacement and slaughter of European Jewry resulting from the Nazi regime. Terminology is not a question of numbers or intent or suffering, none of which should, or can, be compared. The "Holocaust" is a matter of definition, which is commonly misused, including by the media, such as in the following *HuffPost* headline: "The Holocaust's Forgotten Victims: The 5 Million Non-Jewish People Killed by the Nazis."[20]

"Porajmos" is the Romani (Gypsy) term for their unique experience during World War II, especially in Auschwitz. Documentaries and narrative films have been made about Porajmos, including *The Last Stage—The Last Stop—Ostatni etap* (1948), *And the Violins Stopped Playing* (1988), *Korkoro* (2009) and *Porraimos: Europe's Gypsies in the Holocaust* (2002).* Korean and other Asian women in countries occupied by Imperial Japan were referred to as "Comfort Women," a euphemism that minimizes these women's treatment as sex slaves at the hands of the Japanese during World War II. Wikipedia

---

* Roma have been portrayed in several Holocaust films, including: Edward James Olmos co-starred as a Roma Kapo in *Triumph of the Spirit* (1989); a scene in *Train of Life—Train de vie* (1998); a pregnant Roma inmate was briefly featured in *Out of the Ashes* (TV 2003). See also: "Porrajmos: The Romani and the Holocaust with Ian Hancock—Holocaust Living History," https://www.youtube.com/watch?v=tAEJb-p6SOE.

lists seven films about these War victims, including *Spirits' Homecoming* (2016) and *Herstory* (2018) and several documentaries. And the Chinese speak of "The Rape of Nanking" to uniquely identify the apex of Japanese aggression in China during the War, which is depicted in many films including *Iris Chang: The Rape of Nanking* (2007) and *City of Life and Death—Nanjing! Nanjing!* (2009) and the documentary *Nanking* (2007). And certainly, Communists suffered at the hands of the Germans, as expressed in many Soviet films, as well as in *The Photographer of Mauthausen—El fotógrafo de Mauthausen* (2018) about Spanish Communists handed over to Germany by the Franco government.

Yet, no ethnic or national experience other than that of the Jews is "The Holocaust," regardless of the dearth of ways to describe the suffering of others. In other words, suffering during World War II, or in Europe in particular, does not define a Holocaust victim, unless the victim was persecuted because they were Jewish. Even more specifically, Jews persecuted by the Germans explicitly for being homosexuals are not Holocaust victims, but victims of German homophobic policies. Likewise, handicapped Jews who were euthanized as part of the Aktion T4 program were not Holocaust victims. Polish POWs— even if Jewish—murdered at Katyń by the Soviets during World War II are not victims of the Holocaust. Political prisoners throughout the German-occupied lands who suffered in any way for any reason, other than because they were Jewish, were not victims of the Holocaust. And what of non–Jews who suffered for trying to save Jews from the Holocaust? Although these heroes suffered as a result of trying to help Jews, and while these righteous Gentiles should always be recognized as martyrs, these War victims were still correctly classified by Germany as "political prisoners." The political act of civil disobedience does not confer upon an activist the status of the underlying victim.

For example, in 1964 two Jewish boys from New York, Andrew Goodman and Michael Schwerner, were abducted and murdered in Mississippi while trying to register African American voters. These two men, and many other non–African Americans, made a political choice to fight post–Reconstruction institutional racism known as "Jim Crow." Goodman and Schwerner were not victims of Jim Crow, but political casualties of it. Any attempt to impart upon those two men the status of victims of American slavery and its aftermath is a mischaracterization. Yet, a third man who was murdered with them, James Chaney, was African American. Was Chaney a victim of Jim Crow or a political victim? I would defer to others for the answer. But, as for Goodman and Schwerner, they were political martyrs who were fighting American racism; by definition, they could not have been victims of Jim Crow.

This leads to *The Hiding Place* (1975), a film produced by World Wide Pictures— Billy Graham Evangelistic Association. *The Hiding Place* is the true story of a Dutch Gentile, Corrie ten Boom, and her sister who hid Jews from the Germans. Corrie ten Boom has rightfully been honored by the State of Israel at Yad Vashem with the title "Righteous Among the Nations." The Billy Graham Evangelistic Association website states about *The Hiding Place*:

> The book and film tell the story of Holocaust survivor Corrie ten Boom and her family in the years leading up to and during World War II. Their faithful and courageous efforts to save the lives of Jewish families pre-war ultimately landed them in one of the worst Nazi concentration camps. *The Hiding Place* is the most requested production released by World Wide Pictures.[21]

The official description of *The Hiding Place* reveals an obvious failure to learn basic Holocaust history. First, Corrie ten Boom was an evangelical political prisoner of the

Germans, who was arrested for suspicion of aiding Jews. As a Gentile, she could not have been a "Holocaust survivor" as described by Billy Graham's organization. Second, Jewish families in the Netherlands did not need to be saved "pre-war" because the Netherlands was invaded by Germany during the War, on May 10, 1940. Third, while concentration camps are typically beyond comparisons, the lesser-known Ravensbrück camp, which was operated in Germany, was certainly not "one of the worst Nazi concentration camps," let alone the implied death camps. Most of the inmates were political prisoners; few of the inmates were Jews.

But these quibbling objections aside, Billy Graham used the Holocaust through *The Hiding Place* to promote Christianity. The characters praise or speak the word "Jesus" 16 times and "Christ" five times. The dialogue includes, "Jesus knows everything we feel. He promised that when two or three get together in His name He would be there with them, even in Ravensbrück!" What is the exact message here? Are we to believe that Christian piety should prevail at the specific time that Christians attempted to kill millions of European Jews based on those Christians' belief in Christian superiority espoused for 2000 years in Christian theology? As William Nicholls (1933–2003), Professor of Religious Studies at the University of British Columbia, wrote in his seminal 1993 book *Christian Antisemitism: A History of Hate*, "No uncritical reader of the New Testament could easily come away with any but the most negative opinion of Jews."[22] Yet, *The Hiding Place* was intended to rehabilitate or excuse Christianity's responsibility for the historic European antisemitism that culminated in the Holocaust.

Unfortunately, *The Hiding Place* was not the only film that consoled Christianity for its complicity in the Holocaust. *A Rose in Winter* (2018) and *The Seventh Room—A hetedik szoba* (1996) also known as *Edith Stein, The Interior Castle and Auschwitz,* both tell the true story of a Jewish woman (Edith Stein) who converts to Catholicism, dies in Auschwitz because of her Jewish blood, and then is designated as a saint by Pope John Paul II. While not as grotesque as *The Hiding Place*, Edith Stein's story is also an unnecessary Christocentric view of the Holocaust.

Elsewhere, in *Bonhoeffer—Agent of Grace* (TV 2000) and *Amen.* (2002) a few Christian protagonists set out to suggest that some Christians did not agree with German racial policies, while remaining steadfastly faithful to their Christianity. Even if agnosticism or atheism had been the response of Jews in *God on Trial* and *The Quarrel*, their filmmakers certainly were not advocating adherence to the religion that was at the root of Holocaust oppression. And while I cannot suggest any theological answer for Holocaust victims, most assuredly the answer to the misery caused by the "master race" cannot be the "glory of Christ," which is the message of *The Hiding Place, Amen.* and *Bonhoeffer*. These three films attempted to hijack the Holocaust to justify Christian theology. The unspoken cherry on top of *The Hiding Place* is that it has helped fund evangelical ministries, which, at their core, espouse the bedrock belief that all Jews will burn in Hell for eternity at the time of the rapture. Had *The Hiding Place* been Elie Wiesel's target instead of *Sophie's Choice*, Wiesel would not have needed to recant.

But some bright notes with Christian content in Holocaust films do exist. *Conspiracy of Hearts* (1960), about Italian nuns saving Jewish children, was good and included minimal theology. *The Scarlet and the Black* (TV 1983), starring Christopher Plummer, John Gielgud and Gregory Peck as righteous Gentile Monsignor Hugh O'Flaherty, is mostly cute, as well as light on religion. And *Miracle at Moreaux* (TV 1986), which is an unbearably formulaic righteous Gentile film in the style of an "afternoon special," depicts a nun, delicately played by Loretta Swit, who runs a Catholic boarding school. The nun helps three Jewish children escape the Germans, yet does not preach Christian theology, except regarding the need to help people of all faiths. The same light touch is evident in the otherwise unremarkable *Edges of the Lord* (2001), where the local Catholic minister (Willem Dafoe) does not try to proselytize the hidden Jewish boy.

Free Men—Les hommes libres (2011), a French film that portrays the suffering of Muslims in Paris during the War, is less offensive than the above-mentioned Christo-centric films. While some of the Muslims in *Free Men* go out of their way to hide a North African Jew, *Free Men*, too, ignores the indelible alliance between the Germans and Arabs, especially in the British territory of Palestine.

Although less tone-deaf than the above-listed Christian films, the following Holocaust productions suggest that the reason to persevere is for a Gentile soul mate: *Return from the Ashes* (1965), *The Night Porter—Il portiere di notte* (1974), *QB VII* (Miniseries 1974), *The Last Metro—Le dernier métro* (1980), *For Those I Loved—Au nom de tous les miens* (1983), *Life Is Beautiful—La Vita è bella* (1997), *The Poet—Hearts of War* (2007), *Death in Love* (2008), *Remembrance* (2011), *Walk on Water* (2004) and *Phoenix* (2014). In several of these films, the Gentile is also the antagonist/persecutor. Without passing judgment on intermarriage in any way whatsoever, none of these films considers the societal taboo of intermarriage during and for 50 years after the War. By ignoring the topic, these films use the Holocaust to normalize intermarriage, which, although not as egregious as *The Hiding Place*'s message, is still inherently deceptive by omission.

There are also Holocaust-related films that are less about Jewish suffering and more about German persecution of homosexuals, including: *November Moon—November-mond* (1985), *Aimée & Jaguar* (1999), *Bent* (1997), *The Singing Forest* (2003), *Facing Windows—La Finestra di fronte* (2003), *A Love to Hide—Un amour à taire* (TV 2005) and *In Hiding—W ukryciu* (2013). While there is nothing inherently objectionable about films that depict gay love during World War II, each of the homosexuals in these films suffered at the hands of the Germans due to the victims' sexual orientation, not because they were Jews. That being said, *Bent*, in particular, portrays Dachau appropriately.

4

The Unavoidables

Elie Wiesel, Anne Frank,
Oskar Schindler and Oscar Bait

Elie Wiesel: The Elephant in the Room

There was a time, especially in the West, when portraying the Holocaust's inner workings in film was rare. The scarcity of graphic representations for more than 30 years after the Holocaust cannot be overstated. From today's perspective, with representations on television having no boundaries, it is difficult to imagine the shock in 1978 when seeing in NBC's extremely ambitious Holocaust miniseries: Kristallnacht, the Warsaw Ghetto, Babi Yar, Jewish resistance, torture, killing vans, euthanasia/eugenics, the Wannsee Conference, the Sobibor revolt, war crimes' investigations, and Auschwitz—including a gas chamber—all on primetime television. The breadth and specificity of this four-part, seven-hour docudrama was extraordinary for most viewers, their first significant exposure to the Holocaust—but unacceptable for some.

On April 16, 1978, the day that NBC aired the first *Holocaust* episode, *The New York Times* published an op-ed entitled "Trivializing the Holocaust: Semi-Fact and Semi-Fiction." The op-ed was written by Elie Wiesel (1928–2016), the most iconic Holocaust survivor in history. Wiesel asserted that *Holocaust* was "Untrue, offensive, cheap."[1] For Wiesel, who was a stranger to Holocaust films, the miniseries must have been as dismaying as if Mozart were forced to hear his most cherished work debuted by schoolchildren, conducted by an amateur who mixed up the pages and had no sense of rhythm; the notes were there, but somewhat out of place and lacking soul, even when played correctly. Perhaps partly because of the publicity generated by Wiesel's harsh criticism, one out of every two Americans watched part of the *Holocaust* miniseries.[2] Most did not know about the errors and few cared that *Holocaust* was overtly melodramatic. The American public was spellbound.

Wiesel's patience broke again in 1989, eleven years after *Holocaust* aired, three years after Wiesel won the Nobel Peace Prize. He lashed out this time against ABC's miniseries *War and Remembrance* (Miniseries 1988) in another *New York Times*' op-ed entitled "Art and the Holocaust: Trivializing Memory."[3] In this second round, Wiesel penned 1,700 words that boiled down to his assertion that the Holocaust was becoming commercialized and fictionalized by people who had no business writing about or profiting from the Holocaust.*

---

* Permission to reprint in the Appendix of this book both of Elie Wiesel's op-eds about Holocaust films was repeatedly sought from the copyright holder, The Elie Wiesel Foundation for Humanity. Alas, permission had not been granted when this book went to press.

Elie Wiesel's attack on the quality of made-for-television Holocaust depictions was somewhat justified, even if sanctimonious. By 1988, 17 American television films and miniseries had been produced (or co-produced). (See Table 19.)

TABLE 19: AMERICAN-MADE (OR CO-PRODUCED) HOLOCAUST TELEVISION PRODUCTIONS

Recommended in **Bold** (2 of 52). "One of the Best" in **Bold and Underlined** (1 of 15).
Unavailable films in ~~Strikeout~~ (3).

1946–1988	1989–2018
The Diary of Anne Frank (TV 1967)	~~*Murderers Among Us: The Simon Wiesenthal Story* (TV 1989)~~
QB VII (Miniseries 1974)	*Max and Helen* (TV 1990)
Holocaust (Miniseries 1978)	*Never Forget* (TV 1991)
The House on Garibaldi Street (TV 1979)	*Forget Me Not: The Anne Frank Story* (TV 1996)
The Diary of Anne Frank (TV 1980)	*The Man Who Captured Eichmann* (TV 1996)
Playing for Time (TV 1980)	*A Call to Remember* (TV 1997)
Skokie—Once They Marched Through a Thousand Towns (TV 1981)	*In the Presence of Mine Enemies* (TV 1997)
The Wave (TV 1981)	*Miracle at Midnight* (TV 1998)
Remembrance of Love (TV 1982)	*The Devil's Arithmetic* (TV 1999)
The Wall (TV 1982)	*Bonhoeffer: Agent of Grace* (TV 2000)
The Scarlet and the Black (TV 1983)	*Nuremberg* (TV 2000)
~~*The Execution* (TV 1985)~~	**<u>Anne Frank: The Whole Story</u>** (TV 2001)
Wallenberg—A Hero's Story (TV 1985)	**Conspiracy** (TV 2001)
Miracle at Moreaux (TV 1986)	*Haven* (TV 2001)
~~*Lena: My 100 Children* (TV 1987)~~	*Uprising* (TV 2001)
The Attic: The Hiding of Anne Frank (TV 1988)	*Varian's War: The Forgotten Hero* (TV 2001)
War and Remembrance (Miniseries 1988)	*Out of the Ashes* (TV 2003)
	The Courageous Heart of Irena Sendler (TV 2009)

While many of these TV films were successful—financially and educationally—most were also, in retrospect, amazingly offensive. Indeed, some were horrifyingly bad. It would be hopeful to imagine that Wiesel's criticism raised the bar. Since 1989, 18 other American-produced or co-produced television films or miniseries were made. All but a few were vast improvements on their predecessors. Two were superb: *Anne Frank: The Whole Story* (TV 2001) and *Conspiracy* (TV 2001). Portions of *Haven* (TV 2001), *Uprising* (TV 2001) and *Varian's War: The Forgotten Hero* (TV 2001) were excellent or good enough. Most of the other programs were deeply flawed, clueless as to their offensiveness. Objectively, the quality of made-for-television Holocaust films improved after Wiesel's op-eds, which also tracked with the overall improvement in Holocaust film generally.

The networks, however, were impervious to Wiesel's fundamental criticisms; the sponsors continued to buy commercials and producers continued to invest in non-miniseries, made-for-television Holocaust films. In an America that was eating up whatever Holocaust television was being produced, few agreed enough with Wiesel to turn off Holocaust TV. Except for a handful of intellectuals, Jewish America—which regarded any Holocaust representations as a victory—tacitly rejected Wiesel's condemnations.

Although Wiesel rightly assailed the low quality of television productions, he also attacked several films, including the renowned *Sophie's Choice* (1982), the only American-made feature film on his hit list of "exploitative" films. At the same time,

Wiesel ignored many inconceivably inept films. His pontificating—without even knowing which films deserved censure—undermined his credibility as the arbiter of all-things-Holocaust. While it is arguable that American Holocaust film was indirectly changed by Wiesel's op-eds, his attacking such a well-regarded and celebrated film as *Sophie's Choice* undercut his legacy outside of literary circles.

Wiesel's wide-ranging assault on Holocaust films went beyond criticisms of specific productions. Most of his positions were untenable, especially since, as he admitted years later, at the time he wrote the op-eds he did not know, like or understand films altogether. At the time, Wiesel was arguing that he and other Holocaust victims, alone, had a monopoly on the Holocaust, and on the product thereof. Wiesel tried to erect a fence around Holocaust fiction. As he argued, "Auschwitz is something else, always something else. It is a universe outside the universe, a creation that exists parallel to creation."[4] Yes, for Elie Wiesel, this is all true; however, for prisoners at Majdanek, for whom Auschwitz was considered an upgrade, their stories, too, needed to be told, whether firsthand, allegorically, or fictionalized. As for other writers of fiction, whose job it is to expose places that have heretofore been indescribable, Auschwitz is no different from Dresden or Hiroshima, or, for that matter, Manzanar, one of ten American concentration camps holding more than 120,000 Japanese Americans from December 1942 to November 1945.

And then there is the matter of the miniseries *War and Remembrance*, the trigger for Wiesel's second tirade. In the same paragraph where Wiesel denounces the *War and Remembrance* miniseries, he praises the underlying eponymous 1978 novel by his friend Herman Wouk as being "shattering and sensitive."[5] Yet Wiesel surely knew that Herman Wouk was not in the camps. Indeed, Wouk was not even born in Europe, but in the Bronx, and eventually served in the U.S. Navy during the War. In that single comment, Wiesel accidentally acknowledged that suffering in Auschwitz is not, in fact, a prerequisite for writing about Auschwitz, or anything else.

Cecil B. DeMille was not at Mount Sinai. George Lucas was never in a star cruiser. Steven Spielberg never met an alien. And Norman Jewison was never in Anatevka circa 1905. In fact, Jewison, who directed the most famous Jewish film of all time—*Fiddler on the Roof* (1971), which won three and was nominated for eight more Oscars—is neither Jewish nor of Jewish ancestry. Indeed, the best-selling 1994 novel *Snow Falling on Cedars* (recipient of the PEN/Faulkner Award for Fiction), is the story of Japanese-Americans' imprisonment in a California "internment camp," an American concentration camp (not death camp). *Snow Falling on Cedars* fictionalized and revealed—for countless otherwise uninterested readers—the American war crime perpetrated against Japanese-Americans. *Snow Falling on Cedars* was written by David Guterson, an Ashkenazi Jew born 11 years after the end of the War, in 1956. Accepting Wiesel's dual notions—that first-hand knowledge and skin-in-the-game are required to write about the Holocaust or anything—would eliminate all but a tiny fraction of fiction.

Wiesel, who made his reputation and fortune by writing historical Holocaust fiction, some more and some less autobiographical, also argued that non-fiction textbooks and documentaries are the only acceptable sources of Holocaust information. As a purely academic exercise, his argument may have been correct; that second-hand knowledge should be ingested in its purest form. But that is not our world. Although Holocaust intellectuals have relied on many of the scholarly sources Wiesel recommended in his second op-ed—including books by Raul Hilberg, Lucy Davidowicz and

Martin Gilbert, along with Claude Lanzmann's 9½ hour *Shoah*—the MTV generation and beyond were not realistic candidates for Wiesel's syllabus, outside of a collegiate course.

Further, while Elie Wiesel was the biggest stick in Holocaust pop culture, he was not the only voice. Other Auschwitz survivors used their experiences to create art, outside of literature. Indeed many Auschwitz survivors/filmmakers did not agree with Wiesel's pronouncements and denouncements of Holocaust filmmaking, as can be seen in their work. For instance, Auschwitz survivor Wanda Jakubowska (1907–1998) not only filmed *The Last Stage—The Last Stop—Ostatni etap* (1948) in Auschwitz, but also used Holocaust survivors as cast members. Jakubowska also made the Tangential Holocaust films *The End of Our World—Koniec naszego swiata* (1964) and *Invitation—Zaproszenie* (1986). And Auschwitz survivor Branko Lustig (1932–2019), who donated to Yad Vashem his Best Picture Oscar for producing *Schindler's List*, obviously was not on Wiesel's non-narrative Holocaust film bandwagon. Nor was director and Holocaust survivor Yoram Gross (1926–2015), who was on Schindler's real list, but who escaped independently, and who made the animated Holocaust film *Sarah and the Squirrel—The Seventh Match* (1982). Nor was Holocaust survivor Artur "Atze" Brauner, a producer of the Best Foreign Language Oscar winner *The Garden of the Finzi-Continis—Il Giardino dei Finzi-Contini* (1970), one of 13 Holocaust films produced by Brauner. Nor was Auschwitz survivor Robert Clary (1926–), who co-starred in the Holocaust television film *Remembrance of Love* (TV 1982) and who was also a cast member of *Hogan's Heroes* (TV 1965–1971), along with three other Holocaust survivors/refugees: Werner Klemperer (1920–2000), "Colonel Klink"; John Banner (1910–1973), "Sergeant Schultz"; and Leon Askin (1907–2005), "General Burkhalter." Each of these survivors, each of these members of the filmmaking community (and many others) tacitly rejected Wiesel's uncompromising premise that fictionalizing the Holocaust should be the exclusive domain of literature. These survivors and refugees, too, had just as much a right to make a living from their experiences as did Wiesel.

In retrospect, it was Wiesel's condescension that was most galling in his op-eds. One week after the initial attack, the following rejoinder was fired back at Wiesel in a 900-word op-ed to the same *New York Times*: "Mr. Wiesel has trodden his wine press [*sic*] alone. Apart from John J. O'Connor, the *Times* TV critic, … every major newspaper and magazine critic, every major religious group, every important educational group that viewed *Holocaust* has found it stirring, important and of high moral value."[6]

History, too, has repudiated Wiesel's attack. Consider, for example, the impact of the miniseries *Holocaust* in Germany, where the miniseries was joked to have had a greater impact than the original.[7] As stated by the German historian Martin Broszat (1926–1989), "…[*Holocaust*] has brought millions of viewers in the Federal Republic into contact with the Jewish catastrophe during the Nazi tenure more intensively than ever before. Many may now have confronted it for the first time in their lives."[8] And according to Professor Lars Rensmann, Permanent Fellow at the University of Potsdam's Moses Mendelssohn Center for European-Jewish Studies:

> In the course of the last 20 years, Holocaust education has certainly gained importance, not least because of new generations of teachers. This is an effect of the public discourses and memorizations of the Holocaust since 1979 and the first major debates when the TV series *Holocaust* was broadcast in Germany and initiated a new kind of awareness about a subject which was still rather a taboo up until then.[9]

I interviewed former U.S. Ambassador to the European Union Stuart Eizenstat,[10] who, in addition to holding other high government positions, negotiated restitution for Holocaust victims on behalf of the United States government. Eizenstat entered the national stage as President Jimmy Carter's White House Domestic Affairs Advisor. Eizenstat confirmed to me, unequivocally, that immediately after the initial airing of the NBC miniseries *Holocaust*, he had written a memo to President Carter suggesting the formation of the President's Commission on the Holocaust. Within six months of the final episode of *Holocaust*, the President's Commission was established. Less than a year later, the commission recommended the establishment of what became the United States Holocaust Memorial Museum (USHMM) in Washington, D.C., which was funded by Congress by unanimous vote in 1980. As of June of 2019, 45 million people had visited the USHMM, a quarter of whom were schoolchildren. Approximately 90 percent of the USHMM visitors are not Jewish.[11] In 2011, the USHMM established the "Elie Wiesel Award." And who was the chairman of the initial President's Commission on the Holocaust appointed by Jimmy Carter in the wake of the miniseries *Holocaust*? Elie Wiesel, who referred to *Holocaust* as exploitative, "in the most vulgar sense of the word."[12]

Years later, Elie Wiesel renounced his Holocaust film denouncements.[13] Wiesel also admitted that film had not been of interest to him until Harvey Weinstein taught him to love films.[14] Perhaps Wiesel was correct to break the emergency glass (twice) about Holocaust films, if only to pump the brakes. At best, his intellectual exercise was an indictment of inept storytellers. At worst, Wiesel's op-eds were reckless, ignorant, and perhaps examples of old-school literary snobbery in the face of competing media.

Regardless—and notwithstanding the coarseness of many Holocaust productions—although I have no empirical evidence, I am quite sure that, rightly or wrongly, narrative Holocaust film and television have imparted more Holocaust knowledge worldwide than all other sources combined, including Hilberg, Davidowicz, Gilbert, Lanzmann and Wiesel. Although most of Elie Wiesel's arguments and predictions about Holocaust depictions have been disproven, his objections were historically noteworthy. Had his suggestions been fully adopted, however, the world would still be Holocaust-ignorant.

Anne Frank: A Microcosm of Holocaust Film

Anne Frank presents two distinct stories: one story is about an adolescent Jewish girl hiding from the Germans, a vivacious girl who is captured, sent to Auschwitz and dies in Bergen-Belsen just before its liberation; the other story is about Anne Frank's actual diary that she received on her 13th birthday, June 12, 1942, just before the Franks went into hiding. Although Anne Frank was a very real person, she has been relentlessly commodified, including in a video game, t-shirts, and even an ill-fated Halloween costume[15] and cosmetics.[16] But the Anne Frank Diary industry has led a life of its own; subsequent writings and publications have spawned plays, films and controversies.

Anne Frank wrote in her plaid diary for almost two years, chronicling her experiences, thoughts and feelings. Then, on March 29, 1944, Anne Frank heard exiled Dutch Education Minister Gerrit Bolkestein speaking from London on Dutch News Radio. Bolkestein announced that after the war he would collect and publish written stories about Dutch suffering during the German occupation. Bolkestein's request for written accounts of oppression thrilled Anne Frank, who had already dreamt of becoming a famous writer.

Yet, the then almost 15-year-old writer was embarrassed by her 13-year-old writings. So, from March 1944 until her capture on August 4, 1944, Anne Frank edited her original passages for publication. "… [Anne Frank] resolved to write a new book that she called 'The Secret Annex,' based on her diaries, which she hoped to submit after the war. She completed 215 loose pages in a couple of months…."[17] Because the physical diary was filled, Anne Frank continued her writing on scraps of paper. Anne Frank historians refer to the early writings and the edited writings as versions "A" and "B," respectively.

After the family's capture, the scattered papers in the attic were gathered by the Franks' protector, Miep Gies. After the War, she returned the unread papers to the sole survivor of the attic, Otto Frank, upon his return from Auschwitz. Surprisingly, the full version "B" of Anne Frank's diary was never published by Otto Frank. Instead, he created and published a shorter version "C," using passages from "A" and "B."[18] Version "C" was published in 1947 as *Het Achterhuis. Dagboekbrieven 14 Juni 1942–1 Augustus 1944* (*The Annex: Diary Notes 14 June 1942–1 August 1944*) by Contact Publishing in Amsterdam. The English version, *The Diary of a Young Girl*, was published by Doubleday & Company in 1952 and has since been published in more than 70 languages, and has sold more than 25 million copies.[19] In fact, according to Ranker.com, *The Diary of a Young Girl* has actually sold 35 million copies and is the 31st bestselling book of all time (with Dickens' *A Tale of Two Cities* at the top, selling more than 200 million copies).[20]

Otto Frank is believed to have had two reasons to redact versions "A" and "B." First, version "C" was intended to be part of a Contact Publishing series of other Dutch biographies that were much shorter than Anne Frank's complete diary. And second, Otto Frank hoped to protect the reputations of Anne Frank and her mother, Edith Frank. According to the *Independent* in 1998, "[Otto Frank] had excised significant portions of her [Anne Frank's] scribblings, including negative remarks about friends who went into hiding with the family and who later died in concentration camps. At the request of his Catholic publishing house in the Netherlands, he also cut what were then deemed to be sexually graphic passages."[21]

In 1952 America, while some would have been offended by an adolescent girl lashing out at her mother, Anne Frank's "personal" redacted passages are a completely different matter. Take, for example, Anne Frank's diary entry from March 24, 1944, penned just five days before hearing Minister Bolkestein on the radio:

Until I was eleven or twelve, I didn't realize there was a second set of labia on the inside, since you couldn't see them. What's even funnier is that I thought urine came out of the clitoris. I asked Mother one time what that little bump was, and she said she didn't know. She can really play dumb when she wants to! But to get back to the subject. How on earth can you explain what it all looks like without any models? Shall I try anyway? Okay, here goes! When you're standing up, all you see from the front is hair. Between your legs there are two soft, cushiony things, also covered with hair, which press together when you're standing, so you can't see what's inside. They separate when you sit down, and they're very red and quite fleshy on the inside. In the upper part, between the outer labia, there's a fold of skin that, on second thought, looks like a kind of blister. That's the clitoris. Then come the inner labia, which are also pressed together in a kind of crease. When they open up, you can see a fleshy little mound, no bigger than the top of my thumb. The upper part has a couple of small holes in it, which is where the urine comes out. The lower part looks as if it were just skin, and yet that's where the vagina is. You can barely find it, because the folds of skin hide the opening…. That's all there is, and yet it plays such an important role![22]

That passage and many others are conspicuously absent from the original 1952 English edition, skipping from March 23 directly to March 27. There are also deleted entries about Anne Frank's arousal, menstruation, masturbation and her sexual attraction to other girls.

The belief that Otto Frank had redacted his daughter's writings was intensified in 1998 with the discovery of five pages of her writings that had purportedly been given by Otto Frank to a friend, Cor Suijk, to be forever sequestered. According to news reports, "Mr. Suijk, a former employee of the Amsterdam-based Anne Frank Foundation, has told scholars Mr. Frank gave him the missing pages as a gift. Mr. Barnouw [of the Netherlands State Institute for War Documentation] believes he [Otto Frank] wanted to keep their contents private."[23]

Still, Holocaust scholar Laureen Nussbaum, professor emeritus at Portland State University and an acquaintance of Anne Frank's in Amsterdam, suggests that, in fact, the opposite is true: Anne Frank, herself, redacted version "B" and Otto Frank restored some personal portions in version "C":

> When Anne revised her texts, she left out most of her outbursts against her mother. In the light of the prevailing myth, it is interesting that Otto Frank restored several of them in the c-version, for instance in the entry of October 3, 1942. He did the same with a sentence in the a-version in which Anne expresses her longing for her first menstruation. Anne left it out in her rewrite, dated October 29, 1942. Her father reinstated the passage in the c-version.
>
> For the period of December 22, 1943 till March 29, 1944, Otto Frank again had both Anne's a- and b-texts at his disposal. The process of Anne's growing critical introspection can be readily observed if one compares the two versions of her description of a Christmas eve visit by one of the helpers and of the emotional turmoil this visit invokes in her (December 24, 1943). Anne's longing for freedom and a carefree youth has not diminished, but in the b-version her language is more poetic than in the original entry. Moreover, she now adds that she should stop feeling sorry for herself and she ends on a brave and positive note. Here and in subsequent entries Otto Frank deemed it necessary to reinstate the more lachrymose passages Anne had cut out and, occasionally, he even added a sentence or two from other entries Anne had eliminated. As a result much of the coherence of the compositional set-up of Anne's b-version is lost.
>
> The development from a- to b- to c-version can be readily followed by studying a long entry of January 5–6, 1944. In the a-version Anne tells about a psychological wound her mother inflicted on her several years ago. It still hurts, when she thinks of it. In the b-version she eliminates the whole episode and she does the same with another passage of this entry, dealing with her developing body, her menstruation and her "terrible urge" to feel her breasts at night in bed. Otto reinstated both sections of the entry in his c-version, which is again totally at variance with the often repeated statement that he had only left out passages in which Anne had expressed negative feelings about her mother or in which she had written too freely about her own body.[24]

How Otto Frank—who died in 1980—prepared his daughter's original diary became a much bigger discussion six years after his death when *The Critical Edition* of Anne Frank's diary was published (Dutch 1986, English 1989). This newer publication included comparisons from all known versions, both edited and unedited. It also included a discussion about authentication and historical information. *The Critical Edition* is described by Amazon as: "A comparison of the three versions of Anne Frank's diary; Anne's original entries, including never-before-published material; the diary as she herself edited it while in hiding; and the best-known version, edited by her father."[25]

Less than a decade later came 1995's *The Definitive Edition*, which promised: "At last, in a new translation, this definitive edition contains entries about Anne's burgeoning sexuality and confrontations with her mother that were cut from previous editions."[26] And then in 2003, with the discovery of ever more pages, *The Revised Critical Edition* was published, described by Amazon as: "The only complete collection of writings by Anne Frank, this impressive volume contains three of the extant versions of her Diary (including pages that came to light in 1998), *Tales from the Secret Annex* (her lesser-known short stories, fables, and personal reminiscences), and *Cady's Life* (her unfinished novel), along with the latest, most definitive scholarly research into Frank's life."[27]

Doubleday's *Revised Critical Edition* was superseded three years later by Wilco Books' 2006 *Anne Frank: Diary of a Young Girl (Complete and Unabridged)*, which may, in fact, be more complete and unabridged than previous versions that claimed to be completely unabridged—which is completely redundant. Wilco Books was somehow able to publish their 290-page version in 2006, eleven years after Doubleday's 1995 "complete" 340-page *The Definitive Edition*.

As if this were not enough, in 2018 two more pages of Anne Frank's writing containing bawdy material were discovered, having been taped-over. As noted in *The New York Times*, "the teenage diarist who wrote about coming-of-age in a secret attic annex while in hiding from the Nazis during World War II, may have camouflaged the two pages because they contained prurient content that she didn't want her father or someone else in the cramped quarters to discover."[28] This finding comports with Professor Nussbaum's theory.

And finally, in 2019 Bloomsbury Continuum published *Anne Frank: The Collected Works*, a mammoth 752-page foray, which is still not the gravy train's caboose. Indeed, Amazon lists more than 160 soft-cover books authored by Anne Frank (50 just in English), published through 2020. Another 67 Anne Frank-authored hardback and 47 Kindle editions are listed there, including workbooks, graphic novels and "young readers' editions," all seemingly with the consent of the copyright holder, the Anne Frank Foundation (Fonds).

Educators and school districts have almost instinctively used Anne Frank's diary to teach the Holocaust. Hundreds of articles have been written about the educational value of Anne Frank's experiences and thoughts. Lawsuits have also been filed to prohibit the unredacted versions from being in schools and libraries. The entire story of the Anne Frank publications was told thoughtfully by Jessica Landfried in, "Anne Frank, the Holocaust Victim: The Controversy about Her Diary in School Education, and the Controversy about Her Image."[29]

Using Anne Frank to teach the Holocaust boils down to using her words to tell the lighter part of her Holocaust story, while utilizing history books to fill in her post-capture details. Thus, the newer versions include her full biography, which is needed to understand the author's fate. In essence, these complete versions also include de facto history books about how and where Anne Frank died. So, educators teaching with Anne Frank's diary must not only unpack the Holocaust in general, which is muted in her diary, but must also unpack the derivative specific suppositions about Anne Frank's life after she was captured. For this reason, Warren Marcus, director of teacher workshops and conferences in the education division of the United States Holocaust Memorial Museum, also takes issue with The Diary of Anne Frank, suggesting, "Teachers may teach the diary or play and not instruct their students about the last months of her life. Students would be left with many misconceptions about her life as well as about the Holocaust in general."[30]

Plainly, until Anne Frank stopped writing the day she was put on a train, the Holocaust educational component of her story is shallow in relation to most other Holocaust accounts. Notwithstanding the unimaginable suffering described by Anne Frank in hiding, the Franks were unrepresentative of most other Holocaust victims until their discovery; the vast majority of European Jews did not even have the luxury of hiding like rats for years in an attic. As Anne Frank acknowledged in her diary on May 1, 1943, "If I just think of how we live here, I usually come to the conclusion that it is a paradise compared with how other Jews who are not in hiding must be living." So, additionally, educators using Anne Frank must also stress that her diary barely even describes the Holocaust's edge. Indeed, from a Holocaust perspective, Anne Frank's diary only teaches about generic Jewish suffering, which could have occurred at any time, including in 1800s Eastern Europe and during the Spanish Inquisition.

And, frankly, the lesson of the Holocaust must not be Anne Frank's pollyannaish and most famous passage: "In spite of everything I still believe that people are really good at heart." That sentence from *The Diary of a Young Girl* was written on July 15, 1944, just weeks before Anne Frank's capture. To champion this aspirational declaration of Anne Frank, with our knowledge of extermination camps, death squads and genocide—facts unknown to Anne Frank while she was writing her diary—is an example of either acute denial or pathological cognitive dissonance. Indeed, the discipline of psychology is much more relevant than is history or literature when seeking to understand why such a narrative could be promoted in the wake of the Holocaust. Teaching about hope within the context of the Holocaust is merely a validation of the precise human weakness that ignored Hitler's explicit genocidal promises. As lambasted by Ron Rosenbaum in *Tablet Magazine*:

> It's not even clear she wrote this pablum about how good at heart "people" are. Some have said it may have been written by her father to make the diary of her experience more reader-friendly, not the indictment of the populace of Amsterdam, Germany, and indeed all of Europe, who collaborated in her death. Because of course shortly after the upbeat inspiring paragraph was written (or allegedly written) by the young girl, her "secret annex" hiding place was ratted out by Jew-hating neighbors eager to please the mass murderers working for Hitler. All of whom were "truly good of heart" of course. She was shipped off to Bergen-Belsen where she died of typhus or execution by the good-hearted death camp guards.[31]

Tim Blake Nelson's film *The Grey Zone* (2001) was based on Primo Levi's assertion that we are all capable of unthinkable acts. As Nelson wrote, "much of Levi's writing seemed to oppose the themes of Anne Frank. People are not essentially 'good at heart.'"[32] Indeed, the lessons of the Holocaust include that people are *not* necessarily good at heart. The lessons also include that humanity runs the gamut from evil to saintly and that bad adults seldom learn to be good. Further, a lesson from World War II is that non-combatants are fair game in modern war, both tactically (Dresden and Hiroshima) and strategically (genocide). An ancillary lesson of World War II is that enslavement of local populations is not a historical anomaly from the Bible or the New World, but a modern fact from Marseille to Moscow, from Oslo to Athens, and, yes, from Calcutta to California. The ultimate lesson of 1937–1945—during which more people were killed than in all other wars in world history—is that even people who are good at heart act mostly in their own self-interests.

Most assuredly, even the highly enlightened Anne Frank, as she was subjugated in Auschwitz and subsequently dying in Bergen-Belsen, incapacitated by typhus and starvation, feebly fending off rats from eating her sister's body, did not die with the belief, purportedly scribbled in her attic, that people are good at heart. To teach this spurious concept, which was naively written before Anne Frank's deportation, is a disingenuous misappropriation of Anne Frank's innocence. Bluntly, it is preposterous to suggest that the Anne Frank who was either burned or bulldozed at Bergen-Belsen believed at her death that "In spite of everything I still believe that people are really good at heart."

Thus we have arrived at the inescapable dichotomy of relying upon Anne Frank's diary as source material, educationally or theatrically: filmmakers love making stories about "being good at heart" and rarely stray into the unpleasantness of reality, which is the ultimate dilemma of making Holocaust films. As Professor Michael Berenbaum made clear, "Towards the very end of Anne Frank's diary, she says what is emblematically American. The reality is, you cannot come out of understanding the Holocaust by saying that people are good at heart. People may be good at heart, but the Holocaust is certainly no manifestation of that."[33]

As for films, an "Anne Frank" query on the Yad Vashem film database returns 119 titles. IMDb lists 68 titles in many formats, including: feature films, television specials, shorts, miniseries, episodes and one video game, 2010's *Anne Frank: The Game*.[34] While Wikipedia's Holocaust film list includes 10 Anne Frank films (narrative and documentary), a separate Wikipedia page entitled "List of films about Anne Frank"[35] includes more than twice as many Anne Frank films, 22 entries, from 1941 through 2016, with films originating from six of the 12 original NATO members, Japan, several FSU countries—before and after the SU—and Israel.[36] But Wikipedia missed the Spanish version, *El diari d'Anna Frank* (TV 1996) and Wikipedia includes *Freedom Writers* (2007), which mentions Anne Frank's diary and portrays Miep Gies, but is not an Anne Frank film. Whittling down Wikipedia's "List of films about Anne Frank" leaves only about a dozen available narrative Anne Frank films. (See Table 20, which includes "ghosts," films that are not listed or are unavailable or listed on IMDb with almost no user ratings.)

TABLE 20: WIKIPEDIA'S NARRATIVE ANNE FRANK BIOGRAPHY FILMSHY FILMS[37]
Recommended in **Bold** (3 of 52). Unavailable films in ~~Strikeout~~ (5).

Year	Title	Country	Director	Notes
1958	~~The Diary of Anne Frank= Das Tagebuch der Anne Frank~~	East Germany	Emil Stöhr	Television
1959	The Diary of Anne Frank	United States	George Stevens	Film
1959	~~The Diary of Anne Frank= Dnevnik Ane Frank~~	Yugoslavia	Mirjana Samardzic	Television
1962	~~The Diary of Anne Frank= Dagboek van Anne Frank~~	Netherlands	Unknown	Television
1967	~~The Diary of Anne Frank~~	United States	Alex Segal	Television
1980	The Diary of Anne Frank	United States	Boris Sagal	Television
1985	The Diary of Anne Frank— Het dagboek van Anne Frank	Netherlands	Jeroen Krabbé, Hank Onrust	Television
1987	The Diary of Anne Frank	United Kingdom	Gareth Davies	Television
1988	The Attic: The Hiding of Anne Frank	United States	John Erman	Television
1995	The Diary of Anne Frank— Anne no nikki	Japan	Akinori Nagaoka	Anime adaptation of the Diary of Anne Frank
1996	~~The Diary of Anne Frank= El diari d'Anna Frank~~	Spain	Tamzin Townsend	
1999	The Diary of Anne Frank— Le Journal d'Anne Frank	France	Julian Wolff	Film; animated version of Anne Frank's diary. Edited from Anne no nikki.

Year	Title	Country	Director	Notes
2001	***Anne Frank: The Whole Story***	United States—Czech Republic	Robert Dornhelm	Television; some depictions in this version are disputed. Not endorsed by the Anne Frank Foundation.
2009	*The Diary of Anne Frank*	United Kingdom	Jon Jones	Television
2009	*Memories of Anne Frank—Mi Ricordo Anna Frank*	Italy	Alberto Negrin	Television
2015	***My Daughter Anne Frank—Meine Tochter Anne Frank***	Germany	Raymond Ley	Television documentary
2016	***The Diary of Anne Frank—Das Tagebuch der Anne Frank***	Germany	Hans Steinbichler	Cinema

Cynthia Ozick wrote that Anne Frank's story has been "bowdlerized, distorted, transmuted, traduced, reduced; it has been infantilized, Americanized, homogenized, sentimentalized, falsified, kitschified, and, *in fact,* blatantly and arrogantly denied."[38] Certainly, all of this is true when the aggregate of Anne Frank cinema is considered. The changes in Anne Frank's cinematic depiction also track with the overall development of Holocaust film from the Early Era through the Consolidated Era, and film in general. As snapshots, consider the language used in three PG-rated Steven Spielberg films over 43 years: in *Jaws* (1975) the word "shit" was used once, seven years later in *E.T. The Extra-Terrestrial* (1982) the same word was used twice. Thirty-six years after that, in Spielberg's kid-oriented *Ready Player One* (2018), the same word was used 14 times and "douche bag" once. Times have changed, as has the meaning of "acceptable" language, sex and violence in film.

"The Diary of Anne Frank" arrived on Broadway in 1955 and ran for two years and over 700 performances. The play's married playwrights, Frances Goodrich and Albert Hackett, were also hired to write the Anne Frank film adaptation. In fact, Goodrich and Hackett are credited on IMDb with having written every production of Anne Frank in Table 20 from 1958 through 1985.* These Goodrich and Hackett versions were largely devoid of Jewish content, as well as lacking most Holocaust and personal information. According to *The New York Times*' Bernard Weinraub in an article entitled "TV Film Rekindles Dispute Over Anne Frank's Legacy":

> Certainly the most intense controversy over Anne Frank took place in the 1950's when Otto Frank, Anne's father and literary executor, rejected a stage adaptation of the diary by Meyer Levin in favor of one by the husband-and-wife Hollywood screenwriters Frances Goodrich and Albert Hackett, who minimized the Jewish tone and story elements. Garson Kanin, the [Broadway] director of the version by the two screenwriters, went so far as to take out lines about historical persecution of the Jews because it represented what he called "an embarrassing piece of special pleading."[39]

It was from Kanin's Broadway production written by Goodrich and Hackett that George Stevens made his 1959 film version of *The Diary of Anne Frank*, starring Millie Perkins and the thoroughly annoying Shelley Winters, who won the Oscar for Best Supporting Actress. The film also received the statue for Best Cinematography and for Best Art Direction-Set Decoration (Black-and-White), and was nominated for Best Picture,

---

* The married couple Frances Goodrich and Albert Hackett were also posthumously credited with having written the memorable *Father of the Bride* (1991), which starred Steve Martin, Diane Keaton and Martin Short.

Directing, Supporting Actor, Costume Design, and Music (Adaptation Score). The contemporaneous review in the "paper of record" glowed about *The Diary of Anne Frank*, crowing that "Mr. Stevens has produced and directed a minor epic that all but reaches the peak it should."[40] While perhaps this observation was spot-on in 1959, in retrospect the 3-hour "near epic" currently seems like a parody of drawn-out mid-twentieth-century fluff. As a critic wrote 47 years later in 2006 of *The Diary of Anne Frank* (1959), "One of those extremely long and well-meaning adaptations of plays, this doesn't really amount to very much, despite its intrinsically moving subject matter."[41]

The next non-ghost Anne Frank film was the 1980 made-for-television version, featuring 16-year-old Jewish actress Melissa Gilbert, who was in the middle of playing her most famous role, "Laura Ingalls" in *Little House on the Prairie*, which ran from 1974 through 1983. This 1980 version portrayed Anne Frank as relatable and real, which was vastly different from Millie Perkins frolicking around for hours in 1959. The 1980 film alluded to menarche by having Anne Frank wistfully say, "I feel that spring is coming. I feel it in my whole body and soul. I feel utterly confused. I'm longing, so longing for everything. For friends, someone to talk to. Someone who understands. Someone young who feels as I do." All of that ends quietly with a simple kiss on the cheek. "Basically this TV movie version is perky, seriously perky," wrote critic Andy Webb, continuing, "and very American which makes it feel less authentic. In fact the perkiness and energy of it ends up distracting from the depth of the story such as the early scenes of Anne messing around, it's too comedic and so takes away from Anne's messing around coming from being cooped up."[42]

Five years later Dutch actor Jeroen Krabbé co-starred and co-directed with Hank Onrust *The Diary of Anne Frank—Het Dagboek van Anne Frank* (TV 1985). This Dutch television production added nothing to the Anne Frank canon except for the most immature version of Anne Frank ever on film. Not coincidentally, just before the release of the 1986 book *The Diary of Anne Frank: The Critical Edition*, which exposed unfamiliar aspects of Anne Frank, the 1985 film marked the end of Anne Frank films based on Goodrich and Hackett's sterile play.

The four-part 1987 British film *The Diary of Anne Frank* is insufferably English, making no progress. The casting there, too, is lacking. The staging of the closing perp walk out of the front door and into the army truck is embarrassingly theatrical, with each person taking their time to amble along, their specific fate superimposed, with neighbors looking on. Although the video quality and production are better than most previous versions, nothing else recommends this attempt.

Just after, a quite different kind of Anne Frank film was produced in 1988, this time based on the 1987 book *Anne Frank Remembered*, the autobiography of Miep Gies, the Frank family protector: *The Attic: The Hiding of Anne Frank* (TV 1988). The 97-minute made-for-television drama featured Mary Steenburgen as Miep Gies and Paul Scofield as Otto Frank. This Anne Frank film has the least Anne Frank content of any Anne Frank production. As noted in *The Los Angeles Times*, "As largely a celebration of Gies and an expression of her bravery and compassion, it is compelled to continue beyond the climactic arrest of the eight attic occupants, taking this otherwise moving story to a meandering, tedious conclusion."[43]

The Attic was directed by television legend John Erman, who had directed everything from *That Girl* (TV 1966–1971) to the 1968 *Star Trek* (TV 1966–1969) episode "The Empath" to *The Flying Nun* (TV 1967–1970), *Gomer Pyle: USMC* (TV 1964–1969), *Marcus Welby, M.D.* (TV 1969–1976) and one of the four parts of *Roots* (Miniseries 1977). To put it mildly,

Anne Frank and the Holocaust were not in Erman's wheelhouse. The inconsistent accents seem like a Larry David parody, except that the actors were not joking. Anne Frank, in particular, in Erman's production, sounds and acts as though she was developmentally challenged. As a consolation, Steenburgen's Miep Gies was sturdy and got the rest of the job done, despite the generally tacky production, a major characteristic of made-for-television Holocaust productions during the Commercial Era of Holocaust films (1974–1996).

Two identical animated versions of Anne Frank's story were produced in the 1990s, one in Japanese (1995's *Anne no nikki*) and the other voiced in French (1999's *Le Journal d'Anne Frank*). These matching animated versions, clearly intended for children, are difficult to watch with a straight face. It is also hard to believe that animation would be used in Holocaust film after the stunningly flawed *Sarah and the Squirrel—The Seventh Match* (1982). Mercifully, the only salacious portion of the animated Anne Frank pair is when Peter van Pels forces Anne Frank to stare at his cat's penis for about a minute, practically shoving it in Anne Frank's face as the young man chases her around the room. This was hardly an improvement on Goodrich and Hackett.

So, too, *Forget Me Not—The Anne Frank Story* (TV 1996), which is introduced by the real Miep Gies, is a horrifying remnant of the Commercial Era. The utterly forgettable film is not on Wikipedia's list of Anne Frank films (Table 20). IMDb describes *Forget Me Not* as, "A young man intrigued by the Neo-Nazi movement inadvertently takes a time-traveling trip back to the Holocaust and finds himself on a heart-wrenching, eye-opening journey with Anne Frank."[44] *Forget Me Not* is, without doubt, one of the worst Holocaust productions of all time, capping off the 1990s as a floundering period for Anne Frank films.

Near the apex of the Mature Era of Holocaust film (1997–2013), the two-part *Anne Frank: The Whole Story* (TV 2001) changed everything again for Anne Frank films. In the 2001 version, Otto Frank was solidly played by Ben Kingsley, eight years after his famed role as Itzhak Stern in *Schindler's List* (1993). And Anne Frank was terrifically played by 13-year-old Hannah Taylor Gordon, fresh off her role in *Jakob the Liar* (1999), co-starring with Robin Williams, where she alone shone. *The Whole Story* was unlike all previous versions. Nothing substantive was spared in *The Whole Story*, including Anne Frank's capture, her arrival at the Westerbork Concentration Camp, her transport to Auschwitz/Birkenau, her tattooing, shearing, and forced labor, her arrival at Bergen-Belsen, her slow starvation, disease and death with her sister, Margot, just before the camp's liberation. The most fascinating aspect of this superb version is that it was made without the consent of the diary's copyright holders, so none of the actual diary passages could be used.

> There was a disagreement between the filmmakers and the Anne Frank Foundation [Fonds] because the filmmakers wanted to depict in the film that the cleaning lady at 263 Prinsengracht was the one who betrayed the Franks, the van Pels and Mr. Pfeffer, as Melissa Muller wrote in the biography, even though there is no proof to support this claim. In the end, the Anne Frank Foundation denied the filmmakers the rights to *Diary of a Young Girl*, which meant that the filmmakers could not include any quotations from Anne's diary in the film; this explains the absence of any such quotes.[45]

An argument can certainly be made that this version was liberated by the refusal of the Anne Frank Foundation, the filmmakers not needing to be shackled by the letter of Anne Frank's writings. This challenge for the producers, however, facilitated a much more natural story and much less stilted dialogue than in *The Whole Story*'s predecessors.

The 2009 British version of *The Diary of Anne Frank* ends concurrently with Anne Frank's diary entries. This version has a decidedly non-kid-friendly moment, in which Anne Frank fondles her breasts in front of a mirror, stating, "Sometimes, at night, I have the terrible urge to touch my body. I can't tell anyone, even Margot." Apparently the subsequent paragraph in the diary from January 6, 1944, was too controversial to portray, even for the Brits: "Unconsciously, I had these feelings even before I came here. Once when I was spending the night at Jacque's, I could no longer restrain my curiosity about her body, which she'd always hidden from me and which I'd never seen. I asked her whether, as proof of our friendship, we could touch each other's breasts. Jacque refused."

A more interesting Anne Frank film, from Italy, was also released in 2009, *Memories of Anne Frank—Mi ricordo Anna Frank* (TV 2009). This made-for-television Italian-language film also tells the whole story, including Margot and Anne Frank's deaths. It is partly based on the recollections of Anne Frank's dear friend Hannah "Hanneli" Elizabeth Goslar, who was a survivor of Bergen-Belsen and who had spoken with Anne Frank while they were imprisoned there. The same random reconnection had been depicted eight years earlier in *Anne Frank: The Whole Story*, which was twice as long as, and much better than *Memories of Anne Frank*. The sets in *Memories of Anne Frank*, especially at the death camps, do not meet the standards of the later Mature Era, especially of Auschwitz. That being said, *Memories of Anne Frank* is one of the least affected depictions of Anne Frank, and the other Jews in the attic. It also gives scant screen-time to Anne Frank, concentrating mostly on Otto Frank's survival through his liberation at Auschwitz/Birkenau.

Next was the fabulous *My Daughter Anne Frank—Meine Tochter Anne Frank* (TV 2015), which is incorrectly identified on Wikipedia's Anne Frank film list as a "television documentary." *My Daughter Anne Frank* is a riveting German production, directed by Raymond Ley. It uniquely focuses on Otto Frank's efforts to compile and edit Anne Frank's writing just after the War, while devoting half the screen time to hiding in the attic. It uniquely interweaves real interviews with Otto Frank, Miep Gies and Hannah "Hanneli" Elizabeth Goslar. And it has several worthy subplots that include a reenacted interview in 1962 with the Dutch police official who led the SS to the Franks' attic. *My Daughter Anne Frank* is one of the best-produced Holocaust films ever made.

The following year another German-produced Anne Frank film was released, the recommended *The Diary of Anne Frank—Das Tagebuch der Anne Frank* (2016), directed by Hans Steinbichler. It is the least pretentious and finest of all the attic versions. Unlike the 2001's *The Whole Story*, the 2016 version skips Westerbork and Bergen-Belsen, and ends with Anne Frank's shearing at Auschwitz/Birkenau. This version gives the least-romanticized depiction of the principals and their surroundings.

It should be noted, too, that the report about Ari Folman's animated *Where Is Anne Frank*[46] evidently did not foresee that the project would have disappeared into a production void. Despite periodic news about the film's progress, as of the close of 2019, the film *Where Is Anne Frank* has gained the rare distinction of having no date after its IMDb title. This is shorthand for: no one wanted to invest further in another animated version of Anne Frank, described as, "The film follows the journey of Kitty, the imaginary friend to whom Anne Frank dedicated her diary. A fiery teenager, Kitty wakes up in the near future in Anne Frank's house in Amsterdam and embarks on a journey to find Anne, who she believes is still alive, in today's Europe. While the young girl is shocked by the modern world, she also comes across Anne's legacy."[47] The inanity of making yet another time-travel Anne Frank film is beyond comprehension. In July of 2021, *Where Is Anne Frank* was finally screened at the Cannes Film Festival, but, as of publication, has only festival (Jerusalem and Toronto) release dates other than late 2021 in Russia.

As with the general development of cinema, over the past 60 years the portrayal of Anne Frank has increasingly become sexualized, more realistic and more Holocaust-specific. Ironically, these trends have made newer Anne Frank films decreasingly suitable for children. For example, the excellent German version *The Diary of Anne Frank—Das Tagebuch der Anne Frank* (2016) includes a scene with Anne Frank on a bed peering between her legs with a mirror. It also includes a long scene that begins with the following passage from Anne Frank's unredacted diary: "I don't think boys are as complicated as girls. You can easily see what boys look like in photographs or pictures of male nudes, but with women it's different." The scene ends with Anne Frank stating: "The hole is so small I can hardly imagine how a man could get in there, much less how a baby could come out. It's hard enough trying to get your index finger inside."

The contrast between George Stevens' angelic 1959 version and Hans Steinbichler's honest 2016 version is stunning. In 1959, 19-year-old Anne Frank actress Millie Perkins—who was a ringer for Audrey Hepburn—jumped off the screen as an impish ingénue, completely detached from Anne Frank's heritage. That version was supersaturated with a music score seemingly designed to induce diabetes. In 2016, Anne Frank and the attic-dwellers are ordinary looking, practicing, proud Jews. Anne Frank and Peter van Pels make out on a bed. In 2016, the mechanism of genocide is much more than merely implied in a dream. And in the 2016 version, the actress playing Anne Frank, Lea van Acken, was 16 years old during production.

Of the 12 Anne Frank films listed above, three are recommended: The British *Anne Frank: The Whole Story* (TV 2001), the German *My Daughter Anne Frank—Meine Tochter Anne Frank* (TV 2015) and the German *The Diary of Anne Frank—Das Tagebuch Der Anne Frank* (2016). These three are the most realistic, least formulaic Anne Frank films, and they do not limit themselves to being hidden in the attic. They are also the best-produced and least childish.

As the same Anne Frank story is told and re-told, the tastes and standards of each respective period are laid bare; the public's sensibilities that are exposed through the progression of Anne Frank films since 1959 are as clear as tree-rings. For those wanting a more thorough investigation of Anne Frank's impact on culture and history, see Alexandra Zapruder's 2002 book *Salvaged Pages: Young Writers' Diaries of the Holocaust* (Yale University Press) as well as the 15 interdisciplinary essays presented in the 2014 German book, *Anne Frank: Mediengeschichten*. As described by Iwona Guść, Lichtenberg College, Georg August University Göttingen:

> The subjects addressed in "Anne Frank: Mediengeschichten" vary from well-studied dimensions within the Anne Frank research (theatre or film adaptations of the diary, Anne's literary afterlives, and educational projects) to issues that have received little previous attention (Anne Frank in social media, memorials devoted to her, and comic books). The essays are not explicitly separated into sections, but they are effectively organized according to the medium discussed. Essays on photography, theatre and film are gathered together, followed by an essay on music, two on comic books, two on social media, two exploring memorial practices, three on Anne Frank in educational contexts, and a final two articles devoted to Anne's literary afterlives.[48]

Within the context of the entire Anne Frank story—a teenager who is sequestered for two years and then murdered by barbarians—Anne Frank is unquestionably a worthy subject and a dazzling, compelling historic and cultural figure. Her writing is authentic and beautiful. The magnitude of Anne Frank, books about her diary and films cannot be ignored. And Anne Frank's diary can inspire children to journal and to care about their world, to know that many personal struggles are common, and that lemonade can be made from lemons. But, because many of those lessons are independent of the Holocaust, Anne Frank should be used sparingly in Holocaust education.

Addendum

Comedian Ricky Gervais famously quipped that *The Diary of Anne Frank* "ends a bit abruptly and no sequel."[49] Obviously, Gervais has not researched the topic. Anne Frank is the ultimate Holocaust film franchise; since 1958, one new Anne Frank film or television drama has been produced on average every 2½ years.

In 2020, the Anne Frank House in Amsterdam jumped into the game with their *Anne Frank Video Diary* (TV 2020), being delivered weekly in 15 episodes on *YouTube.com*, accompanied by seven educational video extras and a workbook. All episodes rolled-out early May 2020. Like Instagram's selfie-inspired *Eva.Stories* (2019)—where a Hungarian-accented English-speaking actress portrays Holocaust victim Eva Heyman vlogging her 1940s oppression—this new Anne Frank also wields a small unseen video camera.

Strangely, the *Anne Frank Video Diary* cannot be shown in the United States, but is accessible in Israel and 75 other countries, apparently out of deference to the separate "Anne Frank Fonds" (Foundation) in Basil, Switzerland, the copyright holder of all Anne Frank intellectual property, including all Anne Frank writings. The Anne Frank House in Amsterdam has assumed that American copyright commitments are functionally insurmountable vis-à-vis the Anne Frank Fonds. A similarly bizarre clash with the Anne Frank Fonds arose with the incomparable *Anne Frank: The Whole Story* (TV 2001), which was forced to eliminate any of Anne Frank's writings from their script because of a disputed plot point. These petty and counterproductive internecine fights must have sent Anne Frank's father, Otto Frank, spinning in his grave, especially since he was the founder of both the Anne Frank House and the Anne Frank Fonds.

The *Anne Frank Video Diary* star is 13-year-old Luna Cruz Perez, who does not even slightly resemble Anne Frank, aside from her age and a hair-part. This, unfortunately, is not unusual for most Anne Frank productions; except for Hannah Taylor Gordon in *Anne Frank: The Whole Story*, no Anne Frank actress had much of a similarity to Anne Frank, not 1959's Millie Perkins, 1980's Melissa Gilbert or 2015's Mala Emde. But Luna Cruz Perez, is the youngest actress to play Anne Frank in a major production, which is certainly a win for authenticity.

Instead, Luna Cruz Perez was cast because of her acting ability and faithfulness to Anne Frank's spirit, according to the *Anne Frank Video Diary*'s project leader, Tom Brink, Head of Publications & Presentations at the Anne Frank House.[50] The added difficulties, of course, included portraying one of the most famous children in history, an exhaustively documented child during World War II who must simultaneously be a natural voice on social media. Her performance is passable, given the format. The father character, too, was balanced and seemingly true to Otto Frank.

But the Peter van Pels actor, Ezra Blok, was a bit too glamorous for the part, compared to the other attic occupants. He also, curiously, wears a tie and double-breasted suit when cuddling with Anne Frank, which, even if accurate, sets him further apart. The other five people hiding with them—Edith and Margot Frank, Hermann and Auguste van Pels and Fritz Pfeffer—seem like afterthoughts, occasionally bumping around like strangers or, more specifically, like extras, eerily superfluous for named characters. The make-up and lighting were troubling, too, especially with Otto Frank's bald prosthetic and the ultra-close-ups on Anne Frank.

The romantic interactions in *Anne Frank Video Diary* between Anne Frank and Peter van Pels are clumsy, even for the intended age group. Certainly, the innately awkward subject of Anne Frank's sexuality is always a challenge to portray on screen, more difficult to represent appropriately because of the young Anne Frank's unexpected candor revealed in her unabridged diary. Most attempts to portray Anne Frank's sexual awakening in productions reveal filmmakers' inability to distinguish between Holocaust education and adolescent discovery, which are only comingled to make the characters in an otherwise unimaginable world a little bit more relatable. As with most other Anne Frank films, though, the romantic filler in the *Anne Frank Video Diary* misappropriates time that is better spent on Holocaust-specific subplots. Thankfully, this obligatory coming-of-age element is unusually tame in the *Anne Frank Video Diary*.

The sets are identical representations of the Franks' hiding place, including the beams, although this would seem obvious for an Anne Frank House production. Nonetheless, this painstaking authenticity must be lauded and appreciated. Restricting the reproduced annex to the exact dimensions is rare for Anne Frank films, and only possible here because "vlogger" cameras weigh just 300 grams and are 10 centimeters wide by six centimeters deep, thus easily held by a 13-year-old. The benefit is found in the attic's original crampedness; unlike many similar productions, roominess is not implied. And the atmosphere is not frenzied or hyperbolic as had been the hallmark of so many previous attempts. In this Anne Frank world, the inhabitants are calm and measured. Also adding credibility (as opposed to the English-spoken Hungarian-set *Eva.Stories*) is that the *Anne Frank Video Diary* uses Anne Frank's native language, Dutch.

The *Anne Frank Video Diary* ends with the arrest of the Franks and their guests in August of 1944; as in most Anne Frank productions, the filmmakers only focus on the portion of Anne Frank's story before her capture, obfuscating the Franks' total Holocaust experience. The truncated material necessitates much more explanation than that delivered by the annex story and forces others to impart the most difficult exposition. The *Anne Frank Video Diary* episode titles, too, as in episode six's "Quarrelling with dad," drain much of the suspense out of the vignettes.

While the underlying material is the diary, the cast was given leeway to improvise. Even so, the dialogue does not stray significantly from the original text. But that devotion to the spirit of the source material is badly in conflict with the selfie format, which is pedantic here, as in *Eva.Stories*. Neither production trusted its underlying victims' diaries to tell stories within only three walls. Both productions explicitly undermine their veracity, seeming to suggest that today's adolescents are incapable of understanding traditional narrative, which is an inaccurate assumption given the flood of other period-pieces directed at kids, programming that does not debase itself by injecting inauthentic communication technologies into stories. Thank goodness Greta Gerwig, in directing *Little Women* (2019), did not catch the "selfie" bug, and resisted placing a cell phone in the hands of the March Sisters.

The *Anne Frank Video Diary* development began in 2018, a year before *Eva.Stories* was posted. In fact, project leader Tom Brink said that his team was surprised when the Instagram Holocaust drama appeared in the spring of 2019. Brink also suggests that the Anne Frank House had learned from the mistakes of Instagram's distracting overlay set during the Holocaust.[51] Nonetheless, the *Anne Frank Video Diary* regularly bashes the selfie anachronism over viewers' heads, as with the following interspersed dialogue from a few episodes: "And I'm capable [of success], because now I'm working on this project. My video diary." "You want to make an important film?" "Why don't you make him [Otto Frank] a video?" "Hello, dad. I've recorded this video message for you." Although these passages were intended to assure young viewers that the video was not actually true to the era, instead this dialogue was more like a splinter in a wood floor that always draws blood.

This splinter becomes a spike in the "extras," as its narrator proclaims, "Everything about this story is true. The people, the events, the location and the story. All of it. Except for the camera." That is, all of it except for the time machine. Another of the Anne Frank House's promotional supplements suggests, "We all know that Anne Frank kept a diary. Imagine she'd had a video camera." Yes, as if *Eva.Stories*' "What if a girl in the Holocaust had Instagram" was not disturbing enough. Why should anyone have to imagine such things, especially with historical content intended for education? And to be clear, breaking the fourth wall can, in fact, work in Holocaust productions, as with *Genghis Cohn* (1993), *Train of Life—Train de vie* (1998) and *My Führer—Mein Führer—Die wirklich wahrste Wahrheit über Adolf Hitler* (2007). But each of those films was farce, which is certainly not the case here.

Ronald Leopold, Executive Director of the Anne Frank House, posited in his *Anne Frank Video Diary* presser, "…Anne had to appear on camera as she had written her diary: natural, in the moment, sometimes searching for the right words." Of course, the exact opposite is represented in the *Anne Frank Video Diary*: historically natural for Anne Frank was writing in her diary, not speaking to camera. The irony is that this well-intentioned *Anne Frank Video Diary* could have been passable simply by having the Anne Frank character narrate the passages while writing them (ignoring the camera). Its otherwise stellar authenticity to the annex would then have added immeasurably to the Anne Frank canon.

While the *Anne Frank Video Diary*, as it stands, is jaw-dropping for adults who simply cannot ignore its solicitous premise, the video diary still may be accessible to the narrow population of adolescents who purportedly cannot understand stories except as social media. At least, that is the wager of the Anne Frank House. And it may work as a starter on the Anne Frank journey, as merely a supplement to the diary, especially with its educational extras. But hopefully, the *Anne Frank Video Diary* will lead those same viewers to seek out more significant and mature offerings, like 2001's indispensable *Anne Frank: The Whole Story* or the groundbreaking *My Daughter Anne Frank—Meine Tochter Anne Frank* (TV 2015).*

The Black Hole of Holocaust Films: Schindler's List *(1993) & Friends*

Critical understanding of Holocaust films is impossible without explicitly addressing three films that have inordinately deflected light from more worthy Holocaust productions. These are also three of the most successful, yet terribly flawed Holocaust films ever made: *Schindler's List* (1993), *Life Is Beautiful* (1997) and *The Boy in the Striped Pyjamas* (2008).

---

* A portion of this section was first published in the *Jerusalem Post* on April 21, 2020, in an article by this author entitled "A well-intentioned but flawed 'Anne Frank Video Diary.'"

Schindler's List (1993)

The most powerful object in our Holocaust universe is *Schindler's List*; the most dangerous activity in our Holocaust universe is criticizing *Schindler's List*. Its critics are regarded as Darth Vader, not Han Solo. Suggesting that *Schindler's List* is even slightly imperfect, especially during a Holocaust-film lecture, triggers jaw-dropping disappointment, similar to when uttering that George Washington owned slaves.

Without a doubt, *Schindler's List* is a spectacular film, a stunning example of craftsmanship and the pinnacle of its art form. Indeed, as a feature film, *Schindler's List* is almost beyond reproach. Its music, cinematography, casting and storytelling are rightfully celebrated. *Schindler's List* is rated as the 6th greatest film of all time by IMDb users and is similarly regarded on many of the American Film Institute (AFI) lists. And *Schindler's List* is the 37th all-time highest-rated film on Metacritic.[52] It is the highest-grossing Holocaust film of all time: $322 million worldwide, with many free copies having been provided to schools. In some American high school systems, *Schindler's List* has been included as part of a state-mandated study of the Holocaust.[53] *Schindler's List* won 82 awards and was nominated for 49 others, including winning Oscars for Best Picture, Directing, Writer, Cinematography, Art Direction, Editing and Music (Adaptation Score) and nominations for Best Actor, Supporting Actor, Costume Design, Makeup and Sound. The film was also rereleased in 2018.[54] It also should be noted that Steven Spielberg donated his *Schindler's List* profit to create the USC Shoah Foundation and took no salary for his work on the film.

Without proper context, watching the most popular Holocaust film ever made, a film made by the most successful director in history—the first $10 billion director[55]—is a no-brainer. But as a Holocaust film, *Schindler's List* is irredeemably flawed and should be regarded as the ultimate extension of pop culture's power, not as the definitive work of its film genre.

Although Oskar Schindler is the most famous righteous Gentile who ever lived, Oskar Schindler is not the *only* righteous Gentile. In fact, Oskar Schindler is one of 616 Germans recognized by Yad Vashem with the title "Righteous Among the Nations," and one of 27,362 righteous Gentiles worldwide recognized by Yad Vashem, as of this writing.[56] Some people crudely suggest that the sheer number of Jews saved by Oskar Schindler justifies his elevation by Spielberg to demigod status. These people are woefully ill-informed. For example, the number of Jews saved by Oskar Schindler is approximately the same as those saved by the American Jew Ruth Gruber, portrayed in *Haven* (TV 2001). Actually, Oskar Schindler saved fewer Jews than those saved in each of the other 16 films listed in Table 21.

TABLE 21: FILMS DEPICTING MORE THAN 1,000 JEWS SAVED DURING THE HOLOCAUST
Recommended in **Bold** (4 of 52). "One of the Best" in **Bold and Underlined** (1 of 15).

Film	Approx. Jews Saved	Protagonist (Nationality)
The Scarlet and the Black (TV 1983)	6,500 (&POWS)	Monsignor Hugh O'Flaherty (Ireland)
Wallenberg—A Hero's Story (TV 1985)	Tens of thousands.[57]	Raoul Wallenberg (Sweden)
Schindler's List (1993)	1,200	Oskar Schindler (German/Sudeten)
Good Evening, Mr. Wallenberg **(1990)**	Tens of thousands.[58]	Raoul Wallenberg (Sweden)
Miracle at Midnight (TV 1998)	7,220	Dr. Karl Koster (Denmark)

Film	Approx. Jews Saved	Protagonist (Nationality)
Varian's War: The Forgotten Hero (TV 2001)	2,000 to 4,000	Varian Fry (USA)
Perlasca. The Courage of a Just Man (TV 2002)	5,218	Giorgio Perlasca (Italy)
Sugihara Chiune Monogatari (TV 2005)	10,000	Vice Consul Chiune Sugihara (Japan)
Defiance (2008)	1,236	Bielski Brothers (Belarus/USSR)
Akte Grüninger (TV 2013)	3,600	Akte Grüninger (Switzerland)
The Relief of Belsen (TV 2007)	50,000	General James Johnston (U.K.)
Aristides de Sousa Mendes: A Rebel—Désobéir (2008)	10,000	Aristides de Sousa Mendes (Portugal)
The Courageous Heart of Irena Sendler (TV 2009)	2,500	Irena Sendler (Poland)
The Angel of Budapest—El ángel de Budapest (TV 2011)	5,000	Ángel Sanz Briz (Spain)
The Consul of Bordeaux—O Cônsul de Bordéus (2011)	10.000	Aristides de Sousa Mendes (Portugal)
Exodus to Shanghai (2015)	At Least 2,000	Feng-Shan Ho (China)
Persona Non Grata—Sugihara Chiune (2015)	10,000	Vice Consul Chiune Sugihara (Japan)

Suggesting that *Schindler's List* is an unparalleled film simply because Oskar Schindler saved more Jews than any other righteous Gentile is not only tactless, but also false. Further, none of the other righteous Gentiles in Table 21 were Nazis requiring rehabilitation except Oskar Schindler. And, further, more than one of the other righteous Gentiles listed above, like Schindler, lost everything for having helped Jews. In fact, several other righteous Gentiles were disgraced or murdered for having saved Jews. So, neither the number of Jews saved nor the post–War disposition of the protagonist can be rational reasons to pedestal *Schindler's List*.

A much more basic objection to *Schindler's List* is that it is the story of a Nazi saving Jews from Germans. From a storytelling perspective, the premise is perfect; from a moral and historical standpoint, the premise is repulsive. Acclaimed documentary director Claude Lanzmann (1925–2018), whose *Shoah* (1985) is the gold standard of Holocaust exposition, wrote of *Schindler's List*, "The thing I reproach Spielberg is, that he shows the Holocaust through the eyes of a German. Even though it was a German who saved Jews, yet this completely changes the perspective on History. It is the world in reverse."[59]

Peter Farrelly's *Green Book* (2018) is a film made by a White director about a vaguely racist driver making nice with his Black employer. Farrelly's *Green Book* won the 2019 Oscar for Best Picture. Spike Lee, who is Black and whose own *BlacKkKlansman* (2018) lost on Oscar night to Farrelly's *Green Book*, suggested that the world did not need yet another film (*Green Book*) filtered through a White perspective about the Black experience.[60] Lee was similarly vexed in 1989 when a different White director's film about race relations, Bruce Beresford's *Driving Miss Daisy* (1989), outshone Lee's greatly superior *Do the Right Thing* (1989), with *Daisy* winning the Oscars for Best Picture, Actress, Writing and Make-up, while Lee was shut out. Lee's objection both times was simple: why glorify the racists who eventually comprehend their errors? Lee correctly balked at these storybook rehabilitations of White characters who miraculously resolve their underlying residual racism in the aftermath of overt bigotry defeated in World War II, and *Brown v.*

The Board of Education and other American civil rights landmarks. *Schindler's List* used a similar method.

Yet, the arc in *Schindler's List* does not start with a man who is slightly intolerant racially. *Schindler's List* is not about people who were otherwise caring individuals and just needed a little push to see the light, as in *Driving Miss Daisy* or *Green Book*. No, *Schindler's List* celebrates a man who institutionally enabled an ongoing genocide. Oskar Schindler started spying for Nazi military intelligence in 1936 and worked diligently on behalf of his Führer through 1944, during the liquidation of approximately five of six million Jews. "Ignored by the book and film bearing his name," wrote Matt Lebovic in *The Times of Israel,* "Schindler helped Germany lay groundwork for its invasion of Poland 80 years ago. Leading up to the blitzkrieg attack launched on September 1, 1939, Schindler led a network of 25 spies and prepared an infamous false-flag attack called the 'Gleiwitz Incident.'"[61] To understand how thoroughly despicable was Oskar Schindler—a true enemy of the Allies and the Jews, antithetical to the righteous among all nations— read David M. Crowe's 2004 book *Oskar Schindler: The Untold Account of His Life, Wartime Activities, and the True Story Behind the List.*

Schindler and his cohorts profited as cogs in Hitler's machine. For Oskar Schindler to have been analogous to the suddenly woke white protagonists in *Driving Miss Daisy* or *Green Book*, the misguided white protagonists in those two films, instead, would necessarily have been mid-level members of the Klan or some other actively lethal white-power organization. But, even if Oskar Schindler was transformed fully from a Nazi into a righteous Gentile, Oskar Schindler's story is still historically misleading, an outlier who is celebrated in this film for discovering a moral compass, an unnecessary discovery in any rational righteous Gentile portrayal. The recommended films in this book do not depict Nazis as redeemable, even if they were, because such stories skew history by minimizing German culpability.

Especially in light of Spike Lee's astute observation that victims' stories should be told from the perspective of the victims, the central question raised by *Schindler's List* is· why rely on righteous Gentile films at all when learning about the Holocaust? While the chance of finding a German righteous Gentile was less than 1 in 100,000, the chance of finding a Holocaust film that portrays Gentiles saving Jews is about 1 in 6. This criticism was made more subtly by perhaps the greatest filmmaker of modern cinema, Stanley Kubrick, who noted, "The Holocaust is about six million people who get killed. *Schindler's List* is about 600 who don't."[62] Several Holocaust films have been made that portray Jews, themselves, in fact, trying to save Jews. These films include *For Those I Loved—Au nom de tous les miens* (1983), *Hanna's War* (1988), *Korczak* (1990), *All My Loved Ones—Vsichni moji blízcí* (1999), *Haven* (TV 2001), *The Grey Zone* (2001), *Uprising* (TV 2001), *Defiance* (2008) and *Süskind* (2012).

Schindler's List is also 195 minutes, or 3¼ hours long, which may seem to be a petty, almost random complaint. Yet, objectively, *Schindler's List* needed an extra 90 minutes to tell its rather simple story. From a pedagogical standpoint, a film that is 3+ hours is almost abusive, even when broken into several sessions. Specifically in narrative cinema, miniseries-length films telling one story are generally excessive, except with extremely complicated stories, like *The Godfather: Part II* (1974) or *The Lord of the Rings: The Return of the King* (2003), which each tells much more complex stories than does *Schindler's List*.

In fact, *Schindler's List*'s basic plot has been used in more than 30 other righteous Gentile films: someone, somehow becomes overwhelmingly motivated to save Jews ...

and then saves them. Oskar Schindler's story was neither more complicated nor more important than any other righteous Gentile film. As a Holocaust film, there is nothing unique about *Schindler's* plotline. In fact, the plot is, by far, the most consistent story in all Holocaust film, starting with Ralph Thomas' *Conspiracy of Hearts* (1960), a film about a group of Italian nuns who saved hundreds of Jewish children. Yet these other feature films' average running time was 112 minutes, or almost half the length of *Schindler's List*. Three of the righteous Gentile films which are recommended in Chapter 9: Recommended Holocaust Films depict many more Jews being saved than by Oskar Schindler. Those three films were able to tell their important stories in 1¾ hours. These films did not neglect their complicated storylines, but were clever enough to be concise. And, yes, films are partly judged by the economy with which they tell their stories.

Why was *Schindler's List* so long? Even with Steven Spielberg's best intentions, which are not in question here, *Schindler's List* was less about Oskar Schindler than about Steven Spielberg who, after previously directing 14 major films, wanted to be taken seriously, finally. As noted in *The New York Times* upon the film's release, "What better way to goad the Academy into giving Mr. Spielberg the coveted best picture or best director statuette, these cynics say, than to make a long, sober black-and-white film about the Holocaust?"[63] *Schindler's List* is analogous to being stuck in a gallery full of Andy Warhol's paintings for more than three hours: no matter the object, its subject is the artist, lurking behind every turn, seemingly screaming "I'm so deeply embedded in popular culture that you cannot help but regard my brilliance in my art." As noted by critic Jeremy Heilman in 2004, "Spielberg approaches this material with the moronic assumption that a non–Jew would have to search his soul to comprehend the atrocities of the Holocaust in a way that a Jew would not. He seems to see himself as our tour guide on that unnecessary hunt."[64]

I have colleagues who tout *Schindler's List* because of Schindler's transformation, seemingly giving Spielberg extra points for starting with a reprehensible character, as opposed to telling the story of a righteous Gentile who was always righteous. In a word, this inverse scoring system is bizarre. In a rational world, points should not be awarded to people who were filth. Yet *Schindler's List* is so well made, so thoroughly controlling that viewers walk away believing that some Nazis were good. This manipulation is unforgivable, even if a tiny fraction of Nazis were, in fact, good. This also renders the Jews in *Schindler's List* as almost irrelevant, as noted by Liel Leibovitz in *Tablet Magazine,* "Schindler's Jews do not matter. They're abstractions, spiritual currency so that our 'hero' can pay his way toward salvation."[65] Claude Lanzmann concluded, "One is affected by this story of a German swindler, nothing more than that."[66]

A Holocaust educator from South Africa suggested to me that *Schindler's List* is an important film because Oskar Schindler's story is one of redemption, implicitly analogizing Nazis who helped Jews to the South African officials who fought Apartheid. I agreed, but I also asked what lesson she was teaching. If her class was about redemption, then perhaps *Schindler's List* is appropriate. But if the lesson she is teaching is about the Holocaust, then *Schindler's List* tells the most unrepresentative slice of the story. In that regard, promoting Oskar Schindler as the Holocaust poster-boy is similar to a newspaper article about a lifetime smoker's 100th birthday. The story is only interesting because of the anomaly, and, in fact, teaches the wrong lesson about longevity. The de minimis number of righteous Gentile Nazis is not the lesson of the Holocaust, nor is Oskar Schindler's redemption. As noted more generally by Edward Rothstein in *The New York Times*, "…the homiletic approach to the Holocaust has broken down almost all inhibitions in using the Holocaust as an analogy, even though the eagerness to do so is a sure sign of misuse."[67]

Further, the ending of *Schindler's List*, with Oskar Schindler's deification at Schindler's Jerusalem grave, is perhaps the most manipulative scene ever put on film. As if the previous three hours on screen could not adequately exonerate Schindler, Spielberg needed to create an epic spectacle, pairing actors with the people they portrayed. The participants, in the Jewish tradition, put stones on Schindler's grave, as if Oskar Schindler was now a Jew. Spielberg's gravesite grandstanding, with Naomi Shemer's tear-jerking anthem *Yerushalayim Shel Zahav* in the background, was precisely what so many in the Jewish community feared Spielberg would do to the Holocaust. Only the dead could fail to be moved by the final ten minutes of *Schindler's List*, which was remarkably similar to the sublime ending of Tim Burton's fantasy biopic *Big Fish* (2003). Yet, only allegorical protagonists should ever step through the fourth wall into eternal peace accompanied by their own people. In the end, Spielberg was unable to resist another formulaic, schmaltzy finale, capped with shameless, pandering hagiography. Critic Uri Klein's "*Schindler's List* becomes Spielberg's List"[68] astutely delineates Spielberg's brazen destruction of cinematic boundaries at the cemetery.

Roman Polanski turned down directing *Schindler's List*, instead directing a different Holocaust biopic, *The Pianist* (2002), which somewhat reflected Polanski's own life during the Holocaust. *The Pianist* also won Polanski his only Best Director Oscar, after four other Oscar nominations, just like Spielberg's first with *Schindler's List*. But Polanski avoided Spielberg's underlying mistake of Nazi glorification. True, the Jewish protagonist in *The Pianist*, Wladyslaw Szpilman (Adrien Brody) is helped near the end of the film by the very real German army captain Wilhelm Adalbert Hosenfeld, who, like Oskar Schindler, was posthumously honored by Yad Vashem as Righteous Among the Nations. Yet, unlike Spielberg's *Schindler's List*, Polanski's *The Pianist* never rehabilitated or honored Hosenfeld, a German soldier. Polanski, a Holocaust survivor, treats the German soldier as a German soldier, a member of Hitler's army wearing Hitler's uniform, even if Hosenfeld eventually helped a Jew or two. Polanski understood the inherent crassness of glorifying Nazis, under any condition. According to Yad Vashem, it was Wladyslaw Szpilman himself who nominated Captain Hosenfeld in 1998 to be recognized as a righteous Gentile.[69] Imagine that tear-jerking ending—complete with Hosenfeld's tree-planting ceremony at Yad Vashem—had *The Pianist* also been directed by Steven Spielberg.

Further, Spielberg employs the unconscionable Auschwitz shower-fake-out sequence, first seen in *Distant Journey—Daleká cesta* (1950) and then just a few years before *Schindler's List* in *I Was Overtaken by Night—Zastihla me noc* (1986). Spielberg's sequence is among the most deplorable, truly unforgivable, of all Holocaust film scenes ever made. After brutal haircuts upon arrival at Auschwitz/Birkenau, the frightened Jews are led into a shower room. The door and the room are both misleading and historically inaccurate, depicting a shower room that is hermetically closed and functionally ambiguous. To be quite clear, this shower room was created like the snake pit in Spielberg's *Raiders of the Lost Ark* (1981), with the sole intention of frightening the audience, which is expected in a fantasy film. "...Because Spielberg, too, understands that those who enter a gas chamber do not leave it," wrote critic Uri Klein in *HaAretz*, "he uses the scene as a stratagem of tension that befits a cheap horror movie."[70] Ominous music prowls, people hug and cry in terror, driving maximum dramatic tension and incessantly milking the angst. Water finally showers down, instead of, as the audience had feared, deadly gas. Although other films have used this cheap ploy, *Schindler's List*'s is the most obnoxious fake gas/shower scene of any film—replete with 70 seconds of anticipation before water finally flows. Academy Award-nominated German director Michael Haneke wrote of that scene, "I don't want to judge the works of other colleagues in interviews. But taking *Schindler's List* as the most famous example, there's a scene in that film when we don't know if there's gas or water coming out in the showers in the camp…. Spielberg meant well—but it was dumb…."[71]

Haneke's critique, despite his deference to Steven Spielberg, was understated. These starved, displaced, disoriented Jews had just disembarked from cramped, dark cattle cars, where they had been surrounded by the dead and dying during several days of travel without facilities to an unknown destination, the likelihood that these forlorn people could discern that a gas chamber would be disguised as a shower room was zero. Further, the Germans did not make dual-purpose shower rooms; the Auschwitz/Birkenau shower rooms did not resemble gas chambers, with sealed doors or odd mesh columns for the gas. Auschwitz/Birkenau shower rooms were open places lined with windows. Spielberg's morphing of an innocuous shower room into a potential gas chamber is tasteless, creating hyper-cynical Hitchcockian tension, in an otherwise historically accurate Holocaust film.

Rule #1 in the Holocaust universe is to be thoroughly educated about the Holocaust. And, since the shower fake-out never actually could have happened, the scene insults Holocaust victims while minimizing German treachery. Germans intensely guarded information about the gassing process and were exceptionally devious, creating the appearance of normality for the numbed, starved, disoriented victims. And, bluntly, with several million people gassed by the time depicted in *Schindler's List*, the Germans had plenty of practice perfecting deception. While it is possible that late in the war a few arrivees had heard of the gassings, manipulative shower scenes erroneously imply that most Jews knew about gas chambers and that German countermeasures to conceal them had not been taken. In the words of survivor Ernest Lobet, reacting to Spielberg's scene, "Arriving Polish Jews had a stronger premonition that they might not leave the place alive than Jews from other countries, yet they too did not know gassing was the preferred method."[72]

Rule #2 in Holocaust study: never blame the victim. Further, even if foreknowledge of gas were implied to a few characters in *Schindler's List*, the scene erroneously suggested that many in the shower room suspected that gas would flow. The corollary is: fight any insinuation that the Jews were aware of their fate, yet knowingly walked into the gas chambers and did not fight back. In other words, even if most of the slaughtered six million Jews did not fight back, Spielberg's portrayal of Jews meekly walking to their deaths cashes in on and distorts the Holocaust. Finally, in terms of rules, filmmakers should never insult their audience. Together, these exploitative, fake shower scenes are offensive because they assume that the Holocaust film audience cannot perceive fake tension and contrived situations. Depictions like the *Schindler's List* shower scene break all rules, reducing the Holocaust to pulp fiction.

Some supporters of *Schindler's List* validate their fealty to the film by pointing out its decorations from the annual Academy, Golden Globe and BAFTA awards, along with the DGA, PGA and WGA, without realizing that 39 Holocaust films before *Schindler's List* (and 23 after) have also been the object of Oscar's and the trade-guild's love. Likewise, some suggest tautologically that *Schindler's List* should be recommended simply because

Schindler's List has unquestionably raised consciousness about the Holocaust worldwide. With that logic, *Inglourious Basterds* (2009) should be looped in Times Square. Indeed, neither *Holocaust* (Miniseries 1978) nor *Life Is Beautiful* (1997) can be recommended, even though, like *Schindler's List,* both of those productions radically changed the public's Holocaust perception. If awards and raising public awareness about the Holocaust were a criterion for recommending Holocaust films, the list of great films would also include the grotesquely misleading *Jakob the Liar* (1999), *The Reader* (2008) and *The Boy in the Striped Pyjamas* (2008).

Further, *Schindler's List* is so culturally dominant and so famous that it functionally devalues all other Holocaust films. While faulting Steven Spielberg's film for being too successful is unfair to Mr. Spielberg, the effects of the *Schindler's List* black hole of Holocaust films have undeniably absorbed the light of many worthwhile films, especially in the most important Victim genre. This is even more unfair to Mr. Spielberg in light of the many Holocaust films that may have been produced during the Mature Era of Holocaust film (1997–2013) piggybacking on *Schindler's List*'s success. Nonetheless, with or without a recommendation in this book, while *Schindler's List* will continue to be the most highly regarded Holocaust film in history, the above-listed films that tell about Jewish heroism need light.

All of that being said, Steven Spielberg and his film *Schindler's List* have done more to raise Holocaust awareness than, perhaps, anyone other than Anne Frank. Spielberg's USC Shoah Foundation, which has been funded by the profits of *Schindler's List,* is a lasting gift to the world. Regardless, these benefits resulting from *Schindler's List*'s success are irrelevant when recommending films.

Life Is Beautiful (1997)

Life Is Beautiful—La Vita è bella (1997) is the story of an Italian family of three—a Jewish husband, a non–Jewish wife, and their son. The father and son end up in a death camp. Although the camp is not identified, Auschwitz is strongly implied. The father then creates a series of games to distract his son from the horrors of Auschwitz, to keep them both alive so they can reunite with the mother. The father is murdered just before the camp is liberated, but the hidden boy survives. He hitches a ride on an American tank with an American soldier and finds his mother in two screen minutes. Perhaps the liberation by the U.S. Army—which was never in Poland—is a reason Auschwitz is never named. Still, mother and son are reunited, and the father got his wish. As critic Hannah Brown noted in *The Jerusalem Post,* "Starting with Roberto Benigni's *Life Is Beautiful,* a new and very unwelcome genre of movies has emerged: Feelgood Holocaust films…. The death of 6 million people is a bit of a downer, after all. But once Benigni paved the way, it turned out that audiences were willing to see Holocaust movies, as long as they weren't too depressing. If credibility and plausibility had to be sacrificed along the way, well, that's show biz."[73]

Although Hannah Brown's criticism of *Life Is Beautiful* was spot-on, *Life Is Beautiful* did not, in fact, spawn a whole new breed of Holocaust illusions. Actually, only a handful of films since *Life Is Beautiful* have gone down that simplistic path, including *Jakob the Liar* (1999), *The Devil's Arithmetic* (TV 1999), *The Boy in the Striped Pyjamas* (2008) and *Jojo Rabbit* (2019). True, there have been bad Holocaust films other than these since *Life Is Beautiful,* but full-on Holocaust fantasy was mostly extinguished by *Life Is Beautiful.*

Those other films should be considered outliers, brush fires, just like in any other film genre. Roger Ebert wrote in his review of *Life Is Beautiful*:

> The movie actually softens the Holocaust slightly, to make the humor possible at all. In the real death camps there would be no role for Guido [the father]. But *Life Is Beautiful* is not about Nazis and Fascists, but about the human spirit. It is about rescuing whatever is good and hopeful from the wreckage of dreams. About hope for the future. About the necessary human conviction, or delusion, that things will be better for our children than they are right now.[74]

As a general matter in film, the human spirit may be elevated for some by *Life Is Beautiful*. But, in a Victim Holocaust film, Nazis are required. Educationally, *Life Is Beautiful* is devastating, allowing for the notion that the Holocaust was a game and that life during the Holocaust could have been beautiful. It also needs to be noted that Holocaust denial was at its apex around the time that *Life Is Beautiful* won a bucketful of Oscars and earned millions of dollars. To blame this form of antisemitism on an absurd film is equally irrational, yet, for those ignorant enough to be Holocaust deniers, *Life Is Beautiful* is the kind of manure that stimulates growth. *Time Magazine*'s Richard Schickel summed it up well:

> The place is clean, and though the work is hard and the rations are short, no one seems to sicken or die. There are references to mass extermination, but that brutal reality is never vividly presented. Indeed, the prisoners don't seem to see much of their jailers, who, when they do turn up, act as if they've drifted into this film from a *Hogan's Heroes* rerun—barking incomprehensible orders to cover their comic ineptitude … turning even a small corner of this century's central horror into feel-good popular entertainment is abhorrent. Sentimentality is a kind of fascism too, robbing us of judgment and moral acuity, and it needs to be resisted. *Life Is Beautiful* is a good place to start.[75]

Instinctively, one might assume that *Life Is Beautiful*'s thematic downfall is attributable to it being a Holocaust comedy. But most Holocaust comedies successfully told their stories without diminishing the Holocaust's lethality. The question about *Life Is Beautiful* is less about its farcical underpinnings, but more about farcical Auschwitz. John Patterson of the *L.A. Weekly* described it as "…the nauseating fictions peddled by such 'Have-yourself-a-happy-little-Holocaust' films as *Life Is Beautiful* and *Jakob the Liar*."[76] John Patterson got it right.

The ultimate irony here is that a much better Italian Holocaust film—a real story about a boy who survived the camps—was released just a few years before: the recommended *Look to the Sky—Jona che visse nella balena* (1993). That better film is also an example of the blotting out of Holocaust films in 1993 by *Schindler's List*.

The Boy in the Striped Pyjamas (2008)

Since *Life Is Beautiful* in 1997, only one major Holocaust film has been made from a fictional Victim story: *The Boy in the Striped Pyjamas* (2008), an albatross of a film, which features slews of horrifying plot holes and misrepresentations of the Holocaust and Auschwitz.

The Boy in the Striped Pyjamas portrays a perfectly normal family, filled with perfectly normal people speaking the Queen's English, who are displaced from Berlin and forced to move to a mansion in Oswiecim, Poland. The problem is, of course, that the nice daddy had to move the family because of his promotion as the commandant of the largest enterprise in Oswiecim: Auschwitz/Birkenau, the not-so-hidden reeking home of 100,000 slave laborers where thousands were cremated daily. Auschwitz is not revealed through the first quarter of the film, and never explicitly named, although surmised by the details of the gas chamber.

Everyone in the film is nice and reasonable, sympathetic and caring, including mommy and daddy. But their eight-year-old boy, Bruno, is the best. He goes exploring and finds another boy, Shmuel, who is also eight and who seems to be in striped pajamas ("pyjamas" is the British spelling) on the other side of a barbed-wire electrified fenced-in alcove. Bruno thinks this is a farm. The boys become friends, playing games through the fence. *Pyjamas* culminates with Bruno digging under the barbed wire to help Shmuel find Shmuel's missing father. For the prearranged date, Shmuel has miraculously brought an extra set of striped pajamas and a cap for Bruno so that the well-fed, well-groomed German guest will fit right in. Once inside, Bruno asks, "Can we go to the café or something?" Ignoring all of this other inanity, the more basic question is: how was Bruno going to help find Shmuel's dad without knowing what Shmuel's dad looked like? Regardless, they arrive in Shmuel's barracks just in time to join the other prisoners who are suddenly marched to a gas chamber. Bruno's family realizes that their precious German boy is missing and search for him as the boys are being gassed.

The details of the depiction aside, for now, *Pyjamas* is ostensibly two stories. First, it is intended to be understood as the story of friendship and innocence, which does not need the veneer of the Holocaust to be told. Second, *Pyjamas* is about Bruno's mother's realization that her husband is the commandant of a death factory. We are to believe that by 1943—after over a decade of Hitler's rule, after the Nuremberg Laws, Kristallnacht, and the deportation of Berlin's Jews—this dear mother had no idea what was happening to Jews. Or, that being married to an SS-Obersturmbannführer (Colonel), including the lavish trappings, was grand until she realized that the smoke coming out of those chimneys, day and night, was from burning Jews. No, that was too far for the good wife, who then demanded to leave with the kids. Ignorance is hard to plead, even within the internal logic of this film, because the wife's mother-in-law was outwardly hostile to her Obersturmbannführer son because of his immoral job. In fact, the Obersturmbannführer's mother refused to visit her son's family after getting a whiff of his job from Berlin. So, we are left with the Obersturmbannführer's wife and son being heroic out of ignorance or a sudden consciousness, and a loving father who has lost his son to a gas chamber.

Pyjamas is dangerous, like *The Reader*, also released in 2008, because they both humanize the German perpetrators. Germans who committed mass murder in both films start and end as merely flawed functionaries who were just doing their jobs. Of course, the blasphemy of this excuse, made infamous by Adolf Eichmann, can only be understood as objectionable when confronted, not when mitigated by other, non-monstrous behavior. But these films create more sympathy than revulsion for their war criminals.

Although *Pyjamas*, on its face, should be shunned, the myriad of its inauthentic representations are noteworthy, too, not for the sport of a "got you" thrill, but as a further example of why fictional Holocaust films depicting death camps are not merely harmless. Nonetheless, IMDb lists 28 "Goofs" in the film, including that at Auschwitz "…there were double fences, 3 meters apart, around the compound. Too much distance for an outsider to touch an insider."[77] This is just a taste of the absurdity concerning the deadly fencing between the boys, the film's primary set-piece. The fence also has vertical barbed wires which are attached to horizontal cables, which is not only ingenuine, but also would have, most likely, shorted out the system. Early on, for no particular reason when Bruno still thinks it is a farm, he throws a stone at the fence to test it. This causes a spark, which makes little sense. Later, he and Shmuel pass things between the wire, like a soccer ball and clothing, without regard for its lethality. Later, like a commando, Bruno digs a perfect channel under the fence and snakes underneath. All the while 30 meters from the daily meeting spot is a watchtower, which evidently was staffed by blind guards (See 01:16:31). And then there is the basic question of an eight-year-old Shmuel being imprisoned at Birkenau. The child was not hidden; he was part of an adult labor squad. While "impossible" may be too strong, this scenario, if true, would have been exceedingly rare.

Pyjamas is beloved in some countries, including New Zealand and Australia. The film is so tempting to like because it is mind-bogglingly manipulative. As J.R. Jones of the Chicago Reader summarized, "…it reeks of self-righteousness."[78] We want to believe that most people are good, as we are led to believe in Pyjamas. We see this wonderful little German boy who brings food to the starving Jew enslaved by the boy's father. We see the little boy grappling with ethical and dogmatic dilemmas as if he were a superhero. We see the father as human. This is so much more preferable to the truth and oh, so seductive. Sure, the kid dies, as if a sacrifice for daddy's evil deeds, but lessons were learned and they all feel really bad. This cynicism could continue for pages. But, instead, Manohla Dargis of The New York Times is pithy enough to finish it off:

> See Bruno (Asa Butterfield). See Bruno run. See Bruno see a farm. See Bruno see "farmers" in "striped pajamas." See Shmuel (Jack Scanlon). See Shmuel at the farm. See Shmuel run because men are yelling. See Bruno run to his new house. Come home, Bruno, said Mother (Vera Farmiga), in a British accent. Come, Bruno, come. See Bruno and Shmuel meet across an unguarded barbed wire fence. See Bruno and Shmuel laugh, perhaps because there are no soldiers guarding this fence…. See the film's director, Mark Herman, take his camera into a gas chamber where naked men and children huddle, and two little hands clasp before the film cuts to black. Do not see the blood and excrement on the walls or the dead piled on the floor. See Mother howling outside the camp in the rain as the camera hovers over her. See Father (David Thewlis), realizing that his son has been swept away by the Nazi death machine he himself helps run, look horror-stricken. See the Holocaust trivialized, glossed over, kitsched up, commercially exploited and hijacked for a tragedy about a Nazi family. Better yet and in all sincerity: don't.[79]

Pyjamas' director/writer/producer Mark Herman has never made another film after Pyjamas, a rare bit of karma in the otherwise feckless entertainment industry.

As opposed to The Boy in the Striped Pyjamas, Life Is Beautiful is an unfortunate Holocaust film simply because of its misleading representation of life in Auschwitz. Yet, to its credit, Life Is Beautiful, in fact, frames its story as a fantasy. The Boy in the Striped Pyjamas, on the other hand, is the worst kind of Holocaust film, because it shamelessly creates a false perception of the Holocaust and of Germans without ever hinting at the false narrative. Together, these films ravage reality, while manipulating viewers into believing that children could generally be safe in Auschwitz.

Both successful films are brazen examples of Holocaust exploitation, not Nazisploitation, which is set apart as a form of pornography. These films are actual Holocaust exploitations that made hundreds of millions of dollars at the expense of truth. In the end, although Ilsa: She Wolf of the SS (1975) can be dismissed because Ilsa will never be shown in schools or taken seriously, Life Is Beautiful, The Boy in the Striped Pyjamas and Schindler's List are mainstays of education, which is both regrettable and avoidable.

Oscar Bait

"When making Oscar predictions," wrote Anne Thompson in *IndieWire*, "I've learned to never underestimate the Holocaust movie."[80] For generations in Hollywood, there has been widespread murmuring that Holocaust productions are inordinately awarded. The term "Oscar bait" has been associated with the film genre for decades.

Steven Spielberg's *Schindler's List* (1993) is certainly the most famous Holocaust film and garnered the most Oscar nominations with a dozen nods and seven wins, including Best Picture, Director and Writer. But the Holocaust film Oscar champion is actually Bob Fosse's *Cabaret* (1972) with eight wins, including Best Director, Actress and Supporting Actor. However, those two films are just the tip of the Oscar iceberg.

Lucy Mueller estimated in *Review Journal* in 2005 that, of the thousands of films produced generally, the chances of winning any Oscar is approximately 1 in 11,500.[81] Yet, from 1945 to 2020, 361 Holocaust feature films have been produced worldwide, of which 44 have been nominated for 150 Oscars. In fact, of the 77 American-produced Holocaust-related feature films made, 21 have won or been nominated for at least one Oscar, a 27 percent hit rate. Moreover, from 1945 through 1991, one out of every two American Holocaust feature films was Oscar-nominated. Overall, 21 American Holocaust features were nominated for 109 awards, winning 34 Oscars. (See Table 22.)

TABLE 22: HOLOCAUST FILMS THAT WON OR WERE NOMINATED FOR OSCARS
(EXCLUDING THOSE EXCLUSIVELY WINNING
OR NOMINATED FOR BEST FOREIGN LANGUAGE FILM)

Recommended in **Bold** (10 of 52). "One of the Best" in **Bold and Underlined** (3 of 15).

Title	Country	Oscars Winners and Nominations
The Stranger (1946)	U.S.	Nom: Writer
The Search (1948)	U.S.—Switzerland	Win: Juvenile, Writer; Nom: Actor, Director, Writing, Screenplay
The Diary of Anne Frank (1959)	U.S.	Win: Supporting Actress, Cinematography, Art Direction; Nom: Picture, Directing, Supporting Actor, Costume Design, Music (Adaptation Score)
Exodus (1960)	U.S.	Win: Music (Adaptation Score); Nom: Supporting Actor
Judgment at Nuremberg (1961)	U.S.	Win: Writer; Nom: Picture, Directing, Actor, Supporting Actor, Supporting Actress, Cinematography, Art Direction, Costume Design, Editing
The Pawnbroker (1964)	U.S.	Nom: Actor
Ship of Fools (1965)	U.S.	Win: Cinematography, Art Direction; Nom: Picture, Actor, Supporting Actor, Actress, Writer, Costume Design
The Garden of the Finzi-Continis— Il Giardino dei Finzi-Contini (1970)	Italy	Win: Foreign Language Film; Nom: Writer
<u>Cabaret</u> (1972)	U.S.	Win: Directing, Supporting Actor, Actress, Cinematography, Art Direction, Editing, Music (Adaptation Score), Sound; Nom: Picture, Writer
The Man in the Glass Booth (1975)	U.S.	Nom: Actor
Marathon Man (1976)	U.S.	Nom: Supporting Actor

Title	Country	Oscars Winners and Nominations
Voyage of the Damned (1976)	U.K.	Nom: Supporting Actress, Writer, Music (Adaptation Score)
Julia (1977)	U.S.	Win: Actor, Supporting Actress, Writer; Nom: Picture, Directing, Supporting Actor, Actress, Cinematography, Costume Design, Editing, Music (Adaptation Score)
The Boys from Brazil (1978)	U.S.—U.K.	Nom: Actor, Editing, Music (Adaptation Score)
***Sophie's Choice* (1982)**	U.S.	Win: Actress; Nom: Writer, Cinematography, Costume Design, Music (Adaptation Score)
***Au Revoir les Enfants* (1987)**	France—West Germany	Nom: Writer, Foreign Language Film
Enemies: A Love Story (1989)	U.S.	Nom: Supporting Actress, Supporting Actress (II), Writer
Music Box (1989)	U.S.	Nom: Actress
Europa Europa (1990)	Germany—Poland—France	Nom: Writer
Schindler's List (1993)	U.S.	Win: Picture, Directing, Writer, Cinematography, Art Direction, Editing, Music (Adaptation Score); Nom: Actor, Supporting Actor, Costume Design, Makeup, Sound
Shine (1996)	Australia	Win: Actor; Nom: Picture, Actor, Director, Writing, Film Editing, Music
Life Is Beautiful—La Vita è bella (1997)	Italy	Win: Actor, Foreign Language Film, Music (Adaptation Score); Nom: Picture, Directing, Writer, Editing
***The Pianist* (2002)**	U.S.	Win: Directing, Actor, Writer; Nom: Picture, Cinematography, Costume Design, Editing
***Defiance* (2008)**	U.S.	Nom: Music (Adaptation Score)
The Reader (2008)	U.S.	Win: Actress; Nom: Picture, Directing, Writer, Cinematography
***Inglourious Basterds* (2009)**	U.S.	Win: Supporting Actor; Nom: Picture, Directing, Writer, Cinematography, Editing, Sound
Ida (2013)	Poland	Win: Foreign Language Film; Nom: Cinematography
Jojo Rabbit (2019)	U.S.	Win: Screenplay; Nom: Picture, Supporting Actress, Costume Design, Production Design, Editing

With thousands of feature films being produced annually and only a few dozen Oscars being awarded, it is difficult to dismiss as coincidence that so many American Holocaust-related feature films have been Oscar-recognized, especially keeping in mind that the majority of those 77 American-produced or co-produced Holocaust-related feature films are objectively regarded as horrible to subpar, including: *The Hiding Place* (1975), *Death in Love* (2008), *The Substance of Fire* (1996), *The Statement* (2003) *Getting Away with Murder* (1996) and *The Memory Thief* (2007).

Further—except for Foreign Language Film, Documentary Feature and Documentary Short Subject—even to qualify for all other Academy Awards, films must have been advertised and shown in Los Angeles County for at least seven consecutive days during the year of their release. While my research has not yet uncovered the exact number of

Holocaust films that have failed to qualify for an Oscar because they could not afford distribution in Los Angeles, it is a fair guess that at least 80 percent of the 179 non–American produced films did not pass the L.A. hurdle. That being said, aside from *Life Is Beautiful—La Vita è bella* (1997), only five non–American-produced Holocaust feature films not in English have been nominated for Oscars other than Best Foreign Language Film: *The Shop on Main Street—Obchod na korze* (1965) (Actress), *The Garden of the Finzi-Continis—Il Giardino dei Finzi-Contini* (1970) (Writer), *Au Revoir les Enfants* (1987) (Writer), *Europa Europa* (1990) (Writer) and *Ida* (2013) (Cinematography).

As for foreign films and Oscars, from 1960 through 2015, 23 non–American Holocaust-related films were nominated and/or won the Oscar for Best Foreign Language Film. To put that shocking factoid into perspective, on average just foreign (non–American) Holocaust films were celebrated at the Oscars from 1960 through 2015 once every other year. In fact, of the 229 non–American-produced Holocaust-related feature films made during that period, 10 percent have been nominated for Best Foreign Language Film. (See Table 23.)

TABLE 23: HOLOCAUST FILM BEST FOREIGN LANGUAGE OSCAR WINNERS AND NOMINEES
Recommended in **Bold** (6 of 52). "One of the Best" in **Bold and Underlined** (1 of 15).

	Title	*Genre*	*Country*
Winners	**The Shop on Main Street—Obchod na korze (1965)**	Gentile	Czechoslovakia
	The Garden of the Finzi-Continis— Il Giardino dei Finzi-Contini (1970)	Victim	Italy
	A Life Ahead—Madam Rose— Madame Rosa—La Vie devant soi (1977)	Survivor	France
	Life Is Beautiful—La Vita è bella (1997)	Victim	Italy
	Nowhere in Africa—Nirgendwo in Afrika (2001)	Tangential	Germany
	The Counterfeiters—Die Fälscher (2007)	Victim	Austria—Germany
	Ida (2013)	Survivor	Poland
	Son of Saul (2015)	Victim	Hungary
Nominees	*Kapò* (1960)	Victim	Italy—France— Yugoslavia
	The Ninth Circle—Deveti krug (1960)	Gentile	Yugoslavia
	Jacob the Liar—Jakob, der Lügner (1974)	Victim	East Germany— Czechoslovakia
	Lacombe, Lucien (1974)	Gentile	France— West Germany—Italy
	The Last Metro—Le dernier métro (1980)	Tangential	France
	This Boat is Full—Das Boot ist voll (1981)	Victim	Switzerland
	The Revolt of Job—Jób lázadása (1983)	Victim	Hungary
	Angry Harvest—Bittere Ernte (1985)	Gentile	West Germany
	Au Revoir les Enfants (1987)	Gentile	France— West Germany
	The Nasty Girl—Das schreckliche Mädchen (1990)	Gentile	West Germany
	Divided We Fall—Musíme si pomáhat (2000)	Gentile	Czech Republic
	In Darkness (2011)	Gentile	Poland—Germany— Canada

As Roger Ebert wrote about one of those 20 films, "*Angry Harvest* is one of this year's Oscar nominees for best foreign film, again demonstrating the flawed nature of the selection process. It was selected by West Germany, survived the screening process and was nominated…. Until the best foreign film nominees are chosen on the basis of art, not geography and politics, they won't mean very much."[82] Ebert also observed when reviewing *The Notebook—A nagy füzet* (2013): "Such films, whatever their quality, so often end up in U.S. art houses and the Oscars' Best Foreign Film sweepstakes, it's tempting to suspect there's a single factory stamping them out according to formula."[83]

The number of Holocaust films nominated for the Best Foreign Language Oscars is even more impressive considering that the Best Foreign Language Oscar was not even created until 1957. And, until 2006, to be eligible for the Foreign Language Oscar, a submission's dialogue had to be in the official language of the submitting country, which knocked several other Holocaust films out of consideration.

It is worth noting, too, that the (American) Television Academy has been no less generous to Holocaust films when handing out Emmys. From 1974 through 2009, 34 American-produced or co-produced Holocaust-related television programs or miniseries have aired, of which 20 (or nearly 60 percent) have won or been nominated for at least one Emmy. (See Table 24.) Indeed, how bad must those other 14 Holocaust television productions have been not to have received any Emmy nominations?*

TABLE 24: MADE-FOR-TELEVISION EMMY WINNERS AND NOMINATIONS
Recommended in **Bold** (2 of 52). "One of the Best" in **Bold and Underlined** (1 of 15).

Film (Year)	Emmy Winner	Emmy Nomination
QB VII (TV Miniseries 1974)	Single Performance—Supporting Actor—Comedy/Drama Special, Single Performance—Supporting Actress—Comedy/Drama Special, Film Editing for Entertainment Programming—Special, Graphic Design, Music Composition—Special, Film Sound Editing	Special—Drama/Comedy, Single Performance—Supporting Actor—Comedy/Drama Special, Single Performance—Supporting Actress—Comedy/Drama Special, Directing—Special Program—Drama/Comedy, Writing—Special Program—Drama/Comedy—Adaptation, Cinematography for Entertainment Programming—Special, Individual Art Direction/Scenic Design—Single Episode of a Comedy, Drama/Limited Series
Holocaust (Miniseries 1978)	Limited Series, Costume Design—Drama/Comedy Series, Directing—Drama Series, Film Editing—Drama Series, Lead Actor—Limited Series, Lead Actress—Limited Series, Single Performance—Supporting Actress—Comedy/Drama Series, Writing Drama Series	Music Composition—Series (Dramatic Underscore), Art Direction—Drama Series, Continuing Performance—Supporting Actor—Drama Series, Continuing Performance—Supporting Actor—Drama Series, Continuing Performance—Supporting Actress—Drama Series, Lead Actor—Limited Series, Lead Actress—Limited Series
Playing for Time (TV 1980)	Drama Special, Lead Actress—Limited Series/Special, Supporting Actress—Limited Series/Special, Writing—Limited Series/Special	Supporting Actress—Limited Series/Special, Art Direction—Limited Series/Special

---

* The following American-produced or co-produced made-for-television Holocaust films received no Emmy nominations: *The House on Garibaldi Street* (TV 1979), *Remembrance of Love* (TV 1982), *The Execution* (TV 1985), *Miracle at Moreaux* (TV 1986), *Max and Helen* (TV 1990), *Never Forget* (TV 1991), *Forget Me Not: The Anne Frank Story* (TV 1996), *A Call to Remember* (TV 1997), *In the Presence of Mine Enemies* (TV 1997), *Miracle at Midnight* (TV 1998), *Bonhoeffer: Agent of Grace* (TV 2000) and *Varian's War: The Forgotten Hero* (TV 2001).

Film (Year)	Emmy Winner	Emmy Nomination
The Diary of Anne Frank (TV 1980)		Cinematography—Limited Series/Special, Makeup, Individual Achievement—Special Class
Skokie—Once They Marched Through a Thousand Towns (TV 1981)		Actor in a Miniseries or Motion Picture Made for Television
The Wave (TV 1981)	Children's Program	
The Scarlet and the Black (TV 1983)	Sound Mixing for a Limited Series or a Special	Editing for a Limited Series or a Special, Individual Achievement—Graphic Design and Title Sequences
Wallenberg—A Hero's Story (TV 1985)	Directing—Limited Series/Special, Costuming, Film Editing—Limited Series/Special, Film Sound Editing—Limited Series/Special	Drama/Comedy Special, Cinematography—Limited Series/Special, Film Sound Mixing—Limited Series/Special, Lead Actor—Limited Series/Special, Writing—Limited Series/Special
The Attic: The Hiding of Anne Frank (TV 1988)	Writing—Miniseries/Special	Directing—Miniseries/Special, Drama/Comedy Special, Editing—Miniseries/Special—Single Camera Production, Lead Actress—Miniseries/Special, Supporting Actress—Miniseries/Special
War and Remembrance (Miniseries 1988)	Miniseries, Special Visual Effects, Editing—Miniseries/Special—Single Camera Production	Costuming—Miniseries/Special, Hairstyling—Miniseries/Special, Makeup—Miniseries/Special, Makeup—Miniseries/Special, Music Composition—Miniseries/Special (Dramatic Underscore), Art Direction—Miniseries/Special, Cinematography—Miniseries/Special, Directing—Miniseries/Special, Lead Actor—Miniseries/Special, Lead Actress—Miniseries/Special, Sound Editing—Miniseries/Special, Supporting Actress—Miniseries/Special
Murderers Among Us: The Simon Wiesenthal Story (TV 1989)	Writing in a Miniseries or a Special	Drama/Comedy Special, Lead Actor in a Miniseries or a Special
The Man Who Captured Eichmann (TV 1996)		Editing for a Miniseries or a Special—Single Camera Production, Lead Actor in a Miniseries or a Special
The Devil's Arithmetic (TV 1999)	Directing—Children's Special, Writing—Children's Special	Children's Special, Sound Editing
Nuremberg (TV 2000)	Supporting Actor—Miniseries/Movie, Single Camera Sound Mixing—Miniseries/Movie	Miniseries, Sound Editing—Miniseries, Movie/Special
Anne Frank: The Whole Story **(TV 2001)**	Miniseries, Art Direction—Miniseries, Movie/Special	Casting—Miniseries, Movie/Special, Cinematography—Miniseries/Movie, Directing—Miniseries, Movie/Special, Single Camera Picture Editing—Miniseries, Movie/Special, Lead Actor—Miniseries/Movie, Lead Actress—Miniseries/Movie, Supporting Actress—Miniseries/Movie, Sound Editing—Miniseries, Movie/Special. Writing—Miniseries/Movie

Film (Year)	Emmy Winner	Emmy Nomination
Conspiracy (TV 2001)	Lead Actor—Miniseries/Movie, Writing—Miniseries/Movie	Made for Television Movie, Directing—Miniseries, Movie/Special, Cinematography—Miniseries/Movie, Single Camera Picture Editing—Miniseries, Movie/Special, Supporting Actor—Miniseries/Movie, Supporting Actor—Miniseries/Movie, Sound Editing—Miniseries, Movie/Special, Single Camera Sound Mixing—Miniseries/Movie
Haven (TV 2001)		Music Composition—Miniseries, Movie/Special (Dramatic Underscore), Supporting Actress—Miniseries/Movie, Special Visual Effects—Miniseries, Movie/Special
Uprising (TV 2001)	Stunt Coordination	Cinematography—Miniseries/Movie, Supporting Actor—Miniseries/Movie, Sound Editing—Miniseries, Movie/Special
Out of the Ashes (TV 2003)	Cinematography—Miniseries/Movie	
The Courageous Heart of Irena Sendler (TV 2009)	Makeup—Miniseries/Movie (Non-Prosthetic)	Supporting Actress—Miniseries/Movie, Sound Editing—Miniseries, Movie/Special

This heavily awarded art form, however, has had limited demand, which should not be particularly surprising. Without putting too fine a point on it, because few seek entertainment about tragedy, and even fewer about genocide, Holocaust films are much less viewed or commercially successful than most other film genres. In fact, 440 non–Holocaust feature films have grossed more than _Schindler's List_ ($322 million), by far the highest-grossing Holocaust film in history. Indeed, _Avengers: Endgame_ (2019) has grossed more than all Holocaust films combined.[84]

At the same time, the narrow audience of Holocaust filmgoers seems to inflate Holocaust film ratings, perhaps in solidarity with Holocaust victims. For example, the average IMDb user ratings of all Holocaust features is 6.9. This includes the following hideous films with an average IMDb user rating of just 4.3: _Getting Away with Murder_ (1996), _The Singing Forest_ (2003), _The Memory Thief_ (2007), _The Poet—Hearts of War_ (2007), _Death in Love_ (2008), _The Unborn_ (2009) and _Auschwitz_ (2011).

Moreover, although the average IMDb user rating for all 2,600 Oscar-nominated non–Holocaust films produced since 1945 is only 7.17, the average IMDb user rating for all nominated Holocaust films is 7.53. Even those who have not sat through every Holocaust film can intuit that the IMDb user ratings for Holocaust films seem to be gifted with an extra half-point, like on an amateur golfer's handicap scorecard, in deference to the subject matter, not quality.

The epitome of Oscars' overt and relentless fawning over the Holocaust is the 2020 Academy's impulsive recognition of the sophomoric _Jojo Rabbit_. It was nominated for six trophies, including Best Picture, Supporting Actress, Adapted Screenplay, Costume Design, Production Design and Editing. Taika Waititi's _Jojo Rabbit_ is a bad movie, Holocaust or otherwise, and only won for Best Adapted Screenplay. It was the lowest grossing of the seven Best Picture nominees that were released solely in theaters (setting aside the two additional streaming nominees, *Marriage Story* and *The Irishman*). It was also the second lowest-rated of the nine 2020 Best Picture nominees by IMDb users, has the second-lowest number of voters and has the lowest Metascore (aggregate of critical reviews), a shockingly low 58 out of 100. As was noted in *Slant Magazine*, "…Jojo Rabbit suggests what that dapper hipster auteur might generate if he was to remake Elem Klimov's hallucinatory, horrifying World War II epic *Come and See* [*Idi i smotri* (1985)], and that's not a compliment."[85] And as Keith Uhlich noted in *Slant Magazine*:

> This spectacularly wrongheaded "anti-hate satire" (as per the how-the-hell-do-we-market-this-thing ad campaign) is the feature-length equivalent of the "Springtime for Hitler" number from Mel Brooks's *The Producers*, sans context and self-awareness. It takes place in a goofball period la-la land of its own creation, with sets as minutely detailed and shots as precisely composed as those in a Wes Anderson fantasia.[86]

Of course, the real elephant in the room is the tendency to view any attack on Holocaust films as a Trojan horse for antisemitism. The tacit logic has been that any such scrutiny invites accusations that Hollywood is controlled by Jews, suggesting that any discussion about Oscar bait is simply a form of Jew-baiting. But the Oscars are, in fact, as political today as they were in the 1950s when Hollywood blacklisted vulnerable members to appease antisemitic, red-baiting authoritarians in Washington, D.C. A decade later, the ground shifted so fast for the Academy that they had to ditch their repressive Motion Picture Production Code, which they replaced with a homophobic MPAA rating system.

The worst fears of Hollywood's Jews—to need to stand up as Jews—was eventuated in 1978 by Vanessa Redgrave. That night at the 50th Academy Awards, Redgrave marked herself for life as an enemy of Israel with an acceptance speech for the Best Supporting Actress Oscar for her performance in Fred Zinnemann's Holocaust film *Julia* (1977). Redgrave had been claiming that the "Jewish Defense League" had been harassing her because of her pro–Palestinian sympathies exhibited in a film she produced and narrated that same year, *The Palestinian* (1977), which coddled Yasser Arafat and was produced in conjunction with his P.L.O.[87] Redgrave proclaimed on stage:

> You should be very proud that in the last few weeks you have stood firm and you have refused to be intimidated by the threats of a small bunch of Zionist hoodlums whose behavior is an insult to the stature of Jews all over the world, and to their great and heroic record of struggle against fascism and oppression.[88]

Fortunately, an Oscar presenter later that night was famed writer and multiple Oscar-winner Paddy Chayefsky, who would countenance none of Redgrave's vitriol. Chayefsky said before presenting the Best Writing Oscar:

> Before I get on to the writing awards, there's a little matter I'd like to tidy up, at least if I expect to live with myself tomorrow morning. I would like to say—personal opinion, of course—that I'm sick and tired of people exploiting the occasion of the Academy Awards… [applause] …for the propagation of their own personal political propaganda. [applause] I would like to suggest to Miss Redgrave that her winning an Academy Award is not a pivotal moment in history, does not require a proclamation, and a simple "thank you" would have sufficed.[89]

Redgrave, to this day, defends her speech.[90] But her antics were simply another shot across the Academy's bow, just a few years after Marlon Brando sent Native American Sacheen Littlefeather (née Marie Louise Cruz) to accept Brando's Best Actor Oscar for *The Godfather* (1972), saying:

…he [Brando] very regretfully cannot accept this very generous award. And the reasons for this being are the treatment of American Indians today by the film industry—excuse me [boos and cheers]—and on television in movie re-runs, and also with recent happenings at Wounded Knee. I beg at this time that I have not intruded upon this evening, and that we will in the future, our hearts and our understandings will meet with love and generosity. Thank you on behalf of Marlon Brando. [applause][91]

Notwithstanding Paddy Chayefsky's courageous comments, most Jews, who still dominated much of Hollywood production, tried to lay low. But the situation was becoming dicier with overt pressure directed at the Motion Picture Academy for more minority representation. And Oscar is political, meaning that merit is sometimes defeated by guilt. Certainly, since 1990, when Spike Lee was robbed of Best Picture and Director Oscars for his trailblazing *Do the Right Thing* (1989), robbed by the Judeocentric *Driving Miss Daisy* (1989), these questions have been fair game. Was the middling *12 Years a Slave* (2013) better than *Nebraska* (2013), *American Hustle* (2013), *Dallas Buyers Club* (2013) or *Her* (2013), or did (the Black) Steve McQueen's *12 Years a Slave* win Best Picture because Oscar had rebuffed Spike Lee and because no Black director or producer had ever won Best Director or Best Picture until *12 Years a Slave*? Is it racist during these times of immigration politics to point out that Mexicans won the Best Director Oscar five out of six years, from 2014 to 2019?* Are the Oscars solely about art when the headline in *Variety* is "Backlash Grows as Oscars Snub Women Directors Yet Again"? And if there is any doubt that Oscar swings with the times, imagine if *The Pianist* had been released in 2018 instead of in 2002; fat chance that Frances McDormand, Natalie Portman or Salma Hayek would have presented the Best Director statue to Roman Polanski.

In the end, many great Holocaust films have been made, even by Americans. In fact, 12 American-produced Holocaust features are recommended in this book, eight of which have been Oscar-nominated, with four winners. But the specific question remains: why does the Academy nominate and award so many Holocaust films, especially to twaddle like *Jojo Rabbit*? Art is not math. Oscar voters are not computers. And members of the Academy all believe that they are faithfully representing their art form. Objectively, however, despite all the awards and the sometimes-elevated subject matter, Holocaust films are not inherently superior to other film genres; Holocaust films simply have a more avid audience.†

---

* Alfonso Cuarón for *Gravity* (2013); Alejandro González Iñárritu for both *Birdman* (2014) and *The Revenant* (2015); Guillermo del Toro for *The Shape of Water* (2017); and Alfonso Cuarón for *Roma* (2018).

† A portion of this section was first published in the *Jerusalem Post* on February 8, 2020, in an article by this author entitled "'Are Holocaust films Oscar bait?—comment."

5

A Practical History
of Holocaust Filmmaking
in Hollywood

Holocaust filmmakers have challenges beyond those of other filmmakers. Simply put, Holocaust films are uniquely scrutinized. Even filmmakers with the best intentions when making a Holocaust film—like Dustin Hoffman, who executive-produced the terrifyingly misguided and pedagogically ignorant *The Devil's Arithmetic* (TV 1999)—can be disproportionately savaged for their well-meaning choices. The producers of NBC's *Holocaust* miniseries in 1978, who believed they were, in part, undertaking a public service, were clueless about the pending high-minded onslaught. Regardless of whether NBC was blindsided or had been warned that Elie Wiesel and others were lurking upon the moral summit with knives out, NBC should have understood there was a vast difference between producing *Star Trek* (TV 1966–1969), with its periodic portrayals of generic planetary genocides, and producing *Holocaust* less than a decade later. In short, Holocaust filmmakers not only must respect Holocaust memories and history, but also must satisfy the Jewish community's collective expectations.

In Western culture, sensitivity directed toward the Holocaust is more acute than awareness of other genocides and historical injustices, including those perpetrated by Europeans who slaughtered indigenous populations while colonizing the Western Hemisphere and the subsequent enslavement of Africans, as well as the most notorious atrocities of the twentieth-century, including the slaughter of Armenians, Cambodians, former-Yugoslavians, Rwandans and the Communist purges. Holocaust documentation and knowledge towers above that of other cataclysms, which brings, in turn, greater scrutiny upon those producing Holocaust literature and film. Because the Holocaust is the most heavily documented event in human history, Holocaust film veracity is always a question. And skin can be very thin regarding the Holocaust.

For many minorities, any ethnocentric representation is a cause for both celebration and trepidation, especially when portraying tragedies or stereotypes. During the 1970s, Jews became almost giddy with any recognition of the Holocaust, as exemplified in *Annie Hall* (1977), whose protagonist obsesses over the four-hour Holocaust documentary *The Sorrow and the Pity* (1969). But, since the late 1970s, the bar has steadily risen for Holocaust cinema, as has the quality and frequency of Holocaust productions. And Jewish expectations, coupled with apprehension, were seemingly elevated with the release of each new Holocaust film.

Comedian/writer Jenny Yang coined the term "rep sweats," explaining her anxiety when viewing Asian depictions in entertainment, acknowledging that "every time you have the opportunity to see yourself on TV, you hold your breath."[1] This emotion was certainly triggered for many Asians by the release of *Crazy Rich Asians* (2018). In the Jewish world, there were serious rep sweats in anticipation of Norman Jewison's *Fiddler on the Roof* (1971), which opened on Broadway in 1964 and became the longest-running Broadway musical within six months of the film version's release. For the African American community, the release of Ryan Coogler's blockbuster *Black Panther* (2018), was like a national holiday, grossing more in its opening weekend than the total lifetime box office of any Holocaust film. Likewise, the gay community was nervously awaiting *Philadelphia* (1993), starring Tom Hanks and Denzel Washington, made by acclaimed director Jonathan Demme, whose previous feature *The Silence of the Lambs* (1991) had become only the third film in history to win the five major Oscars.*

> By 1993, theater and television had produced many offerings on gay themes and the AIDS crisis, but *Philadelphia* was the first big-budget, major studio movie to center on these themes. As such, it was overburdened with demands. At the time, it was regarded as a "bellwether project" for future AIDS films and was eagerly anticipated both by Hollywood and by the gay community.[2]

Similarly, it is hard to imagine that Francis Ford Coppola or Martin Scorsese also did not feel the burden of Italian-American imagery when making *The Godfather* (1972) and *Goodfellas* (1990), respectively. Certainly, some in their community felt that Coppola and Scorsese had betrayed their own people when portraying Italian-American immigrants as gangsters.

> Joe Colombo, a professed real estate agent who led the Italian-American Civil Rights League in protesting stereotyped depictions of Italians in film … had waged war against the Paramount movie, asserting it propagated an exaggerated fiction about the existence of the mafia.… Four blocks away from the film's location, Colombo had assembled a rally for an Italian-American Unity Day. As he moved to the podium, a photographer with a press pass named Jerome Johnson cut through the crowd and toward the stage. Before Colombo realized what was happening, Johnson had raised a gun and fired three shots, hitting Colombo in the head.[3]

Granted, this violent objection to *The Godfather* extended well-beyond a simple expression of ethnocentric dignity. Yet, judging from Coppola and Scorsese's successive films, Italian-American resistance to their themes must have seemed more like nuisances than crises.

Within the Jewish community, too, there has been angst caused by the Judeocentric antics of proud Jewish cultural icons, such as Philip Roth, Lenny Bruce, Woody Allen, Larry David and Jerry Seinfeld, to name but a few. Their gags (often involving food) were seen as self-hating by many, even if intended as collective self-awareness. But, certainly, if their schtick were replicated by Mel Gibson, the ADL would shift into overdrive. Mel Brooks recently quipped of *The Producers*—both films and the hit Broadway play—that he had received 1,100 letters "from every rabbi that ever saw it."[4]

In fact, Jewish backlash has at times been swift. For example, the common perception is that African American talk-show host Arsenio Hall's career was terminated in 1994 because he insisted upon interviewing the African American virulent antisemite Louis Farrakhan. "Up until that fateful Friday, February 25, 1994, Arsenio Hall had

---

* Best Picture, Actor, Actress, Director and Writing. The other two films to win the five major Oscars: *It Happened One Night* (1934) and *One Flew Over the Cuckoo's Nest* (1975). Interestingly, each of the three films also won only those five awards.

been on the air for over five years, had aired 1,000+ shows, he was the (white) media's darling ... but now he had booked Minister Farrakhan."[5] Regardless of whether such an assertion perpetuates the antisemitic canard concerning "Jewish control of Hollywood," or if that accusation is simply a restatement of Hollywood's very Jewish history,[6] the Jewish outcry to Arsenio Hall's Farrakhan interview was ferocious and effective.[7] Without a doubt, two decades earlier the Jewish community successfully torpedoed CBS's *Bridget Loves Bernie* (TV 1972–1973) because the show featured an intermarried couple:

> Orthodox rabbis met with CBS officials several times. A conservative rabbi organized a boycott by advertisers, and reform rabbis met with CBS staff in secret to have the show cancelled. Rabbi Abraham Gross, president of the Rabbinical Alliance of Orthodox Rabbis and Educators, described the show as a "flagrant insult" to Jews, protesting that intermarriage was strictly forbidden under Jewish law. Threats followed. Meredith Baxter ["Bridget"] said, "We had bomb threats on the show. Some guys from the Jewish Defense League came to my house to say they wanted to talk with me about changing the show." Threatening phone calls [were] made to the home of producer Ralph Riskin....[8]

Whether inordinately or appropriately, the Jewish community is deeply attuned to its representation in the media, especially in television and film. The cliché "but is it good for the Jews?" was a ubiquitous question arising from any Jewish notoriety. So, while no one should have expected Quentin Tarantino to have felt any responsibility toward Holocaust education when making *Inglourious Basterds* (2009), the same indifference was certainly absent leading up to the production of Steven Spielberg's *Schindler's List* (1993), the year after Jonathan Demme's *Philadelphia* (which was only moderately successful*). Indeed, there was colossal nervousness in the Jewish community at the prospect that the Holocaust would be turned into *Raiders of the Lost Ark* (1981) or *Jurassic Park* (1993). As chronicled in *Real Cruelty in Imaginary Gardens*:

> Spielberg had approached the film studio Universal about the possibility of filming Thomas Keneally's novel *Schindler's Ark* on its publication in 1982, but he knew then that he "would need to find considerable maturity as a filmmaker first if he was to meet the emotional challenge that it involved." Spielberg would not begin making the film for ten years. Despite this period of "maturing," there were still huge doubts about Spielberg's ability to tackle such a subject when he did come to make it—"the release of Spielberg's film was awaited with a certain trepidation, encourage by the director's proclivities for the spectacular and his tendencies to excess." This was, after all, the man responsible for *Jaws*, *Jurassic Park* and *The Indiana Jones* trilogy.[9]

Irrespective of my harsh criticisms about *Schindler's List*, Spielberg fully recognized his innate responsibility and committed to make a film that would inform the world about the Holocaust for generations. Perhaps in the entire history of filmmaking, the bar has never been so high as *Schindler's List*'s. Spielberg—the highest-grossing filmmaker in history—waited 10 years to undertake *Schindler's List* because he felt unworthy and ill-prepared.[10] If that anxiety seems exaggerated, consider Jewish director Stanley Kubrick (1928–1999). Only Christopher Nolan, because of three *Batman* films, has more top-250 IMDb titles (8) than does Kubrick (7), who is tied with Martin Scorsese and Steven Spielberg. Kubrick made such renowned films as:

---

* According to Box Office Mojo (which is owned by IMDb which is owned by Amazon), *Philadelphia* was the 12th highest grossing film of 1993, for which Tom Hanks won the Oscar for best actor, the year before he also won for *Forrest Gump* (1994). The ninth grossing film of 1993 was *Sleepless in Seattle* also starring Tom Hanks. The top grossing film was *Jurassic Park*. Further, although *Schindler's List* was officially released in 1994, its "limited release" on December 15, 1993, qualified it on Box Office Mojo as a 1993 release, making it the ninth grossing film of 1993.

- *Paths of Glory* (1957) (62nd on the IMDb all-time list);
- *Spartacus* (1960), four Oscars, two other nominations;
- *Dr. Strangelove or: How I Learned to Stop Worrying and Love the Bomb* (1964) (60th on the IMDb all-time list), four Oscar nominations;
- *2001: A Space Odyssey* (1968) (88th on the IMDb all-time list), one Oscar, three other nominations;
- *A Clockwork Orange* (1971) (92nd on the IMDb all-time list), four Oscar nominations;
- *Barry Lyndon* (1975) (219th on the IMDb all-time list), four Oscars, three other nominations;
- *The Shining* (1980) (63rd on the IMDb all-time list); and
- *Full Metal Jacket* (1987) (96th on the IMDb all-time list), one Oscar nomination;

In 1976, Isaac Bashevis Singer (1902–1991) declined Stanley Kubrick's request to write a Holocaust screenplay. In 1991, with the publication of Louis Begley's semi-autobiographical novel *Wartime Lies*, Kubrick embarked on a Holocaust script, toiling endlessly with the proper way to portray the Holocaust in a film version of *Wartime Lies*. By 1993, Warner Brothers had gotten behind the project, with the screenplay written by Kubrick, then entitled *Aryan Papers*. But the project was killed almost immediately upon the release of *Schindler's List*. According to Kubrick's wife in *Stanley Kubrick's Boxes* (TV 2008) and other sources, the Holocaust project had practically incapacitated her husband:

> The subject he most wanted to make a film about, Stanley Kubrick once said, was the Holocaust—"But good luck putting all of that into a 2-hour movie." … Though the fact of Kubrick's Jewishness is largely unknown among his fans and had little impact in his everyday existence—he never had a bar mitzvah and not one [of] his three marriages was a Jewish ceremony—being a Jew in what he perceived as a largely unfriendly world had a marked effect on his life…. "The reason Stanley gave up on it," said [his widow] Christiane Kubrick in an interview with the Guardian, "is because Steven's [Spielberg] film [*Schindler's List*] is about Jews who lived, and just a few. If you tell the whole truth in the film, which is the only way you could honor all these dead people, and be respectful enough, you would have to tell the whole truth." And that, Christiane concludes, would be "absolutely unsurvivable."[11]

Rep sweats. Like it or not, there is an added burden on filmmakers when dealing with the Holocaust. And, fairly or unfairly, all things Holocaust share this same burden. So, what does it take to make a great narrative Holocaust film? In art, pushing creativity is the only way to ascertain limits; the sweet spot is established by testing and breaking boundaries. Consider, for example, that "Jewish heads explode in *Schindler's List* and at an average rate of one every twelve minutes."[12] Was that too much? Obviously not, judging from *Schindler's List*'s Oscar haul and box office. But, even without the complications of portraying the Holocaust, it has taken many decades of film experimentation to establish taste and limits, mostly through feedback (and pushback).

In 1930, to fend off government regulation of the mostly Jewish owned movie industry, American motion picture studios voluntarily created the "Hays Code" or Motion Picture Production Code (a.k.a. the "Production Code"), which was replaced in 1968 by the current Motion Picture Association of America (MPAA) rating system (G, PG, R, MA). Yet, for almost 50 years, the Production Code was imposed on every film script that was to be produced and released in America. Behind the scenes, the Production Code forced filmmakers to make puritanical changes that eliminated nudity, subdued intimacy, minimized violence, and sterilized language, all the while insisting on "good guy" plots with happy endings. The Production Code was best described as promoting "a Jewish owned business selling Catholic theology to Protestant America."[13] Reading the original list of Production Code objectives in Table 25 is amusing in light of *Schindler's List* or any other graphic Holocaust film:

TABLE 25: PRE-CODE: "DON'TS" AND "BE CAREFULS," AS PROPOSED IN 1927[14]

Resolved, That those things which are included in the following list shall not appear in pictures produced by the members of this Association, irrespective of the manner in which they are treated:

1. Pointed profanity—by either title or lip—this includes the words "God," "Lord," "Jesus," "Christ" (unless they be used reverently in connection with proper religious ceremonies), "hell," "damn," "Gawd," and every other profane and vulgar expression however it may be spelled;
2. Any licentious or suggestive nudity—in fact or in silhouette; and any lecherous or licentious notice thereof by other characters in the picture;
3. The illegal traffic in drugs;
4. Any inference of sex perversion;
5. White slavery;
6. Miscegenation (sex relationships between the white and black races);
7. Sex hygiene and venereal diseases;
8. Scenes of actual childbirth—in fact or in silhouette;
9. Children's sex organs;
10. Ridicule of the clergy;
11. Willful offense to any nation, race or creed;

And be it further resolved, That special care be exercised in the manner in which the following subjects are treated, to the end that vulgarity and suggestiveness may be eliminated and that good taste may be emphasized:

1. The use of the flag;
2. International relations (avoiding picturizing in an unfavorable light another country's religion, history, institutions, prominent people, and citizenry);
3. Arson;
4. The use of firearms;
5. Theft, robbery, safe-cracking, and dynamiting of trains, mines, buildings, etc. (having in mind the effect which a too-detailed description of these may have upon the moron);
6. Brutality and possible gruesomeness;
7. Technique of committing murder by whatever method;
8. Methods of smuggling;
9. Third-degree methods;
10. Actual hangings or electrocutions as legal punishment for crime;
11. Sympathy for criminals;
12. Attitude toward public characters and institutions;
13. Sedition;
14. Apparent cruelty to children and animals;
15. Branding of people or animals;
16. The sale of women, or of a woman selling her virtue;
17. Rape or attempted rape;
18. First-night scenes;
19. Man and woman in bed together;
20. Deliberate seduction of girls;
21. The institution of marriage;
22. Surgical operations;
23. The use of drugs;
24. Titles or scenes having to do with law enforcement or law-enforcing officers;
25. Excessive or lustful kissing, particularly when one character or the other is a "heavy."

Although today's unfettered creative freedom in cinema seems like an inalienable right, the practical acquisition of full artistic license in film has been a relatively recent accomplishment. For filmmakers during the time of the Production Code, it is not hyperbolic to suggest that free speech ended at the gates of Paramount, MGM, Fox, Universal, Disney, Columbia and Warner Brothers, each of which cowered beneath the non-market-driven Production Code. Nonetheless and surprisingly, sexually charged films never ceased to be produced; although the early depictions rarely exceeded a three-second kiss, sexuality has always powered film.

But, by the mid–1960s, with mores changing and an unstoppable entry into America by European films, the fight was taken to the movie studios, which were under increasing pressure by filmmakers to ditch the Production Code. Meanwhile, European films flaunted their creative advantages, as exemplified by Ingmar Bergman's *The Virgin Spring—Jungfrukällan* (1960), which depicted a teen girl being raped and murdered, and which also would have been forbidden to be produced in America. Yet, not only did *The Virgin Spring* win the 1961 Best Foreign Language Oscar, but also, just after the dissolution of the Production Code, *The Virgin Spring* was remade in America as *The Last House on the Left* (1972), launching the storied career of the king of horror films, writer/director Wes Craven.

The Production Code was already teetering, and was ultimately eviscerated in 1968, but not before many anti-authoritarian films by Jewish directors had completely shredded the Code's anachronistic standards, with trailblazing films including Billy Wilder's *The Apartment* (1960), Stanley Kubrick's *Spartacus* (1960) and *Dr. Strangelove or: How I Learned to Stop Worrying and Love the Bomb* (1964), Richard Brooks' (né Reuben Sax) *Elmer Gantry* (1960), Stanley Kramer's *Inherit the Wind* (1960), John Frankenheimer's *The Manchurian Candidate* (1962), Sidney Lumet's *The Pawnbroker* (1964) and *The Hill* (1965), Roman Polanski's (né Raymond Thierry Liebling) *Repulsion* (1965) and *Rosemary's Baby* (1968), Stuart Rosenberg's *Cool Hand Luke* (1967), Mel Brooks' (né Melvyn Kaminsky) *The Producers* (1967) and of course, the very subversive Mike Nichols, with his anti-establishment films *Who's Afraid of Virginia Woolf?* (1966) and *The Graduate* (1967).[15] Not coincidentally, Mike Nichols (1931–2014)—whose films were nominated for 42 Oscars and who was only one of 15 "EGOT" winners (Emmy, Grammy, Oscar, Tony)—was born in Berlin as Mikhail Igor Peschkowsky and fled from Nazi Germany to America in 1939.

After the official demise of the Motion Picture Production Code in 1968, arbitrary moralistic limits imposed by the self-righteous film board were smashed like the Berlin Wall. Concurrently, a new generation of filmmakers was responsible for the real "Golden Age" of cinema. For example, consider the 28 unfettered, groundbreaking films listed in Table 26, all released in the wake of the Production Code's abrogation:

TABLE 26: 28 POST-"PRODUCTION CODE" FILMS THAT WOULD HAVE VIOLATED THE "PRODUCTION CODE"

Film	Director	IMDb Rating	Oscars
Bob & Carol & Ted & Alice (1969)	Paul Mazursky	6.7	Nom: Supporting Actor, Supporting Actress, Writing, Cinematography
Butch Cassidy and the Sundance Kid (1969)	George Roy Hill	8.1	Win: Writing, Cinematography, Music, Score; Nom: Picture, Director, Sound
Cabaret (1972)	Bob Fosse	7.8	Win: Actress, Supporting Actor, Director, Cinematography, Art, Sound, Editing, Music; Nom: Picture, Writing

Film	Director	IMDb Rating	Oscars
Carnal Knowledge (1971)	Mike Nichols	7.0	Nom: Supporting Actress
Catch-22 (1970)	Mike Nichols	7.2	—
A Clockwork Orange (1971)	Stanley Kubrick	8.3	Nom: Picture, Director, Writing, Editing
Deliverance (1972)	John Boorman	7.7	Nom: Picture, Director, Editing
Dirty Harry (1971)	Don Siegel	7.8	—
Easy Rider (1969)	Dennis Hopper	7.4	Nom: Supporting Actor, Writing
*Everything You Always Wanted to Know About Sex * But Were Afraid to Ask* (1972)	Woody Allen	6.8	—
The Exorcist (1973)	William Friedkin	8.0	Win: Writing, Sound; Win: Picture, Actress, Supporting Actor, Supporting Actress, Director, Cinematography, Art, Editing
Five Easy Pieces (1970)	Bob Rafelson	7.5	Nom: Picture, Actor, Supporting Actor, Writing
The French Connection (1971)	William Friedkin	7.8	Win: Picture, Actor, Director, Writing, Editing; Nom: Supporting Actor, Cinematography, Sound
The Godfather (1972)	Francis Ford Coppola	9.2	Win: Picture, Actor, Writing; Nom: Supporting Actor, Supporting Actor (II), Supporting Actor (III), Director, Costume, Sound, Editing, Music
The Godfather: Part II (1974)	Francis Ford Coppola	9.0	Win: Picture, Supporting Actor, Director, Writing, Art, Music; Nom: Actor, Supporting Actor, Supporting Actor (II), Costume
Goodbye, Columbus (1969)	Larry Peerce	6.6	Nom: Writing
Harold and Maude (1971)	Hal Ashby	8.0	—
The Heartbreak Kid (1972)	Elaine May	6.9	Nom: Supporting Actor, Supporting Actress
Kelly's Heroes (1970)	Brian G. Hutton	7.7	—
Klute (1971)	Alan J. Pakula	7.2	Win: Actress; Nom: Writing
The Last Picture Show (1971)	Peter Bogdanovich	8.1	Win: Supporting Actor, Supporting Actress; Nom: Picture, Supporting Actor (II), Supporting Actress (II), Director, Writing, Cinematography
Last Tango in Paris (1972)	Bernardo Bertolucci	7.1	Nom: Actor, Director
Love Story (1970)	Arthur Hiller	6.9	Win: Music; Nom: Picture, Actor, Actress, Supporting Actor, Director, Writing
M.A.S.H. (1970)	Robert Altman	7.6	Win: Writing; Nom: Picture, Supporting Actress, Director, Editing
Midnight Cowboy (1969)	John Schlesinger	7.9	Win: Picture, Director, Writing; Nom: Actor, Actor (II), Supporting Actress, Editing
One Flew Over the Cuckoo's Nest (1975)	Milos Forman	8.7	Win: Picture, Actor, Actress, Director, Writing; Nom: Supporting Actor, Cinematography, Editing, Music

Film	Director	IMDb Rating	Oscars
Summer of '42 (1971)	Robert Mulligan	7.3	Win: Music; Nom: Writing, Cinematography, Editing
Sunday Bloody Sunday (1971)	John Schlesinger	7.2	Nom: Actor, Actress, Director, Writing

Each of these 28 films would have grossly violated many of the red-letter prohibitions of the Production Code, macro and micro. And many of these films significantly impacted everything that followed. For example, without Stanley Kubrick's insanely off-the-rails *A Clockwork Orange*, perhaps Quentin Tarantino wanders off the edge in his extraordinary 1994 *Pulp Fiction*. (Even more likely is that Kubrick's already edgy *The Shining* [1980] might have tipped over without *A Clockwork Orange*'s madness.)

Holocaust films also had to cope with the Production Code, which rendered Holocaust portrayals in American films ridiculously antiseptic. Sidney Lumet, however, fought back in 1964 with *The Pawnbroker*, the story of a concentration camp survivor. *The Pawnbroker* made news for having been given a waiver of Production Code rules, receiving an exception for depicting bare breasts.[16] But accurate depictions of death camps—including violence, nudity, gassing and assuredly unhappy endings—were simply impossible as long as the Production Code ruled.

Another factor in the early scarcity of American-produced Holocaust films was post–War Hollywood Jew-baiting, which was an undercurrent of "the Red Scare," HUAC, and McCarthyism. Through the late 1950s, Jews in Hollywood were inordinately accused of being Communist sympathizers. In large measure, Jewish blacklisting that resulted from these attacks was overseen by the fading immigrant Jewish studio heads, who were increasingly defensive, not wanting to be sullied as un–American or unpatriotic themselves. This period was supercharged by the conviction and execution in 1953 of two American Jews, Julius and Ethel Rosenberg, who had spied for the USSR. Jews did not want to call attention to Jewish subjects in 1950s Hollywood, and the Holocaust was clearly a Jewish subject. Indeed, only non–Jewish directors dared make major Holocaust-related films in 1950s America: Edward Dmytryk's *The Juggler* (1953) and *The Young Lions* (1958), Peter Glenville's *Me and the Colonel* (1958) and George Stevens' *The Diary of Anne Frank* (1959).* Of note, too, *The Great Dictator* (1940), which attacked Hitler's racist policies, was made by Charlie Chaplin, a Gentile.

Filmmakers wanting to address the Holocaust, specifically, also had to grapple with the daunting challenge of creating an entirely new, emotionally charged cinematic genre: depicting the unimaginable recent reality of genocide. Hollywood's track record until the 1960s was far from enlightened and it was ill-prepared to confront the reality emerging from the rubble of Europe. Early Hollywood films featured horrifyingly racist themes, highlighted by D.W. Griffith's overtly racist *The Birth of a Nation* (1915). Hollywood also churned out countless films depicting Native Americans as savages and representing African Americans and Asians as simpletons. For grotesque stereotypes, look no further than Disney's half-man-half-donkey in *Fantasia* (1940) and Disney's Jim Crow crows in *Dumbo* (1941). And, while *Gone with the Wind* (1939) wistfully

---

* Jewish director Max Nosseck's labor-of-love *Singing in the Dark* (1956) was also made during that period, but was produced by a co-star, Joey Adams, and was not a major studio production. It was the swan-song for star of Yiddish theater Moyshe Oysher (1907–1958).

remembered American slavery, its Black winner for Best Supporting Actress, Hattie McDaniel, was not permitted to sit at the 1940 Oscars with her White co-stars, Vivien Leigh and Clark Gable.[17]

Further, during much of the Post-War Era, the Holocaust's details were sketchy, at best. Most of the surviving physical evidence and apparatus remained behind the Iron Curtain. For decades after World War II, many of the details of German atrocities were apocryphal, muddled by rumors, such as the false contentions that Jewish skin had been turned into lampshades[18] and that Jewish fat had been boiled down into soap,[19] as if death ghettos, gas chambers and killing squads were not enough. Not until 1961, with two events, did the Holocaust information spigot open.

First was the worldwide televised trial of German Obersturmbannführer (lieutenant colonel) Adolf Eichmann (1906–1962), the operational overseer of the Holocaust for the Third Reich. From April to December of 1961 in Jerusalem, Eichmann's trial included testimony from 112 witnesses, including many Holocaust survivors.[20] Eichmann was convicted on 15 counts of crimes against humanity, war crimes, crimes against the Jewish people, and membership in a criminal organization. The impact of Eichmann's trial cannot be overstated: no longer could piecemeal snippets be construed as hyperbolic accounts of genocide. Shockingly, Eichmann argued that he was simply following orders, an inoperable argument when committing criminal acts. Further, among others to report on the trial as a sociological landmark was Hannah Arendt, whose 1963 Viking Press book *Eichmann in Jerusalem: A Report on the Banality of Evil* spurred even more discussions about the inner workings of the Nazi program. Both Eichmann-centric phrases—"just following orders" and "the banality of evil"—have become twisted terms-of-art in modern lexicon, shorthand in Holocaust and genocide studies. After exhausting all appeals within the Israeli judiciary, Eichmann was unceremoniously hung in June 1962. Eichmann's audacious capture by Israel in Argentina in May of 1960 and the subsequent spectacle of his trial spawned more than a dozen narrative films, including Oscar winner *Judgment at Nuremberg* (1961) which was timed for release during the apex of Eichmann's trial. As noted by survivor and scholar, Hebrew University Professor Israel Gutman (1923–2013):

> Only in the 1960s did the Eichmann trial, among other factors, prompt a turning point. Survivors' memoirs, the impact of books such as *Anne Frank, Diary of a Young Girl*, and a proliferation of academic literature thrust the Holocaust into the focus of extensive public interest in the United States and other countries. Holocaust research advanced in Israel, Germany, and the United States, and many research and memorial institutes came into being. The magnitude of the crime, the irrationality of its motives, and the unprecedented brutality applied in its perpetration engendered and implanted the anxious feeling that Western civilization had become brittle and wobbly. The Holocaust gradually became an indicator and an integral component of contemporary human consciousness.[21]

The second momentous Holocaust-related event of 1961 was the publication of the first comprehensive historical study of the Holocaust: Raul Hilberg's 1,388-page *The Destruction of the European Jews*, published by Yale University Press. As Christopher Browning, Professor of Holocaust studies at University of North Carolina at Chapel Hill, wrote a quarter-century later:

> If one measure of a book's greatness is its impact, a second is its longevity. For 25 years *The Destruction of the European Jews* has been recognized as the unsurpassed work in its field. While monographic studies of particular aspects of the Final Solution, utilizing archival sources and court records not available to Hilberg before 1961, have extended our knowledge in many areas, *The Destruction of the European Jews* still stands as the preeminent synthesis, the book that put it all together in the framework of an overarching and unified analysis.[22]

Still, it was decades before the world even began to coalesce around a name for the German act of genocide. In Israel and in many Jewish circles, the name is "Shoah." But the common term, "Holocaust," was only cemented into the non–Israeli nomenclature by a TV mini-series. Indeed, "It wasn't until the 1960s," as slightly exaggerated in *The New Republic*, "that scholars and writers began using the term *Holocaust*, and it took the 1978 TV film *Holocaust*, starring Meryl Streep, to push it into widespread use."[23] And with the advent of the new MPAA rating system, as Holocaust films—which always were tacitly intended to be educational—became more violent, their ratings started sliding from PG ("Parental Guidance") to R ("Restricted"). Even trickier were the many Holocaust films that were made for television; they, too, were produced to entertain while educating, yet had to be appropriate for all audiences. So, the obstacles that Holocaust filmmakers had to navigate were very delicate, perched on the edge of violence and suitability.

Early Holocaust films were given much more leeway concerning authenticity. For example, the first Survivor film, *The Search* (1948), starring Montgomery Clift, was courageous, well-intended and unobjectionable. And there is no reason to believe that the subtleties of Holocaust tattoos could have been known to its legendary director, four-time Academy Award winner Fred Zinnemann. However, examining *The Search* historically is a useful exercise. *The Search* depicts an undersized nine-year-old boy, played by Ivan Jandl, who won the now-defunct "Academy Juvenile Award" (or Juvenile Oscar) for his performance. His character, an orphaned Czech boy named Karel (Ivan Jandl), has a tattoo on the outside of his left arm with the number: A24328. The two American soldiers who cared for Karel conclude reductively that "A" was for Auschwitz. (See Picture 1.)

While the placement on Karel's outside forearm was, in fact, possible, Fred Zinnemann could not have

Picture 1: *Search* (1948) tattoo *(top)* and close-up *(bottom)*.

been expected to know that *all* numbered tattoos were from Auschwitz. "A" simply signified a series used to prevent excessively high numbers. The series on males did not exceed 20,000; for women, it continued to 30,000. The "A" series, too, was used on Hungarian prisoners, not Czechs, like Karel.[24] More importantly, of course, children arriving at Auschwitz were either murdered immediately or, on rare occasions, hidden. Either way, children were very rarely tattooed. (While twins used in Josef Mengele's medical experiments were given special tattoos,[25] this explanation for Karel's tattoo would have been tenuous, at best.) However, there is no rational basis to fault Fred Zinnemann's Survivor depiction from 1948.

Ironically, 16 years later in *36 Hours* (1964), an Auschwitz survivor played by Eva Marie Saint is properly numbered as "A-25404," just 1,076 numbers later than Karel's. (See Picture 2.)

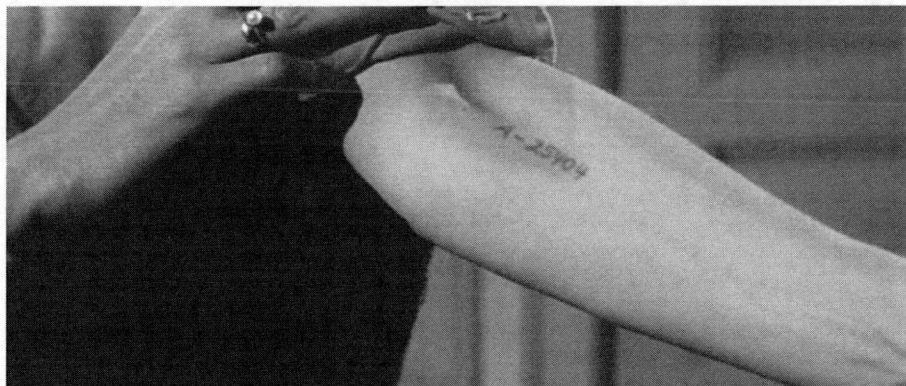

Picture 2: *36 Hours* (1964) tattoo.

But tattooing has been a mixed bag. *Kapò* (1960) depicts the protagonist, played by Susan Strasberg, being tattooed by the camp doctor in a nondescript labor camp. Of all the improbable aspects in *Kapò*, however, tattooing was the least of the film's problems. In *Return from the Ashes* (1965), director J. Lee Thompson not only displayed a tattoo on the protagonist's incorrect (right) arm, but also she was purportedly tattooed in the Dachau Concentration Camp. That mistake was not made in its remake, *Phoenix* (2014), half a century later. On the other hand, a decade after *Return from the Ashes*, director Ronald Neame depicted an Auschwitz tattoo correctly in *The Odessa File* (1974), and the numbering was realistic at "53142," with the first Auschwitz numbering series (without the "A" prefix) ending at 202,499.[26] (See Picture 3.)

And, even as late as 1982, "Sophie" (Meryl Streep) in *Sophie's Choice* succumbed to tattoo issues in a few ways. First, her Auschwitz tattoo, while shown only a few times, is utterly pristine, as if made with a laser printer, vastly more delicate and aligned than real tattoos. On the other hand, her number is possible: "111379," which included the "1" prefix on the first series of the first 90,000 female prisoners, the series that preceded the "A" prefix.[27] Second—and more troubling for a film that hired Auschwitz survivor Kitty Hart as a "technical advisor" before shooting to improve authenticity—is the continuity blunder of only showing her tattoo in one of many sleeveless scenes. (See Picture 4.)*

---

* Tattoo mistakes were also made in television episodes, including *The Pretender* (TV 1996–2000), S02E08, "Hazards" and a 2010 episode of *Nip/Tuck* (TV 2003–2010), S06E18, "Walter & Edith Krieger."

So, it is understandable that, for instance, Gillo Pontecorvo's Post-War Era Holo-caust film *Kapò* lacked the authenticity to which today's filmgoers have become accus-tomed. So soon after the Holocaust, it would have been unfair to have expected anything other than generic German camp depictions produced in the West. Sydney Lumet's *The Pawnbroker* succeeded where *Kapò* failed, by not overreaching, only using a few

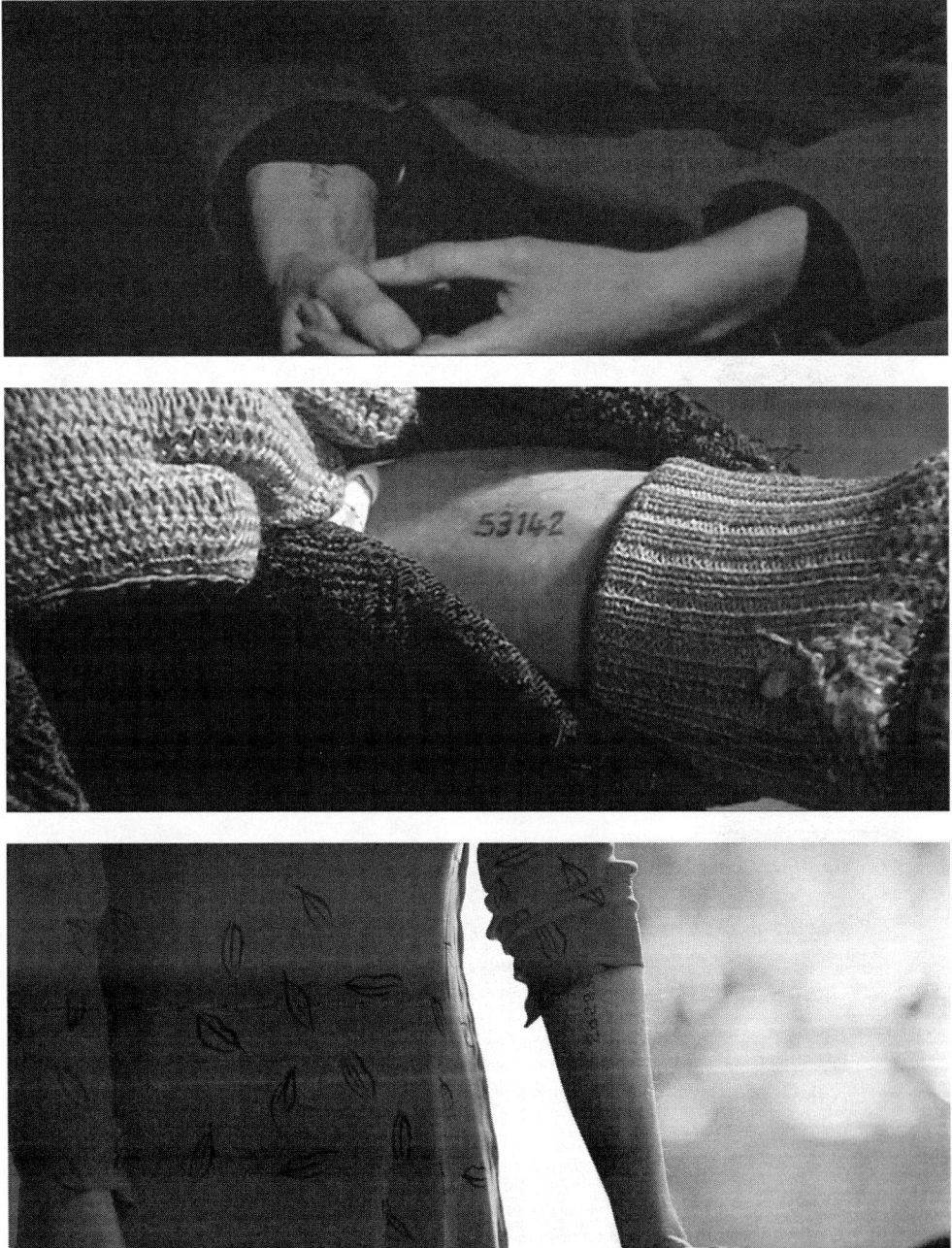

Picture 3: *Return from the Ashes* (1965) tattoo *(top)*, *The Odessa File* (1974) tattoo *(middle)* and *Phoenix* (2014) tattoo *(bottom)*.

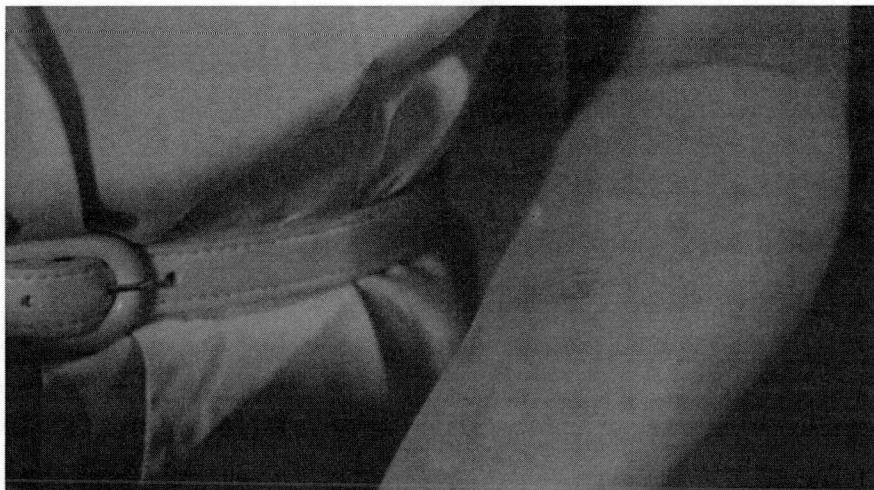

Picture 4: *Sophie's Choice* (1982) tattoo *(top)* and non-tattoo *(middle and bottom)*.

flashbacks from a nondescript concentration camp. Rod Serling, too, succeeded with his courageous 1961 script for *The Twilight Zone* (TV 1959–1964) episode "Deaths-Head Revisited." Directed by Don Medford, the 25-minute episode was a winner, even with its MGM backlot portrayal of Dachau.[28]

Still, America through the mid–1970s was not ready to see a more authentic representation of the Holocaust in theaters or on television. While many of the early Holocaust films depict some of the horrors of the Holocaust, none of those films were dedicated exclusively to the Holocaust's core: mass murder. Instead, early Holocaust films were personal stories about individual struggles to survive, which is not an option in a gas chamber. The most celebrated early Holocaust films all eluded focus on the German killing machine, never showing more than one or two of its many gears. By contrast, many Holocaust films depicted wartime ghetto life, righteous Gentiles, hiding and resistance. Even if Auschwitz or Birkenau were shown in some of these films, even if the films are graphic at times when representing Jewish suffering, their protagonists seldom died (including Anne Frank who, in the 1959 film, only dies in epilogue, not in Bergen-Belsen).

Camp representations, in particular, became trickier as the Holocaust was documented over the decades. A few famous buildings, gates, fences and barracks from German camps that had survived the War have become iconic, making inauthentic sets increasingly obvious. Of the six death camps, only Auschwitz/Birkenau and Majdanek were not razed by the Germans as the Soviets approached. Many of the original buildings at both of these camps have been maintained by Poland as memorials and museums. In fact, for most viewers, the only death camp that is easily identified in pictures and film is Auschwitz/Birkenau. Several identifiable concentration camps also partially survived, including Dachau, Mauthausen and Buchenwald. But apparently, no one told Martin Scorsese when he was making *Shutter Island* (2010) that Auschwitz and Dachau are not interchangeable; Scorsese mistakenly featured the iconic Auschwitz gate with the voiceover, "When we got through the gates at Dachau, the SS guards surrendered." (See Picture 5.)

While dressing random sets in Hollywood sufficed with smaller depictions, as information flowed, the level of detail required for authentic Holocaust fiction grew by magnitudes. American depictions of specific death camps started in full during the Commercial Era. *QB VII* (Miniseries 1974) did not try to reproduce a German camp in flashbacks, but instead visited Leon Uris' mythical "Jadwiga" camp in modern Poland, the remnants of an Auschwitz-inspired camp, complete with reporting of tattoos and medical experiments. Jadwiga, which would be unconvincing by today's standards, was passable in 1974. The depiction of the Ravensbrück Concentration Camp in Billy Graham's *The Hiding Place* (1975) was an improvement over *QB VII*, but still underwhelming, depicting well-fed prisoners in Ravensbrück dressed like housewives who slept on individual metal-framed beds. But by the end of the 1970s, ignorance was no longer a defense for inauthentic portrayals.

Aside from sloppy camp depictions, other more general clues pop up in Holocaust films that challenge authenticity. A prime example of Holocaust ignorance in filmmaking is *The Devil's Arithmetic* (TV 1999). The climax features the impossibility of a gas chamber in a labor camp, that is both technically and aesthetically inept and historically tone-deaf. Similarly, in *The Devil's Arithmetic,* a non–Auschwitz Holocaust tattoo is affixed in a labor camp, a serious historical faux pas by 1999. It is certainly possible that Dustin Hoffman and the other filmmakers responsible for *The Devil's Arithmetic*

Picture 5: "Dachau" Gate in *Shutter Island* (2010) *(top)* with Voiceover "When we got through the gates at Dachau, the SS guards surrendered" and the Actual Auschwitz *(middle)* and Dachau Gates *(bottom)*.

intended these scenes to be an homage, pastiche or amalgamation of the general Holocaust experience. But by 1999 the bar was far too high for such bungles, especially in a film that was touted as educational.

Overall, though, except for Auschwitz, exact architectural reproductions of German camps are, nonetheless, superfluous in cinema; very few other specific camps are depicted in film. For example, *Remembrance* (2011) has many excellent scenes depicting a nondescript concentration/death camp, depictions that are superior to most films listed below in Table 27, a summary of non–Auschwitz camps depicted in Holocaust films.

TABLE 27: GERMAN LABOR AND DEATH CAMPS
(EXCLUDING AUSCHWITZ/BIRKENAU) DEPICTED IN HOLOCAUST FILMS

Camp	*Film*
Bergen-Belsen Concentration Camp	*Pursuit* (TV 1989); *Anne Frank: The Whole Story* (TV 2001); *The Relief of Belsen* (TV 2007)
Buchenwald Concentration Camp	*Naked Among Wolves—Nackt unter Wölfen* (1963); *Naked Among Wolves—Nackt unter Wölfen* (TV 2015); *Fateless—Sorstalanság* (2005)
Dachau Concentration Camp	*Bent* (1997)
Jasenovac Concentration Camp	*The Ninth Circle—Deveti krug* (1960)
Majdanek Death Camp	*Simon Konianski* (2009)
Mauthausen Concentration Camp	*The Counterfeiters—Die Fälscher* (2007); *The Photographer of Mauthausen—El fotógrafo de Mauthausen* (2018)
Ravensbrück Concentration Camp	*The Hiding Place* (1975); *I Was Overtaken by Night—Zastihla me noc* (1986); *Olga* (2004)
Sachsenhausen Concentration Camp	*The Counterfeiters—Die Fälscher* (2007)
Sobibor Death Camp	*Escape from Sobibor* (TV 1987); *Sobibor* (2018)
Theresienstadt Concentration Camp	*Distant Journey—Daleká cesta* (1950); *The Last Butterfly—Poslední motýl* (1991)
Treblinka Death Camp	*For Those I Loved—Au nom de tous les miens* (1983); *Pursuit* (TV 1989)
Westerbork Concentration Camp	*Look to the Sky—Jona che visse nella balena* (1993); *Süskind* (2012)

But, as Elie Wiesel cautioned in 1989, "Auschwitz is something else, always something else. It is a universe outside the universe, a creation that exists parallel to creation."[29] Although Wiesel was making a general plea to fence off Auschwitz/Birkenau from the pablum of modern art and culture—setting aside Auschwitz as untouchable on a sacrosanct plane—Wiesel was also specifically beseeching Hollywood to desist from future Auschwitz productions. Harsh pushback also came from the director of the Holocaust documentary *Shoah* (1985), Claude Lanzmann.[30] Their indictments of Holocaust films ranged from accusations of exploitation to sympathetic portrayals of perpetrators. Before these Holocaust icons lashed out, there was an underlying belief—especially in the Jewish community—that any representation of the Holocaust was a victory.[31] As explained by the German historian Martin Broszat (1926–1989) of *Holocaust*, "The broad impact of this melodramatic film series taught not only conservative historians, but above all the film producers and publicists, a lesson. All of them had dared thus far, if at all, to confront the especially grave issue of the fate of the Jews during the Hitler era with extreme caution and cold practicality. Now, what has happened has happened."[32]

Paradoxically, inauthentic Holocaust films, with their overtly fictional plots and fictionalized characters, also became fuel for armchair Holocaust deniers. So, Holocaust film producers wanting to set their stories in Auschwitz/Birkenau had to navigate many icebergs, including saintly Holocaust icons, antisemites, overt violence, ever-changing standards and the truth. But, of course, even without Wiesel's admonishments, filmmakers comprehended the innate challenges of recreating Auschwitz/Birkenau. Yet, the filmmaking community certainly had neither financial nor moral reasons to heed such a request. On the contrary, Hollywood simply perceived Auschwitz as another challenge to conquer.

Although many early Communist-made films not only depicted Auschwitz/Birkenau, but were shot in the camps, it was not until the late 1970s that any Western film even attempted to portray the Germans' most potent killing machine. But, without access to the locations, among other challenges, depicting Auschwitz was expensive and needed substantial expertise. Together, these factors made Auschwitz representations prohibitive and compromised. This might explain why the otherwise notoriously self-assured Jerry Lewis was so unnerved in 1972 by his Auschwitz-based *The Day the Clown Cried* that he refused to release the film, hiding it from the public, never to be seen in his lifetime, "arguably the most notorious 'lost' film in movie history—a kind of Holy Grail for connoisseurs of presumed bad taste."[33] Six years later—because the producers of the *Holocaust* miniseries were barred from filming in Poland, Czechoslovakia and Hungary—they shot instead mostly in Austria, using the Mauthausen Concentration Camp and its small gas chamber as substitute locations for Auschwitz/Birkenau.[34] Regardless of access, starting in the late 1970s Auschwitz became the subject of many Western films, whether set there exclusively or part of a backstory. In fact, the Austrian film *Gebürtig* (2002) actually partially depicts, to great effect, a film being shot at Birkenau. (See Table 28.)

TABLE 28: WESTERN-PRODUCED AUSCHWITZ/BIRKENAU HOLOCAUST FILMS (NON-EXHAUSTIVE)

Recommended in **Bold** (5 of 52). "One of the Best" in **Bold and Underlined** (3 of 15). Unavailable films in ~~Strikeout~~ (1).

~~The Day the Clown Cried (1972)~~
Death Is My Trade—Aus einem deutschen Leben (1977)
Holocaust (Miniseries 1978)
Playing for Time (TV 1980)
Sophie's Choice (1982)
War and Remembrance (Miniseries 1988)
Triumph of the Spirit (1989)
Schindler's List (1993)
The Truce—La tregua (1997)
Life Is Beautiful (1997)
X-Men (2000)
Anne Frank: The Whole Story (TV 2001)
Grey Zone (2001)
Amen. (2002)
Out of the Ashes (TV 2003)
Fateless—Sorstalanság (2005)
The Last Train—Der Letzte Zug (2006)
The Boy in the Striped Pyjamas (2008)
God on Trial (TV 2008)
Auschwitz (2011)

Colette (2013)	
***Son of Saul* (2015)**	

By today's standards, many of these films seem cheap, melodramatic and ahistorical, despite their more authentic filming locations and sets. Critically, most Auschwitz films relied on inauthentic plots and scenes that simply do not pass the sniff test. And, in a Holocaust film, it only takes a dash of drama to become kitsch. For example, *Playing for Time* (TV 1980)—written by fabled playwright Arthur Miller (1915–2005) and starring Vanessa Redgrave, just a few years after her controversial "Zionist hoodlums" speech when accepting the Best Supporting Actress Oscar for the Tangential Holocaust film *Julia* (1977)—was set in Auschwitz using nonspecific film sets, which could have been set in any generic prison camp worldwide. Many other Auschwitz films are so contrived and formulaic that they step over the line into tastelessness.

Ostensibly, though, the easiest route to instant credibility was filming at Auschwitz/Birkenau, itself. According to Yad Vashem's Online Database, the obscure film *War and Love* (1985) "…was to be made at Auschwitz, an event generating media attention."[35] It is fascinating how many subsequent filmmakers also claimed to have been the first to film at Auschwitz. *Rolling Stone Magazine*'s Peter Travers wrote of *Triumph of the Spirit* (1989), "This earnest but woefully misguided film (*the first major feature to be shot on location at Auschwitz*) [emphasis added]…."[36] Auschwitz/Birkenau, however, had been filmed by many narrative films since just after the War, including those listed in Table 29, several of which have no Jewish content:

TABLE 29: NARRATIVE FILMS SHOT (EVEN PARTIALLY) AT AUSCHWITZ/BIRKENAU

Film	*Genre*
The Last Stage—The Last Stop—Ostatni etap (1948)	Tangential
Passenger—Pasazerka (TV 1963)	Tangential
The End of Our World—Koniec naszego swiata (1964)	Tangential
A Trip to the Unknown—Wycieczka w nieznane (1968)	Non-Holocaust
Remember your name—Pomni imya svoye (1974)	Victim
The Fires Are Still Alive—Ognie sa jeszcze zywe (1976)	Victim
Death Is My Trade—Aus einem deutschen Leben (1977)	Gentile (antisemitic)
Wergili (TV 1977)	Non-Holocaust
The Green Bird—Der grüne Vogel (1980)	Non-Holocaust
Invitation—Zaproszenie (1986)	Tangential
War and Remembrance (Miniseries 1988)	Victim
Kornblumenblau (1989)	Tangential
Triumph of the Spirit (1989)	Victim
Abrahams Gold (1990)	Perpetrator
Walerjan Wrobel's Homesickness (1991)	Non-Holocaust
Schindler's List (1993)	Gentile (Righteous)
Gebürtig (2002)	Survivor
The Birch-Tree Meadow (2003)	Perpetrator
The Aryan Couple (2004)	Victim
In the End Come Tourists—Am Ende kommen Touristen (2007)	Tangential
The Dead and the Living (2012)	Non-Holocaust
Angels in White (2012)	Non-Holocaust
Labyrinth of Lies (2014)	Gentile (antisemitic)

Film	Genre
Pilecki (2015)	Non-Holocaust
Denial (2016)	Tangential

Location alone, however, is not enough to make a film great; simply having a true story shot in its actual location does not guarantee anything, artistically or otherwise. In 1990, Roger Ebert astutely made this point:

> *Triumph of the Spirit* goes to great lengths to establish a basis in fact. It is inspired by a true story, we are told, the story of a Greek Jew who survived the Holocaust because he was an expert boxer. *And it is the first fiction film to be shot on location in the death camp of Auschwitz* [emphasis added]. Every detail is accurate, down to the wooden shoes worn by the prisoners and the crusts of bread thrown onto their dinner plates. I am impressed by the attention to detail demonstrated by the director, Robert M. Young, but I do not consider it a certificate of authenticity.[37]

Dan Curtis' 12-part *War and Remembrance* (Miniseries 1988), which was aired on ABC and was released a year before *Triumph of the Spirit*, was also touted as the first film shot at Auschwitz.[38] Another caveat with *War and Remembrance* foreshadowed a current controversy: Curtis was only allowed to film at Auschwitz if his script did not contain "one word about Polish anti–Semitism."[39] More importantly and more than any other production, Dan Curtis' ambitious *War and Remembrance* tested the limits of depicting Auschwitz. *War and Remembrance* uses several cumulative hours depicting Birkenau, from the conception of gas chambers through their being built and ultimately being used. Director Dan Curtis (né Daniel Mayer Cherkoss) built an exact model of the crematorium from the original plans, just fifty yards from the actual Crematorium IV. Curtis' Holocaust scenes often depicted Jews being bludgeoned, which is exactly how viewers felt after watching the miniseries. "It was very strong," said Steven Spielberg in 2004 about the excessive violence of *War and Remembrance*, continuing, "I've never, before or since, seen anything like it."[40]

War and Remembrance's obsessive Holocaust violence shattered all reasonable boundaries. Still, the film was a spectacle that answered the basic underlying question about Holocaust film production: where is the line that should not be crossed? Overall, the above-listed Auschwitz films and television dramas bank on shock value. For the most part, too, they poorly dissect the Birkenau beast, largely using it as a prop, not a historic setting. These films are autopsies done without scalpels, instead relying on either the patient's chart or a hammer.

Gone were the days when filmmakers could shoot in some nondescript room, call it "Auschwitz" and we give them an unconditional "attaboy." By the end of the twentieth century, there was no excuse for incorrectly depicting the Holocaust, especially Auschwitz/Birkenau, easily the most documented plots of ground in history. With that context, the progression of Holocaust representation from decade to decade comes into focus, from *The Search* (1948), to *The Pawnbroker* (1964), to *Holocaust* (Miniseries 1978), to *Sophie's Choice* (1982), to *War and Remembrance* (Miniseries 1988), to *Schindler's List* (1993). From these films, like skipping a stone on a glassy pond, one marvels at the steady advancement in the representation of the German apparatus. And, finally, the skimming stone arrives at *The Grey Zone* (2001).

6

The Greatest Narrative
Holocaust Film Ever Made

Note: Viewing The Grey Zone *(2001) before continuing is **highly encouraged**.*

Tim Blake Nelson's *The Grey Zone* (2001) is the greatest Holocaust film ever made. Nonetheless, *The Grey Zone,* based on Nelson's own off-Broadway play, has gone almost completely unnoticed, only recognized for one minor honor: the National Board of Review, USA's 2002 "Freedom of Expression Award." (*The Grey Zone* was also nominated for, but lost, the San Sebastián International Film Festival's 2001 "Golden Seashell Award" and the Political Film Society USA's 2003 "PFS Award.") According to Box Office Mojo, *The Grey Zone*'s total lifetime gross was $517,872,[1] despite outstanding performances from a highly respected cast that included Harvey Keitel (who was also one of the film's executive producers), David Arquette, Steve Buscemi, Michael Stuhlbarg, David Chandler, Allan Corduner, Daniel Benzali, Mira Sorvino (who lost 20 pounds for the part), Natasha Lyonne and Lisa Benavides-Nelson.

The Grey Zone's director, writer, producer, and co-editor, Tim Blake Nelson, is not known for directing at all, Holocaust films or otherwise. Nelson—from the tiny Jewish community of Tulsa, Oklahoma (2,300 Jews in 2003[2]) and whose grandparents narrowly escaped certain death in Germany—is best known as an actor, co-starring with George Clooney and John Turturro in the Coen brothers' *O Brother, Where Art Thou?* (2000), and more recently, the title character in the Coen brothers' *The Ballad of Buster Scruggs* (2018) and as "Looking Glass" in *Watchmen* (TV 2019). Nelson's 65+ feature film credits, starting in 1992, also include Steven Spielberg's *Minority Report* (2002) and goofball films like *Meet the Fockers* (2004) and *Scooby-Doo 2: Monsters Unleashed* (2004). Before *The Grey Zone*, Nelson had only directed two feature films, neither of which were highly regarded or had anything to do with the Holocaust or Judaism: the critically acclaimed *Eye of God* (1997)* and *O* (2001),† an adaptation of *Othello.*

A parallel to Nelson's accomplishment with *The Grey Zone* was a feat in the 1968 Olympics in Mexico City. Bob Beaman, an American long jumper, leaped so far that officials did not have a tape long enough to measure his jump. The previous world record had been 27½ feet; Bob Beaman jumped almost two feet further (29 ft. 2½ in.). What Tim

---

* Film Independent Spirit Awards 1998, Nominee, Someone to Watch Award; Seattle International Film Festival 1997, Winner, American Independent Award; Sundance Film Festival 1997, Nominee, Grand Jury Prize, Dramatic; Tokyo International Film Festival 1997, Winner, Bronze Award

† Seattle International Film Festival 2001, Winner, Golden Space Needle Award, Best Director; Tokyo International Film Festival 2001, Nominee, Tokyo Grand Prix

Blake Nelson did with *The Grey Zone* is the equivalent to Beaman's jump—blasting past *Sophie's Choice* (1982)—except no one even knew that Nelson was on the team.

By the time *The Grey Zone* was released in 2001, the mistakes and successes of the previous 55 years and 200 Holocaust feature films had somehow become clear, at least to Tim Blake Nelson. By then, of course, more than 30 years after the demise of the Motion Picture Production Code, tolerance for graphic film had increased dramatically.

Yes, *The Grey Zone* is violent, cutting to the bone, intensely graphic at times. But the violence has purpose, avoiding the random hyperbolic ferocity that had been requisite in many previous Auschwitz films. Only occasionally is *The Grey Zone*'s violence personal. Instead, usually the violence is unemotional for both the victims and perpetrators, as if both parties to the violence are immune from feelings after having seen everything a thousand times in Birkenau. For example, the film opens with a botched suicide, turned murder, which is ultimately explained as a mercy killing. Later, a particularly sadistic guard is overwhelmed and slid alive into an oven by the Jews. And there is torture. *The Grey Zone*'s depiction of violence does not pander. As opposed to the much more gratuitously violent *Schindler's List*, most of the violence in *The Grey Zone* is mundane, both to the viewers and to the numbed characters, furthering our understanding of the dehumanization inherent in the German plan. As Owen Gleiberman of *Entertainment Weekly* wrote, "*The Grey Zone* is a Holocaust drama immersed in the mechanics of mass murder, yet nothing in the film feels exploitative or unnecessarily graphic." Gleiberman added, "...no dramatic feature has ever come quite this close to the matter-of-fact ugliness of the Nazi crimes."[3]

At its core, *The Grey Zone* recounts two historical occurrences at Birkenau: a teenage girl surviving a gas chamber and the Birkenau rebellion in October 1944 that resulted in the permanent destruction of two of Birkenau's four main gas chamber/crematorium complexes. Although the disposition of the surviving girl is dealt with allegorically, *The Grey Zone* is a true story with few fictional characters. And that is the primary lesson about making modern Holocaust Victim films: the stories must be authentic, both in content and depiction. "*The Grey Zone*," wrote John Patterson of the *LA Weekly*, "is honest enough to deny the possibility of hope in Auschwitz. Here everybody dies. Everything comes to zero—a legitimate, if depressing, means of uncovering the nihilism of the Nazi project."[4]

The Grey Zone was based on the memoirs of Jewish pathologist Dr. Miklós Nyiszli (1901–1956), *Auschwitz: A Doctor's Eyewitness Account*,[5] who did much of Josef Mengele's dirty work at Birkenau. Further, while five characters in the film are based on historical figures (Miklos Nyiszli, Erich Muhsfeldt, Josef Mengele, Roza Robota and the young girl), Nelson also based four other characters (Hoffman, Rosenthal, Schlermer and Abramowics) on diaries written by Sonderkommando, the Jews who worked in the crematoria and gas chambers. The Sonderkommandos' writings were discovered long after the War.[6] Nelson also generously credits Dr. Miklós Nyiszli as a co-writer of *The Grey Zone*.

Nelson took no chances with physical authenticity, building two model crematoria near Sofia, Bulgaria, at 80 percent scale using the Germans' original architectural plans kept in the London War Museum.[7] Starting with this level of physical detail, Nelson had enough confidence to faithfully represent in *The Grey Zone* each step of the killing process: Jews packed into boxcars in transit, then arriving at the camp, before being paraded into the undressing room, coerced into the gas chamber, the door closing, the poison dropped in from the roof by Germans in gas masks, then waiting for the 2,000 shrieks to die down before switching on a fan needed for post-death chamber ventilation, Jewish slaves entering with long bibs, loading the corpses onto an elevator, the area where victims were harvested of hair and gold dental-work before burning, smoke billowing, the flames, the pyres needed for excess cremation, coal arriving, ash leaving, chambers cleaned and painted. Rinse and repeat, literally. *The Grey Zone* exhibits the entire process, including the sorting of possessions despoiled from the arriving Jews. Only one moment of the process is left to the imagination: the gassing in the chamber, itself, which must be imagined through the screams and pounding on the door. It is not that no other narrative film revealed everything; it is that no other film gets it all right, including tempo and demeanor.

Every story needs character arc, often with a character who starts repenting after hitting rock bottom. In *The Grey Zone*, this nadir occurs when David Arquette's character "Hoffman" beats a man in the undressing room to a bloody pulp—to death—for a wristwatch, only moments before the dead man would have otherwise been killed in the gas chamber. Just after, Hoffman discovers a girl, who had witnessed the beating, barely alive under a pile of dead bodies in the gas chamber. Hoffman spends the rest of the film desperately trying to save her—and to redeem himself—with full knowledge that he will also be dead within a week. Near the end of the film, when Hoffman is alone with the girl, not knowing if she has been so damaged that she can even understand him, Hoffman confesses everything:

I used to think so much of myself, what I'd make of my life. We can't know what we're capable of, any of us. How can you know what you'd do to stay alive, until you're really asked? I know this now. For most of us, the answer is: anything. It's so easy to forget who we were before … who we'll never be again. There was this old man, he pushed the carts, and on our first day, when we had to burn our own convoy, his wife was brought up on the elevator. Then his daughter, and then both his grandchildren. I knew him. We were neighbors. And in 20 minutes, his whole family, and all its future was gone from this earth. Two weeks later he took pills and was revived. We smothered him with his own pillow, and now I know why. You can kill yourself. That's the only choice. I want them to save you. I want them to save you more than I want anything. I pray to God we save you.

The language choice, here, benefits from generations of failed attempts by many other Holocaust filmmakers to deal with non-native dialogue. In Hoffman's above soliloquy, although David Arquette is portraying a Hungarian, he uses unaccented, common American English, as do the rest of *The Grey Zone*'s Jewish characters, as opposed to the contrived dialects in *Schindler's List* which led to an accent salad tossed with inconsistencies and unidentifiable speech origins. As Philip Gourevitch wrote in *Commentary Magazine* about *Schindler's List*, "…while the Aryans' accents are light, elegant, unidentifiable, the Jews sound fresh off the boat."[8] In *The Grey Zone*, however, Nelson's Jews spoke using their normal American dialect, while the oppressors spoke English with consistent German accents. Although this annoyed some reviewers,[9] Nelson's method seems to be the most effective route, allowing actors to let the script do the work, while also eliminating the ongoing distraction caused by subtitles for the intended English-speaking audience. "Though they're speaking English in the film," Nelson said, "they're meant to be speaking Hungarian, their native tongue. They wouldn't have the silly Jewish accents which never cease to mystify me in Holocaust films."[10] But this method is only effective when used by extraordinary performers who are convincing with every gesture and phoneme, as in *The Grey Zone*.

The dialogue, itself, was stylized and layered. Reviewers noted similarities between

David Mamet's approach and *The Grey Zone*'s dialogue,[11] which is everything that David Mamet intended in *House of Games* (1987) and *Glengarry Glen Ross* (1992), but without Mamet's characters' cartoonishness there. Like Mamet's scripts for *Vanya on 42nd Street* (1994) and *Wag the Dog* (1997), much of *The Grey Zone*'s dialogue speaks on several levels; the characters hear what they want to hear, while we hear everything. It is the kind of dialogue economy that most writers struggle their entire careers to see on screen for even a minute. For example, in the following exchange, Oberscharführer Muhsfeldt (Harvey Keitel) is telling one of the Sonderkommando, Max Rosenthal (David Chandler) that this Sonderkommando group's four-month stint was ending, with both men knowing that the replacements would soon be burning the current group in the same ovens manned by the current Sonderkommando:

> ROSENTHAL: *Our group is happy to remain here.*
> MUHSFELDT: *Happy?*
> ROSENTHAL: *Why kill us now? We're the best kommando you've had.*
> MUHSFELDT: *Did I say kill?*
> ROSENTHAL: *We both know what we're saying.*
> MUHSFELDT: *So, I'm a liar.*
> ROSENTHAL: *You are what you are.*

The dialogue also works because Nelson's ensemble cast does not overreach. Many Jewish characters in the film look bad, either physically or temperamentally. Consider the following outburst by Hesch Abramowics (Steve Buscemi), as he admits his plan to escape during the pending revolt after the gas chamber/crematorium complex is destroyed: "But when we're through with the machinery, I can't run? I have to stay here and be shot or burned alive because that's what you want to do? Because you can't live with it, I can't? Fuck you, Max. It's my fucking life. I hope I live 'til I'm 90." To put a cap on that speech, within moments in the same room, he is casually shot dead by Oberscharführer Muhsfeldt for being in an unauthorized place.

While many filmmakers' insecurities about the subject matter are often revealed through an avalanche of exposition, *The Grey Zone*'s critical facts are meted out only as needed. There is no question that a revolt has been in the works for a while, but the particulars are not rushed. And Nelson never leans on the characters' backstories to make them seem compelling; even the characters' names are mostly irrelevant. In fact, even Josef Mengele, the most infamous personage in the film, appears in a brief early scene, and is unnamed and unglorified. Moreover, Mengele is barely in frame at the beginning of the scene. What would have been a big-wow-moment for most filmmakers—a depiction of the notorious "Angel of Death"—is not allowed to dominate the scene, let alone the film.

The impassive characters bring an understanding of normalcy inside Germany's ultimate death factory. Everyone does their jobs as if in Birkenau, not in a hyperbolic movie. The work has become routine, as dictated by reality. Everyone knows the score and nothing is overblown. For instance, throughout *The Grey Zone*, Harvey Keitel's menacing portrayal of Oberscharführer Erich Muhsfeldt is dispassionately real, as opposed to David Thewlis' sickeningly sympathetic portrayal of the Auschwitz Commandant in *The Boy in the Striped Pyjamas*. In *The Grey Zone*, Keitel played a bluntly nasty Nazi commander, while in *Pyjamas* Thewlis played a heartwarming father, who also just happened to be a top Nazi, despite himself. Because Keitel's performance is so true, most viewers cannot even recognize that Oberscharführer Muhsfeldt is played by the same actor who was "The Wolf" in *Pulp Fiction* (1994). At one point, Oberscharführer Muhsfeldt remarks matter-of-factly about the Jews in a "did he just say that!?" moment:

> I've seen them strike the ones that are slow getting in. They steal, lie to each other. I never fully despised the Jews until I experienced how easily they could be persuaded to do the work here, to do it so well. And to their own people. They'll be dead by week's end, every soul, and we'll replace them with others, no different. Do you know how easy that'll be?

For Harvey Keitel, who had agency as a producer and whose Jewish parents emigrated from Romania and Poland, to have imparted such words and for Tim Blake Nelson to have written these words, alone, elevates their courage as Jewish filmmakers to a rare and lofty space.

Just as *The Grey Zone*'s dialogue does not coddle, the film is also not swaddled in a film score, another lesson learned after decades of sappy Holocaust films. Indeed, one of the most jarring differences between *Schindler's List* and *The Grey Zone* is Steven Spielberg's incessant reliance on John Williams' Oscar-winning score and Itzhak Perlman's violin. Williams' melodic efficacy, with his 51 Oscar nominations, is undeniable; a John Williams score could make infanticide compelling. Yet a syrupy soundtrack did not accompany the Holocaust, and Nelson would have none of it in *The Grey Zone*, rejecting that heretofore ubiquitous, inorganic crutch which props up so many Holocaust films. "There's no soundtrack to dramatize or sentimentalize,"[12] said Liz Smith in *The New York Post* of *The Grey Zone*. It has no score outside of the credits: 25 seconds of a lone clarinet over the opening film title and location; and, at the end, after cards explaining the disposition of the surviving characters, over the final credits is subdued original music written and performed by Jeff Danna. Instead of music, throughout *The Grey Zone* is the ambient churning of Birkenau. Indeed, it is impossible to watch the film and not immediately notice the lack of a score and the correctness of that decision.

Similarly, with a cynicism that should be celebrated, Nelson also carefully picks only two spots for diegetic music, each time the music commencing with a close-up of its source. First, twenty minutes into *The Grey Zone* there is an overhead close-up of a mandolin played by a prisoner. Pulling back, an inmate orchestra is playing Johann Strauss' jolly 1880 "Roses from the South, Opus 388." Nelson pulls back further, revealing that the prisoner orchestra is positioned directly over the entrance to a crematorium complex, with a trainload of Jews slowly walking under the orchestra and into the building. The music continues with shots of the musicians in striped clothing, sprinklers watering the lush Birkenau lawn, guards and Sonderkommando overseeing the orderly procession. The song and scene finish almost two minutes later, with a much higher overhead shot of the long line of Hungarian Jews patiently moving toward their final destination. Meanwhile, the foreground is consumed by the tall crematorium chimney, obstinately billowing, flames shooting from the center. As the next scene starts, the same orchestra can be heard in the background, barely taking a breath before replaying "Opus 388." "I'm still plagued," wrote Rex Reed, "by one Spielbergian shot of long lines of doomed arrivals in civilian clothes marching into a hole in the ground while an orchestra of inmates plays Strauss waltzes."[13]

The only other music in *The Grey Zone* starts ten minutes before the final credits, three minutes into the rebellion: Johannes Brahms' mournful 1869 "Alto Rhapsody, Op. 53," music set over the words of Johann Wolfgang von Goethe's "Harzreise im Winter." In the foreground is a phonograph playing the tinny "Alto Rhapsody" inside Dr. Nyiszli's office. As the shot pans, the simmering music begins to drown out machine-gun fire in the background. With the full audio spectrum of "Alto Rhapsody" restored, the doctor (Allan Corduner) is found cowering under an examination table. The music continues through the end of the rebellion, culminating with the Sonderkommando blowing themselves up along with the crematorium complex they had been force-feeding for four months. The German lyrics being sung include, "First scorned, now a scorner, he secretly feeds on his own merit, in unsatisfying egotism."

Of note, too, the cinematography does not rely on fancy digital effects to suck in viewers. True, Nelson's camera work gets up in people's business when needed, but he does not force the issue. He found the balance between incessant claustrophobic mania and the patient grand shots in *Schindler's List*. As Steven Alan Carr in the journal *Film Criticism* put it, "*The Grey Zone* leaves the visual universe of the Holocaust film intact, its unobtrusive cinematography a handmaiden to the morally charged quest of goal-oriented protagonists in search of personal redemption."[14]

For example, Nelson goes handheld while traversing a long, food-laden table in the Sonderkommando barracks, showing Sonderkommando devouring delicacies that had been gleaned from that day's transport. Even Holocaust aficionados are taken aback by the opulence of the food and drink; more to the point, we are all taken aback when visualizing that material comforts were the currency of mortal cooperation, a concept that, for most of us, is merely a notion until seeing *The Grey Zone*.

In the scene following that meal, a nondescript Sonderkommando walks alone out of a building, toward the camera, which is motionless. The man then turns to the right and the tracking shot begins, following him along a building almost step for step until he enters the same building through a different door. The dolly stops just past the door. Two dozen men are then marched in the opposite direction along the same wall. The dolly tracks them back to position one and is locked down. The men, who are kneeling, are shot with a pistol in the back of the head, one at a time. After two shots, one of the inmates makes a dash for the fence. The camera pans, following the man, closing in ever so slightly, as he is gunned down from behind. But the camera continues to pan past the fallen man to an overflow pyre, from which smoke had been billowing throughout the entire scene.

The theme of *The Grey Zone* is, not surprisingly, grey. Yes, it is shot in color, but grey permeates the palette. Some other colors peek through, but grey is the color of faces and hair and clothing and Birkenau. As with *Big Fish* (2003), *Birdman* (2014) and *The Shape of Water* (2017), *The Grey Zone*'s theme runs deep, far beyond its title and objects. *The Grey Zone*'s Jewish characters live on the precipice between right and wrong, selfishness and empathy, black and white.

The theme is complete when considering the source of the phrase "grey zone" in Holocaust literature. In 1986, just before his death, Auschwitz survivor Primo Levi penned his final work, *The Drowned and the Saved*. In a chapter entitled "Zona Grigia" (the grey area or zone), Levi described Jews who did the Germans' dirty work; the Germans regularly conscripted Jews to make ghetto death lists, police the ghetto, and, most notoriously, be the gears in the death machine. Levy wrote:

The inside of the Lager [camp] was an intricate and stratified microcosm; the "grey zone" … that of the prisoners who in some measure, perhaps with good intentions, collaborated with the authority, was not negligible.… There is not a prisoner who does not remember this and who does not remember his amazement at the time: the first threat, the first insult, the first blow came not from the SS, but from other prisoners, from "colleagues," from these mysterious personages who nevertheless wore the same striped tunic that they, the new arrivals, had just put on.[15]

Nelson acknowledged, "I had to find a way to match Primo Levi's courage in finding nuance and shading in an event where neither is supposed to exist."[16] After Primo Levi's death, Elie Wiesel reportedly said, "Primo Levi died at Auschwitz forty years later."[17] In fact, a part of Primo Levi lives on through Nelson's titular tribute, as well as in two well-made biographical Holocaust films about Primo Levi, *Primo* (TV 2005) and *The Truce—La tregua* (1997), coincidentally starring Nelson's old running-mate John Turturro as Primo Levi.

The Grey Zone theme was seemingly complete after the revolt when all the Jewish characters were killed, except Dr. Nyiszli, including the heretofore surviving girl, who is shot in the back by Muhsfeldt while she ran toward a gate. Indeed, the film could have ended there and still been greater than any other Holocaust film. But Nelson's checkmate, which elicits gasps at each showing, is the dead girl's narration of her physical destruction and disintegration in the final moments, explaining how she, in fact, becomes part of the grey zone (voiced by Portia Reiners):

> After the revolt, half the ovens remain, and we are carried to them together. I catch fire quickly. The first part of me rises in dense smoke that mingles with the smoke of others. Then there are the bones which settle in ash and these are swept up to be carried to the river. And last, bits of our dust simply float there, in air, around the working of the new group. These bits of dust are grey. We settle on their shoes and on their faces and in their lungs. And they become so used to us, that soon they don't cough, and they don't brush us away. At this point, they're just moving, breathing and moving. Like anyone else, still alive in that place. And this is how the work continues.

"Paradoxically," wrote Holocaust film professor Lawrence Baron of the film's closing, "the most moving scene in *The Grey Zone* jettisons the film's graphic realism in favor of a more stylized look and imaginary monologue."[18] Indeed, this girl, this lone known survivor of a gas chamber, had not spoken a word in the film. Only once did the girl even acknowledge that she was capable of comprehension, when she reluctantly nodded to Hoffman during his above-noted confession. The dead girl calmly closes the film, narrating over slow-motion shots of bodies at night moved in carts to another crematorium, fire shooting out from the ovens and from another towering chimney. The ending narration was as necessary and effective as was Michael Corleone being asked by Kay if he had ordered Carlo's murder. The heavenly voice at the end of *The Grey Zone* adds another two feet to Tim Blake Nelson's leap.

Many other films have depicted Jews being forced by the Germans to assist in the Final Solution. Other films have portrayed Sonderkommando, kapos, Jewish police and those in Jewish councils who made lists of prospective deportees. Despite the labor assignment as Sonderkommando of these Jews, we strain to deify them in the face of their seeming cooperation with the Germans; as with many other historical tragedies, holy status is reflexively projected upon Holocaust victims and martyrs.

But what made *The Grey Zone* unique—not rare, but unique—among all other Holocaust films was its unvarnished portrayal of such compromised Jews. Undeniably, most of *The Grey Zone*'s Jewish characters start and remain unlikeable. Until *The Grey Zone*, no other Holocaust film dared allow their victims any meaningful foibles. Even squabbles between Jews of different nationalities are exposed. As Nelson explained, "Conditions in the camps brought out shameful qualities in men, the most benign of which were mistrust, greed, xenophobia, and self-hatred."[19] More than the constant noise of Birkenau devouring its victims throughout *The Grey Zone*, the overriding undercurrent is our dismay that any filmmaker could have showered such imperfections on those from whom we presume purity and righteousness. One feels almost heretical for thinking that Holocaust victims can be anything less than Anne-Frank-angelic.

Yet, the Jewish characters in *The Grey Zone* start imperfect and end imperfect, heroically human. "*The Grey Zone* is the story of people trying desperately to give their lives meaning in a place designed to kill," Nelson said. "And while there are people who act heroically at given points, this is not a film about heroes."[20] Contrast this with the recommended film *Defiance*, for example, where one leaves the theater believing that the Bielski brothers (Daniel Craig and Liev Schreiber) are superhuman, physically and morally. As Sean Axmaker of the *Seattle Post-Intelligencer* summarized about *The Grey Zone*, "Less about heroism than desperation, moral negotiation, sacrifice and remaining human in an inhuman existence, *The Grey Zone* argues that it's also a matter of why and seeks to find meaning in an ordeal that is still, ultimately, unfathomable."[21]

Through this unembellished window into Birkenau, *The Grey Zone* exposes conflicted Jews. Almost without exception, the main characters, themselves, are deeply disturbed by their own actions. All of them—Sonderkommando, women smuggling gunpowder and the Jewish doctor—are raging with conflicts about their respective roles in the death machine. There is nothing subtle about their personal struggles or shame, which seeps out in their actions and their words. The women are pained by endangering the other inmates with the smuggling of gunpowder for the uprising; the doctor is nauseated to be Josef Mengele's workhorse; and the Sonderkommando speak openly of their Faustian bargain, gaining a few months on bedsheets and full stomachs before they, too, go up the chimney. In the following exchange between Sonderkommandos Max Rosenthal (David Chandler) and Hesch Abramowics (Steve Buscemi), this inner rage becomes explicit as the group is considering what to do with the just-found girl.

> ROSENTHAL: *We don't kill people.*
> ABRAMOWICS: *We don't? We put them in the rooms, walk them in and strip them, look them in the face and say it's safe. What the hell is that?*
> ROSENTHAL: *It's not...*
> ABRAMOWICS: *It's not what?*
> ROSENTHAL: *It's not pulling the trigger.*
> ABRAMOWICS: *It's locking them in. You leave the room. Bring them in and leave. Say it's safe. You'll see them when it's over. Who put her inside? Now you think she made it through. God knows how. You're going to be a hero?*
> ROSENTHAL: *Not a hero.*
> ABRAMOWICS: *Not a hero, not a killer. What are you, Max?*

While it is true that *Sophie's Choice* and *The Pianist* and *Defiance* all depict a significant spectrum of torment, the protagonists in those films wrestle with decisions that were immediate, questions of saving themselves, their families and friends. As harrowing as were the personal plights of these characters, their challenges are of a different magnitude than those faced in *The Grey Zone*. Sophie's decisions in *Sophie's Choice*—the fate of her children and Sophie's sexual enslavement—are quite different from the daily torture of stuffing ovens with humans or overseeing ghastly German medical experiments on children.

But, more to the point, as opposed to *The Grey Zone*, the implication in most other Holocaust films is that their protagonists started unfractured and only came upon their imperfections as a result of the Holocaust. It is implied that suicidal Sophie in *Sophie's Choice* became permanently undone only because of Auschwitz; that emotionally-dead Sol Nazerman (Rod Steiger) in *The Pawnbroker* was destroyed by the Holocaust; and that Jewish/Greek middleweight boxing champion Salamo Arouch (Willem Dafoe) became a killer in *Triumph of the Spirit* only by being forced to fight other Jews to the death in Auschwitz, which is ahistorical considering Arouch's pre–War boxing career when he had already knocked out all of his 51 competitors.[22]

Conversely, imperfections are only erased in art. Steven Spielberg has made a career of curing imperfect characters, including Oskar Schindler, who starts *Schindler's List* as an evil, moneygrubbing Nazi, but is rehabilitated by Spielberg's magic touch. But art is unreal, sometimes, perhaps, a derivative of truth, especially in cinema, but unreal nonetheless. And we tend to empathize with those who are cured. This is the difference between Mike Figgis' unflinching *Leaving Las Vegas* (1995) and Gary Marshall's clichéd *Pretty Woman* (1990); between Stuart Rosenberg's uncompromising *Cool Hand Luke* (1967) and Blake Edwards' happy-go-lucky *Breakfast at Tiffany's* (1961). Failure to overcome imperfections and mortal obstacles is not just the difference between comedy and tragedy, but between reality and fiction. Ben Sanderson (Nicolas Cage in *Leaving Las Vegas*) and Lucas "Luke" Jackson (Paul Newman in *Cool Hand Luke*) start imperfect and die imperfect, as do Nelson's Sonderkommando.

Some reviewers got stuck on *The Grey Zone*'s uncompromising insistence that Jews were compromised, surprised that any film would dare depict the dehumanization that the Germans had systematically foisted upon their victims. Sure, many other films have shown brutal Jewish kapos and meandering Sonderkommando, but no film before *The Grey Zone* had depicted these corrupted Jews as protagonists, fully exposed. Indeed, the difference between the violence in other Holocaust films and in *The Grey Zone* is the conspicuous Jewish participation in the process. And, considering how shocking, graphic and stark is *The Grey Zone*, it is not surprising that many reviewers who are not accustomed to this material were shaken by it. Famed critic Rex Reed's opening line in his review of *The Grey Zone* is an acknowledgment of both Reed's respect of the film and his discomfort: "Once in a blue moon, a film comes along that is so powerful and overwhelming that I wish people would see it for its remarkable ability to enlighten and transform, yet so brutal and depressing that I cannot bring myself to recommend it with a clear conscience."[23]

The great Roger Ebert thought so highly of *The Grey Zone* that he reviewed it twice, both times with his highest rating, once after its wide release in 2002[24] and again in 2009[25] as a selection in his "Great Movies" series. Ebert also put *The Grey Zone* on his list of one of the ten best films of 2002.[26] What's more, a few months after his review of *The Grey Zone*, when reviewing *The Pianist* in 2003, Ebert wrote:

> Some reviews of *The Pianist* have found it too detached, lacking urgency. Perhaps that impassive quality reflects what Polanski wants to say. Almost all of the Jews involved in the Holocaust were killed, so all of the survivor stories misrepresent the actual event by supplying an atypical ending. Often their buried message is that by courage and daring, these heroes saved themselves. Well, yes, some did, but most did not and—here is the crucial point—most could not. In this respect Tim Blake Nelson's *The Grey Zone* (2001) is tougher and more honest, by showing Jews trapped within a Nazi system that removed the possibility of moral choice.[27]

Robert Denerstein of the *Rocky Mountain News* wrote, "*The Grey Zone* isn't for everyone, but its riveting power constitutes a stunning (as in it leaves you shattered and shaken) achievement."[28] Indeed, *The Grey Zone* stirs strong emotions. Some educators have been so tied to *Schindler's List* through their curriculum that they dismiss *The Grey Zone* as too violent, although *Schindler's List* is replete with much more gratuitous violence and sex. As suggested in Michael Wilmington's *The Grey Zone* review in the *Chicago Tribune*, "There are better holocaust [*sic*] dramas than *Grey Zone*—*Schindler's List* for one, and due later this year, Roman Polanski's magnificent *The Pianist*. But few will disturb you like *The Grey Zone*—mostly because it won't try for tears."[29]

Others suggest that *The Grey Zone* is inaccurate, pointing to supposed errors in the above-described scene, Johann Strauss' waltz accompanying Hungarian Jews into the gas chamber. First, the real inmate orchestra at Birkenau did not perform upon the entrance to the crematorium complex. However, Rudolf Reder, one of only two Holocaust survivors of the Belzec Death Camp, reported that at Belzec "The band had six members, including a violinist, flutist and accordionist, and usually played in the space between the gas chambers and the massive burial pits."[30] In Birkenau, the orchestra was mostly stationed at the camp's main gate, playing the slave laborers in and out, far from earshot of the crematoria. Second, men and women who were entering the complex would have been separated. And third, these Holocaust victims were depicted with luggage and other personal items, all of which would have been confiscated upon arrival. While each of these observations are correct vis-à-vis Birkenau, Nelson only used 100 minutes to tell the entire story of *The Grey Zone*. To do so required the consolidation of some historical facts, none of which changed or degraded the story or denigrated the Holocaust.

Analogously, Damien Chazelle's dazzling, Oscar-winning *Whiplash* (2014) is the story of a sadistic instructor at a music conservatory. Those who have actually attended music conservatories dislike *Whiplash* because it does not represent their understanding of a music conservatory. Yet *Whiplash* is rated on IMDb as the 44th greatest film of all-time. Similarly, when you are a Holocaust historian, there is no grey zone. But narrative films are not documentaries. And art is an interpretation of facts that are constrained and enhanced to advance a story within the limits of their art form. As opposed to Spielberg's shower fake-out scene and *The Devil's Arithmetic*'s climactic gas chamber debacle, the ahistorical changes made in *The Grey Zone* do not change history or manipulate critical facts. Instead, Nelson creates a referent set of actions to expose the cynical German treachery used to coerce bewildered Jews into the most efficient methods to eventuate the Jews' own murder.

As the cliché goes, imitation is the sincerest form of flattery. That being said, *Son of Saul*, winner of the 2016 Oscar for Best Foreign Language Film, used largely the same story as *The Grey Zone*, including the Sonderkommando and the gas-chamber survivor and the rebellion. *Son of Saul* director László Nemes did not bother to credit either Tim Blake Nelson or Miklós Nyiszli, despite *Son of Saul* being a transparent knockoff of *The Grey Zone*. Nemes was called out about the obvious plagiarism after winning the Cannes Film Festival's Grand Prix, as Karin Badt wrote in the *HuffPost*:

> In fact, when the film began, I had déjà-vu. I had seen some of these scenes already, in a relatively unknown film *The Grey Zone* (2001) by actor-director Tim Blake Nelson. Nelson's film also is about the Sonderkommando rebellion at Auschwitz, based upon the same archival text that Nemes used as source material: *Voices from Beneath the Ashes*. Nelson also filmed the camp from the Sonderkommandos' perspective. In his film as in Nemes,' noise is exceptionally present. In both films, we hear the Sonderkommandos whispering to each other as they walk jerkily about the rooms, close to the frame. In both films, the gas chamber "undressing" room is filmed with a muted color palate [*sic*], intense close-ups, and

loud sound, while men trudge by with cadavers slung over their shoulders. The two films are uncannily similar. I asked the director if he knew *The Grey Zone*, which relatively few people have seen, given its low distribution. "Yes," Nemes said at once, blushing. "But mine is an Anti-*Grey Zone*! Imagine, in *The Grey Zone*, the inmates spoke in English…."[31]

Notwithstanding these concerns and Nemes' unabashed lifting of large parts of *The Grey Zone*, *Son of Saul* is still an above-average Holocaust film and a great representation of Birkenau. However, had *The Grey Zone* never been made, this effusive chapter would still not have been about *Son of Saul*, because, even though it had the same floor routine as *The Grey Zone*, *Son of Saul* did not hit its marks or stick its landing.

In the end, if *The Grey Zone* is, in fact, the last Holocaust film to be shown because almost everything else is a steep disappointment, why is *The Grey Zone* so obscure? While *Schindler's List* has grossed $322 million,[32] *The Grey Zone* has grossed only half a million dollars,[33] which includes the three DVDs I bought. Roughly 10,000 people have rated *The Grey Zone* on IMDb,[34] as compared with 600,000 for *The Pianist*[35] and 36,000 for *Son of Saul*.[36] Objectively, accolades, such as awards, reviews and box office, should be irrelevant, but they are not.

While culture is largely market-driven, many non-artistic factors can also affect a film's success. It is difficult to jump on the bandwagon when you do not even know there is a parade, and *The Grey Zone*'s marketing was suspect. Certainly, the trailer for the film, which can be seen on *YouTube.com*, fails to capture any of the lightning that Nelson got into his bottle, making *The Grey Zone* seem and sound like any other Holocaust melodrama.[37] This point was made clear by Professor Lawrence Baron in his 2012 book *Gray Zones: Ambiguity and Compromise in the Holocaust and its Aftermath*:

> The poster tagline, "The story you haven't seen," was positioned beneath a close-up of the haunting face of the girl. The preview began with this frank voice-over: "We can't know what we're capable of, any of us. How can you know what you'd really do to stay alive, until you're asked? I know now that the answer for most of us is anything." Even the uprising is placed in this defiled perspective: "In order to survive, they did the unthinkable, but it gave them the chance to attempt the impossible." … On its jacket, the recognizable faces of actors Harvey Keitel, Mira Sorvino, David Arquette, and Steve Buscemi hover above the tagline: "While the world was fighting … a secret battle was about to erupt." The narrator on the trailer declares, "Their freedom was lost; their hope was shattered, until the sight of one girl inspired a people to rebel." By fabricating a causal relationship between these two events, the film's distributors obliterated the gray zone between historical authenticity and truth in advertising.[38]

Simply put, while the plot of *The Grey Zone* had to be reduced into a trailer, *The Grey Zone*'s magic is in its pace, which is obliterated in a frenzied two-minute strip-job. While this is true of all great films—given the painful subject material—the gap between the teaser and the real thing, here, was inexorably vast.

It took 23 years for Bob Beamon's long jump record to be broken. *The Grey Zone* is still unmatched, although it has been challenged by three other remarkable Holocaust Victim film releases: the highly decorated *The Pianist* (2002), *Fateless—Sorstalanság* (2005) and Academy Award-winning Best Foreign-Language film *The Counterfeiters— Die Fälscher* (2007). Though vastly different stories, all these films scrupulously portray imperfect Jewish protagonists, mostly in German camps. All four are violent and depict cruelty, but not for shock value. And all these films get to the heart of the Holocaust— Jewish pain—with art and frailty, never pretending that their characters are heroes or suffered uniquely, but rather depicting them as, fractured souls who found themselves on the losing side of genocide.

Perhaps another answer for *The Grey Zone*'s obscurity is found in the date of release: September 13, 2001, just two days after the destruction of the towers in New York City. Given *The Grey Zone*'s purposeful depiction of the deadliest square mile in human history, the timing of its release almost seems perfect. "By the time *The Grey Zone* fades to black," concludes Liz Smith, "people will be stunned into remembering how much evil existed before Sept. 11."[39]

7

Roman Polanski and
The Pianist (2002)

Roman Polanski's *The Pianist* (2002) is not the second-best Holocaust film after Tim Blake Nelson's *The Grey Zone* (2001), but *The Pianist* is certainly in the top five. More importantly, *The Pianist* provides an opportunity to assess ancillary issues that are not necessarily part of a film, but that are impossible to ignore. The core question regarding *The Pianist* is: can Holocaust films be considered independently of their filmmakers?

The Pianist tells the true story of Wladyslaw Szpilman (1911–2000), a famous piano virtuoso, who survived the Warsaw Ghetto. *The Pianist* is a personal look at the destruction and liquidation of Polish Jewry, without venturing into death camps. Szpilman's unlikely survival is reenacted, staged poetically by Polanski, documenting Warsaw's fate, as the Jews are ghettoized and then liquidated, and the city is destroyed by the Germans and the Soviets. Near the end of the War a German officer helps Szpilman, who is so numbed that he barely knows how to react. Their uncomfortable and unidealized interactions provide a great teaching opportunity concerning humanity, role reversal and viewer expectations, asking if human blood flowed through German veins, placing in doubt the expected binary conclusion.

More importantly, Szpilman's diffident relationship with the German officer is also a tacit rebuke to those Hollywood filmmakers who promoted sympathetic Germans and Nazis, directors who tried to make compelling films with irredeemably bad men who are, nonetheless, made redeemable as a cheap filmmaking device. Rather, while Polanski accurately portrays a nuanced world that may contain reprehensible people who occasionally show some compassion, Polanski is one of the few Holocaust filmmakers who did not take Hollywood's bait; Polanski was unwilling to venerate a token Nazi hero.

The Pianist's acting, production, writing and direction are in the top echelon of all film production—not just Holocaust—in rarefied air, along with *Sophie's Choice* (1982), *The Grey Zone* (2001), *Fateless—Sorstalanság* (2005) and *The Counterfeiters—Die Fälscher* (2007). *The Pianist* is breathtaking art, ultra-sensitive to the subject matter, an example of rendering a drop of good from an ocean of evil. That is the bottom line regarding *The Pianist*, itself. Its director is a different story.

The private lives of entertainers and artists affect our perception of their work. Who can watch *Lethal Weapon* (1987) while ignoring Mel Gibson's subsequent antisemitic rantings ("Fucking Jews … the Jews are responsible for all the wars in the world."[1])? Who can listen to Michael Jackson while dismissing the multiple and credible accusations of pedophilia against him?[2] Perhaps the same people who can comfortably watch O.J.

Simpson clown around in David Zucker's *The Naked Gun* (1988), just a few years before Simpson (allegedly) decapitated his ex-wife, Nicole Brown Simpson (1959–1994) and her friend, Ronald Goldman (1968–1994). Yet, for good reason, Simpson was removed entirely from *For Goodness Sake* (1993),* a video about ethics made by the same David Zucker and radio talk-show host Dennis Prager. The video's distributor "began preparing to take Simpson out of the film soon after his ex-wife Nicole and her friend Ronald Goldman were found slain and investigators' attention began concentrating on Simpson."[3] Yet, of course, no one would ever think to remove Simpson from Zucker's *The Naked Gun*, because the film is morally irrelevant.

For better or worse, Holocaust films require more scrutiny than, for example, gangster films, which celebrate bad people doing bad things for glory and money. Is it a dilemma that convicted murderer/gangster Henry Hill was paid $550,000[4] for his story told in *Goodfellas* (1990), the 17th highest-ranked film on IMDb? Within that context, it is trivial that a criminal profited from his crimes. In gangster films such as *Once Upon a Time in America* (1984), *The Departed* (2006) and *The Irishman* (2019) we are not asked to judge characters based on their morality. In these films, as with *The Godfather* (1972), we root for the criminals we like more than other criminals. Except for the horse, nothing is innocent in *The Godfather*, not "Kate" or "Mama" or "Connie" or the police, the newspapers or the baker or the undertaker. Morality is extraneous in these films. It is not good versus evil, but bad versus worse. By contrast, the currency of Holocaust films, fictional or otherwise, is righteousness. And while filmmakers cannot be expected to be saints, watching Roman Polanski's incomparable *The Pianist* (2002) is like knowing that the best sushi chef in the world just left the bathroom without washing.

If screenwriters tried to sell a script based on Roman Polanski's life, they would be laughed out of Hollywood. Polanski's experiences have been wildly unbelievable, uniquely bizarre, and tap into many important swaths of twentieth-century history, much like *Forrest Gump* (1994), except for real. Roman Polanski was born Rajmund Roman Thierry Polański in Paris in 1933 to Jewish parents from Poland. When he was four, the family returned to Poland. From age 6 to 12, during the Holocaust and without his parents, Polanski dodged the Germans and escaped the fate of the vast majority of Polish Jews. As explained by Roger Ebert:

> Polanski himself is a Holocaust survivor, saved at one point when his father pushed him through the barbed wire of a camp. He wandered Krakow and Warsaw, a frightened child, cared for by the kindness of strangers. His own survival (and that of his father) are in a sense as random as Szpilman's, which is perhaps why he was attracted to this story. Steven Spielberg tried to enlist him to direct *Schindler's List*, but he refused, perhaps because Schindler's story involved a man who deliberately set out to frustrate the Holocaust, while from personal experience Polanski knew that fate and chance played an inexplicable role in most survivals.[5]

During the 30 years after World War II, Polanski became a film director in Poland, moved to France and then America, and along the way directed five feature films: *Knife in the Water—Nóz w wodzie* (1962) (Poland), *The World's Most Beautiful Swindlers—Les plus belles escroqueries du monde* (1964) (France—Netherlands—Japan—Italy), *Repulsion* (1965) (U.K.), *Cul-de-sac* (1966) (U.K.) and *Dance of the Vampires* (1967) (U.K.—U.S.). Polanski's sixth film was the Oscar-winning *Rosemary's Baby* (1968), starring

---

* Full disclosure, I was part of the production staff for both *For Goodness Sake* (1993) and Trey Parker's *For Goodness Sake II* (1996), as "Rich 'Shlomo' Brownstein."

Woody Allen's future estranged ex-common-law wife—the fine actress Mia Farrow—who also was the adoptive stepmother of Woody Allen's current wife, Soon-Yi Previn, 35 years Allen's junior. In 1969, while Polanski was in London, members of Charles Manson's "family" broke into Polanski's Los Angeles house and stabbed to death five people, including Polanski's pregnant wife of one year, Sharon Tate (1943–1969).

For most people, surviving the Holocaust, becoming a much-lauded international film director, and having his wife and unborn child slaughtered in one of the most culturally significant crimes in American history would have been enough for many lifetimes. But Polanski was just getting started. He next made *Macbeth* (1971) and the documentary *Weekend of a Champion* (1972). Then came a truly horrible attempt at a comedy called *What?—Che?* (1972), about which Roger Ebert wrote prophetically of its gratuitous nudity, "These and other shots confirm my long-held suspicion that, when it comes right down to it, there's a nasty streak of misogyny in Polanski."[6]

Next was Polanski's spectacular neo-noir *Chinatown* (1974), which is rated among the best 150 films by IMDb users and was nominated for 11 Oscars (winning one, for Best Writing). Polanski also acted in *Chinatown*, his own thug character slicing open the nose of the protagonist (Jack Nicholson). Not only did Polanski star in his own subsequently directed film, *The Tenant—Le locataire* (1976), but IMDb lists Polanski with more than 30 acting credits from 1953 through 2008, including in Andrzej Wajda's Holocaust film *Samson* (1961).

In 1977, Polanski's personal plot significantly thickened when he was arrested and charged with drugging and raping a 13-year-old girl: "…[Roman Polanski] has been a fugitive from the U.S. since 1978. He was arrested and charged with drugging and raping 13-year-old Samantha Geimer in 1977. He pleaded guilty to the lesser charge of unlawful sex with a minor before undergoing 42 days of psychiatric evaluation in prison while awaiting sentencing. Once he learned the judge planned to give him a prison term, he fled to Paris and has been avoiding extradition ever since."[7]

Much has been made in the press about Polanski's almost half-century unsuccessful fight to return to America, either through a pardon or by having the cases (rape and fleeing justice) dismissed.[8] And other accusations have also been made against Polanski. In 2018 he lost a defamation suit against a reporter who alleged that Polanski "sexually assaulted five girls and teenagers."[9] There is also an accusation that Polanski sexually molested a 10-year-old girl in 1975.[10] Yet, his remarkable life continued in exile, including winning the Best Directing Oscar for *The Pianist*, which also garnered the Best Actor award (Adrien Brody) and Best Writer (Ronald Harwood), and was nominated for Best Picture, Cinematography, Costume Design and Editing. *The Pianist* is rated in the top 40 films of all time by IMDb users and has grossed over $120 million.

Polanski has made 25 features, including 14 films since 1986, having worked with many American movie studios that have financed and distributed his steady flow, averaging one release every two years. The critical world, too, gawks in awe as Polanski has not missed a beat working around his geographical prohibitions, recreating places from which he is otherwise prohibited. Since Polanski pled guilty for unlawful sex with a minor and became a fugitive in 1978, the following actors have starred in his films: Jodie Foster, Kate Winslet, Christoph Waltz, Ewan McGregor, Pierce Brosnan, Ben Kingsley, Adrien Brody, Johnny Depp, Lena Olin, Sigourney Weaver, Hugh Grant, Kristin Scott Thomas, Peter Coyote, Harrison Ford, Nastassja Kinski and many others. In 2009, Woody Allen, Martin Scorsese and over 130 other filmmakers signed a petition demanding that

Polanski not be extradited to America to face justice, after he was arrested in Switzerland based on an international warrant from 1978.[11] * In 2017, Polanski's victim in the 1977 drugging and rape, Samantha Geimer, "asked a judge in a Los Angeles court to conclude the case, saying that it had been a '40-year sentence' for both parties,"[12] implying that Polanski's lavish lifestyle in Europe as a celebrated filmmaker has been a prison.

Everything changed in 2017 with the reporting about Harvey Weinstein in *The New Yorker* by Ronan Farrow, Woody Allen's estranged son.[13] Suddenly, Hollywood grew a conscience, as explained in a *Deadline Hollywood* article in 2018 titled "As Cosby and Polanski Exit the Film Academy, Memories of a Past Oscar Linger":

> Inevitably, Hollywood's Great Awakening caught up with Bill Cosby and Roman Polanski on Tuesday night, as the governors of the Academy of Motion Picture Arts and Sciences voted to expel the two in keeping with the group's new ethical conduct rules. Cosby, just convicted on sexual assault charges.... But Polanski is another matter, and not just because he was entangled with Jack Nicholson, at whose house he committed the 1977 unlawful sex with a minor that got him banished, or Anjelica Huston, who was in and out of said house at the time.... More embarrassing, at least for the Academy, is Polanski's Oscar for directing *The Pianist*. The award drew a loud standing ovation at the Kodak Theater on the night of March 23, 2003. Meryl Streep joined in. So did Harvey Weinstein....[14]

One year earlier the same Kodak Theater audience gave Woody Allen a standing ovation when introduced—attending his first and only Academy Awards ceremony—there to present Nora Ephron's 9/11 video, "Love Letter to New York in the Movies." Subsequent to Ronan Farrow's unmasking of Weinstein, both Woody Allen's *A Rainy Day in New York* (2019) and Roman Polanski's *An Officer and a Spy* (2019) had difficulty finding American distributors.[15] Both films were snubbed out of fear of a backlash. It has been reported that "Allen's *A Rainy Day in New York*, which features Timothée Chalamet and Elle Fanning, was first planned to be produced and released by Amazon Studios. But Amazon nixed its $68 million four-film deal with Allen last year allegedly over sexual abuse allegations against the Jewish filmmaker...."[16] Allen then sued Amazon for canceling the deal.[17] Meanwhile, Timothée Chalamet and other stars backed away from Allen,

---

* Petitioners included (according to https://www.indiewire.com/2009/09/over-100-in-film-community-sign-polanski-petition-55821/): Fatih Akin, Stephane Allagnon, Woody Allen, Pedro Almodovar, Wes Anderson, Jean-Jacques Annaud, Alexandre Arcady, Fanny Ardant, Asia Argento, Darren Aronofsky, Olivier Assayas, Alexander Astruc, Gabriel Auer, Luc Barnier, Christophe Barratier, Xavier Beauvois, Liria Begeja, Gilles Behat, Jean-Jacques Beineix, Marco Bellochio, Monica Bellucci, Djamel Bennecib, Giuseppe Bertolucci, Patrick Bouchitey, Paul Boujenah, Jacques Bral, Patrick Braoudé, Andre Buytaers, Christian Carion, Henning Carlsen, Jean-Michel Carre, Patrice Chereau, Elie Chouraqui, Souleymane Cisse, Alain Corneau, Jerome Cornuau, Miguel Courtois, Dominique Crevecoeur, Alfonso Cuaron, Luc et Jean-Pierre Dardenne, Jonathan Demme, Alexandre Desplat, Rosalinde et Michel Deville, Georges Dybman, Jacques Fansten, Joël Farges, Gianluca Farinelli, Jacques Fansten, Etienne Faure, Michel Ferry, Scott Foundas, Stephen Frears, Thierry Fremaux, Sam Gabarski, René Gainville, Tony Gatlif, Costa Gavras, Jean-Marc Ghanassia, Terry Gilliam, Christian Gion, Marc Guidoni, Buck Henry, David Heyman, Laurent Heynemann, Robert Hossein, Jean-Loup Hubert, Alejandro Gonzalez Inarritu, Gilles Jacob, Just Jaeckin, Alain Jessua, Pierre Jolivet, Kent Jones, Roger Kahane, Nelly Kaplan, Wong Kar Waï, Ladislas Kijno, Harmony Korine, Jan Kounen, Diane Kurys, Emir Kusturica, John Landis, Claude Lanzmann, André Larquié, Vinciane Lecocq, Patrice Leconte, Claude Lelouch, Gérard Lenne, David Lynch, Michael Mann, François Margolin, Jean-Pierre Marois, Tonie Marshall, Mario Martone, Nicolas Mauvernay, Radu Mihaileanu, Claude Miller, Mario Monicelli, Jeanne Moreau, Sandra Nicolier, Michel Ocelot, Alexander Payne, Richard Pena, Michele Placido, Philippe Radault, Jean-Paul Rappeneau, Raphael Rebibo, Yasmina Reza, Jacques Richard, Laurence Roulet, Walter Salles, Jean-Paul Salomé, Marc Sandberg, Jerry Schatzberg, Julian Schnabel, Barbet Schroeder, Ettore Scola, Martin Scorcese, Charlotte Silvera, Abderrahmane Sissako, Paolo Sorrentino, Guillaume Stirn, Tilda Swinton, Jean-Charles Tacchella, Radovan Tadic, Danis Tanovic, Bertrand Tavernier, Cécile Telerman, Alain Terzian, Pascal Thomas, Giuseppe Tornatore, Serge Toubiana, Nadine Trintignant, Tom Tykwer, Alexandre Tylski, Betrand Van Effenterre and Wim Wenders.

evidenced by their donations of their salaries from Allen's films to charities that fight sexism in Hollywood.[18]

The backlash against octogenarian Jewish filmmakers Woody Allen and Roman Polanski seems to be converging as "…North American festivals such as Sundance and Toronto have steered to calmer waters, seemingly closing their doors (for now) to filmmakers with MeToo-related baggage."[19] Polanski's film *An Officer and a Spy* is about the Dreyfus Affair, one of the most notorious acts of antisemitism in French history, an event which led to Theodor Herzl's founding of modern Zionism, the precursor to the State of Israel. It is easy to speculate that Polanski is relitigating his exile allegorically through the life of French Army Captain Alfred Dreyfus (1859–1935), who was exiled to Devil's Island in French Guiana after a false conviction for treason, a conviction that was later overturned. In fact, at the 2019 Venice Film Festival, Polanski revealed, "I can see the same determination to deny the facts and condemn me for things I have not done."[20] *Variety*'s Owen Gleiberman quoted Polanski from the same news conference saying, "Most of the people who harass me do not know me and know nothing about the case," to which Gleiberman responded in his review, "I'm sorry, but that comparison is obscene."[21]

While Polanski is suing the Motion Picture Academy to be reinstated,[22] Woody Allen filed "a lawsuit against Amazon for backing out of the [$68 million distribution] deal, claiming their withdrawal was based on 'a 25-year-old, baseless allegation.'"[23] Like clockwork, within hours in November 2019, Polanski was accused by French actress, model, and photographer Valentine Monnier of rape when she was 18 years old in 1975[24]; and Allen settled his lawsuit against Amazon,[25] while reportedly securing for himself North American distribution rights to *A Rainy Day in New York* as part of the settlement.[26]

Finally, in 2019, Roman Polanski was partly the subject of Quentin Tarantino's fantasy *Once Upon a Time … in Hollywood* (2019), which rewrites history by having Polanski's neighbor (instead of Polanski's wife Sharon Tate) murdered by Manson's squad. In the film, Tarantino is both reverential to Polanski as a director, yet is dismissive of Polanski as a man, possibly the greatest insult to one of Hollywood's most notorious womanizers, with one character in the film commenting to Steve McQueen (Damian Lewis), "Sharon absolutely has a type. Cute, short, talented guys who look like 12-year-old boys." So, perhaps the final, lasting impression of Roman Polanski will be Quentin Tarantino's effeminate Polanski who surely would have been emasculated by Sharon Tate, the most fitting homage to Polanski's films. That is Roman Polanski's abridged biography.*

Yet questions remain about how Polanski's filmmaking and history comport with the ideals implicit in Holocaust filmmaking, which should be the unequivocal rejection of evil. Is it fair to examine art within the context of the artist? Where was the outrage before 2017 from the world and a Hollywood community who knew of Polanski's proclivities, at least since his 1977 arrest? Was Polanski given a 40-year pass because he was a Holocaust survivor, a genius, a powerful filmmaker, or because nobody really thought drugging and raping a 13-year-old was a big deal in the 1970s? "It's pretty tough for any person to claim that Polanski is not a dirtbag," critic Tyler Haney wrote in 2009, continuing, "He's a dirtbag of the highest order. But unlike most rapists, Polanski's public image is complicated by the indisputable fact that the man is one of the most talented living film directors."[27] Nor have the fundamental moral underpinnings of Polanski and his

---

* For Polanski's version, at least through 1985, see his autobiography, *Roman by Polanski*, published by Ballantine Books, ISBN: 0345305124.

work suddenly changed after 65 years of filmmaking. In fact, as Roger Ebert suspected in 1976, the degenerate themes in Roman Polanski's work were like a massive oil spill off the coast—visible to all who dared look—a slick that finally made landfall in 2017.

But the same could be said of Woody Allen's past and films. Allen has never lived in exile and never been criminally charged for the child sexual abuse accusations made by one of his adopted children, Dylan Farrow, and her mother, Mia Farrow.[28] Notwithstanding the magnificent *Annie Hall* (1977)—winner of four Oscars, Best Picture, Director (Allen), Writer (Allen) and Actress (Diane Keaton)—Allen has projected many perversions in his movies, which redound to two related themes: first, incessant infidelity and, second, an acute lack of impulse control, including in *Everything You Always Wanted to Know About Sex * But Were Afraid to Ask* (1972), where an elderly orthodox rabbi requests on the imaginary national television game show called "What's My Perversion" to engage in sadomasochism while his wife kneels before him eating pork. Of course, the question remains, whose impulse control is compromised: that of the character or that of the writer/director who created the self-loathing content?

Roman Polanski's films, on the other hand, rely on three different characteristics, each providing a glimpse into his soul. First is coercion, which often takes the form of people trying to leave a place, metaphorically or physically. His protagonists are magically sucked back from the brink, whether exiting a door, a boat, a cabin, a stage, a job or a relationship, and are then metaphorically caged. The second thread in most of Polanski's work is his unabashed indulgence in pathological psychosexual themes, often including rape and psychotic sexuality. The third constant in most of Polanski's creations is non-rape violence against women, with women being assaulted in virtually every film—physically, sexually and verbally. Interestingly, however, random misogyny does not seem to be the goal. And in most of his films, Polanski's abused beautiful women get some classy revenge. Conversely, Polanski's men are often effeminate or cowering, or both, emasculated as they are kicked to the curb by smarter women.

Spun in the most favorable light, the near-ubiquitous misogyny peppered throughout Polanski's catalog is an indictment of humanity, although any two-bit analyst would reduce the theme to its maker's inclinations. Just as mainstream filmgoers cannot help but notice the incessant theme of adultery in almost all of the 50 films directed by Woody Allen, there is no escaping the aberrant themes swimming around Polanski's work, although somewhat moderated in Polanski's later years. In both cases, too, as with all the greats, art follows life, biographies seeping into the corners of their work, as if to rectify—if not justify—their respective checkered pasts. Similarly, Allen's and Polanski's romances have stoked the tabloids, which should also have been flares above the oil spill.

Another juxtaposition between these two filmmaking giants can be distilled down to "character-driven" versus "plot-driven" stories. Because Woody Allen's characters are so interesting and developed, his film plots are practically superfluous; conversely, Roman Polanski's characters seem not to have existed before and are not worth a thought after the curtain. While Polanski's plots are quite developed, the antecedents of Polanski's characters' mental illnesses are generally unexplained, despite the meandering stories that may include some biographical information, but that skimp on any emotional backstory. It is as if Polanski is suggesting that he can carry a story while eliminating the personal exposition needed by other filmmakers, almost without exception, almost without that net. And with the same regularity, Polanski lays out his premises without any foreplay, in the first minutes of the film. His penchant for frontloading the inciting incident again raises the bar, with the only remaining question being: how will Polanski fill the next two hours? Nonetheless, Polanski is a skillful storyteller who successfully uses 95 percent of his films as the second of three acts.

For the most part, too, Polanski's films are difficult to watch, from start to finish, which speaks more to his dark European cinematic origin and script preferences than to his filmmaking ability. Those believing that the world is a happy place will be cured by Roman Polanski's films, which regard frailty as a curse. Happily, sexual deviance and Freudian pathology are absent in *The Pianist*; almost alone in his work, Polanski's Holocaust film has an optimistic ending, an almost-happy ending. Though Polanski's dalliances with the occult in *Rosemary's Baby* and *The Ninth Gate* (1999), together with his tragic association with the Manson murders, might have pigeonholed lesser directors, two dozen other Polanski films have had as much breadth as any of his contemporaries' work, including the very fine films *Tess* (1979), produced by Claude Berri (writer/director of the recommended Holocaust film *The Two of Us* [1967]), *Death and the Maiden* (1994), *Carnage* (2011) and *Venus in Fur—La Vénus à la fourrure* (2013). These films are not only entertaining and impeccably directed, but also relentlessly depressing. In particular, Polanski's gripping *Carnage*—starring Jodie Foster, Kate Winslet, Christoph Waltz and John C. Reilly—checks all the boxes: sublimely made, enthralling dialogue, viciously honest and resolutely disheartening.

Also of note, except for *The Pianist* and *An Officer and a Spy*—and in sharp contrast to Woody Allen's work—none of Roman Polanski's films have any Jewish content. Although aspects of the lives of both of these famous Jewish filmmakers have been self-indulgently hashed out in their films dozens of times for more than half a century, the two men could not be more different in highlighting their ethnicity. In fact, although many of Woody Allen's films are comedies which make fun of Judaism from quip to premise, Allen's Jewish roots are even visible in his serious films. This ethnocentrism is absent in Polanski's work, even in *The Pianist* and *An Officer and a Spy*, where the Jewishness of the Jewish protagonists is barely an afterthought, but simply a reality.

Polanski's nihilistic fetishism is embodied remarkably by the femme fatale characters played by Emmanuelle Seigner (1966–), both in *Bitter Moon* (1992) and *Venus in Fur*. This is less surprising when realizing that, since 1989, Seigner has been Roman Polanski's wife, 33 years his junior, married when she was 24 and he was 56. Seigner could have been Nastassja Kinski's younger sister. (Kinski starred in Polanski's *Tess*.) The Polanskis met during the filming of *Frantic* (1988), starring Harrison Ford. Seigner was positively enchanting as Ford's sidekick, as she was for Johnny Depp in *The Ninth Gate* (1999), and, frankly, in all her films directed by Polanski. Indeed, Seigner's alluring performances in those two meandering films were the only reasons not to walk out of them.

Although Seigner has appeared in more than 35 features, only a handful were directed by her husband. Still, Seigner's career has been overshadowed by being Roman Polanski's wife, which, for better or worse, tacitly justified Polanski's penchant for females half his age. Yet Seigner has been such a force on the screen over the past 30 years that she was rightfully—if not cynically—extended an invitation in 2018 to join the Motion Picture Academy, the year after Mr. Polanski's expulsion, to which she declined in an open letter, writing in part: "I've always been a feminist but how can I ignore the fact that a few weeks ago the Academy showed my husband Roman Polanski the door to satisfy the prevailing mood of the moment. The same Academy that awarded him the best director Oscar for *The Pianist* in 2003. It's a strange case of amnesia!"[29]

So, what is the big deal? The question about *The Pianist* intersects with questions about Woody Allen's *Manhattan* (1979) and classical composer Richard Wagner's prose. When does the artist interfere with the art? There is no question about the brilliance of any of these works. Yet, Woody Allen's Oscar-nominated *Manhattan* normalizes a sexual relationship with a 17-year-old girl, Mariel Hemingway, and a middle-aged man, which bothered nobody in 1979, not in the film and not in Hollywood. Wrote Michael Cieply of *The New York Times* in 2009, "…it remains unclear whether any studio today would make the film, with its matter-of-fact portrayal of an illegal dalliance—or statutory rape—intact."[30]

Richard Wagner (1813–1883), one of the great German composers, wrote prose under the pen name K. Freigedank ("K. Freethought"), prose that contained the explicit antisemitic seeds watered by generations of Germans to sprout and bring forth a forest of antisemites, capped by Wagner's greatest devotee, Adolf Hitler. To this day, it is almost impossible for orchestras to play Wagner's music in the State of Israel, so abhorrent is Wagner's legacy. But, obviously, Wagner was not alone, as noted by Charles McGrath in *The New York Times* in 2009, in his piece "Good Art, Bad People":

> Probably the most frequently cited example is Wagner, whose anti–Semitism was such that he once wrote that Jews were by definition incapable of art. Degas, a painter often praised for his warmth and humanity, was also an anti–Semite and a staunch defender of the French court that falsely convicted Alfred Dreyfus. Ezra Pound was both anti–Semitic and proto-fascist, and if you want to let him off the hook because he was probably crazy as well, the same excuse cannot be made for his friend and protégé T.S. Eliot, whose anti–Semitism, it now seems pretty clear, was more than just casual or what passed for commonplace in those days.[31]

Yet, even considering whether or not to enjoy the art of these antisemites is trivial in relation to supporting the many German companies that enslaved Jews and helped facilitate the Holocaust, companies such as Bayer/IG Farben (which made the Zyklon B gas with Jewish slave labor), Volkswagen (which used Jewish slave labor), Siemens (which used Jewish slave labor) and many others. There, direct culpability for enabling and participating in a war crime is explicit, leaving today's consumers a clear moral choice about supporting Hitler's industrial henchmen, even 75 years later. Similarly, how are we to treat American companies which elected to assist Hitler's genocidal government and thus implicitly participated in the Holocaust? How should we treat Dow Jones' companies that include IBM (which was indispensable to the Germans in tracking and selecting the Jews), Eastman-Kodak (which used slave laborers in Germany) and Ford (whose founder and chairman was openly pro–Nazi and a flagrant antisemite). Should we ignore these awful facts when buying aspirin, a personal computer, a film or a car?

What of the highly celebrated films by D.W. Griffith and Leni Riefenstahl, *The Birth of a Nation* (1915) and *Triumph of the Will* (1935), respectively, features that are essentially racist propaganda that promote subjugation? Is it reasonable to indict these two reprehensible films, at the same time ignoring Polanski? While those horrifyingly bigoted films are plainly set apart from *The Pianist*, which was tacitly intended to fight such prejudice, Griffith's and Riefenstahl's classics are not necessarily morally inferior to many of Polanski's other films and actions, which also seemed to normalize the conquest of the powerless.

The accusations against Polanski et al., too, are different from those against convicted celebrities such as O.J. Simpson, Mike Tyson and Phil Spector. Discussing Polanski, instead, is more like a conversation about supporting the professional endeavors of Bill

Cosby, Michael Jackson, Kobe Bryant, Bryan Singer, R. Kelly, Russell Simmons, Kevin Spacey, Charlie Rose, Woody Allen and many others who were accused of sex crimes, yet famously slipped the punches, especially professionally—some until Harvey Weinstein's fall and the "#MeToo" movement.

Perhaps we laugh today while listening to early Bill Cosby albums, forgetting we are hearing a de facto sex offender. Perhaps we can enjoy the Beatles' album *Let It Be*, produced by a convicted murderer, Phil Spector,[32] and featuring a confessed wife-beater, John Lennon.[33] But the underlying premise of Holocaust film is exposing immorality, whether officially sanctioned acts of genocide, collaboration, despoilment, rape or even neutrality. We watch Holocaust films, alone or with family or students, with the implicit goal of rejecting immorality and wickedness.

Unlike most period-pieces, Holocaust films demand a moral true-north, inherently inviting disproportionate scrutiny, even of their makers. It is naïve to believe that our artists and heroes are flawless. But, before and after watching, it is still our responsibility to consider the context, the message and the messenger. *The Pianist* is a brilliant Holocaust film that becomes more of a teaching tool when considered with the life of its creator, Roman Polanski.

8

Holocaust Film
Curriculum Planning
The "SOFTA" System

Education generally—and Holocaust education specifically—has evolved considerably in 75 years. Although we know implicitly that almost nothing scholarly was documented about the Holocaust as of "VE Day" on May 8, 1945, it must be stated explicitly that the Holocaust is still being documented, even today. Indeed, any expectation of comprehensive Holocaust education during the first 40 years after the War is unrealistic and historically naïve.

Further, revolutionary general theories of education were constantly being rolled out during the post–War generation, undergirded by advancements in both educational psychology and visual media. For example, classrooms from 1945 through the mid–1960s were much less touchy-feely than they became in the wake of the cultural revolution that followed. And just after educational balance seemed to have been attained in the 1980s, the information revolution changed everything again. Gone were the days that age-appropriate materials could be roped off; information now flows everywhere, seemingly without context or attenuation. Unearthing difficult answers by trudging to a library has now been replaced by a Wiki click.

Specific to Holocaust studies, there was once a time, believe it or not, when "shock education" was in vogue. Some well-intentioned educators thought that—to understand the Holocaust—students should be made to "feel" like Holocaust victims, as if that were possible. Some of these misguided attempts to instill empathy included having students write down their dreams, only to see the notes burned, serving students watery soup, locking students in dark rooms, and, at summer camp, awakening campers in the middle of cold nights, forcing these frightened children to stand in lines, all in an effort to teach the Holocaust.

I have witnessed a wide range of techniques since I began teaching Holocaust studies in 1983. Healthy emotions after learning details of cruelty include sadness, disappointment and confusion. Shame, too, is a natural reaction to dishonorable governmental actions. But anger should never be encouraged, whether as an educational technique or a goal. Instilling anger, or its cousins "vengeance" and "retribution," as byproducts of any form of education is dreadfully misguided, particularly in Holocaust education, which is partially intended as a reproach to any authoritarianism, a paradigm intended to incite anger as behavioral leverage. The incitement of anger in Holocaust education is akin to striking a child as a punishment for hitting. An educator's job is to transfer information; our task is assuredly not to instill the antecedent destructive emotions that fueled historical events. And while empathy for victims—in any context—is a critical component of internalization, transference of perpetrators' emotions is an unacceptable form of empathy. Even when teaching about historically immoral acts, the provocation of aggressive emotional reactions in our students is lazy and reckless, indicative of manipulative educators lacking command of their subject matter. While seeing a reaction from our students is gratifying, reaching for the most destructive emotions is shortsighted and educationally weak, which is why we no longer teach the Holocaust by devastating our students.

Earlier Holocaust education also concentrated on trying to comprehend the number 6,000,000, an approach with many drawbacks. First, the number of Jews murdered in the Holocaust is an approximation, which, unlike Avogadro's number, is understood more as a placeholder than as precision. As noted in a *Haaretz* article, "'Six million' is not, and was never intended to be, a precise accounting."[1] Further, not that this was a pedagogical concern, but numerical imprecision has been the perfect red herring for Holocaust deniers, who point to internecine disagreements to bolster deniers' antisemitic arguments. More importantly, objects are not placeholders for people, as analogized in the well-meaning documentary *Paper Clips* (2004), with their collection of six million paperclips amassed by students to symbolize the Holocaust's dead. This early reductionist reflex looked good on paper, mostly because it was relatively uncomplicated, especially since better heuristics were still being developed. Eventually, though, educators and experts recognized that quantifying the Holocaust is counterproductive when teaching the Holocaust as a set of incomprehensible acts. So, in fact, not only is the number 6,000,000 a placeholder, but also the use of the number 6,000,000 in early Holocaust education was as a placeholder that awaited the development of better—more sensitive, appropriate and effective—pedagogical approaches.

Thankfully, the ineffective, ill-informed, discredited and discouraged educational tools that were used to teach the Holocaust have been discarded.[2] As explained to *Education World* by Warren Marcus of the United States Holocaust Memorial Museum, "Many teachers, with the best intentions, present the Holocaust in problematic ways." He outlined the USHMM's prevailing Holocaust educational suggestions:

> First, the education division here feels very strongly that any simulation or role-play in this study is inappropriate and misleading. Students should read and hear testimony to learn about the Holocaust, and not be led by some attempted classroom re-creation to think they know what it felt like.
>
> Second, teachers may spend excessive time trying to have students understand the magnitude of the loss of millions of people through lessons in which objects represent human lives. Individual lives should be studied and individual voices should be heard.
>
> Third, teachers, due to a lack of time, may start their Holocaust study in 1939 or 1941. To provide some context for grappling with how a civilized nation and continent could descend so quickly into this barbarity, it is crucial to start a Holocaust study with the history of antisemitism and with events at least from the end of World War I. Also, if the study starts during World War II, students may see the Jews and other target groups only as victims.
>
> Fourth, teachers may fail to present testimony from individuals and show films that depict the span of experience, including ghetto life and death, camp life, the experiences of hidden children, life before, and so on.
>
> Fifth, teachers may rely on only one text, and students may think that that text depicts what happened to everyone during the period. Another pitfall would be to use only *The Diary of Anne Frank*. Teachers may teach the diary or play and not instruct their students about the last months of her life. Students would be left with many misconceptions about her life and about the Holocaust in general.[3]

Thankfully, the proliferation of Holocaust educational institutions has been accompanied by improved and refined sensibilities. Overall, best-practice Holocaust educational approaches have been codified by Yad Vashem ("The Pedagogical Approach to Teaching the Holocaust"[4]) and by the USHMM ("Guidelines for Teaching about the Holocaust"[5]).

As with every other skill, teaching the Holocaust improves with experience and preparation. And specifically, there is no single correct answer to the question: what is the best film for teaching the Holocaust? Many factors complicate this decision. Although a general set of films is recommended in Chapter 9, the list of recommended films is not a blanket endorsement of any particular film for all educational purposes. In addition, in some cases, tangential or even non–Holocaust films are most effective. For example, when teaching about the rise of fascism, cultural respect, responses to racism or Holocaust denial, these non-core Holocaust films might be recommended: *The Wave* (TV 1981), *Freedom Writers* (2007), *The Memory Thief* (2007), *Labyrinth of Lies— Im Labyrinth Des Schweigens* (2014), *Denial* (2016) and non–Holocaust films *American History X* (1998) and *The Believer* (2001). Or, when studying Holocaust precursors and the rise of Nazism, *Ship of Fools* (1965) and *Julia* (1977) should be considered along with *Cabaret* (1972).

Selecting appropriate Holocaust films requires educators to consider a prescribed set of criteria. To that, I have created the SOFTA Lesson Plan Outline:

> **S**tudents
> **O**bjectives
> **F**ollow-Up
> **T**ime
> **A**dministrative

Properly read, the SOFTA Lesson Plan is a set of suggestions and a checklist to help educators solve the academic puzzle of how to use Holocaust films in the classroom. The SOFTA Lesson Plan is a set of questions that steer educators toward the most effective method of Holocaust film study. Regardless, teaching "The Holocaust" cannot be done with only one film. Using narrative Holocaust films as the primary source for Holocaust education would be educational malpractice, even if a single film could encompass all aspects of the Holocaust. Holocaust film is an educational supplement, which can be used to fill-in and give life to difficult sub-topics within Holocaust study. The SOFTA Lesson Plan explicitly assumes that films are not the lesson plan, but just a portion of a Holocaust topic, woven into the traditional teaching of specific topics in Holocaust study and its follow-up. Below is the complete SOFTA Lesson Plan outline, which will subsequently be expounded upon in this chapter.

Students:
- Environment;
- Age;
- Prior Education;
- Aptitude;
- Emotional Maturity and Uptake;
- Religious/National Orientation and Homogeneity;
- Ability and Willingness to Read Subtitles.

Objectives (and the best-associated films):
- Approximately 60 common teaching objectives are listed, each with examples of films that illuminate these objectives.

Follow-Up:
- Answering Questions;
- Emotional Triage;
- Journaling;
- Workbooks, Further Reading or Watching;
- Academic Examination.

Time:
- Amount of Time Devoted to Holocaust Study;
- Specific Film Preparation Time;
- Follow-Up Time;
- Presentations by Survivors or Other Experts.

Administrative:
- Regulations Concerning Depictions of Sex, Violence and Language;
- Parental Cooperation and/or Consent Forms;
- Technical Capabilities (Venue, Quality of Media, Audio and Projection);
- Mental Health Expert Availability.

Students

Evaluating students' intellectual and emotional abilities must be a priority when teaching the Holocaust. So too, the general characteristics of the students influence Holocaust studies. For example, I started teaching the Holocaust to sixth graders in a Sunday school affiliated with a Conservative Jewish denomination in Portland, Oregon, in 1983. Each of those prepositional phrases impacted my decisions about the curriculum. Imagine how the course changes with the alteration of each descriptor: teaching the Holocaust at a day school affiliated with liberal Methodists in New York City in 2018 to 11th graders. Each of these factors drastically alters the Holocaust curriculum, even before considering the characteristics of classroom demographics: environment; age; prior education; aptitude; emotional maturity and uptake; religious/national orientation and homogeneity; ability; and willingness to read subtitles.

Students: Environment

Students from Berlin, Baltimore, and Jerusalem, even if otherwise sharing the same age, religion and economic class, each require vastly different Holocaust-education planning.

For instance, even informally in Israel, Holocaust education is ubiquitous. As a formal scholastic subject, the Israeli Ministry of Education includes Holocaust education as a required subject for high school graduation. In fact, because the Israeli government subsidizes a journey to death camps and memorials in Poland, in 2018 40,000 (out of 91,000 eligible) high school seniors visited Auschwitz.[6] As a practical matter, the national day of Holocaust remembrance known as "Yom HaShoah" includes a country-wide two-minute siren during which all citizens are encouraged to cease all activity—including driving. It is nearly impossible to avoid the gravity of the Holocaust in Israel when watching people on Yom HaShoah standing next to their cars on freeways for 120 seconds.

The Israeli approach, too, can be understood within the context of when the Jewish State officially memorializes the Holocaust, in contrast to the date used by much of the rest of the world. International Holocaust Remembrance Day is January 27, designated by United Nations General Assembly Resolution 60/7 in 2005, commemorating the liberation of Auschwitz/Birkenau (by the Soviet Army). A dozen European countries also have domestic Holocaust remembrance days that are linked to Holocaust history in their respective localities and their national narratives. For example, Austrian Holocaust Remembrance Day is May 5, the day Mauthausen Concentration Camp was liberated in 1945. The day of Israeli Holocaust remembrance is Yom HaShoah, which was established in 1959 and is equally about its national narrative as is any other commemoration. Yom HaShoah is the 27th of Nisan on the Jewish calendar, corresponding annually to late April or early May. Yom HaShoah is specifically linked to two events: the middle of the Warsaw Ghetto Uprising—which commenced 13 days earlier and lasted 27 days (April 19 to May 16, 1943); and Israel Independence Day, which is the 5th of Iyar, eight days after Yom HaShoah. The notable difference between International Holocaust Remembrance Day and Yom HaShoah is that Israel has linked its official Holocaust remembrance day with two acts of Jewish resistance against Jewish genocide (attempted by the Germans and the Arabs), as opposed to the international Holocaust commemoration of passive Jewish liberation by non–Jews.

Other stark contrasts exist in Israeli culture between the perception of Israeli versus European Jews. Early Israeli society saw Holocaust survivors and victims as weak, vis-à-vis Jews in pre–Israel Palestine who were fighting to create a Jewish State. Israelis see themselves as the brave, mighty and combative Jewish archetype, while Europe's Jews were deemed by Israelis as pathetic for having acquiesced to the Germans' plans. Indeed, unbelievably, "soapy" was a common derisive term used to reference Holocaust survivors in Israel, a name derived from the pervasive myth that Germans had made soap from dead Jews.[7] Some in Israeli society also use the Holocaust as a theological cudgel, an illustration of the consequences of what they believe was German-Jewish godlessness, a sanctimonious approach that denigrates everyone, including the children and pious who constituted the majority of Holocaust victims.[8] And while Israeli society has come a long way in this respect, the Holocaust is still taught nationalistically by many, as exhibit number one of what will happen to Jews without a strong Jewish State.[9] As described by Edward Rothstein in *Mosaic Magazine*:

> True, even Yad Vashem can't resist a homily, in the form of the message silently delivered when, after zigzagging downward and then upward through the exhibition the visitor emerges, after all that carnage, to behold the flowering Judean Hills and the strong, confident state [*sic*] of Israel; but this message, a Zionist one, is itself anchored in the most fundamental Jewish sources and the strongest of the Jewish people's millennial dreams.[10]

Europeans have their own sensibilities, too, which may include shame, guilt or pride for the various actions of previous generations. Some Europeans may derive satisfaction from their countries' maintaining Holocaust memorials, especially at the sites of camps. In 2019, for example, nearly 400,000 of the 2.3 million visitors to Auschwitz/Birkenau were Polish, the most of any nationality.[11] Europe is covered with Holocaust memorials marking thousands of locations and facilities where Jews were murdered or deported.

Then consider American students who might have regular access to the ninety Holocaust memorials (or museums) that have been created in 29 American states, from Washington State to Florida, from California to Maine. Even so, for students and adults, there is an objective difference between, on one hand, standing in Portland's glorious Washington Park at the Oregon Holocaust Memorial, and, on the other hand, touring the remaining Auschwitz gas chamber while wrapped in an Israeli flag. Nonetheless, while American students may have a different, less immediate Holocaust education when compared to Israeli and European students, still these American students may be bringing fewer misconceptions to local lessons that must be unlearned.

Some nationalities, specifically, have disproportional affinity for certain Holocaust films. For instance, many educators in Australia and New Zealand are enamored by *The Boy in the Striped Pyjamas* (2008), where this regrettable film is sometimes used in curriculae. Groups from China that I have taught at Yad Vashem have implied that *Schindler's List* (1993) is more obscure than *The Sound of Music* (1965) (to which they can all sing along), because *The Sound of Music* was one of the first Western films officially shown in China. Yet, most of these Chinese students have never heard of the only Chinese-produced Holocaust film, *A Jewish Girl in Shanghai* (2010). And Germany and France accounted for a quarter of *Inglourious Basterds'* (2009) non–U.S. box office. So, national prevailing attitudes also impact film choices and availability.

Finally, locally made films have a better chance of hitting their marks than do culturally dissonant films. As an example, notwithstanding the differences in language and format, the German sensibilities in their 2016 production *The Diary of Anne Frank—Das Tagebuch Der Anne Frank* could not be more different from the same story told in the Japanese animated *The Diary of Anne Frank—Anne no nikki* (1995). Or maybe the Canadian Survivor film *The Quarrel* (1991) is better suited to European viewers than to Americans. All of which is to say that students' environmental factors can deeply affect the impact of films.

Students: Age

Perhaps reflecting other cultural differences, the United States Holocaust Memorial Museum has a Holocaust lesson plan that is intended for 7th to 12th grades,[12] while Yad Vashem proudly publishes Holocaust teaching guides for the Diaspora for all grades. Yad Vashem's "I Wanted to Fly Like a Butterfly" curriculum is intended for 3rd and 4th grade Holocaust studies. Their "It is because we are Jews" curriculum is intended for 1st and 2nd grades.[13] While not commenting here on the appropriateness of teaching the Holocaust to young children, this chapter assumes that the decision to teach the Holocaust has already been made affirmatively.

The consideration at hand, then, is which, if any, Holocaust films are best suited to the respective ages of intended students. Although the Motion Picture Academy of America (MPAA) ratings, and those of equivalent non–American boards, are provided in the list of Holocaust films in Appendix I, these ratings are analogous to the fast-food industry classifying the healthfulness of its own products. As noted in *ReelRundown*'s excellent 2016 exposé "How the MPAA Movie Rating Scale Fails Our Children":

> …the current system is ambiguous and has been shown to reflect the monetary interests of film studios rather than the values of the average parent. Furthermore, the scale does not distinguish between objectionable elements that are perceived as immoral and those that negatively influence a child's

development. The MPAA rating scale does not adequately fulfill its purpose of helping parents to make informed decisions about what movies are appropriate for their children and must be reformed.[14]

As an example of incomprehensible parental rating by the MPAA is the purported Holocaust film *The Unborn* (2009), rated "PG-13 [parental guidance; some material may be inappropriate for children under age 13] for intense sequences of violence and terror, disturbing images, thematic material and language including some sexual references." The DVD cover features the protagonist in her panties. In the film, she is vividly depicted having sex and is impregnated. A dybbuk (the malicious spirit of a dead person's dislocated soul) reaches into her uterus. But that is just the start; consider the following observations posted by IMDb users for the "MPAA PG-13" rated *The Unborn*[15]:

- One sex scene is briefly shown when a man is on top of a woman and they're kissing passionately (Unrated Version only).
- A man and a woman lie in bed together: she has her head on his bare chest and they talk and kiss (she is mostly covered by a blanket).
- A woman is seen in a shower, her bare back is seen.
- Women are seen wrapped in towels in a locker room scene.
- A woman is seen in low-cut tank tops throughout the film. Some of the tops show cleavage.
- In two scenes, a woman is seen in a bathroom wearing a vest and panties.
- A woman is lying in bed in multiple scenes (in one scene we see her bare back, and in another we see her bare stomach).
- A man tells a woman in a joking manner that she is giving him an erection (using a crude term).
- A woman talks to another woman about a man's porn collection.
- A woman talks to another woman about a man masturbating
- A woman jokes with another woman about her vagina being disease-infested.
- A woman calls another woman a hooker.
- Violence is pretty incredible for a PG-13 movie.
- A woman wakes up on a ceiling and sees herself lying in bed: a pale, sickly-looking child lays next to her, puts his hand on her bare stomach, digs his hand into her stomach, and rips open a hole in her abdomen (her stomach is bloody).
- A woman opens her front door, a child stabs her in the abdomen (she bleeds through her shirt and screams), she struggles to get away from the child, the child's face changes into demonic-looking features, with a wide open mouth and pointed, sharp teeth, and snarls and goes after her; a man rushes the child and gets the knife away (he seems to want to hurt the child but does not).
- A woman lies on the floor after being stabbed, her eyes are open and her face is still, her head begins to jerk from side to side (it makes a cracking and breaking noise) and she makes strange moaning and growling noises; she then starts having what appears to be a seizure, her body shakes, her skin begins changing color and veins appear through it, she screams, her eyes change color also, her mouth opens exposing pointy-looking teeth, and she falls back to the floor and appears to be dead.
- A woman is chased by a man on all fours, he stops at the bottom of a staircase, his head turns completely around and upside down (we hear breaking and cracking noises as his head moves), his spine sticks out through his skin and his

limbs are contorted and twisted, and he continues to chase the woman down a hallway.

- A man grabs a woman by the neck and begins to strangle her; he lifts her body off the ground by the neck, he opens his mouth and insects crawl out, and the woman screams and he has blood and bruises on his face.
- A woman participating in an exorcism turns into a "demon": she bends backward (her back makes a breaking noise, and as she screams, she exposes pointy teeth and yellow eyes).
- A man transforms into a demon: his face changes, and he screams, he smashes his own head into a wall multiple times, and his face changes to demonic features and back again.
- A woman follows a dog into a wooded area and finds a white mask; she picks up the mask, the mask has strings that are buried in the soil, and when she clears away the soil, she find [sic] a fetus in formaldehyde.
- A boy is shown dead, lying on a table, and a man covers the child with a sheet.
- A man falls off a balcony (we see him fall and hit the ground), has blood on his ear, neck, cheek and chin and he dies.
- A man's body writhes and turns to dust.
- A man sees a dog with its head turned upside down on its body, it growls and snarls and shows its teeth, and the man yells at it.
- A young boy unexpectedly hits a woman in the face with a broken mirror shard (in the next scene, she has a small cut under her eye).
- A woman finds a young boy holding a sharp broken mirror shard over the crib of an infant while whispering.
- A dead woman is seen lying on the floor (we see the lower part of her body but her face is obscured by a police officer leaning over the body).
- A young woman walks into a hospital room and sees the back of a woman hunched over in a chair and she is holding something while breathing strangely: the young woman slowly approaches, the woman in the chair looks up, and we see what appears to be a demon-like creature with large teeth and a blue body; it opens its mouth wide and screams and howls at the young woman, who screams out of fear, and the demon drops a large glass jar to the floor (the glass breaks, and liquid spills out on the floor along with a human fetus).
- A woman hits a boy on a tricycle with her car (the child strikes the windshield, but we do not see him hit the ground); the woman exits the car and finds the child standing behind the car, completely unharmed.
- A man breaks through a wall and fights with another man, a woman tries to intervene and the man pushes her down; there is yelling and screaming, the woman jumps on the man's back, and he punches the other man and throws the woman off his back.
- A man hits another man over the head with a piece of metal, knocking him unconscious.
- Two children are seen lying on medical tables, men are shown wrapping straps around the children's heads (they are performing experiments), one man is shown approaching the boy's eye with a large hypodermic needle intending to inject his eye but we do not see the needle go into the eyeball (we hear that the Nazis would inject children's eyes to experiment with iris pigmentation).

- 2 F-words, 7 sexual references, 4 scatological terms, 1 anatomical term, 3 mild obscenities, name-calling (retarded, crazy, freak, hag), 3 religious' exclamations.
- College-aged people drink in a nightclub, a woman says she needs a drink, and a woman blames another woman's hallucinations on being drunk. Later, one of them is seen throwing up in a toilet.
- There are plenty of jump scares and imagery that might scare younger viewers.
- A scene at a concentration camp is shown, and a Nazi scientist is shown poking a needle into a young boy's eye and injecting something. There is [sic] a lot of frightening demonic scenes.
- An old lady is chased by a mutilated (possessed) old man and she falls down the stairs.
- An exorcism is shown at the end that is very intense.

To put it mildly, parents seeking to protect their children from inappropriate material would be ill-advised to rely on the MPAA "PG-13" rating for *The Unborn*. While viewer age is, in fact, the broadest metric for determining film suitability, especially with Holocaust films, age makes a very blunt cut; age and ratings are the first steps of due diligence, not the last.

Since Albert Bandura's 1961 "Bobo Doll Experiment,"[16] a debate has raged about violence in films and on television. The suitability of sex and violence in pop culture was Tipper Gore's signature project when her husband, Al, was a Senator, even before she was second lady.[17] Yet, while few would argue that *Dirty Harry* (1971) spawned a generation of extrajudicial cops or that *The King of Comedy* (1982) led to an uptick in celebrity kidnappings, most adults would argue for imposing some age restrictions in film and on television. The specific question here, of course, is: can the Holocaust be taught without depicting sex or violence? Of the 52 recommended Holocaust films in Chapter 9, 34 titles are MPAA (or non–American equivalent) rated milder than "R" (under age 17 requires accompanying parent or adult guardian).

In the end, however, the objectionable material in all Holocaust films is less jarring than the underlying information about genocide that must be taught. Indeed, the decision to teach the Holocaust is ultimately a choice to teach about inhumanity, regardless of the number of Jewish survivors or rare righteous Gentiles. The Holocaust is objectionable, vile, debasing, sexist, violent, racist and cruel to the extent that it otherwise should be unspeakable, except within the context of education as a method to remember and to prevent the Holocaust from reoccurring. Survivors of other traumas do not need to relive, retell or reenact their experiences, except to heal, to seek justice or as a cautionary tale; we do not learn about the Holocaust to heal or to find justice, but to recognize and prevent future acts of inhumanity. And that lesson is uncomfortable and untidy, regardless of the teaching method. Do students need to see depictions of murder or torture to understand it? That question is not mine to answer. I can simply say that, if the decision has been made to reinforce Holocaust lessons with narrative depictions, many of the recommended films will achieve that goal.

Students: Prior Education

After students' age is considered, educators must ascertain the students' level of prior Holocaust education specifically, and knowledge of history, generally. Holocaust films should not be used to teach history or stories, but to reinforce concepts that have already been taught. For example, without basic knowledge about the Final Solution and without understanding why the Germans occupied the Netherlands, watching many Anne Frank films is no different from watching many non–Holocaust films about hidden families. Without proper preparation, most Holocaust films that are worth using can also be confusing, at best, and damaging, at worst.

Students: Aptitude

Some students have higher intellectual aptitude than others. Some classes are accelerated or AP, while others are less ambitious. The ability to process complex stories is a critical variable when selecting Holocaust films. Some stories are familiar and formulaic, requiring less processing, while others contain so much information that they become white noise. For example, *The Resistance Banker* (2018) tells an extremely complex true story about Dutch bankers who subvert their German occupiers by borrowing a billion dollars which is guaranteed by the exiled Dutch government in London to fund the Dutch resistance. The methods of subterfuge are so complicated that one can easily lose interest in the film. Thankfully, other films, such as the great French *The Two of Us—Le vieil homme et l'enfant* (1967), tell smaller stories that are accessible to all. Except for the most advanced students, because of the additional demands of Holocaust films, it is best to aim slightly lower than presumed, even with the Holocaust films recommended in this book.

Students: Emotional Maturity and Uptake

As opposed to most other historical subjects, Holocaust studies require emotional maturity, which is often an educational bottleneck. Teaching about genocide, if taught well, raises a myriad of questions about national and individual responsibility. Access to victims' stories—whether survivors, literary figures, or in films—is intended to personalize the Holocaust, which, in turn, requires emotional processing. While wars may be taught in history classes, seldom are individuals from such historical events personalized or, in fact, asked to speak to a class. For example, when teaching about World War I, whether in European or American classrooms, seldom were individual testimonies used to personalize those who languished in putrefied trenches for months at a time, perhaps eating their fallen horses, or of those who endured chemical-weapons attacks. The same is true for most historical events, from politics to famines. Conversely, the heuristic tool most identified with Holocaust education is the personalization of the incomprehensible event.

In Holocaust studies, prioritizing academic aptitude over emotional processing ability is a losing proposition. The correct film choice encourages proper emotional processing, while offering an opportunity for educators to observe real-time emotional uptake. Finally, it cannot be stressed enough that showing a Holocaust film should not be regarded as a coffee break for the instructor; students must be monitored as they are escorted into the deep-end of Holocaust representation.

Students: Religious/National Orientation and Homogeneity

Many religions and countries differ in their World War II orientations. Some populations are defensive, tacitly acknowledging culpability, while others dwell on the world's missed opportunity to coalesce to stop the German genocide of European Jews. Others have a sense of pride for fighting back and protecting Jews, while others, obviously, view themselves as victims. Many Chinese students visiting Yad Vashem, for example, view themselves as Holocaust victims, conflating Chinese suffering at the hands of the Japanese with Jewish suffering. The Bulgarians and Danes are proud of their protection of their Jewish citizens. The French and Germans have officially apologized for their respective (and vastly different) roles in the Holocaust. American Jews have a different perspective than do Israeli Jews or Russian Jews, each reflecting different national narratives and collective experiences during the War. So, too, denominational differences in Holocaust perspectives exist. Some view the Holocaust strictly as a theological challenge, while others use the Holocaust as a springboard for Zionism.

When teaching the Holocaust and choosing a Holocaust film, homogeneity (or heterogeneity) of the class must be addressed. For example, a 12th grade Jewish day-school class might properly screen *God on Trial* (TV 2008), which grapples with theological questions, while a theologically heterogeneous class of the same aged students may be overwhelmed with those concepts, and would benefit more from *Conspiracy* (TV 2001), which forthrightly portrays the 1942 Wannsee Conference, where the German leadership coordinated the Final Solution. In short, students' demographics are a critical factor to consider when choosing the correct Holocaust film.

Students: Ability and Willingness to Read Subtitles

Subtitles can be an important factor in the comprehension of a film. Bad subtitling can throw off viewers and be distracting. Even seamless subtitling can be too much for many students and age groups. The Hungarian *Son of Saul* (2015) is a good film, but it is also almost impossible for non–Hungarians to follow because the cinematography pulls eyes away from the subtitles; the plot about a confused, irrational Sonderkommando is hard enough to comprehend, even without a language barrier. Likewise, while the best Anne Frank in hiding film is the 128-minute German version of *The Diary of Anne Frank*—*Das Tagebuch Der Anne Frank* (2016), subtitles are required for non–German-speakers. Although an hour longer, *Anne Frank: The Whole Story* (TV 2001) is a better film for English speakers. Viewers can become so subtitle-fatigued that any educational opportunity can be squandered when screening the wrong film.

Objectives

Although certainly not exhaustive, Table 30 matches approximately 60 specific Holocaust subjects with suitable films. In some cases, many more films exist. In some cases, like "Death and/or concentration camps," only the best of many films are listed. In some cases, such as the "T4 Program," only one film covers the topic. See Appendix I: List of Holocaust Films for more topics and matching films. The films are listed by date, not necessarily by quality.

TABLE 30: SOFTA: OBJECTIVES—MATCHING TOPICS TO FILMS

Objective	Relevant Films
America's Official Response During the Holocaust	*Varian's War: The Forgotten Hero* (TV 2001); *Haven* (TV 2001)

Objective	Relevant Films
Accompanied by Children's Books	*The Island on Bird Street* (1997); *Run Boy Run—Lauf Junge lauf* (2013); Anne Frank
Animated Holocaust Films	*Sarah and the Squirrel* (1982); *The Diary of Anne Frank—Anne no nikki* (1995); *Anne Frank's Diary—Le Journal d'Anne Frank* (1999); *A Jewish Girl in Shanghai* (2010); *Where Is Anne Frank* (2021)
Antisemitic Gentile	*Mr. Klein—Monsieur Klein* (1976); *Aftermath—Poklosie* (2012); *1945* (2017)
Axis Countries' Cooperation with the Germans	*The Shop on Main Street—Obchod na korze* (1965); *The Garden of the Finzi-Continis—Il Giardino dei Finzi-Contini* (1970); *Gloomy Sunday—Ein Lied von Liebe und Tod* (1999); *Divided We Fall—Musíme si pomáhat* (2000); *The Third Half—Treto poluvreme* (2012); *1945* (2017)
Babi Yar	*The Taras' Family—The Unvanquished—Nepokoryonnye* (1945); *Ladies' Tailor—Damskiy portnoy* (1990); *Babij Jar* (2003)
Children in the Holocaust	*The Two of Us—Le vieil homme et l'enfant* (1967); *Korczak* (1990) *Look to the Sky—Jona che visse nella balena* (1993); *Edges of the Lord* (2001); *Run Boy Run—Lauf Junge lauf* (2013)
Christocentric Holocaust	*Conspiracy of Hearts* (1960); *The Hiding Place* (1975); *Miracle at Moreaux* (TV 1986); *Bonhoeffer: Agent of Grace* (TV 2000); *Edges of the Lord* (2001); *Amen.* (2002)
Concentration Camp Liberation	*Band of Brothers*; Episode 9 (TV 2001); *The Relief of Belsen* (TV 2007)
Cultural Sensitivity Vis-À-Vis Antisemitism	*American History X* (1998); *The Believer* (2001) (All Non-Holocaust films)
Death Camp Revolts	*Escape from Sobibor* (TV 1987); *The Grey Zone* (2001); *Son of Saul* (2015); *Sobibor* (2018)
Escaping	*The Pianist* (2002); *Defiance* (2008); *Run Boy Run—Lauf Junge lauf* (2013)
Escaping After Jumping from a Train	*Diamonds of the Night—Démanty noci* (1964); *Angry Harvest—Bittere Ernte* (1985); *The Last Train—Der Letzte Zug* (2006)
Extermination Process	*The Grey Zone* (2001); *Amen.* (2002); *Auschwitz* (2011); *Colette* (2013)
Fascist Individual Tendencies	*The Wave* (TV 1981); *The Memory Thief* (2007); *Non-Holocaust films American History X* (1998); *The Believer* (2001) (Mostly Non-Holocaust films)
German National Guilt	*The Nasty Girl—Das schreckliche Mädchen* (1990); *Three Days in April—Drei Tage im April* (TV 1995); *Labyrinth of Lies—Im Labyrinth Des Schweigens* (2014); *1945* (2017)
Ghettos	*Border Street—Ulica Graniczna* (1948); *For Those I Loved—Au nom de tous les miens* (1983); *Korczak* (1990); *The Island on Bird Street* (1997); *Uprising* (TV 2001); *The Pianist* (2002); *Ghetto—Vilniaus getas* (2005); *In Darkness* (2011); *Süskind* (2012)
Hiding	*The Revolt of Job—Jób lázadása* (1983); *Anne Frank: The Whole Story* (TV 2001); *Edges of the Lord* (2001); *The Diary of Anne Frank—Das Tagebuch Der Anne Frank* (2016)
Hiding Circumcision	*The Two of Us—Le vieil homme et l'enfant* (1967); *A Bag of Marbles—Un sac de billes* (1975); *Au Revoir les Enfants* (1987); *Europa Europa* (1990); *Edges of the Lord* (2001); *Run Boy Run—Lauf Junge lauf* (2013); *A Bag of Marbles—Un Sac De Billes* (2017)
Holocaust Comedies	*Genghis Cohn* (1993); *Train of Life—Train de vie* (1998); *Everything Is Illuminated* (2005); *My Führer—Mein Führer—Die wirklich wahrste Wahrheit über Adolf Hitler* (2007)
Holocaust Denial	*Denial* (2016)

Objective	*Relevant Films*
Holocaust Geography	*Europa Europa* (1990)
Holocaust Time Travel	*The Devil's Arithmetic* (TV 1999); *Forget Me Not: The Anne Frank Story* (TV 1996)
Holocaust Theology	*The Quarrel* (1991); *God on Trial* (TV 2008)
Homosexual Holocaust Film	*Bent* (1997); *A Love to Hide—Un amour à taire* (2005); *Facing Windows—La Finestra di fronte* (2003)
Industrialists Despoiled	*Gloomy Sunday—Ein Lied von Liebe und Tod* (1999); *The Aryan Couple* (2004)
Jewish Resistance	*For Those I Loved—Au nom de tous les miens* (1983); *Hanna's War* (1988); *Korczak* (1990); *Uprising* (TV 2001); *Defiance* (2008); *Süskind* (2012); *Haven* (TV 2001)
Justice and Retribution	*Nuremberg* (TV 2000); *Labyrinth of Lies—Im Labyrinth Des Schweigens* (2014); *The People vs. Fritz Bauer—Der Staat gegen Fritz Bauer* (2015)
Mass Shootings	*War; Remembrance* (Miniseries 1988) (Partial); *Babij Jar* (2003)
Polish National Guilt	*Aftermath—Poklosie* (2012); *Ida* (2013)
Post-War Survivor Aftermath	*The Quarrel* (1991); *Under the Domim Tree—Etz Hadomim Tafus* (1994); *Dear Mr. Waldman—Michtavim Le America* (2006)
Post-War Germany	*Murderers Among Us—Die Mörder sind unter uns* (1946); *The Search* (1948); *Judgment at Nuremberg* (1961); *Nuremberg* (2000); *Relief of Belsen* (TV 2007)
Precursors and the Rise of Nazism	*The Great Dictator* (1940); *Ship of Fools* (1965); *Cabaret* (1972); *Julia* (1977); *Invincible* (2001); *Max* (2002)
Reparations and Restitution	*Woman in Gold* (2015)
Righteous Gentiles—Smaller Stories	*Angry Harvest—Bittere Ernte* (1985); *Au Revoir les Enfants* (1987); *Divided We Fall—Musíme si pomáhat* (2000)
Righteous Gentiles—Larger Stories	*Good Evening, Mr. Wallenberg—God afton, Herr Wallenberg—En Passionshistoria från verkligheten* (1990); *Perlasca. The Courage of a Just Man* (TV 2002); *Akte Grüninger* (TV 2013); *Persona Non Grata—Sugihara Chiune* (2015); *The Zookeeper's Wife* (2017)
French Round Up and Deportation	*Mr. Klein Monsieur Klein* (1976); *The Round Up—La rafle* (2010); *Sarah's Key—Elle s'appelait Sarah* (2010)
T4 Program	*Amen.* (2002)
Transport	*The Last Train—Der Letzte Zug* (2006)
Death Camp Uprisings	*Escape from Sobibor* (TV 1987); *The Grey Zone* (2001); *Son of Saul* (2015); *Sobibor* (2018)
Wannsee Conference and Nuremberg Laws	*The Final Solution: The Wannsee Conference—Die Wannseekonferenz* (TV 1984); *Conspiracy* (TV 2001)
Specific German Camps	*Relevant Films*
Auschwitz/Birkenau Death Camps	*Sophie's Choice* (1982); *Kornblumenblau* (1989); *Triumph of the Spirit* (1989); *The Grey Zone* (2001); *The Birch-Tree Meadow—La petite prairie aux bouleaux* (2003); *Colette* (2013); *Son of Saul* (2015)
Bergen-Belsen Concentration Camp	*Pursuit* (TV 1989); *Anne Frank: The Whole Story* (TV 2001); *The Relief of Belsen* (TV 2007)
Buchenwald Concentration Camp	*Naked Among Wolves—Nackt unter Wölfen* (1963); *Naked Among Wolves—Nackt unter Wölfen* (TV 2015); *Fateless—Sorstalanság* (2005)
Dachau Concentration Camp	*Bent* (1997)
Jasenovac Concentration Camp	*The Ninth Circle—Deveti krug* (1960); *Dara of Jasenovac—Dara iz Jasenovca* (2020)

Specific German Camps	Relevant Films
Majdanek Death Camp	*Simon Konianski* (2009)
Mauthausen Concentration Camp	*The Counterfeiters—Die Fälscher* (2007); *The Photographer of Mauthausen—El fotógrafo de Mauthausen* (2018)
Ravensbrück Concentration Camp	*The Hiding Place* (1975); *Olga* (2004)
Sachsenhausen Concentration Camp	*The Counterfeiters—Die Fälscher* (2007)
Sobibor Death Camp	*Escape from Sobibor* (TV 1987); *Sobibor* (2018)
Theresienstadt Concentration Camp	*Distant Journey—Daleká cesta* (1950); *Distant Journey—Daleká cesta* (1950); *The Last Butterfly—Poslední motýl* (1991)
Treblinka Death Camp	*Pursuit* (TV 1989); *For Those I Loved—Au nom de tous les miens* (1983)
Westerbork Concentration Camp	*Look to the Sky—Jona che visse nella balena* (1993); *Süskind* (2012)
Specific Individuals	**Relevant Films**
Adolf Eichmann	*The Man Who Captured Eichmann* (TV 1996); *Adolf Eichmann* (2007); *The Eichmann Show* (TV 2015); *Operation Finale* (2018)
Adolf Hitler	*Max* (2002); *My Führer—Mein Führer—Die wirklich wahrste Wahrheit über Adolf Hitler* (2007)
Anne Frank	*The Attic: The Hiding of Anne Frank* (TV 1988); *Anne Frank: The Whole Story* (TV 2001); *The Diary of Anne Frank—Das Tagebuch Der Anne Frank* (2016)
Janusz Korczak	*Korczak* (1990); *Uprising* (TV 2001); *The Zookeeper's Wife* (2017)
Josef Mengele	*Playing for Time* (TV 1980); *Out of the Ashes* (TV 2003); *The German Doctor—Wakolda* (2013)
Oskar Schindler	*Schindler's List* (1993)
Primo Levi	*The Truce—La tregua* (1997); *Primo* (TV 2005)
Raoul Wallenberg	*Wallenberg—A Hero's Story* (TV 1985); *Good Evening, Mr. Wallenberg—God afton, Herr Wallenberg—En Passionshistoria från verkligheten* (1990)
Sugihara Chiune	*Nippon no Shindorâ: Sugihara Chiune monogatari* (TV 2005); *Persona Non Grata—Sugihara Chiune* (2015)

Follow-Up

Below are five subcategories of follow-up after having screened a Holocaust film: Answering questions; Emotional Triage; Journaling; Workbooks, Further Reading or Watching; and Academic Examination. Implicitly, these topics are often treated as afterthoughts that should, instead, be forethoughts.

Follow-Up: Answering Questions

The form of this subsection implies the elimination of unstructured or non-moderated "discussion." Allowing students open-ended group conversation after viewing a Victim or Gentile film largely invites non-focused or meandering questions and can become an exercise in peer-interaction that is irrelevant or inappropriate. For example, "socially conscious" discussions can ensue, comparing the treatment of Jews during the Holocaust to the treatment of Jews today or the treatment of any minority during any historical period. While these topics might be relevant when studying the Holocaust within the context of a course about historical minority oppression, for the most part, these discussions can easily devolve into suppositions and aspirations, as opposed to being about the Holocaust or the specific film.

After screening a Holocaust film, care must be taken to answer questions and fill in historical holes, allowing students to absorb the film and process emotions. Consequently, teachers must be well-versed about screened films and should anticipate major questions that will be asked. When time is limited, it is advisable to frontload the discussion by proactively addressing the most frequently asked questions. Historical veracity and artistic meaning can also be preemptively addressed. Educators might also provide index cards for questions, which can be sorted by importance. Questions that might require inordinate time or for which the teacher simply does not know the answer can be set aside and answered in subsequent classes and materials.

With Holocaust film, educators are most effective when knowledgeable about the films shown. Reviews from top critics are generally listed on IMDb, MetaCritic and RottenTomatoes. Reading reviews by top critics is crucial to understanding films. For example, the late Roger Ebert wrote two elucidating reviews about *The Grey Zone*, both of which might be made available to students post-screening. In addition, the primary source material is always useful. To understand *The Grey Zone*, a familiarity with Dr. Miklós Nyiszli's *Auschwitz: A Doctor's Eyewitness Account* is also advisable for educators and older students. Preparation for inevitable post-viewing questions is also worthwhile. Typical questions (and answers) for *The Grey Zone* may include:

QUESTION: *Was the girl who was depicted as surviving the gas chamber based on a true story?*
ANSWER: Yes, according to Dr. Nyiszli's account, one person is reported to have survived the gassing. Unlike the portrayal in *The Grey Zone*, the surviving girl was almost immediately murdered by the Germans.

QUESTION: *Did the Jewish prisoners actually destroy two of the Birkenau gas chambers?*
ANSWER: Yes, and those facilities were never rebuilt.

QUESTION: *What was the relationship between the prisoners at Birkenau and the ammunition factory?*
ANSWER: The women smuggled gunpowder from the Weichsel-Union-Metallwerke munitions factory, which was part of the Auschwitz complex of 45 sub-labor camps. These smugglers were some of the estimated 100,000 slave laborers at Birkenau.

QUESTION: *Why did the Sonderkommando appear to be well-fed and relatively independent? This seems unrealistic at Auschwitz/Birkenau.*
ANSWER: Yes, Sonderkommando, as explained in the film, were given certain privileges in exchange for manning the killing process.

QUESTION: *Did the Jews really operate the killing process for food?*
ANSWER: The Sonderkommando had two choices: work or die.

QUESTION: *Was music really played at the entrance to the gas chamber?*
ANSWER: No, that is an amalgamation. Music was played at Birkenau's main gate and could not be heard at the crematoria complex. But similarly depicted music, in fact, was used in the killing process at the Belzec Death Camp, 350 kilometers away from Auschwitz.

QUESTION: *Then why did the film show an orchestra over the crematoria entrance?*
ANSWER: The filmmaker took artistic license to approximate the general idea that the Germans used live music to distract prisoners.

QUESTION: *Did anyone actually escape during the Birkenau uprising?*
ANSWER: A few prisoners briefly escaped, but all were found and murdered.

QUESTION: *Was the Birkenau uprising the only death camp uprising?*
ANSWER: No, there were uprisings at the Sobibor and Treblinka death camps, and also in the Warsaw Ghetto. Further, there were many smaller and less-celebrated acts of resistance and self-defense, including in Krakow, December 22, 1942, when approximately a dozen Germans were killed.

QUESTION: *How accurate was the depicted killing process?*
ANSWER: It was mostly accurate. However, the arriving Jews had been stuffed into cattle cars for several days, transported from Hungary without food, water or facilities, so the depiction of freshness was inaccurate. Luggage also would have been taken from the prisoners when disembarking the train. And men and women walked into the crematorium complex separately and were murdered separately.

QUESTION: *Why were these inaccuracies in the film?*
ANSWER: Narrative films are assumed to be fictional. Still, the core events depicted in *The Grey Zone* are close enough to the actual circumstances to enable the viewer to understand what happened in Birkenau.

QUESTION: *If the point of* The Grey Zone *was not to depict the conditions at Birkenau, what was the point of* The Grey Zone?
ANSWER: *The Grey Zone* is not an Auschwitz/Birkenau documentary. Instead, *The Grey Zone* was intended to express how some Jews were forced to make the excruciating moral choice between assisting the Germans or being murdered.

Follow-Up: Emotional Triage

During and after a Holocaust film, educators must "read the room," being prepared to pull aside any students who still need time to process the representations. In the case of Holocaust films, however, students lacking any emotional reaction might be a bigger red flag than those tearing-up or otherwise seemingly upset. The mental health professionals within the educational institution might also be consulted before screening, both for input concerning any "at-risk" students and as a post-screening safety-net.

Follow-Up: Journaling

Students should be encouraged to "journal" about their feelings throughout Holocaust education, especially after emotional lessons. Suggest a reasonable minimum number of words or minutes devoted to each entry. Some students might, instead, benefit from "bullet journaling," which is especially easy on smart devices. Students should not be asked to reveal or share private writings. Journaling is intended as a safe space to articulate the emotions that are triggered by difficult information and experiences. Students are often more forthcoming when they are assured that their writings are private.

Follow-Up: Workbooks, Further Reading or Watching

In most cases, additional films and printed resources are useful after Holocaust films. As mentioned above, at a minimum, reviews can fill in many of the holes about a film. Further, although anecdotal, when students believe that they have watched a great film, they internalize it more fully. Culling through reviews for films that are intended for screening is an instructive and necessary exercise to gain mastery over the subject.

Overall, many choices of educational Holocaust literature are also available and resources exist to distinguish them. Students deserve to have the most appropriate materials. While, for example, Anne Frank's teenage observations are important, *The Diary of a Young Girl*, the most-read Holocaust book in history, provides only a tiny fraction of Holocaust education. A great start in the hunt for other Holocaust diaries is Alexandra Zapruder's 2002 book *Salvaged Pages: Young Writers' Diaries of the Holocaust* (Yale University Press). Further, the following (mostly middle-school) books provide a deeper and broader understanding of the Holocaust:

- 1958—Elie Wiesel: *Night*, about a teenager, set in Auschwitz;
- 1969—Hans Peter Richter: *Friedrich,* or in original German *Damals war es Friedrich,* about a Jewish boy's experiences during the War in Germany;
- 1986—Janina Bauman: *Winter in the Morning: A Young Girl's Life in the Warsaw Ghetto and Beyond, 1939–1945* gets to the heart of the Holocaust's terror;
- 1991—Art Spiegelman: *Maus* is a better choice for Holocaust education than Anne Frank's diary;
- 1991—Pearl Benisch: *To Vanquish the Dragon* tells the story of a devoutly religious girl's facing down the Holocaust;
- 1996—Halina Birenbaum: *Hope Is the Last to Die,* about growing up in the Warsaw Ghetto;
- 1999—Livia Bitton-Jackson: *I Have Lived a Thousand Years: Growing Up in the Holocaust,* about being imprisoned in Auschwitz as a teenager;
- 2008—Krystyna Chiger and Daniel Paisner: *The Girl in the Green Sweater: A Life in Holocaust's Shadow,* about evading capture;
- 2009—Ram Oren: *Gertruda's Oath: A Child, a Promise, and a Heroic Escape During World War II*, about a Jewish boy escaping from Poland to Palestine;
- 2013—Leon Leyson: *The Boy on the Wooden Box: How the Impossible Became Possible on Schindler's List,* about life in and after the Krakow Ghetto;
- 2015—Israel Starck: *A Boy Named 68818,* an illustrated memoir that tells a full story of life in Auschwitz.

Additionally, the Jewish Book Council suggests the following 48 "Holocaust Books for Middle-Grade Readers," none of which is Anne Frank's diary, but two of which are her biographies[18]:

A Boy in War	*Bjorn's Gift*
A Friend Called Anne	*Black Radishes*
A Time to Be Brave	*Emil and Karl*
Anne Frank: The Young Writer Who Told the World Her Story	*Escape from Berlin*
Anne Frank: Young Diarist	*Escaping Into the Night*
Beyond Courage: The Untold Story of Jewish Resistance During the Holocaust	*Escaping the Nazis on the Kindertransport*
	Fania's Heart
	Greenhorn

Hana's Suitcase: Anniversary Album
Honey Cake
Irena's Children: A True Story of Courage
Kanada
Like Finding My Twin: How an Eighth-Grade Class
  Reunited Two Holocaust Refugees
Now
Number the Stars: 25th Anniversary Edition
Numbers
Odette's Secrets
Otto: The Autobiography of a Teddy Bear
Prisoner B-3087
Seeking Refuge
Someone Named Eva
Somewhere There Is Still a Sun: A Memoir of the
  Holocaust
Spaghetti Rain
Stones on a Grave
Stumbling on History: An Art Project Compels a
  Small German Town to Face Its Past

Survivors Club
T4: A Novel in Verse
The Dollmaker of Krakow
The End of the Line
The Entertainer and the Dybbuk
The Lily Pond
The Midnight Zoo
The Mozart Question
The Righteous Smuggler
The Tattered Prayer Book
Tuky: The Story of a Hidden Child
Viktor Frankl: A Life Worth Living
What the Night Sings
Whispers from the Camps
Whispers from the Ghettos
Wordwings (Essential Prose)
Would You Salute? One Child's Story of the
  Holocaust

And the Jewish Book Council also recommends 18 "Holocaust Books for Children," none of which is Anne Frank's diary, but includes two Anne Frank biographies. (*Escape from Berlin* is common to both lists)[19]:

A Concert in the Sand
Anne Frank
Anne Frank and the Remembering Tree
Escape from Berlin
Gifts from the Enemy
Hedy's Journey: The True Story of a Hungarian
  Girl Fleeing the Holocaust
Irena Sendler and the Children of the Warsaw
  Ghetto
Janusz Korczak's Children
Jars of Hope

Mister Doctor: Janusz Korczak & the Orphans of
  the Warsaw Ghetto
The Hiding Game
The Magician of Auschwitz
The Orphan Rescue
The Patchwork Torah
The Secret of the Village Fool
The Whispering Town
The Wren and the Sparrow
Through Eva's Eyes

In addition, the Yad Vashem Pedagogical Center* notes other diaries written by young Holocaust victims:

- 1971—Moshe Flinker: *Young Moshe's Diary*, Yad Vashem and the Board of Jewish Education;
- 1974—Éva Heyman: *The Diary of Éva Heyman: Child of the Holocaust by Éva Heyman*, Yad Vashem;
- 2007—Chava Pressburger: *The Diary of Petr Ginz, 1941–1942*, Grove Press.

The Pedagogical Center also notes these stories of Holocaust survivors written for children:

- 2003—Emilie Cohn Roi: *A Different Story, About a Danish Girl in World War II*, Yad Vashem;
- 2007—Naomi Morgenstern: *The Daughter We Had Always Wanted—The Story*

---

 * Special thanks to Nohar Cohen from the *Yad Vashem* Pedagogical Center.

of Marta, Yad Vashem, the Holocaust Martyrs' and Heroes' Remembrance Authority, International School for Holocaust Studies;
- 2015—Henry Foner (Heinz Lichtwitz): *Postcards to a Little Boy: A Kindertransport Story*, Yad Vashem Publications.

And, most importantly, the Pedagogical Center also suggested the following two autobiographical books, both written by Holocaust survivor Uri Orlev, and both produced as recommended films with the same titles:

- 1992—Uri Orlev: *The Island on Bird Street*, HMH Books for Young Readers, *The Island on Bird Street* (1997);
- 2003—Uri Orlev: *Run, Boy, Run*, HMH Books for Young Readers, *Run Boy Run— Lauf Junge lauf* (2013).

Follow-Up: Academic Examination

Very few meaningful questions about the Holocaust are binary or multiple choice. There is no single answer for why the Germans undertook the Holocaust or why the Jews were slaughtered in community after community across Europe. Many factual questions—about names, dates and places—distract from the complexity of the Holocaust. Open-ended queries that are tied to films and their accompanying film reviews can pull together a topic. For example, Roger Ebert's review of *The Pianist* (2002) includes the following passage:

> By showing [Wladyslaw] Szpilman as a survivor but not a fighter or a hero—as a man who does all he can to save himself, but would have died without enormous good luck and the kindness of a few non-Jews—[Roman] Polanski is reflecting, I believe, his own deepest feelings: that he survived, but need not have, and that his mother died and left a wound that had never healed. After the war, we learn, Szpilman remained in Warsaw and worked all of his life as a pianist. His autobiography was published soon after the war, but was suppressed by Communist authorities because it did not hew to the party line (some Jews were flawed and a German was kind). Republished in the 1990s, it caught Polanski's attention and resulted in this film, which refuses to turn Szpilman's survival into a triumph and records it primarily as the story of a witness who was there, saw, and remembers.[20]

With this passage, examination questions for *The Pianist* might include:

- If most of Poland's Jews were murdered by the Germans, what point was being made in *The Pianist*?
- What is *The Pianist* saying by having Szpilman saved by a German soldier?
- How was Szpilman changed by the War?

Time

This section is a guide to academically time-sensitive aspects within Holocaust film study, including: Amount of Time Devoted to Holocaust Study; Specific Film Preparation Time; Follow-Up Time; and Presentations by Survivors or Other Experts.

Time: Amount of Time Devoted to Holocaust Study

Teachers who only have a few classroom days to teach a Holocaust unit are advised to organize an extracurricular event for the screening of an appropriate Holocaust film. Holocaust study demands many hours of standard classroom instruction. When restricted to very brief Holocaust unit-duration (a few days), the best use of time is simply teaching the Holocaust, rather than screening supplemental Holocaust films.

Individual class duration is also the biggest impediment to viewing a Holocaust film. Most recommended Holocaust films run approximately 120 minutes. While "homeroom" classes that span the entire morning or afternoon are ideal for screening films, standard 50-minute classes definitely do not lend themselves to full-length feature films. Breaking up Holocaust films into 45-minute chunks is a work-around, but organizing an extracurricular event is preferable.

With limited time, some educators, too, might opt to use film clips instead of screening entire productions. Using clips can be a more efficient use of time, although such a practice may be jarring or even sacrilegious for film enthusiasts. Cinematic sanctimony aside, using clips can be exceptionally effective. In my lecture to educators, I have strung together a few sets of clips as examples. One set is a three-minute clip called "Find the Jews," which includes scenes from *Gentleman's Agreement* (1947), *Exodus* (1960), *The Two of Us* (1967) and *School Ties* (1992), each scene with an ignorant person being unable to identify the Jewish person in the room, despite rhetoric to the contrary. This clip can be used to illustrate ingrained antisemitism. Another three-minute clip called "Systematic Despoliation," depicts the German practice of collecting and separating the items taken from Jews upon arrival at Auschwitz/Birkenau, with clips from *Colette* (2013), *The Grey Zone* (2001) and *Schindler's List* (1993). And, finally, I show a single clip from *Varian's War: The Forgotten Hero* (TV 2001) which summarizes in two minutes the American State Department's regrettable attitude toward saving the Jews. The 20-minute segment of *Band of Brothers* (Miniseries 2001) "Why We Fight" is also a viable candidate for showing a concentration camp liberation. With the films listed in the above "Objectives" section, innumerable such teaching moments can be gathered. As a film purist, chopping up film is understandably not my preferred method, but using clips is a practical and sometimes necessary alternative when inadequate time can be allocated for comprehensive Holocaust study.

Time: Specific Film Preparation Time

As noted above, educators and students must each prepare for Holocaust films. Students need to understand the context, and teachers must be well-versed about the specific film, including reviews, follow-up questions and permission slips, in many cases.

Time: Follow-Up Time

Also as noted above, the projector must not simply be turned off and class dismissed after a harrowing Holocaust film. If the film has merit, students and educators are advised to set aside time to "unpack" the experience.

Time: Presentations by Survivors or Other Experts

Presentations by Holocaust education specialists and Holocaust survivors are also highly recommended in Holocaust education. Nothing personalizes the Holocaust more than a person. Most major Jewish communities have speakers' bureaus which can make the necessary arrangements. If needing to decide between class time for a Holocaust film or class time for a Holocaust survivor, ditch the film and grab the survivor!

Administrative

Using films to teach the Holocaust requires administrative support regarding the issues listed below. While this does not imply that educators are unable to undertake these tasks, having administrative cover when diverging from a traditional curriculum is usually the safest path. Considered here are: Regulations Concerning the Depictions of Sex, Violence and Language; Parental Willingness and/or Consent Forms; Technical Capabilities (Venue, Quality of Media, Audio and Projection); and Mental Health Expert Availability.

Administrative: Regulations Concerning Depictions of Sex, Violence and Language

Some parents will object to any Holocaust film shown, for many reasons. Some will object to violence, sex and crude language, while others will argue that films are inappropriate tools, altogether, for teaching the Holocaust. One such parent was quoted in a 1998 *New York Times* article entitled "Colorado Board Limits Films in Classrooms to PG and PG-13, and Discontent Arises":

> High school history teachers here are no longer permitted to show the Academy Award-winning film *Schindler's List* to illustrate a lesson on the Holocaust…. "I learned about the Holocaust without watching a movie about it," said Jody Bennett, 41, who has two children in the local schools. "The kids can learn about history without having to see the gore of it all through Hollywood." … The new policy does allow teachers to assign films—even those rated R and NC-17—as homework, with parental approval. But Kennard Z. King, a history teacher at Douglas County High, asked: "Where would there be 100 copies of *Schindler's List*? It's absurd, and it defeats the idea of discussing the film."[21]

Without regard for the veracity of Ms. Bennett's complaint, educators who choose to screen any 195-minute film that includes rape, nudity and a seemingly endless barrage of murders are already asking for trouble.

Administrative: Parental Cooperation and/or Consent Forms

Even in localities that do not require permission slips for violent films, the best practice is to obtain parents' explicit consent when showing a Holocaust film. Included with the slip might be a copy of the film's IMDb page, which lists the MPAA rating, IMDb rating, length, number of awards and many other tidbits. Allow enough time for feedback. And provide an alternative activity for students who opt-out.

Administrative: Technical Capabilities (Venue, Quality of Media, Audio and Projection)

The most neglected component when showing Holocaust films is the technical quality of the screening. Bad audio and/or video can ruin a film. The checklist below is a start, but other issues can always arise:

- Find a video source with the highest resolution;
- Before students arrive, manually set the focus, keystone and screen width while the film is paused on the opening credits. The picture should have no white gaps on the sides and the letters should be crisp. Test the video with at least fifteen seconds from three scenes, beginning, middle and end;
- The room should be completely dark;
- The audio controls should be available, with the volume adjusted periodically. Test the audio by sitting in the middle-front and middle-back;
- For films that require subtitles, the language should be set in advance and subtitle size should be slightly larger than standard (which can be set with many video players);
- Test the A/V system before students arrive;
- Ideally, chairs should be staggered neatly in "theater-style";
- Putting feet up on chairs during Holocaust films is incredibly disruptive and should be strongly discouraged;
- Cell phones should be turned off;
- Students should be encouraged to use the facilities before the film starts;
- Note-taking by students is generally unnecessary during narrative Holocaust films;
- Students should be informed that they will not be tested on film details.

Administrative: Mental Health Expert Availability

If the educational institution is staffed with mental health professionals, that staff should be informed about the proposed screening and given the opportunity to be either present or to be available during and after the screening. On the other hand, the surest sign that an overly ambitious film has been presented is the post-screening need for intervention by a mental health professional.

Summary

Teaching the Holocaust using film instead of primary texts is like taking a bus tour instead of a walking tour: you get there faster on a bus, but the pace and view are determined by your driver (director). Even if you take a bus, at some point you must walk on and off. Similarly, using narrative film is only part of the educational journey. Educators must always know where the film is going and must guide their passengers as they embark, travel and disembark.

9

Recommended
Holocaust Films

Only a tiny percentage of the thousands of non–Holocaust films made each year can be recommended or will win major awards. Perhaps just a few dozen. Using that baseline, only a handful of the 443 Holocaust films should be worthy of recommendation. But, strictly on a percentage basis, finding a good Holocaust film is, in fact, much easier—by magnitudes—than finding a good non–Holocaust film. On the other hand, while many of the recommended Holocaust films here have not received any Oscars or other awards (or even made a profit), they are still good-to-great Holocaust films. In the non–Holocaust world, the same can be true. For example, Harold Ramis' insightful and entertaining *Groundhog Day* (1993) is rightfully considered one of the 250 greatest films of all time by IMDb users, but was not nominated for any 1994 Oscars.*

As with general lists of Holocaust films, external lists of top Holocaust films are fairly unreliable. Like an x-ray of the spine, most lists of top Holocaust films provide recognizable forms, but the details are less obvious. For example, *Ranker.com*'s crowd-sourced list of the top Holocaust films in Table 31 contains many non–Holocaust and/or inaccessible films.

TABLE 31: RANKER.COM THE BEST MOVIES ABOUT THE HOLOCAUST[1]
Recommended in **Bold** (13 of 52). "One of the Best" in **Bold and Underlined** (4 of 15).
Unavailable films in ~~Strikeout~~ (1).

1. *Schindler's List*	2. ***The Pianist***	3. *The Boy in the Striped Pyjamas*
4. *Life Is Beautiful*	5. *The Diary of Anne Frank*	6. *Escape from Sobibor*
7. ***Defiance***	8. *The Book Thief*	9. ***Sophie's Choice***
10. *Surviving with Wolves*	11. *Judgment at Nuremberg*	12. *Naked Among Wolves*
13. *The Reader*	14. *Woman in Gold*	15. *Playing for Time*
16. *The Devil's Arithmetic*	17. ~~*The Day the Clown Cried*~~	18. *Uprising*
19. *Jacob the Liar*	20. ***Son of Saul***	21. *Europa Europa*
22. ***The Grey Zone***	23. ***God on Trial***	24. *Apt Pupil*
25. ***The Shop on Main Street***	26. *Angry Harvest*	27. *Triumph of the Will*
28. ***The Pawnbroker***	29. ***The Counterfeiters***	30. *Murderers Among Us*

---

* Films nominated for Best Picture instead of *Groundhog Day* at the 1994 Academy Awards: Andrew Davis' *The Fugitive* (1993) starring Harrison Ford; James Ivory's *The Remains of the Day* (1993) starring Anthony Hopkins; Jim Sheridan's *In the Name of the Father* (1993) starring Daniel Day-Lewis; Jane Campion's *The Piano* (1993) starring Holly Hunter and Harvey Keitel; and the winner, *Schindler's List* (1993).

31. *Rosenstrasse*	32. **Phoenix**	33. *Kapò*
34. *Landscape After the Battle*	35. *Triumph of the Spirit*	36. **The Island on Bird Street**
37. *The Ninth Day*	38. *Sunshine*	39. *The Aryan Couple*
40. *Amen.*	41. *Army of Shadows*	42. *Seven Beauties*
43. *Bent*	44. *The Truce*	45. *The Stranger*
46. **Fateless**	47. *Edges of the Lord*	48. *Mr. Death: The Rise and Fall of Fred A. Leuchter, Jr.*
49. *Train of Life*	50. *The Boat Is Full*	51. *Geburtig*
52. **Divided We Fall**		

Included in *Ranker*'s top 20 narrative Holocaust films is Jerry Lewis' never released *The Day the Clown Cried* (1972). *Ranker* also lists the documentary *Mr. Death: The Rise and Fall of Fred A. Leuchter, Jr.* (1999). *Ranker*'s list of the greatest Holocaust films also includes many non–Holocaust films such as *Army of Shadows—L'armée des ombres* (1969), *Seven Beauties—Pasqualino Settebellezze* (1975) and *The Book Thief* (2013). Shockingly, *Ranker* also lists as the 27th greatest Holocaust film of all time *The Triumph of the Will* (1935), the infamous Nazi propaganda film commissioned by Hitler, himself. Regarding the actual quality of the films on *Ranker*'s list, over a third of the titles are simply horrible. Indeed, at least one-quarter of their top 20 Holocaust films are among the most offensive and objectionable Holocaust films ever made, including: *The Devil's Arithmetic* (TV 1999), *Jakob the Liar* (1999), *Surviving with Wolves—Survivre avec les loups* (2007), *The Reader* (2008) and *The Boy in the Striped Pyjamas* (2008).

A more accurate ranking of Holocaust films is found by searching the keyword "Holocaust" on IMDb, and then sorting by the top *MetaCritic.com*'s "Metascores," which is provided on IMDb. (See Table 32.) Notably, of the 28 Holocaust films with the highest Metascore, half are recommended in this Chapter 9.

TABLE 32: TOP METASCORE HOLOCAUST FILMS ON IMDb
Recommended in **Bold** (13 of 52). "One of the Best" in **Bold and Underlined** (7 of 15).

	Film	*Rating*	*Metascore*	*Recommended*
1	Schindler's List (1993)	8.9	93	
2	**Son of Saul (2015)**	7.5	89	Yes
3	**Phoenix (2014)**	7.3	89	Yes
4	**Fateless (2005)**	7.0	87	Yes
5	**The Pianist (2002)**	8.5	85	Yes
6	**The Counterfeiters (2007)**	7.6	78	Yes
7	Lore (2012)	7.1	76	
8	**1945 (2017)**	7.3	75	Yes
9	In Darkness (2011)	7.3	74	
10	Nowhere in Africa (2001)	7.6	72	
11	Black Book (2006)	7.8	71	
12	Sunshine (1999)	7.5	71	
13	**Inglourious Basterds (2009)**	8.3	69	Yes
14	**Divided We Fall (2000)**	7.8	69	Yes
15	**Sophie's Choice (1982)**	7.6	68	Yes
16	Walk on Water (2004)	7.4	65	

	Film	Rating	Metascore	Recommended
17	*Denial* (2016)	6.6	63	
18	*Train of Life* (1998)	7.7	62	
19	***The People vs. Fritz Bauer* (2015)**	7.1	61	Yes
20	***This Must Be the Place* (2011)**	6.7	61	Yes
21	*Judgment at Nuremberg* (1961)	8.2	60	
22	*Gloomy Sunday* (1999)	7.9	60	
23	*Life Is Beautiful* (1997)	8.6	59	
24	*Sarah's Key* (2010)	7.5	59	
25	*The Reader* (2008)	7.6	58	
26	***Everything Is Illuminated* (2005)**	7.5	58	Yes
27	***Defiance* (2008)**	7.2	58	Yes
28	***The Grey Zone* (2001)**	7.1	58	Yes
29	*Adam Resurrected* (2008)	6.3	58	
30	*Amen.* (2002)	7.3	57	
31	*The Zookeeper's Wife* (2017)	7.0	57	
32	*A Bag of Marbles* (2017)	7.3	55	
33	*The Boy in the Striped Pyjamas* (2008)	7.8	55	
34	*Remember* (2015)	7.4	52	
35	*Woman in Gold* (2015)	7.3	51	
36	*Apt Pupil* (1998)	6.7	51	
37	*La Rafle* (2010)	7.0	49	
38	*Jakob the Liar* (1999)	6.5	40	

Interestingly, film critics—as measured by Metascore—and IMDb user ratings differ considerably, with a correlation of only 0.4 between the Metascore and the IMDb user rating. In other words, roughly speaking, the opinions of those who rate films on IMDb often do not match the opinions of professional film critics. The Metascore list, though, provides a fairly accurate snapshot of great Holocaust films.

No minimum number of titles was established for the recommended Holocaust films in this book; the goal was not to find a certain number of Holocaust films, but simply to find the best. The criteria for recommendation are compelling and respectful stories that are either:

- The best version(s) of a non-fictional Holocaust story;
- Fictional stories that best exemplify one of the 4+1 Holocaust Film Genres;
- High production standards, with an emphasis on plot, dialogue, acting, casting, editing, cinematography and educational value.

Noticeably absent from the above criteria are measures of cultural impact: popularity, box office, budget, aggregate user reviews and awards. Ranking Holocaust films strictly by success, fame and reputation is a wholly different undertaking, requiring only a spreadsheet. Of the 443 Holocaust films in Appendix I, 52 are good enough to be recommended here.

These reviews do not plumb the depths of commercial film reviews (which are generally available at *RottenTomatoes* and *MetaCritic*) but are more focused on why each is recommended as a Holocaust film. Between the IMDb rating and its number of votes, along with Oscars/Emmys, the general public reception of each film can otherwise be surmised. Still, excerpts from outside sources (when available) augment most of the reviews below.

It should be noted, too, that very few excellent Victim or Gentile Holocaust films involve romance during the War; in a world where a blade of grass was nourishment and where dehumanization and humiliation were ubiquitous, wartime romantic storylines have mostly failed in Holocaust films. True, romance was actually found by some victims during the Holocaust, but Holocaust love stories in film seem petty in relation to genocide, symptomatic of indolent writing and wayward artistic intentions. Also, beware of Victim and Gentile films with excessive soundtracks, especially with flutes, timpani or violins. The stories should speak for themselves, not needing to be pampered by amorous notions or overly sappy film scores.

Notwithstanding the theory that Holocaust films have become "Oscar Bait," one of six Holocaust films can be recommended. Further, of the remaining 391 films that are not recommended, many are still very well-made, yet have been rendered redundant or obsolete by superior versions. For example, the first three major American Holocaust films—*The Stranger* (1946), *The Search* (1948) and *The Juggler* (1953)—are all solid films that score high in their respective Holocaust film genres. Still, none of those Post-War Era films made the list of recommended films because better films with similar stories were later produced.

The most conspicuous question (especially for those who skipped ahead to this chapter) is: why is the most famous and highest-grossing Holocaust film in history, *Schindler's List* (1993), not a recommended Holocaust film here? For that answer, see Chapter 4. More broadly, why are no American-made righteous Gentile films recommended in this book? The answers to these two questions are intertwined. All of the nine American-made righteous Gentile films (listed in Table 33) are either made-for-television sappy dramas and/or emphasize the heroism of their Gentile protagonists more than the plight of their Jewish victims.

TABLE 33: AMERICAN-MADE RIGHTEOUS GENTILE FILMS

The Hiding Place (1975)
Wallenberg—A Hero's Story (TV 1985)
Miracle at Moreaux (TV 1986)
The Attic: The Hiding of Anne Frank (TV 1988)
Schindler's List (1993)
Miracle at Midnight (TV 1998)
Varian's War: The Forgotten Hero (TV 2001)
The Courageous Heart of Irena Sendler (TV 2009)
The Zookeeper's Wife (2017)

American righteous Gentile films have overtly personalized, romanticized and glorified the saviors, often depersonalizing Holocaust victims, rendering them as feckless props without agency. Conversely, the five recommended European righteous Gentile films—*Au Revoir les Enfants* (1987), *Good Evening, Mr. Wallenberg* (1990), *Akte Grüninger* (TV 2013), *Divided We Fall* (2000) and *The Relief of Belsen* (TV 2007)—all emphasize the plight of the Jews more than glorifying their Gentile protectors.

Each recommended film also includes my "Suggested Minimum Grade." Table 34 breaks down the grade/age by the number of recommended films:

TABLE 34: AGE/GRADE RECOMMENDATION KEY

Grade Groups	Grades	Ages	Number of Recommended Films
Late Grade School	6th–7th	12–13	7
Middle School	8th–10th	14–16	24
High School	11th–12th	17+	21

In some cases, the suggested ages are less informed by sexuality or nudity than by violence. While MPAA ratings were discussed in Chapter 8, only films made after 1968 are MPAA-rated, and even then, the rules and standards have changed. The MPAA scale has been altered and eased, with films that might have been rated "R" in 1975 being rated PG today. Also, since the mid–1990s additional information has been included with the letter rating. For example, the rating for *Schindler's List* (1993) is not a simple "R," but "R for language, some sexuality and actuality violence" (whatever "actuality violence" means). Finally, while some non–American films have been submitted for MPAA ratings, often the rating from local systems is on record. In most cases, the MPAA or Local Rating is listed with each film below, but all suitability ratings are notoriously unreliable.

Determining the suitability of individual films is the responsibility of the adults who are exposing non-adults to films. Appropriateness of art is always subjective, reliant on many factors, which include age, maturity, previous exposure, preparation and cultural concerns. My "Suggested Minimum Grade" is a starting point.

Inglourious Basterds (2009), which has a suggested minimum age of 17 ("High School") and which is categorized by the MPAA as "Rated R for strong graphic violence, language and brief sexuality," should be used for Suggested Minimum Grade calibration. If the responsible adult believes that *Inglourious Basterds* is inappropriate for their high schoolers, then it is advised to bump up each of the Suggested Minimum Grades by one level, i.e.: "Late Grade School" to "Middle School," "Middle" to "High School" and "High School" to adult.

The average length of the recommended Holocaust films is 111 minutes. Eight are made-for-television and 44 are feature films, of which only 14 won or were nominated for an Oscar, resulting in 42 nominations and 25 trophies, with four Best Foreign Language Film winners. Of the 52 recommended films, 36 primarily take place during or just after the Holocaust. The 52 recommended films in this chapter are ordered by the 4+1 Holocaust film genres (Victim, Gentile, Survivor, Perpetrator and Tangential) and then by year. (See Table 35.)

The 52 Best Holocaust Films

TABLE 35: RECOMMENDED HOLOCAUST FILMS, SORTED BY 4+1 GENRE
Recommended in **Bold** (52 of 52). "One of the Best" in **Bold and Underlined** (15 of 15).

Victim Genre (22 Films)				
Title	Length	Language	MPAA	Rec. Min. Grade
Diamonds of the Night— Démanty noci (1964)	63	German	U.K.-15	Middle School
The Two of Us— Le vieil homme et l'enfant (1967)	87	French	Sweden-15	Late Grade School

Title	Length	Language	MPAA	Rec. Min. Grade
The Garden of the Finzi-Continis—Il Giardino dei Finzi-Contini (1970)	94	Italian	U.K.-14+	Late Grade School
For Those I Loved—Au nom de tous les miens (1983)	145	French	Unrated (PG)	High School
Korczak (1990)	118	Polish	PG	Late Grade School
Look to the Sky—Jona che visse nella balena (1993)	100	Italian	Unrated (R)	High School
The Island on Bird Street (1997)	107	English	PG-13	Late Grade School
Anne Frank: The Whole Story (TV 2001)	190	English	12	High School
The Grey Zone (2001)	108	English	R for strong Holocaust violence, nudity and language.	High School
The Pianist (2002)	150	English	R for violence and brief strong language.	Middle School
Fateless—Sorstalanság (2005)	136	Hungarian	R for some disturbing Holocaust images including nudity.	High School
Primo (TV 2005)	79	English	PG	Middle School
The Last Train—Der Letzte Zug (2006)	123	German	Unrated (R)	Middle School
My Führer—Mein Führer—Die wirklich wahrste Wahrheit über Adolf Hitler (2007)	89	German	Unrated (PG)	Middle School
The Counterfeiters—Die Fälscher (2007)	98	German	R for some strong violence, brief sexuality/nudity and language.	High School
Defiance (2008)	137	English	R for violence and language.	High School
God on Trial (TV 2008)	90	English	Unrated (PG)	Middle School
Süskind (2012)	118	Dutch, German	Unrated (PG)	Middle School
Run Boy Run—Lauf Junge lauf (2013)	107	Germany—France—Poland	Unrated (PG)	Late Grade School
My Daughter Anne Frank—Meine Tochter Anne Frank (TV 2015)	90	Germany	Unrated (PG)	Middle School
Son of Saul (2015)	107	German, Hungarian (and others)	R for disturbing violent content, and some graphic nudity.	High School
The Diary of Anne Frank—Das Tagebuch Der Anne Frank (2016)	128	German	Unrated (PG)	Middle School

Gentile Genre (11 Films)				
Title	Length	Language	MPAA	Rec. Min. Grade
The Shop on Main Street—Obchod na korze (1965) **(Antisemitic)**	125	Slovak	U.K.-14+	Middle School
Mr. Klein—Monsieur Klein (1976) **(Antisemitic)**	123	French	U.K.-14+	Middle School

Title	Length	Language	MPAA	Rec. Min. Grade
Au Revoir les Enfants (1987) (Righteous Gentile)	104	French	PG	Late Grade School
Good Evening, Mr. Wallenberg—God afton, Herr Wallenberg—En Passionshistoria från verkligheten (1990) (Righteous Gentile)	118	Swedish	Unrated (R)	High School
Three Days in April—Drei Tage im April (TV 1995) (Antisemitic)	105	German	Unrated (R)	High School
Divided We Fall—Musíme si pomáhat (2000) (Righteous Gentile)	123	German	PG-13 for some violence and sexual content.	Middle School
Conspiracy (TV 2001) (Antisemitic)	96	English	R for language.	Middle School
The Relief of Belsen (TV 2007) (Righteous Gentile)	101	English	PG-13	High School
Akte Grüninger (TV 2013)	96	German	Unrated (PG)	Middle School
Labyrinth of Lies—Im Labyrinth Des Schweigens (2014) (Antisemitic)	122	German	R for a scene of sexuality.	Middle School
1945 (2017) (Antisemitic)	91	Hungarian	Unrated (PG)	Middle School

Survivor Genre (10 Films)				
Title	Length	Language	MPAA	Rec. Min. Grade
The Pawnbroker (1964)	116	English	Sweden-15	Middle School
Harold and Maude (1971)	91	English	PG	High School
The Man in the Glass Booth (1975)	117	English	Unrated (PG)	High School
The Quarrel (1991)	85	English	PG-13	Late Grade School
Under the Domim Tree—Etz Hadomim Tafus (1994)	102	Hebrew	Unrated (PG)	Middle School
The Birch-Tree Meadow—La petite prairie aux bouleaux (2003)	131	French	Unrated (PG)	Middle School
Everything Is Illuminated (2005)	104	English	PG-13 for disturbing images—violence, sexual content and language.	Middle School
Dear Mr. Waldman—Michtavim Le America (2006)	90	Hebrew	PG-13	High School
This Must Be the Place (2011)	118	English	R for language, some sexual content and brief disturbing images.	High School
Phoenix (2014)	96	German—English	PG-13 for some thematic elements and brief suggestive material.	Middle School

Perpetrator Genre (5 Films)				
Title	Length	Language	MPAA	Rec. Min. Grade
The Odessa File (1974)	130	English	PG	Middle School
Marathon Man (1976)	125	English	R	High School
Genghis Cohn (1993)	79	English	Unrated (R)	Middle School
Made in Israel (2001)	113	Hebrew	12	High School
The People vs. Fritz Bauer—Der Staat gegen Fritz Bauer (2015)	105	German	R for some sexual content	High School

Tangential Genre (4 Films)				
Title	Length	Language	MPAA	Rec. Min. Grade
Cabaret (1972)	124	English	PG	High School
Sophie's Choice (1982)	151	English	15	High School
The Last Butterfly—Poslední motýl (1991)	118	Czech	PG-13 for thematic elements	Middle School
Inglourious Basterds (2009)	153	English	R for strong graphic violence, language and brief.	High School

Victim Films

"Victim" genre films are primarily set during the Holocaust. Their protagonists are Jews who suffer mainly during, and as a result of, the Holocaust. Surprisingly, Victim films are the least formulaic Holocaust film genre. For example, half of the Victim films portray the protagonist surviving the Holocaust, while half die. Approximately half of Victim films are based on true stories, while half are completely fictional, although the trend since 1997 has been to produce true victim stories. To date, 156 Victim Holocaust films have been made, of which 22 are recommended, much more than in any other genre. The number of recommendations of Victim films reflects both the disproportionate number of films made in this genre and their focus on core Holocaust settings.

Diamonds of the Night—Démanty noci (1964)

Genre:	Victim
Sub-Genre:	Escaping
Length:	63
MPAA or Local Rating:	U.K.-15
Language:	German
Country:	Czechoslovakia
Director:	Jan Nemec
Top-Billed:	Ladislav Jánsky, Antonín Kumbera, Ilse Bischofova
From Wikipedia:	Diamonds of the Night (Czech: Démanty noci) is a 1964 Czech film about two boys on the run from a train taking them to a concentration camp, based loosely on Arnošt Lustig's autobiographical novel Darkness Has No Shadow. It was director Jan Němec's first full-length feature film.
IMDb Rating:	7.6
IMDb Votes:	1262
Holocaust Cinema Complete Description:	Diamonds of the Night—Démanty noci (1964) portrays the fate of two young Jewish escapees from a deportation train. Injured, starved and desperate, the boys are ultimately hunted down for sport by vicious Czech locals. There is nothing pleasant about this film: no sweet musical score or happy ending. Diamonds of the Night simply concerns itself with the near-impossibility of survival during the Holocaust.
Recommendation:	With a running time of only 63 minutes, Diamonds of the Night is a stark peek into Eastern European complicity during the Holocaust.
Suggested Minimum Grade:	Middle School

REVIEW

Two Jewish boys escape from a train, presumably from a death camp transport. The boys not only had to survive injuries, starvation and the elements, but, more importantly, they unsuccessfully tried to evade local Czechs who were German sympathizers. The boys are freezing, wet, frightened and, ultimately, hunted. Of the several films that depict Jews who jumped from trains, no other is more realistic or compelling than Jan Nemec's *Diamonds of the Night*. In fact, no other Holocaust film has ever portrayed the terror of Jews on the run better than this very early effort, although many have tried.

Even though *Diamonds of the Night* is only 63 minutes, it was too much for *The New York Times* reviewer, who wrote in 1968, "And for characters on the outer edge of existence, living an extreme of misery, realism is somehow inappropriate. One loses interest. It looks unreal. Two men running, one ceaselessly preoccupied with his foot, the other in a kind of trance, both hounded by a band of toothless German-speaking Czechoslovaks...."[2] Indeed, when that review was published, realistic Holocaust portrayals—especially in the West—were non-existent. In hindsight, with hundreds of Holocaust films that depict graphic violence, yet with less realism, *Diamonds of the Night* is an early masterpiece.

Diamonds of the Night was the first of 15 features directed by Jan Nemec (1936–2016), who continued directing until the year of his death. *Diamonds of the Night* is also Nemec's highest IMDb user-rated film. Reviewer Eric Hynes wrote in 2013:

> Best known as an early salvo of the Czech New Wave, Jan Nemec's debut stunner feels even more potent now that it's been freed of the expectations and delineations of a national movement. In 64 fleet minutes, we're utterly and overwhelmingly immersed in a Jewish fugitive's singular experience, from hunger pains to hallucinatory reveries. Nemec's technique is as emotionally intuitive as it is masterful, purposefully scrambling past and present, handheld realism (a breathless opening tracking shot) and Buñuellian surrealism (fever-dreamed ants colonizing Jánsky's angelic face). It's a torrent of life—and cinema—in the face of death.[3]

Diamonds of the Night should be paired with the recommended antisemitic Gentile genre film *The Shop on Main Street—Obchod na korze* (1965). Both films were made within 20 years of the Holocaust. Both unapologetically expose Czech complicity with the Germans. And both Communist-era films lay bare Jewish peril in rural Europe; homegrown, visceral hatred of Jews that perfectly complemented and was tacitly licensed by the genocidal German ideology. The locals were unsparingly portrayed as down-home antisemites. These remarkable films depict Jew-haters who did not need the Nuremberg Laws to justify persecution.

The Two of Us—Le vieil homme et l'enfant (1967)

Genre:	Victim
Sub-Genre:	Hidden
Length:	87
MPAA or Local Rating:	Sweden-15
Language:	French
Country:	France
Director:	Claude Berri
Top-Billed:	Michel Simon, Roger Carel, Paul Préboist
From Wikipedia:	*The Two of Us* (French: Le vieil homme et l'enfant) is a 1967 French comedy-drama film.
IMDb Rating:	7.8
IMDb Votes:	1639

Holocaust Cinema Complete Description:	*The Two of Us—Le vieil homme et l'enfant* (1967) is an early, small story about a Jewish boy who is hidden in Vichy France by elderly antisemites who do not know that he is Jewish. The film humanizes both the boy and his caregivers, while offering a view of occupied France. *The Two of Us* subtly exposes the Vichy French mentality in the simplest terms. Although no one dies (except for the family dog), the anxiety of being a hidden Jewish child is masterfully recreated.
Recommendation:	As a starter film, *The Two of Us* is a non-violent depiction of life in Vichy France.
Suggested Minimum Grade:	Late Grade School

REVIEW

The Two of Us—Le vieil homme et l'enfant (1967) is the first French Holocaust film, and one of the finest Holocaust films ever made, French or otherwise. It begins with the narration of director Claude Berri (1934–2009) about his childhood in Lyon, France, during German occupation: "In November 1943, I was eight years old, and already a Jew." This unpretentious film is Berri's true story about being hidden during German occupation, sent by his parents to a rural French community. The boy's protectors are an elderly couple who do not know he is Jewish; the child, on the other hand, not only knows that he is Jewish, but also has learned to hide his faith by memorizing Catholic prayers and never letting anybody see his circumcised penis.

Many Holocaust films gain their gravitas by depicting carnage inflicted on the Jews, especially in death camps. *The Two of Us*, however, is the smallest of stories, achieving its gravitas by exposing the vulnerability of an ignorant old man, the protector of the Jewish child. Alan Scherstuhl of *The Village Voice* wrote in his article, "Claude Berri's *The Two of Us* Remains Greatest Film About a Boy Dealing with His Grampa's Noxious Views":

> Unlike, say, Agnieszka Holland's *Europa Europa* (1991), a drama of a Jewish boy passing as German inside the Reich itself, *The Two of Us* never wrings the situation for thriller-movie suspense…. Berri's film is an act of memory rather than an exercise in genre storytelling.[4]

The grandfather, Pépé ("Grandpa") is imbued with generations of French antisemitism and is played by venerated French actor Michel Simon (1895–1975), who had more than 100 screen credits by 1967, including "Shylock" in *The Merchant of Venice* (1953). Upon the re-release of *The Two of Us* in 2005, Roger Ebert wrote his second review of the film, explaining Michel Simon's character Pépé:

> The old man has not given much thought to his prejudices but caught them like a virus in his childhood and has carried them along uncritically into old age. He has no idea the child he has come to love so much is a Jew. I suspect if he did know, he would make an exception for Claude while continuing to harbor his prejudices against theoretical Jews he has the advantage of knowing nothing about.[5]

Midway into the film, the Jewish child and old man are sitting at a table while cutting potatoes. The little boy, Claude, who is fully aware of his own Jewishness and equally aware of the old man's antisemitism, toys with the old man:

> CLAUDE: *What else do they do? Tell me.*
> PÉPÉ: *Every Friday night and Saturday is their Sabbath.*
> CLAUDE: *What's that?*
> PÉPÉ: *The Sabbath is a sort of holiday. They turn off the electricity and use candles. They eat with their hats on. Like if I were to eat with my hat on.*
> CLAUDE: *But you keep your beret on.*

PÉPÉ: *My beret isn't a hat. And listen to this, son. On Saturdays, they close their stores. No work allowed. But believe me, they catch up on Mondays. They make you pay for their Sabbath.*
CLAUDE: *Was Jesus a Jew?*
PÉPÉ: *So they say.*
CLAUDE: *Then God is a Jew too? Granny says Jesus is the son of God. So, if he's a Jew, so is his father.*
PÉPÉ: *If you listen to everything she says, there's no end to it.*
CLAUDE: *What did the Jews do to you?*
PÉPÉ: *To me, nothing. That's all I need.*

On another occasion, the child teases the old man, accusing him of being a Jew, pointing out that Pépé also has self-ascribed Jewish attributes: frizzy hair, big ears, and a hooked nose. Through it all—going to church, feeding the rabbits and playing together like kids—trust is carved out between the precocious child, the collaborationist old man and the audience. But the ending does not let anyone off the hook. As Roger Ebert wrote in his glowing contemporaneous review:

> The ending is happy, but it isn't phony. If Hollywood had done this film, the old man would have discovered at the end that the boy was Jewish. Then there would have been a fine liberal curtain speech about the brotherhood of man. But Claude Berri, who wrote and directed *The Two of Us*, doesn't fall into that trap. The old man never finds out and, what's more, doesn't need to.[6]

This depiction of Marshal Pétain's France has no violence, a little sex and no Nazis. It quietly makes the point that, 50 years after the Dreyfus Affair, the French needed little encouragement to rid themselves of their Jews. Upon its recent Blu-Ray release, reviewer Jeffrey Kauffman wrote, "I just flat out love *The Two of Us*, despite (or in fact maybe because of) what is Berri's unabashed tendency to display his heart on his sleeve…. *The Two of Us* deserves to be celebrated…."[7]

Except for *Mr. Klein—Monsieur Klein* (1976), none of the dozen subsequent French films dealing with the Holocaust so honestly expresses the visceral French antisemitism that resulted in a quarter of all French Jews being murdered during German occupation. Because of the film's limited focus, *The Two of Us* should not be the first Holocaust film to be used in education. But, in many ways, *The Two of Us* is more effective and less affected than most other Holocaust films.

The Garden of the Finzi-Continis—Il Giardino dei Finzi-Contini (1970)

Genre:	Victim
Sub-Genre:	Descending
Length:	94
MPAA or Local Rating:	U.K.–14+
Language:	Italian
Country:	Italy
Director:	Vittorio De Sica
Top-Billed:	Dominique Sanda, Lino Capolicchio, Helmut Berger
From Wikipedia:	*The Garden of the Finzi-Continis* (Italian: Il giardino dei Finzi-Contini) is a 1970 Italian film, directed by Vittorio de Sica. It stars Lino Capolicchio, Dominique Sanda and Helmut Berger. The film is based upon Giorgio Bassani's novel of the same name.
IMDb Rating:	7.5
IMDb Votes:	5228
Oscars:	Winner: Best Foreign Language Film; Nomination: Best Writer.

Holocaust Cinema Complete Description:	*The Garden of the Finzi-Continis—Il Giardino dei Finzi-Contini* (1970) is the first "arthouse" Holocaust film. It is beautifully made, from start to finish. More importantly, as opposed to most Holocaust films, *Finzi-Continis* depicts assimilated European (Italian) Jews who are unashamedly Jewish, yet who do not solely define themselves by their religious heritage. *Finzi-Continis* also effectively argues that, at some point during the War, wealth could no longer save Jews from the Germans.
Recommendation:	*The Garden of the Finzi-Continis* is ideal for understanding the helplessness of wealthy Jews in Axis Europe.
Suggested Minimum Grade:	Middle School

Review

For the most part, countries allied to Germany during World War II ignored, as long as possible, German demands to disenfranchise, despoil and deport their Jewish citizens to German death camps. For example, German allies Japan, Italy, Hungary, Spain and Bulgaria all either protected the Jews in their countries or dragged their feet when responding to German insistence that the local Jewish populations be liquidated. Indeed, until the Germans occupied Italy in September 1943 and Hungary in March 1944, the Jewish citizens of those countries were safe from deportation, although not entirely safe from local racial laws, especially in Italy. As explained by Professor Israel Gutman:

> Italy had been ruled by a Fascist dictatorship since the early 1920s, had been allied with Nazi Germany since the mid–1930s, had passed its own racial laws in 1938, and had joined the war in 1940. However, it has been demonstrated that the Italians refused to participate in certain kinds of actions and to obey certain orders. They refused to hand over Jews to the Germans—knowing the fate that awaited them— either from Italy itself, or from the territories they occupied and controlled, until the German forces overtook parts of the country in September 1943. The Italians continued to balk even after Mussolini, under German duress, endorsed a deportation order.[8]

The Garden of the Finzi-Continis—Il Giardino dei Finzi-Contini (1970) is an intimate story about the slow, systematic destruction of Italian Jewry, as Mussolini's government enacted anti–Jewish racial policies. Director Vittorio De Sica (1901–1974) helmed this film toward the end of his spectacular acting and directing career, which included a Best Supporting Actor Oscar nomination for *A Farewell to Arms* (1957), as well as directing *Bicycle Thieves—Ladri di biciclette* (1948), which is rated 102 on the all-time IMDb best film list. The beautifully directed *The Garden of the Finzi-Continis* won the 1972 Best Foreign Language Film Oscar and was also nominated for the Best Writing Oscar. The film was based on an autobiographical story by Giorgio Bassani (1916–2000), which was part of his novel *Il romanzo di Ferrara*.

The Garden of the Finzi-Continis is about a very wealthy Jewish Italian family that neither shuns nor obsesses about their religious heritage. Like Philip Roth's "Patimkin" family in Larry Peerce's *Goodbye, Columbus* (1969), these people are rich and Jewish, but their ethnicity barely informs their identities. Jewishness for them was not the chicken in their soup, but the broth. Roger Ebert, bestowing on *The Garden of the Finzi-Continis* his highest rating, wrote:

> *The Garden of the Finzi-Continis*, as nearly as I can tell, is not an enclosed space but an enclosed state of mind. Eager for an afternoon of tennis, the young people ride into it on their bicycles one sunny Sunday afternoon. The Fascist government of Mussolini has declared the ordinary tennis clubs off limits for Italian Jews—but what does that matter, here behind these tall stone walls that have faithfully guarded the Finzi-Contini family for generations?[9]

The Garden of the Finzi-Continis was produced by Arthur Cohn (1927–), the same Arthur Cohn referred to positively by Elie Wiesel in his 1989 *New York Times* rant against Holocaust films, writing, "An authentic documentary-like 'The Final Solution,' by the four-time Oscar winner Arthur Cohn, cannot find a distributor, but people fall all over themselves for cheap and simplistic melodramas."[10] Apparently Mr. Wiesel did not realize in 1989 that Mr. Cohn had also been responsible for a fictionalized Holocaust melodrama, *The Garden of the Finzi-Continis*, made in 1970. The film was also produced by Holocaust survivor Artur "Atze" Brauner. Reviewer Tim Robey wrote in *The Telegraph* of the film upon its release:

De Sica's skill is such that you vividly imagine the (unheard) stomp of jackboots outside these stately garden walls. A silent farewell between a file of departing aristocrats and their little gaggle of loyal retainers is just devastating, piercing you to the core without a single close-up. It's a remarkably economical film—just 94 minutes—and in that time explores a vanished nirvana you won't easily forget. An abandoned great dane [*sic*] is glimpsed for a microsecond; a tennis court filled with beaming ghosts, then left to echo.[11]

Richard Shickel's contemporaneous review in *Life Magazine* inferred a more global message:

About genocide we learned to be articulate only after the fact. At the time it was unbelievable, even to its victims, and there was no vocabulary in which to express the pain and shock. Perhaps more to De Sica's point, pains caused by other human beings are most immediate to us. While we try to avoid dealing with those that derive from the faceless institutional madness that afflicts life in our time. We may be wrong, but that is the truth about us. And this is a film of painful truth most poignantly put.[12]

For Those I Loved—Au nom de tous les miens (1983)

Genre:	Victim
Sub-Genre:	Caught
Length:	145
MPAA or Local Rating:	Unrated (PG)
Language:	French
Country:	Canada—France—Hungary
Director:	Robert Enrico
Top-Billed:	Michael York, Brigitte Fossey, Jacques Penot
From Wikipedia:	*For Those I Loved* (French: *Au nom de tous les miens*) is a drama film from 1983 with Michael York, about a Polish Jewish Holocaust survivor who emigrated to the United States in 1946. It was directed by Robert Enrico for the Les Productions Mutuelles Ltée.
IMDb Rating:	7.1
IMDb Votes:	419
***Holocaust Cinema Complete* Description:**	Although ill-served by its unnecessary contemporary bookends, *For Those I Loved—Au nom de tous les miens* (1983) is one of the finest cinematic portrayals of the Warsaw Ghetto and is one of the only Holocaust film depictions of Treblinka. Produced between *Holocaust* (Miniseries 1978) and *War and Remembrance* (Miniseries 1988), *For Those I Loved* strikes the best early balance between Holocaust depiction and excessive violence. While not as celebrated as *Sophie's Choice* (1982), which was released the previous year, *For Those I Loved* is unabashedly about Jewish suffering and resistance.
Recommendation:	For graphic Warsaw Ghetto resistance and Treblinka portrayal.
Suggested Minimum Grade:	High School

REVIEW

For Those I Loved—Au nom de tous les miens (1983) is the first excellent on-screen depiction of any Jewish ghetto and of any death camp, as well. Its nonlinear story opens with a suicidal survivor, Martin Gray (Michael York), several decades after the war, followed by about an hour and a half flashback to the Warsaw Ghetto and Treblinka. The young man is a crafty smuggler and a fierce resistance leader. He gets captured in the Warsaw Ghetto and is sent to Treblinka, but finds his way back to the ghetto to fight in the famous Warsaw Ghetto uprising. Like the protagonist in *Europa Europa* (1990), Martin Gray somehow can slip between Germany and Russia at will. He survives with only one eye, and then, without explanation, becomes a Soviet soldier conquering Germany and then becomes a wealthy American businessman. The last 30 minutes of the film are the weakest and are superfluous.

For Those I Loved, alone among Holocaust films, also depicts Treblinka and its killing method, carbon monoxide. The 20 minutes of the film at Treblinka are balanced, neither sugarcoated nor excessively harsh. Nonetheless, these camp scenes are still devastating, not sparing the reality of the German death machine. While loading looted Jewish property into a returning boxcar, Martin Gray hides inside and arrives back in the Warsaw Ghetto to participate in the first on-screen uprising or Jewish armed resistance ever portrayed in a Western Holocaust feature film, seen by nobody. Nearly 40 years after the Holocaust, *For Those I Loved* was a groundbreaking Western film, creating a fighting Jewish hero.

For Those I Loved has nonfictional roots, based on a book by Holocaust survivor Martin Gray (né Mieczysław Grajewski) (1922–2016), which details Gray's life from 1922 through 1970, and, as in the film, his post–War wife and four children being killed in a fire. French director Robert Enrico (1931–2001)—who made a few dozen features including *The French Revolution—La révolution française* (1989) with Jane Seymour—apparently made little effort, in a film based on exposition, to explain many lingering, significant issues. For example, how did Martin Gray suddenly become a Russian officer? How did Martin Gray simply walk away from Russia? What happened to his grandmother in America? Are we to understand that in 1970 a former Nazi found Martin Gray, set his family afire and then called Martin Gray after the fire in the first minutes of the film to taunt him? How did Martin Gray become wealthy? What was his obsession throughout the film with Gentile women?

Amazingly, there are no critical reviews of *For Those I Loved* online. (Twelve IMDb users, however, reviewed it.) It received no awards attention, aside from the French César nominations for Most Promising Actor and Best Adapted Screenplay. And fewer than 500 people rated the film on IMDb, despite its starring Michael York, whose career has spanned from *Cabaret* (1972) through *The Simpsons* ("Dr. Lionel Budgie / Nigel / Mason Fairbanks") and *Austin Powers: The Spy Who Shagged Me* (1999; "Basil Exposition").

Despite its faults, *For Those I Loved* is a worthy film that can be used in Holocaust education, especially when showing only the Wartime portion (00:07:46 through 01:50:48).

Korczak (1990)

Genre:	Victim
Sub-Genre:	Caught
Length:	118

MPAA or Local Rating:	PG
Language:	Polish
Country:	Poland—Germany
Director:	Andrzej Wajda
Top-Billed:	Wojciech Pszoniak, Ewa Dalkowska, Teresa Budzisz-Krzyzanowska
From Wikipedia:	*Korczak*, is a 1990 film by Andrzej Wajda shot in black-and-white, about Polish-Jewish humanitarian Janusz Korczak.
IMDb Rating:	7.5
IMDb Votes:	905
Holocaust Cinema Complete Description:	Janusz Korczak is celebrated as the force behind a Warsaw Ghetto orphanage. He has been portrayed in many Holocaust films. *Korczak* (1990), however, is the only film solely about him. It is a no-nonsense retelling of his heroic commitment to care for Jewish orphans who he ultimately accompanied to their deaths at Treblinka, where he meets the same fate. *Korczak* is an unheralded film that portrays Jewish honor and resistance in the face of unmatchable odds.
Recommendation:	A great biopic to learn about non-violent Jewish resistance in the Warsaw Ghetto.
Suggested Minimum Grade:	Late Grade School

REVIEW

Non-Jewish director Andrzej Wajda (1926–2016) helmed more Holocaust films than any other filmmaker, titles including *Samson* (1961), *Landscape After Battle—Krajobraz po bitwie* (1970) and *Holy Week—Wielki tydzien* (1995). He also directed the Best Foreign Language Film Oscar nominee *Katyń* (2007), a masterpiece depicting the slaughter of 22,000 Polish POWs by the Soviets during the War, a war crime that claimed Andrzej Wajda's own father as a victim. From 1955 through 2016, Andrzej Wajda directed 42 feature films. He received the "Honorary Award" at the 2000 Academy Awards "for five decades of extraordinary film direction." The idea that a director in Soviet-controlled Poland could have made so many films that did not toe the Communist Party line illustrates Andrzej Wajda's greatness.

Agnieszka Holland (1948–) directed three Oscar-nominated Holocaust films, *Angry Harvest—Bittere Ernte* (1985), *Europa Europa* (1990) and *In Darkness* (2011). The same year that Holland directed *Europa Europa*, her script for *Korczak* (1990) was directed by Andrzej Wajda.

Korczak tells the story of Dr. Janusz Korczak, who maintained an orphanage in the Warsaw Ghetto. *Korczak* is shot in black-and-white. Its tone and message emphasize a moment where selflessness and sacrifice for others are taught and practiced. Korczak (né Henryk Goldszmit) (1878–1942)—to whom a substantial monument has been dedicated at Yad Vashem—is depicted in several other Holocaust films: *The Martyr—Dr. Korczak and His Children—Sie sind frei, Doktor Korczak* (1975), *L'adieu aux enfants* (TV 1982), *For Those I Loved—Au nom de tous les miens* (1983), *Uprising* (TV 2001), *The Courageous Heart of Irena Sendler* (TV 2009) and *The Zookeeper's Wife* (2017). Korczak is consistently portrayed as selfless in all these films. However, only director Wajda's *Korczak* is features Korczak as the protagonist (and is generally available).

Within 1.3 square miles, the Germans crammed 400,000 Jews into a walled-off portion of Warsaw. The majority of victims were ultimately shipped off and murdered in Treblinka. Only approximately 11,000 of these nearly half-million Warsaw Jews survived to liberation. *Korczak* painstakingly reenacts one man's compassion and drive to allow 200 children to live and die in dignity. The doctor arranged volunteers, begged the Jewish Council for funds and provisions and shamed the local gangsters into supporting his orphans. The children were educated in the orphanage and imbued with the Zionist dream and pride.

Vincent Canby wrote in *The New York Times'* of the film, "Korczak is played soberly by Wojtek Pszoniak, who was so fine as Robespierre in Mr. Wajda's 'Danton.' Korczak's only distinguishing features are his nobility and his occasional losses of temper, as when he attempts to stop a German soldier who is beating an innocent man (which, of course, amounts to more nobility)."[13]

Wajda's *Korczak* is unadorned and blunt. Gruesome footage of dead, emaciated ghetto residents filmed by the Germans is interspliced. Resistance is not a matter of guns, but of maintaining one's humanity. Throughout the film (and in life), Korczak was offered safe passage out of Poland, yet refused to abandon his children. Instead, he marched with his wards to the trains that carried them all to their death at Treblinka. As noted by Rita Kempley in *The Washington Post*, "Stunningly photographed in black-and-white by Robby Muller and deftly scripted by Agnieszka Holland, *Korczak* also serves as a richly detailed, hugely tragic document of Warsaw Ghetto life. And like so many Holocaust films, it portrays the ultimate triumph of human dignity over incomprehensible barbarity."[14]

As with most Victim Holocaust films, there is nothing fun about *Korczak*, yet few Holocaust films are more honest and effective. Korczak's story is worth re-telling and *Korczak* is up to the task.

Look to the Sky—Jona che visse nella balena (1993)

Genre:	Victim
Sub-Genre:	Span
Length:	100
MPAA or Local Rating:	Unrated (R)
Language:	Italian
Country:	Italy—France
Director:	Roberto Faenza
Top-Billed:	Jean-Hugues Anglade, Juliet Aubrey, Jenner Del Vecchio
From Wikipedia:	*Jonah Who Lived in the Whale* (Italian: *Jona che visse nella balena*), in the United States released as *Look to the Sky* is a 1993 Italian-French drama film directed by Roberto Faenza, based on the autobiographical novel by the writer Jona Oberski entitled *Childhood*, focused on the drama of the Holocaust.
IMDb Rating:	6.7
IMDb Votes:	245
***Holocaust Cinema Complete* Description:**	Four years before *Life Is Beautiful* farcically portrayed a boy playing in Auschwitz, *Look to the Sky—Jona che visse nella balena* (1993) told the true story of a young boy who survived the Westerbork Concentration Camp. *Look to the Sky* is a far better choice for those tempted by *Life is Beautiful;* the ending of *Look to the Sky* is correct and the depictions are much more realistic.
Recommendation:	A very good alternative for those tempted to screen *Life Is Beautiful.*
Suggested Minimum Grade:	High School

REVIEW

Look to the Sky—Jona che visse nella balena (1993) a.k.a. *Jonah Who Lived in the Whale* is a sturdy film that depicts a Jewish family of three that becomes a family of one, the little boy Jonah. This Italian-spoken autobiography of Dutch-born Jona Oberski (1938–) starts in Amsterdam just after the commencement of German occupation, when Jonah is four years old.

He and his parents are rounded up and sent to the Westerbork Concentration Camp in northeastern Netherlands. The family members are assigned jobs. Jonah and the other children in the camp are given the task of finding money and jewels that were regularly hidden in arrivees' shoes. Jonah and the other children are allowed by the camp cook to dive into empty vats for scraps. Jonah's parents have their jobs, too, but are primarily trying to protect their son. The father dies from illness in Westerbork. The mother and son, near the end of the War, are put on a transport, presumably to their death. But the train tracks are bombed by the Soviets, who liberate the cargo. The mother and boy are taken to a center for survivors, where the mother dies. Jonah is adopted by a local family.

There is nothing wrong with this unnoticed film. Of the 22 victim films recommended in this book, the protagonist in *Look to the Sky* is the youngest and least melodramatic. It is a strong, yet tender story about luck and survival. Further, more than any other film about children in the Holocaust, *Look to the Sky* depicts the greatest breadth of Holocaust experience, from pre–War to capture to internment to freedom. Perhaps *Look to the Sky*'s lack of success can be attributed to its having been in the shadow of the most-anticipated Holocaust film ever made, *Schindler's List*, which was also released in 1993. Indeed, no critical reviews can be found for *Look to the Sky* and only 245 users have rated it on IMDb (as opposed to more than a million for *Schindler's List*).

Aside from Jonah's parents stealing a moment of passion, *Look to the Sky* is ideal for younger students. In fact, although I rarely advocate editing a film to lower the recommended age, *Look to the Sky* is worth an educator's time to make the rest of this film accessible.

In terms of film study, a fascinating juxtaposition is screening the forgotten *Look to the Sky* followed by the lionized *Life Is Beautiful*, two Italian films (directed by men named "Roberto") about kids surviving the Holocaust. *Look to the Sky* is not only a much better film than *Life Is Beautiful*, but it is also honest; it does not rely on cute fantasy to tell the story of a boy living through the Holocaust. For those who laud *Life Is Beautiful*—or, worse, who use *Life Is Beautiful* in schools—*Look to the Sky* (edited) is the superior choice.

The Island on Bird Street (1997)

Genre:	Victim
Sub-Genre:	Caught
Length:	107
MPAA or Local Rating:	PG-13
Language:	English
Country:	Denmark
Director:	Søren Kragh-Jacobsen
Top-Billed:	Patrick Bergin, Jordan Kiziuk, Jack Warden
From Wikipedia:	*The Island on Bird Street* (Hebrew: האי ברחוב הציפורים; The Island on Birds Street) is a 1981 semi-autobiographical children's book by Israeli author Uri Orlev, which tells the story of a young boy, Alex, and his struggle to survive alone in a ghetto during World War II.
IMDb Rating:	7.2

IMDb Votes:	1208
Holocaust Cinema Complete Description:	*The Island on Bird Street* (1997) portrays a child surviving the War by hiding in the Warsaw Ghetto, in the same manner as in the protagonist's favorite book, *Robinson Crusoe*. The story is more formulaic than most recommended Holocaust films, the ending is mushy, and the film suffers from a lack of realism, but *The Island on Bird Street* can be used as a starter film for younger students learning about the Warsaw Ghetto. Based on a book, is useful for comparative or complimentary lessons.
Recommendation:	One of the few films that depict violence and can be screened by younger students.
Suggested Minimum Grade:	Late Grade School

REVIEW

The Island on Bird Street (1997) and *Run Boy Run—Lauf Junge lauf* (2013) are two recommended semi-autobiographical films based on books by prolific Israeli author Uri Orlev (né Jerzy Henryk Orlowski) (1931–). Both films/books provide a rare opportunity to compare and contrast Holocaust literature with good Holocaust films. (The stories are so incompatible, however, that the emphasis should be placed on "semi" in semi-autobiographical.)

The Island on Bird Street is one of many films about a Jewish boy who must survive the Holocaust without his parents. Alex is stuck in the Warsaw Ghetto after its liquidation and is told by his father to hide until he returns. At that point, *The Island on Bird Street* becomes "Swiss Family Robinstein." Alex builds a hideaway and figures out how to survive and be isolated, complete with a rope ladder. He has one book: *Robinson Crusoe,* written in 1719 by Daniel Defoe. Alex leaves his perch occasionally to hunt for food, rescue people, venture out into the forbidden parts of Warsaw, meet a doctor and little girl. Several times, of course, Alex is almost caught. Finally, his father returns, and they live happily ever after.

The Island on Bird Street was directed by Søren Kragh-Jacobsen, who primarily works in television. His film is one of the rare English-language Holocaust films produced by a non–English-speaking country (Denmark). Some characters speak with American accents and others with British accents. The German-speaking German actors speak German, except when they need to say something understandable in English. *The Island on Bird Street* has a perky score that does not try too hard. The acting, which is mostly Alex (Jordan Kiziuk), is respectable and the sets are adequate. And there is a curious cameo by veteran Hollywood Oscar nominee Jack Warden (né John Warden Lebzelter, Jr.) (1920–2006), who appeared in many legendary films including *12 Angry Men* (1957), *Heaven Can Wait* (1978) and *Being There* (1979). As Dutch reviewer Daphna Berger (translated) noted:

> *The Island on Bird Street* is a pretty good film, here and there a touch of moving and of course supported by the necessary music playing on the emotions. The film is a bit slow, but yes, it is not an exciting war film filled with action and battle scenes where (too) many people fall. It is a special story, seen through the eyes of a child. No ordinary war film. Not even one that needs to be at the top of your must see list.[15]

The *San Francisco Examiner*'s reviewer Edvins Beitiks was frustrated by a slew of unanswered questions that threaten to undermine *The Island on Bird Street* if the film is taken too seriously as great cinema. Beitiks asks rhetorically:

Would you like to know if the doctor crosses into the ghetto because of that roll of money or his own sense of decency? The movie won't tell you. Would you like to know why Alex stops appearing at a regular rendezvous with a girl who is taking a risk to be with him? The movie is silent on that score. Would you like Alex to say, in his own words, why he'll stay behind in the ruins of the ghetto rather than accept an offer to escape to the country? He won't.[16]

My underwhelming review may seem misplaced in this chapter of recommended films because *The Island on Bird Street* is not actually recommended for adults. Instead, *The Island on Bird Street* is a starter film for younger kids. This may seem like a backhanded compliment, but, in fact, to have made a meaningful Holocaust film for kids other than *The Diary of Anne Frank* is not just an accomplishment, but unique. To understand the great difficulty of this accomplishment, compare *The Island on Bird Street* with another film that was expressly made for students, *The Devil's Arithmetic* (TV 1999), which has a plodding, fatuous premise executed with artistic vulgarity. Admittedly, *The Island on Bird Street* is in this chapter precisely because it is the best Victim Holocaust film that can be recommended for younger students.

Anne Frank: The Whole Story (TV 2001)

Genre:	Victim
Sub-Genre:	Hidden
Length:	190
MPAA or Local Rating:	12
Language:	English
Country:	U.S.
Director:	Robert Dornhelm
Top-Billed:	Ben Kingsley, Hannah Taylor Gordon, Tatjana Blacher, Joachim Król
From Wikipedia:	*Anne Frank: The Whole Story* is a two-part mini-series based on the book *Anne Frank: The Biography* by Melissa Müller.
IMDb Rating:	8.0
IMDb Votes:	4401
Emmy:	Winners: Best Miniseries, Art Direction for a Miniseries & Movie or a Special; Nominations: Best Casting for a Miniseries, Movie or a Special, Cinematography for a Miniseries or a Movie, Directing for a Miniseries, Movie or a Special, Single Camera Picture Editing for a Miniseries, Movie or a Special, Lead Actor in a Miniseries or a Movie, Lead Actress in a Miniseries or a Movie, Supporting Actress in a Miniseries or a Movie, Sound Editing for a Miniseries, Movie or a Special & Writing for a Miniseries or a Movie.
***Holocaust Cinema Complete* Description:**	*Anne Frank: The Whole Story* (TV 2001) is the most complete of all Anne Frank films, following Anne and her sister, Margot, to Auschwitz and then to their graphically portrayed deaths in Bergen-Belsen. Unlike all other cinematic depictions of Anne Frank, this one stands alone as complete. Little of the horror experienced by the Franks is hidden in this excellent three-hour version, which answers many of the questions that have been avoided in most of the other 20 cinematic versions of Anne Frank films. *Anne Frank: The Whole Story* lives up to its name.
Recommendation:	For those who are prepared to see the unvarnished fate of Anne Frank.
Suggested Minimum Grade:	High School

REVIEW

The two-part, three-hour *Anne Frank: The Whole Story* (TV 2001) is the most complete Anne Frank film ever made. Instead of being constrained by Anne Frank's famous diary, *The Whole Story* was based on *Anne Frank: The Biography* by Melissa Müller. In fact, none of the diary writings could be used in *The Whole Story* because of a dispute with the Anne Frank Foundation.[17] It was the Foundation's loss. According to *The New York Times*:

> The two major organizations that oversee the Anne Frank estate are sharply divided over this television film. On one side is the Anne Frank House in Amsterdam, whose executive director, Hans Westra, has endorsed it and assisted the production.... "We believe this is an impressive and serious effort to understand Anne Frank." On the other hand the Anne Frank Fonds, or Foundation, in Basel, Switzerland, which oversees the copyright of the diary, receives revenue from its publication and is the legal heir to the estate, has repudiated the Müller book, on which the television movie is based.[18]

Director Robert Dornhelm (1947–) has a sure hand in *The Whole Story*, sure enough to get him hired six years later to direct the four-part, 6½ hour *War and Peace* (Miniseries 2007). *The Whole Story*'s fine cast included Holocaust film veterans Hannah Taylor Gordon playing Anne Frank (*Jakob the Liar* [1999]), Ben Kingsley playing Otto Frank (*Schindler's List* [1993]), Joachim Król playing Hermann van Pels (*Gloomy Sunday—Ein Lied von Liebe und Tod* [1999]), Tatjana Blacher playing Edith Hollander-Frank (*Bonhoeffer: Agent of Grace* [2000]) and Lili Taylor as Miep Gies (non–Holocaust *Mystic Pizza* [1988]).

Anne Frank: The Whole Story spends nearly the first hour framing the Franks' lives before and at the beginning of German occupation, the period preceding the family's retreat to the attic in the middle hour. This portion portrays a less cutesy, more relatable Anne Frank than in all previous versions, still growing into her body and kissing, but more real. The final hour tracks Anne Frank and her sister Margot (Jessica Manley) to their deaths in Bergen-Belsen, and Otto Frank's return to Amsterdam and receipt from Miep Gies of the diary.

The Whole Story does not rely on the pubescent writings in the diary. There is nothing terribly salacious about the film, which received the informative seal of approval from the *Christian Spotlight on Entertainment*:

> There are a few profanities, a scene in which Anne asks if she could touch another girl's breasts (though not in a homosexual way), a couple of scenes of nudity (in the camps) and the violence, although not as explicit as *Schindler's List*, was still there. I would not recommend this film for children, but would wholeheartedly recommend that this film be viewed by teens and adults to remind them of what really happened, lest it should ever happen again. Not a film you will easily forget, but let's face it—Anne's story is one we don't want to ever forget.[19]

Although *The Whole Story* was made for television, it does not feel like a television drama. The accents do not get in the way, nor does the musical score. And, undeniably, part of *The Whole Story*'s success is that it realistically completed the famous story of a young girl that has begun countless times in print and film, but rarely finished in Bergen-Belsen. Anne Frank's journey after the attic is based on research and some conjecture, but no less conjecture than Raoul Wallenberg's (*Wallenberg—A Hero's Story* [TV 1985] and *Good Evening, Mr. Wallenberg—God afton, Herr Wallenberg—En Passionshistoria från verkligheten* [1990]).

The Whole Story avoids Anne Frank's simplistic platitudes and optimism that predated her death camp experience and which surely framed Anne Frank's ultimate beliefs, which were absent from her diary. *Anne Frank: The Whole Story* is the best Anne Frank treatment available. (For more about Anne Frank films, see Chapter 4.)

The Grey Zone (2001)

Genre:	Victim
Sub-Genre:	Caught
Length:	108
MPAA or Local Rating:	R for strong Holocaust violence, nudity and language.
Language:	English
Country:	U.S.
Director:	Tim Blake Nelson
Top-Billed:	David Arquette, Velizar Binev, David Chandler
From Wikipedia:	*The Grey Zone* is based on the book *Auschwitz: A Doctor's Eyewitness Account* written by Dr. Miklós Nyiszli.
IMDb Rating:	7.1
IMDb Votes:	9482
***Holocaust Cinema Complete* Description:**	*The Grey Zone* (2001) is the finest Holocaust film ever made. It depicts two events at Birkenau: the survival of a girl in a gas chamber and the revolt that destroyed two of the crematorium complexes. Few other films capture the ethical dilemmas faced by Jews who were forced either to assist the Germans or to be murdered.
Recommendation:	"TOP THREE" IN GENRE. The final film in Holocaust study.
Suggested Minimum Grade:	High School

REVIEW

See Chapter 6: The Greatest Narrative Holocaust Film Ever Made.

The Pianist (2002)

Genre:	Victim
Sub-Genre:	Escaping
Length:	150
MPAA or Local Rating:	R for violence and brief strong language.
Language:	English
Country:	U.S.
Director:	Roman Polanski
Top-Billed:	Adrien Brody, Thomas Kretschmann, Frank Finla
From Wikipedia:	*The Pianist* is a 2002 biographical drama film co-produced and directed by Roman Polanski, scripted by Ronald Harwood, and starring Adrien Brody. It is based on the autobiographical book *The Pianist*, a Holocaust memoir by the Polish-Jewish pianist and composer Władysław Szpilman, a Holocaust survivor himself.
IMDb Rating:	8.5
IMDb Votes:	603378
Oscar:	Winners: Best Directing, Actor & Writer; Nominations: Best Picture, Cinematography, Costume Design & Editing.
***Holocaust Cinema Complete* Description:**	*The Pianist* (2002) is one of the most beautifully made and highly decorated Holocaust films ever made. It does not create any heroes or embellish any villains, but paints the picture of a solitary man who survives Warsaw—from the creation of the Ghetto through its destruction, and to the end of the War—on little but dumb luck. *The Pianist,* which is based on a true story, is deserving of all its accolades. It is artistic, cinematically brilliant, and educational, without over sentimentalizing.
Recommendation:	To be used as an explanation of how a few Jews survived the Holocaust.
Suggested Minimum Grade:	Middle School

REVIEW

See Chapter 7: Roman Polanski and *The Pianist* (2002).

Fateless—Sorstalanság (2005)

Genre:	Victim
Sub-Genre:	Caught
Length:	136
MPAA or Local Rating:	R for some disturbing Holocaust images including nudity, and brief strong language.
Language:	Hungarian
Country:	U.K.—Hungary—Germany
Director:	Lajos Koltai
Top-Billed:	Marcell Nagy, Béla Dóra, Bálint Péntek
From Wikipedia:	*Fateless* (Hungarian: *Sorstalanság*) is a Hungarian film based on the semi-autobiographical novel *Fatelessness* by the Nobel Prize-winner Imre Kertész, who also wrote the screenplay. It tells the story of a teenage boy who is sent to Auschwitz and Buchenwald.
IMDb Rating:	7.0
IMDb Votes:	6102
***Holocaust Cinema Complete* Description:**	*Fateless—Sorstalanság* (2005) is the breathtaking true account of a teenage boy living through internment at Auschwitz and then in the Buchenwald Concentration Camp. Although the story is more character-driven than *The Grey Zone* (2001), *Fateless* is every bit as pitch-perfect in its production and effectiveness. *Fateless*, the depiction of the journey from an innocent child to a young Holocaust survivor, is peerless.
Recommendation:	"TOP THREE" IN GENRE. For a comprehensive story of a young man enduring some of the most notorious aspects of the Holocaust.
Suggested Minimum Grade:	High School

REVIEW

Like *The Grey Zone* (2001), the Hungarian film *Fateless—Sorstalanság* (2005) is among the most unknown and underrated of all Holocaust films. *Fateless* stands alone presenting one person's journey from innocent young man to death camp survivor. Certainly, part of *Fateless'* greatness resulted from the authentic screenplay by Nobel Laureate for Literature Imre Kertész (1929–2016), based on his semi-autobiographical novel from 1975: *Fatelessness*. And perhaps *Fateless'* beauty resulted from the gorgeous cinematography of first-time director Lajos Koltai (1946–), who is best known as an Oscar-nominated cinematographer, with more than 60 films under his belt from 1970 through 2006. And *Fateless* could be great also because of the acting of newcomer Marcell Nagy, whose character moves seamlessly through the Holocaust with dignity and grace. (Daniel Craig also has a cameo.)

Fateless depicts a 14-year-old boy's journey from Budapest, Hungary, to Auschwitz briefly until transferred to Buchenwald, framed by a prologue and epilogue of family, friends and devastation. Within the camps, the boy's friendships and alliances are not based on power, greed or violence, but on character, kindness and humanity. Each gripping scene is punctuated by unadorned dialogue, which is not stylized, but almost poetic, emanating unpretentiously from the young actor.

The camp scenes are genuine, unique and realistic. This boy is not hidden in a barn or a bombed-out building. He says no Catholic prayers. He is not the outlier who sings or boxes or swindles or operates or kills to survive. He is not on the run. We watch as he simply outlives his German camp, with poise and humility. Below are a few observations from others about *Fateless*.

The Christian Science Monitor: This is a Holocaust movie that is so relentlessly observed and so aware of woe that it never feels like it belongs to a genre. As the boy, Marcell Nagy has a heartbreakingly expressive face.[20]

Variety: Exquisitely modulated and superbly mounted, the directing debut of skilled cinematographer Lajos Koltai went through an extended, unpredictable production history to emerge as a genuinely new way of looking *at* the Holocaust that is markedly different in tone from other such stories including *Schindler's List* and *The Pianis*t.... What elevates *Fateless* to a riskier level in confronting the horrors of the Holocaust is its makers' clear disinterest in the shock-value brutality employed by other directors to illustrate the ordeal.[21]

The New York Times: The visual beauty of Lajos Koltai's *Fateless* is unmistakable, and also a bit disconcerting.... For films in this genre—which has grown steadily since Steven Spielberg's *Schindler's List* was released in 1993—the test of verisimilitude is usually the ostentatiously accurate rendering of horror. There is plenty of that in *Fateless*, and yet one finds oneself noticing, along with the emaciated bodies and ambient cruelty, the delicacy of the light and the painterly composition of the frames.... *Fateless* bears no resemblance to Roberto Benigni's *Life Is Beautiful*, which turned a death camp into a theater of sentimental kitsch.[22]

The Guardian: Former cinematographer Lajos Koltai has stunned the [Berlin Film] festival with this harrowing second world war drama about Hungarian Jews deported to concentration camps. In style and substance it owes something to *Schindler's List,* but has a disquieting ambiguity and sense of unresolved pain different from Spielberg.... This is an extremely powerful film that has captured the imagination of festivalgoers.[23]

For those who believe that *The Grey Zone* is too graphic and difficult, *Fateless* is a worthy replacement. It presents a different form of redemption and courage, yet is equally uncompromising.

Primo (TV 2005)

Genre:	Victim
Sub-Genre:	Caught
Length:	79
MPAA or Local Rating:	PG
Language:	English
Country:	U.K.
Director:	Richard Wilson
Top-Billed:	Antony Sher
From Wikipedia:	*Primo* is a 2005 broadcast by HBO and the BBC. This film is a recording of the Royal National Theatre production of the play *Primo*. It is a monologue told as a memoir by an older Primo looking back at his life in Auschwitz.
IMDb Rating:	7.3
IMDb Votes:	138
BAFTA:	Nomination: Best Actor.
Holocaust Cinema Complete Description:	*Primo* (TV 2005) is a great starter film for the study of Auschwitz. One man stands on an empty stage and describes Auschwitz, exclusively relying on the words of Holocaust survivor Primo Levi. *Primo* reenacts nothing visually. Without any violence, *Primo* is an excellent primer before watching graphic Auschwitz films.
Recommendation:	To start the process of understanding the horror of Auschwitz.
Suggested Minimum Grade:	Middle School

REVIEW

Antony Sher stands alone as a principal Holocaust film actor, literally. He was not only in the thoughtful *God on Trial* (TV 2008), but also starred in the wildly unconventional (and recommended) *Genghis Cohn* (1993). In *Primo* (TV 2005), Antony Sher actually stands alone on a bare stage for over an hour, forcing viewers to try to imagine the unimaginable.

Primo, which was broadcast on the BBC and HBO, is a monologue derived from survivor Primo Levi's writings; the script was adapted, largely by Sher, from Primo Levi's 1947 memoir *If This Is a Man*. *Primo* is the second Holocaust film based on Primo Levi's life. The first was *The Truce—La tregua* (1997), starring John Turturro, which depicted Levi's Auschwitz liberation and return journey to Italy, and was based on Levi's sequel to *If This Is a Man*, his 1963 *The Truce—La tregua* a.k.a. *The Reawakening*.

Primo is a unique Holocaust film in three ways. First, it was shot on an empty theater stage. Second, there is only one actor (and only one character, Levi). And third, it is a soliloquy from start to finish, intense and evocative. *Primo* is a brilliant interpretation that aims to convey the emotional intensity of something that should not be remembered. The many details of sounds and smells and people and activities transcend this one-man-show format.

The script and performance of *Primo* were essentially the same performance as Anthony Sher's 2004 play performed in London's Cottesloe Theatre a year earlier, also called *Primo* and also directed by Richard Wilson. Sher has said that the role was so emotionally taxing that he could not perform it indefinitely. Although no reviews are available for *Primo*, the review of the play is dead-on for the film as well:

> It is best not to look on Antony Sher's adaptation of Primo Levi's *If This Is a Man* as a plain piece of theatre. It is far too powerful and affecting for that, this description of a period—mercifully quite short—of imprisonment in Auschwitz. Jewish Sher is obviously the right man to interpret Levi's words and feelings.... A major part of the success of this—one can only call it a recital rather than a play—is due to the director Richard Wilson, with the help of the designer Hildegard Bechtler, the lighting designer Paul Pyant and the composer of the stark and spare cello score, Jonathan Goldstein. The minimalism they provide is the only way to make this a true experience.[24]

For years I have recommended *Primo* to educators, but because the film is such an oddity, it has been unrealistic to suggest the film as anything other than as a supplement to others. On the other hand, because no violence is portrayed, it might be better to consider *Primo* as a background piece. In the end, however, the uncomfortable *Primo* works on enough levels to be unconditionally recommended.

The Last Train—Der Letzte Zug (2006)

Genre:	Victim
Sub-Genre:	Caught
Length:	123
MPAA or Local Rating:	Unrated (R)
Language:	German
Country:	Germany—Czech Republic
Director:	Joseph Vilsmaier and Dana Vávrová
Top-Billed:	Gedeon Burkhard, Lale Yavas, Lena Beyerling
From Wikipedia:	*The Last Train* (German: *Der letzte Zug*) depicts the fate of some of the last remaining Jews in Berlin, who in April 1943 were rounded up at the Berlin-Grunewald station and sent to the Nazi concentration camp at Auschwitz. The film stands out due to its proximity as well as the unsparing realism with which the brutality of a transport to the Auschwitz concentration camp appears.

IMDB Rating:	6.6
IMDb Votes:	1212
Holocaust Cinema Complete Description:	*The Last Train—Der Letzte Zug* (2006) depicts what is allegorically the final train of Jews deported from Berlin, a birthday present for Hitler in 1943. While most of the film takes place in a boxcar to Auschwitz, flashbacks give color to the Jews on the train. Although little suffering is hidden, the violence is not gratuitous.
Recommendation:	The only film that fully depicts the horror of a deportation train (boxcar).
Suggested Minimum Grade:	Middle School

REVIEW

Film production stories can sometimes be more interesting than the films themselves. Certainly, this was the case with Francis Ford Coppola's (non–Holocaust film) *Apocalypse Now* (1979), which was so maniacally made that the production—that mirrored the plot of the film—had to be exposed in the documentary *Hearts of Darkness: A Filmmaker's Apocalypse* (1991); just as Captain Benjamin L. Willard (Martin Sheen) had to be sent on a harrowing journey in Indochina to neutralize Colonel Walter E. Kurtz (Marlon Brando), Paramount had to navigate both Indochina and Hollywood to neutralize Francis Ford Coppola to end production, and edit and release *Apocalypse Now*. Although much less harrowing than the making of *Apocalypse Now*, the backstory of *The Last Train—Der Letzte Zug* (2006) is also fascinating.

The late Czech actress Dana Vávrová (1967–2009) has over 50 acting credits listed in IMDb, including in one of Milos Forman's Best Picture winners, *Amadeus* (1984), rated the 85th all-time best film on IMDb, winner of seven other Oscars. Vávrová, who died of cancer at age 41, was rarely the headliner, except when directed by German cinematographer and director Joseph Vilsmaier (1939–), her husband. Vilsmaier has over a hundred credits behind the camera, starting in 1970. While Vilsmaier was directing *The Last Train*, a camera fell on him, severely injuring him. Vilsmaier's wife, Vávrová, finished the film, one of three directed or co-directed by Vávrová, who succumbed to cancer three years later. Vilsmaier continued directing until 2015.

Another key to *The Last Train* is its writer and producer, centenarian Artur "Atze" Brauner, who produced over 300 films and specifically produced, co-produced or wrote more than a dozen Holocaust films before *The Last Train*, including: *The Garden of the Finzi-Continis* (1970), *Europa Europa* (1990) and *Babi Yar: The Forgotten Crime—Babij Jar* (2003).

Together, these three filmmakers—Vávrová, Vilsmaier and Brauner—made an admirable film. *The Last Train* artfully depicts what is allegorically the final trainload of Jews deported from Berlin during the War. Unlike Samuel Maoz's Israeli film *Lebanon* (2009), which brilliantly tells its entire story from inside an Israeli tank during combat in the First Israel-Lebanon War, *The Last Train* does not solely rely on the train *mise-en-scène*. While most of *The Last Train* takes place in a boxcar to Auschwitz, flashbacks to life before the War are interspersed, giving color to the characters. However, the scenes outside the train—the capture, flashbacks and the ending—were much less compelling than the boxcar scenes.

The Last Train does not sanitize the transport experience, other than perhaps portraying 50 Jews in the boxcar instead of 150, which did not diminish the film's impact. *The Last Train* also portrays Jews escaping from moving trains, as does *Long Is the Road— Lang ist der Weg* (1949), *Diamonds of the Night—Démanty noci* (1964), *War and Love*

(1985) and *Angry Harvest—Bittere Ernte* (1985). Like *Long Is the Road*, *The Last Train* shows the entire escape and has a happy ending for the escapee. And, like the final moments of *Kapò* (1960), where Susan Strasberg ekes out the Shema prayer, the little girl who escaped the train here also ends on that note, albeit with a much more convincing recitation and a far happier ending than for Strasberg's character.

The Last Train is not as polished as most of the other recommended Holocaust films. The flashbacks are too wistful, which results in slightly hollow characters, as opposed to the intended hallowed characters. Some flashbacks are just short of sentimentality. The German soldiers, too, are unconvincing, especially the few who try to feed the Jews through the windows; the "bad Nazis" and Ukrainians are more caricature than character. The Polish partisans in the forest, too, are atypical, to say the least. As critic Patricia Smagge wrote in *Cinemagazine*: "*Der letzte Zug* is certainly not a film without flaws and does not stand out in originality either. However, this does not detract from the fact that you are caught by your throat by the tragic fate of the poor Jews on the inhuman train transport towards the concentration camps."[25]

But, while certainly imperfect, no other film—including *Schindler's List* (1993)— reaches the realism of a transport better than *The Last Train*. It convincingly portrays the deterioration of Jews on a transport, transformed from well-coiffed Germans into subhuman captives in a boxcar. And, if a few Jews surviving on a transport of a thousand condemned souls can be deemed uplifting, then *The Last Train* also works very well, especially for younger audiences.

"The drama," wrote reviewer Marcus Small about *The Last Train*, "which is often hard to bear compared to other films about the Holocaust, sends the viewer on a journey of no return, leaving one empty and exhausted."[26] That being said, "leaving one empty and exhausted" at the end of a Holocaust film is much better than leaving one emotionally unchallenged. With that in mind, *The Last Train* is a fitting legacy for its late director Dana Vávrová.

My Führer—Mein Führer—Die wirklich wahrste Wahrheit über Adolf Hitler (2007)

Genre:	Victim
Sub-Genre:	Caught
Length:	89
MPAA or Local Rating:	Unrated (PG)
Language:	German
Country:	Germany
Director:	Dani Levy
Top-Billed:	Helge Schneider, Ulrich Mühe, Sylvester Groth
From Wikipedia:	*My Führer—The Really Truest Truth about Adolf Hitler* (German: *Mein Führer—Die wirklich wahrste Wahrheit über Adolf Hitler*) is a 2007 German comedy film. The setting is World War II, around New Year's of 1945. This comedy tells the story of Adolf Hitler and his preparation for a big New Year's speech. Hitler is too depressed to speak, so a Jewish acting coach is called in to tutor him.
IMDb Rating:	5.4
IMDb Votes:	3728

Holocaust Cinema Complete Description:	*My Führer* (2007) is a farcical look at the final days of Adolf Hitler as seen through the eyes of a Jewish acting coach. The premise is wild, but is executed perfectly. This forgotten little film makes fun of the Third Reich while never losing its bearings. While very much in the spirit of Charlie Chaplin's *The Great Dictator* (1940), *My Führer* has a satisfying and appropriate ending.
Recommendation:	A slightly more lighthearted look at the Holocaust and Hitler.
Suggested Minimum Grade:	Middle School

REVIEW

When in doubt about Holocaust comedy, remember the following joke: Hitler went to a fortune-teller who told him that he would die on a Jewish holiday. Hitler asked, "Which Jewish holiday." The fortune-teller responded, "Whenever you die will be a Jewish holiday."

Charlie Chaplin's *The Great Dictator* (1940), which is rated 53rd on IMDb's greatest film list, is regarded as a classic for two reasons: it was Chaplin's first talking film and also Chaplin made merciless fun of Hitler while Hitler was still perceived as a laughing matter. As a film, however, by today's standards, *The Great Dictator* had a few significant faults, including the superfluous Mussolini schtick with "Napaloni—Dictator of Bacteria," and the fourth-wall ending, where Chaplin basically goes all Rodney King, "Can't we all just get along?" *My Führer—Mein Führer—Die wirklich wahrste Wahrheit über Adolf Hitler* (2007), which is roughly translated, "The Really Truest Truth about Adolf Hitler" could just as roughly be considered an homage to *The Great Dictator*. In the case of *My Führer*, however, lessons were learned, notwithstanding another fourth-wall ending.

The premise of *My Führer* is that, near the end of the War, when Hitler was falling apart along with the Third Reich, Hitler just needed to regain his mojo. And what better way to inspire the Fuhrer than to annoy him with a famous Jewish acting coach "Grünbaum" (Ulrich Mühe of the non-Holocaust masterpiece *The Lives of Others* [2006]), who was retrieved from the Sachsenhausen Concentration Camp. (This Sachsenhausen-to-Hitler plot was also somewhat borrowed in flashback in Sam Garbarski's inferior Survivor film *Bye Germany—Es war einmal in Deutschland…* [2017].) While Grünbaum's job is to prepare Hitler to deliver a rousing speech intended to rekindle the German war effort, Grünbaum, instead turns into Hitler's therapist and confidant. Grünbaum's wife and family also are a boon. And the other German characters are just whacky enough to be entertaining. *Mein Führer* is an excellent choice for a lighter, lesser-known Holocaust film that touches on many important topics.

The film unquestionably has the potential to run off the rails, but fiercely clings to them even while almost tipping over. *My Führer* was directed and written by Swiss filmmaker Dani Levy, who most famously made the absolutely insane *Go for Zucker—Alles auf Zucker!* (2004), which rivals the Jewish self-loathing of Woody Allen's *Deconstructing Harry* (1997), which infamously featured Demi Moore's character saying before fellating Stanley Tucci's character: "…borei p'ri ha-blow-job." The frenetic *Go for Zucker*, which was Dani Levy's film previous to *My Führer*, did not portend anything good vis-à-vis Levy's treatment of the Holocaust. But, unlike the completely disrespectful, ham-fisted *Go for Zucker*, Levy held it together in *My Führer*. Others disagree.

In fact, of all the Holocaust films recommended in this book, few have such consistently unhappy reviews. For example, Robert Levin wrote in *Critic's Notebook* of *My Führer*, "Totally concept-driven, the picture turns on the humor inherent in the notion of a Jewish man struggling to help his chief antagonist. While the fresh irony permeates the first few scenes between Grünbaum and Hitler, eventually the novelty wears off and it becomes clear that Mr. Levy has made little more than a sitcom-y rehash of an age-old shrink-patient premise."[27]

New York Times critic Stephen Holden was also disappointed that Levy did not go even wackier, perhaps also imagining that the film should have descended into the craziness of *The Mad Adventures of Rabbi Jacob—Les aventures de Rabbi Jacob* (1973). Holden complained:

> Tonally *My Führer* is divided against itself. The protracted, mostly serious scenes of Grünbaum and his family suggest that Mr. Levy, whose cynical 2004 satire *Go for Zucker!* carried a sharp bite, felt obliged to acknowledge the pain and suffering of the Holocaust. Forsaking the merciless ridicule that might have sent *My Führer* into the same comic orbit as *The Great Dictator* and *The Producers*, he played it too safe.[28]

In any case, *My Führer*'s portrayal of Hitler is more nuanced than Chaplin's in *The Great Dictator*. *My Führer* also serves as an especially important reality check for those who inordinately venerate Chaplin's film. This is not reason enough to recommend *My Führer*; the recommendation is based instead, on the film's unique portrayal of the collapse of Hitler and the Third Reich, made with the kind of joy that such an event should generate, while at the same time, most importantly, insisting that the Holocaust was no joke.

The other obvious comparison to *My Führer* is *Jojo Rabbit* (2019), which is also a comedy set in Berlin during the fall of Nazi Germany. In tone and message, these films are remarkably similar, including with their cartoonish representations of Hitler. But, where *My Führer* clung to the tracks, *Jojo Rabbit* flipped off, meandering into sketch-like bits that may have looked good on a storyboard, but that were flat and obvious on the screen. The clearest difference between the films is their best ten minutes: *Jojo Rabbit*'s best ten minutes were its first ten minutes, which will doom any film; the best ten minutes of *My Führer* were, by contrast, the last ten minutes, which has been the goal of storytelling in any form from the beginning.

Producing Holocaust farce is a difficult task, but not impossible, as evidenced by *Genghis Cohn* (1993), *Train of Life—Train de vie* (1998), *Divided We Fall—Musíme si pomáhat* (2000) and *Inglourious Basterds* (2009). *My Führer* squarely pokes at us from the success column.

The Counterfeiters—Die Fälscher (2007)

Genre:	Victim
Sub-Genre:	Caught
Length:	98
MPAA or Local Rating:	R for some strong violence, brief sexuality/nudity and language.
Language:	German
Country:	Austria—Germany
Director:	Stefan Ruzowitzky
Top-Billed:	Karl Markovics, August Diehl, Devid Striesow
From Wikipedia:	*The Counterfeiters* (German: *Die Fälscher*) fictionalizes Operation Bernhard, a secret plan by Nazi Germany during World War II to destabilize the United Kingdom by flooding its economy with forged Bank of England pound notes. The film centers on a Jewish counterfeiter, Salomon "Sally" Sorowitsch, who is coerced into assisting the operation at the Sachsenhausen concentration camp.
IMDb Rating:	7.6
IMDb Votes:	40087

Oscar:	Winner: Best Foreign Language Film.
Holocaust Cinema Complete Description:	*The Counterfeiters—Die Fälscher* (2007) is one of the finest core Holocaust films ever made. The true story, which is set in both Mauthausen and Sachsenhausen Concentration Camps, portrays Jewish counterfeiters who are forced, upon penalty of death, to cooperate long-term with their German captors. Although not as graphically violent as many other Holocaust films, *The Counterfeiters* tells a compelling story in an excellent film.
Recommendation:	"TOP THREE" IN GENRE. To see a great story about a man who survived the Holocaust by undertaking a unique task.
Suggested Minimum Grade:	High School

REVIEW

The Counterfeiters—Die Fälscher (2007), winner of the Best Foreign Language Oscar, is a representation of the Nazi "Operation Bernhard," the fascinating true story of a counterfeiting program at Sachsenhausen Concentration Camp. "Operation Bernhard" flooded the British and American economies with counterfeit money, thus destabilizing the Allied economies while "generating" needed funds for the Nazi war effort. Estimates of the amount of forged British currency range from £132 million to £300 million (£13 billion today when adjusted for inflation). *The Counterfeiters'* final narration suggests that four times more than the total British bank reserves were produced by "Operation Bernhard."

The Counterfeiters is loosely based on the biography of Adolf Burger, who is called Sorowitsch or "Sally" in the film. He is a Jewish forger who was caught in 1936 and sent to the Mauthausen Concentration Camp in 1939 to work in a quarry. He is a tough guy who, after a stint working the quarry, survives in the camp by painting portraits for German officers. After five years, Sorowitsch is transferred to Sachsenhausen by his original arresting officer, to oversee the ongoing counterfeiting program. *The Counterfeiters* depicts a balance struck by the inmates between satisfying the Germans while sabotaging and hindering the counterfeiting project.

Stefan Ruzowitzky, the Austrian writer/director of *The Counterfeiters*, has made an exceptional picture, worthy of its Oscar and then some. There is nothing cheesy here. Instead, Ruzowitzky has painted a Holocaust story of men who were treated with relative care, merely because of their irreplaceable skills. Nothing is forsaken in *The Counterfeiters*. The cinematography, casting, acting, pacing, storyline and dialogue are first-rate. The music, in particular, is an inspired choice, often featuring just a harmonica accompanied by an acoustic guitar. The score is spot-on, intended to convey the mood of the scenes, as opposed to the all-too-usual substitution of sloppy music for good storytelling.

Devid Striesow, who portrays the believably cruel commandant, is charmingly cunning, keeping his eyes on everyone's fate, especially his own. But the film belongs to star Karl Markovics, who portrays Sorowitsch as shrewd and compassionate, less interested in the loot than the game. Five years later, Markovics also co-starred in *Süskind* (2012), playing the unhinged Nazi antagonist responsible for deporting the Jews of Amsterdam. Two years after that, Wes Anderson cast Markovics in *The Grand Budapest Hotel* (2014).

Markovics absolutely owns the screen in *The Counterfeiters*, from start to finish. As reviewer Adam Bernstein wrote in *The Washington Post*, "The story's most compelling personality—and the best reason to see the film—is Sorowitsch, a character of no particular virtue other than the pride he takes in being an artist of criminality and survival. He is uneasy in the role of protagonist, and when his dignity is shattered, it is fascinating to watch him use his outlaw instincts to maneuver and manipulate."[29] Peter Howell of *The Toronto Star* also credits Markovics and the director for the film's preeminence:

> It is here where the film makes its greatest impact, and where the skills of Ruzowitzky and Markovics are most apparent. Neither man is willing to invest Sally with much in the way of redemptive features, no clue to how his attitude might shift. It's a brave choice that makes us consider the possibility that Sally is completely amoral and contemptible. On the other hand, he could be stalling for time, looking for a way out of the situation.[30]

The Counterfeiters ranks at the top of all Victim Holocaust films, along with *The Grey Zone* (2001), *The Pianist* (2002) and *Fateless—Sorstalanság* (2005), all films about genuine moral choices, survival and redemption. Yet none of these films are suggesting that their answer is any more correct than the choices made by other Holocaust victims. Like *The Grey Zone*, the final scene of *The Counterfeiters* is the cherry atop an already-perfect sundae, a scene that wraps back around to the opening post–War scene in *The Counterfeiters* with Sally in a Monte Carlo casino, entering with piles of counterfeit loot.

Many Victim Holocaust films are difficult to watch, painful, plodding, virtuous spectacles which seem more intent on dramatizing pain than inviting viewers into their world. *The Counterfeiters* is an exception, allowing us to see a complicated, taciturn character's story with style and sensitivity.

Defiance (2008)

Genre:	Victim
Sub-Genre:	Escaping
Length:	137
MPAA or Local Rating:	R for violence and language.
Language:	English
Country:	U.S.
Director:	Edward Zwick
Top-Billed:	Daniel Craig, Liev Schreiber, Jamie Bell
From Wikipedia:	*Defiance* is a 2008 American War film set during the occupation of Belarus by Nazi Germany, based on Nechama Tec's 1993 book *Defiance: The Bielski Partisans*, an account of the Bielski partisans, a group led by Belarusian Jewish brothers who saved and recruited Jews in Belarus during the Second World War.
IMDb Rating:	7.3
IMDb Votes:	127214
Oscar:	Nomination: Best Music (Adaptation Score).
***Holocaust Cinema Complete* Description:**	*Defiance* (2008) is a well-cast story about a large group of Jews who hide from the Germans in the Belarus forests. Unlike most Holocaust films, *Defiance* depicts Jews resisting and successfully subverting the Germans throughout the War. Unlike *Schindler's List*, *Defiance* portrays over a thousand Jews saving themselves, without the need of a German savior. Rightfully, *Defiance* is regarded as one of the greatest Holocaust stories.
Recommendation:	A great story of Jewish resistance and perseverance.
Suggested Minimum Grade:	*High School*

REVIEW

Defiance (2008) is one of those films with a cast and director who are greater and more famous than their film. Start with the director of *Traffic* (2000), the Oscar winner for Best Picture, director Edward Zwick, who also co-created the groundbreaking TV series *Thirtysomething* (TV 1987–1991). Zwick also directed 14 feature films as diverse as *About Last Night…* (1986), *Legends of the Fall* (1994), *The Last Samurai* (2003) and *Glory* (1989). Next is four-time "James Bond," Daniel Craig, whose Bond *Quantum of Solace* (2008) was released the same year he was speaking Russian in *Defiance*. And then the also Russian-speaking "Ray Donovan" aka Liev Schreiber, star of *Spotlight* (2015) and director/writer of the great Holocaust Survivor film *Everything Is Illuminated* (2005). Add to the mix Allan Corduner, who played Dr. Miklós Nyiszli in *The Grey Zone* (2001).

With pedigree established, *Defiance* is one of the important Holocaust films that prompts the seldom-asked question: why do we need righteous Gentile films when we have Jewish resistance films? *Defiance* provides real Jewish heroes who saved 1,200 Jews and killed Germans and antisemitic locals. *Defiance* is the retelling of the Bielski Brothers story about creating a refuge and community in the Belarusian forest, accumulating other Jewish and Gentile refugees along the way. These heroic Jews formed a militia with some Soviet partisans and meted out justice as needed. Roger Ebert wrote of the film:

> As a Nazi observes, not without admiration, the Bielskis set up a self-sustaining village in the wilderness. Their situation is more precarious because they are surrounded by anti–Semites not only from Germany but from Russia and Poland. They cooperate with Soviet forces out of necessity, but cannot delude themselves. Their efforts prevailed, and today there are thousands who would not have been born if they had not succeeded.[31]

Unfortunately, the production is wanting. Cinematically, *Defiance* is mediocre, not much better than *Uprising* (TV 2001). The scenarios are predictable and most performances are stilted. The formulaic dialogue, filled with biblical references, is tiresome, such as, "Tuvia, I almost lost my faith. But you were sent by God to save us." And the battle scenes are little better, with the final combat featuring Craig and Schreiber magically dodging and dancing through thousands of rounds of automatic gunfire, as well as tank shells. And then the battle and all German soldiers are magically silenced when a grenade is dropped into a tank. *The New York Times*' reviewer A.O. Scott got to the heart of the *Defiance* conundrum, asking if inauthentic filmmaking ruins an important story. Scott is dubious, leveling a solid rebuke to Zwick's implicit message:

> His [Zwick's] film furthermore implies that if only more of the Jews living in Nazi-occupied Europe had been as tough as the Bielskis, more would have survived. This may be true in a narrow sense, but it also has the effect of making the timidity of the Jews, rather than the barbarity of the Nazis and the vicious opportunism of their allies, a principal cause of the Shoah. What the Bielskis did is treated not as the extraordinary, odds-defying feat it was, but rather as an ideal that those who did not survive failed to live up to. Death and victimization can be, and have been, treated with sentimentality, but so too can toughness. *Defiance* celebrates strong men (who in real life sought no such glory) at the expense of those whose weakness—whose inability to fight back, or to stay alive—was not a moral failure but a fact of history. It's not exactly false, but it's more than a little inauthentic.[32]

Roger Ebert gave *Defiance* only 2½ out of four stars, which is correct. He also wrote, "…the drama tends to focus on issues, conflicts and romances within the group, and in that sense could be a very good reality show…."[33] Regardless, even if *Defiance* is less artistic or creative than many Holocaust features of the Mature Era of Holocaust film, the story needs to be told before most other stories. As art, *Defiance* could have been more interesting; as a Holocaust story, *Defiance* is essential.

God on Trial (TV 2008)

Genre:	Victim
Sub-Genre:	Caught
Length:	90
MPAA or Local Rating:	Unrated (PG)
Language:	English
Country:	U.K.
Director:	Andy De Emmony
Top-Billed:	Joseph Muir, Josef Altin, Ashley Artus, Antony Sher
From Wikipedia:	*God on Trial,* a 2008 British television play takes place in Auschwitz during World War II. The Jewish prisoners put God on trial in absentia for abandoning the Jewish people. The question is whether God has broken his covenant with the Jewish people by allowing the Nazis to commit genocide.
IMDb Rating:	7.7
IMDb Votes:	2571
BAFTA:	Nomination: Best Sound Fiction—Entertainment.
Holocaust Cinema Complete Description:	Although *God on Trial* (TV 2008) is overtly didactic, it is also one of the few Holocaust films that grapple directly in Auschwitz with the question of how the Holocaust could have happened to God's "Chosen People." *God on Trial* makes almost no effort to recreate Auschwitz/Birkenau, but does have a nice current-day wraparound to open and close the film. For those studying Holocaust theology, *God on Trial* is ideal. For those wanting more of a story, most of the other recommended Victim films are advised.
Recommendation:	For those interested in theological responses to the Holocaust.
Suggested Minimum Grade:	Middle School

Review

A tour bus pulls into the Birkenau parking lot. Within a minute of the tour, the premise is muttered in voiceover: "You know there is a story that the prisoners made a court here and held a trial. They tried the person they thought was most responsible for what happened to them." The rest of *God on Trial* (TV 2008) is a completely fictitious flashback, a theological discussion and verbal jousting in a Birkenau barracks by Jewish prisoners who are moments away from "selection" to the gas chambers. God is ultimately convicted of violating His covenant made to Moses and the Jews. *God on Trial* is based on the 1979 Elie Wiesel play, "The Trial of God (as it was held on February 25, 1649, in Shamgorod)" (Le procès de Shamgorod tel qu'il se déroula le 25 février 1649).

No serious effort is made to represent Auschwitz/Birkenau in *God on Trial*, other than the barracks, which is a bit like staging a film in a hut that overlooks the Grand Canyon, but avoiding the spectacle on the other side of the wall. But this issue mostly disappears as the arguments begin. Despite the ponderous set-up, the questions asked and the answers suggested are vital and thoughtful. The responses are gripping, based on biblical and historical examples of Jewish suffering. The acting is theatrical. The casting is praiseworthy. The dialogue and subplots are gripping. And, aside from the wanting Auschwitz depiction, *God on Trial* hits its marks impeccably. As Mary McNamara of *The Los Angeles Times* concluded, "They are big topics addressed with a striking lack of sentimentality, quite a feat considering the setting. You will weep, but you will also think. And although the weeping will stop fairly soon after the credits role [*sic*], with any luck, the thinking will not."[34]

Meshulam Gotlieb of the Lookstein Center for Jewish Education wrote 6,500 words of criticism about the theological underpinning of *God on Trial*, particularly and unfairly focusing on its Catholic writer, Frank Cottrell-Boyce. In part, Gotlieb concludes: "Unfortunately, Cottrell-Boyce has created a powerful, troubling, and moving movie, which not only fails to do justice to the Jewish tradition and those who were martyred in Auschwitz but actually misinterprets, misrepresents, and defames both in the most callous, unprofessional, and if I may say so, illogical of ways."[35]

Gotlieb's quibbles are like a French-pastry chef who complains about the quality of vanilla extract used by common bakers. While Gotlieb may be correct about some tiny notes near the end of *God on Trial*, the film is much better than any other regarding the most basic theological questions that must be raised about the Holocaust. And, bluntly, voicing these plaintive questions about God and the Holocaust is much more important and memorable than are the answers, which can never be known anyway. For a serious cinematic inquiry of the Holocaust, *God on Trial* is essential.

Süskind (2012)

Genre:	Victim
Sub-Genre:	Caught
Length:	118
MPAA or Local Rating:	Unrated (PG)
Language:	Dutch, German
Country:	Netherlands
Director:	Rudolf van den Berg
Top-Billed:	Jeroen Spitzenberger, Karl Markovics, Nyncke Beekhuyzen
From Wikipedia:	*Süskind* is a Dutch war film directed by Rudolf van den Berg. The film is based on the life of Walter Süskind and is set in Amsterdam during the Second World War.
IMDb Rating:	6.9
IMDb Votes:	1916
Holocaust Cinema Complete Description:	*Süskind* (2012) tells the true story of Jewish resistance in occupied Amsterdam where Walter Süskind saved more than 1,000 Jews. Although slightly melodramatic, though not to the point of being offensive, *Süskind* gets its point across without humanizing the German officer who directs the deportation. *Süskind* also provides a rare glimpse of the Westerbork Concentration Camp.
Recommendation:	A good example of lesser-known Jewish resistance in Amsterdam.
Suggested Minimum Grade:	Middle School

REVIEW

Director Rudolf van den Berg's *Süskind* (2012) is an excellent Dutch film that details the efforts of Walter Süskind (1906–1945), a member of the Amsterdam Jewish Council, who saved 600 Jews from deportation (although a card at the end of the film states he saved "more than a thousand.") *Süskind*, with a runtime of under two hours, is a well-made film that portrays Jews saving Jews from Germans. *Süskind*, which also depicts a ghetto and a concentration camp, is not overly sentimental and does not rely on dubious scenarios.

Jeroen Spitzenberger plays the hero "Walter Süskind" flawlessly, a real person fighting for his family and his people. And Karl Markovics, who was spectacular as the Jewish protagonist in *The Counterfeiters—Die Fälscher* (2007), is equally great as the nuanced German antagonist in *Süskind*. Critic Martijn Scheepers of *Cinemagazine* wrote:

With *Süskind*, director Rudolf van den Berg delivers—after previously *Tirza*—again a very strong film. A conscious choice has been made to tell a compelling story and not so much to give a history lesson and in this the film has succeeded. The basis of the story is historically correct and that is very important. In addition, there is no lack of drama and you notice that the film is working towards a beautiful climax as the grid around Walter begins to close. Despite the fact that many other films about the Second World War have been made, the film feels innovative.[36]

Variety's critic Van Boyd Hoeij also appreciated *Süskind*, writing:

Mostly male-dominated film nonetheless offers strong femme roles to Nyncke Beekhuyzen as Sueskind's unsure wife; Olga Zuiderhoek as one of his accomplices; and Chava Voor in 't Holt in a small but pivotal role as a Jewish prostitute. Some 600 children were smuggled to safety in the Dutch countryside but thankfully, van den Berg focuses on the adults and their more complex moral quandaries, mostly avoiding histrionics or facile, tear-jerking melodrama. The orchestral score similarly shows restraint, relying on fewer instruments in the film's tensest moments, though the baroque use of the violin in the home stretch is not exactly subtle.[37]

The Westerbork Concentration Camp is depicted in *Süskind* without any specificity. Life in the Amsterdam Ghetto was also too antiseptic. But the portrayals, situations and outcomes were measured and appropriate. *Süskind* is a better-made film than *Korczak* (1990) and *Defiance* (2008), both of which also depict Jewish heroism. It is a watchable, yet difficult Holocaust film, that makes the most of an important story.

Run Boy Run—Lauf Junge lauf (2013)

Genre:	Victim
Sub-Genre:	Escaping
Length:	107
MPAA or Local Rating:	Unrated (PG)
Language:	German, Polish, Yiddish, Russian
Country:	Germany—France—Poland
Director:	Pepe Danquart
Top-Billed:	Andrzej Tkacz, Kamil Tkacz, Elisabeth Duda
From Wikipedia:	*Run Boy Run* (German: *Lauf Junge lauf*, Polish: *Biegnij, chłopcze, biegnij*, French: *Cours sans te retourner*) is an adaptation of the 2000 novel *Run, Boy, Run* by Uri Orlev, based on the life of Yoram Fridman, who as an eight-year-old Jewish boy in 1942, escaped the Warsaw Ghetto and survived, largely on his own, for the next three years in rural Nazi-occupied Poland.
IMDb Rating:	7.1
IMDb Votes:	1434
***Holocaust Cinema Complete* Description:**	*Run Boy Run—Lauf Junge lauf* (2013) is the most genuine of many films made about young Jewish boys hiding during the War. It is based on the autobiography of a Holocaust survivor who lost an arm while in hiding, but was able to persevere. The acting is compelling and the ending is perfect. *Run Boy Run* is based on a book that can also be used as a companion lesson with the film.
Recommendation:	A great film for younger audiences that does not pander.
Suggested Minimum Grade:	Late Grade School

Review

The very well-made *Run Boy Run—Lauf Junge lauf* (2013) is the second Victim Holocaust film based on an autobiography of survivor Uri Orlev (né Jerzy Henryk Orlowski) (1931–), following his Warsaw Ghetto story told in *The Island on Bird Street* (1997). *Run*

Boy Run, especially in comparison to *The Island on Bird Street,* is the difference between the beginning and end of the Mature Era of Holocaust film, which also spans 1997 through 2013.

Run Boy Run is the story of a little Jewish boy who is saved in the Polish countryside by a series of locals and a vast amount of luck. The boy is played by twins Andrzej and Kamil Tkacz, who are impeccably cast as a Jewish child trying to assimilate into rural Catholic Poland. Jewish boys on the run or hiding alone during the Holocaust is not a new cinematic idea. The first film to depict boys on the run was *Diamonds of the Night—Démanty noci* (1964), which was more graphic and difficult. In comparison to *Run Boy Run,* the film *Europa Europa* (1990) is almost silly, with its antics, travel, love interest and focus on sexuality. And *The Island on Bird Street* (1997) is more like an afternoon special.

But *Run Boy Run* tells its story with confidence and pride. As noted by reviewer Dorota Hartwich in *Cineuropa, Run Boy Run* gets the job done, not needing to stray off into inorganic plot points:

> What matters is that the spectator can identify with the character. Finally, what is also crucially important is that the truth was not distorted in any way, neither by shameless didacticism, generalizations, nor a pathos filled tone, which could easily have happened in this context. The story and human behaviours are complex (those of the Polish people, the Germans and the Jews) and younger audiences can sense this because the director avoided clichés.[38]

The closest comparison to *Run Boy Run* is *Edges of the Lord* (2001), which is a slightly more complicated story with more moving parts. Both films feature little boys on the run in Poland. Both little boys pretend that they are Catholic and learn basic Catholic liturgy. Both boys are adorable. But *Run Boy Run* is more cinematographically accomplished and more genuine than *Edges of the Lord. Run Boy Run* is also based on a true story with a perfect ending. *Run Boy Run*'s Oscar-winning director Pepe Danquart put it all together, making a complete film about one small miracle amid a devastated world.

My Daughter Anne Frank—Meine Tochter Anne Frank (TV 2015)

Genre:	Victim
Sub-Genre:	Hidden
Length:	90
MPAA or Local Rating:	Unrated (PG)
Language:	German
Country:	Germany
Director:	Raymond Ley
Top-Billed:	Mala Emde, Götz Schubert, Lion Wasczyk
From Wikipedia:	The life story of Anne Frank is told from the perspective of her father Otto Frank. After his release from the Auschwitz concentration camp, he returns to Amsterdam to visit his company at Prinsengracht 263. There he receives the diary of his daughter Anne from his clerk Miep Gies, who helped the hidden occupants in the rear building. Miep Gies had picked up the loose pages and books spread out on the backyard floor and hid them in a desk drawer to return them to Anne after the war.
IMDb Rating:	6.5
IMDb Votes:	170

Holocaust Cinema Complete Description:	*My Daughter Anne Frank—Meine Tochter Anne Frank* (TV 2015) is a dazzlingly produced Holocaust film that tells broader Anne Frank stories, about her father's efforts to get her diary published. In *My Daughter Anne Frank,* the Franks' informant is exposed and several of Anne Frank's contemporaries are interviewed. This film is a 90-minute treasure.
Recommendation:	This film is recommended as a unique Anne Frank angle.
Suggested Minimum Grade:	Middle School

REVIEW

Director Raymond Ley's *My Daughter Anne Frank—Meine Tochter Anne Frank* (TV 2015) is one of the best-produced Holocaust films ever made. Half of the film depicts Otto Frank's post–War quest to assemble, edit and publish Anne Frank's diary. The other half reenacts many familiar scenes from the Franks' attic. This version of Anne Frank is much more creatively portrayed than the dozen Goodrich & Hackett classic screenplay versions. For example, *My Daughter Anne Frank* is appropriately somber in the attic, not with a prancing Anne Frank, not overflowing with irrelevant melodramatic screeching and personal tussles. The cinematography is brilliant, far from the tired staging of most Anne Frank films. This version also respectfully retells Otto Frank's pain. According to the director, Raymond Ley, when asked why he based the film on Otto Frank's perspective, he responded:

> I would have thought there would already be at least 52 television films and three series on the topic, but that wasn't the case. Maybe it has to do with the significance of the literature and the discussion about it as "girls' literature." But that's just a presumption. Telling the story through Otto was an idea that developed between me, the producer and the editorial department.[39]

My Daughter Anne Frank also, uniquely for Anne Frank films, intersplices newsreel footage and many real interviews with people who knew Anne Frank, including Miep Gies, Hannah "Hanneli" Elizabeth Goslar and the real Otto Frank. Indeed, of all Holocaust films to use the technique of adding documentary images and interviews to the narrative body of a film, *My Daughter Anne Frank* is, by light-years, the most effective.

The film also has another fascinating plotline involving a journalist in 1962 tracking down the Dutch police official who was responsible for deporting the Franks. Minister Bolkestein's speech encouraging journaling is also uniquely replayed. The reviewer from *Fernsehserien* noted: "The film looks at a small part of the world through the eyes of Anne Frank. Through impressive screen projections, however, the world outside the hiding place also finds its way into the descriptions of the girl. In the confines of her chamber, the images of the times are storming past her: the German invasion, the arbitrary arrests on the street, the kidnapping of Jewish families."[40]

The only drawbacks to *My Daughter Anne Frank* are, like most earlier Anne Frank films, this version also minimizes the Franks' Jewishness. Also, the 19-year-old actress, Mala Emde, who plays Anne Frank seems more like a beauty queen than a Holocaust victim, a cross between Courteney Cox and Julia Louis-Dreyfus, much more regal than the 15-year-old Anne Frank could have been. But the performance is not showy, which is refreshing for an Anne Frank film. And, with a 90-minute runtime, *My Daughter Anne Frank* is, indeed, a treasure. (For more about Anne Frank films, see Chapter 4.)

Son of Saul (2015)

Genre:	Victim
Sub-Genre:	Caught
Length:	107
MPAA or Local Rating:	R for disturbing violent content, and some graphic nudity.
Language:	German, Hungarian, Polish, Yiddish, Russian, Slovak, Czech, Greek
Country:	Hungary
Director:	László Nemes
Top-Billed:	Géza Röhrig, Levente Molnár, Urs Rechn
From Wikipedia:	*Son of Saul* (Hungarian: *Saul fia*) is set in the Auschwitz concentration camp during World War II, and follows a day and a half in the life of Saul Ausländer, a Hungarian member of the Sonderkommando.
IMDb Rating:	7.5
IMDb Votes:	36269
Oscar:	Winner: Best Foreign Language Film.
Holocaust Cinema Complete Description:	*Son of Saul* (2015) is a Hungarian remake of *The Grey Zone* (2001). *Son of Saul,* however, only portrays one Sonderkommando, as opposed to the larger Sonderkommando crew portrayed in *The Grey Zone.* The one Sonderkommando in *Son of Saul* finds a surviving child after a gassing. The Germans examine how the child survived the gas and then kill him. The Sonderkommando then spends the rest of the film trying to ritually bury the child. The Birkenau revolt is barely portrayed. *Son of Saul* is recommended as a great representation of Auschwitz/Birkenau and of one Sonderkommando.
Recommendation:	As a comparative film to *The Grey Zone* (2001).
Suggested Minimum Grade:	High School

Review

Oscar winner for Best Foreign Language Film *Son of Saul* (2015) and its director, László Nemes, are the pride of Sam Spiegel Film & Television School in Jerusalem, which was recently named one of the top 15 film schools in the world.[41] *Son of Saul* has been critically successful. In addition to its Oscar, *Son of Saul* won 59 other awards and was nominated for 55 more. It has grossed approximately $9.7 million[42] and has an astronomical Rotten Tomatoes critics' score of 96 percent.[43]

Although rarely noted outside of this book, *Son of Saul* is a derivative of Tim Blake Nelson's *The Grey Zone* (2001). More than derivative, for the most part, *Son of Saul* is a Hungarian version of *The Grey Zone.* Although some criticism is leveled in this book against *Son of Saul,* especially in Chapter 6: The Greatest Narrative Holocaust Film Ever Made as compared to *The Grey Zone, Son of Saul* is still one of the finest representations of Birkenau.

Vis-à-vis *The Grey Zone,* like the cloned brothers in *The Boys from Brazil* (1978), when identical twins are raised in different countries and cultures, the differences are conspicuous. The minor variances with *The Grey Zone* include: *Son of Saul'*s language, Hungarian; the camerawork in *Son of Saul* is relentless handheld close-ups; *Son of Saul* is only about one Sonderkommando; and *Son of Saul'*s finale after the revolt follows a handful of escapees who are hunted down and murdered. *Flickering Myth'*s Joshua Gill understated his observation of *Son of Saul* in relation to *The Grey Zone,* noting, "*Son of Saul* is a more extensive re-imagining of Dr. Miklós Nyiszli's book."[44] This straying from the book includes that the surviving child was, in fact, a boy, which is ahistorical. At one point, when the child is being carried to the doctor's office, the question is asked if anyone had ever survived the gas before. "I only saw it once, this girl," a man answered, referring to either the truth or to *The Grey Zone*. In *Son of Saul*, however, the surviving child is almost immediately suffocated by the Germans, which is closer to the truth.

László Nemes' story is about a member of a Sonderkommando, Saul, flawlessly played by Hungarian actor Géza Röhrig, who finds a surviving little boy in a gas chamber. Saul tried to save the child, but, unlike the girl in *The Grey Zone*, this boy is murdered soon after and examined by the Germans. From that point forward, Saul adopts the dead child as his own, seeking its proper burial. The ending also differs from *The Grey Zone*, treating the Birkenau uprising as a nuisance for Saul, only useful as a way to escape with the corpse to bury it.

Saul fixates on finding a rabbi to say Kaddish—the prayer for the dead—for the boy. This swirling premise is completely fallacious: rabbis are no more qualified than any other Jew to say Kaddish. Further, virtually every Eastern European Jew knew how to say Kaddish. Finally, by Jewish law, the Kaddish would not have been proper or effective without at least 10 Jewish men present. At the same time, on the brink of the rebellion, because Saul has become so lost in this child, Saul also loses a package of smuggled gunpowder that was intended for the uprising and would be a red flag for the Germans if found. Justin Chang of *Variety* wrote:

> The prolonged assault of the filmmaking won't be to all tastes—particularly the sound work by Tamas Zanyi, who almost seems to be overcompensating for the picture's visual restrictions with its cacophonous layering of screams, shouts, frenzied whispers, gunshots and unplaceable background noise. But few will argue with the sustained grip and power of the film's central performance: Rohrig, an amazing find, requires no grand speeches or overtly introspective moments to hold our attention for nearly every second of the 107-minute running time. His eyes seem to radiate a determination and moral clarity that extends beyond the here and now, his actions suggesting a desperate will to believe in a God who could scarcely seem more absent. For Saul, and for Nemes' galvanizing film, the acceptance of death is no excuse for the rejection of meaning.[45]

Notwithstanding Justin Chang's conclusion ("…no excuse for the rejection of meaning"), Saul's plainly psychotic obsession with the dead boy renders the film's message meaningless. *Son of Saul* vaguely implies a lot, yet says nothing outright. Even the motivation for Saul's obsession with the dead boy is ambiguous. As Joshua Gill put it in *Flickering Myth*, "he chooses to do so not for any redemptive purpose. Instead, it is suggested that because he also sees himself as dead, by burying the boy he is in some way granting him what he believes he wasn't granted himself."[46] It was as if Nemes said, "let's just follow this crazy guy around Birkenau to discover which of 100 ways he will perish." But because we are repelled by crazy protagonists in films who have irrational goals, sussing out *Son of Saul*'s meaning is a fool's errand, a rabbit hole that viewers instinctively avoid; even if we can feel empathy from the mentally ill, we do not seek meaning from their irrationality. As Steven Alan Carr, Purdue University's Director of the Institute for Holocaust and Genocide Studies, harshly concluded, "The Holocaust film is dead. *Son of Saul* has temporarily found a way to turn its style and form inside out."[47]

True, Holocaust film is replete with pathological and mentally imbalanced characters, including the protagonists in *The Juggler* (1953), *The Pawnbroker* (1964), *Harold and Maude* (1971), *The Man in the Glass Booth* (1975), *Sophie's Choice* (1982), *Under the Domim Tree* (1994), *Adam Resurrected* (2008), *The Unborn* (2009) and *Ida* (2013). Yet all these protagonists portray mentally ill Holocaust survivors in Survivor Films after the

War. As for deranged protagonists in Holocaust Victim films, for good reason, almost none except for *Son of Saul* has ever portrayed a delusional protagonist *during* the War, except for Robin Williams' quirky character in the misguided *Jakob the Liar* (1999), and that plot was mishandled as well. But at least in the case of *Jakob the Liar*, the protagonist was trying to give others in the ghetto hope, as opposed to Saul's counterproductive mania. In the words of *New York Magazine*'s David Edelstein, "…we measure works that center on human atrocities by different standards, and deluded Saul ends up a poor vessel for a journey of this magnitude."[48]

Moreover, Saul's form of redemption is the ritual burial of a dead child, not saving a living child. Saul's manic quest turns the plot into an abstract parable. Hoffman and his cohorts in *The Grey Zone* are trying to save a living girl while organizing an uprising; Saul is figuratively trying to atone for all, while, in fact, obstructing the uprising. Symbolic finales can be crucial in films, like when "Chief" escapes at the end of Milos Forman's *One Flew Over the Cuckoo's Nest* (1975) or when "Chance" walks on water at the end of Hal Ashby's *Being There* (1979). But *Son of Saul*'s symbolism requires a psycho-pathological Holocaust victim, a concept which, in twenty-first-century Holocaust Victim film, is obsolete. In contrast, *The Grey Zone*'s Jewish characters—despite the insanity of Birkenau—are disturbing but not disturbed. Furthermore, no protagonist in any Victim Holocaust film—fictional or true—aside from Saul, focuses on a symbolic goal, as opposed to surviving, saving others' lives, escaping from or disrupting the Germans. This does not make *Son of Saul* uniquely bold, but rather uniquely flawed. And let's not forget that Milos Forman's "Chief" succeeds symbolically by destroying part of the asylum and indeed by escaping the cuckoo's nest; Saul fails at everything except trying.

Pau Bosch Santos, who wrote 9,000 words about *Son of Saul* in the *East European Film Bulletin*, suggests that "Saul's madness consists in his refusal against all odds to become a mere victim…."[49] Santos also contrasts *Son of Saul* with *The Grey Zone*, writing, "*Son of Saul* is a catalog of heroic deeds," while "*The Grey Zone* tells the story *Son of Saul* leaves in the background…."[50] Yet, Santos' definition of heroism is only correct if sacrificing to honor one dead Jew is more heroic than destroying half of Birkenau's crematoria.

Even after spilling the forgoing 1,500 words of red ink on *Son of Saul*, in a world that commercially supports such dubious films as *Jakob the Liar* (1999), *The Devil's Arithmetic* (TV 1999), *The Reader* (2008), *Life Is Beautiful* (1997), *The Boy in the Striped Pyjamas* (2008) and *Jojo Rabbit* (2019), any film that tries to emulate *The Grey Zone* (even without attribution) and any sincere account of Birkenau is laudable. *Son of Saul* is successful and stands alone as the champ of Holocaust films that spoon-feed apprehension throughout, followed closely by *Diamonds of the Night—Démanty noci* (1964). *Son of Saul*'s cloistered depiction of a death camp is incomparable. Nemes' oppressive camerawork never allows the viewer any comfort. It is akin to visiting Auschwitz today in the dead of Polish winter, where one is unable to concentrate on the tour because of the oppressive cold, wind and icy footing. *Son of Saul* is also the cinematic equivalent to inducing role-playing in Holocaust education, which, although pedagogically discredited, still proves quite effective in this film.

The Diary of Anne Frank—Das Tagebuch Der Anne Frank (2016)

Genre:	Victim
Sub-Genre:	Hidden
Length:	128

MPAA or Local Rating:	Unrated (PG)
Language:	German
Country:	Germany
Director:	Hans Steinbichler
Top-Billed:	Lea van Acken, Martina Gedeck, Ulrich Noethen
From Wikipedia:	*Das Tagebuch der Anne Frank* (Anne Frank's diary) is the story of Anne Frank, the Jewish girl who went into hiding with her family in Amsterdam and became a victim of the Holocaust. The film is based on Anne Frank's famous diary.
IMDb Rating:	6.7
IMDb Votes:	700
Holocaust Cinema Complete Description:	*The Diary of Anne Frank—Das Tagebuch Der Anne Frank* (2016) is the best Anne Frank in hiding film ever made. It is not sterilized or anodyne like many of the first 20 versions and is much more revealing of Anne Frank's ordeal. Although not as complete as *Anne Frank: The Whole Story* (TV 2001), the hiding portion of this 2016 version is far more convincing. Because this film is more realistic than most previous versions, it is only appropriate for older audiences.
Recommendation:	A great companion to the book, *The Diary of Anne Frank*.
Suggested Minimum Grade:	Middle School, but possibly better for Senior High because of sexuality.

REVIEW

The Diary of Anne Frank—Das Tagebuch Der Anne Frank (2016) is the most mature Anne Frank version of all Anne Frank films. The cast of this 2016 version, finally, is filled with ordinary looking people, with Anne Frank only slightly more attractive. The pettiness expressed by Anne Frank in her diary and faithfully redirected toward the adults who populate her world in most other versions is, thankfully, minimized in this 2016 version. Although still occasionally impudent and petulant, Anne's hallmark cuteness in the other versions has also been toned down to a reasonable level here. The spacious set, although larger and thus less authentic than in other Anne Frank films, places greater emphasis on the actors than on the scenery to depict the angst of those living in the attic. This version also includes Anne Frank's arrival and head-shaving at Auschwitz/Birkenau, after which it chronicles the fates of all the Franks and their guests. Critic Christian Boy of the *NZZ Media Group* noted:

> The 16-year-old Lea van Acken credibly embodies the title heroine as an idiosyncratic girl between cheerfulness and despair. It is also good that Steinbichler shows Anne Frank's deportation to Auschwitz, where her hair is shaved. The scenes are sober, free of pathos and almost documentary. George Stevens' [*The Diary of Anne Frank* (1959)] had cut out the concentration camp after spectators at test shows said they did not like the scene.[51]

The dream sequences, too, in the 2016 version are vibrant, as is Anne's sexuality. She also has extended kissing sessions with Peter. She wistfully speaks of feminine hygiene, stuffs her bra, gazes through a mirror to see her genitals and muses about the geometry of sex. Reviewer Andreas Staben of *Filmstarts* found the same qualities that set this version apart:

> The 16-year-old Lea van Acken even outperforms her film debut *Kreuzweg*. Her Anne is talented, charismatic and modern, but at the same time completely normal; A teenager arguing with her mother (sadly sad: Martina Gedeck), experiencing the first menstruation, being interested in the male anatomy as well as the female and yearning for freedom and understanding…. And it is quite consistent that he

is content after the last diary entry not with text overlays on the fate of Anne, but still some scenes on it and reinforces the contrast: It is almost unbearable to have to watch, like Anne and the other women to be shorn by the Nazis of hair. Conclusion: This independent remake of the famous diary of Anne Frank impresses with her humanity.[52]

Of all the Anne Frank films, this version, *The Diary of Anne Frank—Das Tagebuch Der Anne Frank* is the most genuine. It also feels the most like a feature film, as opposed to made-for-television. It also stands out as the most sexual of Anne Frank films, which is neither a criticism nor a bonus, but simply a fact. And it is in German. Artistically, the English version *The Diary of Anne Frank* (TV 2009) is a steep step down, which may not matter to most English-speaking high schoolers for whom the 2009 version might be more appropriate. And the three-hour *Anne Frank: The Whole Story* (TV 2001) is better produced than the 2009 version, but it is also much more violent and graphic. Although most critics found this 2016 version to be either unnecessary or too lewd, credit Swiss director Hans Steinbichler for making the most sincere version of Anne Frank in hiding in this 2016 production. (For more about Anne Frank films, see Chapter 4.)

Gentile Films

To date, 86 Gentile Holocaust films have been made, which break down into two sub-categories: righteous Gentile films and antisemitic Gentile films. Thirty-nine Righteous Gentile (or "upstander") films have been made, while 18 films have been about antisemitic Gentiles.

Righteous Gentile films are primarily set during the tail-end of the Holocaust and always feature a Gentile protagonist who helps at least one Jew during the Holocaust, as in *Schindler's List* (1993), *Varian's War* (TV 2001), *The Courageous Heart of Irena Sendler* (TV 2009) and *The Zookeeper's Wife* (2017). While there is a temptation to assign "Righteous Gentile" status whenever a Jew is helped in a film by a Gentile during the Holocaust—as with most of the Anne Frank films, *The Pianist* (2002) and *Run Boy Run* (2013)—if the protagonist is a Holocaust victim, as in those examples, then it is nonetheless a Victim film.

The remaining quarter of Gentile films, however, portray antisemitic Gentiles who persecuted, hindered or despoiled Jews during or just after the War. Some of these antisemitic Gentile films include *The Shop on Main Street—Obchod na korze* (1965), *The Nasty Girl—Das schreckliche Mädchen* (1990), *Conspiracy* (TV 2001), *Aftermath—Poklosie* (2012) and *1945* (2017). None are solely American-made.

Both righteous Gentile and antisemitic Gentile films in the Gentile Holocaust genre are mostly based on true stories. Eleven Gentile films are recommended in this chapter, five righteous Gentile and six antisemitic Gentile films.

The Shop on Main Street—Obchod na korze (1965)

Genre:	Gentiles
Sub-Genre:	Antisemitic
Length:	125
MPAA or Local Rating:	U.K.-14+
Language:	Slovak
Country:	Czechoslovakia
Director:	Ján Kadár and Elmar Klos

Top-Billed:	Ida Kaminska, Jozef Kroner, Hana Slivková
From Wikipedia:	*The Shop on Main Street* (Czech—Slovak: Obchod na korze, in the U.K. A Shop on the High Street) is a 1965 Czechoslovak film about the Aryanization program during World War II in the Slovak State.
IMDb Rating:	8.1
IMDb Votes:	6913
Oscar:	Winner: Best Foreign Language Film; Oscar nomination: Best Actress.
Holocaust Cinema Complete Description:	*The Shop on Main Street—Obchod na korze* (1965) is an uncompromising depiction of Czech antisemitism and collaboration with the Germans. It portrays with great honesty the systematic, brazen "appropriation" of Jewish businesses by the local Czech community as the Jews are being deported. Given that depictions of Soviet suffering were the Communism party line until the fall of Communism, *The Shop on Main Street* is even more impressive considering that it was made behind the "Iron Curtain."
Recommendation:	For those studying despoilment of Jews by local populations.
Suggested Minimum Grade:	Middle School

REVIEW

The best Post-War Era Holocaust films did not attempt to depict death camps in epic productions. Instead, the best early films concentrated on smaller stories about individual victims and their difficult moral decisions, as with the first recommended antisemitic Gentile film *The Shop on Main Street—Obchod na korze* (1965). This Communist Czech winner of the 1966 Oscar for Best Foreign Language Film also featured a remarkable performance from then 66-year-old Ida Kaminska (1899–1980), who was nominated for the Best Actress Oscar for her performance in *The Shop on Main Street* (losing to Elizabeth Taylor in *Who's Afraid of Virginia Woolf?* [1966]). *The Shop on Main Street* was co-directed by Hungarian Ján Kadár (1918–1979) and Czech Elmar Klos (1910–1993). Ten years later, Ján Kadár directed the charming Oscar-nominated (non–Holocaust) *Lies My Father Told Me* (1975), about a Jewish family in Montreal, Canada, circa 1920.

The Shop on Main Street is about the days leading up to the deportation of a small community of Jews in a rural Czech town. A widowed shop owner (Kaminska) is oblivious to the pending catastrophe. The town's Gentiles are busy divvying up the Jews' property even before the Jews are taken away. One man, a good-hearted simpleton, poignantly played by Jozef Kroner, has been proactively assigned ownership of the old woman's button and thread shop, which is often terribly busy. In her senility, the woman comes to believe this despoiler is her nephew. He is increasingly torn, not knowing how to protect or save her, and ultimately, accidentally kills her. Gary Tooze of *DVDBeaver* wrote: "Moving effortlessly from drama to humour to tragedy, *The Shop on Main Street* is a complex political morality tale of common lives disturbed and destroyed by war. A story of loyalty, betrayal, cowardice and heroism, it is a scathing exploration of how minor compromises can lead to complicity in the horrors of a totalitarian regime. It asks every spectator: 'If it had been you, what would you have done?'"[53] In a review entitled "One of the more memorable films about the Holocaust," critic Dennis Schwartz wrote:

> Through the magnificent performances of Kroner and Kaminska, a star in the Yiddish theater who was born in Odessa, the film reaches great heights by showing how the ordinary person gets caught up in the conflicts of his time and is stuck trying to make the right choices. The pathetic carpenter, a Christian who just wants to be left alone to play with his dog and work with wood, becomes so confused

when things are out of his control, that he's not sure at the end if he's capable of doing the morally right thing or of even knowing his own identity.[54]

The Shop on Main Street would be half of a seamless double-feature when paired with the outstanding Hungarian film *1945* (2017). Made 52 years later, *1945* depicts two Jews returning to their village just after the War, ostensibly to their former store which was taken by locals as the Jews were deported, with the new owners having no intention of returning the ill-gotten property and business. Both films mercilessly portray the avarice of rural antisemitic communities, their two-fisted feasting on Jewish property, and their enthusiastic complicity with Nazi Germany. Both films suggest that anyone with a moral compass was regarded by their compatriots as aberrant busybodies, weaklings who should have stuck with the program and taken what the Lord had "given" them. And both films expose the endemic antisemitism upon which the Germans banked when occupying Europe.

Mr. Klein—Monsieur Klein (1976)

Genre:	Gentiles
Sub-Genre:	Antisemitic
Length:	123
MPAA or Local Rating:	U.K.-14+
Language:	French
Country:	France
Director:	Joseph Losey
Top-Billed:	Alain Delon, Jeanne Moreau, Francine Bergé
From Wikipedia:	*Monsieur Klein* (Mr. Klein) is a 1976 French film directed by Joseph Losey, with Alain Delon starring in the title role.
IMDb Rating:	7.6
IMDb Votes:	4408
***Holocaust Cinema Complete* Description:**	*Mr. Klein—Monsieur Klein* (1976) is a sophisticated story about a French Gentile who profits from the misfortunes of the French Jewish community at the start of German occupation. As Jews were being deported, Paris was a buyer's market for art dealers. Mr. Klein lives the good life until he is misidentified as a Jew, at which time his fortunes change. The premise is marvelous, and the filmmaking is excellent.
Recommendation:	A provocative look at French complicity in Paris during German occupation.
Suggested Minimum Grade:	Middle School

REVIEW

The French *Mr. Klein—Monsieur Klein* (1976), like *Hair* (Broadway 1968), features a man who is killed during war due to mistaken identity. The difference, though, is that the nice guy who dies in *Hair* is tragic, while Mr. Klein's dying is closer to justice. American Gentile director Joseph Losey (1909–1984) made *Mr. Klein* during his exile from America, long after Losey's blacklisting caused by a HUAC probe. Like Losey's experience in 1950s America, *Mr. Klein*'s plot loosely indicts the authoritarian penchant for convenience in place of working to discover the messy truth. The irony here is that Losey's protagonist, Mr. Klein, is a smarmy Catholic Alsatian who is completely unsympathetic, despite his ultimate plight.

Mr. Klein has no moral crisis when acquiring art at vastly distressed prices from the downward spiraling Jews. Mr. Klein is perfectly depicted as a French parasite, prospering from the desperate Jews during German occupation just before the infamous roundup of French Jews into the Vel' d'Hiv (Paris velodrome) in July 1942. On one level, it is remarkable that an American could have made such an authentic French film. *Mr. Klein* is a better Holocaust film than any other solo French production, with the exception of Claude Berri's autobiographical *The Two of Us—Le vieil homme et l'enfant* (1967).* But perhaps only a non–French director had enough distance to admonish the French so acutely for their complicity. Further, Losey's dispassionate accuracy was especially rare during the Commercial Era of Holocaust film.

Two much lesser films in 2010 also focused on the Paris roundup, *The Round Up— La rafle* (2010) and *Sarah's Key—Elle s'appelait Sarah* (2010). Both of those films use the cataclysmic round up as a starting point for their meandering films; *Mr. Klein* ends with Mr. Klein being rounded up to be sent to his death. Alain Delon, who plays Mr. Klein, is also perfectly cast. "Great acting by Delon," wrote critic Dennis Schwartz, "a great premise and great atmosphere, make this nearly a great film."[55] As reviewed by *Cinemagazine*'s Patricia Smagge in 2009:

> *Mr. Klein* is an intense psychological thriller that passes you by at a moderate pace. Although the storyline is not always easy to follow, it does not take Losey and Delon any effort to hold the viewer's attention. Delon's performance is subtle and precisely balanced with the overall atmosphere that this film wants to convey. *Mr. Klein* is a complex character study with nightmarish traits and a brilliant twist at the end where the shivers will be on your back. This film by Joseph Losey deserves a much larger audience than he has received so far.[56]

Mr. Klein is not the kind of film one might expect from a victim of political persecution. It rightfully does not allow for even the slightest sympathy for Mr. Klein. *Mr. Klein* is a gem for those wanting to see the French portrayed at their worst during the War, which is a theme in many French films. *Mr. Klein*'s tight focus on one man is compelling, as is François Truffaut's larger *The Last Metro—Le dernier métro* (1980), starring French cinematic titans Catherine Deneuve, Gérard Depardieu and Jean Poiret. That film also takes many big swings at their native country. The tone of *Mr. Klein* supports the notion that European Gentiles had little love for their Jews and were all too happy to have their unexpected German "guests" do a little housecleaning before Germany's ultimate checkout.

Au Revoir les Enfants (1987)

Genre:	Gentiles
Sub-Genre:	Righteous
Length:	104
MPAA or Local Rating:	PG
Language:	French
Country:	France—West Germany
Director:	Louis Malle
Top-Billed:	Gaspard Manesse, Raphael Fejtö, Francine Racette
From Wikipedia:	*Au Revoir les Enfants* (meaning "Goodbye, Children") is an autobiographical 1987 film written, produced and directed by Louis Malle.
IMDb Rating:	8.0
IMDb Votes:	27179
Oscar:	Nominations: Best Writer & Foreign Language Film.

* *Au Revoir les Enfants* (1987) was a French co-production with West Germany.

Holocaust Cinema Complete Description:	After *Conspiracy of Hearts* (1960), *Au Revoir les Enfants* (1987) is the first major righteous Gentile film. *Au Revoir les Enfants* was worth the wait. Loosely based on the director Louis Malle's wartime experience, it tells the true story of French Jewish schoolchildren who are hidden in a Catholic boarding school. *Au Revoir les Enfants* is a rich, poignant film that is understandably sentimental, yet that does not descend into mawkishness.
Recommendation:	A classy alternative to commercialized righteous Gentile stories.
Suggested Minimum Grade:	Late Grade School

REVIEW

French director Louis Malle (1932–1995) had a storied career, directing 24 feature narrative films, including the idiosyncratic *My Dinner with Andre* (1981), the coarse *Atlantic City* (1980), the salacious *Pretty Baby* (1978), featuring 12-year-old Brooke Shields as a prostitute, *Vanya on 42nd Street* (1994), which is the most underrated film I have ever seen, and the frank Holocaust film *Lacombe, Lucien* (1974), about a young dimwit in occupied France who embraces the power of being a gangster for the occupiers. For the last 15 years of his life, Malle was also the husband of prominent actress Candice Bergen, who gained fame in Mike Nichols' *Carnal Knowledge* (1971) and later as the star of *Murphy Brown* (TV 1988–2018).

Malle's greatest professional accomplishment was his autobiographical *Au Revoir les Enfants* (1987) ("Goodbye Children"), which was Oscar-nominated for both the Best Foreign Language Film and Best Writing. As Vincent Canby noted in *The New York Times* upon the film's release: "Every film that Mr. Malle made in those intervening years has been preparation for *Au Revoir les Enfants*. Like *The Dead*, which it resembles in no other way, it's a work that has the kind of simplicity, ease and density of detail that only a film maker [*sic*] in total command of his craft can bring off, and then only rarely."[57]

There is nothing outrageous or fancy about *Au Revoir les Enfants*. Nothing flashy happens. It is simply the story of Malle as a young student named Julien at a Catholic boarding school in occupied France and three Jewish boys who are welcomed there as students in an attempt to save them from the Germans. Ultimately, an angry kitchen boy who has had his black-market side business disrupted, reports the Jews for a bounty. The Jews are taken, certainly to their deaths, along with the priest in charge, who states as he is being led away, "Au Revoir les Enfants." In a world where clever people strive to identify double entendre where none may exist, Malle is clearly stating through the priest that the young witnesses can never be children again. Roger Ebert wrote in his "Great Films" series:

> The film ends in a long closeup of Julien, reminding us of the last shot of Truffaut's *The 400 Blows*, and we hear Malle's voice on the soundtrack: "More than 40 years have passed, but I'll remember every second of that January morning until the day I die." After the speech ends, the camera stays on Julien's face for 25 more seconds, and on the soundtrack the piano is heard once again, this time quiet, sad and correct.[58]

Au Revoir les Enfants is one of only five righteous Gentile films recommended in this book. It and the fine Czech film *Divided We Fall—Musíme si pomáhat* (2000) are also the only recommended righteous Gentile films that do not reenact masses of Jews being saved. Even so, *Au Revoir les Enfants* is most similar to the recommended French Victim film *The Two of Us—Le vieil homme et l'enfant* (1967), whose Jewish protagonist is also a child, a young boy hidden in occupied France and who had much better luck than Malle's classmates.

With an IMDb rating of 8.0, *Au Revoir les Enfants* is Malle's top-rated film and one of his last, made 33 years into an accomplished career. Malle rarely made audacious or grandstanding epics. He preferred to pull authentic performances from the stories of those with little agency. Louis Malle's autobiographical *Au Revoir les Enfants* is a lesson for film lovers and filmmakers alike, that art works best when it is authentic and heartfelt.

Good Evening, Mr. Wallenberg—God afton, Herr Wallenberg— En Passionshistoria från verkligheten (1990)

Genre:	Gentiles
Sub-Genre:	Righteous
Length:	118
MPAA or Local Rating:	Unrated (R)
Language:	Swedish
Country:	Sweden
Director:	Kjell Grede
Top-Billed:	Stellan Skarsgård, Katharina Thalbach, Károly Eperjes
From Wikipedia:	*Good Evening, Mr. Wallenberg* (Swedish: God afton, Herr Wallenberg— En Passionshistoria från verkligheten) is a 1990 film about Swedish World War II diplomat Raoul Wallenberg, who was instrumental in saving the lives of thousands of Hungarian Jews from the Holocaust.
IMDb Rating:	6.8
IMDb Votes:	870
***Holocaust Cinema Complete* Description:**	*Good Evening, Mr. Wallenberg* (1990) tells the story of Raoul Wallenberg who saved many tens of thousands of Jews. This screen version of his story is uncompromising in its depiction of German savagery and Jewish powerlessness. Wallenberg, who was later captured and murdered by the Soviets, is portrayed as a goodhearted man who never sought glory or thanks. Of films that depict Gentiles who save many Jews, *Good Evening, Mr. Wallenberg* is the most genuine and non-commercial.
Recommendation:	"TOP THREE" IN GENRE. For those seeking an ambitious righteous Gentile story that keeps the victims in perspective.
Suggested Minimum Grade:	High School

REVIEW

Until *Schindler's List* (1993), Raoul Wallenberg was easily the most famous righteous Gentile in history. His exploits, when saving tens of thousands of Hungarian Jews before his abduction and then disappearance by the Soviets during the liberation of Budapest, were legendary.[59] A majority of Western countries have at least one monument dedicated to Wallenberg, who was also posthumously awarded the United States Congressional Gold Medal in 2012 in recognition of his achievements and heroic actions during the Holocaust.

In 1985, the 200-minute American made-for-television *Wallenberg—A Hero's Story* was aired, starring heartthrob Richard Chamberlain as Raoul Wallenberg. This micro-miniseries—produced between *Holocaust* (Miniseries 1978) and *War and Remembrance* (Miniseries 1988)—suffered from the same overt melodramatic treatment as those two more famous miniseries. Fortunately, the Swedish take on Raoul Wallenberg, *Good Evening, Mr. Wallenberg—God afton, Herr Wallenberg—En Passionshistoria från verkligheten* (1990), avoided the many temptations that befell the American biopic.

Director Kjell Grede's *Good Evening, Mr. Wallenberg* does not glorify Raoul Wallenberg as a man seeking anything other than the safety of as many Jews as possible. The film is not sentimental, but a humble depiction of a humble man who gave his life to save thousands of strangers. As noted extensively in Chapter 4, *Schindler's List* is successful partly because it rehabilitated a loathsome man. This deceptive crutch is unnecessary in *Good Evening, Mr. Wallenberg*, which, although not as artful, is a much braver story about a far better man. Starring Swedish actor Stellan Skarsgård, best known as Professor Lambeau in *Good Will Hunting* (1997), *Good Evening, Mr. Wallenberg* portrays Raoul Wallenberg as selfless and determined. "The acting as a whole in the film was superb," noted critic Haley Harris.[60] The violence, too, in *Good Evening, Mr. Wallenberg* is well-placed, harsh and makes no bones about being in a warzone filled with genocidal psychopaths, held together by a bankrupt Nazi ideology as the Soviets were closing in. As *The New York Times'* critic Stephen Holden wrote:

> A film of epic ambitions, *Good Evening, Mr. Wallenberg* is particularly good at evoking a feeling of absolute chaos at a moment when the world is in a state of collapse. The eerily silent back street [*sic*] in which a rapidly diminishing group of survivors and their captor wait for their fate to descend is like an apocalyptic eye of the storm.[61]

This moment in World War II—when the Germans on the Eastern front realized that all was lost, that the "Master Race" was about to become subservient, and that accountability would not come from some austere Western court, but by a bullet to the back of the head—is usually satisfying in Holocaust films. It is sour here, in the fine *Good Evening, Mr. Wallenberg*, because of the same fate of Raoul Wallenberg doled out by the same Soviets. With a runtime of 1¼ hours shorter than *Schindler's List,* and with a protagonist who is a good man from start to finish, in a perfect world *Good Evening, Mr. Wallenberg* would replace *Schindler's List* in classrooms and on must-see lists.

Three Days in April—Drei Tage im April (TV 1995)

Genre:	Gentile
Sub-Genre:	Antisemitic
Length:	105
MPAA or Local Rating:	Unrated (PG)
Language:	German
Country:	Germany
Director:	Oliver Storz
Top-Billed:	Karoline Eichhorn, April Hailer, Eva Michel
From Wikipedia:	*Three days in April* is a German-French-Austrian film by director Oliver Storz from 1995 about the events in a German village at the end of the Second World War. The plot is based on a true story.
IMDb Rating:	7.6
IMDb Votes:	60
***Holocaust Cinema Complete* Description:**	*Three Days in April—Drei Tage im April* (TV 1995) captures the moment just before German transition from supremacy to submission. It portrays the German despair near the end of the War when all is lost. Just then, cattle cars full of Jews in transit from one concentration camp to another are abandoned in a little German village. What, if anything, should the locals do with or for these dying Jews? If all is lost, what is gained by helping these people who, for more than a decade, have officially been deemed subhuman enemies of the German State.
Recommendation:	For those wanting to contemplate the perspective of the vanquished common people in the "Master Race" at the end of the Third Reich.
Suggested Minimum Grade:	High School

REVIEW

Three Days in April—Drei Tage im April (TV 1995) does a nice job with a great premise: what to do with an abandoned trainload of Jews in Germany just before the end of the War. Regrettably, the film is based on a true story. *Three Days in April* exposes all of this in a film that was also explicitly intended by the filmmakers to be a memorial to those Jews who suffered 50 years earlier in the event portrayed. This German film succeeded on all levels.

Three Days in April is lugubrious, with no hint of sympathy for the failing Reich, no glory for the would-be war-criminals in German uniforms. It is just some last-minute German rutting and fretting during the final days of supremacy, the most tenuous for all: the six-pointed star that was a death sentence becomes a life-saving source of identification; the Nazi uniform that made the world cower in January is shed in April; the woman who slept with the local SS officer for a few extra rations in occupied Europe is shorn of her hair and beaten during liberation. As noted in the German review site *Tittelbach*:

> The story takes place in the last days of the war. The Americans are not far off. Between hope and fear, most of the inhabitants of the small Swabian village go about their daily business. In the tavern squats meanwhile the Schwemmgut of the war, scattered Landser, the survivors of a front theater. You sing enemy music, let yourself drift—soon the whole haunt is over anyway. But then, the people in the most terrible way catch up with the reality of the Third Reich: A cattle car with hundreds of inmates to be transferred to a concentration camp, safe from the Allies, is parked at the station of the village.[62]

With the wartime belief in racial superiority being extinguished, what is a southern German town to do with three cattle cars full of Jews from camps in Poland? The moral questions raised are more pragmatic than those in *God on Trial* (TV 2008). And like *God on Trial*, *Three Days in April* is bookended by scenes from the present. *Three Days in April* is an extraordinarily thoughtful film that lets none of the antagonists off the hook. It also proves once again that valid Holocaust films can be made without special effects, massive budgets, miles of film and interminable plots.

Divided We Fall—Musíme si pomáhat (2000)

Genre:	Gentiles
Sub-Genre:	Righteous
Length:	123
MPAA or Local Rating:	PG-13 for some violence and sexual content.
Language:	German
Country:	Czech Republic
Director:	Jan Hrebejk
Top-Billed:	Bolek Polívka, Csongor Kassai, Jaroslav Dusek
From Wikipedia:	[Translated Czech, Edited] During German occupation, a Czech couple hides a Jewish escapee of a concentration camp in their home.
IMDb Rating:	7.8
IMDb Votes:	4509
Oscar:	Nomination: Best Foreign Language Film.
***Holocaust Cinema Complete* Description:**	*Divided We Fall—Musíme si pomáhat* (2000) is a small story about a Jew who is hidden by a married couple in occupied Czechoslovakia. Like most Czech Holocaust films, *Divided We Fall* is subtle, never overreaching. It is a charming film that makes its points without making a big fuss.
Recommendation:	A small righteous Gentile story set in Eastern Europe.
Suggested Minimum Grade:	Middle School

REVIEW

The Czechs have a knack for making honest, smaller Holocaust films. Academy Award nominee for Foreign Language Film *Divided We Fall—Musíme si pomáhat* (2000) is exemplary. It is the story of a darling young Gentile couple without children who inadvertently are pressed into hiding a Jewish stranger in their apartment for two years. The twist is that their best friend—who bears a striking resemblance to Hitler—is an enthusiastic local henchman for the German occupiers. The film is a series of "almost-caught" moments, with the friend seemingly always a step behind. Ultimately the Nazi sympathizer catches on and they all save each other in a nice set of twists.

Richard Schickel wrote in *Time Magazine* of *Divided We Fall*: "A biblically named couple, Josef and Marie (Boleslav Polivka and Anna Siskova), who, during World War II, agree to hide David (Csongor Kassai), a concentration-camp escapee. Josef and Marie desperately want a child, which, for medical reasons, they are unable to conceive."[63] Director Jan Hrebejk's *Divided We Fall* is not violent. It is not flashy. It lost out on the Foreign Language Film Oscar to *Crouching Tiger, Hidden Dragon* (2000), the highest-grossing non–American film in history. But *Divided We Fall* gets the job done using as much humor as *Life Is Beautiful,* without embarrassing itself when trying to get a laugh.

As noted by *The New York Times'* critic A.O. Scott: "The film's climax is a crescendo of mortal suspense that also includes elements of farce. Unlike the meretricious *Life Is Beautiful, Divided We Fall* is pervaded with humor that serves not to sentimentalize or sugarcoat the monstrosity of Naziism [sic], but to explain it. The filmmakers explore not only the banality of evil, but also the banality of goodness, and the ridiculousness, as well as the tragedy, of their collision."[64]

Divided We Fall and Louis Malle's *Au Revoir les Enfants* (1987), also a Best Foreign Language Film Oscar nominee, are the only two righteous Gentile films recommended in this book that are not about saving thousands of Jews. Although completely different in tone, both films tell modest, plausible stories about simple people trying to do the right thing despite the very real possibility of being murdered for their trouble. And, laudably, neither film depicts its hidden Jews as lesser than their protectors. *Au Revoir les Enfants* ends badly for a righteous Gentile and his wards, while *Divided We Fall* has a happy ending. On the other hand, while the tragic *Au Revoir les Enfants* was a true story that represented the overwhelming common outcome of such heroism, *Divided We Fall* allows a fictional ray of light without glorifying or stepping all over itself.

Finally, it is worth noting that this slot could have been devoted to the also very well made *Protector—Protektor* (2009), which is, overall, a better Czech film, but not as good a Holocaust film.

Conspiracy (TV 2001)

Genre:	Gentiles
Sub-Genre:	Antisemitic
Length:	96
MPAA or Local Rating:	R for language.
Language:	English
Country:	U.S.—U.K.
Director:	Frank Pierson
Top-Billed:	Kenneth Branagh, Clare Bullus, Stanley Tucci

From Wikipedia:	*Conspiracy* is a 2001 BBC–HBO war film which dramatizes the 1942 Wannsee Conference. The film delves into the psychology of Nazi officials involved in the "Final Solution of the Jewish Question" during World War II.
IMDb Rating:	7.8
IMDb Votes:	15701
Emmy:	Winners: Best Lead Actor in a Miniseries or a Movie & Writing for a Miniseries or a Movie; Nominations: Made for Television Movie, Directing for a Miniseries, Movie or a Special, Cinematography for a Miniseries or a Movie, Single Camera Picture Editing for a Miniseries, Movie or a Special, Supporting Actor in a Miniseries or a Movie, Supporting Actor in a Miniseries or a Movie, Sound Editing for a Miniseries, Movie or a Special & Single Camera Sound Mixing for a Miniseries or a Movie.
Holocaust Cinema Complete Description:	*Conspiracy* (TV 2001) vividly depicts the chillingly sterilized 1942 Wannsee Conference where, in one afternoon outside of Berlin, Reinhard Heydrich and his top assistant, Adolf Eichmann, codified the "Final Solution." The made-for-television film explains that the Germans had concluded that, because shooting the first million Jews in fields had been inefficient and had demoralized German soldiers who pulled the trigger, a better method of mass murder had been developed. The solution that day was revealed as Auschwitz and its gas chambers. The film brilliantly portrays German heartlessness exhibited at the conference.
Recommendation:	"TOP THREE" IN GENRE. Ideal for teaching about the German decision to implement the "Final Solution"
Suggested Minimum Grade:	Middle School

REVIEW

On January 20, 1942, in an ornate villa, Am Großen Wannsee 56–58, in the Wannsee suburb of Berlin, 15 men gathered around a large conference table for a few hours. The typical understanding of the infamous Wannsee Conference was that the fate of European Jews was decided then and there. Laura Fries in *Variety* began her review of *Conspiracy* (TV 2001), the reenactment of Wannsee, by asserting:

> It could be a boardroom at any Fortune 500 company where stockholders bicker over inventory and storage. Instead, the 15 men gathered in this lakeside resort home outside of Berlin are discussing the details of a "Final Solution" to purge all Jews from Europe. In this disturbing original movie, co-produced by HBO and BBC Films, director Frank Pierson recreates the less than two hours it took for high-ranking Third Reich officials to agree to the eradication of an entire race.[65]

This is a slight misreading of history. By the time of the conference, largely as a result of German mass murders by death squads after the invasion of Poland, approximately 2 million Jews had already been murdered. More broadly, the fate of Europe's Jews had been cast with Hitler's ascension to power nine years earlier, in 1933. If not then, certainly after the Nuremberg Laws in September 1935, when the status of German Jews was reduced to subhuman. If not then, the fate of Europe's Jews was sealed when British Prime Minister Neville Chamberlain capitulated to Hitler by signing the 1938 Munich Agreement, giving the Sudetenland region of Czechoslovakia to Hitler. Other events arguably could demarcate when the fate of Europe's Jews was decided.

Yet, there is a pervasive belief that the Wannsee Conference was the beginning of the Final Solution. In fact, the Wannsee Conference was simply an example of vaunted German efficiency and process, serving two specific housekeeping objectives: first, the political consolidation of the power by Obergruppenführer (three-star general) Reinhard

Heydrich to oversee the Final Solution, per his boss, Reichsführer Heinrich Himmler; and, second, the notification to the German politicians, military and civil servants that the remaining 11 million Jews within Germany's reach would be gassed, starved and worked to death at a rate of many thousands per day—millions per year—per Reinhard Heydrich. In short, the real story of the Wannsee Conference is the successful power-grab of Reinhard Heydrich, eliminating any doubt by those at the meeting who may have technically been Heydrich's superiors or lateral to him, that they were either going to play genocide ball with him or be eliminated.

Frank Pierson's 96-minute BBC/HBO *Conspiracy* is a breathtaking reenactment of the Wannsee Conference, written from a once-hidden transcript of the event. It is also rare for having a running time that approximates the length of the event being reenacted. *Conspiracy* is perfect. "Every aspect works," wrote critic Charles Tatum, continuing, "you may find yourself in utter disbelief, as I was, when you see how many of the participants survived the war and returned to civilian life, living decades after the meeting's subjects."[66]

Reinhard Heydrich is played by five-time Oscar nominee Kenneth Branagh, whose performance is astounding, shockingly effective and one of the most memorable of all the thousands of Holocaust film performances. Branagh's Heydrich is penetrating, like a javelin dropped from an airplane into a lake. No less effective is Stanley Tucci as Adolf Eichmann, Heydrich's right-hand man, entrusted with the execution of the plan. *The New Yorker*'s critic Melvin Backman wrote a review entitled "*Conspiracy*, a Withering Study of the Bureaucracy of the Holocaust," where he noted:

> With the softer hearts cowed, the men take their leave. Outside, Stanley Tucci's *Adolf Eichmann* catches the guards indulging in a snowball fight. He finds the superior officer and slaps him. "It just seemed to happen," the soldier stammers. "Not in uniform," Eichmann replies. "Nothing ever just happens."[67]

Colin Firth was magnificent, as was the rest of the cast. If nothing else, the film is worth watching simply for the performances. Tacitly, this film also asks some basic questions about the Holocaust. For example, could Germany have prevailed—or at least not been required to capitulate to "total surrender"—had they not directed their resources to the Holocaust? Why didn't the Germans simply exploit the majority of Jews as laborers instead of killing them? How did the German judiciary respond to extrajudicial planning? And most strikingly, how was it possible for the Final Solution to be accomplished without any paper trail from Adolf Hitler or his Reichsführer Heinrich Himmler? *Conspiracy* also features a subtle mini-epilogue allegory, suggesting that the Germans should be careful what they ask for; they will ultimately miss their Jews, not for moral or societal reasons, but for the simple loss of their raison d'être.

The story of *Conspiracy* is also told well in the Austrian/West German *The Final Solution: The Wannsee Conference—Die Wannseekonferenz* (TV 1984). The earlier attempt is also well-made, but not as artistic or as focused. *Conspiracy* is an amazing film that should be mandatory for all English-speaking high school students.

The Relief of Belsen (TV 2007)

Genre:	Gentiles
Sub-Genre:	Righteous
Length:	101
MPAA or Local Rating:	PG-13

Language:	English
Country:	U.K.
Director:	Justin Hardy
Top-Billed:	Iain Glen, Nigel Lindsay, Jemma Redgrave
From Wikipedia:	*The Relief of Belsen* is a feature-length drama that was first shown on Channel 4 in the United Kingdom on 15 October 2007. It depicts events that unfolded at Bergen-Belsen concentration camp following the liberation of the camp by British troops in April 1945. Written by Justin Hardy and Peter Guinness, it nevertheless cites its sources from eye witness accounts of people who were there at the time.
IMDb Rating:	7.3
IMDb Votes:	252
BAFTA:	Nomination: Best Specialist Factual.
Holocaust Cinema Complete Description:	*The Relief of Belsen* (TV 2007) is a historical reenactment of British efforts to save 60,000 dying Jews in the just liberated Bergen-Belsen Concentration Camp. No other Holocaust film comes close to depicting the challenges faced by the liberators of German camps. Although some of the side plots are superfluous, *The Relief of Belsen* is an absolute triumph in its difficult portrayal of the War's aftermath.
Recommendation:	For those interested in the Allied efforts to save Jews after liberation.
Suggested Minimum Grade:	High School

REVIEW

Stories abound about emaciated death camp survivors dying just after having been given food by their liberators; these survivors of starvation in German camps died because they could not digest real food. Some films portray a few Holocaust victims during liberation, such as *Naked Among Wolves—Nackt unter Wölfen* (1963), *The Truce—La tregua* (1997), *Life Is Beautiful—La Vita è bella* (1997), *The Counterfeiters—Die Fälscher* (2007) and *Naked Among Wolves—Nackt unter Wölfen* (TV 2015). But only one film deals directly with the unprecedented humanitarian crisis faced by camp liberators in the aftermath of the defeat of Germany, *The Relief of Belsen* (TV 2007). (*Band of Brothers* [Miniseries 2001, Episode 9] also laudably deals with the subject, but more briefly and with much less detail.) That reason, alone, recommends *The Relief of Belsen*.

This British film reenacts British efforts to solve historically difficult medical issues. At all liberated camps, thousands of survivors were dying daily from typhus and years of malnutrition. At Bergen-Belsen, a concentration camp in northern Germany (where Anne Frank died), quarantines, bulldozers, chemical showers, razing infected areas with flame throwers, forced feeding and compassion were all tried. Ultimately, a protein formula was utilized, which was also useless until it was made edible. Certainly, the most interesting moment in the film was when the Brits forced the local Germans and POWs to help care for some of the survivors, deconstruct the disease-riddled camp and bury the dead. Also, in a rarely successful maneuver, stock footage of Bergen-Belsen was used, albeit sparingly, but effectively.

The only fault of *The Relief of Belsen* was the manipulative personal storylines, which were unnecessary and trite, even if true. Nonetheless, learning of this British intrepidness—especially that of Major-General James Johnston—was worth wading through some melodrama and romance. Of passing interest to film buffs is that two lesser-known members of the Redgrave acting clan star in *The Relief of Belsen*: Corin Redgrave, brother of both Lynn and Vanessa Redgrave, and uncle of Natasha

Richardson, and Corin's daughter, Jemma—all five of whom appeared in at least one Holocaust film, as did the grandfather, Sir Michael Redgrave in *The 25th Hour—La vingt-cinquième heure* (1967).

The Relief of Belsen is an obscure film, with no professional reviews. Nonetheless, *The Relief of Belsen* is the only film for learning in-depth about the challenges of camp liberation. More than 60,000 out of approximately 75,000 Jews were saved after the War by dozens of Gentiles at Belsen, compassionate individuals who risked typhus and lived in intolerable conditions to save Jews. *The Relief of Belsen* deserves to be watched and these Brits deserve our gratitude, both the liberators and filmmakers.

Akte Grüninger (TV 2013)

Genre:	Gentiles
Sub-Genre:	Righteous
Length:	96
MPAA or Local Rating:	Unrated (PG)
Language:	Swiss German, German
Country:	Switzerland—Austria
Director:	Alain Gsponer
Top-Billed:	Helmut Förnbacher, Aaron Hitz, Pascal Holzer
From Wikipedia:	*Akte Grüninger* is a Swiss-Austrian feature film that was produced in 2013 for the Swiss television SRF. The television film focuses on the events in late summer 1938, when Paul Grüninger saved the lives of up to 3,600 Jewish refugees from Germany and Austria by pre-dating their visas, enabling them to migrate "illegally" to Switzerland.
IMDb Rating:	6.8
IMDb Votes:	180
Holocaust Cinema Complete Description:	*Akte Grüninger* (TV 2013) is about a Swiss police commander on the German border who disobeyed orders, saving 3,600 Jews. Grüninger found a way to allow entry to Jews in 1938 when no other haven was available to them. Grüninger's Swiss government never forgave him for forging the documents needed to subvert their laws. The film, although made-for-television, feels like a feature film. *Akte Grüninger* is an outstanding righteous Gentile film.
Recommendation:	A relatively unknown story about Swiss attitudes leading up to and during the Holocaust.
Suggested Minimum Grade:	Middle School

REVIEW

Paul Grüninger (1891–1972) was a Swiss police commander stationed on the Swiss/German border. In 1938, as Jews were trying to escape Germany into Switzerland, Grüninger was faced with a dilemma: turn away thousands of fleeing Jews who would likely be murdered if they stayed in Germany, or violate Swiss law by allowing these refugees to cross into his safe country and then harbor them. Fortunately, for thousands of Jews, Grüninger chose the latter.

To save Jews, Paul Grüninger manipulated municipal records, found housing for refugees, and made sure they had food and dignity. His reward by Swiss authorities, almost until his death in 1972, was to live out his life as disgraced and insubordinate. According to Yad Vashem, which designated Grüninger as "Righteous Among the Nations," Paul Grüninger saved 3,600 Jews. A documentary about Paul Grüninger was made, called *Grüninger's Fall* (1997).

The narrative film about this righteous Gentile *Akte Grüninger* (TV 2014), was late in coming, but worth the wait. The filmmakers do not minimize the foul deeds of other Swiss functionaries who attempted to thwart Grüninger's efforts. And, more importantly, *Akte Grüninger* portrays Grüninger as a normal, good man, but does not deify him. Although the film was made-for-television by Swiss/Austrian production companies, director Alain Gsponer made a film that is more of an art house offering than a TV production. Reviewer Mohan Mani wrote, "Director Alain Gsponer has the great talent of transporting viewers directly into those gritty times of World War II. The proof is that you will never feel that this movie was originally planned for TV release only."[68] Star Stefan Kurt is not trite, but genuine and believable. Film critic Ellinor Lori at *Rockstar. ch* wrote, "Although a documentary has already been published, as well as several books on the subject, the Swiss director Alain Gsponer has succeeded in creating a movie with *Akte Grüninger*, which emotionally demonstrates the fight for humanity and more than once presses on the lacrimal gland [tear duct]."[69]

Akte Grüninger is far less graphic than the other two recommended films about righteous Gentiles who saved many thousands of Jews, *Good Evening, Mr. Wallenberg—God afton, Herr Wallenberg—En Passionshistoria från verkligheten* (1990) and *The Relief of Belsen* (TV 2007). *Akte Grüninger* is quieter and less complicated, which accounts for its 96-minute running time.

Labyrinth of Lies—Im Labyrinth Des Schweigens (2014)

Genre:	Gentiles
Sub-Genre:	Antisemitic
Length:	122
MPAA or Local Rating:	R for a scene of sexuality.
Language:	German
Country:	Germany
Director:	Giulio Ricciarelli
Top-Billed:	André Szymanski, Alexander Fehling, Friederike Becht
From Wikipedia:	[Edited] In post-War Germany, federal prosecutor-general Fritz Bauer assigns the investigation of former workers at Auschwitz.
IMDb Rating:	7.3
IMDb Votes:	9781
***Holocaust Cinema Complete* Description:**	*Labyrinth of Lies—Im Labyrinth Des Schweigens* (2014) tells the story of a young prosecutor in post–War West Germany who functionally knew nothing about the Holocaust, yet eventually roots out Nazis in German civil service. The film is a remarkable portrayal of protected Nazis in post–War West German society. As with other antisemitic Gentile films, *Labyrinth of Lies* succeeds in exposing the lesser-known criminals who aided in the Final Solution.
Recommendation:	A look into post–War West German attitudes toward Holocaust perpetrators.
Suggested Minimum Grade:	Middle School

REVIEW

Twelve minutes into Giulio Ricciarelli's *Labyrinth of Lies—Im Labyrinth Des Schweigens* (2014), the young West German prosecutor protagonist in post–War Germany is admonished by a colleague, "Mankind's biggest atrocity is simply denied and forgotten." To which the star replies, "What are you talking about?" The prosecutor's answer to this naïve question becomes the premise of *Labyrinth of Lies*: "A German prosecutor not knowing what happened at Auschwitz is a disgrace."

Labyrinth of Lies is a brave film that tells two stories: it exposes the massive number of Nazis who were integrated into post–War West German civil service; and it reveals the cultivated ignorance of post–War Germans who were raised to be oblivious of their beloved country's monstrous past. The film addresses both issues, aided by a visit to Auschwitz/Birkenau. As a bonus, in the end, the star gets his girl and the world is a little less ignorant.

That cursory synopsis does not do justice to the excellence and sensitivity of *Labyrinth of Lies*. The synopsis is also far too coy about failed denazification, which is genuinely addressed in the film. This is especially impressive for the first feature film directed and written by Giulio Ricciarelli, who is principally an actor, but who stayed behind the camera in *Labyrinth of Lies*. André Szymanski stars as the fictional Johann Radmann, who is an amalgamation of West German officials Joachim Kügler (1926–2012) and Georg Friedrich Vogel (1926–2007). As noted by Boyd van Hoeij in *The Hollywood Reporter*'s review, with the subheading, "German newbie director Giulio Ricciarelli casts Alexander Fehling as a 1950s public prosecutor who wants to sue the 8,000 people that worked at Auschwitz":

> The film deftly explores the story's complex moral issues from several sides and credibly shows how they start hitting closer and closer to home for the increasingly disturbed Radmann. Generally, the screenplay's extremely rich, from its throwaway particulars that shed a light on the position of women in post-war Germany to its unexpected flashes of humor, which ensure the film doesn't collapse under the weight of heavy themes. Less successful are a subplot involving a visit to the death camp itself and the prosecutor's chase of the elusive [failed] Dr. Mengele, which are both too short to make anything but very superficial points yet drag on the proceedings in the film's closing reels.[70]

André Szymanski is particularly effective in the lead role, traversing the fine line between naïveté and ignorance. As Oleg Ivanov wrote in his review in *Slant*:

> Still, *Labyrinth of Lies* remains an important reminder of the evil that lurks within all men, ready to be unleashed under the proper circumstances. If its ultimate stance on the nature of this evil is muddled, it displays a subtle enough understanding of how Cold War politics allowed Nazi criminals to go largely unpunished after the war. With many former Nazis still in positions of vital political and economic importance as a result of both American and Soviet resistance or indifference to large-scale denazification, what these prosecutors were able to accomplish remains nothing short of heroic.[71]

While *Labyrinth of Lies* documents post–War antisemitic Gentiles, it focuses less on the Holocaust than on the society that enabled it. The complementary recommended film, *The People vs. Fritz Bauer—Der Staat gegen Fritz Bauer* (2015), is based on much of the same material as *Labyrinth of Lies*, but is less fictional. In fact, Fritz Bauer is a significant character in *Labyrinth of Lies*, which is much easier and more effective for general audiences than the more complicated (and better-produced) *The People vs. Fritz Bauer*.

1945 (2017)

Genre:	Gentiles
Sub-Genre:	Antisemitic
Length:	91
MPAA or Local Rating:	Unrated (PG-13)
Language:	Hungarian
Country:	Hungary

Director:	Ferenc Török
Top-Billed:	Péter Rudolf, Bence Tasnádi, Tamás Szabó Kimmel
From Wikipedia:	*1945* is a 2017 Hungarian drama film co-written by Török and Gábor T. Szántó. It concerns two Jewish survivors of the Holocaust who arrive in a Hungarian village in August 1945, and the paranoid reactions of the villagers, some of whom fear that these and other Jews are coming to reclaim Jewish property.
IMDb Rating:	7.3
IMDb Votes:	1578
Holocaust Cinema Complete Description:	While *The Shop on Main Street* (1965) concentrated on the brazenly systematic taking of Jewish property by individuals in a rural Czech community during the War, *1945* (2017) depicts the return of two despoiled Holocaust survivors just after the War to their rural Hungarian village. The question of communal culpability is overshadowed by greed. This excellent post–War slice of life makes its case with the pace of a Western showdown.
Recommendation:	"TOP THREE" IN GENRE. An excellent story about Jews returning to their previous eastern European home town just after the Holocaust.
Suggested Minimum Grade:	Middle School

REVIEW

Hungarian Ferenc Török's *1945* (2017) is simply startling. The plot is startling. The filmmaking is startling. The style is startling. In the Consolidated Era of Holocaust film production, Török's *1945* gives hope that original stories can still be written and great new Holocaust films can still be made. With the feel of a Western showdown, two religiously observant Jewish survivors of the Holocaust arrive at a Hungarian village train station and start walking. These black-clad men, Sámuel and his son, are heading home, behind a carriage that hauls two large trunks, back to the place where they had owned the local pharmacy, which had been "appropriated" by a Gentile family at the time of Jewish deportation. Although none of the townsfolk know why these men have returned, the belief in the community is that the men intend to reclaim their property, which, as it is made clear by the locals, is not going to happen. Both the current "owners" and townspeople increasingly panic, fearing that the return of any property would be a lethal slippery slope.

The acting, cinematography and staging in *1945* are superior to all but a handful of Holocaust films. Co-star Marcell Nagy (1991–) who played the Jewish son—and whose virtuosity was on full display when starring in the unrivaled *Fateless—Sorstalanság* (2005)—is two for-two in his brief Holocaust film acting career. (His only other feature was the non–Holocaust *Tüskevár* [2012]). True, Nagy had almost no lines and little to do in *1945* except be reticent in a black suit. But like Robert Horry—seven-time NBA champ on three different teams—Nagy picks winners.

Since the passing of the great film critic Roger Ebert (1942–2013), I have sometimes almost lamented the release of great films such as *1945*, because Ebert has not been here to enjoy them with us and to explain their greatness. *1945* is one such film that we can appreciate vicariously for him. Nonetheless, the following excerpts from four reviews all come close to hitting the spot:

New York Times: Ferenc Torok's lean, suggestive Hungarian feature, *1945*, shot in gorgeous, high-contrast black-and-white, is a Holocaust film built, consciously or not, on a reversal of the tropes of the western, down to ticking clocks that might as well be nearing high noon. The visiting men in black hats—a father (Ivan Angelus) and his adult son (Marcell Nagy)—aren't villains out for revenge, but Orthodox Jews, who have come to the village at the end of the war. They are transporting trunks said to be filled with perfume or cosmetics. The purpose of their journey is obscure.[72]

Los Angeles Times: Simple, powerful, made with conviction and skill, *1945* proceeds as inexorably as Sámuel and his son on their long walk into town. It's a potent messenger about a time that is gone but whose issues and difficulties are not even close to being past.[73]

Christian Science Monitor: Movies shot in black and white, especially in the modern era, are often described as "stark," but there's no other way to characterize the visuals in the marvelous Hungarian movie *1945*, the look of the film perfectly emblematizes the story. Set a few months after V-E Day, it takes place in a single summer afternoon in a small village.[74]

Variety: Nothing in helmer Török's previous filmography would predict his virtuosity here. In a film with surprisingly little dialogue, a fine ensemble cast, including real-life married couple Rudolph and Nagy-Kálózy, convincingly enables this dissection of village life and matters of conscience to be more shown than told. Key to the impact is the superb lensing of veteran DP Elemér Ragályi. The mirrored opening shot, a close-up of István shaving with a straight razor, establishes a sustained tone of impending doom, while his beautifully composed images, frequently framed through gauzy linen curtains, windows, doors, and fences, heighten visual interest.[75]

The simplicity of the premise is equally genius and righteous, never approaching the self-righteousness of so many other Holocaust films; the audacity of the filmmakers to cast stones and indict innate European rural antisemitism is desperately needed. This film answers the question: why were the locals in occupied Europe so happy to see the Germans arrive? But the overarching message of *1945* is about Jewish honor and memory. And, aside from a brief prelude to oral sex which can easily be skipped, *1945* is appropriate for all ages.

While I have largely disregarded film spoilers in this book, in the case of *1945*, little more needs to be revealed. *1945* can be viewed as the sequel or epilogue to the great Czech Holocaust film *The Shop on Main Street—Obchod na korze* (1965), which depicts Czechs' seizing a Jewish shop during the War as the Jews are deported to be slaughtered.

Survivor Films

"Survivor" genre films are primarily set after the Holocaust and are mainly about a Jewish protagonist who suffered (or whose ancestors suffered) during the Holocaust. The formula for Survivor films spuriously suggests that adult Holocaust survivors or their progeny are pathologically damaged, incapable of normal social function and frequently suicidal. Almost all Survivor films are fiction, with the notable exception of *Woman in Gold* (2015) and possibly *Bye Germany—Es war einmal in Deutschland…* (2017). Typically, Survivor films are adorned with Holocaust flashbacks. To date, there have been 86 Survivor films, of which 10 are recommended below.

The Pawnbroker (1964)

Genre:	Survivor
Sub-Genre:	Post Post-War
Length:	116
MPAA or Local Rating:	Sweden-15
Language:	English
Country:	U.S.
Director:	Sidney Lumet

Top-Billed:	Rod Steiger, Geraldine Fitzgerald, Brock Peters
From Wikipedia:	The film was the first produced entirely in the United States to deal with the Holocaust from the viewpoint of a survivor. It earned international acclaim for Steiger, launching his career as an A-list actor. It was among the first American films to feature nudity during the Production Code, and was the first film featuring bare breasts to receive Production Code approval. Although it was publicly announced to be a special exception, the controversy proved to be first of similar major challenges to the Code that ultimately led to its abrogation.
IMDb Rating:	7.8
IMDb Votes:	6981
Oscar:	Nomination: Best Actor.
Holocaust Cinema Complete Description:	The Pawnbroker (1964) is not the first Survivor film, but it was the first Holocaust film to depict an older Holocaust survivor twenty years after the War. The survivor in The Pawnbroker has disintegrated emotionally under the weight of his memories. There is nothing joyful or easy about the story, which implies that the pawnbroker can never recover. The allegorical style of memory suppression was innovative and extremely effective.
Recommendation:	A great look at the first Holocaust survivors in the 1960s.
Suggested Minimum Grade:	Middle School

REVIEW

The Pawnbroker (1964) is one of many socially conscious films made by fearless American director Sidney Lumet (1924–2011), who was nominated for Best Director Oscar for four of his other groundbreaking films: *12 Angry Men* (1957), *Dog Day Afternoon* (1975), *Network* (1976) and *The Verdict* (1982). The Academy also bestowed upon Lumet its "Honorary Award" in 2005 for a 50-year career during which Lumet directed 44 feature films, which had garnered 46 Oscar nominations. Lumet grew up in the Lower East Side of New York, the son of Yiddish theater veterans.

But it was Lumet's first film, *12 Angry Men*, rated on IMDb as the fifth greatest film of all-time, produced by and starring Henry Fonda, that set the tone. Lumet went on to direct films about losers and the downtrodden, fighting what Lumet perceived as injustice. His protagonists have been disfigured by their circumstances and society, like rocks that catch a waterfall. The most famous line from Lumet's films, written for *Network* by three-time Oscar winner Sidney Aaron "Paddy" Chayefsky (1923–1981), is the iconic, "I'm as mad as hell, and I'm not going to take this anymore!" *Network* won four Oscars and is also ranked in IMDb in the top 250 best films, as is *Dog Day Afternoon*. And no one who has ever seen Lumet's *The Verdict*—written by David Mamet, and nominated for five Oscars—can forget the pathetic, washed-up lawyer played by Paul Newman, a performance and temperament that exemplifies Lumet's power as a director.

Less renowned, but equally poignant, was *The Pawnbroker*, starring Rod Steiger, whose portrayal of Sol Nazerman, a Holocaust survivor 20 years after liberation, garnered Steiger a nomination for Best Actor Oscar. Nazerman lived on Long Island, but owned and operated a pawn shop in East Harlem (aka Spanish Harlem). *The Pawnbroker*'s plotline is mostly irrelevant. Instead, it is a series of interactions with customers, employees and friends, all of whom remind Nazerman that his soul died in Auschwitz, despite his physical survival. As summarized by Gary Tooze in *DVDBeaver Blu-ray*, "With the rise of Hitler, Prof. Sol Nazerman, a Jew, and his family were dragged to a concentration camp, where he saw his two children die and his wife raped by Nazi officers.

Now he operates a pawnshop in Spanish Harlem. Numbed by the horrors of his past, he considers himself conditioned against any emotion."[76]

All is laid bare 47 minutes into the film when Nazerman is admonished in the following soliloquy by Nazerman's bedridden friend, Mendel, played by Baruch Lumet (1898–1992), Sidney Lumet's father:

> I was in Auschwitz, too. I came out alive. You came out dead.... Guilt. And there it is. Guilt to find yourself alive. And so you wrap yourself in a kind of shroud and feel you share the dignity of death with those who really died. Tell me, does blood ever flow through you, Sol Nazerman? Can you feel pain? [Nazerman: "No."] You are a fake. You breathe, you eat, you walk. You make money. You take a dream and give a dollar. And give no hope. [Nazerman: "I survive."] Survive? A coward's survival, and at what a price! No love. No passion. No pity! Dead! Sol Nazerman, the walking dead!

Lumet's point throughout *The Pawnbroker*, however, is not only that Nazerman has been emptied by the Holocaust, but also that nothing Nazerman does allows him to escape his memories. Triggered by everyday events, Nazerman's repressed Holocaust memories spill out in a series of increasingly longer flashbacks that erupt interspliced onto the screen. Why they all come flooding out suddenly in the mid–1960s is not clear, but soon enough they are overwhelming, providing enough backstory to humanize the stone-cold pawnbroker. Critic Emanuel Levy wrote, "Artistically and thematically, Sidney Lumet's *The Pawnbroker* is a significant film as it is one of the first Hollywood movies to deal with the Holocaust and its aftermath. The film tackles this difficult subject in an innovative style, which borrows devices from the French New Wave."[77]

The Pawnbroker ends with Lumet's kumbaya moment of intercultural empathy when one of Nazerman's Puerto Rican employees, Jesus, dies in a botched robbery. During the climax, with Jesus cradled and dying in Nazerman's arms, the emotionless Holocaust survivor emits a famous silent scream, for which Rod Steiger took creative credit.[78] The same silent scream—perhaps as an homage 18 years later—is mimed by Meryl Streep's "Sophie" in *Sophie's Choice* (1982) when her daughter is taken upon arrival at Auschwitz to be murdered. Nazerman wanders away unchanged from the bloody mess during the last few moments of *The Pawnbroker*, still deadened by the Holocaust, Lumet informing the world that there can be no happy ending and no consolation after Auschwitz. As David Blakeslee wrote in his review in *Criterioncast*:

> In addition to the engrossing story that keeps first time viewers guessing as to how it will all turn out (though the cover art functions as a significant giveaway), *The Pawnbroker* features a vibrant, jazzy soundtrack by Quincy Jones (his first major film assignment in that capacity) and several extended scenes of vintage New York City streetscapes, an environment that Lumet spent a lot of time filming over the course of his distinguished career. This movie even played an important role in the final dismantling of the Motion Picture Production (Hays) Code, as the first Hollywood film granted an exception from the guidelines to show naked female breasts (the exposure of which was integral to a key scene, hardly for erotic arousal—indeed, quite the opposite effect was intended and achieved.)[79]

As with most Holocaust Survivor films, the particularly important *The Pawnbroker*'s depiction of an irreparably damaged Holocaust survivor is at odds with the actual condition of most real survivors, who pulled themselves together and led productive, healthy lives after the defeat of Germany. Nonetheless, normal people without significant problems are rarely the subject of films. But *The Pawnbroker*'s point—that difficult memories are even more difficult to forget—is well-taken. And the cultural significance of this difficult film was substantial.

Harold and Maude (1971)

Genre:	Survivor
Sub-Genre:	Post Post-War
Length:	91
MPAA or Local Rating:	PG
Language:	English
Country:	U.S.
Director:	Hal Ashby
Top-Billed:	Ruth Gordon, Bud Cort, Vivian Pickles
From Wikipedia:	*Harold and Maude* is a 1971 American romantic black comedy drama. It incorporates elements of dark humor and existentialist drama. The plot revolves around the exploits of a young man named Harold Chasen who is intrigued with death. Harold drifts away from the life that his detached mother prescribes for him, and slowly develops a strong friendship, and eventually a romantic relationship, with a 79-year-old woman named Maude who teaches Harold about living life to its fullest and that life is the most precious gift of all.
IMDb Rating:	8.0
IMDb Votes:	36209
Holocaust Cinema Complete Description:	*Harold and Maude* (1971) is a cult classic and a masterpiece. *Harold and Maude* is also rarely regarded as a Survivor Holocaust film. It is the story of an eccentric old woman who lives in a converted train-car in California. She refuses to dwell on the past. Not until 70 minutes into the 90-minute film is it even made clear that she is a survivor, and only then with a brief glimpse of her Auschwitz tattoo. Nothing is wasted in this classic, the subtlest of all Holocaust films.
Recommendation:	"TOP THREE" IN GENRE. For those seeking a lighter Holocaust film, which still has great meaning.
Suggested Minimum Grade:	High School

REVIEW

A search on IMDb of American-made non-animated comedies produced from 1967 until 2013 with a user rating of at least 8.0 (with at least 10,000 votes) yields only 16 feature films. (See Table 36.) Most of those films are extraordinary and heralded, including two films each by Woody Allen, Peter Weir and Hal Ashby. Most have iconic lines or gestures.

TABLE 36: AMERICAN-MADE NON-ANIMATED COMEDY FEATURES MADE SINCE 1967 WITH A USER RATING OF AT LEAST 8.0 ON IMDb (WITH AT LEAST 10,000 VOTES)

Director	Film
Hal Ashby (1929–1988)	*Being There* (1979)
	Harold and Maude (1971)
Woody Allen (1935–)	*Annie Hall* (1977)
	Manhattan (1979)
Peter Bogdanovich (1939–)	*Paper Moon* (1973)
Mel Brooks (1926–)	*Young Frankenstein* (1974)
Bob Clark (1939–2007)	*A Christmas Story* (1983)
Joel Coen (1954–) & Ethan Coen (1957–)	*The Big Lebowski* (1998)
George Roy Hill (1921–2002)	*The Sting* (1973)
Mike Nichols (1931–2014)	*The Graduate* (1967)
Rob Reiner (1947–)	*This Is Spinal Tap* (1984)

Director	Film
Harold Ramis (1944–2014)	*Groundhog Day* (1993)
Guy Ritchie (1968–)	*Snatch* (2000)
Peter Weir (1944–)	*Dead Poets Society* (1989)
	The Truman Show (1998)
Robert Zemeckis (1951–)	*Back to the Future* (1985)

In his brief 16-year directing career, Hal Ashby (1929–1988) helmed fewer than a dozen narrative features, of which two obscure films are on the above list. Most of Hal Ashby's films were amazingly iconic in the 1970s, including: *Coming Home* (1978), which garnered Oscars for stars Jane Fonda and Jon Voight; *The Last Detail* (1973) with Jack Nicholson and Randy Quaid, which was nominated for three Oscars; *Shampoo* (1975), starring Warren Beatty, Julie Christie and Goldie Hawn, winning one Oscar and nominated for three others; *Bound for Glory* (1976), the Woody Guthrie story starring David Carradine, winning two Oscars and nominated for four more; and the Oscar-winning *Being There* (1979), which is on the list in Table 36 (and is, in my opinion, the greatest film ever made.*) Hal Ashby's films were often about deeply naïve men.

Enter Hal Ashby's incomparable *Harold and Maude* (1971), one of the greatest cult classics of all time,[80] which took the moviegoing world years to appreciate and now resides in Table 36. For example, Roger Ebert gave *Harold and Maude* only 1½ (out of four) stars, writing contemporaneously, "And so what we get, finally, is a movie of attitudes."[81] But eventually the American Film Institute recognized *Harold and Maude* on many of its lists, including: 2000's AFI's 100 Years … 100 Laughs—#45; 2002's AFI's 100 Years … 100 Passions—#69; 2006's AFI's 100 Years … 100 Cheers—#89; and 2008's AFI's 10 Top 10: #9 Romantic Comedy Film. Of Hal Ashby's first seven films, which were all made in the 1970s, all but *Harold and Maude*, his second film, were Oscar-nominated.

Harold and Maude is outrageous and radical, absolutely the kind of film that could never have been made while the Motion Picture Production Code repressed American filmmaking. Harold is a draft-aged young man during the Vietnam War, born into a very wealthy family. Harold has nothing better to do than attend strangers' funerals and to shock his bon vivant mother by regularly and graphically faking his suicide. Soon enough, Harold meets Maude at a funeral, just days before her 80th birthday. These two vastly different eccentrics are separated by 60 years, by breeding and by class. They ultimately fall in love—as do we with them—aided by Cat Stevens' resplendent soundtrack, including his picture-perfect song "If You Want to Sing Out, Sing Out," which was written for the film.

I have shown *Harold and Maude* to hundreds of college students during my teaching career. For the first 20 minutes of the film, between the "suicides" and the age difference of the two protagonists, most viewers are simply slack-jawed, staring in disbelief. Then there is a certain point when giggles can be heard, followed by unfettered laughter, gasps and then tears.

The characters in this film are so overwhelming that the actors who portrayed them were typecast for the rest of their careers. First is Ruth Gordon (1896–1985), whose first

---

* *Being There* was also the last major film of Peter Sellers' spectacular career, which included *Dr. Strangelove or: How I Learned to Stop Worrying and Love the Bomb* (1964) and *The Pink Panther* series (1963, 1975, 1976, 1978). *Being There* also featured Shirley MacLaine, Melvyn Douglas near the end of his 50-year career, capped with an Oscar for Best Supporting Actor.

IMDb credit is in 1915, plays Maude to perfection: vulnerable, but steadfast in her paci-fist beliefs. Gordon not only won the Best Supporting Actress Oscar in Roman Polanski's *Rosemary's Baby* (1968), but was also a three-time Best Writer Oscar nominee, including for *Adam's Rib* (1949). Then there is Bud Cort (1946–), who was also flawlessly cast as Harold, an exposed young adult who starts with very few beliefs, but who ends with just enough.

Maude makes it her business to teach the morbid boy about trust and love, which he ultimately accepts. She lives in a converted train car, filled with art and instruments, packed with endless miscellaneous stuff. About 43 minutes into the film, Harold enquires about an umbrella mounted above Maude's fireplace mantel. Maude explains:

> Oh, that's just a relic. I found it when I was packing to come to America. It used to be my defense on picket lines and rallies and political meetings, being dragged off by the police and attacked by thugs of the opposition. [Harold: What were you fighting for?] Oh, big issues. Liberty. Rights. Justice. Kings died. Kingdoms fell. I don't regret the kingdom—what sense in borders and nations and patriotism—but I miss the kings. When I was a little girl I was taken to the palace in Vienna, to a garden party. I can still see the sun shining, the parasols, the flashing uniforms of the young officers. I thought then that I would marry a soldier. Later on Frederick would chide me about it. He was so serious. A doctor at the university and in the government. [Thirteen-second pause.] But that was all before.

Maude tears up. Harold does not ask "who is Frederick" or "before what?" And, just as quickly, the reveal flies past viewers, who attribute the ramblings to a batty old lady. Then, 70 minutes into the 90-minute film, "The camera zooms in and, for a moment, lingers on Maude's wrist—so slightly that it's easy to miss the six-digit number tattooed there."[82] (See Picture 6.)

The half-second take on Maude's Auschwitz tattoo, her living in a converted train car and the above passage are the only obvious references to Maude's being a Holocaust survivor, let alone being Jewish. As noted in *MoviePooper*, "Maude talks about having survived political unrest in her past and has a numbered tattoo on her arm. Though never expressly stated, these clues suggest that Maude is a Holocaust survivor."[83]

Just after Harold notices the tattoo, Maude ignores the reveal and notes a seaside flock of seagulls, explaining to the shocked boy, "Dreyfus once wrote from Devil's Island that he would see the most glorious birds. Many years later in Brittany, he realized they had only been seagulls." This reference to French Army Captain Alfred Dreyfus (1859–1935)—who was exiled after a false conviction for treason and is the archetypal victim of European antisemitism—had been lost on me, even after dozens of viewings. So jarring is the tattoo scene that I had never heard Maude's astonishing Alfred Dreyfus dialogue until examining the scene to select images for publication.

The themes of individuality and universal love, the idea of life needing to be lived to its fullest and of the waste of war and hatred, these subjects are implied as the lessons learned and lived by Maude resulting from her oppression. The film is neither preachy nor self-important, but honest. *Harold and Maude* has become a cult classic because it is intensely quirky and because of Cat Stevens' soundtrack. Scott Tobias sums it up for *AV Club*:

> So how does *Harold and* [sic] *Maude* look today, seen with fresh eyes? Mostly terrific, but also more than a little familiar. As I said, the film is the birth of modern indie quirk, full of elements and attitudes that have become cliché: Heroes who are more whimsical conceits than real-life, flesh-and-blood creations; an offbeat and slightly twee pop soundtrack (here by Cat Stevens); authority figures painted as stiff, clueless, and completely devoid of humanity; and some vague leftist political references thrown in

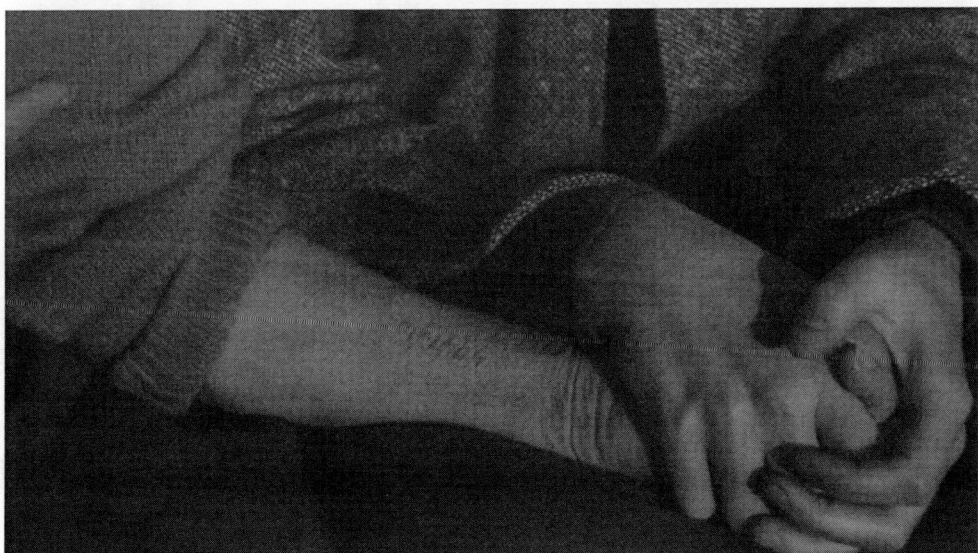

Picture 6: *Harold and Maude* (1971). **Ruth Gordon and Bud Cort** *(top).* **Maude's tattoo** *(bottom).*

for good measure. It may sound like I'm being snarky and dismissive here—and I'll be the first to admit that familiarity has bred some contempt—but there's good quirk and bad quirk, and *Harold and* [*sic*] *Maude* still falls on the right side of the line.[84]

As a Holocaust film, *Harold and Maude* is rarely mentioned and often dismissed by Holocaust film scholars. In fact, Professor Judith E. Doneson (1947–2002) in her excellent 2002 book *The Holocaust in American Film* states outright that *Harold and Maude* is not a Holocaust film.[85] I respectfully disagree with the late Professor Doneson; *Harold and Maude* is unshakably a Holocaust film, checking all the Survivor film boxes. Irrespective, Hal Ashby's superb *Harold and Maude* should be considered as mandatory for basic and Holocaust film literacy.

The Man in the Glass Booth (1975)

Genre:	Survivor
Sub-Genre:	Post Post-War
Length:	117
MPAA or Local Rating:	Unrated (PG)
Language:	English
Country:	U.S.
Director:	Arthur Hiller
Top-Billed:	Maximilian Schell, Lois Nettleton, Lawrence Pressman
From Wikipedia:	*The Man in the Glass Booth* is a 1975 American drama film. The film was produced and released as part of the American Film Theatre, which adapted theatrical works for a subscription-driven cinema series. The screenplay was adapted from Robert Shaw's 1967 novel and 1968 stage play, both of the same name. The plot was inspired by the kidnapping and trial of the German Nazi SS-Obersturmbannführer (lieutenant colonel) Adolf Eichmann, who was one of the major organizers of the Holocaust.
IMDb Rating:	7.4
IMDb Votes:	925
Oscar:	Nomination: Best Actor.
Holocaust Cinema Complete Description:	*The Man in the Glass Booth* (1975) is a hyperbolic parody of the Eichmann trial, with many more twists than the real story. This masterfully made film defies logic, which is part of its appeal. While *The Man in the Glass Booth* conveys a fair amount of Holocaust history, the story is a quirky character-driven tragedy. *The Man in the Glass Booth* is one of the few Holocaust films that benefits from its overacting.
Recommendation:	For those particularly interested in an Eichmann juxtaposition.
Suggested Minimum Grade:	High School

REVIEW

Vienna-born Maximilian Schell (1930–2014) has starred in more Holocaust films than any other actor. Among other roles in his exceedingly long career, Schell played a young defense attorney in *Judgment at Nuremberg* (1961), a conniving husband in *Return from the Ashes* (1965), Anne Frank's father in *The Diary of Anne Frank* (TV 1980), an anti–Nazi German partisan in *Julia* (1977) and the ringleader of a neo–Nazi organization in post–War West Germany in *The Odessa File* (1974). Maximilian Schell epitomized what it meant to be a Holocaust actor, a keen task for a Roman Catholic Austrian who grew up in Switzerland after the 1938 Anschluss (the annexation of Austria by Nazi Germany).

"Wackadoodle" would be the term used today for the protagonist Schell plays in Arthur Hiller's *The Man in the Glass Booth* (1975), and for which Schell was nominated for the Best Actor Oscar. In fact, to Schell's credit, it is often unclear in *The Man in the Glass Booth* if Schell's character is the protagonist or the antagonist. Robert Shaw's novel and screenplay, *The Man in the Glass Booth*, takes many of the details of Adolf Eichmann's capture and trial to tell a bizarre story.

Madcap films seemed to have been Arthur Hiller's brand during the heart of his feature film directorial career, including the zany films *The In-Laws* (1979), *Romantic Comedy* (1983), and the Gene Wilder and Richard Pryor films *Silver Streak* (1976) and *See No Evil, Hear No Evil* (1989). But the kind of crazy in Hiller's *The Man in the Glass Booth* is not because of pratfalls or comedians in their prime, but because the protagonist—an extremely wealthy Holocaust survivor in New York—convinces the Mossad that he is a facsimile of Eichmann, an infamous Nazi war criminal. As Noel Megahey wrote in 2003 about *The Man in the Glass Booth Review* in *The Digital Fix*:

> Maximilian Schell—nominated for an Oscar, maybe more for the edgy duality of his role as a Nazi-Jew than for his actual performance here—chews up the scenery, spits it out and has the script for dessert. Hiller clearly felt that the filmed version of the play needed to spell its madness out a little more obviously for a cinema audience, so Schell (perhaps intentionally) treats us to complete caricatures of both his Jewish and Nazi roles.[86]

Truth and delusion ultimately sort themselves out in the film's surprising climax, but little in this plot can be taken seriously, especially the over-churned death scene, which seems lifted from Stanley Kramer's *Inherit the Wind* (1960). Yet, many of the underlying stories told in the set-piece trial are fully in the spirit of German behavior and attitudes during the Holocaust. As for its implied relationship to the actual Eichmann trial, *The Man in the Glass Booth* is a natural and interesting cinematic comparison, but it is almost entirely irrelevant to the trial, except for the titular booth. More interesting is thinking about *The Man in the Glass Booth* in relation to *Inglourious Basterds* (2009), which is also fictionalized so passionately that only the completely naïve could believe that it is true. In tone, too, the films are kindred spirits.

The Man in the Glass Booth continued the tradition of portraying very unstable Holocaust survivors, from *The Juggler* (1953) to *The Pawnbroker* (1964) through *Harold and Maude* (1971) and *The Night Porter—Il portiere di notte* (1974). *The Man in the Glass Booth*, however, provides much more Holocaust content than almost any other Survivor film; on the other hand, it employs a whole lot more theatrics to get there.

As a fitting analog/postscript to *The Man in the Glass Booth*, its writer Robert Shaw (1927–1978)—better known for his acting roles in such films as *The Sting* (1973), *Jaws* (1975), *A Man for All Seasons* (1966) and *From Russia with Love* (1963)—"requested that his name be removed from the film adaptation because 'he was unhappy with Edward Anhalt's script.'"[87] After seeing the film, Shaw implored Hiller to reinstate his name, but, by then it was too late.[88] Which is to say, everything about *The Man in the Glass Booth* is unsettling.

The Quarrel (1991)

Genre:	Survivor
Sub-Genre:	Post-War
Length:	85
MPAA or Local Rating:	PG-13
Language:	English
Country:	Canada
Director:	Eli Cohen
Top-Billed:	R.H. Thomson, Saul Rubinek, Merlee Shapiro
From Wikipedia:	[Edited] Two estranged friends—one a rabbi and the other an agnostic writer, both Holocaust survivors—resume an old argument.
IMDb Rating:	7.0
IMDb Votes:	232

Holocaust Cinema Complete Description:	*The Quarrel* (1991) is the smallest of stories, about two Eastern European Holocaust survivors who meet just after the War in Montreal. These former best friends, who had been estranged before the War, both believed that the other had died in the Holocaust. The secular/observant theological questions concerning the Holocaust are argued between these two men, more organically than in *God on Trial*. There is nothing flashy about *The Quarrel*. As opposed to most other Survivor films, however, these survivors are functional, healthy members of society.
Recommendation:	This is a great starter Holocaust film, particularly when learning about Holocaust theology.
Suggested Minimum Grade:	Late Grade School

REVIEW

Canadian-directed and solo-produced Holocaust productions have been either utterly abysmal or have simply disappeared, including *The Lucky Star* (1980), *Charlie Grant's War* (TV 1984), *Two Men* (TV 1988), *The Poet—Hearts of War* (2007) and *Autumn Hearts: A New Beginning—Emotional Arithmetic* (2007). Even Canadian Norman Jewison's Perpetrator Holocaust film *The Statement* (2003), a U.S./Canadian co-production, is among the worst Holocaust films in its genre, despite starring Michael Caine and Tilda Swinton, and despite being helmed by Jewison, who also directed the most famous Jewish film ever made, *Fiddler on the Roof* (1971). As merely an academic exercise, finding anything cinematically virtuous in these offerings would be an interesting (yet futile) task for students of Canadian film. Canada's consistently miserable Holocaust film record is odd considering the number of great Canadian film directors, including Jewison, James Cameron, Ted Kotcheff, Ivan and Jason Reitman and even Arthur Hiller, who directed the recommended Survivor film *The Man in the Glass Booth* (1975), which was American-produced. Even the magnificent Jewish Canadian film *Lies My Father Told Me* (1975) was directed by a non–Canadian, Czech Ján Kadár (*The Shop on Main Street—Obchod na korze* [1965]).

The particularly good Survivor film *The Quarrel* (1991), although a solo-Canadian production, was made by Israeli director Eli Cohen, who also made other particularly good Israeli Survivor films in Hebrew: *The Summer of Aviya* (1988) and the recommended *Under the Domim Tree* (1994). *The Quarrel* was based on a short story by Chaim Grade, which was turned into a play by ethicist and Rabbi Joseph Telushkin, with the screenplay by David Brandes.

The film's backstory, which is provided in exposition, is that two Holocaust survivors in their 30s had been best friends in Eastern Europe before the War. They studied at the same yeshiva (seminary) and were inseparable until one of the friends walked away from Orthodoxy, a particularly difficult choice in light of Jewish communal expectations. The other friend had become the head rabbi of a Canadian yeshiva. The two men bump into each other in a park and spend most of the film discussing their past and what can roughly be reduced to arguing Holocaust theology. As in *God on Trial* (TV 2008), weighty issues are raised that can never be solved, whether in a ninety 90-minute film or in eternity. *The Quarrel* is simple enough to be set anywhere at any time. Here, it is set in Montreal on Rosh Hashanah in 1948. Regardless, no matter the fineness of the sandpaper, it still abrades. "This adaptation," wrote Hal Hinson of *The Washington Post*, "is serious, well-intentioned and intelligent; in other words, it isn't merely shallow or crude. But it is deadly serious. *The Quarrel* comes to us exactly as advertised; it's one long Talmudic spat between a pair of Jewish stereotypes."[89]

The Quarrel hones in on its target, deals with it respectfully and then lets the film finish without too much drama or sententiousness. One man thinks that Holocaust survival is a miracle and that miracles, by definition, are acts of God, and, thus warrants celebrating His glory; the other friend, like Primo Levi, suggests that, since any God who would allow the Holocaust is not worth loving, the better path is to excuse God from the man's life. *The New York Times* critic Stephen Holden wrote that *The Quarrel* "...is commendable simply for having the temerity to grapple with serious ideas in a form not usually given to intellectual discourse."[90]

The success of the film is found in the dialogue, which could easily have been contrived and unnatural. Canadian stars R.H. Thomson and Saul Rubinek (who was born in a post–War German refugee camp) were completely at ease with their lines and soliloquies. *The Quarrel* is ideal for those wanting to start a theological conversation about the Holocaust, yet who would prefer it be staged in a beautiful post–War Canadian park than in Birkenau, as in *God on Trial*. It is the difference between kneeling on fine versus coarse sandpaper.

Under the Domim Tree—Etz Hadomim Tafus (1994)

Genre:	Survivor
Sub-Genre:	Post-War
Length:	102
MPAA or Local Rating:	Unrated (PG)
Language:	Hebrew
Country:	Israel
Director:	Eli Cohen
Top-Billed:	Gila Almagor, Juliano Mer-Khamis, Uri Avrahami
From Wikipedia:	*Under the Domim Tree* (Hebrew: עץ הדומים תפוס) is a 1994 Israeli film based on the 1992 book of the same name by Gila Almagor. Both the book and the film are sequels to Almagor's 1985 autobiographical book, *Summer of Aviya*, about the protagonist's childhood in the 1950s in Israel. Under the Domim Tree tells of Aviya's years in the Oudim boarding school and about the relations that are formed between the Israeli–born students and the students who survived the holocaust [*sic*].
IMDb Rating:	7.2
IMDb Votes:	202
Holocaust Cinema Complete Description:	*Under the Domim Tree—Etz Hadomim Tafus* (1994) is a vivid window into the lives of adolescent Holocaust survivors and of Israel in the early 1950s. The young survivors struggle with normal issues of teenage life while grappling with memories of the War and trying to remember their former lives in eastern Europe. While some of the story concerns a custody battle, *Under the Domim Tree* is mostly a testament to those adults and Israeli institutions which cared for child survivors and orphans from the Holocaust.
Recommendation:	Mainly for studying the development of Israeli children who were Holocaust survivors.
Suggested Minimum Grade:	Middle School

REVIEW

A few years after directing the recommended Canadian Survivor film *The Quarrel* (1991), Israeli actor/director Eli Cohen (1940–) made *Under the Domim Tree—Etz Hadomim Tafus* (1994), one of several collaborations between Cohen and with Israeli writer/actress Gila Almagor (née Gila Alexandrovich) (1939–), who is regarded as the "first lady of Israeli cinema and theater."[91] *The Summer of Aviya—Ha-Kayitz Shel Aviya* (1988), too, was an earlier collaboration by the two about Holocaust survivors. Both of the Israeli films were based on Almagor's autobiography and both featured Kaipu Cohen in starring roles.*

Under the Domim Tree is set in a boarding school responsible for raising and loving orphaned Holocaust survivors. While a plot involving custody and identity is somewhat the focus, the film is mostly about a communal approach used to rehabilitate these otherwise forsaken children. Although many Israelis have believed that European Jews were weak by purportedly not fighting the Germans, as opposed to Israelis who fought the Arabs when attacked and threatened, *Under the Domim Tree* does not go there. Instead, we are left with the kinder side of a harsh 1950s Israel, that cares for its own and has started to become disabused of its unfair criticism of European Jewry.

Most of *Under the Domim Tree* is about children who are so genuine that it is impossible to imagine that these kids were simply playing roles. The adults, too, do not overreach, but the kids are the stars. Director Eli Cohen, who is also a fine actor, must be very proud of these performances. As *New York Times*' critic Stephen Holden wrote: "What holds the movie together are its heartfelt, natural performances by a mostly nonprofessional cast. These young actors evoke a tightly knit community collectively caught between an irretrievable past and a problematic future they must invent together."[92] And critic Mary Weems wrote in *Movie Magazine International*:

> This film, which is the sequel to the 1988 film *The Summer of Aviya*, is based on the autobiography of Israel's Queen of the Silver Screen, Gila Almagor. She wrote the screenplay, and plays the role of her own mother in the psychiatric ward. This film, in Hebrew and Polish with English subtitles, offers powerful drama, an unusual glimpse of life, and a unique perspective on a historical moment. Most important, with its final image of the enduring domim tree, and newly planted tulips spring up in the desert, it gives an inspiring view of the human potential for survival and for generosity.[93]

Cohen's steady hand and experience with the subject keeps the film from wandering off into madness, even if that is the apparent destination of some of its characters. Most Israeli films about Holocaust survivors are honest and compelling, but none deal specifically with this forgotten cohort of Hitler's victims. *Under the Domim Tree* works on many levels, but especially for high school students who are learning about the aftermath of the Holocaust.

The Birch-Tree Meadow—La petite prairie aux bouleaux (2003)

Genre:	Survivor
Sub-Genre:	Post Post-War
Length:	131
MPAA or Local Rating;	Unrated (PG)
Language:	French
Country:	Germany—France—Poland
Director:	Marceline Loridan-Ivens
Top-Billed:	Anouk Aimée, August Diehl, Marilu Marini
From Wikipedia:	Myriam, who has lived in New York for about fifty years, returns to Europe for the annual commemoration of the Auschwitz alumni. She decides to return to Birkenau where she once lived in the hell of concentration camps.

* An entry in IMDb falsely claims that Kaipu Cohen is the daughter of the film's director Eli Cohen. https://www.imdb.com/name/nm0169529/bio?ref_=nm_ov_bio_sm.

IMDb Rating:	6.8
IMDb Votes:	129
Holocaust Cinema Complete Description:	*The Birch-Tree Meadow—La petite prairie aux bouleaux* (2003) is the most honest Holocaust Survivor film ever made. Sixty years after her imprisonment in Birkenau, a woman returns to get some answers and closure. Remarkably, she leaves with both, as do the viewers. This is not the "crazy" Holocaust survivor from most other films, but a mature, thoughtful woman who seeks and attains some peace when leaving Birkenau again so many years later.
Recommendation:	"TOP THREE" IN GENRE. This film is recommended to those seeking an understanding of the travails of Holocaust survivors.
Suggested Minimum Grade:	Middle School

REVIEW

French director Marceline Loridan Ivens (née Marceline Rozenberg) (1928–2018), who survived Auschwitz, Bergen-Belsen and Theresienstadt, directed several documentaries in the 1970s, but only directed one narrative film—and that late in her life— the intensely autobiographical *The Birch-Tree Meadow—La petite prairie aux bouleaux* (2003).

Since 1944, French actress Anouk Aimée (née Nicole Françoise Florence Dreyfus) has acted in more than 70 feature films, including in Federico Fellini's Oscar-decorated *La Dolce Vita* (1960) and *8½* (1963). Aimée, born in 1932 Paris, was the first actress Oscar-nominated for a French-speaking role for her performance in Claude Lelouch's *A Man and a Woman* (1966), in which she is thoroughly enchanting, simply unforgettable.

Ivens wrote and directed her own story about a excruciating return to Birkenau sixty years later, performed exquisitely by Aimée. *The Birch-Tree Meadow* flawlessly blends the documentary mentality to a narrative film, creating scripted drama with a cathartic visit. It depicts a sophisticated Holocaust survivor in her sixties who shimmies into Birkenau through a fence that once was electrified and represented the end of her world. She remembers. She ponders. She finds closure. "This is a film," wrote *Variety's* David Stratton, "of contemplation rather than action, a film which mostly concentrates on the experiences of an aging woman who forces herself to come to terms with the most painful memories of the past."[94]

She also visits the home that belonged to her parents in an adjacent town. The apartment is now occupied by a Polish woman who freely admits that her grandparents came into possession of the apartment during the War. The Polish woman's reflex, however, upon opening the door, is to ask defensively if the survivor intends to reclaim the property. A picture of the survivor's father is presented, posed in front of the same hearth that is in this home. Leaving no doubt, on the hearth next to the survivor's father is the same vase that sits on the same present-day hearth.

The film also faithfully portrays Israeli kids in a disco, probably in Krakow, blowing off steam after their Auschwitz/Birkenau tour, a common occurrence and an interesting juxtaposition with the somber daytime experience and our tendency to compartmentalize and process difficult experiences. After achieving her goal, the survivor is asked by her de facto guide if she returned to Birkenau to testify. She replies, "Survivors don't come back to testify. They are diseased with suffering, like me. They are afraid to come back here, like me. They only think of one thing: to get the hell out of here."

This storyline, told in documentaries such as *Kitty: Return to Auschwitz* (1979) and

Pizza in Auschwitz (2008), is the fire around which all other Holocaust Survivor films dance, but never approach. All others meander with flashbacks—some more and some less authentic—but at no time jump into the fire or walk over the coals. The characters and plots in most other Survivor Holocaust films are caricatures. But Anouk Aimée portrays the kind of Holocaust survivor whom we have all met, a woman who has gone on with her life with grace despite her pain, not allowing Hitler another victory.

As a film, *The Birch-Tree Meadow* is great; as a Holocaust film, *The Birch-Tree Meadow* is indispensable. It is also the most honest Survivor Holocaust film ever made. In fact, *The Birch-Tree Meadow* is the only Survivor film that ever needed to be made; the rest, although perhaps entertaining and somewhat elucidating, are mere contrivances in comparison.

Everything Is Illuminated (2005)

Genre:	Survivor
Sub-Genre:	Second Generation
Length:	104
MPAA or Local Rating:	PG-13 for disturbing images—violence, sexual content and language.
Language:	English
Country:	U.S.
Director:	Liev Schreiber
Top-Billed:	Elijah Wood, Eugene Hutz, Boris Lyoskin
From Wikipedia:	*Everything Is Illuminated* is a 2005 biographical comedy-drama film. It was adapted from the novel of the same name by Jonathan Safran Foer, and was the debut film of Liev Schreiber both as a director and as a screenwriter.
IMDb Rating:	7.5
IMDb Votes:	54110
***Holocaust Cinema Complete* Description:**	*Everything Is Illuminated* (2005) is a fabulously entertaining film about the American grandson of a Holocaust survivor who travels to Ukraine to solve a family mystery. Like most fish-out-of-water/roadshow films, the protagonist, who exhibits signs of obsessive-compulsive behavior, only interacts with odd characters, who are later humanized. The Holocaust tie-in, complete with a passable wartime reenactment, is the least compelling aspect of this fine film.
Recommendation:	For those who are interested in Eastern European family roots.
Suggested Minimum Grade:	Middle School

REVIEW

Liev Schreiber (1967–) has had a fascinating career. He is best known as the consummate fixer starring in (and producing) *Ray Donovan* (TV 2013–2020). Schreiber also starred in *Spotlight* (2015), a top 250 IMDb-rated film, *The Manchurian Candidate* (2004), *X-Men Origins: Wolverine* (2009), did voice work in a half dozen animated features and co-starred with Robin Williams and Daniel Craig respectively in the Holocaust films *Jakob the Liar* (1999) and *Defiance* (2008). Schreiber is one of the most recognizable actors and narrators of his generation. But arguably he exercised his greatest professional magic behind the camera for the only film he wrote and directed: *Everything Is Illuminated* (2005), which stars Elijah Wood, who is best known for his headlining (and recurring) role as "Frodo" in *The Lord of the Rings* trilogy (2001–2003). Wood also had a small but memorably creepy role in the transcendent *Eternal Sunshine of the Spotless Mind* (2004).

Based on the book of the same name by Jonathan Safran Foer, *Everything Is Illuminated* is a "second-generation" Holocaust Survivor film, surrounded by quotation marks because "second-generation" is a sub-genre here that includes all descendants of Holocaust victims; Jonathan, the protagonist of *Everything Is Illuminated*, is actually third-generation. Jonathan's idiosyncratic trappings in his novel were transformed to obsessive-compulsive behavior in Schreiber's film. The cinematic version of Jonathan Safran Foer puts things of interest in Ziploc bags, which Jonathan compulsively keeps handy in his pockets, like a germaphobe might carry a hand sanitizer in case of an unintended handshake. *Variety*'s Todd McCarthy suggested that Wood's character may have been pushed too far, which is a minority opinion:

> In general, Schreiber's approach is one of reducing the rich, if sometimes overwrought, material down to its most accessible, audience-pleasing elements. Jonathan's uptight, humorless mien blocks the development of any further character traits; role's rigid conception might have worked had the rest of the picture been similarly stylized, a la Jarmusch or the Coen Brothers. As it is, Wood's powerlessness to break out of the emotive straightjacket [sic] hands the picture to his Russian costars on a platter, and they run with it.[95]

The mystery in *Everything Is Illuminated* concerns something given to Jonathan as a child by his dying grandmother, an item that, of course, was immediately sealed in a plastic bag. As an adult, Jonathan has a large wall in his home festooned like a genealogical crime map with bagged items. Quick enough, most of the film becomes a road trip through Ukraine. Jonathan tracks down some family history and the mystery object's origin, which is hardly a unique cinematic device. His stylized Ukrainian tour guides—Alex (Eugene Hutz) and Alex's grandfather (Boris Lyoskin)—steal the show. The tour guide Alex is peculiar and gripping, using hilarious bastardized English, which grows on Jonathan. Alex's very offensive grandfather, too, is ostensibly a virulent antisemite. Together they find all the answers, plus a few more that had not even been asked. Then *Everything Is Illuminated* is wrapped up, with the aid of Holocaust flashbacks, imparting the kind of cultural enlightenment expected in most road-show films.

The magic of *Everything Is Illuminated* has almost nothing to do with the story. The film is great because of the performances, the dialogue, the fish-out-of-water elements, the editing and the titles. A good story is required for a good film, but these other elements are required to make a good story into a great film. As Roger Ebert noted:

> *Everything Is Illuminated* is a film that grows in reflection. The first time I saw it, I was hurtling down the tracks of a goofy ethnic comedy when suddenly we entered dark and dangerous territory. I admired the film but did not sufficiently appreciate its arc. I went to see it again at the Toronto Film Festival, feeling that I had missed some notes, had been distracted by Jonathan's eyeglasses and other relative irrelevancements (as Alex might say). The second time, I was more aware of the journey Schreiber was taking us on, and why it is necessary to begin where he begins in order to get where he's going.[96]

Like Ray Donovan at a target range, Liev Schreiber hit every bullseye with style and grace in his *Everything Is Illuminated*. It is a long way to go to find limited Holocaust content, but *Everything Is Illuminated* is a fine film, nonetheless.

***Dear Mr. Waldman—Michtavim Le America* (2006)**

Genre:	Survivor
Sub-Genre:	Post-War
Length:	90
MPAA or Local Rating:	PG-13

Language:	Hebrew
Country:	Israel
Director:	Hanan Peled
Top-Billed:	Rami Heuberger, Evgenia Dodina, Ido Port
From Wikipedia:	[Hebrew translated edited] Hilik Waldman, 10, and his brother grow up with Holocaust survivor parents, each of whom lost his spouse and previous children in the Holocaust. The longing for the dead undermines the relationship between parents and children living in constant fear of family breakup.
IMDb Rating:	7.2
IMDb Votes:	68
Holocaust Cinema Complete Description:	*Dear Mr. Waldman—Michtavim Le America* (2006) is an exceptional Israeli film about Israeli Holocaust survivors in the early 1960s. The characters are damaged, but forward-looking, trying to make the best of their new lives with their new families in a new country. The father holds onto the dream that his dead brother works in Washington for President Kennedy. *Dear Mr. Waldman*'s portrayal of 1960s Israeli society is particularly moving.
Recommendation:	A happier than normal Holocaust survivor film in early Israel.
Suggested Minimum Grade:	High School

REVIEW

Israeli television writer Hanan Peled (1951–) has directed one feature film: *Dear Mr. Waldman—Michtavim Le America* (2006). Hanan Peled is one-for-one. Peled also produced and wrote *Dear Mr. Waldman*, a project that clearly came from his heart. His autobiographical film has a simple premise that reveals Peled's pain as the son of Holocaust survivors: an adult survivor in Israel desperately believes that a man with the same name as his brother who unquestionably died in Auschwitz works in Washington, D.C., for President John F. Kennedy. The survivor, who has been told by eyewitnesses that his brother perished, grasps onto this tiny strand—or shard, depending on perspective—which is the survivor's final post–Holocaust hurdle to recovery. Peled's story symbolizes the final, symbolic leap needed to move on from the Holocaust.

One of many Survivor films set in Israel, *Dear Mr. Waldman* is sweeter than most; so too, in contrast to most Survivor Holocaust films, the plot is often playful. The survivor writes a letter to his supposed brother in America. He obsessively awaits the return letter, sometimes stalking the mail carrier. The 10-year-old son, Hilik, sees his father's anguish and seeks to put an end to it by paying a man with an English typewriter to forge an answer to the father. Hilik's older brother, who is learning English, reads the letter to the family:

> Dear Mr. Waldman. I was very pleased to receive your letter. My family, too, came from Radom [Poland]. I don't know much about my childhood because I jumped off the train and spent the war in hiding. I just wanted you to know that I'm alive. I know it would make you happy. We must meet sometime. Have a nice day. Sincerely yours. Jacob Waldman.

The dialogue and acting in *Dear Mr. Waldman* are first-rate. Evgenia Dodina, who also co-starred in *Made in Israel* (2001), proves again she is a national treasure. But Hilik, played by Ido Port—whose adult character narrates the open and close—is the most compelling character, sparkling with every scene, whether taking abuse, or making a friend, or loving his parents or pulling his father from the abyss. As summarized by Prairie Miller in *NewsBlaze*:

Hilik's solution, to fabricate a pretend correspondence between Jack Waldman and Moishe, is at the heart of Hanan Peled's compassionate yet candid autobiographical tale, and the search of his own father to find his son missing in the Holocaust. *Dear Mr. Waldman* is ultimately a wise and affectionate story about the positive powers of the imagination to cope in surprising ways, with an often troublesome and far from perfect human existence.[97]

Reviewer Richard Propes in *The Independent Critic* put it differently, writing:

Despite its occasional dip into melodrama and a story that may ring a tad familiar, *Dear Mr. Waldman* is a hidden jewel among this year's independent cinema and a sure sign of the growth and potential of the Israeli film scene. A beautifully paced film featuring characters you will most definitely care about, *Dear Mr. Waldman* is worth the effort to find whether that be on the film festival circuit or upon its eventual release on home video.[98]

In a terrific climactic sequence, Hilik finally informs his father that he had written the letter, and that he had done so to make the father feel better. Soon after, the father confronts another survivor who had just conned the father out of his life savings. The survivor responds, referring to the father's dead brother, "Is it my fault he died? Did I send him to the crematorium? What do you want from me? You think you'll be left with nothing? You've got two children. What have I got? A Chevy and a wife who didn't stop crying for the last 20 years."

There are many other subplots in *Dear Mr. Waldman* regarding affairs and swindles and pubescent kids getting into trouble. For example, Holocaust memories spill out of the father and his paramour during sex, with each of the lovers cathartically yelling out the names of a different partner who died in Auschwitz. Without the sex scenes, this film would be suitable for all ages. But the sex scenes necessarily reveal the pervasive pain suffered by survivors, reminding us that those who walked out of Auschwitz did so with horrifying memories. *Dear Mr. Waldman* is a remarkable gem, especially for those also seeking representations of early Israel.

This Must Be the Place (2011)

Genre:	Survivor
Sub-Genre:	Second Generation
Length:	118
MPAA or Local Rating:	R for language, some sexual content and brief disturbing images.
Language:	English
Country:	Italy—France—Ireland
Director:	Paolo Sorrentino
Top-Billed:	Sean Penn, Frances McDormand, Judd Hirsch
From Wikipedia:	*This Must Be the Place* is a 2011 European drama film written by Sorrentino and Umberto Contarello and released in the United States in late 2012. The film deals with a middle-aged wealthy rock star who becomes bored in his retirement and takes on the quest of finding his father's tormentor, a Nazi war criminal who is a refugee in the United States.
IMDb Rating:	6.7
IMDb Votes:	29463

Holocaust Cinema Complete Description:	Like the Survivor film *Harold and Maude,* 40 years later, *This Must Be the Place* (2011) is intensely quirky and beautifully made. *This Must Be the Place* features the estranged adult son of a just-deceased Auschwitz survivor. The son, a retired rock star, sets out to settle his father's score against a 90-year-old Auschwitz guard. While far more Holocaust-oriented than *Harold and Maude, This Must Be the Place* also is a celebration of life and growth.
Recommendation:	"TOP THREE" IN GENRE. For those interested equally in great film-making and Holocaust studies
Suggested Minimum Grade:	High School

REVIEW

Imagine a coming-of-age film featuring a 50ish retired rock star, played by Sean Penn, who is also an avenging second-generation Holocaust survivor and who daily paints his face and lips to maintain his rocker persona. Throw in his firefighter wife played by Frances McDormand, a feeble Nazi, a teenaged female sidekick, a missing child, the head Talking Head and a half-dozen versions of their titular song "This Must Be the Place (Naive Melody)," two continents and a slew of fascinating characters. What you get is Italian director/writer Paolo Sorrentino's wonderful *This Must Be the Place* (2011), which was nominated at the 2011 Cannes for the "Palme d'Or," but lost to the misguided and inferior *The Tree of Life* (2011) which also starred Sean Penn (and Brad Pitt). *This Must Be the Place* did, however, win the Cannes "Prize of the Ecumenical Jury," whose mandate is to "honor works of artistic quality which witnesses to [sic] the power of film to reveal the mysterious depths of human beings...."[99]

This Must Be the Place is Cheyenne's (Sean Penn) story. He is a retired international rocker who lives in sincere affectation. Cheyenne is stalwartly genuine, whether at the mall, playing handball, pleasuring his wife or chasing his father's tormentor. The black sheep of an Orthodox Jewish family, Cheyenne decided at 15 to be different. He left Brooklyn with talent and became a rock star and European zillionaire. Cheyenne is evocative of The Cure's Robert Smith, with jet-black teased hair, gaudy lipstick, pretentious glasses and alarming makeup. He maintains this mask in everyday life, the same grotesque stage façade which he used while performing. Cheyenne is also not short of idiosyncrasies, which include: blowing his obnoxious hair out of his eyes; pulling a cart or luggage, as if they are security blankets; and fear of flying, which causes Cheyenne to take a boat to America from his Dublin home, missing his father's death. Cheyenne uncontrollably reveals his self-view during a peculiarly staged soliloquy directed at Talking Heads' David Byrne (who also gets the "Music By" credit):

> I was a fucking pop star. And I just wrote dreary songs because they were all the rage and made tons of money. Just depressed songs for depressed kids. And two of them, more fragile than the rest, ended up doing themselves in as a result of it. And now I go to the cemetery once a week to appease my guilt. And it doesn't make it better. It makes it fucking worse. And then my wife asks me why I don't play anymore. And I think she must be a fool, because then, but then maybe she just loves me very much, which makes her more of a fool, because she doesn't know what a disaster her husband is. And that's it David. That's it.

And so it is. At his core, Cheyenne is still the 15-year-old kid who ran away from Brooklyn and Jewish Orthodoxy. In another powerful scene, a neighborhood friend voices her pain to Cheyenne about her missing son, her Tony, who has disappeared. The woman accuses Cheyenne of not trying to find the boy. She then lashes out at him for abandoning his own family a generation earlier. Not finished chastising her guest, this mother chides Cheyenne, saying "You never took up smoking because you remained a child. Children are the only ones who never get the urge to smoke." Therein lies the challenge: can Cheyenne grow up?

The inciting incident comes with the death of Cheyenne's estranged father, a Holocaust survivor, complete with an Auschwitz tattoo. Cheyenne returns to New York just after his father's death, learns about his father's German wartime antagonist, sets out across America to track down this German guard who humiliated the father in Auschwitz, a man whom the father had been hunting for 40 years. In what one critic attacked as "jarringly, cripplingly wrong,"[100] in the next 90 minutes of screen time, 10 days of searching, with a modicum of clues, Cheyenne finds the Nazi guard, whom Cheyenne's father, with all his resources, could not find in decades.

The main elements in *This Must Be the Place* are splendid, especially the cast. Sean Penn birthed a wholly new person with the character of Cheyenne, similar in originality to the characters created by Dustin Hoffman in *Rain Man* (1988), Daniel Day-Lewis in *My Left Foot* (1989), and Johnny Depp in *Edward Scissorhands* (1990). As aptly noted by reviewer Ed Whitfield, "we get as lost in Penn's character as he does."[101] Cheyenne's wife Jane is played impeccably by Frances McDormand, who never gives a bad performance in anything. Cheyenne's best friend Mary is played by Eve Hewson (U2 frontman Bono's daughter), and veteran actors Harry Dean Stanton and Judd Hirsch have solid roles. Further, the cinematography is gorgeous, not just filming but also seemingly capturing parts of America on screen. The pacing and dialogue are enchanting, as when Cheyenne mutters the beginning of a question, "Why is Lady Gaga…" which is, in fact, his entire question.

And there are several important Holocaust moments, such as when Cheyenne is speaking with the Nazi's wife, a retired high school history teacher, as Cheyenne digs for clues about her supposedly dead husband. Cheyenne, posing as an ex-student, practically teases her purportedly having taught about the Holocaust. "I remember," Cheyenne says, "it was very … touching." Her answer? "Well naturally … it was a tragedy … for children. No one should ever touch the children." She implies, of course, that killing millions of adult Jews was not a tragedy. Not satisfied, Cheyenne continues baiting her, asking why the Germans killed the Jews. Her answer is so nonchalantly antisemitic that it could have been uttered in a 1938 Munich beer hall: "They wanted their money." Aghast, Cheyenne presses, "But not all Jews were rich." To which the old woman coolly replies, "All of them had something."

Importantly, the ultimate disposition of the Nazi, too, is perfectly just, not overblown or bloodthirsty, but spot-on appropriate, leaving the Nazi revealed, humiliated and vulnerable, but alive. Further, the circumstances at Auschwitz described by the Nazi are historically accurate and fascinating. *Variety*'s critic Jay Weissberg agreed, writing that the film deals with "the Holocaust, in ways most films devoted to the subject can't touch with anything approaching this deep-seated honesty."[102] Director/writer Paolo Sorrentino made great art in this film.

Most satisfying is the transformation of Cheyenne from pop star caricature to full-fledged adult. Growth is most obvious in the last scene when a graying, clean-cut, un–Goth, luggageless Cheyenne appears outside Mary's mother's house, smiling, perhaps giving hope that someday Tony, too, will return. Cheyenne's transformation is more subtly demonstrated by his taking a cigarette while waiting for an airplane—not a boat—on his way back home to Ireland. More for the pure joy of finding fine, yet obscure, cinema, than as a Holocaust Survivor film—especially for fans of Sean Penn and/or Talking Heads—*This Must Be the Place* is a passionate, must-see film.

Phoenix (2014)

Genre:	Survivor
Sub-Genre:	Post-War
Length:	96
MPAA or Local Rating:	PG-13 for some thematic elements and brief suggestive material.
Language:	German—English
Country:	Germany
Director:	Christian Petzold
Top-Billed:	Nina Hoss, Ronald Zehrfeld, Nina Kunzendorf
From Wikipedia:	*Phoenix* is set in Germany in the aftermath of World War II, where Nelly, a Jew who managed to survive Auschwitz concentration camp, decides to go back to her husband Johnny in Berlin. She has had to have her face reconstructed owing to a bullet wound, and her husband does not recognize her.
IMDb Rating:	7.3
IMDb Votes:	13628
***Holocaust Cinema Complete* Description:**	*Phoenix* (2014) is a remake of the 1965 film *Return from the Ashes*, in which a disfigured Holocaust survivor returns after the War to reunite with her husband, who does not recognize her. She eventually discerns that he had betrayed her during the War. Like most films that depict just-post–War Europe, *Phoenix* is uplifting, with a protagonist who is eventually empowered and who can start anew.
Recommendation:	A rare film about a female Holocaust survivor's perseverance and empowerment.
Suggested Minimum Grade:	Middle School

REVIEW

German director Christian Petzold's *Phoenix* (2014) is a remake of the fairly well-regarded film *Return from the Ashes* (1965), based on Hubert Monteilhet's 1961 novel *Le Retour des cendres* ("The Return of the Ashes"). Maximilian Schell starred in the original 1965 version as a conniving husband of a rich woman who Schell's character believed died in the Holocaust, but the gold-digging husband is unable to put his hands on her fortune. Petzold's much better version had 50 years of technical advantages. But Petzold also makes the film more about the returning, unrecognizable wife, portrayed touchingly by veteran German film star Nina Hoss playing "Nelly Lenz," than about the lecherous husband who betrayed her to the Nazis. Petzold crafted a compelling story from a novel and earlier version that can be used at film schools to demonstrate how to transform a good film (*Return from the Ashes*) into a great film.

The film opens with Nelly, her head almost completely bandaged, a passenger in a car at an American checkpoint into Berlin. She is recuperating from reconstructive surgery, which, as she heals steadily throughout the film, returns Nelly back to her recognizable beauty. While still disfigured, Nelly, a Jewish cabaret singer, finds her Gentile husband Johnny (Ronald Zehrfeld), who is a slimeball working in the local nightclub. Johnny takes pity on her and eventually perceives a distant resemblance to his wife. He enlists her in his plan, convincing Nelly to pretend to be his wife so he can have some papers signed to inherit the wife's estate. He cluelessly trains her to emulate his wife's mannerisms and handwriting. Both Nelly and the audience are practically bursting with the expectation that Johnny will eventually recognize that she is, in fact, his wife. But it is not until the exceptional climax that all is revealed to him. *Slant*'s James Lattimer wrote, "If this melodramatic setup sounds implausible to the point of incredulity, that's probably because it is an exercise in the sort of willing suspension of disbelief that cinema itself is built on. For as Petzold repeatedly demonstrates, this story isn't beholden to the laws of reality, but rather unfolds in an imaginary realm pieced together from cinematic references...."[103]

Nelly's experience in Auschwitz is not an afterthought in *Phoenix*, as it was in the original *Return from the Ashes*; Nelly's tattoo becomes part of the story. Throughout, the friend who nurses Nelly back to health encourages her to move to Palestine and forget Johnny. There is no reason to believe that Nelly was not on that boat by the final credits. *Hollywood Reporter* critic Jordan Mintzer wrote:

> Both a powerful allegory for post-war regeneration and a rich Hitchcockian tale of mistaken identity, *Phoenix* once again proves that German filmmaker Christian Petzold and his favorite star, Nina Hoss, are clearly one of the best director-actor duos working in movies today. Like their last collaboration, *Barbara*, this pared-down, classically helmed period piece uses one woman's harrowing story to explore Germany's troubled past, though in this case the setting is WWII and the heroine is a concentration camp survivor returning to Berlin in search of her lost husband.[104]

Phoenix's climax is staged at a small party that ends with the star singing her most famous song. Nelly's serenade is so soulful—so obviously her unique styling—that no one in the room doubts her identity, especially with her tattoo finally revealed. The culmination is Johnny's reaction. He starts by accompanying her on the piano and then stops as he realizes what has actually happened, paralyzed by abject humiliation, as she continues acapella. Nelly controls the room and the moment as only an artist can, an impeccable few minutes that ends all subterfuge without a word of dialogue, away from which she walks liberated, ditching the contemptible man she once adored. Eric Kohn of *IndieWire* noted, "Hoss' portrayal of a woman at odds with her surroundings is in a class by itself. Similar to last year's *Ida*, in which a young nun discovers she's Jewish and explores her family's past in war-torn Poland, *Phoenix* hovers in a dreamlike plane between the dark past and uncertain present."[105] *Phoenix* hits all the right notes while making many important points about subjugation and empowerment. *Phoenix* is perhaps the final great Holocaust Survivor film.

Perpetrator Films

"Perpetrator" Holocaust films are about Germans or their collaborators who persecuted Jews during the War and then escaped justice. These perpetrators are usually hiding or on-the-run long after the War. Almost all Perpetrator films are either fiction or historical reenactments about Adolf Eichmann or Josef Mengele. Perpetrator films are the most formulaic of the genres: the Germans are portrayed as cunning, having been able to escape and hide, for at least one generation; the hidden German perpetrator is forced out of hiding by some external event; artificial tension is usually sprinkled in by having the perpetrator spotted by one of his victims in public, which rarely amounts to anything; the story ends with the German perpetrator committing suicide or being killed by someone who had nothing to do with the Holocaust. To date, 47 Perpetrator films have been made; five of the best are recommended below.

The Odessa File (1974)

Genre:	Perpetrator
Sub-Genre:	Post-War
Length:	130
MPAA or Local Rating:	PG
Language:	English
Country:	US—West Germany
Director:	Ronald Neame
Top-Billed:	Jon Voight, Maximilian Schell, Maria Schell
From Wikipedia:	*The Odessa File* is an Anglo-German 1974 espionage thriller film, adaptation of the novel *The Odessa File* by Frederick Forsyth, about a reporter's investigation of a neo–Nazi political-industrial network in post–Second World War West Germany.
IMDb Rating:	7.0
IMDb Votes:	8647
Holocaust Cinema Complete Description:	*The Odessa File* (1974) is one of the few Perpetrator Holocaust films to include meaningful Holocaust flashbacks, which not only frame the motivation for killing the hidden Nazi, but also exposes the underground of Nazis who are still plotting in West German society.
Recommendation:	A Perpetrator film with some historical meat on its bones.
Suggested Minimum Grade:	Middle School

REVIEW

The year before Maximilian Schell (1930–2014) starred as a deranged Holocaust survivor in *The Man in the Glass Booth* (1975), he played the fictionalized SS-Obersturmführer Eduard Roschmann, who was based on a real Nazi in hiding in 1963. In the fictionalized *The Odessa File* (1974), directed by Ronald Neame (1911–2010), and the 1972 novel of the same name by Frederick Forsyth (1938–), Roschmann is also the ringleader of a neo–Nazi organization in post–War West Germany.

Forsyth's Roschmann in *The Odessa File* novel is a case study in fictionalization, with just enough truth about Roschmann's real character to cause some historians to set the record straight. For example, Forsyth refers in his novel to Roschmann as the "Butcher of Riga," which has been debunked, although the actual Roschmann certainly oversaw war crimes and inconceivable butchery as the commandant of the Riga Ghetto in 1943. Other details of Eduard Roschmann's life were purposely embellished for Forsyth's novel by famed Nazi hunter Simon Wiesenthal (1908–2005), who intended to flush Roschmann out with pseudo-information.[106] As famed Professor Deborah Lipstadt wrote, "Wiesenthal's claims about tracking war criminals in the post-war years are likewise riddled with exaggerations, if not outright falsehoods."[107] Nonetheless and astonishingly, Roschmann was actually smoked out by *The Odessa File*, as explained by Forsyth in 2011:

> They made it into a film, which was screened in a little fleapit cinema south of Buenos Aires, where a man stood up and said, "I know that man, he lives down the street from me," and denounced him. He [Roschmann] decided to make a run for it to Paraguay and died of a heart attack on the river crossing. They buried him in an unmarked gravel pit. I hope they tossed a copy of the book in on top of him.[108]

Despite Simon Wiesenthal's fictional liberties, he was not only credited in the film as "Documentary Advisor," but also exaltedly portrayed as a main character. Of note, too, is the co-starring role of Maximilian Schell's sister, Maria Schell (1926–2005), who also had a significant film career, with over 100 acting credits on IMDb, including as "Vond-Ah" in

Superman (1978). Among other oddities, the opening song in Neame's creepy West Germany on the day of JFK's assassination is Perry Como singing "Christmas Dream," written for the film by a very young Andrew Lloyd Webber.

But *The Odessa File*'s star is Jon Voight, in the middle of his remarkable career, which has included his co-starring in *Deliverance* (1972), winning the Best Actor Oscar for *Coming Home* (1978), and Oscar nominations for Best Actor in *Midnight Cowboy* (1969), *Runaway Train* (1985), and *Ali* (2001), and more recently playing the iconic slimeball patriarch "Mickey" in *Ray Donovan* (TV 2013–2020).

Voight also portrays the ineffectual SS-Gruppenführer (General) Jürgen Stroop in *Uprising* (TV 2001), the German commander responsible for crushing the famed Warsaw Ghetto Uprising, where 150 German soldiers were killed by the Jewish inhabitants. The real Stroop was tried, convicted and executed in 1947 by the Soviets in Warsaw's Mokotów Prison (a location that differs from the film's version). In *Uprising*, which seems to depict far more than a few hundred bad guys cut down, Voight is the least plastic of all the characters, especially David Schwimmer. Voight's accent and demeanor almost lift *Uprising* from trite to passable. Likewise, Voight saved the otherwise formulaic *The Odessa File* from itself, with his boyish innocence mixed with just enough cunning. "Voight is able to shine in a manner that isn't showy," wrote reviewer Peter Martin in 2011. "He displays oodles of quiet, probing intelligence with little more than a firm set to his chin."[109]

In *The Odessa File*, Voight plays a young reporter who stumbles onto the death of a Holocaust survivor. He connects the dots with the help of Wiesenthal and the Mossad (Israeli intelligence), discovering a fictitious underground network responsible for hiding Nazis, a group called "ODESSA," an acronym for "Organisation der ehemaligen SS-Angehörigen" (Organization of Former SS Members). The Mossad transforms the reporter into an undercover former SS sergeant so the reporter can infiltrate ODESSA, where Voight finds another gear in his performance. The Mossad, however, is mostly interested in subverting a plot by Roschmann and ODESSA to deliver a missile guidance system to Egypt, which is to be used to destroy Israel with combined biological and radioactive warheads. The ending involves an unusually good plot twist, delightfully orchestrated by director Neame on the heels of his manic *The Poseidon Adventure* (1972).

Neame's Holocaust flashback scenes are good but too brief. There is also some confusing language about the "Riga Concentration Camp," instead of the Riga Ghetto. So too, a killing field with a ravine is depicted, which was unlikely at a camp or in a ghetto. Further, the film attributes to Roschmann the invention of gas vans—mobile killing trucks with the exhaust pumped in the rear compartment—which also were not in Latvia and which Roschmann certainly did not invent. But just as certainly, in 1974 these historical discrepancies were intended as Holocaust composites. On the other hand, a survivor character was depicted with an accurate Auschwitz tattoo. Overall, however, these errors do not outweigh the general information imparted. And, although Voight's German accent is consistent, the oddity of these purported Germans speaking English in West Germany is abrasive throughout. So, too, the Mossad's plotline is heavy-handed.

The interesting phenomenon of *The Odessa File* is that it was not well-respected when released. Although few saw it in theaters, *The Odessa File* soon became a mainstay of video rentals. Contemporaneous reviewers were not thrilled with the film, either. Don Druker in the *Chicago Reader* chided, "Frederick Forsyth's thriller gets a more pedestrian treatment from Ronald Neame than his *Day of the Jackal* got from Fred Zinnemann, and the surprises increasingly fail to surprise … but Voight has rarely been better."[110] Richard T. Jameson in *Parallax View* also cast a few stones, writing, "Despite an earnest and doggedly intelligent personification by Jon Voight, the protagonist, a freelance journalist trying to find a certain notorious Nazi in 1963 West Germany, makes little sense."[111] And Nora Sayre in *The New York Times* was even more dismissive:

> When a thriller is built entirely around one star, you know that he's not going to vanish, that he simply can't get bumped off—hence the suspense sags. And that's one of the many flaws in Ronald Neame's "The Odessa File".… The movie is so dependent on Jon Voight's presence that he's hardly allowed off the screen.… Mr. Voight is not at his best—he's just too thoughtful a performer for a mere action part, which offers too little scope for the variety of his talents. He hasn't much to do beyond conveying worry, weariness and patience; he's rarely allowed to smile—and it's a deprivation not to see this actor smile.[112]

Like most filmgoers, I also did not watch *The Odessa File* when it was released, but only years later. I can imagine that viewers in the 1970s may have been uncomfortable with content that included an authentically tattooed Holocaust survivor who ultimately stands with Jon Voight's character in Yad Vashem's Hall of Remembrance saying Kaddish (the prayer for the dead) for the man killed in the first act. And the reenactments, which were mostly graphic hangings and shootings, were also unusually harrowing for the 1970s. Further, Maximilian Schell's impassioned speech defending his atrocities were disturbingly evocative of Adolf Eichmann: "A soldier is given orders. He obeys those orders. He doesn't ask if they are right or wrong. You know that as well as I do. All I did was to obey my orders." However, time has been kind to *The Odessa File*, as exemplified by the following two reviews written within the last ten years:

> *The Odessa File* is both an entertaining thriller and a textbook example of the "invisible" style of directing that has largely disappeared. As you watch the film, you're unaware of Neame's directorial guidance, and yet it's there at all times. It *has* to be for the film to sustain suspense so successfully for its 128-minute running time, despite the lack of major action scenes and a story that unfolds almost entirely through dialogue. Neame keeps his takes short and cuts frequently but not abruptly. He has people moving in the frame, but in casual motions that fit naturally with what they're engaged in at the moment, and he has the actors deliver their lines in a heightened, urgent style that's almost theatrical (it helps that they all have accents).[113]
>
> Jon Voight makes for a personable and credible lead. It's easy enough to imagine him as a driven journalist and, while there are action sequences, has the everyman quality that we see less and less of in these days of virtually superhuman leads. The journey he embarks on, both professionally and personally, is never less than fascinating and his sympathetic playing is a large part of what makes it work. Maximilian Schell is the other big name in the cast, the malign presence of his venal character haunting the picture even when he's off screen for long stretches. And the climactic confrontation between Voight and Schell is both revelatory and satisfying.[114]

The Odessa File is less meandering than the recommended Perpetrator film *Marathon Man* (1976)—which stars Jon Voight's co-star from *Midnight Cowboy* (1969), Dustin Hoffman—but is not nearly as compelling. *The Odessa File* is more of a period piece that still delivers. More importantly, *The Odessa File* is much more Holocaust-specific than is *Marathon Man*. But, like many outcomes in Hollywood, perhaps the biggest reason *The Odessa File* has been forgotten is timing: it was released in the shadow of the first blockbuster Holocaust miniseries, *QB VII* (Miniseries 1974), a splash that sunk the retrospectively better production.

Marathon Man (1976)

Genre:	Perpetrator
Sub-Genre:	Post Post-War

Length:	125
MPAA or Local Rating:	R
Language:	English
Country:	U.S.
Director:	John Schlesinger
Top-Billed:	Dustin Hoffman, Laurence Olivier, Roy Scheider
From Wikipedia:	*Marathon Man* is a 1976 American suspense-thriller film. It was adapted by William Goldman from his 1974 novel of the same name.
IMDb Rating:	7.5
IMDb Votes:	50533
Oscar:	Nomination: Best Supporting Actor.
Holocaust Cinema Complete Description:	*Marathon Man* (1976) is the classic Perpetrator film, with a Nazi, evocative of Josef Mengele, who tortures a Jew. The film's directing and acting are so good that the large plot-holes and blatant misdirection are simply forgotten. Of note, too, is the implication that even those Jews who did not identify with their heritage were not immune from persecution. *Marathon Man* is a grand roller-coaster ride, which is both terrifying and—despite its lapses—is still satisfying.
Recommendation:	The classic Perpetrator film, for those wanting a thrill.
Suggested Minimum Grade:	High School

REVIEW

From 1950 until 2000, John Schlesinger (1926–2003) directed 19 films, of which only two will be remembered: Best Picture, Director and Writing Oscar-winner *Midnight Cowboy* (1969), which was also nominated for Best Editing, Best Actress, and received Best Actor nominations for both stars, Dustin Hoffman and Jon Voight.* Schlesinger's other memorable film is *Marathon Man* (1976), which also starred Hoffman and co-starred Laurence Olivier (1907–1989), Roy Scheider (1932–2008) and William Devane (1939–). Olivier, who had already been nominated for a dozen other Oscars, was nominated for Best Supporting Actor for his performance in *Marathon Man*. Hoffman was in the prime of his career, in the middle of a period where he was nominated for six Oscars in 21 years, having won two. Roy Scheider and William Devane never got the big awards, but always made their teams better in their 100 feature films.

Marathon Man is the prototypical Perpetrator film. Sure, the groundwork had been laid in American cinema by Orson Welles' *The Stranger* (1946) and Ronald Neame's *The Odessa File* (1974), which also was cast with all-stars Jon Voight and Maximilian Schell. But *Marathon Man* is the archetype regarding tone, its terrifying Nazi, the fake tension, gratuitous violence, misdirection and themes. As for the ending, after Dustin Hoffman demanded a rewrite, *Marathon Man*'s antagonist still met the same fate as most other fictional Nazis in Perpetrator films: a dead Nazi who is not killed by a Jew. Roger Ebert started his review of the film with the following:

> I'm not a purist when it comes to thrillers, and with *Marathon Man*, that's just as well. If a movie like this is going to work, it has to work moment by moment and scene by scene—and *Marathon Man* does. There are all sorts of unanswered questions when the film's over, but I'm not inclined to hold that against it. I enjoy thrillers for the people and predicaments in them, not for their clockwork plots.[115]

---

* John Wayne's performance in *True Grit* (1969) beat them out, as well as Richard Burton in *Anne of the Thousand Days* (1969) and Peter O'Toole in *Goodbye, Mr. Chips* (1969).

Marathon Man was written by a master, two-time Oscar-winner William Goldman (1931–2018), who certainly knew what he was doing, having been credited with screenplays of 30 feature films, including many of the most iconic of any generation, from *Butch Cassidy and the Sundance Kid* (1969) to *The Princess Bride* (1987), from *Papillon* (1973) to *All the President's Men* (1976), *Misery* (1990) and *Chaplin* (1992). Films Goldman wrote were nominated for 26 Oscars, of which 10 trophies were won. Goldman also wrote the underlying novels *The Princess Bride* and *Marathon Man*. Certainly, of the above-listed gems, very few merited Roger Ebert's backhanded compliment, that *Marathon Man* is excellent despite itself.

That is a kind way of saying that about 20 minutes of this 125-minute film are filled with exciting and captivating scenes that have nothing to do with the story, which is about: (1) the Nazi "Zell" (Laurence Olivier), who has been hiding in South America since the war, and who decides to retrieve billions of dollars' worth of Jewish-looted diamonds from a safety deposit box in New York City; (2) a CIA handler, played by Roy Scheider, who has been paying Zell for information about other Nazis in hiding; (3) Zell's killing the CIA handler because Zell thinks he will be robbed of his diamonds; (4) the CIA handler's brother, Babe Levy (Dustin Hoffman), who gets caught in the middle because the CIA handler somehow manages to die in Babe's arms; (5) Babe is suspected of having been told about the diamonds and is tortured. *Variety* was even more dismissive:

> Film spends literally half of its length getting some basic plot pieces fitted and moving. By which time it's asking a lot if anybody still cares why Dustin Hoffman's brother Roy Scheider is a mysterious globe-trotter; why Laurence Olivier as an ex-Nazi disguises his appearance to leave a jungle hideaway to go to NY; why U.S. secret agent William Devane seems in league with Olivier and his goons, Richard Bright and Marc Lawrence; why Marthe Keller throws herself at Hoffman; why the memory of Hoffman's dishonored professor-father, a victim of the McCarthy era, relates to anything.[116]

As Roger Ebert assured us, none of this seems to matter. The acting in *Marathon Man* is not *Hamlet*, but it is still plenty good, and led to a story about a lesson given to method-actor Hoffman by the old pro, Olivier, on the *Marathon Man* set: "Upon being asked by his co-star how a previous scene had gone, one in which Hoffmann's character had supposedly stayed up for three days, Hoffmann admitted that he too had not slept for 72 hours to achieve emotional verisimilitude. 'My dear boy,' replied Olivier smoothly, 'why don't you just try acting?'"[117]

Marathon Man's familiar music score is also noteworthy. Unfortunately, it is familiar and reminiscent of the other 44 feature film scores also composed by Michael Small (1939–2003) from 1969 through 2000. Some of Small's other movies are *Jaws: The Revenge* (1987), *Pumping Iron* (1977) and *The Postman Always Rings Twice* (1981). Small also scored nine of director Alan J. Pakula's 16 features, including *Klute* (1971) and *The Parallax View* (1974), both of which are embarrassingly similar to *Marathon Man*'s score.

Nonetheless, no one who has ever seen *Marathon Man* will forget when William Devane's character "Janeway" orchestrates Babe's capture so that Babe can be tortured by Zell, who made a name for himself during the Holocaust for drilling into prisoners' teeth. For old times' sake, Zell has a few sessions with Babe in the chair, constantly asking him, "Is it safe?" While Zell wants to know if Babe's brother told Babe about Zell's diamond stash at the bank, Babe has no idea why he is being tortured. If you want to scare a baby boomer, take a drill and say to them with your best German accent, "Is it safe?" As a Holocaust film, *Marathon Man* provides the roadmap for all Perpetrator films; it is better as a Holocaust Perpetrator film than a general flick. Regardless, no one who sees *Marathon Man* forgets *Marathon Man*.

Genghis Cohn (1993)

Genre:	Perpetrator
Sub-Genre:	Post-War
Length:	79
MPAA or Local Rating:	Unrated (R)
Language:	English
Country:	U.S.—U.K.
Director:	Elijah Moshinsky
Top-Billed:	Antony Sher, Robert Lindsay, Matthew Marsh
From Wikipedia:	—
IMDb Rating:	6.8
IMDb Votes:	123
Holocaust Cinema Complete Description:	*Genghis Cohn* (1993) is a Holocaust comedy about a West German police commissioner in 1958 who is also a former SS officer. The former Nazi is tormented by an apparition, the ghost of a Jew the Nazi killed. Tonally, like in *My Führer* (2007), thematically like *The Twilight Zone*'s episode "Deaths-Head Revisited" (1961), this delightful film belittles post–War West German civil service as the home of so many former Nazis. The film is whimsical and ghoulish, culminating seamlessly.
Recommendation:	"TOP THREE" IN GENRE. A Jewish ghost story that makes its point with Jewish cynicism.
Suggested Minimum Grade:	Middle School

REVIEW

On a German talk show, comedian Robin Williams (1951–2014) was asked why there is so little comedy in Germany, to which he replied, "Did you ever think you killed all the funny people?"[118] *Genghis Cohn* (1993) is an extension of Williams' cutting observation.

Genghis Cohn is an exceptionally good, but forgotten Holocaust comedy, a forerunner to the recommended Victim film *My Führer—Mein Führer—Die wirklich wahrste Wahrheit über Adolf Hitler* (2007). *Genghis Cohn*'s name, alone, is funny. But the film has slipped so far through the cracks that no summary of it has been written for IMDb or Wikipedia. Yad Vashem's Online Movie Database describes it simply as "Based on a novel by Romain Gary, a Jewish comedian, who was shot a [*sic*] Dachau, returns to haunt his executioner and exact an ironic revenge." Even that description is incorrect: the comedian was murdered in a pit with the rest of the Jews from his village by a death squad, not in Dachau.

Genghis Cohn is about fictional police commissioner Otto Schatz, who has become the face of a post–War West German city and is celebrated for having eliminated crime in his town. Schatz is also quite the Teutonic social climber and womanizer. And, of course, this West German police commissioner is also a former Nazi officer who commanded an Einsatzgruppen (death squad) in Eastern Europe. In an early flashback, Schatz oversees the slaughter of Jews. One of those murdered was an accomplished comedian named "Genghis Cohn" who, just before being murdered, shouts at Schatz in Yiddish, "kish mir in tuchas" (kiss my ass). Ken Tucker of *Entertainment Weekly* was enthralled by *Genghis Cohn*:

> A deliriously complicated little trifle, *Genghis Cohn* ... stars Antony Sher as Genghis Cohn, a Jewish music-hall comedian whose World War II death was ordered by Nazi officer Otto Schatz (Robert

Lindsay). Years later, Schatz is living the life of a highly respected police commissioner in the small town of Licht when Cohn's ghost returns to haunt him. And not just haunt him—to taunt him, to ridicule him unmercifully, to turn him into a suicidal laughingstock. There's a subplot about a series of murders Schatz is investigating, and a religious conversion that has to be seen to be believed. All this, plus ["Bond girl"] Diana Rigg as a wittily zaftig widow pursuing Schatz—what more could you want? A-[119]

Everything is going swimmingly for Schatz until 1958, when a serial murderer is on the loose in his town. As the body count rises, the ghost of Genghis Cohn increasingly haunts the German with a barrage of jokes and schtick, some of it in Yiddish. Director Elijah Moshinsky cleverly stages the appearances of the comedian whose ghost progressively torments the German, culminating in Schatz's suicide, but not before Schatz assimilates many of Genghis Cohn's mannerisms and Yiddish vocabulary into his personality. "A loopy idea," wrote Derek Elley in *Variety*, "diffused by a loose script and even looser direction, *Genghis Cohn* should attract some offshore attention from the sheer outrageousness of its premise and the roster of name players. But this BBC telemovie, about a former Nazi haunted by the pesky ghost of a Dachau victim, is more fitted to fests and Jewish events than broader theatrical situations."[120]

Genghis Cohn is about guilt, retribution and Jewish humor. It also directly indicts West German society for knowingly promoting the careers of war criminals. Interestingly, while some German films tackle the covert acceptance of Nazis in West German civil service—including the recommended *Labyrinth of Lies—Im Labyrinth Des Schweigens* (2014) and *The People vs. Fritz Bauer—Der Staat gegen Fritz Bauer* (2015)—*Genghis Cohn* and *The Odessa File* (1974) are the only Holocaust films made by non–Germans that take serious jabs at West Germany's Nazi-filled bureaucracy. *Genghis Cohn* is a British-American co-production, the only feature film directed by Elijah Moshinsky (1946–), who spent his first five years in Shanghai, China, with his parents, three of the 22,000 given refuge, first by the occupying power (Imperial Japan) and later by the post–War Chinese government. Many of the Shanghai Jews left for Israel after the establishment of the State. (Although few Jews remain, the story of the Shanghai Jews is retold in the Chinese film *A Jewish Girl in Shanghai* [2010]). Moshinsky's family, however, immigrated to Australia, where he became a director of opera, theater and television. It is no coincidence that Moshinsky's only film was Holocaust-related.

Genghis Cohn was written by Romain Gary (né Roman Kacew) (1914–1980). Gary was a French Jewish novelist, diplomat, film director and World War II aviator. He was the only author to have won the Prix Goncourt (the Académie Goncourt's prize in French literature) under two names. This was scandalous because the Prix Goncourt's rules explicitly prohibit an author from winning more than once. Gary used the pseudonym "Émile Ajar" to fool the committee and then sent a relative to accept the prize as the fictional author "Émile Ajar." Gary wrote 17 feature films, including the Holocaust Survivor film *A Life Ahead—Madam Rose—Madame Rosa—La Vie devant soi* (1977), which, although not recommended in this book, won the Oscar for Best Foreign Language Film.

Genghis Cohn's screenplay was written by British-Jewish Stanley Price (1931–2019), who was an accomplished British television writer. The unctuous Nazi Otto Schatz is played by Tony Award-winning British actor Robert Lindsay, who has made a fine name for himself in the U.K. with a broad range of performances, from dramatic to comedy to farce, on stage, screen and television.

The humor in *Genghis Cohn* is thoroughly Jewish, as expressed by the actor playing

Genghis Cohn, Antony Sher, who is no Holocaust lightweight. The South African-born British-Jewish Sher also sparkled in the recommended and brave one-man-show *Primo* (TV 2005), where he stood on a bare stage for 75 minutes reciting passages from Primo Levi's Auschwitz/Birkenau remembrances. Sher also had a supporting part in the ambitious British-produced *God on Trial* (TV 2008). As the crowbar of Schatz's unhinging, Sher is delightful and very funny. His performance is wholly nuanced, with just the right amount of glee spilling out while destroying his killer, and a dash of solemnity about the underlying truth and circumstance. Sher's performance is obnoxiously ethnic, a cross between a meth-addled Alvy Singer (*Annie Hall*) and a go-for-broke Max Bialystock (*The Producers*).

Another interesting nugget about *Genghis Cohn* is that its premise is similar to Rod Serling's deadly serious *The Twilight Zone* (TV 1959–1964) 25-minute episode "Deaths-Head Revisited," which was bravely aired on network television in 1961 (and was set in Dachau, although on a Hollywood set). The basic plot is similar, told melodramatically in *The Twilight Zone* and hilariously in *Genghis Cohn*. In both cases, a Holocaust apparition causes the death of an SS officer who has flourished in post–War West Germany.

Put it all together and *Genghis Cohn* becomes a courageous, yet overlooked film that should be remembered kindly as one of the best Holocaust comedies. Where most films could have overshot their short and stormy runway because of such tantalizing distractions as a big-mouthed Jewish comedian and a pompous ex-Nazi, *Genghis Cohn* noses up, trims its wings and gracefully touches down safely, dumping its odious passenger lifeless on the tarmac.

Made in Israel (2001)

Genre:	Perpetrator
Sub-Genre:	Post Post-War
Length:	113
MPAA or Local Rating:	12
Language:	Hebrew
Country:	Israel
Director:	Ari Folman
Top-Billed:	Menashe Noy, Evgenia Dodina, Jürgen Holtz
From Wikipedia:	*Made in Israel* is a 2001 Israeli drama film directed by Ari Folman.
IMDb Rating:	6.8
IMDb Votes:	131
***Holocaust Cinema Complete* Description:**	*Made in Israel* (2001) portrays a time so far in the future that, as part of an Israeli/Syrian peace deal, the last surviving Nazi war criminal is handed over to Israel as part of the Golan Heights exchange. From there, Israeli police are entrusted to transport the German to Jerusalem to stand trial. Meantime, others, who have their own sense of justice, have put a bounty on the German's head. *Made in Israel* is a unique and astute Israeli perspective, a meaningful stab at an otherwise stale Perpetrator genre.
Recommendation:	"TOP THREE" IN GENRE. A fine Israeli take on vengeance and justice in a beautiful film.
Suggested Minimum Grade:	High School

REVIEW

Israeli director Ari Folman made one of the most controversial major Israeli films in history, the Oscar-nominated *Waltz with Bashir* (2008), an animated film that was extremely critical of Israelis during the First Israel-Lebanon War. The animation style was superb, as was Folman's attack on the Israeli politicians and commanders responsible for the war, and especially their tacit responsibility for allowing Israel's Lebanese Christian allies to slaughter as many as 3,500 Palestinians. The film was so innovative that Folman was asked to use the same technique when he wrote and directed *The Congress* (2013), a mostly biographical acid trip about actress Robin Wright, who has since shot to stratospheric status in *House of Cards* (TV 2013–2018). Folman also directed the animated *Where Is Anne Frank* (2021), which almost died the death of a thousand cuts. But Folman's best film to date is *Made in Israel* (2001).

The Perpetrator genre is so formulaic—with really bad villains and equally sympathetic heroes—that Folman's take, long before his animation detour, was fresh and needed. The premise is that, far in the future, the last Nazi would be turned over to Israel for trial. The entire film is shot during the Nazi's transport from the Golan Heights to Jerusalem. But there is a bounty on the Nazi because some would like him as a trophy and others believe he will evade justice in the Israeli legal system. So a whole series of colorful characters track the Nazi.

Nothing is wasted in *Made in Israel*, perhaps the most genuine Perpetrator film. The expected never occurs and the unexpected works on many levels. Even *Made in Israel*'s most jarring scenes are compelling and engrossing. At times the film is very funny and cynical; at other times it is endearing and even romantic, especially with co-star Evgenia Dodina, who plays a Russian assassin and who also lit up the screen in the recommended *Dear Mr. Waldman—Michtavim Le America* (2006). *Made in Israel* shows Israelis at their best and at their most vulnerable. It transmits a loving, but accurate picture of modern Israel, a purity in representation without any of the controversy or stylistic gymnastics of *Waltz with Bashir*.

For example, there is a charming scene in English where the police commander must take the Nazi to a diner in the Golan Heights for a meal. The commander is told by the owner that the Nazi cannot eat there. The commander replies, "You see sir, the Nazi has to eat. This is justice, law-and-order made in Israel. Even Nazi convicts get their meal. He wants a double cheeseburger with two eggs on top. Bacon and sausage with a big pile of fries and mayonnaise and a large Coke with ice, no lemon." The commander then just orders coffee, stating, "eating pigs makes me jealous." During the meal the Nazi asks if he can be taken to the Sea of Galilee—the place where the Nazi insists that Jesus walked on water—so the Nazi can be purified before facing trial in Jerusalem.

COMMANDER: *Jesus did not walk on the water.*
NAZI: *He did.*
COMMANDER: *He did not.*
NAZI: *If he didn't walk on water, then Moses didn't split the sea.*
COMMANDER: *Yes, he did.*
NAZI: *He did not.*
COMMANDER: *He did.*
NAZI: *How would you know?*
COMMANDER: *I learned about it in school…. Now shut up and eat your meat.*

The Israel Film Fund initially declined to subsidize *Made in Israel*, so Folman used his own resources and connections. After Katriel Schory, director of the Israel Film Fund, and others viewed the rough cut, they changed their minds. According to *Haaretz*: "'When we saw the rough cut,' says [Katriel] Schory, 'it was deserving, at the very least on the basis of all the effort that went into it. I believe that this group of filmmakers, the producer and the director and the actors, are real cinema people who will stay in the sector, and it is our duty to encourage them.'"[121]

The Israel Film Fund ultimately made a great decision. Director Ari Folman has certainly continued writing and directing notable films. But *Made in Israel* is his least pretentious and most laudable. *Made in Israel* ends correctly in every way; the many subplots are resolved with the ease of an assassin's trigger pull (although that is not, actually, how it goes down). Those who lived, deserved to live; those who died either were bad people or martyrs for the State. And filming in the snowy Golan Heights in the middle of winter with exposition provided by hourly Israeli national radio news were masterstrokes. The casting and acting are superb, as is the score. No Perpetrator film is better or more essential than *Made in Israel*.

The People vs. Fritz Bauer—Der Staat gegen Fritz Bauer (2015)

Genre:	Perpetrator
Sub-Genre:	Post-War
Length:	105
MPAA or Local Rating:	R for some sexual content.
Language:	German
Country:	Germany
Director:	Lars Kraume
Top-Billed:	Rüdiger Klink, Burghart Klaußner, Andrej Kaminsky
From Wikipedia:	*The People vs. Fritz Bauer* (German: *Der Staat gegen Fritz Bauer*) is a 2015 German drama film.
IMDb Rating:	7.1
IMDb Votes:	3196
***Holocaust Cinema Complete* Description:**	*The People vs. Fritz Bauer—Der Staat gegen Fritz Bauer* (2015), much like *Labyrinth of Lies* (2014) the previous year, is about the post–War West German bureaucracy hiding former Nazis. While *Labyrinth of Lies* is primarily about exposing a German Gentile to the actions of the previous generation, *The People vs. Fritz Bauer* concentrates on the perspective of a post–War Jewish German state prosecutor who is willing to violate West German laws to help Israel capture Adolf Eichmann. *The People vs. Fritz Bauer* thoroughly exposes racism and homophobia in post–War Germany.
Recommendation:	"TOP THREE" IN GENRE. A terrific representation of post–War West Germany, from the point of view of a gay, German Jewish prosecutor.
Suggested Minimum Grade:	High School

REVIEW

Just as *The Odessa File* (1974), *Genghis Cohn* (1993) and *Labyrinth of Lies—Im Labyrinth Des Schweigens* (2014) exposed the integration of Nazis into civil service in post–War West Germany, *The People vs. Fritz Bauer—Der Staat gegen Fritz Bauer* (2015) takes a very deep and personal autobiographical dive into Nazis in West German bureaucracy. This time it is from the point of view of a German Jewish Holocaust survivor, who returns to Germany and becomes a West German prosecutor, the very real Fritz Bauer (1903–1968).

Director Lars Kraume's *The People vs. Fritz Bauer* is a classy movie with a savvy protagonist, the kind of mature professional who we all would want in our corner. He passionately roots out Nazis in West German bureaucracy and even gets a tip concerning the whereabouts of both Adolf Eichmann and Josef Mengele. He risked being arrested for conveying information to the Mossad about Eichmann, which was a violation of West German law. In fact, it was Bauer's information that ultimately led to Eichmann's capture by the Mossad.

Through it all was a sub-plot about Bauer being a suicidal homosexual, both of which were also illegal in West Germany. Although he was closeted, Bauer had a protégé who was set-up and compromised after having been photographed in the act with a transvestite. This co-star, Ronald Zehrfeld, was a good fit, playing a vastly different character than he did the year before as the evil husband in the recommended Survivor film *Phoenix* (2014). The climax of *The People vs. Fritz Bauer* was Bauer being responsible for the "Frankfurt Auschwitz trials" from 1963 to 1965, which led directly to the indictment of approximately ten percent of the 8,200 German personnel who served at Auschwitz/Birkenau.

"Fritz Bauer," wrote Ken Jaworowski in *The New York Times*, "is a mass, and a mess, of contradictions: crafty yet principled, loyal yet friendless, brooding yet driven. Sometimes he charges ahead, other times he bumbles along, usually engulfed in a cloud of tobacco smoke."[122] As noted by Kenneth Turan in *The Los Angeles Times*:

> It's called *The People vs. Fritz Bauer*, but this involving, based-on-fact German drama is really about Fritz Bauer versus everybody else, not the other way around. All but unknown in this country, Bauer was a major crusader against Nazi influence in post–World War II Germany and the key player in 1963's Auschwitz trials, the first time German criminal cases were brought against Holocaust perpetrators. Bauer has been the subject of major museum exhibitions and numerous books, and this film was a considerable success in its homeland, winning six Lolas (the German Oscars), including best picture and best director for Lars Kraume.[123]

Although the protagonist, Fritz Bauer, was a real Jewish survivor, *The People vs. Fritz Bauer* is a Perpetrator film, because it is primarily about tracking down Nazis. Further, Bauer hid in Denmark and Sweden during the War; his experiences as a victim of German persecution during the Holocaust are irrelevant in this film. Oktay Ege Kozak wrote for *The Playlist* of *The People vs. Fritz Bauer*:

> Kraume almost goes out of his way to make his visual style as unsexy and unappealing as possible. These meetings about extremely important decisions that could forever alter the world's perception of what happened during World War II took place in dry, grayscale offices, and Kraume's admirable concentration on realism is what gives his film such an admirable political procedural aesthetic. By letting us focus more on the performances and the dialogue, he manages to create an emotionally engaging, important, and yes, cinematically alluring story. [A-][124]

Another made-for-television version of the same story aired the following year, *The General Case—Die Akte General* (TV 2016). But the original, *The People vs. Fritz Bauer*, is a serious film that is beautifully produced and executed. With or without the Holocaust angle, the film is a success. For those wishing to know about the many failures of denazification, and a few victories, *The People vs. Fritz Bauer* is a great start. Either way, it is a fine film.

Tangential Films

The "plus one" genre of the 4+1 system is "Tangential" Holocaust films, which includes Holocaust representations, but which are not, at their core, about the Holocaust. For example, *Sophie's Choice* (1982) is not a Victim Holocaust film because the Victim film genre is defined by having Jewish protagonists who suffered during the Holocaust. Sophie is not Jewish. Further, Victim Holocaust films are set primarily during the Holocaust, which is not the case with *Sophie's Choice*, which spent only about 20 minutes in an Auschwitz flashback. *Sophie's Choice* is also not a Gentile film because Sophie did not save or harm Jews during the Holocaust. And, although Sophie is clearly a survivor of German oppression during the Holocaust and her story mostly is about her post–War fate, because Sophie is not Jewish, by definition she is not a Holocaust survivor, thus *Sophie's Choice* cannot be a Survivor film. And of course, Sophie is not a Holocaust perpetrator. Yet, undeniably, *Sophie's Choice* is a Holocaust film; anyone who splits hairs by suggesting that *Sophie's Choice* is not a Holocaust film because Sophie is not Jewish is being unreasonably didactic. Indeed, grappling with the question of how to account for the Holocaust-themed *Sophie's Choice* vis-à-vis the four core genres was my original reason for adding the Tangential plus-one genre.

Most of the 68 Tangential Holocaust films are either not primarily about the Jewish experience during the Holocaust or are not primarily Holocaust depictions. Some are pre–War depictions of the rise of Nazism. Four Tangential Holocaust films are recommended below.

Cabaret (1972)

Genre:	Tangential
Sub-Genre:	Pre-War
Length:	124
MPAA or Local Rating:	PG
Language:	English
Country:	U.S.
Director:	Bob Fosse
Top-Billed:	Liza Minnelli, Michael York, Helmut Griem
From Wikipedia:	Situated in Berlin during the Weimar Republic in 1931, under the presence of the growing Nazi Party. The musical numbers are entirely diegetic, taking place inside the club, with one exception. In the sexually charged "Two Ladies," about a ménage à trois, the Master of Ceremonies is joined by two of the Kit Kat girls.
IMDb Rating:	7.8
IMDb Votes:	41673
Oscar:	Winners: Best Directing, Supporting Actor, Actress, Cinematography, Art Direction, Editing & Music (Adaptation Score), Sound; Nominations: Best Picture & Writer.
Holocaust Cinema Complete Description:	*Cabaret* (1972) portrays homosexuals, transvestites and Jews during the rise of Nazism in Germany. As a musical, *Cabaret* is great. As a peek into the early Third Reich, the film is uncompromising and rarely leans on violence to make its point. As a Holocaust film, *Cabaret* is worth watching for two songs, "Tomorrow Belongs to Me" and "If You Could See Her."
Recommendation:	An excellent portrayal of pre–War Germany during the rise of Nazism.
Suggested Minimum Grade:	High School

REVIEW

Many films give color to the rise of Hitler and the disintegration of the Weimar Republic, including *The Great Dictator* (1940), *Ship of Fools* (1965), *The Sound of Music* (1965), *Julia* (1977), *Invincible* (2001), *Nowhere in Africa—Nirgendwo in Afrika* (2001) and

Max (2002). Some of these films, like *Nowhere in Africa* and *Invincible,* play around the edges about the rise of the Third Reich, while others, such as *The Great Dictator* and *Max,* are squarely about Adolf Hitler. Many of these films have rich histories, both pre- and post-release. For example, Charlie Chaplin's *The Great Dictator* absolutely infuriated Hitler and was banned in Germany. And Stanley Kramer's *Ship of Fools* was robbed of its rightful Best Picture Oscar by the eternally overrated *The Sound of Music* (1965).

Cabaret (1972) also has a richly intricate history. British aristocrat Christopher William Bradshaw Isherwood (1904–1986) wrote two novellas in his 1945 semi-autobiographical *The Berlin Stories* (1935–39). In 1951, British playwright John William Van Druten (1901–1957) turned Isherwood's work into the Broadway play *I Am a Camera* (Broadway 1951–1952), starring Julie Harris (1925–2013), who also starred in the film version of Isherwood's story *I Am a Camera* (1955). Eleven years later, the story was again on Broadway, this time as a musical called *Cabaret* (Broadway 1966–1969), starring Joel Grey and Jill Haworth (1945–2011) lasting 1,165 performances. At that point, the great Bob Fosse (1927–1987), who was best known as a Broadway choreographer, heard that a film version of *Cabaret* was in the works. He grand jetéd to the opportunity. *Cabaret,* which was filmed mainly in West Germany, was one of only five films directed by Fosse; the others are *Sweet Charity* (1969), *Lenny* (1974), the excruciatingly autobiographical *All That Jazz* (1979) and *Star 80* (1983).* The controversial film *Cabaret* made big waves, according to AMC's *Filmsite.org*:

> The sexually-charged, semi-controversial, kinky musical was the first one ever to be given an X rating (although later re-rated) with its numerous sexual flings and hedonistic club life. There was considerable sexual innuendo, profanity, casual sex talk (homosexual and heterosexual), some evidence of anti–Semitism, and even an abortion in the film.[125]

By 1972 *Cabaret* was able to strike the right balance, retelling the Weimar Republic's fall and highlighting the rise and implications of Nazism, yet without needing Hitler's character to make its point about the pending danger to the Jews of Europe and to world peace. Even after the above summary, volumes more could be written about *Cabaret*'s origins, performances and reception, which started on Broadway and ended with eight Oscars and two other nominations, which is more Oscar statuettes than any other Holocaust film ever won, including *Schindler's List* (7).

This review will serve as a "two-fer," a chance to compare a great musical, *Cabaret,* which is fearlessly stylized, featuring mature songs, serious themes and masterful performances, direction and editing, with *The Sound of Music*—an iconic film about the same period and political realities—that is childish and mindless, especially when objectively viewed by adults without the drummed-in baggage of generations who fetishize a perky failed nun serving a stilted master and his annoying charges.

First, *Cabaret* is about diverse characters who navigate complex adult relationships that are complicated by cataclysmic political and social change. The disparate group of men and women in Berlin uses thoughtful themes to express themselves with an impressive array of songs that speak to impassable issues. *Cabaret*'s fully developed characters are not exuberantly singing about diatonic scales or twittering pruriently about being 16 and then realizing that next year will sequentially render one 17, as if boastfully announcing the discovery of nonlinear Euclidean string theory. *Cabaret* is intentionally uncomfortable, a biting indictment of Hitler's ascension, without retreating to *The Sound of*

---

* For more about Bob Fosse, see FX Network's wonderful *Fosse/Verdon* (Miniseries 2019).

Music's pyrrhic victory of a pretty, young nun taming a bunch of children or glorifying their father, Georg von Trapp, a historically real man who served Austria/Germany in World War I, a killer who sank more than a dozen British and American ships, a point that the filmmakers conveniently ignore. In the starkest terms, *Cabaret* showcases a female protagonist, Sally, who portrays a classic feminist progenitor. Sally does not need a man to solve her problems. And, in fact, Sally is not the problem, as is Maria, who has been given by the church to a military commander in an authoritarian society to care for his progeny and to breed new ones, which was the real Von Trapp story, and which is also the plot of Margaret Atwood's dystopic *The Handmaid's Tale*. That this unwitting young woman, Maria, is blissfully unaware of her subjugation neither changes the moral equation nor diminishes the analogy. Although this may seem harsh, consider the following monologue from Jay Roach's *Coastal Elites* (2020):

> I'd like you to close your eyes and envision a beautiful hillside lush with wildflowers and overlooking a peaceful, undisturbed valley. You're like Julie Andrews singing *The Sound of Music* with her arms open wide and never dreaming she'd soon be trafficked by the Catholic Church into becoming an unpaid nanny under a Nazi regime and ultimately marrying an employer twice her age in a scenario that could more rightly be termed #EdelweissMeToo, #NoneOfMyFavoriteThings, and #SoonYeVonTrapp.

If Julie Andrews' maudlin performance of a dependent, helpless woman/child who could not cut it in the abbey succeeds, it is only by the power of Andrews' personal appeal. A few of the songs about goats and bees and deer are catchy, but infantile. As Robert Glatzer (1932–2010) of *Movies 101* wrote in a review entitled "Can We Ever Forget 'The Sound of Music?' Let's Try":

> Should we blame Rodgers and Hammerstein? Well, why not? They wrote the songs, which to the adult ear sound like the first murmurings of late onset Alzheimer's. Take a minute and try reciting the lyrics to "Doe, A Deer" out loud and see what I mean. Of course, blame is easy. Rodgers and Hammerstein had written themselves out years before and were raiding the old songbook for anything they could steal and rewrite....[126]

Then there is "Edelweiss," a song written for the film by the same Jewish icons, Richard Rodgers (1902–1979) and Oscar Hammerstein (1895–1960). Edelweiss urges glorification of Austria—Hitler's homeland—forever. Austria, which had also been responsible for World War I, when Austrians slaughtered a quarter of all Serbian civilians, was so disdained internationally that post–War Austria was forbidden by international treaties to become allied with NATO or the Warsaw Pact, and forbidden to reunite with Germany forever. Making "Edelweiss" the climax of *The Sound of Music*, a song that has mistakenly been assumed to have been an authentic Austrian anthem, was so sickening to star Christopher Plummer that he admitted on the DVD commentary that he needed to be drunk to film the scene.[127] Plummer hated *The Sound of Music* so much that he referred to it—his most famous film—as "The Sound of Mucus" and "S&M."[128] Robert Glatzer concluded, "In 1998 a group of crack-addicted monkeys in an experimental lab at the University of Minnesota were allowed to watch television. Their favorite tape? *The Sound of Music*."[129]

So why is *The Sound of Music* so beloved? We can learn so much from Roger Ebert's honest approach to understanding cherished films. As Ebert wrote of *Triumph of the Will* (1935), another film that whitewashes the history of an Austrian World War I soldier, Adolf Hitler:

> But how fresh was my memory of *Triumph of the Will*? I believe I saw it as an undergraduate in college, and my memory would have been old and fuzzy even in 1994, overlaid by many assertions of the film's

"greatness." Now I have just seen it again and am stunned that I praised it. It is one of the most historically important documentaries ever made, yes, but one of the best? It is a terrible film, paralyzingly dull,
simpleminded, overlong and not even "manipulative," because it is too clumsy to manipulate anyone
but a true believer. It is not a "great movie" in the sense that the other films in this group are great, but it
is "great" in the reputation it has and the shadow it casts.[130]

Likewise, most viewers of *The Sound of Music* are so convinced the film they saw
as a child is magical that they are not willing to subject it to Ebert's refocused scrutiny.
Indeed, Roger Ebert was famously willing to reexamine his opinions, never relying on
his cuddly memory of films or his ego, but strictly on the silver screen. Interestingly, Jay
Ruud started his review of *The Sound of Music* by invoking Ebert:

Roger Ebert claimed never to have seen *The Sound of Music*. To my knowledge he never expanded on
that statement, but it might be inferred that the great critic was suggesting he had no interest in seeing
the film, perhaps because the tremendous affection that the movie has enjoyed in the fifty years since its
first release might be reason to suspect it of appealing to the lowest common denominator in the audience—sacrificing art for popularity.[131]

As for the lesser-known *Cabaret*, Ebert wrote, "This is no ordinary musical. Part of
its success comes because it doesn't fall for the old cliché that musicals have to make you
happy. Instead of cheapening the movie version by lightening its load of despair, director
Bob Fosse has gone right to the bleak heart of the material and stayed there well enough
to win an Academy Award for Best Director."[132]

Liza Minnelli, who received the Best Actress Oscar for her portrayal of "Sally" in
Cabaret, uses honesty and hopelessness to elevate her character into a rare place in American film history. Minnelli became a legitimate movie star in *Cabaret*, as a performer in a
Berlin nightclub, singing about the dire times with the veracity of a participant, not like
a flimsy prize from a cereal box. Sally is vulnerable, sassy, compassionate and real. Sure,
the beloved Julie Andrews is especially adored by those who grew up watching her as
the delightful authority figure in her Oscar-nominated role in *The Sound of Music,* and a
year earlier in her Best Actress-winning role in *Mary Poppins* (1964), a woman who we
all wished could have mothered us with a spoonful of sugar. But nothing about Andrews'
performance in *The Sound of Music* or her character Maria yields any meaningful perspective about the times they intended to represent, nor about life itself. Unless the point
of *The Sound of Music* was to learn about how a vapid 22-year-old woman can capture the
heart of a heartless 47-year-old man, nothing but Julie Andrews' beauty matters in comparison to the full-throated *Cabaret*.

The 26-year-old *Cabaret* star, Liza Minnelli, had issues of her own to overcome,
including being the daughter of the acutely narcissistic Judy Garland (1922–1969), who
had died of a Seconal overdose just a few years before Minnelli starred in *Cabaret*. Until
Cabaret, to be Liza Minnelli—to be the daughter of "Dorothy" from *The Wizard of Oz*
(1939)—was no different from being Sean Lennon or Lorna Luft. But Minnelli's performance in *Cabaret* lifted her from the homely little girl who had sung with her mother on
television, to a place that did not care about rainbows or lollipops. Minnelli's Sally has
more than enough power to break free of her mother's gravity and is every bit as rich as
her mother's Dorothy. Truth be told, the triple-threat performance of the kid required
serious hoofing skills never demonstrated by Garland.

Cabaret, too, dabbled in fairy tales about love and devotion, but settled on more
important topics than raindrops on roses and whiskers on kittens. Beyond explicitly
fleshing out why one would want to escape from Europe, *Cabaret* pushed theretofore

taboo limits with its depiction of homosexuals, transsexuals and free women who needed answer to no one. Michael York's unaffected portrayal of a gay man does not drag the film through uncomfortable moments, but it exposed moviegoers in the 1970s to something rarely portrayed as ordinary. This is even more thought-provoking considering that another *Cabaret* co-star, Joel Grey (né Joel David Katz) (1932–), father of Jennifer Grey, was closeted for most of his life, one of the worst-kept secrets in Hollywood. That it would take another 40 years for Grey to come out is another indication of the bravery of *Cabaret*'s filmmakers, who did not hesitate to normalize homosexuality in their film. All of *Cabaret*'s accomplishments would have been impossible just five years earlier, before the demise of the Motion Picture Production Code.

Contrast *Cabaret*'s real lives of little people struggling to survive in an increasingly hellish society with the *Sound of Music*'s only moment of serious conflict, almost three hours in, when Rolfie, Liesel's Nazi dreamboat, pulls a pistol on a few people for a moment or two. Who in that film had earned being spared? The little Nazi, Rolfie? The fallen nun? The World War I war criminal whose deeds were papered over with the trill of a flute? Civilized people have always pondered how other civilized people can become uncivilized, whether individually or as a nation, which is completely glossed over in the *Sound of Music*. Whatever happened to their glorious Austria that would have caused the Von Trapp exodus is conspicuously absent from the *Sound of Music*, aside from a vague swastika here or there, without context or meaning.

Cabaret, on the other hand, offers significant insight into the pending cataclysm, not necessarily with individual character arcs that go south, but with the gradual buy-in of German society. Just the scene where Sally's friends watch a young German boy lead the rousing "Tomorrow Belongs to Me," a chillingly passionate ode to Hitler and Hitlerism, shatters any misconception that the Holocaust was perpetrated by Nazis, not Germans. The German people's embrace of Nazism is laid bare in that scene with their love song to the revitalized Fatherland. And, not to beat a dead Austrian horse, but the intensely fervent "Tomorrow Belongs to Me" scene, alone, outclasses everything in *The Sound of Music*. The essence of these two films boils down to the "Edelweiss" scene's fully excusing the perpetrators, while "Tomorrow Belongs to Me" exposes them. The *Cabaret* song "If You Could See Her" is equally complex and compelling.

Cabaret should not be shown to kids, not so much because of sexuality and a few violent scuffles as because children cannot comprehend *Cabaret*. To understand the emotions, relationships and politics revealed in *Cabaret* requires that moment when people realize that doing the right thing can, at times, be dissonant with one's own welfare. Even though that very concept—that people and societies can turn bad—is a central lesson of the Holocaust, a child cannot become an adult without fully coming to grips with the reality that evil is not just a storybook concept. *Cabaret* is the best Holocaust film about pre–War Germany, without the skewed biographies depicted in *Julia* and *Max*, without the farce of Chaplin, and without the frivolity of Maria.

Sophie's Choice (1982)

Genre:	Tangential
Sub-Genre:	Post Post-War
Length:	151
MPAA or Local Rating:	15
Language:	English

Country:	U.S.
Director:	Alan J. Pakula
Top Billed:	Meryl Streep, Kevin Kline, Peter MacNicol
From Wikipedia:	The film stars Meryl Streep as Zofia "Sophie" Zawistowski, a Polish immigrant with a dark secret from her past who shares a boarding house in Brooklyn with her tempestuous lover, Nathan, and a young writer, Stingo.
IMDb Rating:	7.6
IMDb Votes:	34643
Oscar:	Winners: Best Actress; Nominations: Best Writer, Cinematography & Costume Design, Music (Adaptation Score).
Holocaust Cinema Complete Description:	Sophie's Choice (1982) is among the most famous of all Holocaust films, yet it tells the post–War story of a Gentile woman who survived Auschwitz. Although less than a fifth of the film is a depiction of Sophie's life in Auschwitz, Sophie's Choice was the first Western Holocaust film to represent the death camp with cinematic respect. Sophie's Choice is an essential link in the chain of must-see Holocaust films.
Recommendation:	"TOP THREE" IN GENRE. A beautifully acted iconic film that provides a non–Jewish perspective of Auschwitz.
Suggested Minimum Grade:	High School

REVIEW

Sophie's Choice (1982) was the first Western Holocaust film to portray Auschwitz with cinematographic respect. Although less than a quarter of the film is set in Auschwitz, director Alan J. Pakula's flashback of Sophie's world in the most infamous spot on earth suddenly elevated Holocaust film from amorphous, ill-informed, bottom-line representations, to the genuine article. That being said, *Sophie's Choice*'s greatness is a function of everything except its Auschwitz depiction.

Sophie's Choice starts with William Styron's novel's hick, Stingo, who moves to New York City to become a writer. Stingo quickly finds himself living in a house with an American-born Jewish man and his Polish lover, Sophie, who endured Auschwitz as a political prisoner. The vortex of their pain is enough to doom the couple, but provides Stingo with the perspective needed to be a novelist.

Like "Catch-22," the phrase "Sophie's Choice" has become part of our vocabulary. Sophie, because she is not Jewish, is given the choice upon her arrival at Auschwitz as to which one of her two children will be allowed to live. The two-minute scene is etched indelibly in viewers' minds: Sophie's dismay when asked to decide which of her children will be murdered; her refusal to choose between them; and her ultimate betrayal of her baby girl, in nothing but a sadistic game by the German officer who happened upon the beautiful woman. But, no matter, Sophie is ruined. Although she survives, mostly because of her beauty and guile, Sophie's soul has been irreparably punctured and her life seeps out over the ensuing decade. Few tragedies in film are more predictable and foretold than Sophie's ultimate demise. Yet the film is so pitch-perfect that her death is almost a relief. Roger Ebert wrote:

> Sometimes when you've read the novel, it gets in the way of the images on the screen. You keep remembering how you imagined things. That didn't happen with me during *Sophie's Choice*, because the movie is so perfectly cast and well-imagined that it just takes over and happens to you. It's quite an experience…. *Sophie's Choice* is a fine, absorbing, wonderfully acted, heartbreaking movie. It is about three people who are faced with a series of choices, some frivolous, some tragic. As they

flounder in the bewilderment of being human in an age of madness, they become our friends, and we love them.[133]

Each of *Sophie's Choice*'s three stars shines brightly, near the beginning of three note-worthy careers that are as easy to predict from *Sophie's Choice* as was Dustin Hoffman's in *The Graduate* (1967) and John Travolta's in *Saturday Night Fever* (1977). Although Sophie was not Meryl Streep's first big role, she delivered one of the greatest performances of all time in *Sophie's Choice*, for which she was awarded her first Best Actress Oscar.* *The New York Times* reviewer, Janet Maslin, noted:

> The chief thing Stingo must do, though, is to lead the reader or audience toward an unqualified fascina-tion with Sophie. That part is easy. The character's halting, Polish-accented speech; her charming (and, in one instance, hilariously obscene) malapropisms; her frank sexuality (something Miss Streep con-veys easily without any need for nudity); her long, haunted reminiscences—these are the components of an unforgettable heroine, and the work of the astonishing actress who brings her to life…. After Auschwitz.[134]

Co-stars Kevin Kline and Peter MacNicol have never stopped working since *Sophie's Choice,* playing memorable characters in movies and on episodic television. The great-ness of *Sophie's Choice* is not due to the veracity of places or plotlines, but to the glimpses of humanity shared by Sophie, Nathan and Stingo as they try to fend off the inevitable. Only Stingo walks away, knowing that the flicker of joy he witnessed, as the other two flamed out together for eternity, was less of a consolation prize than the grand prize. Their memories, love and tiny triumphs lived on through Stingo, experiences created by three dissimilar people who absorbed and reflected the goodness that they found in each other.

The Last Butterfly—Poslední motýl (1991)

Genre:	Tangential
Sub-Genre:	Wartime
Length:	118
MPAA or Local Rating:	Rated PG-13 for thematic elements
Language:	Czech
Country:	Czechoslovakia—France—U.K.
Director:	Karel Kachyna
Top Billed:	Tom Courtenay, Brigitte Fossey, Ingrid Held
IMDb Rating:	7.0
IMDb Votes:	228
From Wikipedia:	—
***Holocaust Cinema Complete* Description:**	*The Last Butterfly—Poslední motýl* (1991) is an excellent fictional film that depicts the very real Theresienstadt Concentration Camp, the sham "model" concentration camp, which was created to fool the international community and, specifically, the Red Cross. The Czech film *The Last Butterfly* is told from the perspective of a fictional famous Gentile per-former who is forced to participate in a show for the Red Cross in Ther-esienstadt with Jewish prisoners, all of whom are to be shipped out after the show and murdered.

---

* Meryl Streep's first Oscar was for Best Supporting Actress in *Kramer vs. Kramer* (1979). She was nomi-nated for the same award in *The Deer Hunter* (1978). She was nominated for Best Actress for her work in *The French Lieutenant's Woman* (1981), the year before *Sophie's Choice* (1982). In the 39 years from 1979 through 2018, Meryl Streep has been nominated for 21 Oscars, winning only for *Kramer vs. Kramer, Sophie's Choice* and *The Iron Lady* (2011).

Recommendation:	"TOP THREE" IN GENRE. This film is recommended for those wanting to learn about Theresienstadt Concentration Camp.
Suggested Minimum Grade:	Junior High School

Review

The Last Butterfly—Poslední motýl (1991) is beguiling. It depicts a fictional, famous non–Jewish French comic/actor/mime who takes part in the French Resistance against German occupation. He is ultimately handled and then eliminated by the Germans with great precision. One can easily imagine that *The Last Butterfly* is everything that Jerry Lewis intended for his clown-in-Auschwitz film, the aborted *The Day the Clown Cried* (1972).

The protagonist performer is arrested and told that he will be paid handsomely for a performance at Theresienstadt, the model concentration camp near Prague. His performance with Jews from the camp is intended to convince the Red Cross that Theresienstadt is representative of all German camps and that the rumors of Jews being mistreated, shot and gassed were simply Allied propaganda. Theresienstadt was famous for this subterfuge to fool the world, replete with building facades and an emphasis on the arts and classrooms. Unlike many camps, Theresienstadt remains intact today and is worth a visit if one is near Prague. A famous book was published of drawings and poetry by the children of Theresienstadt called "I Never Saw Another Butterfly," which certainly played into the film's title. *New York Times'* reviewer Stephen Holden wrote:

> *The Last Butterfly* is one of the quietest movies about the Holocaust ever made. Although many of its characters are Jews caged in the Czechoslovak ghetto city of Theresienstadt and face imminent deportation to death camps, you wouldn't know it from the way they talk. Musing on their fate, they adopt the sorrowful-to-sardonic tone of Chekhov aristocrats lamenting the boorishness of modern life.... The mood of calm despair that hangs over the film lends it a disquietingly surreal aura. But it also plays into the story, which describes an attempt to deliver a horrifying message without stating it in words.[135]

Tangential films such as *The Last Butterfly* and *Sophie's Choice* (1982) would belong in the Victim genre had their protagonists been Jewish, as opposed to many other Holocaust films in the Tangential genre that of lack of enough Holocaust content. In terms of learning about and understanding the Holocaust, regarding *The Last Butterfly* and *Sophie's Choice*, Tangential versus Victim films is almost a distinction without a difference; including the majority of Anne Frank titles, both *The Last Butterfly* and *Sophie's Choice* teach much more about the Holocaust than do many Victim films.

The Last Butterfly also could be paired with the great *Mr. Klein—Monsieur Klein* (1976), which was similarly about a French Gentile who died with the Jews. The contrast between the protagonist in *The Last Butterfly*, who is a member of the French Resistance, and *Mr. Klein*'s slimy lead character is unambiguous. Both films, however, are cleverly made and unencumbered by sentimentality. Yet, the message together is clear: when in doubt, the Germans murdered with impunity.

Ultimately, the protagonist falls in love with the kids in the camp as they prepare together for their performance. The only real question is whether he will be deported to a death camp after the performance with children, of whom most did not survive. The less obvious question is the quality of his act in the camp. *The Last Butterfly* has the courage to show his performance which star Sir Tom Courtenay pulls off and then some. Which is to say, many films portray actors and musicians who are purportedly at the top of their art, but avoid showing actual performances because the act will never match the hype, as with Jesse Eisenberg's empty performance as Jewish mime Marcel Marceau during the Holocaust in *Resistance* (2020). Because Courtenay is spectacular and in his element, *The Last Butterfly* is a wonderful film that delivers when it counts and takes no prisoners.

Inglourious Basterds (2009)

Genre:	Tangential
Sub-Genre:	Wartime
Length:	153
MPAA or Local Rating:	R for strong graphic violence, language and brief sexuality.
Language:	English
Country:	U.S.
Director:	Quentin Tarantino
Top Billed:	Brad Pitt, Diane Kruger, Eli Roth
From Wikipedia:	The film tells an alternate history story of two plots to assassinate Nazi Germany's leadership, one planned by Shosanna Dreyfus, a young French Jewish cinema proprietor, and the other by a team of Jewish American soldiers led by First Lieutenant Aldo Raine.
IMDb Rating:	8.3
IMDb Votes:	1061435
Oscar:	Winners: Best Supporting Actor; Nominations: Best Picture, Directing, Writer, Cinematography, Editing & Sound.
Holocaust Cinema Complete Description:	*Inglourious Basterds* (2009), for better or worse, is the Holocaust touchstone for many. It is the fictional story of Jewish revenge during the Holocaust. As an educational film, *Inglourious Basterds* is dangerously misleading; as a fictional Tangential Holocaust film, it is not only smart, but immensely entertaining and satisfying.
Recommendation:	"TOP THREE" IN GENRE. For those who want to see the millennials' hallmark of Holocaust film.
Suggested Minimum Grade:	High School

REVIEW

From the opening bell, *Inglourious Basterds* (2009) is captivating. Every scene is compelling and entertaining. Every major character—good or evil—is insanely gripping, convincing even in the most absurd situations. Director Quentin Tarantino's total cinematic command during his 2½ hour the film has earned him a spot as one of the greatest storytellers of his generation, although, to be accurate, Tarantino was already regarded as such after making *Pulp Fiction* (1994). But unlike *Pulp Fiction*'s untraditional serialized format, Tarantino proved with *Inglourious Basterds* that he could form a film to his wit and sensibilities without the gimmickry of television-like segmentation and characters who seemed more like extensions of the campy *Batman* television series starring Adam West than like real people. Moreover, while Tarantino flirted with greatness by mocking justice and morality in *Pulp Fiction*, *Inglourious Basterds* was hyper-conjugal with those concepts. As Mick LaSalle of the *Houston Chronicle* wrote:

> It's not enough to say that *Inglourious Basterds* is Quentin Tarantino's best movie. It's the first movie of his artistic maturity, the film his talent has been promising for more than 15 years. The picture contains all the things his fans like about Tarantino—the wit, the audacity, the sudden violence—but this movie's emotional core and bigness of spirit are new.[136]

With *Inglourious Basterds*, Tarantino was absolute in his villainization of all Germans, his glorification of American vigilantes and his veneration of Jewish victims. He gave voice to the story that we all had wanted to see for the previous 65 years: unbridled vengeance against the Nazis, delivered with the precision of a crossbow's strike between the eyes. His completely untenable tale had been available to generations of filmmakers. Only Tarantino had the guts to say it out loud: let's just man-up one time in our politically correct crucible and, as long as we are going there, screw it all and to hell with the Nazis and reality. *Basterds* unapologetically left everything on the screen, reducing World War II to the kind of absolute ethics required when watching professional wrestling. Nuanced characters need not have applied. Roger Ebert opined:

> After I saw *Inglourious Basterds* at Cannes, although I was writing a daily blog, I resisted giving an immediate opinion about it. I knew Tarantino had made a considerable film, but I wanted it to settle, and to see it again. I'm glad I did. Like a lot of real movies, you relish it more the next time. Immediately after *Pulp Fiction* played at Cannes, QT asked me what I thought. "It's either the best film of the year or the worst film," I said. I hardly knew what the hell had happened to me. The answer was: the best film. Tarantino films have a way of growing on you. It's not enough to see them once.[137]

A shred of *Inglourious Basterds*' truth might be inferred from the secret U.S. intelligence team called "The Ritchie Boys," so-called because they were trained at Fort Ritchie in Maryland. This group of approximately 15,000 German-speaking American soldiers specializing in the interrogation of German prisoners of war included 2,200 Jewish refugees from Germany and Austria, and is the subject of two documentaries: *The Ritchie Boys* (2004) and *About Face: The Story of the Jewish Refugee Soldiers of World War II* (2005).[138] Included among the ranks of the Ritchie Boys were Richard Schifter, former Assistant Secretary of State for Human Rights and Humanitarian Affairs, and author J.D. Salinger. But to suggest that the Ritchie Boys were factually represented in the farcical *Inglourious Basterds* is foolhardy, as with believing anything in a Tarantino flick.

And, indeed, that is the underlying issue with *Inglourious Basterds* (and *Once Upon a Time … in Hollywood* [2019]): some viewers actually leave the theater believing that *Basterds* is a true story. Ironically, this is a smaller danger than believing that *Life Is Beautiful* (1997) and *The Boy in the Striped Pyjamas* (2008) depict historical reality. With their distorted Auschwitz representations, *Beautiful* and *Pyjamas* erode important facts about Holocaust perpetrators, in particular, and the German killing machine, in general; both films minimize the lethality and brutality of the Germans, while distorting significant critical facts about Auschwitz/Birkenau. Conversely, the most damage that could be done by *Basterds* is to glorify heroic characters, which is a more innocuous message than that Auschwitz was a playground. Tarantino's fictionalization does not distort the Holocaust, but, instead, distorts the American reaction to the Holocaust. True, *Inglourious Basterds* is misleading about the circumstances of Hitler's demise and of the overall behavior of American troops. But from a Holocaust perspective, these are not issues, especially in relation to *Pyjamas*' implication that the Germans were all good-hearted and that Auschwitz/Birkenau was porous enough for a child to slip through the deadly electrified fence and wander into a gas chamber.

After two generations of filmmakers walking on eggshells in Holocaust cinema, afraid to showcase more than one bad Nazi per film, I applaud Quentin Tarantino's unique take-no-prisoners approach to the subject and characters. Like a Marvel or DC Comics franchise, perhaps the sequel to *Inglourious Basterds* could be for his crew to time-travel back to *Pyjamas* and vanquish those bastards, too.

The Very Best Holocaust Films

There is a difference between good, entertaining films and the unqualified greatest films, Holocaust or otherwise. What are the greatest Holocaust films? The answer to that is found in Table 37, which is ordered by genre and then chronologically, not necessarily by greatness.

TABLE 37: THE BEST HOLOCAUST FILMS (THREE FILMS PER GENRE)
"One of the Best" in **Bold and Underlined** (15).

Victim	*The Grey Zone* (2001)	*Fateless—Sorstalanság* (2005)	*The Counterfeiters— Die Fälscher* (2007)
Gentile	*Good Evening, Mr. Wallenberg* (1990)	*Conspiracy* (TV 2001)	*1945* (2017)
Survivor	*Harold and Maude* (1971)	*The Birch-Tree Meadow— La petite prairie aux bouleaux* (2003)	*This Must Be the Place* (2011)
Perpetrator	*Genghis Cohn* (1993)	*Made in Israel* (2001)	*The People vs. Fritz Bauer* (2015)
Tangential	*Sophie's Choice* (1982)	*The Last Butterfly— Poslední motýl* (1991)	*Inglourious Basterds* (2009)

Curriculum-planning for many academic situations is fleshed out generally in Chapter 8. But, below in Table 38 is my specific ordered recommendation of Holocaust films for a standard 15-week *university*-level Holocaust film class based on the above-listed best films:

TABLE 38: FULL SEMESTER HOLOCAUST FILM CLASS SCHEDULE
"One of the Best" in **Bold and Underlined** (15).

Week	Film	Length
1	*Conspiracy* (TV 2001)	96
2	*Sophie's Choice* (1982)	151
3	*Good Evening, Mr. Wallenberg* (1990)	118
4	*The Last Butterfly—Poslední motýl* (1991)	118
5	*The Counterfeiters—Die Fälscher* (2007)	98
6	*Fateless—Sorstalanság* (2005)	136
7	*The Grey Zone* (2001)	108
8	*1945* (2017)	91
9	*The People vs. Fritz Bauer* (2015)	105
10	*Made in Israel* (2001)	113
11	*Harold and Maude* (1971)	91
12	*The Birch-Tree Meadow—La petite prairie aux bouleaux* (2003)	104
13	*This Must Be the Place* (2011)	118
14	*Genghis Cohn* (1993)	79
15	*Inglourious Basterds* (2009)	153

Epilogue

Eva.Stories *and Holocaust Film Trends*

When lecturing to educators at Yad Vashem, I always ask: what is your students' "go to" Holocaust film? For years, the answer has been either Steven Spielberg's *Schindler's List* (1993) or Quentin Tarantino's *Inglourious Basterds* (2009). Yet, briefly teachers from North American Jewish day schools surprised me with a different film: Instagram's *Eva. Stories* (2019), which came complete with the tagline, "What if a girl in the Holocaust had Instagram?"

Eva Heyman was a 13-year-old Hungarian Jewish girl who was murdered at Birkenau and who wrote a diary until she was rounded up for transport in 1944. Her diary was first published in Hungarian in 1947. It was republished by Yad Vashem in Hebrew as *Yomanah shel Evah Hayman* in 1964 and in an English translation first as *The Diary of Eva Heyman* in 1974, then as *The Diary of Eva Heyman: Child of the Holocaust* in 1988.[1] Eva Heyman was precocious, wrote about her interest in boys, could not connect with her mother, parted her hair on the side, and rarely hesitated to express herself; her diary entries ceased before she arrived at Auschwitz/Birkenau. Yes, Eva Heyman's story is, essentially, "Anne Frank 2.0" as some have quipped. Regardless of the similarities in these stories, unraveling the *Eva.Stories'* cinematic approach to Holocaust representation in 2019 provides an excellent opportunity to tie together what has worked and what has failed in 75 years of Holocaust portrayals, as well as the current trajectory of the art form.

After an analysis of most Holocaust feature films and made-for-television productions, the overriding trends since 1945 are that Holocaust stories in films have become increasingly genuine and far more realistic. Most Holocaust filmmakers have rejected outlandish premises that pander to audiences. The big-name outliers—*Life Is Beautiful*— *La Vita è bella* (1997), *The Devil's Arithmetic* (TV 1999), *The Boy in the Striped Pyjamas* (2008), *Inglourious Basterds* (2009) and *Jojo Rabbit* (2019)—are notable because they are so peculiar, so ahistorical, inauthentic and flashy, not because they have been imitated or have altered the Holocaust film trendline. So, too, while Holocaust educators have tried many new approaches since the 1970s, the most successful component of Holocaust education when using films remains authenticity, in story and production. Because teaching about genocide is not enhanced by introducing inorganic elements and meandering plots, most Holocaust filmmakers and educators have largely rejected outlandish premises.

Enter Instagram's *Eva.Stories*, the first test-tube baby of a supposedly new Holocaust cinema species: the social media Holocaust film. According to *The Guardian, Eva.Stories* was "Produced with a multi-million dollar budget, 400 staff and actors, and elaborate sets including tanks and trains [*sic*] carriages...."[2] *Eva.Stories* also had a substantial advertising budget, enough for billboards in Israel, publicists, marketing, and celebrity endorsements including from Gal Gadot, Bar Refaeli, Netta Barzilai, Sarah Silverman, the official Instagram account of the White House and Israeli Prime Minister Benjamin Netanyahu, who tweeted that *Eva.Stories* "exposes the immense tragedy of our people through the story of one girl."[3] Purportedly, *Eva.Stories* has 1.6 million followers, according to its Instagram homepage. Yet, as *The New York Times* pointed out, "Even before the fictional Instagram account was activated, it had more than 200,000 followers, the result of an aggressive marketing campaign involving billboards and online promotions by celebrity social media influencers."[4]

The actual number of *Eva.Stories'* viewers is a trickier question. Most articles written about the project state that *Eva.Stories* has received 120 million views. In a flurry of dubious press reports, this blatantly misleading number—approximately a hundred times greater than the total world population of Jewish adolescents—has been left unchallenged. To put that claim in perspective, the highest American viewership of any live event in history was approximated as 114,442,000 for Super Bowl XLIX in 2015.[5] Interestingly, Instagram's segment-oriented view-count methodology and the total number of *Eva.Stories'* hundreds of individually viewed segments (each counted as "views") within more than 30 "posts" suggests that fewer than a hundred thousand individuals, at most, actually viewed the entire series, which raises a host of ancillary issues about generous reporting on all sides: journalists, producers and Instagram. In any event, it appears that *Eva.Stories* quickly peaked just after its release on Yom HaShoah (Israeli Holocaust Remembrance Day) 2019, and has since been largely forgotten.

Eva.Stories was a big production that went out of its way to dumb down quality, both to appear to have been made by a child and to attract children. The actors in *Eva.Stories* are ingenuine, almost plastic. British actress Mia Quiney, who played the Hungarian Eva Heyman, leads a parade of unrecognizable and exaggerated accents. The dialogue is particularly stilted, wildly inauthentic and historically difficult. The wardrobe is distracting. The cinematography makes occupied Europe seem festive and foolish. The Instagram titles and effects are ridiculous, even if that was intentional. Only a handful of Holocaust productions have been more artificial, less believable and as poorly developed as *Eva.Stories*, regardless of its true source.

Artistic license ends at the exact spot where belief can no longer be suspended, which includes "What if a girl in the Holocaust had Instagram?" Yet the overwhelming reaction to the Instagram contrivance is: if *Eva.Stories* helps teach the Holocaust by "moderning things up," then welcome aboard, as if it is perfectly natural to tell a true Holocaust story with an anachronistic premise propped up by silly graphics, emojis, hashtags and an inverted aspect ratio. In a Jewish world which is desperate for new child-friendly Holocaust content, these issues have largely been ignored due to fear of being crushed by *Eva.Stories'* runaway bandwagon and any potential backlash from a giant social media platform.

Eva.Stories enthusiasts, who heralded it as the vanguard of Holocaust storytelling, insist that the anachronism is irrelevant to the story's effectiveness. They suggested that the Instagram/Holocaust non sequitur is quickly ignored by young viewers, accepted as normal contemporary storytelling. But the Instagram platform makes ignoring its framework impossible. Instagram is not *Eva.Stories'* fourth wall, but part of the story, with its onscreen tools that include ways of sending love to Eva. So, as long as Eva has wandered into the land of prop madness by posting to Instagram in 1944 from a cattle car bound for Auschwitz, what is there to lose by Eva also using Google to map out Birkenau for partisans, ordering arms and drones from Amazon, and distributing iPads to the guards that loop *Inglourious Basterds* and *Judgment at Nuremberg* (1961)?

Eva.Stories' producers would, of course, argue that such idiocy needlessly changes the underlying story and ruins Eva's historical integrity, as if that had not already been accomplished by the Instagram overlay. Assuredly, supporters also acknowledge that the Instagram angle would have been disdainful if portraying Anne Frank, Hannah Senesh or Elie Wiesel, because we all know that they did not have Instagram. This bizarre argument implies that inauthentically portraying the equally real Eva Heyman is fair game because of her obscurity. Nonetheless, had Instagram simply been used to post Eva Heyman's story episodically, the producers could have faithfully transmitted the essence of her diary; tweaking the tag to "Messages from the Holocaust" would have avoided needlessly adding the platform's framework into the story.

For viewers who already have garnered basic Holocaust literacy about Hitler's rise to power, about Germany's military conquests and about the Final Solution, *Eva.Stories* might fill in some blanks or add color. But for most, who simply stumbled across the *Eva. Stories* Instagram postings because of Wonder Woman or FOMO, *Eva.Stories* will be no more meaningful than any other visual media tragedy. Sure, if the goal of *Eva.Stories* were merely to seed the concept of the Holocaust in children's heads, it may have been a temporary success, but without context or follow-up, the lesson only lasts until the next shiny object jumps to the top of a child's memory stack. And, of course, for those who believe that Holocaust education is so fundamental that it should be government-mandated—as in 11 American states, constituting almost half of the U.S. population—the first Holocaust lesson should not be an unsupervised, passive introduction via a 4-inch screen, especially without explanations.

Eva.Stories has been spuriously compared to the 2017 Pulitzer Prize winner for fiction, Colson Whitehead's *The Underground Railroad*. But there, the escape grid used by American slaves in the mid–1850s, which was contemporaneously regarded metaphorically as "the underground railroad," was given its own life in Whitehead's book, set on a fictional underground interstate American railway system, an economic impossibility even now. Yet, in today's parlance, the underground railway was actually "a thing" during slavery, even if simply metaphorical then. Conversely, Instagram was obviously nothing during the Holocaust, metaphorically or otherwise. *Eva.Stories* inauthentically molded itself around the characteristics of a social media platform that has no historical antecedent, unless spuriously assuming that private journaling was the forerunner to social media.

Some have also fatuously suggested that criticizing *Eva.Stories* would somehow have a chilling effect on real Instagram postings from war zones. The theory is that any pushback against Instagram will deter those who have found a platform to share their pain. In truth, of course, condemning *Eva.Stories* will only affect those who might similarly be planning on sucking the Holocaust and other pre-twenty-first-century events into an ahistorical social media paradigm.

Can new ways of teaching the Holocaust emerge, even through social media? Perhaps. Holocaust education and media are constantly evolving. For instance, there was once a time when Holocaust education included having children write down their ambitions and then forcing the same students to watch their dreams burn in a pyre. Further, in the late 1980s and the 1990s, Holocaust films were so gratuitously violent that, according to *Commentary Magazine*, "Jewish heads explode in *Schindler's List* and at an average rate of one every twelve minutes."[6] Today, few would argue that *Schindler's List* (1993) would have been less effective without most of the violence, a de facto reality for teachers who regularly edit down *Schindler's List,* and for most twenty-first-century Holocaust filmmakers not named Tarantino.

The great American Holocaust miniseries have also gone the way of dinosaurs since *War and Remembrance* (Miniseries 1988). Even more starkly, although approximately 60 Holocaust feature films have been made since 2004, no solely American-produced made-for-television Holocaust films have been released since 2004, despite more than 30 American made-for-television Holocaust productions made in the quarter-century from 1978 through 2003. Why? Can anyone imagine why viewers trended away from watching made-for-television Holocaust films that were interrupted to sell Volkswagens, Bayer or soap. Is there even a good product to sell after showing a gas chamber? Not really. The crass framework of commercial television often distracted from the storytelling and timing, making it much more difficult to plunge oneself into a Holocaust storyline. Instagram, with its hundreds of distinct segments buried in 30 postings in *Eva.Stories* and its tools framing the video, is like network television on steroids. By design, Instagram interrupts the full story and tries to distract with its overlay tools. Far more insidious than television, Instagram's goal is enticing viewers into clicking here and there, like subjects in a Skinner box.

The final argument made by some proponents of *Eva.Stories* and its Instagram platform is that, because social media is omnipresent, other delivery systems have become the preferred content-viewing source. While adolescents living on cell phones is a reality, social media has not extinguished other content platforms. Feature film grosses are at an all-time high, with the three-year average always increasing. Television is cranking out new series at an unprecedented rate, filling in gaps that were once the home of reruns, and adding supplemental networks. The Walt Disney Company, alone, owns or has a stake in more than 60 cable channels, in addition to the ABC broadcast network. Original programming is constantly being produced by HBO, Showtime, VH1 and many others. And broadcast on demand (or streaming video) is flourishing, with Netflix, Hulu, Amazon Prime, HBO Max, Apple TV, Peacock TV, Disney Plus, Paramount Network, YouTube.com and many other platforms. So, instead of regarding Instagram Holocaust movies as needed, new or unique, it should be regarded as trying to play catch-up in the streaming-video market, as is Facebook, which has also started streaming.

Despite all of *Eva.Stories'* hype, the media did not really take *Eva.Stories'* bait, preferring to report on it as an event, as opposed to lauding the production. Some in the Jewish press, however, did bite on the flavor-of-the-month, proclaiming *Eva.Stories* to be something that it was not: groundbreaking. "If innovation were a third-rail for Holocaust education," wrote Gabe Kahn of *New Jersey Jewish News* about *Eva.Stories,* "we'd never have films like Kirsten Dunst's *The Devil's Arithmetic* [TV 1999], the play *Anne Frank & Me* [performed at a middle school in 1996], or Art Spiegelman's hugely influential graphic novel *Maus* [Serialized from 1980 to 1991]."[7] But Mr. Kahn confused "innovation" with "trail blazing." In that light, his references, too, did not raise the bar for subsequent Holocaust representations. For instance, all of Mr. Kahn's examples are at least 20 years old, with the heyday of graphic Holocaust novels ending—not commencing—almost 30 years ago with *Maus*, which was the only mainstream success of the entire Holocaust graphic novel genre, if you can even call a few series a "genre." Mr. Kahn's two other examples of groundbreaking Holocaust representations, and dozens of additional forays, are now obsolete because they were ultimately regarded as novelties by an efficient market that rejected those prototypes as inauthentic. In fact, in the pantheon of Holocaust representations—in a world that will produce almost anything that even approximates Anne Frank—the play *Anne Frank & Me*, having never been performed on a major stage, is barely even noise, a fate that has already befallen *Eva. Stories*.

As for genuine innovation, new and better ways of depicting the Holocaust have been the energy that has powered Holocaust education, generally, and Holocaust films specifically, since their inception. Most of the 15 films listed at the end of Chapter 9 are fabulously innovative, pushing limits of storytelling, quality, presentation and content far beyond many of their predecessors. No cinematic genre has been more welcoming of innovation than Holocaust film, which has included drama, melodrama, docudrama, comedy, farce and science fiction, using live-action, animation and newsreel footage in all combinations, producing features, shorts, episodic television, made-for-television movies and miniseries, focusing on many different ranges of viewers by age and other demographics.

Indeed, the lethal third rail of Holocaust education has not been innovation. In fact, there is no "third-rail" of Holocaust film production: not Nazi porn, not brainless comedies, not time-warped premises, not bad acting, not blaming the Jews, not graphic violence, not rape or even the view inside an operating gas chamber. Almost everything has been tried, with differing results, over 75 years of Holocaust film production. And now we can check social media off the list, too.

In reality, no genre of film has been more complete and more unbridled than has been Holocaust films. The only catches have been films that have been inauthentic or of poor quality. Many such films have been weeded out over time. This additional layer of scrutiny, which is attracted by Holocaust films, kicks garbage to the curb, based on the sanctity of the underlying event. It is now understood that, with very few chances to reach audiences inundated with choices, Holocaust content can no longer afford the messiness of a fictional Holocaust story or a dubious premise.

Because of *Eva.Stories*, a few more Holocaust productions will be made for social media. They will likely refrain from placing 2020 technology into 1944 lives, backing away from the "looking-glass." The year after *Eva.Stories*, the Anne Frank House in Amsterdam released the 15-part *Anne Frank Video Diary* (TV 2020) on YouTube.com, a production that had been in the pipeline at least a year before the Instagram volley. The *Anne Frank* plot settled into a more normative representation, and without all the bells and whistles and inverted aspect ratio.

In 2013, in a visit to the Anne Frank Museum in Amsterdam, Justin Bieber wrote in the guest book, "Anne was a great girl. Hopefully she would have been a belieber." *Eva.Stories* is an extension of that narcissistic stupor, essentially putting a smartphone in Anne Frank's hands, calling her "Eva" and then grasping for

Justin Bieber's attention. Even when viewed on a cell phone, the core lessons of the Holocaust taught through all the above-recommended films will be remembered much longer than the flash of *Eva.Stories*. And, soon enough, for better or worse, *Schindler's List* and *Inglourious Basterds* will again be the Holocaust film placeholders.*

---

* A portion of this Epilogue was first published in the *Jerusalem Post* on October 2, 2019, in an article by this author entitled "'Eva.Stories' and Holocaust film trends."

Appendix I
List of Holocaust Films

LIST OF HOLOCAUST FILMS
(GENRE, SUB-GENRE, LENGTH, A SOURCE)
Recommended in **Bold** (52). "One of the Best" in **Bold and Underlined** (15).
Unavailable films in ~~Strikeout~~ (48). At publication time, most films in strikeout
are functionally unavailable. This status may change for a few films that may become
digitized and made available online. However, the vast majority of the unavailable titles
were never reproduced after their initial limited release.

Title	Genre	Sub-Genre	Length	Source
~~Abraham's Gold (1990)~~	Perpetrator	Post-War	95	
Across the Waters—Fuglene over sundet (2016)	Gentile	Righteous	94	YouTube.com
~~The Actress—Die Schauspielerin (1988)~~	Tangential	Pre-Holocaust	88	
Adam Resurrected (2008)	Survivor	Post Post-War	106	Amazon Prime
Adolf Eichmann (2007)	Perpetrator	Post-War	100	Amazon Prime
~~After the Truth—Nichts als die Wahrheit (1999)~~	Perpetrator	Post Post-War	128	
After Your Decrees aka Fair Game—Wedle wyroków twoich... (1984)	Victim	Escaping	95	DailyMotion.com
Aftermath—Poklosie (2012)	Gentile	Antisemitic	107	jfi.org
Aimée & Jaguar (1999)	Victim	Disguised	125	DailyMotion.com
Akte Grüninger (TV 2014)	Gentile	Righteous	96	Amazon
Alan and Naomi (1992)	Survivor	Wartime	96	Tubitv.com
All My Loved Ones—Vsichni moji blízcí (1999)	Victim	Escaping	91	DailyMotion.com
Almost Peaceful—Un monde presque paisible (2002)	Survivor	Post-War	94	YouTube.com
Amen. (2002)	Gentile	Antisemitic	132	Amazon Prime
And Now My Love—Toute une vie (1974)	Survivor	Post Post-War	150	Ok.Ru
...and the Fifth Horseman Is Fear—...a pátý jezdec je Strach (1965)	Victim	Descending	100	YouTube.com
The Angel of Auschwitz (2019)	Victim	Camp	101	Ok.Ru
~~The Angel of Budapest—El ángel de Budapest (TV 2011)~~	Gentile	Righteous	120	
~~Angels in White—Mal'akhiyot Be-lavan (2012)~~	Victim	Caught	120	
Angry Harvest—Bittere Ernte (1985)	Gentile	Righteous	105	CDA.pl
Anna's Return—Annas Heimkehr (TV 2003)	Gentile	Righteous	128	WorldCat.org
Anne Frank: The Whole Story (TV 2001)	Victim	Hidden	190	YouTube.com
Apt Pupil (1998)	Perpetrator	Post Post-War	111	Amazon Prime

Title	Genre	Sub-Genre	Length	Source
Aristides de Sousa Mendes: A Rebel—Désobéir (TV 2008)	Gentile	Righteous	104	YouTube.com
The Aryan Couple (2004)	Victim	Wartime	120	Amazon
Ascension Day—Wniebowstapienie (1969)	Victim	Hiding	85	CDA.pl
The Assisi Underground (1985)	Gentile	Righteous	115	Youtu.be
At First Sight—Entre Nous—Coup de foudre (1983)	Victim	Hiding	110	Ok.Ru
The Attic: The Hiding of Anne Frank (TV 1988)	Gentile	Righteous	95	Amazon Prime
***Au Revoir les Enfants* (1987)**	Gentile	Righteous	104	YouTube.com
Auschwitz (2011)	Victim	Caught	73	YouTube.com
The Auschwitz Report (2020)	Victim	Escaping	94	
Autumn Hearts A New Beginning—Emotional Arithmetic (2007)	Survivor	Post Post-War	99	Amazon
Babi Yar: The Forgotten Crime—Babij Jar (2003)	Victim	Wartime	112	DailyMotion.com
A Bag of Marbles—Un sac de billes (1975)	Victim	Escaping	105	Ok.Ru
A Bag of Marbles—Un sac de billes (2017)	Victim	Escaping	110	WorldCat.org
~~*Baranski* (1979)~~	Perpetrator	Post Post-War	68	
Bent (1997)	Tangential	Not Primarily a Jewish Experience	105	DailyMotion.com
Bernhard Lichtenberg (TV 1965)	Gentile	Righteous	90	Gloria.tv
***The Birch-Tree Meadow—La petite prairie aux bouleaux* (2003)**	Survivor	Post Post-War	131	WorldCat.org
The Birth Certificate—Swiadectwo urodzenia (1961)	Victim	Hiding	99	YouTube.com
Bittersweet—Het bittere kruid (1985)	Victim	Ghetto	89	YouTube.com
Black Book—Zwartboek (2006)	Victim	Hidden	145	WorldCat.org
Black Thursday—Les guichets du Louvre (1974)	Gentile	Righteous	95	WorldCat.org
Blessed Is the Match: The Life and Death of Hannah Senesh (2008)	Victim	Caught	86	jfi.org
~~*Blind Hero: Otto Weidt—Ein blinder Held—Die Liebe des Otto Weidt* (TV 2014)~~	Gentile	Righteous	90	
The Bloom of Yesterday—Die Blumen von gestern (2016)	Tangential	Not Primarily Holocaust Depiction	125	Ok.Ru
Bolero Dance of Life—Les uns et les autres (1981)	Tangential	Not Primarily Holocaust Depiction	184	Amazon
Bonhoeffer: Agent of Grace (TV 2000)	Tangential	Not Primarily a Jewish Experience	88	YouTube.com
Border Street—Ulica Graniczna (1948)	Victim	Wartime	115	CDA.pl
The Boy in the Striped Pyjamas (2008)	Victim	Caught	93	Amazon
The Boys from Brazil (1978)	Perpetrator	Post Post-War	125	YouTube.com
~~*Brussels Transit—Bruxelles-transit* (1982)~~	Survivor	Post-War	80	
Bye Germany—Es war einmal in Deutschland... (2017)	Survivor	Post-War	102	CDA.pl
***Cabaret* (1972)**	Tangential	Pre-Holocaust	124	Amazon Prime
A Call to Remember (TV 1997)	Survivor	Post Post-War	110	Amazon
The Cellar—Ha-Martef (1963)	Survivor	Post-War	76	WorldCat.org
~~*Charlie Grant's War* (TV 1984)~~	Gentile	Righteous	125	
Charlotte (1981)	Victim	Hiding	96	WorldCat.org

Title	Genre	Sub-Genre	Length	Source
The Children of Chance— Les enfants de la chance (2016)	Victim	Hiding	95	Ok.Ru
Chosen (2016)	Gentile	Righteous	105	
Closed Season—Ende der Schonzeit (2012)	Gentile	Righteous	100	YouTube.com
Cloudy Sunday—Ouzeri Tsitsanis (2015)	Victim	City	116	YouTube.com
Cold Days—Hideg napok (1966)	Perpetrator	Post-War	96	Vimeo.com
Colette (2013)	Victim	Caught	126	CDA.pl
The Condemned of Altona—I sequestrati di Altona (1962)	Perpetrator	Post-War	114	YouTube.com
Conspiracy (TV 2001)	Gentile	Antisemitic	96	Amazon Prime
Conspiracy of Hearts (1960)	Gentile	Righteous	113	Youtu.be
The Consul of Bordeaux—O Cônsul de Bordéus (2011)	Gentile	Righteous	90	YouTube.com
The Counterfeiters—Die Fälscher (2007)	Victim	Caught	98	Amazon Prime
The Courageous Heart of Irena Sendler (TV 2009)	Gentile	Righteous	95	YouTube.com
The Customer of the Off Season— Ore'ach B'Onah Metah (1970)	Perpetrator	Post Post-War	90	
Dara of Jasenovac—Dara iz Jasenovca (2020)	Tangential	Not Primarily a Jewish Experience	130	
Darkness in Daytime—Nappali sötétség (1963)	Gentile	Righteous	104	
David (1979)	Victim	Descending	125	
Dawn (2014)	Survivor	Post-War	95	
A Day in October—En dag i oktober (1991)	Gentile	Righteous	97	Yad Vashem
The Day the Clown Cried (1972)	Victim	Caught	90	
Dear Mr. Waldman—Michtavim Le America (2006)	Survivor	Post-War	90	Moviesplace4u.com
Death in Love (2008)	Survivor	Second Generation	100	Solarmovie.to
Death Is My Trade—Aus einem deutschen Leben (1977)	Gentile	Antisemitic	145	DailyMotion.com
The Debt—Ha-Hov (2007)	Perpetrator	Post Post-War	100	Amazon Prime
The Debt (2010)	Perpetrator	Post Post-War	113	Amazon Prime
Defiance (2008)	Victim	Escaping	137	Amazon Prime
Denial (2016)	Tangential	Not Primarily Holocaust Depiction	110	Amazon Prime
Der Passagier—Welcome to Germany (TV 1988)	Survivor	Post Post-War	102	
The Devil's Arithmetic (TV 1999)	Victim	Caught	95	Linkedfilm.com
Diamonds of the Night—Démanty noci (1964)	Victim	Escaping	63	YouTube.com
The Diary of Anne Frank—Anne no nikki (1995)	Victim	Hidden	102	YouTube.com
The Diary of Anne Frank— Dagboek van Anne Frank (TV 1962)	Victim	Hidden	90	
The Diary of Anne Frank— Das Tagebuch Der Anne Frank (2016)	Victim	Hidden	128	Amazon Prime
The Diary of Anne Frank— Das Tagebuch Der Anne Frank (TV 1958)	Victim	Caught	--	
The Diary of Anne Frank—Dnevnik Ane Frank (TV 1959)	Victim	Hidden	--	

Title	Genre	Sub-Genre	Length	Source
~~The Diary of Anne Frank—El diari d'Anna Frank (TV 1996)~~	Victim	Hidden	--	
The Diary of Anne Frank— Het dagboek van Anne Frank (TV 1985)	Victim	Hidden	140	hilversumtv.nl
The Diary of Anne Frank—Le Journal d'Anne Frank (1999)	Victim	Hidden	88	YouTube.com
The Diary of Anne Frank (1959)	Victim	Hidden	170	YouTube.com
~~The Diary of Anne Frank (TV 1967)~~	Victim	Hidden	124	
The Diary of Anne Frank (TV 1980)	Victim	Hidden	109	YouTube.com
The Diary of Anne Frank (TV 1987)	Victim	Hidden	112	YouTube.com
The Diary of Anne Frank (TV 2009)	Victim	Hidden	150	YouTube.com
Distant Journey—Daleká cesta (1950)	Victim	Span	108	WorldCat.org
Dita Saxová (1968)	Survivor	Post-War	103	YouTube.com
Divided We Fall—Musíme si pomáhat (2000)	Gentile	Righteous	123	Amazon
~~Drancy Avenir (1997)~~	Survivor	Post Post-War	84	
The Earth Cries Out—Il grido della terra (1949)	Tangential	Not Primarily Holocaust Depiction	90	YouTube.com
Edges of the Lord (2001)	Victim	Hidden	95	Ok.Ru
The Eichmann Show (TV 2015)	Perpetrator	Post-War	90	Amazon
~~Elysium (1987)~~	Victim	Camp	118	
~~Enclosure—L'enclos (1961)~~	Victim	Caught	105	
The End of Our World—Koniec naszego swiata (1964)	Tangential	Not Primarily a Jewish Experience	138	CDA.pl
Enemies: A Love Story (1989)	Survivor	Post-War	119	Amazon
Escape from Sobibor (TV 1987)	Victim	Caught	176	YouTube.com
Europa Europa (1990)	Victim	Escaping	112	Amazon Prime
Everything Is Illuminated (2005)	Survivor	Second Generation	104	Amazon Prime
~~Ewa (2016)~~	Survivor	Post Post-War	85	
The Execution (TV 1985)	Perpetrator	Post Post-War	90	YouTube.com
Exodus (1960)	Tangential	Not Primarily Holocaust Depiction	208	Videa.hu
Exodus to Shanghai (2015)	Gentile	Righteous	79	Filmfreeway.com
~~Falsch (1987)~~	Survivor	Post Post-War	82	
Fanny's Journey—Le voyage de Fanny (2016)	Victim	Escaping	94	CDA.pl
Fateless—Sorstalanság (2005)	Victim	Caught	136	Amazon Prime
~~Father (1990)~~	Perpetrator	Post Post-War	100	
Fatherland (TV 1994)	Perpetrator	Post Post-War	106	YouTube.com
The Fed One—Hranjenik (1970)	Victim	Caught	88	DailyMotion.com
Fever at Dawn—Hajnali láz (2015)	Survivor	Post-War	114	Videa.hu
The Final Solution: The Wannsee Conference— Die Wannseekonferenz (TV 1984)	Gentile	Antisemitic	85	YouTube.com
For Those I Loved—Au nom de tous les miens (1983)	Victim	Caught	145	DailyMotion.com
Forbidden (1984)	Gentile	Righteous	114	YouTube.com
Forbidden Dreams—Death of the Beautiful Robucks—Smrt krásných srncu (1987)	Victim	Escaping	91	DailyMotion.com

Title	Genre	Sub-Genre	Length	Source
Forget Me Not: The Anne Frank Story (TV 1996)	Victim	Hidden	60	YouTube.com
~~*Forgiveness—Esther's Diary* (2008)~~	Survivor	Post Post-War	75	
Free Men—Les hommes libres (2011)	Tangential	Not Primarily a Jewish Experience	99	Ok.Ru
Freedom Writers (2007)	Tangential	Not Primarily Holocaust Depiction	122	Amazon Prime
From Hell to Hell—Iz ada v ad (1996)	Tangential	Not Primarily Holocaust Depiction	101	YouTube.com
Fugitive Pieces (2007)	Survivor	Post Post-War	104	Amazon
The Garden of the Finzi-Continis— Il Giardino dei Finzi-Contini (1970)	Victim	Descending	94	YouTube.com
Gebürtig (2002)	Survivor	Post Post-War	110	Amazon Prime
The General Case—Die Akte General (TV 2016)	Perpetrator	Post-War	92	WorldCat.org
Genghis Cohn (1993)	Perpetrator	Post-War	79	Amazon
The German Doctor—Wakolda (2013)	Perpetrator	Post-War	94	DailyMotion.com
Getting Away with Murder (1996)	Perpetrator	Post-War	91	Amazon
Ghetto—Vilniaus getas (2005)	Victim	Caught	110	YouTube.com
~~*Gitel* (2015)~~	Survivor	Post-War	115	
~~*The Glass Cage—La cage de verre* (1965)~~	Survivor	Post-War	85	
Gloomy Sunday—Ein Lied von Liebe und Tod (1999)	Victim	Descending	112	YouTube.com
God on Trial (TV 2008)	Victim	Caught	90	DailyMotion.com
Gold of Rome—L'oro di Roma (1961)	Victim	Descending	96	YouTube.com
The Gold Rimmed Glasses—Gli occhiali d'oro (1987)	Victim	Span	110	Ok.Ru
Good (2008)	Gentile	Antisemitic	96	Amazon Prime
Good Evening, Mr. Wallenberg— God afton, Herr Wallenberg— En Passionshistoria från verkligheten (1990)	Gentile	Righteous	118	Ok.Ru
~~*The Great Promise— Dim'at Ha'Nehamah Ha'Gedolah* (1947)~~	Tangential	Not Primarily Holocaust Depiction	50	
The Grey Zone (2001)	Victim	Caught	108	Amazon Prime
Gruber's Journey—Calatoria lui Gruber (2008)	Tangential	Not Primarily Holocaust Depiction	100	YouTube.com
The Guard of Auschwitz (2018)	Gentile	Righteous	102	Aaparat.com
Hanna's Journey—Hannas Reise (2013)	Tangential	Not Primarily Holocaust Depiction	100	DailyMotion.com
Hanna's Sleeping Dogs—Hannas schlafende Hunde (2016)	Survivor	Post-War	120	YouTube.com
Hanna's War (1988)	Victim	Caught	148	WorldCat.org
Harold and Maude (1971)	Survivor	Post Post-War	91	Amazon Prime
Haven (TV 2001)	Survivor	Post-War	180	YouTube.com
Heartbeat Detector—La question humaine (2007)	Tangential	Not Primarily Holocaust Depiction	143	Ok.Ru

Title	Genre	Sub-Genre	Length	Source
~~Hidden Children—La fuga degli innocenti (TV 2004)~~	Victim	Escaping	200	
The Hiding Place (1975)	Gentile	Righteous	150	YouTube.com
High Street—Rue haute (1977)	Tangential	Not Primarily a Jewish Experience	94	YouTube.com
Holy Week—Wielki tydzien (1995)	Gentile	Righteous	93	WorldCat.org
~~The Hour of Truth—L'heure de la vérité (1965)~~	Survivor	Post-War	101	
The House in Karp Lane— Das Haus in der Karpfengasse (TV 1965)	Victim	Escaping	110	YouTube.com
~~House of the Generals (2003)~~	Victim	Span	111	
The House on Garibaldi Street (TV 1979)	Perpetrator	Post-War	101	Amazon
How A Hirschberger Learned Danish— Wie ein Hirschberger Dänisch lernte (TV 1968)	Victim	Escaping	95	Yad Vashem
I Do Not Care If We Go Down in History as Barbarians—Îmi este indiferent daca în istorie vom intra ca barbari (2018)	Gentile	Antisemitic	140	YouTube.com
~~I Know Why I Live—Ich weiß, wofür ich lebe (1955)~~	Gentile	Righteous	100	
I Was Overtaken by Night—Zastihla me noc (1986)	Tangential	Not Primarily a Jewish Experience	135	YouTube.com
Ida (2013)	Survivor	Post-War	82	Ok.Ru
The Illegals—Lo Tafhidenu (1947)	Tangential	Not Primarily Holocaust Depiction	47	YouTube.com
I'm Alive and I Love You— Je suis vivante et je vous aime (1998)	Gentile	Righteous	95	WorldCat.org
In Another Lifetime— Vielleicht in einem anderen Leben (2011)	Gentile	Righteous	90	WorldCat.org
In Darkness (2011)	Gentile	Righteous	144	YouTube.com
In Hiding—W ukryciu (2013)	Gentile	Righteous	103	YouTube.com
In the End Come Tourists— Am Ende kommen Touristen (2007)	Tangential	Not Primarily Holocaust Depiction	85	YouTube.com
In the Presence of Mine Enemies (TV 1997)	Victim	Caught	100	Amazon
In the Shadow of Hate—W cieniu nienawisci (TV 1986)	Gentile	Righteous	111	YouTube.com
Inglourious Basterds (2009)	Tangential	Not Primarily Holocaust Depiction	153	Amazon Prime
~~The Interpreter—Tlmocník (2018)~~	Survivor	Second Generation	113	
~~The Interrogation (2016)~~	Perpetrator	Post-War	83	
The Investigation—Die Ermittlung (TV 1966)	Perpetrator	Post-War	155	YouTube.com
Invincible (2001)	Tangential	Pre-Holocaust	133	Amazon Prime
Invitation—Zaproszenie (1986)	Tangential	Not Primarily a Jewish Experience	92	CDA.pl
The Island on Bird Street (1997)	Victim	Caught	107	DailyMotion.com
It Will Never Happen Again—Unzere Kinder (1951)	Survivor	Post-War	80	JewishFilm.org
Jacob the Liar—Jakob, der Lügner (1974)	Victim	Caught	100	Amazon
Jakob the Liar (1999)	Victim	Caught	120	Amazon Prime
Jew Boy Levi—Viehjud Levi (1999)	Tangential	Pre-Holocaust	95	WorldCat.org

Title	Genre	Sub-Genre	Length	Source
A Jewish Girl in Shanghai (2010)	Victim	Hidden	80	YouTube.com
Joanna (2010)	Gentile	Righteous	110	YouTube.com
Jojo Rabbit (2019)	Gentile	Righteous	108	Amazon Prime
~~Journey to Jerusalem—Patuvane kam Yerusalim (2003)~~	Victim	Escaping	112	
Judgment at Nuremberg (1961)	Perpetrator	Post-War	179	Ok.Ru
Judith (1966)	Survivor	Post-War	109	YouTube.com
The Juggler (1953)	Survivor	Post-War	84	Ok.Ru
Julia (1977)	Tangential	Pre-Holocaust	118	Amazon Prime
Just an Ordinary Jew—Ein ganz gewöhnlicher Jude (2005)	Survivor	Second Generation	89	WorldCat.org
Just Beyond That Forest—Jeszcze tylko ten las (1991)	Gentile	Righteous	86	Freedisc.pl
Kapò (1960)	Victim	Caught	116	YouTube.com
Kapo in Jerusalem—Kapo be'Yerushalaim (2015)	Survivor	Post-War	98	Yad Vashem
Keep Away from the Window—Daleko od okna (2000)	Gentile	Righteous	104	DailyMotion.com
Korczak (1990)	Victim	Caught	118	YouTube.com
Kornblumenblau (1989)	Tangential	Not Primarily a Jewish Experience	88	YouTube.com
Labyrinth of Lies—Im Labyrinth Des Schweigens (2014)	Gentile	Antisemitic	122	Amazon
Lacombe, Lucien (1974)	Gentile	Righteous	138	Ok.Ru
Ladies' Tailor—Damskiy portnoy (1990)	Victim	Descending	89	DailyMotion.com
~~Ladieu aux enfants (TV 1982)~~	Victim	Ghetto	95	
Landscape After Battle—Krajobraz po bitwie (1970)	Tangential	Not Primarily a Jewish Experience	109	Amazon
~~The Last (2019)~~	Perpetrator	Post Post-War	123	
The Last Butterfly—Poslední motýl (1991)	Tangential	Not Primarily a Jewish Experience	118	Amazon
The Last Chance—Die letzte Chance (1945)	Gentile	Righteous	113	YouTube.com
~~The Last Hole—Das letzte Loch (1981)~~	Gentile	Antisemitic	92	
~~The Last Letter—La dernière lettre (2002)~~	Victim	Caught	61	
~~The Last Mensch—Der letzte Mensch (2014)~~	Survivor	Post Post-War	89	
The Last Metro—Le dernier métro (1980)	Tangential	Not Primarily a Jewish Experience	131	Amazon Prime
The Last Stage—The Last Stop—Ostatni etap (1948)	Tangential	Not Primarily a Jewish Experience	105	YouTube.com
The Last Suit—El último traje (2017)	Survivor	Post Post-War	91	Ok.Ru
~~The Last Supper—Das letzte Mahl (2018)~~	Tangential	Pre-Holocaust	80	
The Last Train—Der Letzte Zug (2006)	Victim	Caught	123	YouTube.com
Late Season—Utószezon (1967)	Perpetrator	Post-War	119	DailyMotion.com
Left Luggage (1998)	Survivor	Second Generation	100	Amazon
Lena: My 100 Children (TV 1987)	Survivor	Post-War	100	Tubitv.com
~~Leni (TV 1994)~~	Victim	Escaping	80	
Les Misérables (1995)	Victim	Descending	175	Amazon Prime
Les violons du bal (1974)	Victim	Escaping	110	WorldCat.org

Title	Genre	Sub-Genre	Length	Source
~~Let Me Go (2017)~~	Perpetrator	Post Post-War	101	
~~Let's Go! (TV 2014)~~	Survivor	Second Generation	90	
The Life Ahead—La vita davanti a sé (2020)	Survivor	Post Post-War	94	Netflix
A Life Ahead—Madam Rose—Madame Rosa—La Vie devant soi (1977)	Survivor	Post Post-War	105	Amazon
Life for Life: Maximilian Kolbe—Zycie za zycie (1991)	Tangential	Not Primarily a Jewish Experience	90	CDA.pl
Life Is Beautiful—La Vita è bella (1997)	Victim	Caught	116	Amazon Prime
~~The Light of Hope—La llum d'Elna (2017)~~	Gentile	Righteous	96	
Lili Marleen (1981)	Victim	Escaping	112	Amazon
Living Goods—Lebende Ware (1969)	Gentile	Antisemitic	96	YouTube.com
Long Is the Road—Lang ist der Weg (1949)	Victim	Span	77	YouTube.com
Look to the Sky—Jona che visse nella balena (1993)	Victim	Caught	100	Amazon
Lore (2012)	Gentile	Antisemitic	109	DailyMotion.com
~~Louise's Diary 1942—Les amours secrètes (2010)~~	Victim	Hiding	85	
A Love to Hide—Un amour à taire (TV 2005)	Tangential	Not Primarily a Jewish Experience	102	YouTube.com
~~The Lucky Star (1980)~~	Victim	Hidden	110	
Made in Israel (2001)	Perpetrator	Post Post-War	113	WorldCat.org
Malou (1981)	Survivor	Second Generation	95	WorldCat.org
The Man in the Glass Booth (1975)	Survivor	Post Post-War	117	Amazon Prime
The Man Who Captured Eichmann (TV 1996)	Perpetrator	Post-War	96	YouTube.com
Marathon Man (1976)	Perpetrator	Post Post-War	125	Amazon Prime
Marriage in the Shadows—Ehe im Schatten (1947)	Victim	Hidden	105	WorldCat.org
The Martyr—Dr. Korczak and His Children—Sie sind frei, Doktor Korczak (1975)	Victim	Caught	99	Yad Vashem
Max (2002)	Tangential	Pre-Holocaust	106	Amazon Prime
Max and Helen (TV 1990)	Survivor	Post-War	100	YouTube.com
Max and Helen—Max e Hélène (TV 2015)	Survivor	Post-War	99	CDA.pl
Me and the Colonel (1958)	Tangential	Not Primarily Holocaust Depiction	109	YouTube.com
Memories of Anne Frank—Mi ricordo Anna Frank (TV 2009)	Victim	Caught	92	YouTube.com
The Memory Thief (2007)	Tangential	Not Primarily Holocaust Depiction	95	Amazon Prime
Mendel (1997)	Survivor	Post-War	94	YouTube.com
Miracle at Midnight (TV 1998)	Gentile	Righteous	90	WorldCat.org
Miracle at Moreaux (TV 1986)	Gentile	Righteous	58	YouTube.com
Mr. Klein—Monsieur Klein (1976)	Gentile	Antisemitic	123	Ok.Ru
Monastero di Santa Chiara (1949)	Gentile	Righteous	90	YouTube.com
Monsieur Batignole (2002)	Gentile	Righteous	100	YouTube.com
Morituri (1948)	Tangential	Not Primarily a Jewish Experience	88	Amazon
~~The Mover (2018)~~	Gentile	Righteous	90	

Title	Genre	Sub-Genre	Length	Source
Murderers Among Us—Die Mörder sind unter uns (1946)	Perpetrator	Post-War	91	DailyMotion.com
Murderers Among Us: The Simon Wiesenthal Story (TV 1989)	Survivor	Post-War	160	YouTube.com
~~*Murer. Anatomy of a Trial= Murer. Anatomie eines Prozesses (2018)*~~	Perpetrator	Post-War	110	
Music Box (1989)	Perpetrator	Post Post-War	124	YouTube.com
My Daughter Anne Frank— Meine Tochter Anne Frank (TV 2015)	Victim	Hidden	90	YouTube.com
~~*My Father's House=Beit Avi (1947)*~~	Survivor	Post-War	84	
My Führer—Mein Führer—Die wirklich wahrste Wahrheit über Adolf Hitler (2007)	Victim	Caught	89	WorldCat.org
My Mother's Courage—Mutters Courage (1995)	Victim	Escaping	88	Amazon
Naked Among Wolves—Nackt unter Wölfen (1963)	Tangential	Not Primarily a Jewish Experience	124	Amazon
Naked Among Wolves—Nackt unter Wölfen (TV 2015)	Tangential	Not Primarily a Jewish Experience	105	YouTube.com
The Nasty Girl—Das schreckliche Mädchen (1990)	Gentile	Antisemitic	94	Ok.Ru
~~*Natalia (1988)*~~	Victim	City	116	
Never Forget (TV 1991)	Survivor	Post Post-War	94	YouTube.com
Newland—Aretz Hadasha (1994)	Tangential	Not Primarily Holocaust Depiction	105	WorldCat.org
The Night Porter—Il portiere di notte (1974)	Survivor	Post Post-War	118	Amazon Prime
Nina's Journey—La Maison De Nina (2005)	Victim	Caught	112	Amazon
1945 (2017)	Gentile	Antisemitic	91	YouTube.com
The Ninth Circle—Deveti krug (1960)	Gentile	Righteous	107	YouTube.com
Nippon no Shindorâ: Sugihara Chiune monogatari (TV 2005)	Gentile	Righteous	129	YouTube.com
Not All Were Murderers—Nicht alle waren Mörder (TV 2006)	Victim	Descending	92	Vimeo.com
November Moon—Novembermond (1985)	Victim	Span	108	WorldCat.org
Nowhere in Africa—Nirgendwo in Afrika (2001)	Tangential	Pre-Holocaust	141	Amazon Prime
Nuremberg (TV 2000)	Perpetrator	Post-War	180	YouTube.com
The Odessa File (1974)	Perpetrator	Post-War	130	Amazon Prime
Of a Thousand Delights—Sandra— Vaghe stelle dell'Orsa... (1965)	Survivor	Second Generation	105	YouTube.com
Olga (2004)	Tangential	Not Primarily Holocaust Depiction	141	WorldCat.org
One Day You'll Understand—Plus tard (2008)	Survivor	Second Generation	90	WorldCat.org
The Only Way (1970)	Gentile	Righteous	86	YouTube.com
Operation Eichmann (1961)	Perpetrator	Post-War	92	YouTube.com
Operation Finale (2018)	Perpetrator	Post-War	122	Amazon Prime
Operation Stadium—Akcija Stadion (1977)	Victim	City	90	YouTube.com
~~*Our Father in Heaven=Otche nash=Pater Noster (1989)*~~	Victim	Caught	87	

Title	Genre	Sub-Genre	Length	Source
Out of Evil—Mi Klalah L'Brahah (1950)	Tangential	Not Primarily Holocaust Depiction	80	JewishFilmFestivals.org
Out of the Ashes (TV 2003)	Victim	Caught	113	Amazon
The Painted Bird (2019)	Victim	Escaping	169	Amazon
Passenger—Pasazerka (TV 1963)	Tangential	Not Primarily a Jewish Experience	62	Ok.Ru
The Passerby—La passante du Sans-Souci (1982)	Perpetrator	Post Post-War	110	Amazon
Past Life (2016)	Perpetrator	Post Post-War	109	Ok.Ru
The Pawnbroker (1964)	Survivor	Post Post-War	116	YouTube.com
The People vs. Fritz Bauer— Der Staat gegen Fritz Bauer (2015)	Perpetrator	Post-War	105	Amazon
Perlasca. The Courage of a Just Man— Perlasca. Un eroe italiano (TV 2002)	Gentile	Righteous	197	WorldCat.org
Persian Lessons (2020)	*Victim*	*Camp*	*127*	
Persona Non Grata—Sugihara Chiune (2015)	Gentile	Righteous	139	Amazon
Phoenix (2014)	Survivor	Post-War	96	Amazon Prime
The Pianist (2002)	Victim	Escaping	150	Amazon Prime
Playing for Time (TV 1980)	Victim	Caught	150	YouTube.com
The Poet—Hearts of War (2007)	Gentile	Righteous	100	Amazon
Postcard from a Journey—Kartka z podrózy (1984)	Victim	Ghetto	78	YouTube.com
The Pracht Inn (2014)	Survivor	Post Post-War	92	WorldCat.org
Prague (1992)	Survivor	Second Generation	90	YouTube.com
Prayer for Katerina Horovitzova— Modlitba pro Katerinu Horovitzovou (TV 1965)	Victim	Captured	60	YouTube.com
Primo (TV 2005)	Victim	Caught	79	Amazon Prime
Private Resistance—De ijssalon (1985)	Victim	City	92	YouTube.com
Professor Mamlock (1961)	Tangential	Pre-Holocaust	99	YouTube.com
Protector—Protektor (2009)	Gentile	Righteous	102	Ok.Ru
Punch Me in the Stomach (1997)	Survivor	Second Generation	72	JewishFilm.org
The Quarrel (1991)	Survivor	Post-War	85	WorldCat.org
~~*Quezon's Game* (2018)~~	Gentile	Righteous	125	
Raindrops—Regentropfen (1981)	Victim	City	93	Yad Vashem
The Reader (2008)	Perpetrator	Post-War	124	Amazon Prime
Redemption Road—Landgericht (TV 2017)	Victim	Span	203	YouTube.com
The Relief of Belsen (TV 2007)	Gentile	Righteous	101	YouTube.com
Remember (2015)	Perpetrator	Post Post-War	94	Amazon
Remember Your Name—Pomni imya svoye (1974)	Tangential	Not Primarily a Jewish Experience	96	WorldCat.org
Remembrance—Die verlorene Zeit (2011)	Victim	Span	105	Amazon Prime
Remembrance of Love (TV 1982)	Survivor	Post Post-War	100	YouTube.com
The Resistance—The Invisibles—Die Unsichtbaren (2017)	Victim	Hidden	110	Amazon
Resistance (2020)	Victim	Escaping	120	Amazon Prime
Return from the Ashes (1965)	Tangential	Not Primarily Holocaust Depiction	105	YouTube.com

Title	Genre	Sub-Genre	Length	Source
The Revolt of Job—Jób lázadása (1983)	Victim	Hidden	105	DailyMotion.com
Riphagen—Riphagen: The Untouchable (2016)	Gentile	Antisemitic	131	YouTube.com
Romeo, Juliet and Darkness—Romeo, Julie a tma (1960)	Gentile	Righteous	92	Amazon
The Rose Garden—The Rosegarden (1989)	Survivor	Post-War	112	Amazon Prime
~~*A Rose in Winter* (2018)~~	Victim	Hiding	135	
Rosenstrasse (2003)	Survivor	Second Generation	136	Amazon Prime
Rose's Songs—A Rózsa énekei (2003)	Tangential	Not Primarily Holocaust Depiction	98	Videa.hu
The Round Up—La rafle (2010)	Gentile	Righteous	115	Amazon Prime
Rua Alguem 5555: My Father (2003)	Perpetrator	Post Post-War	100	YouTube.com
Run Boy Run—Lauf Junge lauf (2013)	Victim	Escaping	107	Amazon Prime
Salad Days—Zielone lata (1980)	Gentile	Righteous	102	YouTube.com
Samson (1961)	Victim	Escaping	117	DailyMotion.com
The Samuel Project (2018)	Survivor	Second Generation	92	Tubitv.com
Sarah and the Squirrel—The Seventh Match (1982)	Victim	Hidden	70	YouTube.com
Sarah's Key—Elle s'appelait Sarah (2010)	Tangential	Not Primarily Holocaust Depiction	111	Amazon
Saviors in the Night—Unter Bauern (2009)	Victim	Hiding	95	WorldCat.org
The Scarlet and the Black (TV 1983)	Gentile	Righteous	143	YouTube.com
Schindler's List (1993)	Gentile	Righteous	195	Amazon Prime
The Search (1948)	Survivor	Post-War	105	YouTube.com
A Secret—Un secret (2007)	Tangential	Not Primarily Holocaust Depiction	105	YouTube.com
Sergeant Schmidt—Feldwebel Schmid (TV 1968)	Gentile	Righteous	100	Yad Vashem
Seven Journeys—In Those Days—In jenen Tagen (1947)	Gentile	Antisemitic	111	YouTube.com
The 17th Bride—Ha-Kala (1985)	Victim	Descending	95	WorldCat.org
The Seventh Room—A hetedik szoba (1996)	Victim	Hidden	108	YouTube.com
~~*Shades of Truth* (2015)~~	Gentile	Righteous	--	
~~*Shepherd: The Hero Dog* (2019)~~	Victim	Escaping	93	
Shine (1996)	Survivor	Second Generation	105	Amazon Prime
Ship of Fools (1965)	Tangential	Pre-Holocaust	149	Ok.Ru
The Shop on Main Street—Obchod na korze (1965)	Gentile	Antisemitic	125	YouTube.com
Simon Konianski (2009)	Survivor	Second Generation	100	WorldCat.org
The Singing Forest (2003)	Tangential	Not Primarily Holocaust Depiction	72	WorldCat.org
Singing in the Dark (1956)	Survivor	Post-War	84	JewishFilm.org
Skipper Next to God—Maître après Dieu (1951)	Gentile	Righteous	92	Gloria.tv

Title	Genre	Sub-Genre	Length	Source
Skokie—Once They Marched Through a Thousand Towns (TV 1981)	Tangential	Not Primarily Holocaust Depiction	125	YouTube.com
The Sky Is Falling—Il cielo cade (2000)	Tangential	Not Primarily a Jewish Experience	102	WorldCat.org
Sobibor (2018)	Victim	Caught	115	Amazon Prime
Son of Saul (2015)	Victim	Caught	107	Amazon Prime
The Song and the Silence (1968)	Victim	City	80	Yad Vashem
~~*The Song of Names* (2019)~~	Victim	Escaping	113	
Sophie's Choice (1982)	Tangential	Not Primarily a Jewish Experience	151	Amazon Prime
Spring 1941 (2007)	Victim	Hidden	120	Amazon Prime
Spring of Life—Pramen zivota (TV 2000)	Tangential	Not Primarily a Jewish Experience	107	DailyMotion.com
Springtime in Budapest—Budapesti tavasz (1955)	Gentile	Righteous	109	DailyMotion.com
The Square of St. Elizabeth— Námestie svätej Alzbety (1966)	Victim	City	85	YouTube.com
Stars—Sterne (1959)	Victim	Caught	91	YouTube.com
The Statement (2003)	Perpetrator	Post Post-War	120	Amazon Prime
Stielke, Heinz, Fifteen—Stielke, Heinz, fünfzehn... (1987)	Victim	Hiding	95	YouTube.com
~~*A Story About a Bad Dream* (2000)~~	Victim	Span	49	
~~*The Story of a Murder—Chronik eines Mordes* (1965)~~	Perpetrator	Post-War	91	
The Stranger (1946)	Perpetrator	Post-War	95	YouTube.com
~~*Stream Line—La linea del fiume* (1976)~~	Victim	Escaping	105	
The Substance of Fire (1996)	Survivor	Post Post-War	97	WorldCat.org
The Summer of Aviya—Ha-Kayitz Shel Aviya (1988)	Survivor	Post-War	95	WorldCat.org
Sunshine (1999)	Tangential	Not Primarily Holocaust Depiction	180	YouTube.com
Surviving with Wolves—Survivre avec les loups (2007)	Victim	Escaping	118	YouTube.com
Süskind (2012)	Victim	Caught	118	Amazon Prime
The Taras' Family—The Unvanquished—Nepokoryonnye (1945)	Tangential	Not Primarily a Jewish Experience	107	YouTube.com
~~*A Tear in the Ocean—Une larme dans l'océan* (1973)~~	Victim	Ghetto	86	
~~*Tel Aviv-Berlin* (1987)~~	Survivor	Post-War	90	
Temporary Paradise—Ideiglenes paradicsom (1981)	Victim	Hiding	92	Vimeo.com
~~*The Testament* (2017)~~	Survivor	Second Generation	88	
~~*There Is Many Like Us* (2015)~~	Victim	Escaping	85	
The Third Half—Treto poluvreme (2012)	Victim	Descending	113	WorldCat.org
~~*38* (1986)~~	Tangential	Pre-Holocaust	97	
36 Hours (1965)	Tangential	Not Primarily Holocaust Depiction	115	Ok.Ru
This Boat Is Full—Das Boot ist voll (1981)	Victim	Escaping	96	Amazon Prime

Title	Genre	Sub-Genre	Length	Source
***This Must Be the Place* (2011)**	Survivor	Second Generation	118	Amazon Prime
Those Who Remained—Akik maradtak (2019)	Survivor	Post-War	83	YouTube.com
***Three Days in April—Drei Tage im April* (TV 1995)**	Gentile	Antisemitic	105	WorldCat.org
~~*Toman* (2018)~~	Gentile	Righteous	142	
Tomorrow's a Wonderful Day—Adamah (1947)	Survivor	Post-War	47	YouTube.com
Train of Life—Train de vie (1998)	Victim	Escaping	103	YouTube.com
~~*Transit* (1980)~~	Survivor	Post-War	87	
Treason—Prodosia (1964)	Tangential	Not Primarily Holocaust Depiction	96	YouTube.com
Triumph of the Spirit (1989)	Victim	Caught	120	Amazon
The Truce—La tregua (1997)	Survivor	Post-War	125	YouTube.com
The 25th Hour—La vingt-cinquième heure (1967)	Tangential	Not Primarily a Jewish Experience	130	Ok.Ru
25 Firemen's Street—Tüzoltó utca 25. (1973)	Gentile	Righteous	97	YouTube.com
Twist of Fate—Pursuit (TV 1989)	Perpetrator	Post-War	180	YouTube.com
Two Men (TV 1988)	Survivor	Post-War	116	Yad Vashem
***The Two of Us—Le vieil homme et l'enfant* (1967)**	Victim	Hidden	87	Amazon Prime
The Unborn (2009)	Tangential	Not Primarily Holocaust Depiction	87	Amazon Prime
***Under the Domim Tree—Etz Hadomim Tafus* (1994)**	Survivor	Post-War	102	WorldCat.org
Unfair Competition—Concorrenza sleale (2001)	Victim	Descending	110	WorldCat.org
Uprising (TV 2001)	Victim	Caught	151	Amazon Prime
Valentina's Mother—Ima shel Valentina (2008)	Survivor	Post-War	76	Yad Vashem
Varian's War: The Forgotten Hero (TV 2001)	Gentile	Righteous	121	Amazon
Victor Young Perez (2013)	Victim	Camp	110	YouTube.com
Voyage of the Damned (1976)	Victim	Descending	155	YouTube.com
~~*Voyages* (1999)~~	Survivor	Post-War	115	
Walk on Water (2004)	Perpetrator	Post Post-War	103	Ok.Ru
Walking with the Enemy (2013)	Victim	City	124	YouTube.com
The Wall (TV 1982)	Victim	Ghetto	135	YouTube.com
Wallenberg—A Hero's Story (TV 1985)	Gentile	Righteous	200	WorldCat.org
The Wandering Jew—L'ebreo errante (1948)	Victim	Wartime	110	YouTube.com
War and Love (1985)	Victim	Span	108	WorldCat.org
Warsaw: Year 5703—Warszawa. Année 5703 (1992)	Victim	Hidden	110	Yad Vashem
The Wave (TV 1981)	Tangential	Not Primarily Holocaust Depiction	44	YouTube.com
~~*Welcome in Vienna—Wohin und zurück* (1986)~~	Victim	Escaping	118	
~~*We'll Go to the City—Andremo in città* (1966)~~	Victim	Hiding	104	
When Day Breaks—Kad svane dan (2012)	Tangential	Not Primarily Holocaust Depiction	95	DailyMotion.com
~~*When Hitler Stole Pink Rabbit— Als Hitler das rosa Kaninchen stahl* (2019)~~	Victim	Escaping	119	

Title	Genre	Sub-Genre	Length	Source
~~Where to and Back—Part 1. God Doesn't Believe in Us—Ferry or How It Was—Wohin und zurück= Teil 1: An uns glaubt Gott nicht mehr= Ferry oder Wie es war (TV 1982)~~	Victim	Escaping	110	
Who Will Write Our History (2018)	Victim	Caught	95	Amazon Prime
Witness Out of Hell—Zeugin aus der Hölle (1966)	Survivor	Post-War	83	WorldCat.org
~~Witnesses—Svideteli (2018)~~	Victim	Caught	104	
Woman in Gold (2015)	Survivor	Post Post-War	109	Amazon Prime
A Woman's Pale Blue Handwriting— Eine blaßblaue Frauenschrift (TV 1984)	Tangential	Pre-Holocaust	105	JewishFilm.org
The Wooden Gun—Roveh Huliot (1979)	Survivor	Post-War	95	WorldCat.org
Wunderkinder (2011)	Tangential	Not Primarily a Jewish Experience	100	Amazon
X-Men (2000)	Survivor	Post Post-War	104	Amazon Prime
X-Men: First Class (2011)	Survivor	Post Post-War	132	Amazon Prime
The Zookeeper's Wife (2017)	Gentile	Righteous	126	Amazon Prime

LIST OF HOLOCAUST FILMS
(DIRECTOR, OSCAR/EMMY WINS
AND OSCAR/EMMY NOMINATIONS)

Recommended in **Bold** (52). "One of the Best" in **Bold and Underlined** (15).
Unavailable films in ~~Strikeout~~ (48). At publication time, most films in strikeout
are functionally unavailable. This status may change for a few films that may become
digitized and made available online. However, the vast majority of the unavailable titles
were never reproduced after their initial limited release.

Title	Director	Oscar/Emmy Winner	Oscar/Emmy Nomination
~~Abraham's Gold (1990)~~	Jörg Graser		
Across the Waters—Fuglene over sundet (2016)	Nicolo Donato		
~~The Actress—Die Schauspielerin (1988)~~	Siegfried Kuehn		
Adam Resurrected (2008)	Paul Schrader		
Adolf Eichmann (2007)	Robert Young		
~~After the Truth—Nichts als die Wahrheit (1999)~~	Roland Suso Richter		
After Your Decrees aka Fair Game— Wedle wyroków twoich... (1984)	Jerzy Hoffman		
Aftermath—Poklosie (2012)	Wladyslaw Pasikowski		
Aimée & Jaguar (1999)	Max Färberböck		
Akte Grüninger (TV 2014)	Alain Gsponer		
Alan and Naomi (1992)	Sterling Van Wagenen		
All My Loved Ones—Vsichni moji blízcí (1999)	Matej Minac		
Almost Peaceful— Un monde presque paisible (2002)	Michel Deville		
Amen. (2002)	Costa-Gavras		
And Now My Love—Toute une vie (1974)	Claude Lelouche		

Title	Director	Oscar/Emmy Winner	Oscar/Emmy Nomination
...and the Fifth Horseman Is Fear— ...a pátý jezdec je strach (1965)	Zbynek Brynych		
The Angel of Auschwitz (2019)	Terry Lee Coker		
~~*The Angel of Budapest— El ángel de Budapest* (TV 2011)~~	Luis Oliveros		
~~*Angels in White—Mal'akhiyot Be-lavan* (2012)~~	Tali Avrahami		
Angry Harvest—Bittere Ernte (1985)	Agnieszka Holland		Foreign Language Film
Anna's Return—Annas Heimkehr (TV 2003)	Xaver Schwarzenberger		
Anne Frank: The Whole Story (TV 2001)	Robert Dornhelm	Miniseries, Art Direction for a Miniseries, Movie or a Special	Casting for a Miniseries, Movie or a Special, Cinematography for a Miniseries or a Movie, Directing for a Miniseries, Movie or a Special, Single Camera Picture Editing for a Miniseries, Movie or a Special, Lead Actor in a Miniseries or a Movie, Lead Actress in a Miniseries or a Movie, Supporting Actress in a Miniseries or a Movie, Sound Editing for a Miniseries, Movie or a Special, Writing for a Miniseries or a Movie
Apt Pupil (1998)	Bryan Singer		
Aristides de Sousa Mendes: A Rebel— Désobéir (TV 2008)	Joël Santoni		
The Aryan Couple (2004)	John Daly		
Ascension Day—Wniebowstapienie (1969)	Jan Rybkowski		
The Assisi Underground (1985)	Alexander Ramati		
At First Sight—Entre Nous— Coup de foudre (1983)	Diane Kurys		
The Attic: The Hiding of Anne Frank (TV 1988)	John Erman	Writing in a Miniseries or a Special	Directing in a Miniseries or a Special, Drama—Comedy Special, Editing for a Miniseries or a Special—Single Camera Production, Lead Actress in a Miniseries or a Special, Supporting Actress in a Miniseries or a Special
Au Revoir les Enfants (1987)	Louis Malle		Writer, Foreign Language Film
Auschwitz (2011)	Uwe Boll		

Title	Director	Oscar/Emmy Winner	Oscar/Emmy Nomination
The Auschwitz Report (2020)	Peter Bebjak		
Autumn Hearts A New Beginning—Emotional Arithmetic (2007)	Paolo Barzman		
Babi Yar: The Forgotten Crime—Babij Jar (2003)	Jeff Kanew		
A Bag of Marbles—Un sac de billes (1975)	Jacques Doillon		
A Bag of Marbles—Un sac de billes (2017)	Christian Duguay		
~~*Baranski* (1979)~~	Werner Masten		
Bent (1997)	Sean Mathias		
Bernhard Lichtenberg (TV 1965)	Peter Beauvais		
The Birch-Tree Meadow—La petite prairie aux bouleaux (2003)	Marceline Loridan-Ivens		
The Birth Certificate—Swiadectwo urodzenia (1961)	Stanislaw Rózewicz		
Bittersweet—Het bittere kruid (1985)	Kees Van Oostrum		
Black Book—Zwartboek (2006)	Paul Verhoeven		
Black Thursday—Les guichets du Louvre (1974)	Michel Mitrani		
Blessed Is the Match: The Life and Death of Hannah Senesh (2008)	Roberta Grossman		
~~*Blind Hero. Otto Weidt—Ein blinder Held—Die Liebe des Otto Weidt* (TV 2014)~~	Kai Christiansen		
The Bloom of Yesterday—Die Blumen von gestern (2016)	Chris Kraus		
Bolero Dance of Life—Les uns et les autres (1981)	Claude Lelouch		
Bonhoeffer: Agent of Grace (TV 2000)	Eric Till		
Border Street—Ulica Graniczna (1948)	Aleksander Ford		
The Boy in the Striped Pyjamas (2008)	Mark Herman		
The Boys from Brazil (1978)	Franklin J. Schaffner		Actor, Editing, Music (Adaptation Score)
~~*Brussels Transit—Bruxelles-transit* (1982)~~	Samy Szlingerbaum		
Bye Germany—Es war einmal in Deutschland... (2017)	Sam Garbarski		
Cabaret (1972)	Bob Fosse	Directing, Supporting Actor, Actress, Cinematography, Art Direction, Editing, Music (Adaptation Score), Sound	Picture, Writer
A Call to Remember (TV 1997)	Jack Bender		
The Cellar—Ha-Martef (1963)	Natan Gross		
~~*Charlie Grant's War* (TV 1984)~~	Martin Lavut		
Charlotte (1981)	Frans Weisz		
The Children of Chance—Les enfants de la chance (2016)	Malik Chibane		

Title	Director	Oscar/Emmy Winner	Oscar/Emmy Nomination
~~Chosen (2016)~~	Jasmin Dizdar		
Closed Season—Ende der Schonzeit (2012)	Franziska Schlotterer		
Cloudy Sunday—Ouzeri Tsitsanis (2015)	Manousos Manousakis		
Cold Days—Hideg napok (1966)	András Kovács		
Colette (2013)	Milan Cieslar		
The Condemned of Altona—I sequestrati di Altona (1962)	Vittorio De Sica		
Conspiracy (TV 2001)	Frank Pierson	Lead Actor in a Miniseries or a Movie, Writing for a Miniseries or a Movie	Made for Television Movie, Directing for a Miniseries, Movie or a Special, Cinematography for a Miniseries or a Movie, Single Camera Picture Editing for a Miniseries, Movie or a Special, Supporting Actor in a Miniseries or a Movie, Supporting Actor in a Miniseries or a Movie, Sound Editing for a Miniseries, Movie or a Special, Single Camera Sound Mixing for a Miniseries or a Movie
Conspiracy of Hearts (1960)	Ralph Thomas		
The Consul of Bordeaux—O Cônsul de Bordéus (2011)	João Correa, Francisco Manso		
The Counterfeiters—Die Fälscher (2007)	Stefan Ruzowitzky	Foreign Language Film	
The Courageous Heart of Irena Sendler (TV 2009)	John Kent Harrison	Makeup for a Miniseries or a Movie (Non-Prosthetic)	Supporting Actress in a Miniseries or Movie, Sound Editing for a Miniseries, Movie or a Special
~~The Customer of the Off Season—Ore'ach B'Onah Metah (1970)~~	Moshé Mizrahi		
Dara of Jasenovac—Dara iz Jasenovca (2020)	Predrag Antonijevic		
~~Darkness in Daytime—Nappali sötétség (1963)~~	Zoltán Fábri		
~~David (1979)~~	Peter Lilienthal		
~~Dawn (2014)~~	Romed Wyder		
A Day in October—En dag i oktober (1991)	Kenneth Kort Madsen		
~~The Day the Clown Cried (1972)~~	Jerry Lewis		
Dear Mr. Waldman—Michtavim Le America (2006)	Hanan Peled		
Death in Love (2008)	Boaz Yakin		

Title	Director	Oscar/Emmy Winner	Oscar/Emmy Nomination
Death Is My Trade—Aus einem deutschen Leben (1977)	Theodor Kotulla		
The Debt—Ha-Hov (2007)	Assaf Bernstein		
The Debt (2010)	John Madden		
Defiance (2008)	Edward Zwick		Music (Adaptation Score)
Denial (2016)	Mick Jackson		
~~*Der Passagier—Welcome to Germany* (TV 1988)~~	Thomas Brasch		
The Devil's Arithmetic (TV 1999)	Donna Deitch	Directing in a Children's Special, Writing in a Children's Special	Children's Special, Sound Editing
Diamonds of the Night—Démanty noci (1964)	Jan Nemec		
The Diary of Anne Frank—Anne no nikki (1995)	Akinori Nagaoka		
~~*The Diary of Anne Frank—Dagboek van Anne Frank* (TV 1962)~~	--		
The Diary of Anne Frank—Das Tagebuch Der Anne Frank (2016)	Hans Steinbichler		
~~*The Diary of Anne Frank—Das Tagebuch Der Anne Frank* (TV 1958)~~	Emil Stöhr		
~~*The Diary of Anne Frank—Dnevnik Ane Frank* (TV 1959)~~	Mirjana Samardzic		
~~*The Diary of Anne Frank—El diari d'Anna Frank* (TV 1996)~~	Tamzin Townsend		
The Diary of Anne Frank—Het dagboek van Anne Frank (TV 1985)	Jeroen Krabbé & Hank Onrust		
The Diary of Anne Frank—Le Journal d'Anne Frank (1999)	Julian Y. Wolff		
The Diary of Anne Frank (1959)	George Stevens	Supporting Actress, Cinematography, Art Direction	Picture, Directing, Supporting Actor, Costume Design, Music (Adaptation Score)
~~*The Diary of Anne Frank* (TV 1967)~~	Alex Segal		
The Diary of Anne Frank (TV 1980)	Boris Sagal		Cinematography for a Limited Series or a Special, Achievement in Makeup, Individual Achievement—Special Class
The Diary of Anne Frank (TV 1987)	Gareth Davies		
The Diary of Anne Frank (TV 2009)	Jon Jones		Sound in a Non-Series (OFTA)
Distant Journey—Daleká cesta (1950)	Alfréd Radok		
Dita Saxová (1968)	Antonín Moskalyk		
Divided We Fall—Musíme si pomáhat (2000)	Jan Hrebejk		Foreign Language Film
~~*Drancy Avenir* (1997)~~	Arnaud des Pallières		

Title	Director	Oscar/Emmy Winner	Oscar/Emmy Nomination
The Earth Cries Out—Il grido della terra (1949)	Duilio Coletti		
Edges of the Lord (2001)	Yurek Bogayevicz		
The Eichmann Show (TV 2015)	Paul Andrew Williams		
~~*Elysium* (1987)~~	Erika Szántó		
~~*Enclosure—Lenclos* (1961)~~	Armand Gatti		
The End of Our World— Koniec naszego swiata (1964)	Wanda Jakubowska		
Enemies: A Love Story (1989)	Paul Mazursky		Supporting Actress, Supporting Actress (II), Writer
Escape from Sobibor (TV 1987)	Jack Gold		Drama—Comedy Special, Art Direction for a Miniseries or a Special, Directing in a Miniseries or a Special, Lead Actor in a Miniseries or a Special, Writing in a Miniseries or a Special
Europa Europa (1990)	Agnieszka Holland		Writer
Everything Is Illuminated (2005)	Liev Schreiber		
~~*Ewa* (2016)~~	Haim Tabakman		
The Execution (TV 1985)	Paul Wendkos		
Exodus (1960)	Otto Preminger	Music (Adaptation Score)	Supporting Actor
Exodus to Shanghai (2015)	Anthony Hickox		
~~*Falsch* (1987)~~	Jean-Pierre Dardenne		
Fanny's Journey—Le voyage de Fanny (2016)	Lola Doillon		
Fateless—Sorstalanság (2005)	Lajos Koltai		
~~*Father* (1990)~~	John Power		
Fatherland (TV 1994)	Christopher Menaul		
The Fed One—Hranjenik (1970)	Vatroslav Mimica		
Fever at Dawn—Hajnali láz (2015)	Péter Gárdos		
The Final Solution: The Wannsee Conference—Die Wannseekonferenz (TV 1984)	Heinz Schirk		
For Those I Loved— Au nom de tous les miens (1983)	Robert Enrico		
Forbidden (1984)	Anthony Page		
Forbidden Dreams—Death of the Beautiful Robucks—Smrt krásných srncu (1987)	Karel Kachyna		
Forget Me Not: The Anne Frank Story (TV 1996)	Fred Holmes		

Title	Director	Oscar/Emmy Winner	Oscar/Emmy Nomination
~~Forgiveness—Esther's Diary (2008)~~	Mariusz Kotowski		
Free Men—Les hommes libres (2011)	Ismaël Ferroukhi		
Freedom Writers (2007)	Richard LaGravenese		
From Hell to Hell—Iz ada v ad (1996)	Dmitriy Astrakhan		
Fugitive Pieces (2007)	Jeremy Podeswa		
The Garden of the Finzi-Continis— Il Giardino dei Finzi-Contini (1970)	Vittorio De Sica	Foreign Language Film	Writer
Gebürtig (2002)	Robert Schindel & Lukas Stepanik		
The General Case—Die Akte General (TV 2016)	Stephan Wagner		
<u>Genghis Cohn (1993)</u>	Elijah Moshinsky		
The German Doctor—Wakolda (2013)	Lucía Puenzo		
Getting Away with Murder (1996)	Harvey Miller		
Ghetto—Vilniaus getas (2005)	Audrius Juzenas		
~~Gitel (2015)~~	Robert Mullan		
~~The Glass Cage—La cage de verre (1965)~~	Philippe Arthuys, Jean-Louis Levi-Alvarès		
Gloomy Sunday— Ein Lied von Liebe und Tod (1999)	Rolf Schübel		
God on Trial (TV 2008)	Andy DeEmmony		Best Sound Fiction—Entertainment (BAFTA)
Gold of Rome—L'oro di Roma (1961)	Carlo Lizzani		
The Gold Rimmed Glasses— Gli occhiali d'oro (1987)	Giuliano Montaldo		
Good (2008)	Vicente Amorim		
<u>Good Evening, Mr. Wallenberg— God afton, Herr Wallenberg— En Passionshistoria från verkligheten (1990)</u>	Kjell Grede		
~~The Great Promise— Dim'at Ha'Nehamah Ha'Gedolah (1947)~~	Joseph Lejtes		
<u>The Grey Zone (2001)</u>	Tim Blake Nelson		
Gruber's Journey—Calatoria lui Gruber (2008)	Radu Gabrea		
The Guard of Auschwitz (2018)	Terry Lee Coker		
Hanna's Journey—Hannas Reise (2013)	Julia von Heinz		
Hanna's Sleeping Dogs— Hannas schlafende Hunde (2016)	Andreas Gruber		
Hanna's War (1988)	Menahem Golan		
<u>Harold and Maude (1971)</u>	Hal Ashby		

Title	Director	Oscar/Emmy Winner	Oscar/Emmy Nomination
Haven (TV 2001)	John Gray		Music Composition for a Miniseries, Movie or a Special (Dramatic Underscore), Supporting Actress in a Miniseries or a Movie, Special Visual Effects for a Miniseries, Movie or a Special
Heartbeat Detector—La question humaine (2007)	Klotz Nicolas		
~~*Hidden Children—La fuga degli innocenti* (TV 2004)~~	Leone Pompucci		
The Hiding Place (1975)	James F. Collier		
High Street—Rue haute (1977)	André Ernotte		
Holy Week—Wielki tydzien (1995)	Andrzej Wajda		
~~*The Hour of Truth—L'heure de la vérité* (1965)~~	Henri Calef		
The House in Karp Lane— Das Haus in der Karpfengasse (TV 1965)	Kurt Hoffmann		
~~*House of the Generals* (2003)~~	Dan Spigel		
The House on Garibaldi Street (TV 1979)	Peter Collinson		
How a Hirschberger Learned Danish— Wie ein Hirschberger Dänisch lernte (TV 1968)	Rolf Busch		
I Do Not Care If We Go Down in History as Barbarians—Îmi este indiferent daca in istorie vom intra ca barbari (2018)	Radu Jude		
~~*I Know Why I Live— Ich weiß, wofür ich lebe* (1955)~~	Paul Verhoeven		
I Was Overtaken by Night— Zastihla me noc (1986)	Juraj Herz		
Ida (2013)	Pawel Pawlikowski	Foreign Language Film	Cinematography
The Illegals—Lo Tafhidenu (1947)	Meyer Levin		
I'm Alive and I Love You— Je suis vivante et je vous aime (1998)	Roger Kahane		
In Another Lifetime— Vielleicht in einem anderen Leben (2011)	Elisabeth Scharang		
In Darkness (2011)	Agnieszka Holland		Foreign Language Film
In Hiding—W ukryciu (2013)	Jan Kidawa-Blonski		
In the End Come Tourists— Am Ende kommen Touristen (2007)	Robert Thalheim		
In the Presence of Mine Enemies (TV 1997)	Joan Micklin Silver		
In the Shadow of Hate— W cieniu nienawisci (TV 1986)	Wojciech Zóltowski		

Title	Director	Oscar/Emmy Winner	Oscar/Emmy Nomination
Inglourious Basterds (2009)	Quentin Tarantino	Supporting Actor	Picture, Directing, Writer, Cinematography, Editing, Sound
~~*The Interpreter—Tlmocník* (2018)~~	Martin Sulík		
~~*The Interrogation* (2016)~~	Erez Pery		
The Investigation—Die Ermittlung (TV 1966)	Peter Schulze-Rohr		
Invincible (2001)	Werner Herzog		
Invitation—Zaproszenie (1986)	Wanda Jakubowska		
The Island on Bird Street (1997)	Søren Kragh-Jacobsen		
It Will Never Happen Again— Unzere Kinder (1951)	Natan Gross		
Jacob the Liar—Jakob, der Lügner (1974)	Frank Beyer		Foreign Language Film
Jakob the Liar (1999)	Peter Kassovitz		
Jew Boy Levi—Viehjud Levi (1999)	Didi Danquart		
A Jewish Girl in Shanghai (2010)	Wang Genfa & Zhang Zhenhui		
Joanna (2010)	Feliks Falk		
Jojo Rabbit (2019)	Taika Waititi	Screenplay	Picture, Supporting Actress, Costume Design, Production Design, Editing
~~*Journey to Jerusalem— Patuvane kam Yerusalim* (2003)~~	Ivan Nichev		
Judgment at Nuremberg (1961)	Stanley Kramer	Writer	Picture, Directing, Actor, Supporting Actor, Supporting Actress, Cinematography, Art Direction, Costume Design, Editing
Judith (1966)	Daniel Mann		
The Juggler (1953)	Edward Dmytryk		
Julia (1977)	Fred Zinnemann	Actor, Supporting Actress, Writer	Picture, Directing, Supporting Actor, Actress, Cinematography, Costume Design, Editing, Music (Adaptation Score)
Just an Ordinary Jew— Ein ganz gewöhnlicher Jude (2005)	Oliver Hirschbiegel		
Just Beyond That Forest— Jeszcze tylko ten las (1991)	Jan Lomnicki		
Kapò (1960)	Gillo Pontecorvo		Foreign Language Film
Kapo in Jerusalem—Kapo be'Yerushalaim (2015)	Uri Barbash		
Keep Away from the Window— Daleko od okna (2000)	Jan Jakub Kolski		
Korczak (1990)	Andrzej Wajda		

Title	Director	Oscar/Emmy Winner	Oscar/Emmy Nomination
Kornblumenblau (1989)	Leszek Wosiewicz		
Labyrinth of Lies— Im Labyrinth Des Schweigens (2014)	Giulio Ricciarelli		
Lacombe, Lucien (1974)	Louis Malle		Foreign Language Film
Ladies' Tailor—Damskiy portnoy (1990)	Leonid Gorovets		
~~*L'adieu aux enfants* (TV 1982)~~	Claude Couderc		
Landscape After Battle— Krajobraz po bitwie (1970)	Andrzej Wajda		
~~The Last (2019)~~	Jeff Lipsky		
The Last Butterfly—Poslední motýl (1991)	Karel Kachyna		
The Last Chance—Die letzte Chance (1945)	Leopold Lindtberg		
~~*The Last Hole—Das letzte Loch* (1981)~~	Herbert Achternbusch		
~~*The Last Letter—La dernière lettre* (2002)~~	Frederick Wiseman		
~~*The Last Mensch—Der letzte Mensch* (2014)~~	Pierre-Henry Salfati		
The Last Metro—Le dernier métro (1980)	François Truffaut		Foreign Language Film
The Last Stage—The Last Stop— Ostatni etap (1948)	Wanda Jakubowska		
The Last Suit—El último traje (2017)	Pablo Solarz		
~~*The Last Supper—Das letzte Mahl* (2018)~~	Florian Frerichs		
The Last Train—Der Letzte Zug (2006)	Joseph Vilsmaier & Dana Vávrová		
Late Season—Utószezon (1967)	Zoltán Fábri		
Left Luggage (1998)	Jeroen Krabbé		
Lena: My 100 Children (TV 1987)	Ed Sherin		
~~*Leni* (TV 1994)~~	Leo Hiemer		
Les Misérables (1995)	Claude Lelouch		
Les violons du bal (1974)	Michel Drach		
~~*Let Me Go* (2017)~~	Polly Steele		
~~*Let's Go!* (TV 2014)~~	Michael Verhoeven		
The Life Ahead—La vita davanti a sé (2020)	Edoardo Ponti		
A Life Ahead—Madam Rose— Madame Rosa—La Vie devant soi (1977)	Moshé Mizrahi	Foreign Language Film	
Life for Life: Maximilian Kolbe— Zycie za zycie (1991)	Krzysztof Zanussi		
Life Is Beautiful—La Vita è bella (1997)	Roberto Benigni	Actor, Foreign Language Film, Music (Adaptation Score)	Picture, Directing, Writer, Editing
~~*The Light of Hope—La llum d'Elna* (2017)~~	Sílvia Quer		
Lili Marleen (1981)	Rainer Werner Fassbinder		
Living Goods—Lebende Ware (1969)	Wolfgang Luderer		

Title	Director	Oscar/Emmy Winner	Oscar/Emmy Nomination
Long Is the Road—Lang ist der Weg (1949)	Herbert B. Fredersdorf & Marek Goldstein		
Look to the Sky— Jona che visse nella balena (1993)	Roberto Faenza		
Lore (2012)	Cate Shortland		
~~*Louise's Diary 1942—Les amours secrètes* (2010)~~	Franck Phelizon		
A Love to Hide—Un amour à taire (TV 2005)	Christian Faure		
~~*The Lucky Star* (1980)~~	Max Fischer		
Made in Israel (2001)	Ari Folman		
Malou (1981)	Jeanine Meerapfel		
The Man in the Glass Booth (1975)	Arthur Hiller		Actor
The Man Who Captured Eichmann (TV 1996)	William A Graham		Editing for a Miniseries or a Special—Single Camera Production, Lead Actor in a Miniseries or a Special
Marathon Man (1976)	John Schlesinger		Supporting Actor
Marriage in the Shadows— Ehe im Schatten (1947)	Kurt Maetzig		
The Martyr—Dr. Korczak and His Children—Sie sind frei, Doktor Korczak (1975)	Aleksander Ford		
Max (2002)	Meyjes Menno		
Max and Helen (TV 1990)	Philip Saville		
Max and Helen—Max e Hélène (TV 2015)	Giacomo Battiato		
Me and the Colonel (1958)	Peter Glenville		
Memories of Anne Frank—Mi ricordo Anna Frank (TV 2009)	Alberto Negrin		
The Memory Thief (2007)	Gil Kofman		
Mendel (1997)	Alexander Røsler		
Miracle at Midnight (TV 1998)	Ken Cameron		
Miracle at Moreaux (TV 1986)	Paul Shapiro		
Mr. Klein—Monsieur Klein (1976)	Joseph Losey		
Monastero di Santa Chiara (1949)	Mario Sequi		
Monsieur Batignole (2002)	Gérard Jugnot		
Morituri (1948)	Eugen York		
~~*The Mover* (2018)~~	Davis Simanis Jr.		
Murderers Among Us— Die Mörder sind unter uns (1946)	Wolfgang Staudte		
Murderers Among Us: The Simon Wiesenthal Story (TV 1989)	Brian Gibson	Writing in a Miniseries or a Special	Drama/Comedy Special, Lead Actor in a Miniseries or a Special
~~*Murer: Anatomy of a Trial— Murer: Anatomie eines Prozesses* (2018)~~	Christian Frosch		
Music Box (1989)	Costa-Gavras		Actress

Title	Director	Oscar/Emmy Winner	Oscar/Emmy Nomination
My Daughter Anne Frank—Meine Tochter Anne Frank (TV 2015)	Raymond Ley		
~~*My Father's House—Beit Avi* (1947)~~	Herbert Kline, Ben Oyserman, and Joseph Lejtes		
My Führer—Mein Führer—Die wirklich wahrste Wahrheit über Adolf Hitler (2007)	Dani Levy		
My Mother's Courage—Mutters Courage (1995)	Michael Verhoeven		
Naked Among Wolves—Nackt unter Wölfen (1963)	Frank Beyer		
Naked Among Wolves—Nackt unter Wölfen (TV 2015)	Philipp Kadelbach		
The Nasty Girl—Das schreckliche Mädchen (1990)	Michael Verhoeven		Foreign Language Film
~~*Natalia* (1988)~~	Bernard Cohn		
Never Forget (TV 1991)	Joseph Sargent		
Newland—Aretz Hadasha (1994)	Orna Ben-Dor Niv		
The Night Porter—Il portiere di notte (1974)	Liliana Cavani		
Nina's Journey—La Maison De Nina (2005)	Lena Einhorn		
<u>*1945* (2017)</u>	Ferenc Török		
The Ninth Circle—Deveti krug (1960)	France Štiglic		Foreign Language Film
Nippon no Shindorâ: Sugihara Chiune monogatari (TV 2005)	Takayoshi Watanabe		
Not All Were Murderers—Nicht alle waren Mörder (TV 2006)	Jo Baier		
November Moon—Novembermond (1985)	Alexandra von Grote		
Nowhere in Africa—Nirgendwo in Afrika (2001)	Caroline Link	Foreign Language Film	
Nuremberg (TV 2000)	Yves Simoneau	Supporting Actor in a Miniseries or a Movie, Single Camera Sound Mixing for a Miniseries or a Movie	Miniseries, Sound Editing for a Miniseries, Movie or a Special
The Odessa File (1974)	Ronald Neame		
Of a Thousand Delights—Sandra—Vaghe stelle dell'Orsa... (1965)	Luchino Visconti		
Olga (2004)	Jayme Monjardim		
One Day You'll Understand—Plus tard (2008)	Amos Gitai		
The Only Way (1970)	Brent Christensen		
Operation Eichmann (1961)	R.G. Springsteen		
Operation Finale (2018)	Chris Weitz		
Operation Stadium—Akcija Stadion (1977)	Dusan Vukotic		

Title	Director	Oscar/Emmy Winner	Oscar/Emmy Nomination
~~Our Father in Heaven—Otche nash—Pater Noster (1989)~~	Boris Yermolayev		
Out of Evil—Mi Klalah L'Brahah (1950)	Joseph Krumgold		
Out of the Ashes (TV 2003)	Joseph Sargent	Cinematography for a Miniseries or a Movie	
The Painted Bird (2019)	Václav Marhoul		
Passenger—Pasazerka (TV 1963)	Andrzej Munk & Witold Lesiewicz		
The Passerby—La passante du Sans-Souci (1982)	Jacques Rouffio		
Past Life (2016)	Avi Nesher		
The Pawnbroker (1964)	Sidney Lumet		Actor
The People vs. Fritz Bauer—Der Staat gegen Fritz Bauer (2015)	Lars Kraume		
Perlasca. The Courage of a Just Man—Perlasca. Un eroe italiano (TV 2002)	Alberto Negrin		
Persian Lessons (2020)	Vadim Perelman		
Persona Non Grata—Sugihara Chiune (2015)	Cellin Gluck		
***Phoenix* (2014)**	Christian Petzold		
***The Pianist* (2002)**	Roman Polanski	Directing, Actor, Writer	Picture, Cinematography, Costume Design, Editing
Playing for Time (TV 1980)	Daniel Mann	Drama Special, Lead Actress in a Limited Series or a Special, Supporting Actress in a Limited Series or a Special, Writing in a Limited Series or a Special	Supporting Actress in a Limited Series or a Special, Art Direction for a Limited Series or a Special
The Poet—Hearts of War (2007)	Damian Lee		
Postcard from a Journey—Kartka z podrózy (1984)	Waldemar Dziki		
The Pracht Inn (2014)	Tamar Yarom		
Prague (1992)	Ian Sellar		
Prayer for Katerina Horovitzova—Modlitba pro Katerinu Horovitzovou (TV 1965)	Antonin Moskalyk		
***Primo* (TV 2005)**	Richard Wilson		Best Actor (BAFTA)
Private Resistance—De ijssalon (1985)	Dmitri Frenkel Frank		
Professor Mamlock (1961)	Konrad Wolf		
Protector—Protektor (2009)	Marek Najbrt		
Punch Me in the Stomach (1997)	Francine Zuckerman		
***The Quarrel* (1991)**	Eli Cohen		
~~*Quezon's Game* (2018)~~	Matthew Rosen		
Raindrops—Regentropfen (1981)	Michael Hoffmann		

Title	Director	Oscar/Emmy Winner	Oscar/Emmy Nomination
The Reader (2008)	Stephen Daldry	Actress	Picture, Directing, Writer, Cinematography
Redemption Road—Landgericht (TV 2017)	Matthias Glasner		
The Relief of Belsen (TV 2007)	Justin Hardy		Specialist Factual (BAFTA)
Remember (2015)	Atom Egoyan		
Remember Your Name—Pomni imya svoye (1974)	Sergey Kolosov		
Remembrance—Die verlorene Zeit (2011)	Anna Justice		
Remembrance of Love (TV 1982)	Jack Smight		
The Resistance—The Invisibles— Die Unsichtbaren (2017)	Claus Räfle		
Resistance (2020)	Jonathan Jakubowicz		
Return from the Ashes (1965)	J. Lee Thompson		
The Revolt of Job—Jób lázadása (1983)	Imre Gyöngyössy		Foreign Language Film
Riphagen—Riphagen: The Untouchable (2016)	Pieter Kuijpers		
Romeo, Juliet and Darkness— Romeo, Julie a tma (1960)	Jiří Weiss		
The Rose Garden—The Rosegarden (1989)	Fons Rademakers		
~~*A Rose in Winter* (2018)~~	Joshua Sinclair		
Rosenstrasse (2003)	Margarethe von Trotta		
Rose's Songs—A Rózsa énekei (2003)	Andor Szilágyi		
The Round Up—La rafle (2010)	Roselyne Bosch		
Rua Alguem 5555: My Father (2003)	Egidio Eronico		
Run Boy Run—Lauf Junge lauf (2013)	Pepe Danquart		
Salad Days—Zielone lata (1980)	Stanislaw Jedryka		
Samson (1961)	Andrzej Wajda		
The Samuel Project (2018)	Marc Fusco		
Sarah and the Squirrel— The Seventh Match (1982)	Yoram Gross		
Sarah's Key—Elle s'appelait Sarah (2010)	Gilles Paquet-Brenner		
Saviors in the Night—Unter Bauern (2009)	Ludi Boeken		
The Scarlet and the Black (TV 1983)	Jerry London	Sound Mixing for a Limited Series or a Special	Editing for a Limited Series or a Special, Individual Achievement—Graphic Design and Title Sequences
Schindler's List (1993)	Steven Spielberg	Picture, Directing, Writer, Cinematography, Art Direction, Editing, Music (Adaptation Score)	Actor, Supporting Actor, Costume Design, Makeup, Sound

Title	Director	Oscar/Emmy Winner	Oscar/Emmy Nomination
The Search (1948)	Fred Zinnemann	Juvenile, Writer	Actor, Director, Writing, Screenplay
A Secret—Un secret (2007)	Claude Miller		
Sergeant Schmidt—Feldwebel Schmid (TV 1968)	Nathan Jariv		
Seven Journeys—In Those Days—In jenen Tagen (1947)	Helmut Käutner		
The 17th Bride—Ha-Kala (1985)	Nadav Levitan		
The Seventh Room—A hetedik szoba (1996)	Márta Mészáros		
~~*Shades of Truth* (2015)~~	Liana Marabini		
~~*Shepherd: The Hero Dog* (2019)~~	Lynn Roth		
Shine (1996)	Scott Hicks	Actor	Picture, Supporting Actor, Director, Writing, Film Editing, Music
Ship of Fools (1965)	Stanley Kramer	Cinematography, Art Direction	Picture, Actor, Supporting Actor, Actress, Writer, Costume Design
The Shop on Main Street—Obchod na korze (1965)	Ján Kadár and Elmar Klos	Foreign Language Film	Actress
Simon Konianski (2009)	Micha Wald		
The Singing Forest (2003)	Jorge Ameer		
Singing in the Dark (1956)	Max Nosseck		
Skipper Next to God—Maître après Dieu (1951)	Louis Daquin		
Skokie—Once They Marched Through a Thousand Towns (TV 1981)	Herbert Wise		Actor in a Miniseries or Motion Picture Made for Television
The Sky Is Falling—Il cielo cade (2000)	Andrea Frazzi & Antonio Frazzi		
Sobibor (2018)	Konstantin Khabensky		
Son of Saul (2015)	László Nemes	Foreign Language Film	
The Song and the Silence (1968)	Nathan Cohen		
~~*The Song of Names* (2019)~~	François Girard		
Sophie's Choice (1982)	Alan J. Pakula	Actress	Writer, Cinematography, Costume Design, Music (Adaptation Score)
Spring 1941 (2007)	Uri Barbash		
Spring of Life—Pramen zivota (TV 2000)	Milan Cieslar		
Springtime in Budapest—Budapesti tavasz (1955)	Félix Máriássy		
The Square of St. Elizabeth—Námestie svätej Alzbety (1966)	Vladimir Bahna		
Stars—Sterne (1959)	Konrad Wolf		
The Statement (2003)	Norman Jewison		
Stielke, Heinz, Fifteen—Stielke, Heinz, fünfzehn... (1987)	Michael Kann		

Title	Director	Oscar/Emmy Winner	Oscar/Emmy Nomination
~~A Story About a Bad Dream (2000)~~	Pavel Stingl		
~~The Story of a Murder— Chronik eines Mordes (1965)~~	Joachim Hasler		
The Stranger (1946)	Orson Welles		Writer
~~Stream Line—La linea del fiume (1976)~~	Aldo Scavarda		
The Substance of Fire (1996)	Daniel J. Sullivan		
The Summer of Aviya— Ha-Kayitz Shel Aviya (1988)	Eli Cohen		
Sunshine (1999)	István Szabó		
Surviving with Wolves— Survivre avec les loups (2007)	Véra Belmont		
Süskind (2012)	Rudolf van den Berg		
The Taras' Family—The Unvanquished— Nepokoryonnye (1945)	Mark Donskoy		
~~A Tear in the Ocean— Une larme dans l'océan (1973)~~	Henri Glaeser		
~~Tel Aviv-Berlin (1987)~~	Tzipi Trope		
Temporary Paradise— Ideiglenes paradicsom (1981)	András Kovács		
~~The Testament (2017)~~	Amichai Greenberg		
~~There Is Many Like Us (2015)~~	Josh Webber		
The Third Half—Treto poluvreme (2012)	Darko Mitrevski		
~~38 (1986)~~	Wolfgang Gluck		
36 Hours (1965)	George Seaton		
This Boat Is Full—Das Boot ist voll (1981)	Markus Imhoof		Foreign Language Film
This Must Be the Place (2011)	Paolo Sorrentino		
Those Who Remained—Akik maradtak (2019)	Barnabás Tóth		
Three Days in April—Drei Tage im April (TV 1995)	Oliver Storz		
~~Toman (2018)~~	Ondrej Trojan		
Tomorrow's a Wonderful Day—Adamah (1947)	Helmar Lerski		
Train of Life—Train de vie (1998)	Radu Mihaileanu		
~~Transit (1980)~~	Daniel Wachsmann		
Treason—Prodosia (1964)	Costas Manoussakis		
Triumph of the Spirit (1989)	Robert M. Young		
The Truce—La tregua (1997)	Francesco Rosi		
The 25th Hour—La vingt-cinquième heure (1967)	Henri Verneuil		
25 Firemen's Street—Tüzoltó utca 25. (1973)	Istvan Szabo		
Twist of Fate—Pursuit (TV 1989)	Ian Sharp		
Two Men (TV 1988)	Gordon Pinsent		

Title	Director	Oscar/Emmy Winner	Oscar/Emmy Nomination
The Two of Us— *Le vieil homme et l'enfant* **(1967)**	Claude Berri		
The Unborn (2009)	David S. Goyer		
Under the Domim Tree— *Etz Hadomim Tafus* **(1994)**	Eli Cohen		
Unfair Competition—Concorrenza sleale (2001)	Scola Ettore		
Uprising (TV 2001)	Jon Avnet	Stunt Coordination	Cinematography for a Miniseries or a Movie, Supporting Actor in a Miniseries or a Movie, Sound Editing for a Miniseries, Movie or a Special
Valentina's Mother—Ima shel Valentina (2008)	Matti Harari, Arik Lubetzki		
Varian's War: The Forgotten Hero (TV 2001)	Lionel Chetwynd		
Victor Young Perez (2013)	Jacques Ouaniche		
Voyage of the Damned (1976)	Rosenberg Stuart		Supporting Actress, Writer, Music (Adaptation Score)
~~*Voyages* (1999)~~	Emmanuel Finkiel		
Walk on Water (2004)	Eytan Fox		
Walking with the Enemy (2013)	Mark Schmidt		
The Wall (TV 1982)	Robert Markowitz		
Wallenberg—A Hero's Story (TV 1985)	Lamont Johnson	Directing in a Limited Series or a Special, Achievement in Costuming, Film Editing for a Limited Series or a Special, Film Sound Editing for a Limited Series or a Special	Drama—Comedy Special, Cinematography for a Limited Series or a Special, Film Sound Mixing for a Limited Series or a Special, Lead Actor in a Limited Series or a Special, Writing in a Limited Series or a Special
The Wandering Jew—L'ebreo errante (1948)	Goffredo Alessandrini		
War and Love (1985)	Moshé Mizrahi		
Warsaw: Year 5703— Warszawa. Année 5703 (1992)	Janusz Kijowski		
The Wave (TV 1981)	Alexander Grasshoff	Children's Program	
~~*Welcome in Vienna—Wohin und zurück* (1986)~~	Axel Corti		
~~*We'll Go to the City—Andremo in città* (1966)~~	Nelo Risi		
When Day Breaks—Kad svane dan (2012)	Goran Paskaljevic		
~~*When Hitler Stole Pink Rabbit— Als Hitler das rosa Kaninchen stahl* (2019)~~	Caroline Link		

Title	Director	Oscar/Emmy Winner	Oscar/Emmy Nomination
~~Where to and Back—Part 1: God Doesn't Believe in Us—Terry or How It Was—Wohin und zurück—Teil 1: An uns glaubt Gott nicht mehr—Terry oder Wie es war (TV 1982)~~	Axel Corti		
Who Will Write Our History (2018)	Roberta Grossman		
Witness Out of Hell—Zeugin aus der Hölle (1966)	Zika Mitrovic		
~~Witnesses—Svideteli (2018)~~	Konstantin Fam		
Woman in Gold (2015)	Simon Curtis		
A Woman's Pale Blue Handwriting—Eine blaßblaue Frauenschrift (TV 1984)	Axel Corti		
The Wooden Gun—Roveh Huliot (1979)	Ilan Moshenson		
Wunderkinder (2011)	Markus Rosenmüller		
X-Men (2000)	Bryan Singer		
X-Men: First Class (2011)	Matthew Vaughn		
The Zookeeper's Wife (2017)	Niki Caro		

List of Holocaust Films (Language, Country, IMDb Rating & Votes and Top-Billed Cast)

Recommended in **Bold** (52). "One of the Best" in **<u>Bold and Underlined</u>** (15). Unavailable films in ~~Strikeout~~ (48). At publication time, most films in strikeout are functionally unavailable. This status may change for a few films that may become digitized and made available online. However, the vast majority of the unavailable titles were never reproduced after their initial limited release.

Title	Country	Language	IMDb Rating	IMDb Votes	Top-Billed Cast
~~Abraham's Gold (1990)~~	Germany	German	7.6	71	Hanna Schygulla, Günther Maria Halmer, Daniela Schötz
Across the Waters—Fuglene over sundet (2016)	Denmark	Danish	6.2	640	David Dencik, Danica Curcic, Jakob Cedergren
~~The Actress—Die Schauspielerin (1988)~~	East Germany	German	7.3	29	Corinna Harfouch, André Hennicke, Michael Gwisdek
Adam Resurrected (2008)	US–Germany–Israel	English	6.3	3358	Jeff Goldblum, Willem Dafoe, Cristian Motiu
Adolf Eichmann (2007)	UK	English	5.9	2733	Avner W. Less, Thomas Kretschmann, Troy Garity
~~After the Truth—Nichts als die Wahrheit (1999)~~	Germany	German	7.3	806	Kai Wiesinger, Götz George, Karoline Eichhorn

Title	Country	Language	IMDb Rating	IMDb Votes	Top-Billed Cast
After Your Decrees aka Fair Game—Wedle wyroków twoich... (1984)	West Germany	Polish, German	6.9	48	Sharon Brauner, Anna Dymna, Günter Lamprecht
Aftermath—Poklosie (2012)	Poland	Polish	7.3	2906	Maciej Stuhr, Ireneusz Czop, Zbigniew Zamachowski
Aimée & Jaguar (1999)	Germany	German	7.3	5688	Maria Schrader, Juliane Köhler, Johanna Wokalek
Akte Grüninger (TV 2014)	Switzerland–Austria	Swiss, German, German	6.8	180	Helmut Förnbacher, Aaron Hitz, Pascal Holzer
Alan and Naomi (1992)	US	English	6.8	359	Lukas Haas, Vanessa Zaoui, Michael Gross
All My Loved Ones—Vsichni moji blízcí (1999)	Czech Republic	Czech	7.3	429	Rupert Graves, Josef Abrhám, Jiří Bartoska
Almost Peaceful—Un monde presque paisible (2002)	France	French	6.8	336	Simon Abkarian, Zabou Breitman, Vincent Elbaz
Amen. (2002)	Germany–Romania–France	English	7.3	12228	Ulrich Tukur, Mathieu Kassovitz, Ulrich Mühe
And Now My Love—Toute une vie (1974)	France–Italy	French, English	7.1	644	Marthe Keller, André Dussollier, Charles Denner
...and the Fifth Horseman Is Fear—...a pátý jezdec je Strach (1965)	Czechoslovakia	Czech	7.2	382	Miroslav Machácek, Olga Scheinpflugová, Zdenka Procházková
The Angel of Auschwitz (2019)	UK	English	6.5	737	Noeleen Comiskey, Steven Bush, Hayley-Marie Axe
~~*The Angel of Budapest—El ángel de Budapest* (TV 2011)~~	Spain–Hungary	Spanish	6.3	134	Francis Lorenzo, Ana Fernández, János Bán
~~*Angels in White—Mal'akhiyot Be-lavan* (2012)~~	Israel	Hebrew	--	--	Liat Azar, Eynat Baranovsky, Moshki Bornstein
Angry Harvest—Bittere Ernte (1985)	West Germany	German	7.3	659	Armin Mueller-Stahl, Elisabeth Trissenaar, Wojciech Pszoniak
Anna's Return—Annas Heimkehr (TV 2003)	Germany	German	6.9	80	Veronica Ferres, Julia Krombach, Herbert Knaup
Anne Frank: The Whole Story (TV 2001)	US	English	8.0	4401	Ben Kingsley, Hannah Taylor Gordon, Tatjana Blacher, Joachim Król
Apt Pupil (1998)	US	English	6.7	32059	Ian McKellen, Brad Renfro, Joshua Jackson
Aristides de Sousa Mendes: A Rebel—Désobéir (TV 2008)	France	French	8.3	43	Bernard Le Coq, Nanou Garcia, Lionel Lingelser

Title	Country	Language	IMDb Rating	IMDb Votes	Top-Billed Cast
The Aryan Couple (2004)	US–UK	English	6.3	981	Martin Landau, Kenny Doughty, Caroline Carver
Ascension Day—Wniebowstapienie (1969)	Poland	Polish	5.4	9	Malgorzata Braunek, Andrzej Antkowiak, Piotr Wysocki
The Assisi Underground (1985)	US	English	5.9	274	Ben Cross, James Mason, Irene Papas
At First Sight—Entre Nous—Coup de foudre (1983)	France	French	7.1	1680	Miou-Miou, Isabelle Huppert, Guy Marchand
The Attic: The Hiding of Anne Frank (TV 1988)	US	English	6.9	277	Mary Steenburgen, Paul Scofield, Huub Stapel
Au Revoir les Enfants (1987)	France–West Germany	French	8.0	27179	Gaspard Manesse, Raphael Fejtö, Francine Racette
Auschwitz (2011)	Germany	German	3.2	1269	Steffen Mennekes, Arved Birnbaum, Maximilian Gärtner
The Auschwitz Report (2020)	Slovakia—Czech Republic—Germany	Slovak	8.5	24	Noel Czuczor, Peter Ondrejicka, John Hannah
Autumn Hearts A New Beginning—Emotional Arithmetic (2007)	Canada	English	6.1	1206	Susan Sarandon, Christopher Plummer, Gabriel Byrne
Babi Yar: The Forgotten Crime—Babij Jar (2003)	Germany–Belarus	German	6.2	141	Michael Degen, Barbara De Rossi, Katrin Saß
A Bag of Marbles—Un sac de billes (1975)	France	French	6.7	216	Richard Constantini, Paul-Eric Shulmann, Joseph Goldenberg
A Bag of Marbles—Un sac de billes (2017)	France–Canada–Czech Republic	French	7.3	2685	Dorian Le Clech, Batyste Fleurial, Patrick Bruel
~~*Baranski* (1979)~~	West Germany	German	--	--	Wolf Ackva, Jan Groth, Thussy Marini
Bent (1997)	UK–Japan	English	7.3	6992	Lothaire Bluteau, Clive Owen, Mick Jagger
Bernhard Lichtenberg (TV 1965)	West Germany	German	9.8	10	Paul Verhoeven, Karl Striebeck, Klausjürgen Wussow
The Birch-Tree Meadow—La petite prairie aux bouleaux (2003)	Germany–France–Poland	French	6.8	129	Anouk Aimée, August Diehl, Marilu Marini
The Birth Certificate—Swiadectwo urodzenia (1961)	Poland	Polish	7.5	294	Henryk Hryniewicz, Beata Barszczewska, Andrzej Banaszewski
Bittersweet—Het bittere kruid (1985)	Netherlands	Dutch	5.9	245	Ester Spitz, Gerard Thoolen, Kitty Courbois

Title	Country	Language	IMDb Rating	IMDb Votes	Top-Billed Cast
Black Book—Zwartboek (2006)	UK–Netherlands–Germany–Belgium–Myanmar	Dutch	7.8	66373	Carice van Houten, Sebastian Koch, Thom Hoffman
Black Thursday—Les guichets du Louvre (1974)	France	French	6.7	53	Christian Rist, Christine Pascal, Judith Magre
Blessed Is the Match: The Life and Death of Hannah Senesh (2008)	US	English	7.0	123	Peter Hay, Judy Baumel-Schwartz, Michael Berenbaum
~~*Blind Hero: Otto Weidt—Ein blinder Held—Die Liebe des Otto Weidt* (TV 2014)~~	Germany	German	7.5	45	Edgar Selge, Henriette Confurius, Julia Goldberg
The Bloom of Yesterday—Die Blumen von gestern (2016)	Germany–Austria	German	6.6	753	Lars Eidinger, Adèle Haenel, Jan Josef Liefers
Bolero Dance of Life—Les uns et les autres (1981)	France	French	7.4	2118	Robert Hossein, Nicole Garcia, Geraldine Chaplin
Bonhoeffer: Agent of Grace (TV 2000)	US	English	6.3	505	Ulrich Tukur, Johanna Klante, Robert Joy, Tatjana Blacher
Border Street—Ulica Graniczna (1948)	Poland	Polish	7.3	153	Mieczyslawa Cwiklinska, Jerzy Leszczynski, Wladyslaw Godik
The Boy in the Striped Pyjamas (2008)	US–UK	English	7.8	160268	Asa Butterfield, David Thewlis, Rupert Friend
The Boys from Brazil (1978)	US–UK	English	7.0	22777	Gregory Peck, Laurence Olivier, James Mason
~~*Brussels Transit—Bruxelles-transit* (1982)~~	Belgium	English, Yiddish	8.4	24	Hélène Lapiower, Boris Lehman, Jeremy Wald
Bye Germany—Es war einmal in Deutschland... (2017)	Belgium–Germany–Luxembourg	German, English	6.5	1029	Moritz Bleibtreu, Antje Traue, Tim Seyfi
Cabaret (1972)	US	English	7.8	41673	Liza Minnelli, Michael York, Helmut Griem
A Call to Remember (TV 1997)	US	English	6.8	210	Blythe Danner, Joe Mantegna, David Lascher
The Cellar—Ha-Martef (1963)	Israel	Hebrew	--	--	Zaharira Harifai, Hannah Kahane, David Smadar
~~*Charlie Grant's War* (TV 1984)~~	Canada	English	7.0	25	R.H. Thomson, Jean Archambault, Chris Bark

Title	Country	Language	IMDb Rating	IMDb Votes	Top-Billed Cast
Charlotte (1981)	Netherlands–West Germany–UK–Italy	German	7.1	102	Birgit Doll, Elisabeth Trissenaar, Brigitte Horney
The Children of Chance— Les enfants de la chance (2016)	France	French	6.3	117	Philippe Torreton, Pauline Cheviller, Matteo Perez
~~*Chosen* (2016)~~	UK	English	5.2	787	Luke Mably, Ana Ularu, Tomasz Aleksander
Closed Season—Ende der Schonzeit (2012)	Germany-Israel	German	6.9	236	Brigitte Hobmeier, Hans-Jochen Wagner, Christian Friedel
Cloudy Sunday—Ouzeri Tsitsanis (2015)	Greece	Greek, German, Ladino	6.4	1471	Andreas Konstantinou, Haris Fragoulis
Cold Days—Hideg napok (1966)	Hungary	Hungarian	7.8	374	Zoltán Latinovits, Iván Darvas, Tibor Szilágyi
Colette (2013)	Czech Republic–Slovakia–Netherlands	English	6.0	379	Jirí Mádl, Clémence Thioly, Juraj Adamík
The Condemned of Altona— I sequestrati di Altona (1962)	Italy-France	English	6.7	471	Sophia Loren, Maximilian Schell, Fredric March
Conspiracy (TV 2001)	US-UK	English	7.8	15701	Kenneth Branagh, Clare Bullus, Stanley Tucci
Conspiracy of Hearts (1960)	UK	English	7.1	395	Lilli Palmer, Sylvia Syms, Yvonne Mitchell
The Consul of Bordeaux— O Cônsul de Bordéus (2011)	Portugal	Portuguese	6.3	314	Vítor Norte, Carlos Paulo, João Nunes Monteiro
The Counterfeiters—Die Fälscher (2007)	Austria–Germany	German	7.6	40087	Karl Markovics, August Diehl, Devid Striesow
The Courageous Heart of Irena Sendler (TV 2009)	US–Poland	English	7.3	3337	Anna Paquin, Marcia Gay Harden, Goran Visnjic
~~*The Customer of the Off Season— Ore'ach B'Onah Metah* (1970)~~	Israel–France	French	7.5	11	Claude Rich, Hénia Suchar, Hans Christian Blech
Dara of Jasenovac—Dara iz Jasenovca (2020)	Serbia	Serbian, Croatian	8.4	31954	Biljana Cekic, Zlatan Vidovic, Anja Stanic
~~*Darkness in Daytime— Nappali sötétség* (1963)~~	Hungary	Hungarian	7.8	30	Gyula Benkö, Lajos Básti, Ilona Béres
~~*David* (1979)~~	West Germany	German	6.7	114	Mario Fischel, Walter Taub, Irena Vrkljan
~~*Dawn* (2014)~~	Switzerland–UK–Germany–Israel	Hebrew, English, French	6.4	46	Sarah Adler, Joel Basman, Moris Cohen

Title	Country	Language	IMDb Rating	IMDb Votes	Top-Billed Cast
A Day in October—En dag i oktober (1991)	Denmark	English	6.3	277	D.B. Sweeney, Kelly Wolf, Tovah Feldshuh
~~*The Day the Clown Cried* (1972)~~	Sweden–France	English	--	--	Jerry Lewis, Peter Ahlm, Lars Amble
Dear Mr. Waldman— Michtavim Le America (2006)	Israel	Hebrew	7.2	68	Rami Heuberger, Evgenia Dodina, Ido Port
Death in Love (2008)	US	English	5.0	928	Josh Lucas, Jacqueline Bisset, Lukas Haas
Death Is My Trade— Aus einem deutschen Leben (1977)	West Germany	German	7.1	241	Götz George, Elisabeth Schwarz, Kurt Hübner
The Debt—Ha-Hov (2007)	Israel	Hebrew	6.9	840	Gila Almagor, Yuriy Chepurnov, Oleg Drach
The Debt (2010)	US–UK	English, German, Russian	6.9	59630	Helen Mirren, Sam Worthington, Tom Wilkinson
Defiance (2008)	US	English	7.3	127214	Daniel Craig, Liev Schreiber, Jamie Bell
Denial (2016)	US–UK	English	6.6	14805	Rachel Weisz, Tom Wilkinson, Timothy Spall
~~*Der Passagier—Welcome to Germany* (TV 1988)~~	West Germany–UK–Switzerland	German	6.8	60	Tony Curtis, Katharina Thalbach, Matthias Habich
The Devil's Arithmetic (TV 1999)	US	English	6.5	3359	Kirsten Dunst, Brittany Murphy, Paul Freeman
Diamonds of the Night— Démanty noci (1964)	Czechoslovakia	German	7.6	1262	Ladislav Jánsky, Antonín Kumbera, Ilse Bischofova
The Diary of Anne Frank— Anne no nikki (1995)	Japan	Japanese	6.6	116	Fumie Kashiyama, Gô Katô, Tetsuko Kuroyanagi
~~*The Diary of Anne Frank— Dagboek van Anne Frank* (TV 1962)~~	Netherlands	Dutch	5.3	11	Kitty Courbois, Martine Crefcour, Rob de Vries
The Diary of Anne Frank— Das Tagebuch Der Anne Frank (2016)	Germany	German	6.7	700	Lea van Acken, Martina Gedeck, Ulrich Noethen
~~*The Diary of Anne Frank— Das Tagebuch Der Anne Frank* (TV 1958)~~	East Germany	German	--	--	Ursula Burg, Karola Ebeling, Wolfgang Heinz
~~*The Diary of Anne Frank— Dnevnik Ane Frank* (TV 1959)~~	Yugoslavia	Serbo-Croatian	7.2	11	Milena Dapcevic, Rada Djuricin, Dejan Djurovic
~~*The Diary of Anne Frank— El diari d'Anna Frank* (TV 1996)~~	Spain	Spanish	--	--	Alex Brendemühl, Imma Colomer, Santi Ibáñez

Title	Country	Language	IMDb Rating	IMDb Votes	Top-Billed Cast
The Diary of Anne Frank— Het dagboek van Anne Frank (TV 1985)	Germany	Dutch	7.4	66	Jip Wijngaarden, Jeroen Krabbé, Truus te Selle
The Diary of Anne Frank— Le Journal d'Anne Frank (1999)	UK–Ireland– Netherlands– Luxembourg	French	6.1	152	Miep Gies, Hannah Pick-Goslar
The Diary of Anne Frank (1959)	US	English	7.4	10629	Millie Perkins, Shelley Winters, Joseph Schildkraut
~~The Diary of Anne Frank (TV 1967)~~	US	English	6.5	82	Peter Beiger, Theodore Bikel, Diana Davila
The Diary of Anne Frank (TV 1980)	US	English	6.8	513	Maximilian Schell, Joan Plowright, James Coco
The Diary of Anne Frank (TV 1987)	UK	English	5.5	104	Janet Amsbury, Elizabeth Bell, Emma Bowe
The Diary of Anne Frank (TV 2009)	UK	English	7.5	2568	Kate Ashfield, Geoffrey Breton, Ron Cook
Distant Journey—Daleká cesta (1950)	Czechoslovakia	Czech	7.3	195	Blanka Waleská, Otomar Krejca, Viktor Ocásek
Dita Saxová (1968)	Czechoslovakia	Czech	7.2	74	Krystyna Mikolajewska, Bohus Záhorský, Karel Höger
Divided We Fall— Musíme si pomáhat (2000)	Czech Republic	German	7.8	4509	Bolek Polívka, Csongor Kassai, Jaroslav Dusek
~~Drancy Avenir (1997)~~	France	French, German	7.5	28	Aude Amiot, Thierry Bosc, Anna-Lisa Nathan
The Earth Cries Out— Il grido della terra (1949)	Italy	Italian	6.9	46	Marina Berti, Andrea Checchi, Vivi Gioi
Edges of the Lord (2001)	US–Poland	English	7.0	3195	Haley Joel Osment, Willem Dafoe, Richard Banel
The Eichmann Show (TV 2015)	UK	English	6.6	3605	Martin Freeman, Anthony LaPaglia, Rebecca Front
~~Elysium (1987)~~	Hungary	Hungarian	7.2	33	Ferenc Bács, Zoltán Nagy, Klaus Abramowsky
~~Enclosure—L'enclos (1961)~~	France– Yugoslavia	French	7.4	64	Hans Christian Blech, Jean Négroni, Herbert Wochinz
The End of Our World— Koniec naszego swiata (1964)	Poland	Polish	7.6	15	Jan Adamski, Piotr Augustyniak, Andrzej Balcerzak
Enemies: A Love Story (1989)	US	English	6.8	1758	Ron Silver, Anjelica Huston, Lena Olin

Title	Country	Language	IMDb Rating	IMDb Votes	Top-Billed Cast
Escape from Sobibor (TV 1987)	UK–Yugoslavia	English	7.5	7040	Alan Arkin, Joanna Pacula, Rutger Hauer
Europa Europa (1990)	Germany–Poland–France	German, Russian, Polish, Hebrew, Yiddish	7.6	13240	Solomon Perel, Marco Hofschneider, René Hofschneider
***Everything Is Illuminated* (2005)**	US	English	7.5	54110	Elijah Wood, Eugene Hutz, Boris Lyoskin
~~*Ewa* (2016)~~	Israel	Hebrew	5.1	48	Avi Kushnir, Efrat Ben-Zur, Gil Frank
The Execution (TV 1985)	US	English	5.5	86	Loretta Swit, Rip Torn, Jessica Walter
Exodus (1960)	US	English	6.8	7858	Paul Newman, Eva Marie Saint, Ralph Richardson
Exodus to Shanghai (2015)	Austria	English	6.5	59	Yaara Benbenishty, Alexandre Nguyen, Markus von Lingen
~~*Falsch* (1987)~~	Belgium	French	5.5	57	Bruno Cremer, Jacqueline Bollen, Nicole Colchat
Fanny's Journey—Le voyage de Fanny (2016)	France–Belgium	French	7.0	1087	Léonie Souchaud, Fantine Harduin, Juliane Lepoureau
***Fateless—Sorstalanság* (2005)**	UK–Hungary–Germany	Hungarian	7.0	6102	Marcell Nagy, Béla Dóra, Bálint Péntek
~~*Father* (1990)~~	Australia	English	6.9	119	Max von Sydow, Carol Drinkwater, Julia Blake
Fatherland (TV 1994)	UK	English	6.5	5032	Rutger Hauer, Miranda Richardson, Peter Vaughan
The Fed One—Hranjenik (1970)	Yugoslavia	Serbo-Croatian	7.8	44	Fabijan Sovagovic, Nikola-Kole Angelovski, Giuseppe Addobbati
Fever at Dawn—Hajnali láz (2015)	Hungary–Sweden–Israel	Hungarian	6.7	218	Gila Almagor, Anna Azcárate, Gábor Máté
The Final Solution: The Wannsee Conference—Die Wannseekonferenz (TV 1984)	Austria–West Germany	German	7.9	800	Dietrich Mattausch, Gerd Böckmann, Friedrich G. Beckhaus
***For Those I Loved—Au nom de tous les miens* (1983)**	Canada–France–Hungary	French	7.1	419	Michael York, Brigitte Fossey, Jacques Penot
Forbidden (1984)	UK–West Germany	English	6.7	160	Jacqueline Bisset, Jürgen Prochnow, Irene Worth
Forbidden Dreams—Death of the Beautiful Robucks—Smrt krásných srncu (1987)	Czechoslovakia	Czech	7.6	490	Karel Hermánek, Rudolf Hrusínský, Jirí Krampol

Title	Country	Language	IMDb Rating	IMDb Votes	Top-Billed Cast
Forget Me Not: The Anne Frank Story (TV 1996)	US	English	7.6	33	Reg Grant, Ivan Borodin, Jenny Krochmal
~~Forgiveness—Esther's Diary (2008)~~	US	English	5.4	16	Juli Erickson, Shelley Calene-Black, Sydney Barrosse
Free Men—Les hommes libres (2011)	France	French	6.6	1202	Tahar Rahim, Michael Lonsdale, Mahmud Shalaby
Freedom Writers (2007)	US	English	7.5	59783	Hilary Swank, Imelda Staunton, Patrick Dempsey
From Hell to Hell—Iz ada v ad (1996)	Belarus	German, Russian, Yiddish	6.7	82	Valeria Valeeva, Anja Kling, Gennadi Svir
Fugitive Pieces (2007)	Canada–Greece	English	7.1	2059	Robbie Kay, Monika Schurmann, Nina Dobrev
The Garden of the Finzi-Continis— Il Giardino dei Finzi-Contini (1970)	Italy	Italian	7.5	5228	Dominique Sanda, Lino Capolicchio, Helmut Berger
Gebürtig (2002)	Austria	German	6.5	197	Peter Simonischek, Ruth Rieser, August Zirner
The General Case—Die Akte General (TV 2016)	Germany	German	6.8	244	Ulrich Noethen, David Kross, Bernhard Schütz
Genghis Cohn (1993)	US–UK	English	6.8	123	Antony Sher, Robert Lindsay, Matthew Marsh
The German Doctor—Wakolda (2013)	Argentina– France–Spain– Norway	Spanish, German	6.8	5214	Alex Brendemühl, Diego Peretti, Guillermo Pfening
Getting Away with Murder (1996)	US	English	4.5	1110	Jack Lemmon, Dan Aykroyd, Lily Tomlin
Ghetto—Vilniaus getas (2005)	Lithuania	German	6.9	1138	Heino Ferch, Sebastian Hülk, Erika Marozsán
~~Gitel (2015)~~	UK	Lithuanian	7.2	46	Nikolaj Antonov, Josif Baliukevic, Valentinas Kaplunas
~~The Glass Cage—La cage de verre (1965)~~	France	French	--	--	Georges Rivière, Jean Négroni, Françoise Prévost
Gloomy Sunday— Ein Lied von Liebe und Tod (1999)	Germany– Hungary	German	7.9	6424	Joachim Król, Erika Marozsán, Stefano Dionisi
God on Trial (TV 2008)	UK	English	7.7	2571	Joseph Muir, Josef Altin, Ashley Artus, Antony Sher
Gold of Rome—L'oro di Roma (1961)	Italy	Italian	6.8	105	Gérard Blain, Anna Maria Ferrero, Jean Sorel

Title	Country	Language	IMDb Rating	IMDb Votes	Top-Billed Cast
The Gold Rimmed Glasses—Gli occhiali d'oro (1987)	Italy–France–Yugoslavia	Italian	7.2	514	Philippe Noiret, Rupert Everett, Valeria Golino
Good (2008)	UK–Germany–Hungary	English	6.2	6264	Viggo Mortensen, Jason Isaacs, Jodie Whittaker
Good Evening, Mr. Wallenberg—God afton, Herr Wallenberg—En Passionshistoria från verkligheten (1990)	Sweden	Swedish	6.8	870	Stellan Skarsgård, Katharina Thalbach, Károly Eperjes
~~*The Great Promise—Dim'at Ha'Nehamah Ha'Gedolah (1947)*~~	Israel	Hebrew	--	--	Abraham Sofaer, Alexander Sarner, Dan Lustig
The Grey Zone (2001)	US	English	7.1	9482	David Arquette, Velizar Binev, David Chandler
Gruber's Journey—Calatoria lui Gruber (2008)	Romania	Romanian, German, Italian	7.0	148	Iorin Piersic Jr., Marcel Iures, Udo Schenk
The Guard of Auschwitz (2018)	UK	English	4.6	591	Lewis Kirk, Claudia Grace Mckell, Michael McKell
Hanna's Journey—Hannas Reise (2013)	Germany–Israel	German, English, Hebrew	6.3	367	Karoline Schuch, Doron Amit, Leah Koenig
Hanna's Sleeping Dogs—Hannas schlafende Hunde (2016)	Germany–Austria	German	6.4	47	Hannelore Elsner, Nike Seitz, Franziska Weisz
Hanna's War (1988)	US	English	6.3	334	Ellen Burstyn, Maruschka Detmers, Anthony Andrews
Harold and Maude (1971)	US	English	8.0	36209	Ruth Gordon, Bud Cort, Vivian Pickles
Haven (TV 2001)	US	English	6.2	378	Natasha Richardson, Colm Feore, Henry Czerny
Heartbeat Detector—La question humaine (2007)	France	French	6.2	1098	Mathieu Amalric, Michael Lonsdale, Edith Scob
~~*Hidden Children—La fuga degli innocenti (TV 2004)*~~	Italy	Italian	7.0	97	Ken Duken, Jasmine Trinca, Ennio Fantastichini
The Hiding Place (1975)	US	English	7.6	1548	Julie Harris, Jeannette Clift, Arthur O'Connell
High Street—Rue haute (1977)	Belgium	French	7.4	26	Annie Cordy, Mort Shuman, Bert Struys
Holy Week—Wielki tydzień (1995)	Poland	Polish	6.0	140	Beata Fudalej, Wojciech Malajkat, Jakub Przebindowski
~~*The Hour of Truth—L'heure de la vérité (1965)*~~	France	French	7.2	39	Karlheinz Böhm, Brett Halsey, Corinne Marchand

Title	Country	Language	IMDb Rating	IMDb Votes	Top-Billed Cast
The House in Karp Lane—Das Haus in der Karpfengasse (TV 1965)	West Germany	German	7.9	18	Edith Schultze-Westrum, Frantisek Filipovský, Ladislav Kríz
House of the Generals (2003)	US	English	7.2	17	Farah White, Michelle Irving, Elena Burunova
The House on Garibaldi Street (TV 1979)	US	English	7.1	259	Topol, Nick Mancuso, Janet Suzman
How A Hirschberger Learned Danish—Wie ein Hirschberger Dänisch lernte (TV 1968)	East Germany	German	--	--	Josef Schaper, Ruth Hellberg, Günther Wille
I Do Not Care If We Go Down in History as Barbarians—Îmi este indiferent daca in istorie vom intra ca barbari (2018)	Romania–Czech Republic–Germany–Bulgaria–France	Romanian	7.3	1096	Ioana Iacob, Alex Bogdan, Alexandru Dabija
I Know Why I Live—Ich weiß, wofür ich lebe (1955)	West Germany	German	6.0	6	Luise Ullrich, Robert Freitag, Lil Dagover
I Was Overtaken by Night—Zastihla me noc (1986)	Czechoslovakia	Czech	7.0	40	Jana Riháková, Jana Brejchová, Rudolf Hrusínský
Ida (2013)	Poland	Polish	7.4	43090	Agata Kulesza, Agata Trzebuchowska, Dawid Ogrodnik
The Illegals—Lo Tafhidenu (1947)	Israel	Hebrew	3.5	6	Dahn Ben Amotz, Yankel Mikalovitch, Tereska Torres
I'm Alive and I Love You—Je suis vivante et je vous aime (1998)	France	French	5.8	65	Jérôme Deschamps, Dorian Lambert, Agnès Soral
In Another Lifetime—Vielleicht in einem anderen Leben (2011)	Austria–Germany–Hungary	German, Hungarian, Yiddish	6.6	63	Ursula Strauss, Johannes Krisch, Orsolya Tóth
In Darkness (2011)	Poland–Germany–Canada	Polish	7.3	9042	Robert Wieckiewicz, Benno Fürmann, Agnieszka Grochowska
In Hiding—W ukryciu (2013)	Poland	Polish	5.6	207	Magdalena Boczarska, Julia Pogrebinska, Tomasz Kot
In the End Come Tourists—Am Ende kommen Touristen (2007)	Germany	German	6.9	993	Alexander Fehling, Ryszard Ronczewski, Barbara Wysocka
In the Presence of Mine Enemies (TV 1997)	US	English	6.1	274	Armin Mueller-Stahl, Charles Dance, Elina Löwensohn
In the Shadow of Hate—W cieniu nienawisci (TV 1986)	Poland	Polish	5.1	10	Bozena Adamek, Henryk Bista, Barbara Brylska
Inglourious Basterds (2009)	US	English	8.3	1061435	Brad Pitt, Diane Kruger, Eli Roth

Title	Country	Language	IMDb Rating	IMDb Votes	Top-Billed Cast
~~The Interpreter—Tlmočník (2018)~~	Slovakia–Czech Republic–Austria	Slovene	6.7	441	Peter Simonischek, Jiří Menzel, Zuzana Mauréry
~~The Interrogation (2016)~~	Israel–Germany	German, Polish	6.9	61	Joan Blackham, Romanus Fuhrmann, Maciej Marczewski
The Investigation—Die Ermittlung (TV 1966)	West Germany	German	9.3	23	Horst Beck, Karl Bockx, Viktor Stefan Görtz
Invincible (2001)	US–UK–Germany–Ireland	English	6.5	3787	Jouko Ahola, Tim Roth, Anna Gourari
Invitation—Zaproszenie (1986)	Poland	Polish	5.9	7	Antonina Gordon-Górecka, Maria Probosz, Kazimierz Witkiewicz
The Island on Bird Street (1997)	Denmark	English	7.2	1208	Patrick Bergin, Jordan Kiziuk, Jack Warden
It Will Never Happen Again— Unzere Kinder (1951)	Poland	Yiddish	7.0	18	Shimen Dzigan, Ysrael Szumacher, Niusia Gold
Jacob the Liar—Jakob, der Lügner (1974)	East Germany–Czechoslovakia	German	7.3	1046	Vlastimil Brodský, Erwin Geschonneck, Henry Hübchen, Armin Mueller-Stahl
Jakob the Liar (1999)	US	English	6.5	13832	Robin Williams, Hannah Taylor Gordon, Éva Igó, Armin Mueller-Stahl, Liev Schreiber, Alan Arkin
Jew Boy Levi—Viehjud Levi (1999)	Austria–Switzerland–Germany	German	7.0	159	Bruno Cathomas, Bernd Michael Lade, Ulrich Noethen
A Jewish Girl in Shanghai (2010)	China	Chinese	6.6	19	Cui Jie, Zhao Jing, Ma Shaohua
Joanna (2010)	Poland	Polish	6.9	421	Urszula Grabowska, Sara Knothe, Stanislawa Celinska
Jojo Rabbit (2019)	US	English	7.9	284013	Roman Griffin Davis, Thomasin McKenzie, Scarlett Johansson
~~Journey to Jerusalem— Patuvane kam Yerusalim (2003)~~	Bulgaria	Bulgarian	6.0	105	Elena Petrova, Aleksandr Morfov, Vasil Vasilev-Zueka
Judgment at Nuremberg (1961)	US	English	8.2	58028	Spencer Tracy, Burt Lancaster, Richard Widmark, Maximilian Schell
Judith (1966)	US–Israel–UK	English	5.6	322	Sophia Loren, Peter Finch, Jack Hawkins
The Juggler (1953)	US	English	6.5	417	Kirk Douglas, Milly Vitale, Paul Stewart

Title	Country	Language	IMDb Rating	IMDb Votes	Top-Billed Cast
Julia (1977)	US	English	7.3	7739	Jane Fonda, Vanessa Redgrave, Jason Robards, Maximilian Schell, Meryl Streep
Just an Ordinary Jew— Ein ganz gewöhnlicher Jude (2005)	Germany	German	7.0	244	Ben Becker, Siegfried Kernen, Samuel Finzi
Just Beyond That Forest— Jeszcze tylko ten las (1991)	Poland	Polish	7.5	65	Ryszarda Hanin, Joanna Friedman, Marta Klubowicz
Kapò (1960)	Italy–France–Yugoslavia	Italian	7.7	1589	Susan Strasberg, Laurent Terzieff, Emmanuelle Riva
Kapo in Jerusalem— Kapo be'Yerushalaim (2015)	Israel	Hebrew	7.4	7	Icho Avital, Abraham Celektar, Aryeh Cherner
Keep Away from the Window— Daleko od okna (2000)	Poland	Polish	6.8	143	Dorota Landowska, Dominika Ostalowska, Bartosz Opania
Korczak (1990)	Poland–Germany	Polish	7.5	905	Wojciech Pszoniak, Ewa Dalkowska, Teresa Budzisz-Krzyzanowska
Kornblumenblau (1989)	Poland	Polish	7.1	87	Adam Kamien, Marcin Tronski, Piotr Skiba
Labyrinth of Lies— Im Labyrinth Des Schweigens (2014)	Germany	German	7.3	9781	André Szymanski, Alexander Fehling, Friederike Becht
Lacombe, Lucien (1974)	France–West Germany–Italy	French, German	7.8	5542	Pierre Blaise, Aurore Clément, Holger Löwenadler
Ladies' Tailor—Damskiy portnoy (1990)	USSR	Russian	7.3	27	Innokentiy Smoktunovskiy, Tatyana Vasileva, Yelena Kozelkova
~~L'adieu aux enfants (TV 1982)~~	France	French	--	--	Herve Aiem, Stéphane Andréi, Pierre Baton
Landscape After Battle— Krajobraz po bitwie (1970)	Poland	Polish	7.1	649	Daniel Olbrychski, Stanislawa Celinska, Aleksander Bardini
~~The Last (2019)~~	US	English	3.4	59	Rebecca Schull, Jill Durso, AJ Cedeno
The Last Butterfly—Poslední motýl (1991)	Czechoslovakia–France–UK	Czech	7.0	228	Tom Courtenay, Brigitte Fossey, Ingrid Held

Title	Country	Language	IMDb Rating	IMDb Votes	Top-Billed Cast
The Last Chance—Die letzte Chance (1945)	Switzerland	German, Italian, English, French, Yiddish, Dutch, Polish	6.7	261	Ewart G. Morrison, John Hoy, Ray Reagan
The Last Hole—Das letzte Loch (1981)	West Germany	German	7.4	47	Herbert Achternbusch, Annamirl Bierbichler, Franz Baumgartner
The Last Letter—La dernière lettre (2002)	France	French	7.1	131	Catherine Samie
The Last Mensch—Der letzte Mentsch (2014)	Germany	German	6.7	141	Mario Adorf, Katharina Derr, Hannelore Elsner
The Last Metro—Le dernier métro (1980)	France	French	7.4	10565	Catherine Deneuve, Gérard Depardieu, Jean Poiret
The Last Stage—The Last Stop— Ostatni etap (1948)	Poland	Polish, Russian, German	7.1	191	Tatjana Gorecka, Antonina Gordon-Górecka, Barbara Drapinska
The Last Suit—El último traje (2017)	Argentina	Spanish	7.0	520	Miguel Ángel Solá, Ángela Molina, Martín Piroyansky
The Last Supper—Das letzte Mahl (2018)	Germany	German	8.7	383	Bruno Eyron, Sharon Brauner, Michael Degen
The Last Train—Der Letzte Zug (2006)	Germany–Czech Republic	German	6.6	1212	Gedeon Burkhard, Lale Yavas, Lena Beyerling
Late Season—Utószezon (1967)	Hungary	Hungarian	7.1	124	Antal Páger, Noémi Apor, Lajos Básti
Left Luggage (1998)	Netherlands	English	7.4	2678	Laura Fraser, Adam Monty, Isabella Rossellini, Maximilian Schell
Lena: My 100 Children (TV 1987)	US	English	6.5	116	Linda Lavin, Torquil Campbell, Lenore Harris
Leni (TV 1994)	Germany	German	9.2	12	Johannes Thanheiser, Johanna Thanheiser, Christa Berndl
Les Misérables (1995)	France	French	7.5	3425	Jean-Paul Belmondo, Michel Boujenah, Alessandra Martines
Les violons du bal (1974)	France	French	6.8	95	Jean-Louis Trintignant, Marie-José Nat, Gabrielle Doulcet
Let Me Go (2017)	UK	English	5.7	207	Juliet Stevenson, Jodhi May, Lucy Boynton

Title	Country	Language	IMDb Rating	IMDb Votes	Top-Billed Cast
~~Let's Go! (TV 2014)~~	Germany	German	6.2	33	Maxim Mehmet, Karin Hanczewski, Milton Welsh
The Life Ahead—La vita davanti a sé (2020)	US–Italy	English	6.9	4211	Renato Carpentieri, Francesco Cassano, Ibrahima Gueye
A Life Ahead—Madam Rose—Madame Rosa—La Vie devant soi (1977)	France	French	7.3	883	Simone Signoret, Michal Bat-Adam, Samy Ben-Youb
Life for Life: Maximilian Kolbe—Zycie za zycie (1991)	Poland–Germany	German	6.3	191	Edward Zentara, Christoph Waltz, Artur Barcis
Life Is Beautiful—La Vita è bella (1997)	Italy	Italian	8.6	518795	Roberto Benigni, Nicoletta Braschi, Giorgio Cantarini
~~The Light of Hope—La llum d'Elna (2017)~~	Spain–Switzerland	Spanish, Catalan, French	6.8	80	Noémie Schmidt, Nausicaa Bonnín, Natalia de Molina
Lili Marleen (1981)	West Germany	English	7.2	3227	Hanna Schygulla, Giancarlo Giannini, Mel Ferrer
Living Goods—Lebende Ware (1969)	West Germany	German	--	--	Horst Schulze, Marion van de Kamp, Hannjo Hasse
Long Is the Road—Lang ist der Weg (1949)	West Germany	German, Polish, Yiddish	7.5	25	Israel Becker, Bettina Moissi, Berta Litwina
Look to the Sky—Jona che visse nella balena (1993)	Italy–France	Italian	6.7	245	Jean-Hugues Anglade, Juliet Aubrey, Jenner Del Vecchio
Lore (2012)	Austria–Germany–UK	Polish	7.1	12986	Saskia Rosendahl, Kai-Peter Malina, Nele Trebs
~~Louise's Diary 1942—Les amours secrètes (2010)~~	France	French	5.3	32	Anémone, Deborah Durand, Grégory Barboza
A Love to Hide—Un amour à taire (TV 2005)	France	French	8.2	2636	Jérémie Renier, Louise Monot, Bruno Todeschini
~~The Lucky Star (1980)~~	Canada	English	6.5	114	Rod Steiger, Louise Fletcher, Lou Jacobi
<u>Made in Israel (2001)</u>	Israel	Hebrew	6.8	131	Menashe Noy, Evgenia Dodina, Jürgen Holtz
Malou (1981)	West Germany	German	6.9	35	Ingrid Caven, Grischa Huber, Helmut Griem
The Man in the Glass Booth (1975)	US–Italy	English	7.4	925	Maximilian Schell, Lois Nettleton, Lawrence Pressman

Title	Country	Language	IMDb Rating	IMDb Votes	Top-Billed Cast
The Man Who Captured Eichmann (TV 1996)	US	English	6.5	626	Robert Duvall, Arliss Howard, Jeffrey Tambor
Marathon Man (1976)	US	English	7.5	50533	Dustin Hoffman, Laurence Olivier, Roy Scheider
Marriage in the Shadows— Ehe im Schatten (1947)	East Germany	German	7.0	125	Paul Klinger, Ilse Steppat, Alfred Balthoff
The Martyr—Dr. Korczak and His Children—Sie sind frei, Doktor Korczak (1975)	West Germany– Israel	German	6.8	12	Leo Genn, Orna Porat, Efrat Lavie
Max (2002)	UK–Hungary– Canada	English	6.6	6807	John Cusack, Noah Taylor, Leelee Sobieski
Max and Helen (TV 1990)	US–UK	English	6.7	134	Treat Williams, Alice Krige, Martin Landau
Max and Helen—Max e Hélène (TV 2015)	Italy	English	6.1	141	Alessandro Averone, Carolina Crescentini, Ennio Fantastichini
Me and the Colonel (1958)	US	English	7.0	544	Danny Kaye, Curd Jürgens, Nicole Maurey
Memories of Anne Frank— Mi ricordo Anna Frank (TV 2009)	Italy	Italian	5.9	207	Rosabell Laurenti Sellers, Emilio Solfrizzi, István Hirtling
The Memory Thief (2007)	US	English	5.8	217	Mark Webber, Rachel Miner, Jerry Adler
Mendel (1997)	Norway	Norwegian	6.4	189	Thomas Jüngling Sørensen, Teresa Harder, Hans Kremer
Miracle at Midnight (TV 1998)	US	English	7.1	320	Sam Waterston, Mia Farrow, Justin Whalin
Miracle at Moreaux (TV 1986)	US–Canada	English	7.6	92	Loretta Swit, Robert Joy, Ken Pogue
Mr. Klein—Monsieur Klein (1976)	France	French	7.6	4408	Alain Delon, Jeanne Moreau, Francine Bergé
Monastero di Santa Chiara (1949)	Italy	Italian	--	--	Edda Albertini, Massimo Serato, Nyta Dover
Monsieur Batignole (2002)	France	French	7.0	2924	Jules Sitruk, Gérard Jugnot, Michèle Garcia
Morituri (1948)	West Germany	German	7.1	48	Lotte Koch, Hilde Körber, Winnie Markus
The Mover (2018)	Latvia	Latvian, Russian, German, Yiddish	7.2	385	Arturs Skrastins, Ilze Blauberga, Matiss Kipluks

Title	Country	Language	IMDb Rating	IMDb Votes	Top-Billed Cast
Murderers Among Us— *Die Mörder sind unter uns* (1946)	East Germany	German	7.5	1698	Hildegard Knef, Elly Burgmer, Erna Sellmer
Murderers Among Us: The Simon Wiesenthal Story (TV 1989)	US	English	7.6	268	Ben Kingsley, Renée Soutendijk, Craig T. Nelson
~~Murer: Anatomy of a Trial— Murer: Anatomie eines Prozesses (2018)~~	Austria– Luxembourg	German, Yiddish, Hebrew	7.2	394	Ursula Ofner, Karl Fischer, Alexander E. Fennon
Music Box (1989)	US	English	7.3	5940	Jessica Lange, Armin Mueller-Stahl, Frederic Forrest
My Daughter Anne Frank— Meine Tochter Anne Frank (TV 2015)	Germany	German	6.5	170	Mala Emde, Götz Schubert, Lion Wasczyk
~~My Father's House—Beit Avi (1947)~~	Israel	English	4.8	6	Y. Adaki, Irene Broza, Michael Cohen
My Führer—Mein Führer— Die wirklich wahrste Wahrheit über Adolf Hitler (2007)	Germany	German	5.4	3728	Helge Schneider, Ulrich Mühe, Sylvester Groth
My Mother's Courage— *Mutters Courage* (1995)	UK–Germany– Austria–Ireland	English	6.9	164	Pauline Collins, George Tabori, Ulrich Tukur
Naked Among Wolves— *Nackt unter Wölfen* (1963)	East Germany	German	7.3	632	Erwin Geschonneck, Armin Mueller-Stahl, Krystyn Wójcik
Naked Among Wolves— *Nackt unter Wölfen* (TV 2015)	Germany	German	7.2	3087	Florian Stetter, Peter Schneider, Sylvester Groth
The Nasty Girl— *Das schreckliche Mädchen* (1990)	West Germany	German	7.4	2195	Lena Stolze, Hans-Reinhard Müller, Monika Baumgartner
~~Natalia (1988)~~	France	French	5.1	19	Pierre Arditi, Philippine Leroy-Beaulieu, Gérard Blain
Never Forget (TV 1991)	US	English	6.9	230	Leonard Nimoy, Dabney Coleman, Blythe Danner
Newland—Aretz Hadasha (1994)	Israel	Hebrew	6.7	52	Etti Ankri, Louise Asher, Gedalia Besser
The Night Porter—Il portiere di notte (1974)	US–Italy	Italian	6.8	9524	Dirk Bogarde, Charlotte Rampling, Philippe Leroy
Nina's Journey—La Maison De Nina (2005)	Poland–Sweden	Polish, Swedish	6.7	330	Agnieszka Grochowska, Maria Chwalibóg, Andrzej Brzeski
_1945 (2017)_	Hungary	Hungarian	7.3	1578	Péter Rudolf, Bence Tasnádi, Tamás Szabó Kimmel

Title	Country	Language	IMDb Rating	IMDb Votes	Top-Billed Cast
The Ninth Circle—Deveti krug (1960)	Yugoslavia	Croatian	8.0	293	Dusica Zegarac, Boris Dvornik, Branko Tatic
Nippon no Shindorâ: Sugihara Chiune monogatari (TV 2005)	Japan	Japanese	--	--	Takashi Sorimachi, Naoko Iijima, Kazue Fukiishi
Not All Were Murderers— Nicht alle waren Mörder (TV 2006)	Germany	German	7.2	275	Nadja Uhl, Aaron Altaras, Hannelore Elsner
November Moon—Novembermond (1985)	Germany–France	German	5.8	181	Maurice Arama, Daniel Berlioux, Denise Boulet
Nowhere in Africa— Nirgendwo in Afrika (2001)	Germany	English	7.6	11465	Juliane Köhler, Merab Ninidze, Matthias Habich
Nuremberg (TV 2000)	US–Canada	English	7.4	5018	Alec Baldwin, Brian Cox, Christopher Plummer
The Odessa File (1974)	US– West Germany	English	7.0	8647	Jon Voight, Maximilian Schell, Maria Schell
Of a Thousand Delights—Sandra— Vaghe stelle dell'Orsa... (1965)	Italy	Italian	7.2	1685	Claudia Cardinale, Jean Sorel, Michael Craig
Olga (2004)	Brazil	Portuguese	6.5	2808	Camila Morgado, Caco Ciocler, Luís Melo
One Day You'll Understand— Plus tard (2008)	France	French	5.7	298	Jeanne Moreau, Hippolyte Girardot, Emmanuelle Devos
The Only Way (1970)	US	English	6.2	115	Ebbe Rode, Helle Virkner, Jane Seymour
Operation Eichmann (1961)	US	English	6.3	254	Werner Klemperer, Ruta Lee, Donald Buka
Operation Finale (2018)	US	English	6.7	1115	Oscar Isaac, Ben Kingsley, Mélanie Laurent
Operation Stadium—Akcija Stadion (1977)	Yugoslavia	Serbo-Croatian	6.5	106	Igor Galo, Franjo Majetic, Zvonimir Crnko
~~*Our Father in Heaven—Otche nash— Pater Noster* (1989)~~	USSR	Russian	7.5	20	Margarita Terekhova, Aleksandr Ignatyev, Valentin Nikulin
Out of Evil—Mi Klalah L'Brahah (1950)	Israel	Hebrew	--	--	Mordechai Ben-Ze'ev, Nahum Buchman, Roberta Hodes
Out of the Ashes (TV 2003)	US	English	6.9	995	Christine Lahti, Bruce Davison, Jonathan Cake

Title	Country	Language	IMDb Rating	IMDb Votes	Top-Billed Cast
The Painted Bird (2019)	Czech Republic–Slovakia–Ukraine	Slovak	7.3	627	Harvey Keitel, Stellan Skarsgård, Barry Pepper
Passenger—Pasazerka (TV 1963)	Poland	Polish	7.6	1229	Aleksandra Slaska, Anna Ciepielewska, Jan Kreczmar
The Passerby—La passante du Sans-Souci (1982)	France–West Germany	French	6.8	751	Romy Schneider, Michel Piccoli, Helmut Griem
Past Life (2016)	Israel	Hebrew	6.4	503	Nelly Tagar, Joy Rieger, Doron Tavory
The Pawnbroker (1964)	US	English	7.8	6981	Rod Steiger, Geraldine Fitzgerald, Brock Peters
The People vs. Fritz Bauer—Der Staat gegen Fritz Bauer (2015)	Germany	German	7.1	3196	Rüdiger Klink, Burghart Klaußner, Andrej Kaminsky
Perlasca. The Courage of a Just Man—Perlasca. Un eroe italiano (TV 2002)	Italy	Italian	7.2	473	Luca Zingaretti, Jérôme Anger, Amanda Sandrelli
Persian Lessons (2020)	Belarus	English, French, German, Italian, Persian	7.1	499	Nahuel Pérez Biscayart, Lars Eidinger, Jonas Nay
Persona Non Grata—Sugihara Chiune (2015)	Japan	Japanese	6.4	157	Toshiaki Karasawa, Koyuki, Borys Szyc
Phoenix (2014)	Germany	German, English	7.3	13628	Nina Hoss, Ronald Zehrfeld, Nina Kunzendorf
The Pianist (2002)	US	English	8.5	603378	Adrien Brody, Thomas Kretschmann, Frank Finla
Playing for Time (TV 1980)	US	English	7.7	1479	Vanessa Redgrave, Jane Alexander, Maud Adams
The Poet—Hearts of War (2007)	Canada	English	5.2	936	Jonathan Scarfe, Nina Dobrev, Zachary Bennett
Postcard from a Journey—Kartka z podrózy (1984)	Poland	Polish	5.4	22	Wladyslaw Kowalski, Rafal Wieczynski, Maja Komorowska
The Pracht Inn (2014)	Israel	Hebrew	5.6	10	Michaela Elkin, Michaela Eshet, Vladimir Friedman
Prague (1992)	UK	English	6.4	67	Alan Cumming, Sandrine Bonnaire, Bruno Ganz
Prayer for Katerina Horovitzova—Modlitba pro Katerinu Horovitzovou (TV 1965)	Czechoslovakia	Czech	8.0	63	Jirí Adamíra, Jirí Bruder, Lenka Fiserová
Primo (TV 2005)	UK	English	7.3	138	Antony Sher

Title	Country	Language	IMDb Rating	IMDb Votes	Top-Billed Cast
Private Resistance—De ijssalon (1985)	Netherlands	Dutch	6.4	149	Gerard Thoolen, Bruno Ganz, Renée Soutendijk
Professor Mamlock (1961)	East Germany	German	7.0	105	Wolfgang Heinz, Ursula Burg, Hilmar Thate
Protector—Protektor (2009)	Czech Republic	Czech, German	7.2	772	Matthias Brandt, Jan Budar, David Czesany
Punch Me in the Stomach (1997)	US	English	5.8	6	Deb Filler, Francine Zuckerman
The Quarrel (1991)	Canada	English	7.0	232	R.H. Thomson, Saul Rubinek, Merlee Shapiro
~~Quezon's Game (2018)~~	Philippines	English	8.3	81	Raymond Bagatsing, Rachel Alejandro, Kate Alejandrino
Raindrops—Regentropfen (1981)	West Germany	German	6.1	8	Elfriede Irrall, Walter Renneisen, Jack Geula
The Reader (2008)	US	English	7.6	211305	Kate Winslet, Ralph Fiennes, Bruno Ganz
Redemption Road—Landgericht (TV 2017)	Germany	German	7.1	198	Ronald Zehrfeld, Johanna Wokalek, Saskia Reeves
The Relief of Belsen (TV 2007)	UK	English	7.3	252	Iain Glen, Nigel Lindsay, Jemma Redgrave
Remember (2015)	Canada–Germany	English	7.4	17467	Christopher Plummer, Kim Roberts, Amanda Smith, Martin Landau
Remember Your Name—Pomni imya svoye (1974)	Poland–USSR	Polish	7.5	88	Lyudmila Kasatkina, Tadeusz Borowski, Ryszarda Hanin
Remembrance—Die verlorene Zeit (2011)	Germany	German, Polish, English	7.2	1781	Alice Dwyer, Mateusz Damiecki, Dagmar Manzel
Remembrance of Love (TV 1982)	US	English	6.4	76	Kirk Douglas, Robert Clary, Pam Dawber
The Resistance—The Invisibles—Die Unsichtbaren (2017)	Germany	German	7.1	906	Max Mauff, Alice Dwyer, Ruby O. Fee
Resistance (2020)	US–UK–Germany	English	6.2	3265	Jesse Eisenberg, Clémence Poésy, Matthias Schweighöfer
Return from the Ashes (1965)	UK	English	7.0	633	Maximilian Schell, Samantha Eggar, Ingrid Thulin
The Revolt of Job—Jób lázadása (1983)	Hungary	Hungarian	7.6	414	Hédi Temessy, Ferenc Zenthe, Gábor Fehér

Title	Country	Language	IMDb Rating	IMDb Votes	Top-Billed Cast
Riphagen—Riphagen: The Untouchable (2016)	Netherlands	Dutch	7.1	6161	Sigrid ten Napel, Huub Smit, Steef de Bot
Romeo, Juliet and Darkness—Romeo, Julie a tma (1960)	Czechoslovakia	Czech	7.5	320	Ivan Mistrík, Daniela Smutná, Jirina Sejbalová
The Rose Garden—The Rosegarden (1989)	US–West Germany–Austria	English	7.0	316	Liv Ullmann, Maximilian Schell, Peter Fonda
~~*A Rose in Winter* (2018)~~	US	English	5.6	26	Zana Marjanovic, Christian Cooke, Ken Duken
Rosenstrasse (2003)	Germany	German	6.8	2132	Katja Riemann, Maria Schrader, Svea Lohde
Rose's Songs—A Rózsa énekei (2003)	Hungary	Hungarian	6.6	134	Franco Castellano, Viktor Baradlay, David Zum
The Round Up—La rafle (2010)	France	French	7.0	7405	Jean Reno, Mélanie Laurent, Gad Elmaleh
Rua Alguem 5555: My Father (2003)	Italy	English	6.7	195	Thomas Kretschmann, Charlton Heston, F. Murray Abraham
Run Boy Run—Lauf Junge lauf (2013)	Germany–France–Poland	German, Polish, Yiddish, Russian	7.1	1434	Andrzej Tkacz, Kamil Tkacz, Elisabeth Duda
Salad Days—Zielone lata (1980)	Poland	Polish	6.3	10	Tomasz Jarosinski, Jacek Bryniarski, Agnieszka Konopczynska
Samson (1961)	Poland	Polish	6.4	146	Serge Merlin, Alina Janowska, Elzbieta Kepinska
The Samuel Project (2018)	US	English	7.3	101	Liza Lapira, Ken Davitian, Hal Linden
Sarah and the Squirrel—The Seventh Match (1982)	Australia	English	7.0	47	Mia Farrow, Joan Bruce, John Faasen
Sarah's Key—Elle s'appelait Sarah (2010)	France	French	7.5	14705	Kristin Scott Thomas, Mélusine Mayance, Niels Arestrup
Saviors in the Night—Unter Bauern (2009)	Germany–France	German	6.4	244	Veronica Ferres, Armin Rohde, Lia Perez
The Scarlet and the Black (TV 1983)	US	English	7.7	2279	Gregory Peck, Christopher Plummer, John Gielgud
Schindler's List (1993)	US	English	8.9	1026681	Liam Neeson, Ralph Fiennes, Ben Kingsley

Title	Country	Language	IMDb Rating	IMDb Votes	Top-Billed Cast
The Search (1948)	US–Switzerland	English	7.9	3317	Montgomery Clift, Ivan Jandl, Aline MacMahon
A Secret—Un secret (2007)	France	French	6.8	2774	Cécile de France, Patrick Bruel, Ludivine Sagnier
Sergeant Schmidt—Feldwebel Schmid (TV 1968)	West Germany	German	9.3	6	Karl Michael Vogler, Sylvie Beck, Helmut Förnbacher
Seven Journeys—In Those Days— In jenen Tagen (1947)	Germany	German	7.4	271	Gert Schäfer, Erich Schellow, Winnie Markus
The 17th Bride—Ha-Kala (1985)	Israel	English	4.7	18	Lisa Hartman, Rosemary Leach, John Grillo
The Seventh Room—A hetedik szoba (1996)	Italy–Hungary	Hungarian	6.9	124	Maia Morgenstern, Elide Melli, Jan Nowicki
~~*Shades of Truth* (2015)~~	Italy–UK	Italian	5.7	34	Christopher Lambert, Giancarlo Giannini, Gedeon Burkhard
~~*Shepherd: The Hero Dog* (2019)~~	US–Hungary	English	4.6	141	August Maturo, Ken Duken, Ayelet Zurer
Shine (1996)	Australia	English	7.7	47314	Geoffrey Rush, Armin Mueller-Stahl, Justin Braine
Ship of Fools (1965)	US	English	7.2	4402	Vivien Leigh, Simone Signoret, José Ferrer
The Shop on Main Street— Obchod na korze (1965)	Czechoslovakia	Slovak	8.1	6913	Ida Kaminska, Jozef Kroner, Hana Slivková
Simon Konianski (2009)	Belgium–France– Canada	Italian	6.2	264	Jonathan Zaccaï, Popeck, Nassim Ben Abdelmoumen
The Singing Forest (2003)	US	English	1.8	527	Jon Sherrin, Erin Leigh Price, Eric Morris
Singing in the Dark (1956)	US	English	6.9	7	Moyshe Oysher, Phyllis Hill, Joey Adams
Skipper Next to God— Maître après Dieu (1951)	France	French	6.8	12	Pierre Brasseur, Jacques François, Jean Mercure
Skokie—Once They Marched Through a Thousand Towns (TV 1981)	US	English	7.3	306	Danny Kaye, John Rubinstein, Carl Reiner
The Sky Is Falling—Il cielo cade (2000)	Italy	Italian	6.6	404	Isabella Rossellini, Jeroen Krabbé, Barbara Enrichi
Sobibor (2018)	Russia	Russian, German, Polish, Yiddish	6.4	770	Konstantin Khabenskiy, Christopher Lambert, Mariya Kozhevnikova

Title	Country	Language	IMDb Rating	IMDb Votes	Top-Billed Cast
Son of Saul (2015)	Hungary	German, Hungarian, Polish, Yiddish, Russian, Slovak, Czech, Greek	7.5	36269	Géza Röhrig, Levente Molnár, Urs Rechn
The Song and the Silence (1968)	US	English	--	--	Mary Antoianette, Nana Austin, Felix Fibich
~~*The Song of Names* (2019)~~	Canada–Germany–Hungary–UK	English	6.4	2328	Eddie Izzard, Gerran Howell, Stanley Townsend
Sophie's Choice (1982)	US	English	7.6	34643	Meryl Streep, Kevin Kline, Peter MacNicol
Spring 1941 (2007)	Poland	English	5.9	512	Katarzyna Al Abbas, Miroslaw Baka, Stanislaw Brejdygant, Joseph Fiennes
Spring of Life—Pramen zivota (TV 2000)	Czech Republic	Czech	6.8	290	Monika Hilmerová, Michal Sieczkowski, Johana Tesarová
Springtime in Budapest— Budapesti tavasz (1955)	Hungary	Hungarian	7.0	88	ábor Rajnay, Miklós Gábor, Mária Mezei
The Square of St. Elizabeth— Námestie svätej Alzbety (1966)	Slovenia	Slovene	7.0	23	Emília Vásáryová, Bronislav Krizan, Ctibor Filcík
Stars—Sterne (1959)	East Germany–Bulgaria	German, Bulgarian, Ladino	7.5	259	Shimen Dzigan, Ysrael Szumacher, Niusia Gold
The Statement (2003)	US–UK–Canada–France	English	6.2	4522	Michael Caine, Tilda Swinton, Alan Bates, Charlotte Rampling
Stielke, Heinz, Fifteen— Stielke, Heinz, fünfzehn… (1987)	East Germany	German	6.9	18	Marc Lubosch, Jens Müller, Gert Gütschow
~~*A Story About a Bad Dream* (2000)~~	Czech Republic	Czech	--	--	--
~~*The Story of a Murder= Chronik eines Mordes* (1965)~~	East Germany	German	7.6	15	Angelica Domröse, Ulrich Thein, Jirí Vrstála
The Stranger (1946)	US	English	7.4	16421	Orson Welles, Edward G. Robinson, Loretta Young
~~*Stream Line=La linea del fiume* (1976)~~	Italy	Italian	5.3	18	Philippe Leroy, Riccardo Cucciolla, Lea Massari
The Substance of Fire (1996)	US	English	5.9	565	Tony Goldwyn, Benjamin Ungar, Timothy Hutton
The Summer of Aviya— Ha-Kayitz Shel Aviya (1988)	Israel	Hebrew, Polish	7.1	322	Gila Almagor, Kaipu Cohen, Eli Cohen

Title	Country	Language	IMDb Rating	IMDb Votes	Top-Billed Cast
Sunshine (1999)	Germany–Austria–Hungary–Canada	English	7.5	12067	Ralph Fiennes, Rosemary Harris, Rachel Weisz
Surviving with Wolves—Survivre avec les loups (2007)	Belgium–France	French	6.7	854	Mathilde Goffart, Yaël Abecassis, Guy Bedos
Süskind (2012)	Netherlands	Dutch, German	6.9	1916	Jeroen Spitzenberger, Karl Markovics, Nyncke Beekhuyzen
The Taras' Family—The Unvanquished—Nepokoryonnye (1945)	USSR	Russian	7.2	26	Amvrosi Buchma, Venyamin Zuskin, Lidiya Kartashyova
~~A Tear in the Ocean—Une larme dans l'océan (1973)~~	France	French	8.6	10	Alexandre Stere, Dominique Rollin, Armand Abplanalp
~~Tel Aviv-Berlin (1987)~~	Israel	Hebrew	7.6	5	Zohar Aloni, Yosef Carmon, Anatol Constantin
Temporary Paradise—Ideiglenes paradicsom (1981)	Hungary	Hungarian	7.8	10	André Dussollier, Edit Frajt, László Szabó
~~The Testament (2017)~~	Israel	Hebrew	7.0	354	Ori Pfeffer, Rivka Gur, Hagit Dasberg
~~There Is Many Like Us (2015)~~	US–Canada–Israel	English	8.2	92	Eric Roberts, Tyler Mauro, Kayleigh Gilbert
The Third Half—Treto poluvreme (2012)	Macedonia	Macedonian, German	7.9	7912	Katarina Ivanovska, Sasko Kocev, Richard Sammel
~~38 (1986)~~	West Germany–Austria	German	6.4	127	Tobias Engel, Sunnyi Melles, Heinz Trixner
36 Hours (1964)	US	English	7.4	3191	James Garner, Eva Marie Saint, Rod Taylor
This Boat Is Full—Das Boot ist voll (1981)	Switzerland	German	7.2	426	Tina Engel, Hans Diehl, Martin Walz
This Must Be the Place (2011)	Italy–France–Ireland	English	6.7	29463	Sean Penn, Frances McDormand, Judd Hirsch
Those Who Remained—Akik maradtak (2019)	Hungary	Hungarian	7.2	998	Károly Hajduk, Abigél Szőke, Mari Nagy
Three Days in April—Drei Tage im April (TV 1995)	Germany	German	7.6	60	Karoline Eichhorn, April Hailer, Eva Michel
~~Toman (2018)~~	Czech Republic–Slovakia	Czech	6.5	309	Jirí Machácek, Katerina Winterová, Stanislav Majer
Tomorrow's a Wonderful Day—Adamah (1947)	Israel	Hebrew	7.3	25	Sam Balter, Benjamin Hildesheimer, Jimmie Lipton

Title	Country	Language	IMDb Rating	IMDb Votes	Top-Billed Cast
Train of Life—Train de vie (1998)	France–Belgium–Netherlands–Israel–Romania	French	7.7	8026	Lionel Abelanski, Rufus, Clément Harari
~~Transit (1980)~~	Israel	Hebrew	6.7	9	Fitcho Ben-Zur, Gedalia Besser, Yair Elazar
Treason—Prodosia (1964)	Greece	Greek	7.1	66	Petros Fyssoun, Manos Katrakis, Dimitris Myrat
Triumph of the Spirit (1989)	US	English	6.9	1932	Willem Dafoe, Edward James Olmos, Robert Loggia
The Truce—La tregua (1997)	Italy	English	6.7	1415	John Turturro, Rade Serbedzija, Massimo Ghini
The 25th Hour—La vingt-cinquième heure (1967)	France–Italy–Yugoslavia	French, English, Romanian	7.6	1504	Anthony Quinn, Virna Lisi, Grégoire Aslan
25 Firemen's Street—Tüzoltó utca 25. (1973)	Hungary	Hungarian	6.7	252	Lucyna Winnicka, Margit Makay, Károly Kovács
Twist of Fate—Pursuit (TV 1989)	UK	English	7.4	291	Branko Blace, Mirko Boman, Trevor Byfield
Two Men (TV 1988)	Canada	English	5.6	5	Martha Gibson, Lila Kedrova, Anne Kokot
The Two of Us—Le vieil homme et l'enfant (1967)	France	French	7.8	1639	Michel Simon, Roger Carel, Paul Préboist
The Unborn (2009)	US	English	4.8	45763	Odette Annable, Gary Oldman, Cam Gigandet
Under the Domim Tree—Etz Hadomim Tafus (1994)	Israel	Hebrew	7.2	202	Gila Almagor, Juliano Mer-Khamis, Uri Avrahami
Unfair Competition—Concorrenza sleale (2001)	Italy	Italian	6.9	1274	Diego Abatantuono, Sergio Castellitto, Gérard Depardieu
Uprising (TV 2001)	US	English	7.3	4256	Leelee Sobieski, Hank Azaria, David Schwimmer, Jon Voight
Valentina's Mother—Ima shel Valentina (2008)	Israel	Hebrew	6.2	8	Eyal Cohen, Silvia Drori, Liat Ekta
Varian's War: The Forgotten Hero (TV 2001)	US–UK–Canada	English	6.4	755	William Hurt, Howard Ryshpan, Carol Shamy, Alan Arkin
Victor Young Perez (2013)	France	French	6.3	480	Brahim Asloum, Steve Suissa, Isabella de Ligne-La Trémoïlle

Title	Country	Language	IMDb Rating	IMDb Votes	Top-Billed Cast
Voyage of the Damned (1976)	UK	English	6.5	2154	Faye Dunaway, Oskar Werner, Lee Grant
~~*Voyages* (1999)~~	France	French	7.1	304	Shulamit Adar, Liliane Rovère, Esther Gorintin
Walk on Water (2004)	Israel	English	7.4	6205	Lior Ashkenazi, Knut Berger, Caroline Peters
Walking with the Enemy (2013)	US	English	6.4	1949	Jonas Armstrong, Ben Kingsley, Hannah Tointon
The Wall (TV 1982)	US	English	7.0	172	Tom Conti, Lisa Eichhorn, Gerald Hiken
Wallenberg—A Hero's Story (TV 1985)	US	English	7.4	305	Richard Chamberlain, Alice Krige, Kenneth Colley
The Wandering Jew—L'ebreo errante (1948)	Italy	Italian	7.7	18	Vittorio Gassman, Valentina Cortese, Inga Gort
War and Love (1985)	US–Israel	English	7.7	42	Sebastian Keneas, Kyra Sedgwick, David Spielberg
Warsaw: Year 5703— Warszawa. Année 5703 (1992)	Poland–West Germany–France	German	6.4	120	Lambert Wilson, Hanna Schygulla, Julie Delpy
The Wave (TV 1981)	US	English	7.1	2704	Bruce Davison, Lori Lethin, John Putch
~~*Welcome in Vienna— Wohin und zurück* (1986)~~	Austria	German	7.7	96	Valda Aviks, Gabriel Barylli, Monica Bleibtreu
~~*We'll Go to the City— Andremo in città* (1966)~~	Italy–Yugoslavia	Italian	6.4	73	Geraldine Chaplin, Nino Castelnuovo, Federico Scrobogna
When Day Breaks—Kad svane dan (2012)	Serbia	Serbian	7.1	634	Mustafa Nadarevic, Predrag Ejdus, Meto Jovanovski
~~*When Hitler Stole Pink Rabbit— Als Hitler das rosa Kaninchen stahl* (2019)~~	Germany–Switzerland	German	7.1	1054	Riva Krymalowski, Marinus Hohmann, Carla Juri
~~*Where to and Back—Part 1: God Doesn't Believe in Us—Ferry or How It Was—Wohin und zurück—Teil 1: An uns glaubt Gott nicht mehr—Ferry oder Wie es war* (TV 1982)~~	Austria	German	7.8	127	Johannes Silberschneider, Barbara Petritsch, Armin Mueller-Stahl
Who Will Write Our History (2018)	US	English	7.8	48	Jowita Budnik, Piotr Glowacki, Piotr Jankowski
Witness Out of Hell— Zeugin aus der Hölle (1966)	West Germany	German	7.2	46	Irene Papas, Daniel Gélin, Heinz Drache

Title	Country	Language	IMDb Rating	IMDb Votes	Top-Billed Cast
~~Witnesses—Svideteli (2018)~~	Russia–Belarus–Ukraine–Poland–France–Czech Republic–Israel	Russian	6.8	98	Oksana Fandera, Filipp Yankovskiy, Lenn Kudrjawizki
Woman in Gold (2015)	US–UK	English	7.3	45904	Helen Mirren, Ryan Reynolds, Daniel Brühl
A Woman's Pale Blue Handwriting—Eine blaßblaue Frauenschrift (TV 1984)	Austria	English	8.3	67	Friedrich von Thun, Gabriel Barylli, Krystyna Janda
The Wooden Gun—Roveh Huliot (1979)	Israel	Hebrew	6.6	61	Nadav Brenner, Nissim Eliaz, Michael Kafir
Wunderkinder (2011)	Germany	German	6.8	703	Gedeon Burkhard, Catherine Flemming, Natalia Avelon
X-Men (2000)	US	English	7.4	515161	Patrick Stewart, Hugh Jackman, Ian McKellen
X-Men: First Class (2011)	US	English	7.7	586020	James McAvoy, Michael Fassbender, Jennifer Lawrence
The Zookeeper's Wife (2017)	US–UK	English	7.0	27472	Jessica Chastain, Johan Heldenbergh, Daniel Brühl

List of Holocaust Films
(Summaries and MPAA or Equivalent Ratings)

Note: Summaries are reproduced from the sources indicated in brackets, with spellings Americanized and various small errors corrected. In translated summaries, some additional editing has been done for clarity.

Recommended in **Bold** (52). "One of the Best" in **Bold and Underlined** (15). Unavailable films in ~~Strikeout~~ (48). At publication time, most films in strikeout are functionally unavailable. This status may change for a few films that may become digitized and made available online. However, the vast majority of the unavailable titles were never reproduced after their initial limited release.

Title	Summary	MPAA or Local Rating
~~Abraham's Gold (1990)~~	[Yad Vashem] A chest full of gold teeth extracted from Holocaust victims reveals terrible secrets. This revelation forever changes the lives of Abraham, his family members and other inhabitants of a sleepy village in Bavaria. The hero of the film, Hunzinger, arrives with his friend in Poland. Their final destination—Auschwitz is carefully kept secret. Hunzinger was a guard in Auschwitz during the German occupation of Poland and he's buried there a box with golden teeth of the victims.	Unrated
A Woman's Pale Blue Handwriting—Eine blaßblaue Frauenschrift (TV 1984) — *Across the Waters—Fuglene over sundet (2016)*	[Wikipedia, translated from Danish] The year is 1943, and Arne Itkin is a famous Jewish jazz musician who lives in Copenhagen with his wife Miriam and their 5-year-old son Jacob. Rumors are beginning to circulate that the Germans will deport all Danish Jews, and *(cont.)*	15

Title	Summary	MPAA or Local Rating
	as this becomes a reality, the family must flee their homes. They are told that they can be sailed to Sweden from Gilleleje by local fishermen, but local collaborators and the Gestapo quickly get on the trail of them. Now it's about survival for the little family, who hope the people who can help are trustworthy.	
~~The Actress—Die Schauspielerin~~ ~~(1988)~~	[Wikipedia, translated from German] Maria Rheine, actress at a provincial theater, falls in love with her colleague Mark Löwenthal. To show him this, she accuses him on the rehearsal stage of only marking and not playing with the heart in a shared love scene in the play *Amphitryon*. During the next rehearsal of the scene, the two get closer and become a couple. They now spend their free time together, going for a walk and swimming. During a walk in early April 1933, Maria wanted to buy a pair of shoes in a Jewish shoe shop that was guarded by an SA man because of the boycott of the Jews. Since Mark himself is Jewish, he does not want to provoke this and pulls Maria away from the business.	15
Adam Resurrected (2008)	[Wikipedia] The film, part of which is told through a series of flashbacks, follows the story of Adam Stein, a charismatic patient of a fictitious psychiatric asylum for Holocaust survivors in Israel, in 1961. Adam was a comedian in Berlin prior to the Second World War, during which he was sent to a concentration camp. Adam manages to survive the war only because his pre-war act was recalled by an SS officer, who takes Adam as his "pet," insisting he act like a dog. His humiliation was his ticket to survival, as he was even forced to play the fiddle as his wife and daughter were led to the gas chambers. While he is outwardly charming and witty, Adam is tormented by survivor's guilt and delusions that he is a dog.	R for some disturbing behavior, sexuality, nudity and some language.
Adolf Eichmann (2007)	[Wikipedia] The film is based on manuscripts of the interrogations of Adolf Eichmann before he was tried and hanged in a prison in Israel. Eichmann recounts events from his past to a young Israeli officer, Captain Avner Less, who is faced with the immense task of tricking the skilled manipulator into self-incrimination. While the world waits, Less's countrymen call for immediate execution, forcing him and Eichmann to confront each other in a battle of wills.	TV-MA
~~After the Truth—~~ ~~Nichts als die Wahrheit (1999)~~	[Wikipedia] The infamous Nazi doctor Josef Mengele, who performed unethical medical experiments and is considered to be personally responsible for the selection of mass groups of detainees to be murdered in the gas chambers at the Auschwitz concentration camp, comes back from his hideout in Argentina as an 87-year-old man who is in his last days. Back in Germany, he must face trial for his crimes. Peter Rohm, a young solicitor and expert on Mengele, has to defend him. But Rohm feels unable to do so; when he decides to take on the case he endangers not only the relationship to his wife but also their very lives.	Unrated

Title	Summary	MPAA or Local Rating
After Your Decrees aka *Fair Game—Wedle wyroków twoich...* (1984)	[Yad Vashem] In this drama, a German-Polish copro-duction, a young Jewish girl in Nazi occupied Poland during WWII tries to escape the Nazi persecution. The film contains short segments of archival films from the period of the Holocaust.	Unrated (PG)
Aftermath—Poklosie (2012)	[Wikipedia] The fictional Holocaust-related thriller and drama is inspired by the July 1941 Jedwabne pogrom in occupied north-eastern Poland during Operation Barbarossa, in which 340 Polish Jews of Jedwabne were locked in a barn later set on fire by a group of Polish males who were motivated by antisem-itism.	Unrated (PG)
Aimée & Jaguar (1999)	[Wikipedia] The film explores the lives of Felice Schragenheim, a Jewish woman who has assumed a false name and belongs to an underground organiza-tion, and Lilly Wust, a married mother of four who is unsatisfied with her philandering Nazi officer husband. The film begins in 1997, with an 83-year-old Lilly tak-ing up residence in a dilapidated flat that once served as an underground hideout. Brought to a retirement home, Lilly encounters her old maid Ilse, who was rounded up during 1945, and is already a tenant.	Unrated (MA)
Akte Grüninger (TV 2014)	*Akte Grüninger* (TV 2014) is about a Swiss police commander on the German border who disobeyed orders, saving 3,600 Jews. Grüninger found a way to allow entry to Jews in 1938 when no other haven was available to them. Grüninger's Swiss government never forgave him for forging the documents needed to sub-vert their laws. The film, although made-for-television, feels like a feature film. *Akte Grüninger* is an outstand-ing righteous Gentile film. [Wikipedia] The television film focuses on the events in late summer 1938, when Paul Grüninger saved the lives of up to 3,600 Jewish refugees from Germany and Austria by pre-dating their visas, enabling them to migrate 'illegally' to Switzerland.	Unrated (PG)
Alan and Naomi (1992)	[Wikipedia] After initial urging from his parents, 14-year-old Alan develops an emotional friendship with Naomi, who has been deeply troubled since see-ing her father killed by the Nazis in Europe.	PG
All My Loved Ones—Vsichni moji blízcí (1999)	[Wikipedia] It is the story of an upwardly-mobile Jew-ish-Czech family before the Nazi invasion of Czecho-slovakia. After initial denial about the looming danger, the family is unable to find a way out of the country upon realizing the reality of the imminent Nazi threat. An uncle in the family meets Nicholas Winton, the British humanitarian who, just before the start of the Second World War, organized the rescue of several hundred Jewish children from German-occupied Czechoslovakia and likely death in the Holocaust.	Unrated
Almost Peaceful—Un monde presque paisible (2002)	[Wikipedia, translated from French] A clothing work-shop decides to resume its activities in the district of Jewish tailors in Paris, just after the war in 1946. Five men, four women and a few children try to learn to live again.	Unrated

Title	Summary	MPAA or Local Rating
Amen. (2002)	[Wikipedia] During World War II, Kurt Gerstein, a Waffen-SS officer employed in the SS Hygiene Institute, designs programs for the purification of water and the destruction of vermin. He is shocked to learn that the process he has developed to eradicate typhus, by using a hydrogen cyanide mixture called Zyklon B, is now being used for killing Jews and other "undesirables" in extermination camps. Gerstein attempts to notify Pope Pius XII about the gassings, but is appalled by the lack of response he gets from the Catholic hierarchy.	PG
And Now My Love—Toute une vie (1974)	[Wikipedia] The story begins in France with a black-and-white, silent film-style sequence in the pre-World War I era, where a woman meets a man operating a prototypical Lumiere movie camera in a park. After being charmed into taking a turn operating the crank on his camera, she is next seen bearing his child while he is enlisted in the French army, documenting soldiers in a trench. He receives a telegram announcing the birth of his son, but is killed by enemy fire quickly after. His widow and young son are given posthumous medals for his service by a general.	X
...and the Fifth Horseman Is Fear—...a pátý jezdec je Strach (1965)	[Wikipedia] Set in Prague during the German occupation of Czechoslovakia, the film follows Dr. Braun, a Jewish doctor forbidden to practice medicine who instead works for German officials cataloging confiscated Jewish property. All Braun wants to do is survive, but his pragmatic mentality is challenged when an injured resistance fighter stumbles into his apartment building. A quest for morphine leads Dr. Braun through his tortured city, where fear eats away at the social structure.	Unrated (PG)
The Angel of Auschwitz (2019)	[Yad Vashem, translated from Hebrew] Auschwitz 1944, a Polish midwife is imprisoned in the infamous concentration camp, and soon enlists the help of Dr. Mengele at the camp hospital. She delivers 3,000 babies in appalling conditions and earns for herself the name Angel from Auschwitz.	15
~~*The Angel of Budapest—El ángel de Budapest* (TV 2011)~~	[Wikipedia] The plot focuses on Ángel Sanz Briz, a Spanish ambassador in Hungary during World War II. Operating until early 1944 in Budapest, he helped to save the lives of thousands of Jews from the Holocaust. He issued them protective papers and lodged them in Spanish safe houses, covered by the embassy's sovereignty. At that time, the Hungarian government was persecuting and deporting Jews to Nazi death camps. A romantic storyline follows the lovelife of Antal, a Hungarian Jew who falls in love with the daughter of an Arrow Cross official of the Fascist government. Antal slowly turns to the resistance movement to save the couple.	Unrated
~~*Angels in White—Mal'akhiyot Be-lavan* (2012)~~	[Wikipedia] The story takes place in the women's camp in Auschwitz concentration camp, in 1945. Haya arrives with her daughter Inuchka. During the selection process, the two are separated, and Haya promises *(cont.)*	Unrated

Title	Summary	MPAA or Local Rating
	her daughter that she will do anything and everything to make sure they reunite. In the children's section, Inuchka is terrified of the cruel kapo, Maria, and runs away from her. She is found crying by Reysy, a prisoner who works as a nurse in the infirmary, who takes her to the clinic and tries to hide her there. Another nurse, Shifra, objects to this plan, but the head nurse, Nechama, convinces Shifra to keep the secret, in exchange for part of her daily food rations. Reysy is fired from the infirmary when she is discovered trying to organize a Yom Kippur prayer.	
Angry Harvest—Bittere Ernte (1985)	[Wikipedia] In the winter of 1942–43, a Jewish family leaps from a train going through Silesia. They are separated in the woods, and Leon, a local peasant who's now a farmer of some wealth, discovers the woman, Rosa, and hides her in his cellar. Leon's a middle-aged Catholic bachelor, tormented by his sexual drive. He doesn't tell Rosa he's seen signs her husband is alive, and he begs her to love him. Rosa offers herself to Leon if he'll help a local Jew in hiding who needs money. Leon pays, and love between Rosa and him does develop, but then Leon's peasant subservience and his limited empathy lead to tragedy.	R
Anna's Return—Annas Heimkehr (TV 2003)	[Wikipedia, translated from Dutch] Anna's Homecoming, a TV drama by Xaver Schwarzenberger from 2003, describes how the Catholic maid Anna Schweighofer saved the Jewish child Franziska Goldberg from deportation in Munich in 1942 when her parents were picked up for a transport to the Auschwitz concentration camp. Anna then passes Franziska off as her illegitimate child and brings her to her family in the fictional Drachselreuth in the Bavarian Forest in relative safety.	Unrated
Anne Frank: The Whole Story (TV 2001)	*Anne Frank: The Whole Story* (TV 2001) is the most complete of all Anne Frank films, following Anne and her sister, Margot, to Auschwitz and then to their graphically portrayed deaths in Bergen-Belsen. Unlike all other cinematic depictions of Anne Frank, this one stands alone as complete. Little of the horror experienced by the Franks is hidden in this excellent three-hour version, which answers many of the questions that have been avoided in most of the other 20 cinematic versions of Anne Frank films. *Anne Frank: The Whole Story* lives up to its name. [Wikipedia] *Anne Frank: The Whole Story* is a two-part mini-series based on the book *Anne Frank: The Biography* by Melissa Müller.	12
Apt Pupil (1998)	[Wikipedia] In Southern California in 1984, 16-year-old high school student Todd Bowden discovers that his elderly neighbor, Arthur Denker, is in reality Kurt Dussander—a former Sturmbannführer in the SS who is now a fugitive war criminal hiding from justice. Todd blackmails Dussander by threatening to turn him in to the police. However, the teenager is fascinated with Nazi atrocities perpetrated during World War II, and forces Dussander to share disturbing *(cont.)*	R for scenes of strong violence, language and brief.

Title	Summary	MPAA or Local Rating
	stories of what it was like working at Nazi extermination camps, and how it felt to participate in genocide.	
Aristides de Sousa Mendes: A Rebel—Désobéir (TV 2008)	[Wikipedia, translated from French] In June 1940, as German troops invaded French territory, "the largest single-person rescue action during the Holocaust" took place: more than thirty thousand people, including ten thousand Jews, were able to escape Nazi barbarism. A lonely man, defying his hierarchy and the orders of dictator Salazar, chooses in his soul and conscience to allow tens of thousands of refugees to reach his country, Portugal, by organizing an uninterrupted visa distribution for several days. This man is Aristides de Sousa Mendes, consul of Bordeaux.	Unrated
The Aryan Couple (2004)	[Wikipedia] The film's story line is set in 1944, during World War II, and is about a Jewish Hungarian industrialist who, in order to ensure his large family's safe passage out of the Third Reich, is forced to hand over his business and his enormously valuable possessions to the Nazis. The plot is loosely based on the life events of Hungarian Jewish industrialist Manfred Weiss and his Manfréd Weiss Steel and Metal Works.	Rated PG-13 for violence, disturbing images and thematic elements
Ascension Day—Wniebowstapienie (1969)	A Jewish woman married a non-Jewish Polish man during Nazi Occupation.	Unrated
The Assisi Underground (1985)	[Wikipedia] In 1943, Franciscan priest Rufino Niccacci is asked by the bishop of Assisi Giuseppe Placido Nicolini to covertly rescue Italian Jews from the Nazis.	PG
At First Sight—Entre Nous—Coup de foudre (1983)	[Wikipedia, translated from French] The story describes the meeting and then the friendship between two women who are opposed to everything, one a tormented artist, the other a *petit bourgeois* conformist with vague dreams, in the aftermath of a Second World War fraught with intimate dramas for the two women.	15
The Attic: The Hiding of Anne Frank (TV 1988)	[Wikipedia]. It is based on Miep Gies's book *Anne Frank Remembered*.	PG
Au Revoir les Enfants (1987)	After *Conspiracy of Hearts* (1960), *Au Revoir les Enfants* (1987) is the first major righteous Gentile film. *Au Revoir les Enfants* was worth the wait. Loosely based on the director Louis Malle's wartime experience, it tells the true story of French Jewish schoolchildren who are hidden in a Catholic boarding school. *Au Revoir les Enfants* is a rich, poignant film that is understandably sentimental, yet that does not descend into mawkishness. [Wikipedia] During the winter of 1943–44, Julien Quentin, a student at a Carmelite boarding school in occupied France, is returning to school from vacation. He acts tough to the students at the school, but he is actually a pampered boy who misses his mother deeply. Saddened to be returning to the monotony of boarding school, Julien's classes seem uneventful until Père Jean, the headmaster, introduces three new pupils. One of them, Jean Bonnet, is the same age as Julien. Like the other students, Julien at first despises *(cont.)*	PG

Title	Summary	MPAA or Local Rating
	Bonnet, a socially awkward boy with a talent for arithmetic and playing the piano. One night, Julien wakes up and discovers that Bonnet is wearing a kippah and is praying in Hebrew.	
Auschwitz (2011)	[Wikipedia] The film attempts to depict the harsh reality of the process inside the Auschwitz concentration camp by using brutal imagery. Book-ended by documentary footage as well as interviews with German teenagers about what they know about the Holocaust, Boll's intention is to show viewers just how depraved and sadistic life in the camp was.	Unrated (R)
The Auschwitz Report (2020)	[Wikipedia] Two prisoners in the Auschwitz concentration camp manage to escape with a document about the camp's operation.	Unrated
Autumn Hearts A New Beginning—Emotional Arithmetic (2007)	[Wikipedia] *Emotional Arithmetic* focuses primarily on three people who formed a bond in the Drancy internment camp, where they were imprisoned by the Nazis during World War II: Jakob Bronski, who saw goodness in two orphaned children in the camp, Melanie and Christopher, and who helped them to survive. Decades after their release from Drancy, their emotional wounds still affect their lives in different ways when they meet again.	PG-13 for thematic elements and brief strong language.
Babi Yar: The Forgotten Crime—Babij Jar (2003)	Filmed in Europe and given a limited theatrical release, the film recounts the mass murders in September 1941 of thousands of Jews, Soviet POWs, communists, Gypsies (Romani people) and civilian hostages by German Einsatzgruppen, and Ukrainian nationalist collaborators in the title location, a ravine in Kyiv (the capital of Ukraine).	Unrated
A Bag of Marbles—Un sac de billes (1975)	[Wikipedia, translated from French] In 1942, the anti-Semitic laws of the Vichy government forced the two elders of a Jewish hairdresser in Paris to flee to the free zone. A little later, the two other brothers also flee to reach the South of France. They succeed in crossing the demarcation line and join Menton where they will find their brothers and soon their parents.	Unrated (PG)
A Bag of Marbles—Un sac de billes (2017)	[Wikipedia] In occupied France during World War II, two young Jewish brothers, Maurice and Joseph, are sent by their parents to the Italian Zone, and display courage, intelligence and ingenuity as they escape the occupiers and try to reunite their family.	Unrated (PG)
~~Baranski (1979)~~	[ww.bfi.org.uk] A former concentration camp victim meets up with his tormentor whom he had long considered dead.	Unrated
Bent (1997)	[Wikipedia] Max is a promiscuous gay man living in 1930s Berlin. He is at odds with his wealthy family because of his homosexuality. One evening, much to the resentment of his boyfriend, Rudy, Max brings home a handsome Sturmabteilung man. Unfortunately, he does so on the Night of the Long Knives, when Hitler ordered the assassination of upper echelon SA corps. The Sturmabteilung man is discovered and killed by SS men in Max and Rudy's apartment, and the two have to flee Berlin.	NC-17 for a strong scene of graphic sexuality.

Title	Summary	MPAA or Local Rating
Bernhard Lichtenberg (TV 1965)	[Wikipedia, translated from German] Berlin 1941. Provost Bernhard Lichtenberg receives a visit from a married couple who tell him a terrible story about their son Rudolf, who was admitted to a mental institution, where he died suddenly, although he finally seemed perfectly healthy. It was here that Lichtenberg learned personally for the first time that the Nazi regime had apparently launched a program to destroy so-called "life unworthy of life." The church man discusses with his faithful from the church and family how best to react to this unheard of barbarism.	Unrated
The Birch-Tree Meadow— ***La petite prairie aux bouleaux*** ***(2003)***	*The Birch-Tree Meadow—La petite prairie aux bouleaux* (2003) is the most honest Holocaust Survivor film ever made. Sixty years after her imprisonment in Birkenau, a woman returns to get some answers and closure. Remarkably, she leaves with both, as do the viewers. This is not the "crazy" Holocaust survivor from most other films, but a mature, thoughtful woman who seeks and attains some peace when leaving Birkenau again so many years later. [Wikipedia, translated from French] Myriam, who has lived in New York for about 50 years, returns to Europe for the annual commemoration of Auschwitz alumni. She decides to return to Birkenau where she once lived in the hell of the concentration camps.	Unrated (PG)
The Birth Certificate— *Świadectwo urodzenia* (1961)	[Wikipedia, translated from Polish] The film consists of three different short stories told from the perspective of children who experienced the events of World War II... "On the Road" takes place in September 1939, when, amid the conflagration of war, after the destruction of his regiment, [a man] carries the documents of the staff office... "Letter from the Camp" focuses on the fate of three brothers during the occupation... "A Drop of Blood" begins when little Mirka wakes up in an abandoned Jewish tenement house whose inhabitants were deported by the Nazis.	Unrated
Bittersweet—Het bittere kruid (1985)	[Wikipedia, translated from Dutch] *Het Bittere Kruid* is about the Jewish girl Sara and the demise of her family during the Second World War. Sara is suddenly released from the sanatorium where she is being treated for tuberculosis in 1942. It turns out that her friend's father, her best friend in the sanatorium, as an NSB member, has demanded that Sara be removed.	Unrated
Black Book—Zwartboek (2006)	[Wikipedia] In 1944, Dutch-Jewish singer Rachel Stein is hiding from the Nazi regime in the occupied Netherlands. When the farmhouse where she has been hiding is destroyed by an Allied bomber, she goes to see a lawyer named Smaal, who has been helping her family. He arranges for her to escape to the liberated southern part of the country. Aided by a man named Van Gein, Rachel is reunited with her family and boards a boat that is to take them and other refugees to the south. However, they are ambushed on the river by members of the German SS, who kill them and rob the bodies of valuables. Rachel alone survives, but does not manage to escape from occupied territory.	R for some strong violence, graphic nudity, sexuality and language.

Title	Summary	MPAA or Local Rating
Black Thursday— *Les guichets du Louvre* (1974)	[Wikipedia] On 16 July 1942 in Paris, Paul, a young student on the Left Bank, hears that the French authorities are rounding up the Jewish inhabitants of the city for deportation. To make a gesture against the evil of the German occupation and the collaborationist French régime, he goes to a Jewish quarter on the Right Bank determined to save someone. French police are there in force, herding Jewish people out of apartments and hustling them into commandeered buses. They already have the names and addresses, and can easily recognize Jewish people by the compulsory yellow star sewn to their clothes.	Unrated (PG)
Blessed Is the Match: The Life and Death of Hannah Senesh (2008)	[Yad Vashem] Narrated by three-time Academy Award nominee Joan Allen, *Blessed Is the Match* is the first documentary feature about Hannah Senesh, the World War II-era poet and diarist who became a paratrooper, resistance fighter and modern-day Joan of Arc. Safe in Palestine in 1944, Hannah joined a mission to rescue Hungary's Jews. Shockingly, it was the only outside rescue mission for Jews during the Holocaust. Hannah parachuted behind enemy lines, was captured, tortured and ultimately executed by the Nazis. Incredibly, her mother Catherine witnessed the entire ordeal—first as a prisoner with Hannah and later as her advocate, braving the bombed-out streets of Budapest in a desperate attempt to save her daughter. With unprecedented access to the Senesh family archive, this powerful story unfolds through the writings and photographs of Hannah and Catherine Senesh.	Unrated
~~Blind Hero: Otto Weidt—~~ ~~Ein blinder Held—~~ ~~Die Liebe des Otto Weidt~~ ~~(TV 2014)~~	[Wikipedia, translated from German] The film begins in 1941 in Weidt's Berlin brush factory at Rosenthaler Strasse 39, Berlin-Mitte: the Gestapo is in the house and is harassing the Jewish workforce. Weidt pretended to do so, but was able to bribe the Gestapo officer to let the employees of the "war-important company" work for him until further notice. Similar scenes are repeated, whereby Weidt always knows how to preserve the lives of his Jewish employees through a mixture of deception, drama, flattery, apparent submissiveness, persistence, cunning and bribery towards the Gestapo, who returns more and more frequently.	Unrated
The Bloom of Yesterday— *Die Blumen von gestern* (2016)	[Wikipedia, translated from German] The film portrays the Holocaust researcher Totila Blumen, known as Toto. The grandson of a prominent general of the Waffen-SS suffers from his background, his career and his misanthropy.	Unrated
Bolero Dance of Life— *Les uns et les autres* (1981)	[Wikipedia] The film follows four families, with different nationalities (French, German, Russian, and American) but with the same passion for music, from the 1930s to the 1980s. The various story lines cross each other time and again in different places and times, with their own theme scores that evolve as time passes.	Unrated (PG)
Bonhoeffer: Agent of Grace (TV 2000)	[Yad Vashem] Television movie about the Lutheran pastor Dietrich Bonhoeffer who fought Nazi tyranny during World War II and was eventually hanged in *(cont.)*	Unrated (PG)

Title	Summary	MPAA or Local Rating
	1945. Lutheran minister Dietrich Bonhoeffer is in the United States in the 1930s exploring the spiritual vitality of the African American church. Eschewing the safety of America, he returns to his native Germany. An outspoken critic of Hitler and the Nazis from the start, he rebels against church leaders complicit in the rise of the Third Reich…	
Border Street—Ulica Graniczna (1948)	[Wikipedia] The film depicts the Nazis' purge of Warsaw Jews by following the fates of five families, representative of the various social, political, and ethnic strata in Warsaw, through the war, and culminates in the Warsaw Ghetto Uprising.	Unrated
The Boy in the Striped Pyjamas (2008)	[Wikipedia] Set in World War II, the Holocaust drama relates the horror of a Nazi extermination camp through the eyes of two 8-year-old boys: Bruno, the son of the camp's Nazi commandant, and Shmuel, a Jewish inmate.	PG-13 for some mature thematic material involving the Holocaust.
The Boys from Brazil (1978)	[Wikipedia] Young, well-intentioned Barry Kohler stumbles upon a secret organization of Third Reich war criminals holding clandestine meetings in Paraguay and finds that Dr. Josef Mengele, the infamous Auschwitz doctor, is with them. He phones Ezra Lieberman, an aging Nazi hunter living in Vienna, Austria, with this information. A highly skeptical Lieberman tries to brush Kohler's claims aside, telling him that it is well known that Mengele is living in Paraguay.	R
~~*Brussels Transit—Bruxelles-transit* (1982)~~	A child's memories of emigrating from Poland to Belgium.	Unrated
Bye Germany— Es war einmal in Deutschland… (2017)	[Wikipedia] Having survived the war and everything the Third Reich wanted to throw at them, David Berman and his friends have only one plan in mind: to get to the States as soon as possible. But for that, they need money. Just when this design seems almost within his grasp, David gets fleeced of all his savings— and, all the dodgy shenanigans in his past finally catch up with him!	Unrated (PG)
Cabaret (1972)	*Cabaret* (1972) portrays homosexuals, transvestites and Jews during the rise of Nazism in Germany. As a musical, *Cabaret* is great. As a peek into the early Third Reich, the film is uncompromising and rarely leans on violence to make its point. As a Holocaust film, *Cabaret* is worth watching for two songs, "Tomorrow Belongs to Me" and "If You Could See Her." [Wikipedia] In 1931 Berlin, young American Sally Bowles performs at the Kit Kat Klub. A new British arrival in the city, Brian Roberts, moves into the boarding house where Sally lives. A reserved academic and writer, Brian wants to give English lessons to earn a living while completing his doctorate. Sally tries to seduce Brian, but he tells her that on three previous occasions he has tried to have sexual relationships with women, all of which failed. They become friends, and Brian witnesses Sally's bohemian life in the last days of the Weimar Republic.	PG

Title	Summary	MPAA or Local Rating
A Call to Remember (TV 1997)	Holocaust survivors use their experiences to try to prevent their son from serving in Vietnam.	Rated R for language and sexuality
The Cellar—Ha-Martef (1963)	[Yad Vashem] A mono-drama dealing with a Holocaust survivor who is haunted by fears. *The Cellar* is one of the first Israeli films dealing with the Holocaust. The director of the film Natan Gross, born in Krakov and one of the pioneers of Israeli cinema, is himself a victim of the Nazi experience. He managed to survive as a Christian Aryan by using forged papers.	Unrated
~~*Charlie Grant's War* (TV 1984)~~	[Wikipedia] Set during World War II, the film stars R. H. Thomson as Charlie Grant, a Canadian activist and humanitarian who was living in Austria at the time of the war, and helped to smuggle Jews out of the country for their safety.	Unrated (PG)
Charlotte (1981)	[Wikipedia] It is a biography about German-Jewish painter Charlotte Salomon, who died in the Holocaust.	Unrated
The Children of Chance—Les enfants de la chance (2016)	[Wikipedia, translated from French] In 1942, Maurice Gutman, a 12-year-old Jewish child, was separated from his family following an accident. During his stay in the pediatric service of the Garches hospital, his family was taken to the Drancy camp, then deported to the Auschwitz camp. He spent two years in the hospital, escaping the police inquisition thanks to the head doctor; friendships are established in the group of children where he is, some of whom recover and others die. On his release, after the Liberation, he finds his aunt and understands that she is, of his family, the only survivor of the Nazi massacre.	Unrated
~~*Chosen* (2016)~~	[Wikipedia] An unassuming young lawyer leads a fight against the Nazis near the end of the Second World War.	15
Closed Season—Ende der Schonzeit (2012)	[Wikipedia, translated from German] Bruno, a solitary student, travels from Germany to Israel in 1970 to a remote kibbutz to look for his biological father. He has a letter from his late mother in his luggage that he is supposed to hand over to his father. But the Holocaust survivor Avi brusquely rejects Bruno. He doesn't want the young German bothering him and his family with the past. Only with great persistence does Bruno Avi break his silence and remember.	Unrated
Cloudy Sunday—Ouzeri Tsitsanis (2015)	[Wikipedia] The film is set during the occupation of Thessaloniki, Greece's second largest city and home to the largest population of Jews in Greece, by Nazi Germany during WWII.	Unrated
Cold Days—Hideg napok (1966)	[Wikipedia, translated from Hungarian] In 1946, three men await a court verdict in prison investigating their role in the 1942 Novi Sad massacre. One day they bring a new prisoner into their cell, Corporal Szabó, with whom they begin to talk about which of them did what in the three days of the massacre. Their narration culminates in the tragedy of the wife of Major Büky. Major Büky lives in the knowledge that his wife was taken away by the Germans on the third day of the *(cont.)*	A

Title	Summary	MPAA or Local Rating
	massacre to be used as a witness in the lawsuit, proving that they had nothing to do with the excesses of the Hungarian soldiers. However, the narrative reveals exactly what the fate of the woman became.	
Colette (2013)	[csfd.cz, translated from Czech] The love story of the prisoners of Vili and the beautiful Belgian Jew Colette tells of the fate of secret love in an environment of horror and death, of the thin line between good and evil and truth and falsehood. a world of daily struggle for survival. There is a strict hierarchy even among the prisoners themselves. He trades in everything that can save lives, or at least delay death. Colette, a Jew, arrives in Auschwitz by transport from Belgium. Prisoner Vili advises her on what to say during the selection, thus saving her from death in a gas chamber. Colette's beauty will soon be noticed by a fanatical SS officer Weisacker who employs her in his workshop. He inexorably falls under her spell and at the same time intoxicated with the cruelty and power over the life and death of a racially inferior being. Despite their daily suffering, Vili and Colette get closer. Their love gives them the strength to endure the hell of a concentration camp. In a desperate fight for life, they plan a risky escape together … (official text of the distributor)	Unrated (R)
The Condemned of Altona— I sequestrati di Altona (1962)	[Wikipedia] A father, who is dying, calls together his family, to go over his last wishes.	A
Conspiracy (TV 2001)	*Conspiracy* (TV 2001) vividly depicts the chillingly sterilized 1942 Wannsee Conference where, in one afternoon outside of Berlin, Reinhard Heydrich and his top assistant, Adolf Eichmann, codified the "Final Solution." The made-for-television film explains that the Germans had concluded that, because shooting the first million Jews in fields had been inefficient and had demoralized German soldiers who pulled the trigger, a better method of mass murder had been developed. The solution that day was revealed as Auschwitz and its gas chambers. The film brilliantly portrays German heartlessness exhibited at the conference. [Wikipedia] On 20 January 1942, as Nazi Germany's war effort sours due to the failure of Operation Barbarossa, the entrance of the United States into World War II, and the death of Walther von Reichenau, a meeting is held to determine the method by which the government is to implement Adolf Hitler's policy, that the German sphere of influence should be free of Jews, including those in the occupied territories of Poland, Latvia, Estonia, Czechoslovakia and France.	R for language.
Conspiracy of Hearts (1960)	[Wikipedia] In 1943 Italy, nuns hide and protect Jewish children who have escaped from a concentration camp. The Italian camp has been taken over by German forces with a colonel and his sadistic lieutenant in command. When the colonel and lieutenant threaten to execute some of the nuns, including Mother Katharine, for helping the Jewish children to escape, the *(cont.)*	UK-PG

Title	Summary	MPAA or Local Rating
	Italian soldiers block the execution and shoot the Germans dead. The Italian soldiers then leave the camp to join Italian partisans in the nearby hills.	
The Consul of Bordeaux— O Cônsul de Bordéus (2011)	[Wikipedia, translated from German] The film tells the life story of the Portuguese diplomat Aristides de Sousa Mendes, who as consul general in Bordeaux saved the lives of around 30,000 people during the Second World War. Woven into the real story is the fictional story of a refugee who becomes a famous conductor.	Unrated
The Counterfeiters— Die Fälscher (2007)	*The Counterfeiters—Die Fälscher* (2007) is one of the finest core Holocaust films ever made. The true story, which is set in both Mauthausen and Sachsenhausen Concentration Camps, portrays Jewish counterfeiters who are forced, upon penalty of death, to cooperate long-term with their German captors. Although not as graphically violent as many other Holocaust films, *The Counterfeiters* tells a compelling story in an excellent film. [Wikipedia] It fictionalizes Operation Bernhard, a secret plan by Nazi Germany during World War II to destabilize the United Kingdom by flooding its economy with forged Bank of England pound notes. The film centres on a Jewish counterfeiter, Salomon "Sally" Sorowitsch, who is coerced into assisting the operation at the Sachsenhausen concentration camp.	R for some strong violence, brief sexuality/ nudity and language.
The Courageous Heart of Irena Sendler (TV 2009)	[Wikipedia] Irena Sendler is a Catholic social worker who has sympathized with the Jews since her childhood, when her physician father died of typhus contracted while treating poor Jewish patients. When she initially proposes saving Jewish children from the Warsaw Ghetto, her idea is met with skepticism by fellow workers, her parish priest, and even her own mother Janina.	TV-PG
~~*The Customer of the Off Season— Oreach B'Onah Metah* (1970)~~	After World War II, a couple visits Eilat, Israel. The husband is recognized by a stranger as a Nazi.	Unrated
Dara of Jasenovac— Dara iz Jasenovca (2020)	[Wikipedia] it deals with war crimes and atrocities that took place at Jasenovac concentration camp, which was a part of the Holocaust and the wider genocide of Serbs in the Independent State of Croatia.	Rated R for strong and disturbing violent content, and some sexual content
~~*Darkness in Daytime— Nappali sötétség* (1963)~~	[Wikipedia, translated from Hungarian] *The Darkness of the Living Room* is a Hungarian film made in 1963, in which a writer meets a girl, Ágnes. They fall in love with each other in 1944. Then the man finds out that his love is a persecuted Jewish girl. As a father and daughter, they pull themselves together in a village on Lake Balaton. However, after a few days, Agnes is arrested for distributing an illegal press product. During the confrontation, the writer confesses the truth, but Agnes insists that she is the writer's daughter.	Unrated

Title	Summary	MPAA or Local Rating
~~David (1979)~~	[Wikipedia] *David* follows an adolescent Jewish boy, David Singer, who comes of age in Nazi Berlin. The film reveals the struggles for identity and survival that often overlapped among the Jews of war-torn Europe, particularly the young.	Unrated (PG)
~~Dawn (2014)~~	[Wikipedia] *Dawn* is a psychological drama behind closed doors, in which four comrades in arms pressure the young Elisha to overcome his moral qualms and fully commit to the armed struggle. The story is set in Palestine in 1947, during the British mandate period. The Zionists are fighting for the establishment of a Jewish state. A member of the armed Jewish underground has been sentenced to death by the British authorities. In return, the resistance has kidnapped a British officer, trying to redeem their friend.	Unrated
A Day in October—En dag i oktober (1991)	A reenactment of the rescue of the Danish Jewish community during World War II.	Unrated
~~The Day the Clown Cried (1972)~~	[Wikipedia] [Jerry] Lewis plays a washed-up German circus clown named Helmut Doork during the beginning of World War II and the Holocaust. Although he was once a famous performer who toured North America and Europe with the Ringling Brothers, Doork is now past his prime and receives little respect. After Doork causes an accident during a show, the head clown convinces the circus owner to demote Doork. Upon returning home, Doork confides his problems to his wife Ada, and she encourages him to stand up for himself. After going back to the circus, Helmut overhears the circus owner agreeing to fire him after the head clown issues an ultimatum. A distraught Helmut is arrested later by the Gestapo for ranting about Germany and drunkenly mocking Adolf Hitler in a bar. Following an interrogation at the Gestapo headquarters, he is imprisoned in a Nazi camp for political prisoners. For the next three to four years, he remains there while hoping for a trial and a chance to plead his case.	Unrated
Dear Mr. Waldman—Michtavim Le America (2006)	*Dear Mr. Waldman—Michtavim Le America* (2006) is an exceptional Israeli film that portrays adult Holocaust survivors in Israel in the early 1960s. The characters are damaged, but forward-looking, trying to make the best of their new lives with their new families in a new country. The father holds onto the dream that his dead brother is alive and working in Washington for President Kennedy. When the dream is finally crushed, the survivor can move on. *Dear Mr. Waldman's* portrayal of 1960s Israeli society is particularly moving. [Wikipedia, Hebrew translated edited] Hilik Waldman, 10, and his brother grow up with Holocaust survivor parents, each of whom lost his spouse and previous children in the Holocaust. The longing for the dead undermines the relationship between parents and children living in constant fear of family breakup.	PG-13

Title	Summary	MPAA or Local Rating
Death in Love (2008)	[Wikipedia] *Death in Love* is a psychosexual-thriller about a love affair between a Jewish woman and a doctor overseeing human experimentation at a Nazi German concentration camp, and the impact this has on her sons' lives in the 1990s.	R for disturbing violent and graphic sexual content, nudity and language.
Death Is My Trade— Aus einem deutschen Leben (1977)	[Wikipedia] Like the novel, the film is partly based on interrogation records of the trial against Rudolf Höß, SS-officer and commander of the Nazi concentration and extermination camp Auschwitz, as well as on his autobiographical notes. He made these notes first during his time as British POW, then, after he was extradited, as Polish prisoner in 1946/47, before he was executed as a convicted war criminal. Instead of using the name Rudolf Höß, whose life was the model for the film, the pseudonym Franz Lang is used, in order that he remain anonymous.	Unrated
The Debt—Ha-Hov (2007)	[Wikipedia] The film is not based on actual fact, and centers on an Israeli-Mossad Kidon team who in 1964 capture a notorious Nazi doctor Josef Mengele who had performed human experimentation in a German extermination camp, and, when he escapes from them, they report him as being shot once in the head and killed during his attempted escape. In the following years, the agents receive numerous accolades for their actions, with none suspecting the truth, but in the late 1990s, they learn he may be alive, repentant, and likely to expose the truth of the events.	Unrated (PG)
The Debt (2010)	[Wikipedia] *The Debt* is a 2010 British-American remake of the 2007 Israeli alternate history-thriller film *Ha-Hov*.	R for some violence and language.
Defiance (2008)	*Defiance* (2008) is a well-cast story about a large group of Jews who hide from the Germans in the Belarus forests. Unlike most Holocaust films, *Defiance* depicts Jews resisting and successfully subverting the Germans throughout the War. Unlike *Schindler's List*, *Defiance* portrays over a thousand Jews saving themselves, without the need of a German savior. Rightfully, *Defiance* is regarded as one of the greatest Holocaust stories. [Wikipedia] The film is based on events which began in August 1941. Nazi Einsatzgruppen are sweeping through Eastern Europe, systematically killing Jews. Among the survivors not killed or restricted to ghettoes are the Polish Jewish Bielski brothers: Tuvia, Zus, Asael and Aron. Their parents are dead, killed by local police under orders from the German occupiers. The brothers flee to the Naliboki Forest, vowing to avenge the deaths of their parents.	R for violence and language.
Denial (2016)	[Wikipedia] Deborah Lipstadt is an American professor of Holocaust studies whose speaking engagement is disrupted by David Irving, a writer on Nazi Germany. He files a libel lawsuit in the United Kingdom against Lipstadt and her publisher for declaring him a Holocaust denier in her books. As the burden of proof in UK libel cases lies with the accused, Lipstadt and her legal team, led by solicitor Anthony Julius and barrister Richard Rampton, must prove that Irving lied about the Holocaust.	G-13 for thematic material and brief strong language.

Title	Summary	MPAA or Local Rating
~~*Der Passagier—Welcome to Germany* (TV 1988)~~	[Wikipedia] Mr. Cornfield, a film director from Hollywood, arrives in Berlin to make a film about an episode from the Holocaust that is set in a Berlin film studio: In 1942 the Ministry of Propaganda gave a director by the name of Körner permission to choose thirteen Jewish prisoners from a concentration camp for his anti-Semitic film, who would be employed as small actors, would be housed on the studio premises and would be allowed to emigrate to Switzerland after the filming was finished.	Unrated
The Devil's Arithmetic (TV 1999)	[Wikipedia] The film opens with Hannah, a teen girl, in a tattoo parlor with her friends, contemplating what tattoo she wants. Before she can decide, she notes the time and realizes she is late for a Passover dinner. Hannah hates going to her family seder as her family tells the same stories and Hannah is tired of hearing about the past. Her aunt tells her every year that Hannah looks like her namesake, Chana, but won't tell Hannah who Chana was or what she did. During the seder Hannah opens the front door to let in the prophet Elijah, but she sees a Polish village instead of the outside of the apartment. All of a sudden she is not only in a new place but also in the year 1941.	12
Diamonds of the Night—Démanty noci (1964)	*Diamonds of the Night—Démanty noci* (1964) portrays the fate of two young Jewish escapees from a deportation train. Injured, starved and desperate, the boys are ultimately hunted down for sport by vicious Czech locals. There is nothing pleasant about this film: no sweet musical score or happy ending. *Diamonds of the Night* simply concerns itself with the near-impossibility of survival during the Holocaust. [Wikipedia] *Diamonds of the Night* begins with two teenage boys fleeing from a train and shedding, as they run, long black coats, on the backs of which are painted in white the letters "KL," the abbreviation for Konzentrationslager. Behind them are the sounds of shouting and shooting. The film employs little dialogue, and the boys' escape through forests and swamps and across rocky terrain is interpolated with the dreams, memories, hallucinations, fantasies, and flashbacks of the younger of the two boys.	UK-15
The Diary of Anne Frank—Anne no nikki (1995)	[Wikipedia] *Anne no Nikki* (アンネの日記), also known as *The Diary of Anne Frank*, is a 1995 Japanese anime film based on Anne Frank's *The Diary of a Young Girl*.	Unrated (PG)
~~*The Diary of Anne Frank—Dagboek van Anne Frank* (TV 1962)~~	Based on the standard Anne Frank screenplay by Frances Goodrich and Albert Hackett.	Unrated (PG)
The Diary of Anne Frank—Das Tagebuch Der Anne Frank (2016)	*The Diary of Anne Frank—Das Tagebuch Der Anne Frank* (2016) is the best Anne Frank in hiding film ever made. It is not sterilized or anodyne like many of the first 20 versions and is much more revealing of Anne Frank's ordeal. Although not as complete as *Anne Frank: The Whole Story* (TV 2001), the hiding portion of this 2016 version is far more convincing. *(cont.)*	Unrated (PG)

Title	Summary	MPAA or Local Rating
	Because this film is more realistic than most previous versions, it is only appropriate for older audiences. [Wikipedia, translated from German] At first, Anne Frank lives as a happy, lively girl. She is happy to be able to visit her relatives in Sils Maria. But the discriminatory measures taken by the National Socialists are making life in her new home, Amsterdam, increasingly difficult. As a Jew, she is increasingly marginalized. On her 13th birthday, she was given a diary, to which she now confides her thoughts in the form of letters to an imaginary friend. A few weeks later, at the beginning of July 1942, the family has to go into hiding after Anne's older sister Margot receives an invitation to "labor service."	
~~The Diary of Anne Frank= Das Tagebuch Der Anne Frank (TV 1958)~~	Based on the standard Anne Frank screenplay by Frances Goodrich and Albert Hackett.	Unrated
~~The Diary of Anne Frank= Dnevnik Ane Frank (TV 1959)~~	Based on the standard Anne Frank screenplay by Frances Goodrich and Albert Hackett.	Unrated
~~The Diary of Anne Frank= El diari d'Anna Frank (TV 1996)~~	Based on the standard Anne Frank screenplay by Frances Goodrich and Albert Hackett.	Unrated
The Diary of Anne Frank— Het dagboek van Anne Frank (TV 1985)	Based on the standard Anne Frank screenplay by Frances Goodrich and Albert Hackett.	Unrated (PG)
The Diary of Anne Frank— Le Journal d'Anne Frank (1999)	[Wikipedia] An animated film based on Anne Frank's 1942–1944 The Diary of a Young Girl.	Unrated (PG)
The Diary of Anne Frank (1959)	[Wikipedia] The Diary of Anne Frank is a 1959 film based on the Pulitzer Prize winning play of the same name, which was based on the diary of Anne Frank. It was directed by George Stevens, with a screenplay by Frances Goodrich and Albert Hackett. It is the first film version of both the play and the original story, and features three members of the original Broadway cast.	UK-Universal
~~The Diary of Anne Frank (TV 1967)~~	[Wikipedia] The Diary of Anne Frank was a 1967 TV film based on the book The Diary of a Young Girl by Anne Frank.	Unrated (PG)
The Diary of Anne Frank (TV 1980)	[Wikipedia] The Diary of Anne Frank is a 1980 American made-for-television biographical drama film which originally aired on NBC on November 17, 1980. Like the 1959 film of the same name, it was written by Frances Goodrich and Albert Hackett and directed by Boris Sagal. Unlike the 1959 film, the TV-film focuses more on character development than suspense, and is considerably shorter than the 1959 version.	Unrated (PG)
The Diary of Anne Frank (TV 1987)	[Wikipedia] The Diary of Anne Frank is 1987 BBC televised miniseries. It was based on The Diary of a Young Girl by Anne Frank.	Unrated
The Diary of Anne Frank (TV 2009)	[Wikipedia] The Diary of Anne Frank is a BBC adaptation, in association with France 2, of The Diary of a Young Girl originally written by Anne Frank and adapted for television.	Unrated (PG)

Title	Summary	MPAA or Local Rating
Distant Journey—Daleká cesta (1950)	[Wikipedia] *Distant Journey* follows Hana, a Jewish eye doctor who falls in love and marries a Gentile named Toník. Their simple love story becomes a nightmare when the government begins the systematized extermination of the Jews. Hana's family is transported to Theresienstadt, and the romance becomes a struggle for survival.	Unrated
Dita Saxová (1968)	[Yad Vashem] Dita, a beautiful, strong 18-year-old girl in communist Prague, lives in a girls' youth hostel with her friends, all of whom, Dita included, are survivors of Nazi concentration camps. Though she appears strong and composed on the outside, her unsure dealings with men reveal her to be full of questions and anxieties. Based on the novel by Arnost Lustig, the film was confiscated immediately after its premiere in Prague in 1968.	Unrated
Divided We Fall— Musíme si pomáhat (2000)	*Divided We Fall—Musíme si pomáhat* (2000) is a small story about a Jew who is hidden by a married couple in occupied Czechoslovakia. Like most Czech Holocaust films, *Divided We Fall* is subtle, never overreaching. It is a charming film that makes its points without making a big fuss. 　　[Wikipedia] The film opens in 1939 Czechoslovakia. Horst, a Czech-German Nazi collaborator married to a German woman and co-worker of Josef, brings food to Josef and his wife Marie, who are Czechs. Josef hates the Nazis. When Josef finds David, who had escaped a concentration camp in occupied Poland after first being sent to the Theresienstadt concentration camp in northern Bohemia, Josef and Marie decide to hide him in their apartment.	PG-13 for some violence and sexual content.
~~*Drancy Avenir* (1997)~~	Three stories: (1) about the last Holocaust survivor; (2) a researcher of the Drancy Concentration Camp, (3) a journey on a boat.	Unrated
The Earth Cries Out— Il grido della terra (1949)	[Wikipedia, translated from Italian] At the end of the war, a group of Jews, freed by the allies from the concentration camps in Germany, clandestinely reached Palestine. Among them, an Israeli surgeon and his future daughter-in-law are transferred to a refugee camp in Puglia and, led by Ariè, they reach Palestine, where the guerrilla war between Jewish partisans and the occupying English is underway.	Unrated
Edges of the Lord (2001)	[Wikipedia] Romek is the son of a wealthy Jewish couple. When the Nazis invade Poland, the family contacts an old friend and tasks him to hide their son. During this plight, Romek poses as the Catholic nephew of a local farmer, with the aid of a compassionate priest.	R for some violence and sexual content.
The Eichmann Show (TV 2015)	[Wikipedia] In 1961, former Nazi Adolf Eichmann is captured by Israeli agents and put on trial. American television producer Milton Fruchtman fervently believes that the trial, with its witness accounts of Nazi atrocities, should be televised to show the world the evils of the Holocaust and to combat any resurgence of Nazism, and joins forces with black-listed director Leo Hurwitz. Despite death threats, reluctance to cooperate from several networks, and even resistance from the Israeli prime minister, David Ben-Gurion, *(cont.)*	Unrated (PG)

Title	Summary	MPAA or Local Rating
	who fears a "show trial," the pair persist and move their cameras into the courtroom.	
Elysium (1987)	A child is sent to a concentration camp and his parents try to find him.	Unrated
Enclosure—L'enclos (1961)	[Wikipedia, translated from French] In 1944, in a concentration camp, an SS officer had two prisoners sentenced to death placed in a special enclosure: Karl, a German political detainee and member of the underground anti-Nazi organization of the camp, and David, a French Jew. They are told that whoever kills his companion will be pardoned.	Unrated
The End of Our World— Koniec naszego swiata (1964)	[Wikipedia, translated from Polish] The film presents the everyday life of the Auschwitz-Birkenau concentration camp as seen through the eyes of one of the surviving prisoners, Henryk, who returns to the museum many years later, showing a couple of Americans around it. For newcomers from the United States, this place is something unusual, not fully understood; they do not know that their guide was once a prisoner. For Henryk, coming back to the camp after nearly 20 years is an avalanche of strong memories of his arrest, struggle for survival, rebellion against the SS and escape.	Unrated
Enemies: A Love Story (1989)	[Wikipedia] In 1949, guilt-ridden Holocaust survivor Herman Broder lives in New York with his wife, Yadwiga. During the war, Yadwiga—the Broders' gentile servant—saved Herman's life by hiding him in a hayloft. Believing his wife, Tamara, to have perished in a concentration camp, Herman took Yadiga with him as his wife when he emigrated to the United States. He tells her that he works as a traveling book-salesman; however, in reality, he is a ghost writer for the avaricious Rabbi Lembeck. He also is having an affair with Masha, whose own experiences in a concentration camp have left her embittered about God and Judaism; she emigrated to New York with her mother and married Leon, an older man from whom she is estranged.	15
Escape from Sobibor (TV 1987)	[Wikipedia] On 14 October 1943, members of the Sobibor camp's underground resistance succeeded in covertly killing 11 German SS-Totenkopfverbände officers and a number of Sonderdienst Ukrainian and Volksdeutsche guards. Of the 600 inmates in the camp, roughly 300 escaped, although all but 50–70 were later re-captured and killed. After the escape, SS Chief Heinrich Himmler ordered the death camp closed. It was dismantled, bulldozed under the earth, and planted over with trees to cover it up.	15
Europa Europa (1990)	[Wikipedia] It is based on the 1989 autobiography of Solomon Perel, a German Jewish boy who escaped the Holocaust by masquerading as a "Nazi" German.	15
Everything Is Illuminated (2005)	*Everything Is Illuminated* (2005) is a fabulously entertaining film about the American grandson of a Holocaust survivor who travels to the Ukraine to solve a family mystery. Like most fish-out-of-water/roadshow films, the protagonist, who exhibits signs of obsessive-compulsive behavior, only interacts with odd *(cont.)*	PG-13 for disturbing images—violence, sexual content and language.

Title	Summary	MPAA or Local Rating
	characters, who are later humanized. The Holocaust tie-in, complete with a passable wartime reenactment, is the least compelling aspect of this fine film. [Wikipedia] Jonathan Safran Foer, a young American Jew, goes on a quest to find the woman, Augustine, who saved his grandfather, Safran Foer, during the Holocaust in a small Ukrainian town called Trachimbrod that was wiped off the map when the Nazis liquidated Eastern European shtetls.	
~~Ewa (2016)~~	An Israeli and a Holocaust survivor marry and have a loving life together. When the survivor/wife falls ill, the husband discovers an unknown apartment that they own together.	Unrated
The Execution (TV 1985)	A women's Mahjong club of Holocaust survivors scheme to execute a Nazi war criminal.	PG-13
Exodus (1960)	[Wikipedia] After the Second World War, Katherine "Kitty" Fremont, a widowed American nurse, is sightseeing in Cyprus following a tour of duty for the U.S. Public Health Service in Greece. Her guide mentions the Karaolos internment camp on Cyprus, where thousands of Jews—many of them Holocaust survivors—are detained by the British, who refuse them passage to Palestine. Kitty visits British General Sutherland, who knew her late husband. When Sutherland suggests she volunteer at the internment camp for a few days, Kitty declines, citing she would feel uncomfortable around Jews.	UK-PG
Exodus to Shanghai (2015)	The Chinese Consul stationed in Vienna, Austria, before the war works with a married couple to issue emigration visas to Shanghai.	15
~~Falsch (1987)~~	[Wikipedia, translated from French] At nightfall, a four-engine aircraft has just landed at a country airport. Only one passenger gets off, Joe, the last survivor of the Falsch Jewish family. It's been forty years since he left Berlin—in 1938. In the arrival hall, his dead family is there: parents, sister, brother, sister-in-law, aunt—who died in the concentration camps—the uncle and his wife—exiles in England, gone to Palestine and returned to die in Berlin—and Lili the young German, daughter of a Nazi, whom he loved and who died under the bombardments of Berlin.	Unrated
Fanny's Journey— Le voyage de Fanny (2016)	[Wikipedia] In Vichy France, 1943, a group of French Jewish children (who had been sheltered by the Œuvre de Secours aux Enfants for three years) must now flee to neutral Switzerland, separated from any adults they can trust.	Unrated
Fateless—Sorstalanság (2005)	*Fateless—Sorstalanság* (2005) is the breathtaking true account of a teenage boy living through internment at Auschwitz and then in the Buchenwald Concentration Camp. Although the story is more character-driven than *The Grey Zone* (2001), *Fateless* is every bit as pitch-perfect in its production and effectiveness. *Fateless*, the depiction of the journey from an innocent child to a young Holocaust survivor, is peerless. (*cont.*)	R for some disturbing Holocaust images including nudity, and brief strong language.

Title	Summary	MPAA or Local Rating
	[Wikipedia, translated from Hungarian] Gyuri Köves is an ordinary boy from Budapest, who lived his life uneventfully in 1944. It's almost like the majority, except for one thing: he is Jewish. Shortly after his father was taken to labor, he was also captured and taken to Auschwitz, from where he was transported to the Buchenwald camp. Gyuri Köves does not rebel against his fate, he is not surprised, he does not seek a way out, he experiences the tribulations of life.	
~~Father (1990)~~	[Wikipedia] The film begins with a scene of an open pit full of shot naked bodies somewhere in Lithuania during the Second World War. A young Iya Zetnick crawls out of the bodies in tears, apparently having survived a massacre. Decades later in modern-day Melbourne we are introduced to Joe Muller and his affable family. His adult daughter Anne lives with him, and one day she receives a phone call from Iya Zetnick, asking her to be sure to watch a television current affairs show coming up. Joe thinks it concerns a trivial matter about his business, but he and his family are shocked when the show instead links him to the massacre of Iya's family in Lithuania.	PG-13
Fatherland (TV 1994)	[Wikipedia] A prologue outlines the story's alternate timeline. The failure of the D-Day invasion causes the United States Armed Forces' withdrawal from the European theater of the Second World War and General Dwight D. Eisenhower's retirement in disgrace. The United States continues its Pacific War against the Empire of Japan, and led by General Douglas MacArthur, it uses atomic bombs for its victory. In Europe, Nazi Germany successfully achieves its invasion of the United Kingdom, which results in King George VI fleeing with his family to Canada and continuing to rule the British Empire. Under Nazi supervision, Edward VIII assumes the throne in the United Kingdom, and Wallis Simpson becomes his queen.	Unrated (PG-13)
The Fed One—Hranjenik (1970)	[Yad Vashem] Group of concentration camp prisoners is being constantly tortured by their Kappo [sic]. Since they are too weak to stand against him, they pick the strongest among themselves and feed him with parts of their rations.	Unrated (PG)
Fever at Dawn—Hajnali láz (2015)	Holocaust survivors fall in love and persevere in a Swedish hospital.	Unrated
The Final Solution: The Wannsee Conference— Die Wannseekonferenz (TV 1984)	[Wikipedia] 1984 German TV film portraying the events of the Wannsee Conference, held in Berlin in January 1942. The script is derived from the minutes of the meeting. Since no verbatim transcription of the meeting exists, the dialogue is necessarily fictionalized. The main theme of the film is the bureaucratic nature of the genocide.	Unrated (PG)

Title	Summary	MPAA or Local Rating
For Those I Loved— *Au nom de tous les miens* (1983)	Although ill-served by its unnecessary contemporary bookends, *For Those I Loved—Au nom de tous les miens* (1983) is one of the finest cinematic portrayals of the Warsaw Ghetto and is one of the only Holocaust film depictions of Treblinka. Produced between *Holocaust* (Miniseries 1978) and *War and Remembrance* (Miniseries 1988), *For Those I Loved* strikes the best early balance between Holocaust depiction and excessive violence. While not as celebrated as *Sophie's Choice* (1982), which was released the previous year, *For Those I Loved* is unabashedly about Jewish suffering and resistance. [Wikipedia] The main character in the book belonged to the Reform Jews, where he lived with his family in Warsaw Ghetto after the Nazi invasion of Poland. The character supports his family with black-market supplies and joins the Resistance. He is deported to the Treblinka camp, where he manages to survive and then escape. Afterwards he joins the partisan forces and then the Red Army, taking part in the capture of Berlin.	Unrated (PG)
Forbidden (1984)	[Wikipedia] German countess Nina von Halder is a student in veterinary medicine in Berlin, Germany on the eve of World War II. Ostracized by her family due to her liberal views and opposition to the Nazi government, she lives alone, independent and strong-willed. The film opens with Nina studying at the library the day Germany invades Poland. She is angered and tells a classmate she knows the reasons Hitler gave for the invasion (to allegedly rescue ethnic Germans from Polish attackers) are a pack of lies.	PG-13
Forbidden Dreams—Death of the Beautiful Robucks— *Smrt krásných srncu* (1987)	[Wikipedia, translated from Czech] The film shows the social atmosphere in Czechoslovakia in the 1930s. The main character is a sales representative and seller of Electrolux vacuum cleaners, who invents new sales methods and thrives thanks to his personal charm. In his free time, he enjoys life and fishing. However, during the Nazi occupation, he was released due to his Jewish origin and his family was in danger of being transported to a concentration camp; he therefore makes a risky trip to the countryside for venison.	Unrated
Forget Me Not: The Anne Frank Story (TV 1996)	An antisemite is sent back in time to Anne Frank's attic and taught a lesson about tolerance.	Unrated (PG)
~~*Forgiveness—Esther's Diary* (2008)~~	[Wikipedia] A Roman Catholic child, Apollonia Kowalski, and a Jewish child, Esther Blumenfeld, were childhood best friends in 1940's Poland. The two girls were separated when Esther was taken away to a Nazi concentration camp. When the war ended, both girls separately emigrated to the United States with their families. They remained separated thereafter.	Unrated

Title	Summary	MPAA or Local Rating
Free Men—Les hommes libres (2011)	[Wikipedia] In occupied Paris, the young unemployed Algerian, Younes Ben Daoud, makes a living on the black market. He is arrested by the police, and to avoid prison he agrees to spy on the Paris Mosque. The police suspect that the mosque leadership, including its rector Si Kaddour Benghabrit, is helping resistance fighters and protecting North African Jews by giving them Muslim birth certificates.	Unrated (PG)
Freedom Writers (2007)	The true story of a high school teacher in California who used Anne Frank's *Diary* and the Holocaust to teach her students about tolerance, empathy and excellence.	PG-13 for violent content, some thematic material and language.
From Hell to Hell—Iz ada v ad (1996)	[Wikipedia] In 1941, the Polish town Kielce is occupied by the Nazis. The main character, before being sent to a concentration camp, gives her daughter to a Polish family whose child has recently died. When the war has passed, the former prisoner returns to his hometown and wants his daughter returned, but she has grown up not knowing who her real parents were. Internal contradictions and deep spiritual experiences put the heroes in a cruel situation of choice.	Unrated
Fugitive Pieces (2007)	[Wikipedia] The film tells the story of Jakob Beer, who is orphaned in Poland during World War II and is saved by a Greek archeologist.	R for some sexuality.
The Garden of the Finzi-Continis— Il Giardino dei Finzi-Contini (1970)	*The Garden of the Finzi-Continis—Il Giardino dei Finzi-Contini* (1970) is the first "arthouse" Holocaust film. It is beautifully made, from start to finish. More importantly, as opposed to most Holocaust films, *Finzi-Continis* depicts assimilated European (Italian) Jews who are unashamedly Jewish, yet who do not solely define themselves by their religious heritage. *Finzi-Continis* also effectively argues that, at some point during the War, wealth could no longer save Jews from the Germans. [Wikipedia] In the late 1930s, in Ferrara, a group of young friends get together for afternoons of tennis and happy times. Some of them are Italian Jews and a rising tide of Fascism has imposed increasingly anti-Semitic restrictions in their lives. Barred from regular tennis clubs, they go to play at the grand, walled estate owned by the Finzi-Continis, a wealthy, intellectual and sophisticated Jewish family. The two young Finzi-Continis, Alberto and his sister Micòl, have organized a tennis tournament. Oblivious to the threats around them, life still seems to be sunny at the large Finzi-Contini estate, keeping the rest of the world at bay.	UK-14+
Gebürtig (2002)	A Holocaust survivor is lured back to Austria to help catch a Nazi.	Unrated
The General Case— Die Akte General (TV 2016)	[Wikipedia, translated from German] The Hessian attorney general Fritz Bauer investigates criminals from the Nazi era in Frankfurt in 1959. He also succeeds in enabling Israel to arrest Adolf Eichmann in Argentina by traveling to Israel privately and giving the Mossad a tip.	Unrated

Title	Summary	MPAA or Local Rating
Genghis Cohn (1993)	*Genghis Cohn* (1993) is a Holocaust comedy about a West German police commissioner in 1958 who is also a former SS officer. The former Nazi is tormented by an apparition, the ghost of a Jew he killed. Tonally, like in *My Führer* (2007), thematically like *The Twilight Zone*'s episode "Deaths-Head Revisited" (1961), this delightful little film belittles post-War West German civil service as the home of so many former Nazis. The film is whimsical and ghoulish, culminating seamlessly.	Unrated (R)
The German Doctor—Wakolda (2013)	[Wikipedia] Josef Mengele is in exile in Argentina in 1960, living under a new identity. He makes a long journey by road to a new location by following a family, as the roads are dangerous. Mengele has his own place to stay in Patagonia, but he takes an interest in Lilith, who is the daughter of the family, and he moves into their hotel by paying six months' rent.	PG-13 for thematic material and brief nudity.
Getting Away with Murder (1996)	[Wikipedia] Jack Lambert's neighbor Max Mueller is revealed on the TV news to be the escaped Nazi war criminal Karl Luger who was sentenced to death by the courts. Under the constant duress of the news media's allegations, Mueller plans to flee to South America. Angered that Mueller might never pay for his crimes, Lambert takes the drastic step of poisoning him by injecting cyanide into some of the fruit in Mueller's apple tree, from which he regularly makes freshly juiced apple juice.	R
Ghetto—Vilniaus getas (2005)	[Wikipedia, translated from Italian] It is a story of fatal love and terrible hatred. The action takes place in Vilnius ghetto during World War II years. Nazi officer Kitelis, a former actor and jazz musician himself, falls in love with the Jewish singer Chaya and helps to establish a theater in the ghetto.	Unrated (R)
~~*Gitel* (2015)~~	A Holocaust survivor struggles with her past.	Unrated
~~*The Glass Cage—La cage de verre* (1965)~~	[Yad Vashem] Deported as a child to a concentration camp in 1942, Pierre has been married for 15 years to Helene, a non-Jewish Frenchwoman. 1961 finds them living in a prosperous bourgeois life in Tel Aviv. Helen works; Pierre is an engineer, currently working on an irrigation scheme in the Negev desert. But the impending trial of Adolf Eichmann disrupts their calm routine.	Unrated
Gloomy Sunday— Ein Lied von Liebe und Tod (1999)	[Wikipedia] In the present day, German industrialist Hans Wieck returns to Budapest with his family on the occasion of his 80th birthday having been stationed there during World War II. During dinner at his favorite restaurant, Szabó's, Hans regales his family and friends with stories of his many visits to the restaurant before and during the war. As he relishes his favorite dish, "Beef Rolls" he suddenly collapses with the song "Gloomy Sunday" being played, at his request, by two musicians. As he dies he sees a portrait of a beautiful woman taken many years before. The film then flashes back to Budapest during the late 1930s.	Unrated (R)

Title	Summary	MPAA or Local Rating
God on Trial (TV 2008)	Although *God on Trial* (TV 2008) is overtly didactic, it is also one of the few Holocaust films that grapple directly in Auschwitz with the question of how the Holocaust could have happened to God's "Chosen People." *God on Trial* makes almost no effort to recreate Auschwitz/Birkenau, but does have a nice current-day wraparound to open and close the film. For those studying Holocaust theology, *God on Trial* is ideal. For those wanting more of a story, most of the other recommended Victim films are advised. [Wikipedia] The play takes place in Auschwitz during World War II. The Jewish prisoners put God on trial in absentia for abandoning the Jewish people. The question is whether God has broken his covenant with the Jewish people by allowing the Germans to commit genocide	Unrated (PG)
Gold of Rome—L'oro di Roma (1961)	[Wikipedia, translated from Italian] After the Italian armistice the Germans occupy Rome. In October 1943 the commander of the German police calls the president of the Jewish community in his presence and orders him to deliver 50 kilos of gold within two days; otherwise he will take 200 household heads hostage. The community is divided between those who decide to give in to blackmail and hand over the little gold left to them and those who do not believe in the word of the Germans. The Jews remaining in the ghetto are impoverished by the Italian racial laws and with enormous difficulty they try to collect the required amount.	Unrated
The Gold Rimmed Glasses— Gli occhiali d'oro (1987)	[Wikipedia] Set in Ferrara and in a nearby seaside resort in 1938, the plot follows a Jewish student and a homosexual doctor who suffer persecution in Fascist Italy.	Unrated
Good (2008)	[Wikipedia] John Halder is a Frankfurt literary professor and an example of the good man: he is apparently devoted to his wife and children and he does his best to look after his aged mother. He even tells his best friend, who is a Jewish psychiatrist, that the anti-Semitism of the National Socialists is "just a balloon they throw up in the air to distract the masses." But this is Germany in 1933, and men can change.	R for language.
***Good Evening, Mr. Wallenberg— God afton, Herr Wallenberg— En Passionshistoria från verkligheten* (1990)**	*Good Evening, Mr. Wallenberg* (1990) tells the story of Raoul Wallenberg who saved many tens of thousands of Jews. This screen version of his story is uncompromising in its depiction of German savagery and Jewish powerlessness. Wallenberg, who was later captured and murdered by the Soviets, is portrayed as a goodhearted man who never sought glory or thanks. Of films that depict Gentiles who save many Jews, *Good Evening, Mr. Wallenberg* is the most genuine and non-commercial. [Wikipedia, translated from Swedish] The film is about Raoul Wallenberg's last weeks in Budapest, from Christmas 1944 to January 1945. It centers on two events; Raoul's attempt to free some twenty captured people on a truck and to rescue 65,000 people trapped in the ghetto.	Unrated (R)

Title	Summary	MPAA or Local Rating
~~The Great Promise=~~ ~~Dim'at Ha'Nehamah Ha'Gedolah~~ ~~(1947)~~	Three stories told by soldiers: (1) a farmer establishes a kibbutz; (2) children of the Holocaust being absorbed in the kibbutz.; settlement on the Jordan River.	Unrated
The Grey Zone (2001)	*The Grey Zone* (2001) is the finest Holocaust film ever made. It depicts two events at Birkenau: the survival of a girl in a gas chamber and the revolt that destroyed two of the crematorium complexes. Few other films capture the ethical dilemmas faced by Jews who were forced either to assist the Germans or to be murdered. [Wikipedia] The film opens in October 1944, in the Auschwitz-Birkenau extermination camp. A small group of Sonderkommando, prisoners assigned to dispose of the bodies of other dead prisoners, are plotting an insurrection that, they hope, will destroy at least one of the camp's four crematoria and gas chambers.	R for strong Holocaust violence, nudity and language.
Gruber's Journey— Calatoria lui Gruber (2008)	[Wikipedia] The film centers on an Italian writer named Curzio Malaparte, who was a member of the Italian Fascist Party. Malaparte is assigned to cover the Russian front for the Italian news service, and travels with Colonel Freitag of the Wehrmacht and the deputy commander of the local Romanian garrison to Romania. He suffers from a serious allergy and is sent to consult world-class allergist Dr. Josef Gruber in Iaşi, but Gruber is missing.	Unrated
The Guard of Auschwitz (2018)	The Holocaust is seen from the perspective of a German soldier at Auschwitz.	15
Hanna's Journey—Hannas Reise (2013)	Several generations after the Holocaust, a German woman named Hanna moves to Israel for work, but also finds romance. Although this non-Jewish young woman is uninformed about the Holocaust and is ignorant about her family's Nazi past, she ultimately determines to learn her history.	Unrated
Hanna's Sleeping Dogs— Hannas schlafende Hunde (2016)	[Wikipedia, translated from German] In the late 1960s, nine-year-old Johanna Berger grew up as a Catholic girl in Wels in Upper Austria, where she lived with her mother Katharina, her father Franz and her brother. She likes to sing, but her parents forbid everything that gives her joy. Her mother always takes care not to attract attention and to adhere to the usual customs, such as going to church on Sundays. Little Hanna is taught modesty, adaptability and restraint as important virtues.	Unrated
Hanna's War (1988)	[Wikipedia] Hannah Senesh was a Hungarian schoolgirl with poetic aspirations. In the face of rising anti-Semitic tensions in Budapest, Hanna leaves her mother Katalin and family behind to work on a kibbutz in then Palestine. There she is recruited by the British Air Force for a dangerous mission: The RAF will train volunteers and parachute them over their native lands if they agree to help downed fliers escape from enemy territory.	PG-13

Title	Summary	MPAA or Local Rating
Harold and Maude **(1971)**	*Harold and Maude* (1971) is a cult classic and a masterpiece. *Harold and Maude* is also rarely regarded as a Survivor Holocaust film. It is the story of an eccentric old woman who lives in a converted train-car in California. She refuses to dwell on the past. Not until 70 minutes into the 90-minute film is it even made clear that she is a survivor, and only then with a brief glimpse of her Auschwitz tattoo. Nothing is wasted in this classic, the subtlest of all Holocaust films. [Wikipedia] *Harold and Maude* is a 1971 American romantic black comedy drama. It incorporates elements of dark humor and existentialist drama. The plot revolves around the exploits of a young man named Harold Chasen who is intrigued with death. Harold drifts away from the life that his detached mother prescribes for him, and slowly develops a strong friendship, and eventually a romantic relationship, with a 79-year-old woman named Maude who teaches Harold about living life to its fullest and that life is the most precious gift of all.	PG
Haven (TV 2001)	[Yad Vashem] This television drama tells the true story of a woman named Ruth Gruber who travels to Europe to help escort 1000 Jewish war refugees to the United States. She comes to love and feel sorry for them all, and fights for their rights to live in America.	PG-13 for thematic elements, violence and disturbing images, and brief sensuality.
Heartbeat Detector— *La question humaine* (2007)	[Wikipedia] The film centers on Kessler, a psychologist in the human resources department of the French branch of a long-established German firm. The firm has recently dismissed 50% of its workforce on criteria devised by Kessler. Rose, the vice-president of the company, requests Kessler to look into whether Jüst, the CEO, is fit to do his job. The CEO discovers Kessler is investigating him and tells him that Rose, whose previous name was Kraus, has a Nazi past.	Unrated (R)
~~*Hidden Children—*~~ ~~*La fuga degli innocenti*~~ ~~(TV 2004)~~	[Yad Vashem] This is a true story about forty Jewish children on their way to Israel, who were blocked by the German and Italian occupation of Yugoslavia in 1941. Before finding a haven at Villa Emma in Nonantola in northern Italy, where they arrived on June 17, 1942, the children spent several adventurous months in Slovenia, caught up in the ongoing fight between the partisans and the Italian army.	Unrated
The Hiding Place (1975)	[Wikipedia] As the Nazis invade the Netherlands in 1940, Corrie and the rest of her family allow Jews to hide in a part of their home that is specially remodeled by members of the Dutch resistance. However, the Nazis eventually discover that the family is hiding Jews, and on February 28, 1944, the entire family and its friends are arrested after their betrayal by a Dutch collaborator. The hidden Jews are never found by authorities. The Nazis send Corrie and her sister, Betsie, to the Ravensbrück concentration camp, Germany, for hiding Jews in their home. At the concentration camp, Betsie encourages Corrie to remain hopeful that God will rescue them from the brutalities they experience.	PG

Title	Summary	MPAA or Local Rating
High Street—Rue haute (1977)	[Yad Vashem] *High Street* is an unusual drama focusing on a woman driven mad by events during World War II. An American expatriate artist living in Brussels becomes obsessed with the woman's imaginary battles, and attempts to discover their root. He discovers she has been "fighting" since the Nazis killed her Jewish husband and young son in 1943, and his life is transformed.	Unrated
Holy Week—Wielki tydzien (1995)	[Wikipedia, translated from Polish] The film takes place in 1943 in occupied Warsaw. Irena Lilien, a young Jewish woman, hides with her friends. Taken by two Gestapo agents, she bribes them. On the street, she meets her ex-fiancé who takes her to his apartment. The presence of a Jewish woman gives rise to various attitudes among Poles living in the tenement house.	Unrated
~~*The Hour of Truth—L'heure de la vérité* (1965)~~	[Wikipedia, translated from French] Jonathan Strauss, a former deportee of German origin, has rebuilt his life in Israel, where he is an engineer. He shares his life with Dahlia Modiano, of Judeo-Spanish origin, who has three brothers, Benjamin (a doctor in a hospital), Haïm (an old independence fighter) and David (a bookseller). Dahlia tells Jonathan that she is pregnant. In the evening, while the whole family celebrates the Jewish Passover, with their friend Moshe Misrahi, who participated in the hunt for Eichmann, Fred Blynt, a young American sociologist, arrives. He is interested in the history of the Gandstadt camp and wants to question Jonathan, who is the only survivor, after all the other prisoners were liquidated by the camp commander, Hans Wernert, who disappeared upon liberation.	Unrated
The House in Karp Lane—Das Haus in der Karpfengasse (TV 1965)	[Wikipedia, translated from German] The Karpfengasse mentioned in the title is located in the old Jewish quarter of Prague. The building at number 115 houses very different people on its three floors: Czechs, Germans and many Jews. A new, terrible time dawned for all of them when on March 15, 1939, the German Wehrmacht invaded the Czech Republic and proclaimed the "Protectorate of Bohemia and Moravia."	Unrated
~~*House of the Generals* (2003)~~	[Yad Vashem] 10 million Ukrainians lost their lives in the first half of the 20th Century. 600,000 Ukrainian Jews perished, victims of Hitler and Stalin. The Ukraine amassed thousands of World War II monuments. Half of the Russian losses occurred in the Ukraine. Based on a true story.	Unrated
The House on Garibaldi Street (TV 1979)	[Wikipedia] Israeli premier David Ben-Gurion approves a Mossad operation to be led by Isser Harel to kidnap Adolf Eichmann, the Nazi mass murder organizer. Harel's team travels to Argentina to track down Ricardo Klement, who they believe is Eichmann. They soon discover that the Klement family moved two months before. Primo, a local contact, goes to their former residence and gets a lead to Dieter, one of Eichmann's sons.	Unrated (PG)

Title	Summary	MPAA or Local Rating
How A Hirschberger Learned Danish— *Wie ein Hirschberger Dänisch lernte* (TV 1968)	[Yad Vashem] This TV drama tell the story of a Jewish lawyer, Wilhelm Heilmann, who escapes Nazi Germany in 1939 to Denmark with his son Helmut and their attempts to assimilate in the foreign country and then, when the Nazis occupy it, to escape once again, this time to neutral Sweden.	Unrated
I Do Not Care If We Go Down in History as Barbarians— *Îmi este indiferent daca in istorie vom intra ca barbari* (2018)	[Wikipedia, translated from Romanian] Theater director Mariana Marin intends to make a comprehensive reconstruction of the Odessa massacre. In 1941, the commander of the Romanian army, Ion Antonescu, ordered the execution of Jewish citizens in retaliation and hundreds of thousands of innocent people were killed. Mariana wants to show all this in front of the Royal Palace in the center of Bucharest, but she faces some unexpected and ridiculous problems, because both amateur actors and city hall representatives have quite strong opinions not only about what really happened, but also about how that reality should be staged and presented to the public.	15
~~*I Know Why I Live—*~~ ~~*Ich weiß, wofür ich lebe* (1955)~~	[Wikipedia, translated from German] Maria Pfluger had worked as a nurse during the Second World War. In the greatest need, Mary, who has always felt committed to the protection and preservation of life, turned out to be a saving angel when she took two small children under her wing. The existence of the two boys is extremely threatened in the Third Reich, because Pit and Jascho are both of Jewish faith. But now, a decade later, the war is long over, and yet Maria has adopted the two now adolescents instead of children and accordingly loved them.	Unrated
I Was Overtaken by Night— *Zastihla me noc* (1986)	[Yad Vashem] The life and slow death of Communist journalist and Prague City Council member Jozka Jaburkova in the Ravensbruck concentration camp is the focus of this wartime drama starring Jana Rihakova as the tragic Jaburkova. Suffering almost from the beginning as an illegitimate child burdened with extreme moral expectations by her fanatically religious mother, Jaburkova suffered at the hands of the teachers and authorities in her all girls' school. Her sympathy for the oppressed or those experiencing unjust hardship or discrimination got her into trouble again and again, both as a student and when she went on to seek employment. As the camera focuses on scenes in the concentration camp, Jaburkova's memories of her past are shown in flashbacks.	Unrated
Ida (2013)	[Wikipedia] In the 1960s Polish People's Republic, Anna, a young novice nun, is told by her prioress that before she takes her vows she must visit her aunt, Wanda Gruz, who is her only surviving relative. Anna travels to Warsaw visit her aunt Wanda, a chain-smoking, hard-drinking, sexually promiscuous judge who reveals that Anna's actual name is Ida Lebenstein; Ida's parents had been Jews who were murdered late in the German occupation of Poland during World War II.	PG-13 for thematic elements, some sexuality and smoking.

Title	Summary	MPAA or Local Rating
The Illegals—Lo Tafhidenu (1947)	[Yad Vashem] Author Meyer Levin joined Haganah men after WWII and described in this semi-documentary film "Aliyah Bet," the underground illegal movement of Holocaust survivors to British mandated Palestine. The story follows a young Polish Jewish couple that makes its winding way to Eretz Israel. Including footage of British soldiers boarding a refugee ship.	Unrated
I'm Alive and I Love You— Je suis vivante et je vous aime (1998)	[Wikipedia, translated from French] During the occupation in France, a railway worker found a message that had fallen from a train of deportees, with a few words "I am alive and I love you—Sarah" as well as an address. He discovers that Sarah's son, who is only four years old, has escaped the roundup.	Unrated
In Another Lifetime— Vielleicht in einem anderen Leben (2011)	[Wikipedia, translated from German] The historical background of the film is formed by the last days of World War II in April 1945. In the course of one of the death marches of those days when the Schutzstaffel and Volkssturm drive thousands of Jews through the crumbling German Reich from the occupied territories in the east towards the concentration camps, the SS-Oberscharführer Schöndorf marches a group of initially 20 Jews from Hungary through eastern Austria. The destination is the Mauthausen concentration camp.	Unrated
In Darkness (2011)	[Wikipedia] *In Darkness* is a dramatization of a rescue of Jewish refugees during World War II in the German-occupied city Lwów. For over a year, a Polish Catholic sewer maintenance worker and burglar, Leopold Socha, along with his friend and co-worker Szczepek Wróblewski, hid and cared for a group of Polish Jews who had escaped the massacres and deportations during the liquidation of the Lwów Ghetto.	R for violence, disturbing images, sexuality, nudity and language.
In Hiding—W ukryciu (2013)	[Wikipedia, translated from Polish] The film is about homosexual love between women, one of whom is a hidden Jewish woman and the other the Polish woman hiding her. The plot takes place at the end of World War II.	Unrated
In the End Come Tourists— Am Ende kommen Touristen (2007)	[Wikipedia, translated from Polish] 19-year-old Sven, who is doing community service, ends up in Oświęcim, Poland, also known as Auschwitz. There he is supposed to work in the international meeting center and above all to take care of the elderly concentration camp survivor Krzemiński.	Unrated
In the Presence of Mine Enemies (TV 1997)	[Wikipedia] The film is a remake of an original TV drama scripted by Rod Serling for *Playhouse 90*, titled "In the Presence of Mine Enemies," starring Charles Laughton. The plot centers on a rabbi and his children. The movie also features Charles Dance as a German officer, and introducing Jason Schwartz as Israel leader of the orphan rebellion.	PG-13
In the Shadow of Hate— W cieniu nienawisci (TV 1986)	A righteous Gentile in Warsaw hides a Jewish child.	Unrated

Title	Summary	MPAA or Local Rating
Inglourious Basterds (2009)	_Inglourious Basterds_ (2009), for better or worse, is the Holocaust touchstone for many. It is the fictional story of Jewish revenge during the Holocaust. As an educational film, _Inglourious Basterds_ is dangerously misleading; as a fictional Tangential Holocaust film, it is not only smart, but immensely entertaining and satisfying. 　[Wikipedia] The film tells an alternate history story of two plots to assassinate Nazi Germany's leadership, one planned by Shosanna Dreyfus, a young French Jewish cinema proprietor, and the other by a team of Jewish American soldiers led by First Lieutenant Aldo Raine.	R for strong graphic violence, language and brief sexuality.
~~_The Interpreter—Tlmocník_ (2018)~~	[Wikipedia] In Vienna, retiree Georg meets an interpreter named Ali. The two men embark on a journey across Slovakia, encountering wartime survivors who will hopefully lead them to the Nazi officer that killed Ali's parents.	Unrated
~~_The Interrogation_ (2016)~~	[Yad Vashem] A feature film. In 1946, Rudolf Franz Ferdinand Höss, the longest serving commander of Auschwitz concentration camp, is awaiting trial in a Polish prison. Albert, a young and successful Polish investigation judge, is appointed to interrogate Höss and get a perfect confession out of him. The encounter between the two men will unveil the frightening routine and banalization of evil that took place in the camp. By introducing the use of Zyklon B in Auschwitz, Rudolf Höss carried out the most efficient mass killing process ever known, which claimed the lives of approximately 1.1 million people. The film is based on the memoirs Höss wrote before his execution.	15
The Investigation—Die Ermittlung (TV 1966)	[Wikipedia, translated from German] _The Investigation_ was to become part of a larger "world theater" project, following the structure of Dante Alighieri's _Divine Comedy_. The three-part drama project should encompass the otherworldly spheres of hell, paradise and the purgatory in between. In reverse of Dante's convictions, _The Investigation_, which takes place during the Frankfurt Auschwitz trials, should correspond to the "Paradiso" of the Dante conception and paradise should be the place of despair for those who suffer.	Unrated
Invincible (2001)	The story of a Jewish strongman in Germany. While basing his story on the real-life figure Zishe Breitbart (a.k.a. Siegmund Breitbart), Herzog uses the bare facts of Breitbart's life to weave fact and fiction (e.g., the story is set in 1932 Berlin, a full seven years after Breitbart's death in 1925) to create an allegory of human strength, knowing oneself with honesty and pride in one's heritage.	PG-13 for some sexual content and thematic elements.
Invitation—Zaproszenie (1986)	[Yad Vashem] Film starts with a flashback, showing us a young couple, celebrating their engagement. But the war disrupts their love. He becomes a soldier, she finally finds herself in Auschwitz. Anna, the main character, finds her memories triggered when her old flame Piotr, who now lives in the US, comes to visit Poland in the 1980s.	Unrated

Title	Summary	MPAA or Local Rating
The Island on Bird Street (1997)	*The Island on Bird Street* (1997) portrays a child surviving the War by hiding in the Warsaw Ghetto, in the same manner as in the protagonist's favorite book, *Robinson Crusoe*. The story is more formulaic than most recommended Holocaust films, the ending is mushy, and the film suffers from a lack of realism, but *The Island on Bird Street* can be used as a starter film for younger students learning about the Warsaw Ghetto. Based on a book, is useful for comparative or complementary lessons. 　　[Wikipedia] … a 1981 semi-autobiographical children's book by Israeli author Uri Orlev, which tells the story of a young boy, Alex, and his struggle to survive alone in a ghetto during World War II.	PG-13
It Will Never Happen Again— Unzere Kinder (1951)	A famous Polish comedy duo, who are Holocaust survivors, entertains child-survivors.	Unrated
Jacob the Liar—Jakob, der Lügner (1974)	[Wikipedia] In a Jewish ghetto in German-occupied Poland, a man named Jakob is caught on the streets after curfew. He is told to report to a German military office where he finds the officer in charge passed out drunk. The radio is running and Jakob hears a broadcast about the advances of the Soviet Army. Eventually, Jakob sneaks out and goes home. Later he tells his friends that the Russians are not very far away. As no one believes he went to the Nazi office and came out alive, Jakob makes up a lie, claiming he owns a radio—a crime punishable by death.	Argentina-13
Jakob the Liar (1999)	[Wikipedia] In Poland of early 1944, a Polish-Jewish shopkeeper named Jakob Heym is summoned to the German headquarters after being falsely accused of being out after curfew. While waiting for the commander, Jakob overhears a German radio broadcast speaking about Soviet offensives. Returned to the ghetto, Jakob shares his information with a friend, sparking rumors that there is a secret radio within the ghetto. After hesitating, Jakob decides to use the chance to spread hope throughout the ghetto by continuing to tell the optimistic, fantastic tales that he allegedly heard from his "secret radio", and his lies keep hope and humor alive among the isolated ghetto inhabitants. He also has a real secret, in that he is hiding a young Jewish girl who escaped from an extermination camp deportation train.	PG-13 for violence and disturbing images.
Jew Boy Levi—Viehjud Levi (1999)	[Yad Vashem] Drama based on a play by Thomas Strittmatter. It is the story of Levy, a Jewish traveling salesman in the area of "The Black Forest" in southwest Germany, in the days of the strengthening of Nazism and outbreak of the latent antisemitism.	Unrated
A Jewish Girl in Shanghai (2010)	[Wikipedia] Set mainly in and around the Shanghai Ghetto in Japanese-occupied Shanghai during the Second World War, the film tells the story of three children. Rina and her younger brother Mishalli are Jewish refugees who escaped Europe but are without their parents. A-Gen is a Chinese orphan boy who *(cont.)*	NR

Title	Summary	MPAA or Local Rating
	meets Rina and helps her and her brother to survive. The children form strong friendships and have adventures as they try and fend off the Japanese army occupying the city, and their allies, the Nazis. In the background, the Second Sino-Japanese War takes place, while the children must face the uncertainty that concerns the fate of Rina and Mishalli's parents in Europe.	
Joanna (2010)	[Wikipedia, translated from Polish] Krakow in the period of Nazi occupation. In the life of Joanna nothing is given forever. A friend suddenly becomes an enemy, and her soft heart turns into a curse. Joanna works in a cafe and one day she takes in a girl she accidentally meets, Róża, whose mother was taken by the Germans.	Unrated (R)
Jojo Rabbit (2019)	[Wikipedia] Johannes "Jojo" Betzler, a ten-year-old Hitler Youth member, finds out that his mother is hiding a Jewish girl in their attic. He must then question his beliefs, while dealing with the intervention of his imaginary friend, a fanciful version of Adolf Hitler with a comedic stand on the politics of the war.	Rated PG-13 for mature thematic content, some disturbing images, violence, and language
~~*Journey to Jerusalem—Patuvane kam Yerusalim* (2003)~~	[Yad Vashem, translated from Hebrew] Two children, German Jews, accompanied by their old uncle, try to escape from the fascists, on their way to Palestine. They must reach Istanbul by train and from there by ship to the land of the fathers. Due to the death of the uncle, the brother and sister find themselves at the train station in Sofia and not in Istanbul. In the end, Bulgaria managed to save all 50,000 Jews during World War II.	Unrated
Judgment at Nuremberg (1961)	[Wikipedia] Set in Nuremberg, Germany, in 1948, the film depicts a fictionalized version of the Judges' Trial of 1947, one of the 12 U.S. military tribunals during the Nuremberg trials.	UK-PG
Judith (1966)	[Wikipedia] In Palestine shortly before the end of the British mandate, the Haganah has learned that a former German tank commander, General Gustav Schiller, is teaching the Arabs battle tactics, but they are unable to locate him. Then they learn of the existence of his Jewish former wife, Judith Auerbach Schiller, and arrange for her to be smuggled into Palestine via the port of Haifa. She is placed in the care of Aaron Stein, a Haganah commander, at a kibbutz.	Unrated
The Juggler (1953)	[Wikipedia] After World War II, German Hans Müller is one of a shipload of Jewish refugees who disembark at Haifa in 1949. Like many other concentration camp survivors, Hans has psychological problems, including survivor guilt. At one point, he mistakes a woman and some children for his murdered family.	UK-14+
Julia (1977)	Julia was a close childhood friend of Lillian Hellman, who would become a famous American author and playwright. Julia moves from America to attend college in England and then medical school in Austria. During Hitler's rise to power, Julia becomes an anti-Nazi activist in Vienna. When Hellman visits Europe, Julia enlists her famous friend to smuggle money into Germany for other anti-Nazi activists.	PG

Title	Summary	MPAA or Local Rating
Just an Ordinary Jew— *Ein ganz gewöhnlicher Jude* (2005)	[Wikipedia, translated from German] The Hamburg journalist Emanuel Goldfarb, the only son of Holocaust survivors, is invited by a teacher to his class so that he can answer the students' questions about Judaism. With the formulation of the rejection, in which Goldfarb reveals his identity and his life as a Jew and German in Germany, a monologue emerges which Goldfarb speaks into a dictation machine—angry about such cautious formulations as "Member of your religious community" or "Jewish fellow citizen" instead of "Jew."	Unrated
Just Beyond That Forest— *Jeszcze tylko ten las* (1991)	[Wikipedia, translated from Polish] Kulgawcowa agrees to lead Rutka, the daughter of her former employer, from the ghetto to her family in the countryside. They are close to their destination when they encounter a German soldier. Rutka's Aryan documents contain a photo of her parents that she had taken secretly.	Unrated
Kapò (1960)	[Wikipedia] Naive 14-year-old Edith and her Jewish parents are sent to a concentration camp, where the latter are killed. Sofia, an older, political prisoner, and a kindly camp doctor save her from a similar fate by giving her a new, non-Jewish identity, that of the newly dead Nichole Niepas.	Hungary-14
Kapo in Jerusalem— *Kapo be'Yerushalaim* (2015)	[Yad Vashem, translated from Hebrew] A drama film set in 1946. Two survivors from Auschwitz arrive in Jerusalem. Bruno is a doctor, singer and pianist. It is rumored in the city that Bruno was a capo who abused Jewish prisoners. Bruno fought for his good name, and for the principles he followed. Doubt also arises in the heart of Sarah trying to support him. With the outbreak of the 1948 Arab-Israeli War, he enlists and is sent to battle over the burning Ramat Rachel from which he never returns. Before the battle, he conducted a mental account of his actions in Auschwitz. In 1950, in Jerusalem licking the wounds of war, in difficult days of austerity, when many Holocaust survivors were absorbed into it, his wife Sarah, along with his lovers and haters, made their mental account.	Unrated (PG)
Keep Away from the Window— *Daleko od okna* (2000)	[Yad Vashem] A once happy marriage begins to fall apart when Jan and Barbara find out that she cannot have children. When the couple hide a young Jewish widow in their house and she becomes pregnant with the husband's child, the couple pass the baby off as their own, setting all the characters onto a complex and dangerous journey. Based on the story "That Girl from Hamburg" by Hanna Krall, this gripping drama is played out against the far greater proportions of the beginning of WWII.	Unrated
***Korczak* (1990)**	Janusz Korczak is celebrated as the force behind a Warsaw Ghetto orphanage. He has been portrayed in many Holocaust films. *Korczak* (1990), however, is the only film solely about him. It is a no-nonsense retelling of his heroic commitment to care for Jewish orphans whom he ultimately accompanied to their *(cont.)*	PG

Title	Summary	MPAA or Local Rating
	deaths at Treblinka, where he meets the same fate. *Korczak* is an unheralded film that portrays Jewish honor and resistance in the face of unmatchable odds. [Wikipedia, translated from German] The film is set in Warsaw during World War II in 1942. It tells the last weeks in the life of the Jewish-Polish doctor, children's book author and educator Janusz Korczak. Korczak runs an orphanage he founded. After the Warsaw Ghetto was established his orphanage has to move to the ghetto with the Jewish children. In the ghetto, too, he sacrificed himself for his children. He looks after around 200 Jewish children under the most adverse circumstances.	
Kornblumenblau (1989)	[Wikipedia, translated from German] In Auschwitz concentration camp there is a block leader nicknamed Kornblaumenblau, who forces musicians to play his favorite music, including the song called "Kornblu-menblau." When Tadeusz Wyczynski arrives as a new prisoner in the camp, he is said to be used for forced labor. However, his musical talent is quickly noticed, which is why he climbs up the warehouse hierarchy and works first as a musician, then as a waiter. The block leader's wife saved him from death with her intercession. When the Red Army liberates Auschwitz, he plays the song "Kalinka" for them.	Unrated
Labyrinth of Lies— Im Labyrinth Des Schweigens (2014)	*Labyrinth of Lies—Im Labyrinth Des Schweigens* (2014) tells the story of a young prosecutor in post-War West Germany who functionally knew nothing about the Holocaust, yet eventually roots out Nazis in German civil service. The film is a remarkable portrayal of pro-tected Nazis in the post-War West German society. As with other antisemitic Gentile films, *Labyrinth of Lies* succeeds in exposing the lesser-known criminals who aided in the Final Solution. [Wikipedia] In 1958, Johann Radmann is a young and idealistic public prosecutor who takes an interest in the case of Charles Schulz, a former Auschwitz extermination camp commander who is now teaching at a school in Frankfurt am Main. Radmann is deter-mined to bring Schulz to justice, but finds his efforts frustrated because of the many former Nazis who are serving in government and looking out for one another.	R for a scene of sexuality.
Lacombe, Lucien (1974)	[Wikipedia] In June 1944, as the Allies are fighting the Germans in Normandy, Lucien Lacombe, a 17-year-old country boy, tries to join the Resistance. The local Resistance leader, the village school teacher, turns him down on grounds of age. Lucien travels back to the town where he works by bicycle and stumbles on the hotel that is the headquarters of the Carlingue, the French auxiliaries of the Gestapo, and is taken into custody. Under the influence of alcohol, he betrays the teacher, who is brought in and tortured. Seeing that Lucien could be useful, the Carlingue recruit him into their lawless regime of extortion and terror.	R

Title	Summary	MPAA or Local Rating
Ladies' Tailor—Damskiy portnoy (1990)	[Wikipedia, translated from Russian] All the Jews of the city of Kiev and its environs must appear on Monday, September 29, 1941, at 8 o'clock in the morning at the corner of Melnikovaya and Dokterivskaya streets (near the cemeteries). They are directed to take their documents and valuables, as well as warm clothes, linen, etc. Any Jew who does not comply with the order and is found elsewhere will be shot. Any citizen who enters the apartments left by the Jews and appropriates their belongings will be shot.	Unrated
~~*L'adieu aux enfants* (TV 1982)~~	About Dr. Janusz Korczak, who cared for hundreds of children in the Warsaw Ghetto.	Unrated
Landscape After Battle— Krajobraz po bitwie (1970)	[Wikipedia] *Landscape After Battle* tells a story of two young concentration camp survivors. In the opening sequence, Vivaldi's "Autumn" can be heard while the prisoners are liberated. A young Polish poet, Tadeusz, is asked by a pretty Jewish girl, Nina, to go with her to the West. His camp experience, however, prevents him from realizing the depth of her love for him, and he is reluctant to commit. Nina is accidentally shot dead by an American soldier, causing Tadeusz to cry for the first time in years.	Unrated
~~*The Last* (2019)~~	A Jewish family discovers that the matriarch was a Nazi nurse at Auschwitz.	Unrated
The Last Butterfly— Poslední motýl (1991)	*The Last Butterfly—Poslední motýl* (1991) is an excellent fictional film that depicts the very real Theresienstadt concentration camp, the sham "model" concentration camp, which was created to fool the international community and, specifically, the Red Cross. The Czech film *The Last Butterfly* is told from the perspective of a fictional famous Gentile performer who is forced to participate in a show for the Red Cross in Theresienstadt with Jewish prisoners, all of whom are to be shipped out after the show and murdered.	Rated PG-13 for thematic elements
The Last Chance— Die letzte Chance (1945)	[Wikipedia] In 1943, the Allies have landed in southern Italy, so Allied prisoners of war are transported north by train. When the train is bombed from the air at night, some of the prisoners escape. Englishman Lieutenant Halliday and American Sergeant Braddock stumble across each other in the dark and team up.	Unrated
~~*The Last Hole—Das letzte Loch* (1981)~~	A bored, delusional man wanders around post-War Munich talking with the dead.	Unrated
~~*The Last Letter— La dernière lettre* (2002)~~	A Jewish mother in Ukraine recounts her life in a final letter written to her child.	Unrated
~~*The Last Mensch— Der letzte Mentsch* (2014)~~	[Wikipedia, translated from German] Marcus Schwartz is an old man who lives in Cologne. He survived the Auschwitz and Theresienstadt concentration camps, but never spoke about them and even took on another name. He has always repressed his past as Menachem Teitelbaum and even rejected the state pension to which he was entitled as a Jew. With the end of his life approaching, he wished to be buried traditionally in a Jewish cemetery.	Unrated

Title	Summary	MPAA or Local Rating
The Last Metro—Le dernier métro (1980)	[Wikipedia] Opening in 1942 during the German occupation of France, it follows the fortunes of a small theatre in the Montmartre area of Paris which keeps up passive resistance by maintaining its cultural integrity, despite censorship, antisemitism and material shortages, to emerge triumphant at the war's end. The title evokes two salient facts of city life under the Germans: fuel shortages led people to spend their evenings in theatres and other places of entertainment, but the curfew meant they had to catch the last Métro train home.	PG
The Last Stage—The Last Stop— Ostatni etap (1948)	[Wikipedia] Marta Weiss, a Polish Jew, arrives by cattle car to the Auschwitz concentration camp. While there, she catches the attention of the guards as she is multilingual and is put to work as a translator. When she inquiries about the factory at the camp, a fellow inmate informs her that it is a crematorium and that the rest of her family likely has been murdered. The character Marta Weiss is based on the true life of Mala Zimetbaum.	Unrated (PG)
The Last Suit—El último traje (2017)	[Wikipedia, translated from Spanish] Abraham Bursztein, an 88-year-old Jewish tailor, who has great-grandchildren to whom his daughters intend to sell the apartment while sending him to a nursing home, travels from Buenos Aires to Lodz in Poland, where he sets out to find a Polish friend, Piotrek, who saved him from certain death at the end of WWII and later helped him escape, to give him that last suit to which the title alludes.	Unrated (PG)
~~*The Last Supper—Das letzte Mahl* (2018)~~	[Wikipedia, translated from German] On the day Hitler came to power, the Jewish Glickstein family met in Berlin for dinner. Surprising rifts open up: While nineteen-year-old Leah tells her parents that she is going to Palestine, her eighteen-year-old brother Michael and his friends want to go to the Nazis' torchlight procession to pay homage to the new era.	Unrated
The Last Train—Der Letzte Zug (2006)	*The Last Train—Der Letzte Zug* (2006) depicts what is allegorically the final train of Jews deported from Berlin, a birthday present for Hitler in 1943. While most of the film takes place in a boxcar to Auschwitz, flashbacks give color to the Jews on the train. Although little suffering is hidden, the violence is not gratuitous. [Wikipedia] The film depicts the fate of some of the last remaining Jews in Berlin, who in April 1943 were rounded up at the Berlin-Grunewald station and sent to the Nazi concentration camp at Auschwitz.	Unrated (R)
Late Season—Utószezon (1967)	[Wikipedia, translated from Hungarian] The film seeks with relentless honesty the answer to the responsibility of a cowardly, compromising intelligentsia drifting helplessly through events for the abduction and slaughter of a family during the Holocaust.	Unrated

Title	Summary	MPAA or Local Rating
Left Luggage (1998)	[Wikipedia] While escaping from Nazis during World War II, a Jewish man buries two suitcases full of things dear to his heart in the ground. The war deprived him of his family, and afterwards he endlessly turns over the soil of Antwerp to find the suitcases, an obsessive compulsion. He keeps checking old maps and keeps digging, trying to find what he lost. His daughter Chaya is a beautiful modern girl looking for a part-time job. She finds a place as a nanny in the strictly observant Hasidic family with many children, although her secular manners clearly fly in the face of their beliefs.	PG
Lena: My 100 Children (TV 1987)	[Yad Vashem] The extraordinary true story of Lena Kuchler-Silberman based on her book *My Hundred Children,* depicting the heroic and harrowing actions she undertook after World War II to save 100 Jewish orphans from starvation, deprivation and abuse.	Unrated
~~*Leni* (TV 1994)~~	[Wikipedia, translated from German] The Jewish girl Leni, whose real name is Gabriele Schwarz, was born on May 24, 1937, in Markt Oberdorf as the daughter of a Jewish singer from Augsburg. When she was three weeks old, the mother hid her daughter with farmers on a remote farm near Stiefenhofen in Westallgäu. After the hiding place became known, Leni first came to the orphanage of the Vincentine Sisters in Munich at the age of five. From there she was sent to the Auschwitz-Birkenau extermination camp in 1943, deported and murdered. A memorial plaque in the Spinner Chapel on the outskirts of Oberstaufen and a glass window in the plague chapel above Stiefenhofen remind us of Leni's fate today.	Unrated
Les Misérables (1995)	[Wikipedia] As the film opens, Henri's father, a chauffeur, is falsely accused of having murdered his boss. During his trial and imprisonment, Henri's mother finds a job in a tavern on a Normandy beach. There Henri sees a film adaptation of *Les Misérables.* His father dies attempting to escape from prison, and upon hearing the news Henri's mother commits suicide. Henri grows up an orphan and learns boxing.	Rated R for violence, brief language and sexuality
Les violons du bal (1974)	[Wikipedia, translated from French] It is the story of a filmmaker who has wanted to make the same autobiographical film for 20 years. With little means, he shoots a chronicle of the present time. All the elements of his childhood life, dream life, transposed and unrealistic memories, merge into the present. Stunned, a nine-year-old boy, Michel, witnesses the collapse of what was his life: jostled furniture, rolled up rugs, trinkets and books missing at the bottom of the boxes, and suitcases in which his family piles up clothes and objects.	Unrated (PG)
~~*Let Me Go* (2017)~~	[letmegomovie.com/about, edited] *Let Me Go* is the true story of Helga Schneider, who was abandoned by her mother—an Auschwitz guard—in 1941 when Helga was only four years old. Seventy years later, both women's emotional histories are explored.	15

Title	Summary	MPAA or Local Rating
~~Let's Go!~~ (TV 2014)	[Yad Vashem] Based on the novel *Von Zuhause wird nicht erzählt* by Laura Waco. 1968—the 20-year-old Laura comes from the U.S, where she has emigrated with her boyfriend Gabriel, back to Munich, to the funeral of her father, and has to deal with her mother and her own history. Laura's parents survived the Holocaust and remained after the war in Germany. The trauma, persecution and concentration camps have shaped not only their lives but also the lives of their children. Can Laura now in the confrontation with her mother understand the fate of her parents and be reconciled with her mother?	Unrated
The Life Ahead— La vita davanti a sé (2020)	[Wikipedia] Madam Rosa is a former prostitute and Holocaust survivor who provides childcare for the children of other "working women" in the port city of Bari, Apulia, Italy. After Momo, a 12-year old Senegalese street kid, robs her, she reluctantly agrees to take him in. They develop a deep bond and she tries to help him find his way in life.	PG-13
A Life Ahead—Madam Rose— Madame Rosa—La Vie devant soi (1977)	[Wikipedia] In Belleville, Paris, Madame Rosa, an elderly French Jew and Holocaust survivor who worked as a prostitute, now runs a boarding home for the children of prostitutes. One of them is Momo, an Algerian boy who is believed to be 11. Although Madame Rosa is Jewish and sometimes makes racist comments about Momo, she remains aloof of the Arab-Israeli conflict and raises Momo as a Muslim in respect of his heritage, taking him to her friend Mr. Hamil for instruction in religion, French literature, and Arabic at the Grand Mosque.	Unrated (R)
Life for Life: Maximilian Kolbe— Zycie za zycie (1991)	[Wikipedia, translated from Polish] The camp in Auschwitz, 1941. One of the prisoners—Jan—made a daring escape though quite accidental. In connection with his escape, the camp commander sentenced 10 prisoners to death in the starvation chamber. Franciscan Maximilian Maria Kolbe decides to give his life for another prisoner. At the end of the war and for many years after it, Jan and the Franciscan Anzelm from Niepokalanów wanted to learn about Kolbe's motives, but both men had different considerations.	Unrated
Life Is Beautiful—La Vita è bella (1997)	[Wikipedia] In 1944 when Northern Italy is occupied by Nazi Germany, Guido, his uncle Eliseo, and Giosuè are seized on Giosuè's birthday. They and many other Jews are forced onto a train and taken to a concentration camp. After confronting a guard about her husband and son, and being told there is no mistake, Dora volunteers to get on the train in order to be close to her family. However, as men and women are separated in the camp, Dora and Guido never see each other during the internment. Guido pulls off various stunts, such as using the camp's loudspeaker to send messages—symbolic or literal—to Dora to assure her that he and their son are safe.	PG

Title	Summary	MPAA or Local Rating
~~The Light of Hope—La llum d'Elna (2017)~~	[Wikipedia, translated from Catalan] It takes place in 1942 and explains the struggle of Elisabeth Eidenbenz to save the Swiss maternity hospital in Elna, a maternity hospital located in Elna, in northern Catalonia, which housed women refugees from the Spanish war, and then World War II.	Unrated
Lili Marleen (1981)	[Wikipedia] The film is set during the Third Reich and is about the forbidden love between the German singer Willie and the Swiss Jewish composer Robert Mendelssohn, who actively seeks to help an underground group of German Jews.	R
Living Goods—Lebende Ware (1969)	SS Major Kurt Becher is appointed by Heinrich Himmler as the Chief of the Economic Department of the SS Command in Nazi-occupied Hungary. Becher commandeers a Budapest villa which had been owned by an executive of a Jewish-owned industrial conglomerate. Becher personally despoils wealthy Hungarian Jews in exchange for their safety.	Unrated
Long Is the Road—Lang ist der Weg (1949)	[Wikipedia] The story examines the Holocaust from the perspective of a Polish Jewish family and a young man who is able to escape while he is transported to a concentration camp.	Unrated
Look to the Sky—Jona che visse nella balena (1993)	Four years before *Life Is Beautiful* farcically portrayed a boy playing in Auschwitz, *Look to the Sky—Jona che visse nella balena* (1993) told the true story of a young boy who survived the Westerbork Concentration Camp. *Look to the Sky* is a far better choice for those tempted by *Life Is Beautiful;* the ending of *Look to the Sky* is correct and the depictions are much more realistic. [Wikipedia] *Jonah Who Lived in the Whale* (Italian: *Jona che visse nella balena*), in the United States released as *Look to the Sky,* is a 1993 Italian-French drama film directed by Roberto Faenza, based on the autobiographical novel by the writer Jona Oberski entitled *Childhood,* focused on the drama of the Holocaust.	Unrated (R)
Lore (2012)	[Wikipedia] In south-west Germany, during the aftermath of World War II, five destitute siblings must travel 900 km to their grandmother's home by the Bay of Husum near Hamburg after their high-level Nazi parents disappear in danger of arrest by Allied occupation authorities. Along the way, they encounter a variety of other Germans, some of whom are helpful while others are antagonistic. Eventually they meet up with a young man presenting himself as Thomas, a young Jewish concentration camp survivor, who joins their group and becomes their unofficial guardian.	Unrated (PG)
~~Louise's Diary 1942—Les amours secrètes (2010)~~	[Yad Vashem, translated from Hebrew] In 1942, Sarah, a young Jew, is in love with Hans, a German officer who opposed Nazi ideology and provided forged documents to Jews. Despite the danger, they manage to meet and the love between them blossoms. Those around them do not accept this and things get out of hand.	Unrated

Title	Summary	MPAA or Local Rating
A Love to Hide— *Un amour à taire* (TV 2005)	[Wikipedia] A young Jewish girl, Sarah, is looking to escape the clutches of the Third Reich after seeing her parents and sister brutally slain by a smuggler who betrayed them while attempting to escape to England. Terrified, she is sheltered by her childhood friend Jean, a homosexual in a clandestine relationship with his lover Philippe.	Unrated (R)
~~*The Lucky Star* (1980)~~	[Wikipedia] A young Jewish boy who escapes from the traumas of the war-torn Netherlands by living in a fantasy world of American westerns.	PG
Made in Israel (2001)	*Made in Israel* (2001) portrays a time so far in the future that, as part of an Israeli/Syrian peace deal, the last surviving Nazi war criminal is handed over to Israel as part of the Golan Heights exchange. From there, Israeli police are entrusted to transport the German to Jerusalem to stand trial. Meantime, others, who have their own sense of justice, have put a bounty on the German's head. *Made in Israel* is a unique and astute Israeli perspective, a meaningful stab at an otherwise stale Perpetrator genre. [Wikipedia, translated from Hebrew] The plot of the film takes place "somewhere in the not too distant future," according to the subtitle at the beginning of the film, and takes place entirely in the Golan Heights in the days following the signing of a peace agreement between Israel and Syria. At the beginning of the film, two parallel stories begin with two pairs of assassins sent by Hoffman, the son of a Holocaust survivor, to bring the last Nazi to Israel in order to bring him to a show trial in Israel, and there is a reward on his head.	12
Malou (1981)	[Yad Vashem] Hannah, otherwise a happily married young woman, is obsessed by the memory of her French-born mother Malou, a mysterious figure, long dead, who existed entirely at the mercy of the men in her life. Hannah loves her husband Martin, an ambitious German architect, but resents her commitment to him. She doesn't want to wind up the sodden, emotional wreck that Malou was when she finally died in Buenos Aires in 1967. Hannah is not especially appealing at first. She is moody, willful and sarcastic. One day, without warning, she sets out to find the ghost of Malou by visiting the places where her mother lived and worked before meeting Hannah's father. It's not an easy search, because Malou's stories were often contradictory. In some stories she works as a maid for a wealthy French family. In others she has some small fame and following as a nightclub chanteuse. Always, however, she is dependent on the kindness of men.	Unrated
The Man in the Glass Booth (1975)	*The Man in the Glass Booth* (1975) is a hyperbolic parody of the Eichmann trial, with many more twists than the real story. This masterfully made film defies logic, which is part of its appeal. While *The Man in the Glass Booth* conveys a fair amount of Holocaust history, the story is a quirky character-driven tragedy. *The Man in the Glass Booth* is one of the few Holocaust films that benefits from its overacting. *(cont.)*	Unrated (PG)

Title	Summary	MPAA or Local Rating
	[Wikipedia] Arthur Goldman is Jewish and a Nazi death camp survivor. Now a rich industrialist, he lives in luxury in a Manhattan high-rise. He banters with his assistant Charlie, often shocking him with his outrageousness and irreverence about aspects of Jewish life. One day, Israeli secret agents kidnap Goldman and take him to Israel for trial on charges of being a Nazi war criminal. Goldman's trial forces his accusers to face not only his presumed guilt, but theirs as well.	
The Man Who Captured Eichmann (TV 1996)	[Wikipedia] Set in 1960, the story follows the efforts of the Mossad, the Israeli Secret Service, to find former SS Colonel Adolf Eichmann, who fled Germany for Argentina and took the name Ricardo Klement. He was wanted for the mass murder of both Jews and non-Jews in Europe during the Holocaust. Learning of Eichmann's living in Argentina, the Mossad sends a team to capture him, led by agent Peter Malkin. The standing order is to bring Eichmann back alive to Israel for trial.	PG
Marathon Man (1976)	*Marathon Man* (1976) is the classic Perpetrator film, with a Nazi who tortures a Jew and who is intended to be evocative of Josef Mengele. The film's directing and acting are so good that the large plot-holes and blatant misdirection are simply forgotten. Of note, too, is the implication that even those Jews who did not identify with their heritage were not immune from persecution. *Marathon Man* is a grand roller-coaster ride, which is both terrifying and—despite its lapses—still satisfying. [Wikipedia] "Babe" Levy, a graduate student, becomes embroiled in a plot by Nazi war criminal Christian Szell to retrieve stolen diamonds from a safety deposit box owned by Szell's dead brother. Babe becomes unwittingly involved due to his brother Doc's dealings with Szell.	R
Marriage in the Shadows— Ehe im Schatten (1947)	[Wikipedia] Actor Hans Wieland refuses to divorce his actress wife, Elisabeth, who is Jewish, even as extreme pressure is applied on him by the Nazi authorities. He even takes her to a premiere of one of his films where she is unwittingly introduced to a high Nazi Party official. Upon later discovering that the charming woman at the premiere was in fact Jewish, he orders her arrest. Hans Wieland is given an ultimatum by his former friend Herbert Blohm, now a Nazi official at the Reichskulturministerium, to save himself by divorcing his wife.	Unrated
The Martyr—Dr. Korczak and His Children—Sie sind frei, Doktor Korczak (1975)	[Wikipedia, translated from German] Poland at the time of the German occupation. In 1942, on the orders of the SS, around half a million Jews were crammed into the Warsaw Ghetto. Here the Polish Jewish doctor and educator Dr. Korczak cares for about 200 orphans. Again and again the physician, who is extremely active and concerned about the welfare of the children entrusted to him, succeeds in saving many of the children from the death that has long been ordered. But at the beginning of August 1942, the order comes from the German occupiers to evacuate the ghetto.	Unrated (PG)

Title	Summary	MPAA or Local Rating
Max (2002)	[Wikipedia] British-Hungarian-Canadian fictional drama film, that depicts a friendship between a Jewish art dealer, Max Rothman, and a young Austrian painter, Adolf Hitler. The film explores Hitler's views which began to take shape under Nazi ideology, while also studying the artistic and design implications of the Third Reich and how their visual appeal helped hypnotize the German people. The film goes on to study the question of what could have been had Hitler been accepted as an artist.	R for language.
Max and Helen (TV 1990)	[Yad Vashem] This drama based on the fact-based novel by Nazi-hunter Simon Wiesenthal tells the story about his 1962 prosecution of the head of a Polish factory who he learns was Werner Schultz, a sadistic Nazi labor camp commandant. To be able to bring him to justice, he must find witnesses who can help him. This leads him to Max Rosenberg, a still tormented man who lost his wife, Helen, in the camps. Initially Max refuses to cooperate, but gradually his story unfolds beginning before the Holocaust.	Unrated
Max and Helen—Max e Hélène (TV 2015)	[Wikipedia, translated from Italian] Max Sereni is a Jewish medical student at the University of Venice. His family was captured and deported to Germany while he hides in an attic. He does not want to leave the city because Hélène lives there, the girl he is in love with, who is the daughter of an anti-Semitic fascist. But one day the SS discovers the hiding place and capture Max. At that point Hélène decides to follow her boyfriend, even though she is not Jewish. While they are deported, the two manage to get married on the train and, when it slows down, they manage to escape into the woods.	Unrated
Me and the Colonel (1958)	[Wikipedia] In Paris during the World War II invasion of France by Nazi Germany, Jewish refugee S.L. Jacobowsky seeks to leave the country before it falls. Meanwhile, Polish diplomat Dr. Szicki gives antisemitic, autocratic Polish Colonel Prokoszny secret information that must be delivered to London by a certain date.	Unrated (PG)
Memories of Anne Frank— Mi ricordo Anna Frank (TV 2009)	[Wikipedia] The film is about diarist Anne Frank and her friendship with Hanneli Goslar. In 1935, Anne and Hanneli, both of whom were little children, meet on their first day of school. From that moment, they become very good friends and their friendship continues until 1942, when Anne and her family go to hiding. A few months after Anne and her family go to hiding, the Goslars are arrested by the Nazis. Hanneli, after being deported to the Bergen-Belsen concentration camp, is reunited with Anne, who is a more unprivileged prisoner in the other side of the camp, which is separated by an electric-wired fence from the side where Hanneli is imprisoned.	R
The Memory Thief (2007)	[Wikipedia] The film chronicles the experiences of a young man who becomes involved in documenting the experiences of survivors of the Holocaust, as his commitment turns into obsession and madness.	Unrated (PG)

Title	Summary	MPAA or Local Rating
Mendel (1997)	[Yad Vashem] Drama of a Jewish family, the Trotzigs, from Germany who, having survived the Nazi concentration camps, relocate to Norway in 1954. Curious nine-year-old Mendel Trotzig, who was born after the war, knows his family is keeping something from him, a secret that seems connected to a mysterious photograph in his mother's pocketbook, but his parents are determined to shield him from the horrors of the past.	Unrated (PG)
Miracle at Midnight (TV 1998)	[Wikipedia] On Wednesday, September 29, 1943, Doctor Koster learns of the imminent arrest of the Danish Jews on midnight Friday from a former government minister, who had been alerted by German maritime attaché Georg Duckwitz. The Kosters start by hiding Rabbi Ben Abrams and his family, but soon realize they can help more Jews and become an integral part of an effort to transport over 7,000 Jews to neutral Sweden.	TV-PG
Miracle at Moreaux (TV 1986)	[Wikipedia] In the film, three Jewish children fleeing the Nazis take refuge in a French convent. The children attend a boarding school run by a Catholic nun, Sister Gabrielle. The children arrive while the school is putting on a Nativity pageant, and in a quick act of thinking, Sister Gabrielle pretends the three children are her students. The Jewish children remain in the school for some time while the Nazis that are patrolling the area, led by an SS Major, hunt for them in the forests surrounding the convent.	Unrated (G)
Mr. Klein—Monsieur Klein **(1976)**	*Mr. Klein—Monsieur Klein* (1976) is a sophisticated story about a French Gentile who profits from the misfortunes of the French Jewish community at the start of German occupation. As Jews were being deported, Paris was a buyer's market for art dealers. Mr. Klein lives the good life until he is misidentified as a Jew, at which time his fortunes change. The premise is marvelous, and the filmmaking is excellent. [Wikipedia] Paris, January 1942. France is occupied by the Nazis. Robert Klein, apparently apolitical, is a well-to-do art dealer, Roman Catholic and Alsatian by birth, who takes advantage of French Jews who need to sell artworks to raise cash to leave the country. One day, the local Jewish newspaper, addressed to him, is delivered to his home. He learns that another Robert Klein who has been living in Paris, a Jew sought by police, has had his own mail forwarded to him in an apparent attempt to destroy his social reputation and make him a target of official anti-Semitism.	UK-14+
Monastero di Santa Chiara (1949)	[Wikipedia] The Jewish singer Ester di Veroli has two admirers: Rudolf, an SS officer, and the Neapolitan Enrico. Rudolf's previous girlfriend, the German Greta, jealous of Ester, arranges for the latter, who has found refuge with a priest, to be arrested. But Rudolf, instead of taking her to prison, entrusts her to the nuns of the Monastery of Santa Chiara, which is destroyed by a bombing, so Ester goes in search of Rudolf, but falls into the hands of her rival and ends up in a concentration camp, where fortunately she is freed thanks to the arrival of the Allies.	Unrated

Title	Summary	MPAA or Local Rating
Monsieur Batignole (2002)	[Wikipedia] The film depicts the story of an ordinary grocer, Edmond Batignole, who helps the young son of his Jewish neighbor, and the boy's two cousins, to reach Switzerland safely.	Unrated
Morituri (1948)	[Wikipedia] As the end of the Second World War approaches and the Soviet Red Army is advancing, a group of concentration camp inmates is helped to escape by a Polish doctor. They hide in a wood where they meet other fugitives, who have been there for months, constantly in fear of being discovered. Out of fear of the German army patrols, they do not dare to leave the forest, even as the food supplies run low. The Polish doctor blows up a bridge, attracting the German troops' attention to the forest.	Unrated
~~*The Mover* (2018)~~	[Wikipedia] Žanis Lipke, a Latvian dock worker, saves 60 Jews during the German occupation of Latvia during World War II by sheltering them in a bunker under his house and transporting them to safety with the help of his family and friends.	Unrated
Murderers Among Us—Die Mörder sind unter uns (1946)	[Wikipedia] Berlin in 1945 after Germany's defeat in the war. The former military surgeon Dr. Hans Mertens stumbles down the street, drunk. He suffers from flashbacks of the war and has an aversion to people in pain, which prevents him from practicing medicine. Instead, he spends his days drinking. An artist and Nazi concentration camp survivor, Susanne Wallner, finds him living in her apartment as she returns home.	UK-PG
Murderers Among Us: The Simon Wiesenthal Story (TV 1989)	[Wikipedia] As Austrian Jews living in Ukraine at the beginning of World War II, Simon Wiesenthal and his family are captured by Nazis and sent to live in a series of prison camps, where Wiesenthal cheats death several times. When he is liberated from Mauthausen in 1945, Wiesenthal provides vital information to the Americans in the Nuremberg War Trials and dedicates his life to hunting down Nazi war criminals, even though doing so comes at a cost to his family.	Unrated
~~*Murer: Anatomy of a Trial—Murer: Anatomie eines Prozesses* (2018)~~	[Official film site: prismafilm.at] Graz [Austria], 1963. The respected local politician and wealthy farmer Franz Murer is on trial for a serious war crime allegedly committed while he was in command of the Vilnius ghetto in 1941–43. The evidence of his guilt is overwhelming. But the powers-that-be want to close this dark chapter of their country's history once and for all.	Unrated
Music Box (1989)	[Wikipedia] American crime drama film that tells the story of a Hungarian-American immigrant who is accused of having been a war criminal. The plot revolves around his daughter, an attorney, who defends him, and her struggle to uncover the truth.	15
My Daughter Anne Frank—Meine Tochter Anne Frank (TV 2015)	*My Daughter Anne Frank—Meine Tochter Anne Frank* (TV 2015) is a dazzlingly produced Holocaust film that tells broader Anne Frank stories, about her father's efforts to get her diary published. In *My Daughter Anne Frank*, the Franks' informant is *(cont.)*	Unrated (PG)

Title	Summary	MPAA or Local Rating
	exposed and several of Anne Frank's contemporaries are interviewed. This film is a 90-minute treasure. [Wikipedia, translated from German] The life story of Anne Frank is told from the perspective of her father Otto Frank. After his liberation and return from the Auschwitz concentration camp, he went back to Amsterdam to his company at Prinsengracht 263. There he received the diary of his daughter Anne from his office worker Miep Gies, who helped the hidden residents in the rear building. Miep Gies had kept the loose pages and books scattered on the floor in the rear building and hidden them in a desk drawer so that she could give them back to Anne after the war.	
~~My Father's House—Beit Avi (1947)~~	[Wikipedia] David Halevy is a ten-year-old Holocaust survivor. He is separated from his father in Nazi-occupied Krakow. His father has told him that they will meet in Palestine. After the war, David goes to Palestine, hoping that he will meet his father there. On the ship he befriends Miryam, who lost her family in an extermination camp. David is taken to Meir Shfeya youth village, but he cannot adapt and makes a journey to find his father. After a long journey he is told that his parents were both murdered in the Holocaust.	Unrated
My Führer—Mein Führer— Die wirklich wahrste Wahrheit über Adolf Hitler (2007)	*My Führer* (2007) is a farcical look at the final days of Adolf Hitler as seen through the eyes of a Jewish acting coach. The premise is wild, but is executed perfectly. This forgotten little film makes fun of the Third Reich while never losing its bearings. While very much in the spirit of Charlie Chaplin's *The Great Dictator* (1940), *My Führer* has a satisfying and appropriate ending. [Wikipedia, translated from German] The film is set during World War II and deals with Adolf Hitler, who is about to give a major New Year's speech. He is to be rhetorically prepared for this by the Jewish actor Adolf Grünbaum.	Unrated (PG)
My Mother's Courage— Mutters Courage (1995)	[Wikipedia, translated from German] The film is set in Budapest in 1944. George Tabori tells the story of his mother Elsa Tabori, who is a passionate rummy player. She regularly meets up with her friends in Budapest for game afternoons. The danger of being captured and deported by the Nazis on the street is of little interest to them.	Unrated (PG-13)
Naked Among Wolves— Nackt unter Wölfen (1963)	[Wikipedia] Buchenwald concentration camp, early 1945. A Polish prisoner named Jankowski, who has been on a death march from Auschwitz, brings a suitcase to the camp. When the inmates in the storage building open it, they discover a three-year-old child. Jankowski tells them he is the son of a couple from the Warsaw Ghetto, both of whom perished. Prisoner Kropinski becomes attached to the boy, and begs Kapo André Höfel to save him.	Unrated
Naked Among Wolves— Nackt unter Wölfen (TV 2015)	[Wikipedia] The film takes place in the years 1944 and 1945 towards the end of World War II in the Buchenwald concentration camp. Prisoners in the Nazi concentration camp risk their lives by taking in a young Jewish boy rescued from a Polish ghetto.	Unrated (R)

Title	Summary	MPAA or Local Rating
The Nasty Girl—Das schreckliche Mädchen (1990)	[Wikipedia] A German high school student, Sonja wins an essay contest and goes on a trip to Paris. Martin Wegmus begins teaching physics at Sonja's school and one of Sonja's classmates falls in love with him. Almost by luck, Mr. Wegmus and Sonja kiss. The teacher promises to return for her. The next year, she enters the contest again. She chooses "My Town During the Third Reich" from the possible topics. Her research leads her to discover that her picture-perfect town had been intimately involved in the Third Reich and that nearly all of the city's prominent families were members of the Nazi party long before it came to power.	PG
~~*Natalia* (1988)~~	[Wikipedia, translated from France] Coming from a Polish Jewish family emigrated to France, Natalia is an actress. During the Second World War, provided with false papers, she continued her career in cinema. While shooting a film, she was arrested and deported. On her return, she refused to collaborate with the film purification commission and could no longer play.	Unrated
Never Forget (TV 1991)	[Wikipedia] Mr. Mermelstein and Mrs. Mermelstein are a true-life California couple thrown into the spotlight of judicial history in the 1980s. He is a Hungarian-born Jew, sole survivor of his family's extermination at Auschwitz, and she is a Southern Baptist from Tennessee. Their four children are good kids, typical Americans, with just enough orneriness to irritate each other, but enough love and class to pull together when it counts. When challenged by a hate group to prove that Jews were actually gassed at Auschwitz, Mel Mermelstein rises to the occasion with the support of his wife and children, in spite of the dangers to himself, his business, and his family.	Unrated
Newland—Aretz Hadasha (1994)	Eight-year-old Anna and fourteen-year-old brother Jan are orphaned Holocaust survivors living in 1950s Israel. They survive as pickpockets. The staff at their absorption camp and local townspeople help the youths adjust to their new lives.	Unrated
The Night Porter—Il portiere di notte (1974)	[Wikipedia] During World War II, Maximilian Theo Aldorfer, a former Nazi Schutzstaffel officer who had posed as a doctor to take sensational photographs in concentration camps, and Lucia Atherton, a teen-age girl interned in a concentration camp due to her father's Socialist political ties, had an ambiguous sadomasochistic relationship. Max tormented Lucia, but also acted as her protector. In 1957, Lucia, now married to an American orchestra conductor, meets Max again by chance.	R
Nina's Journey—La Maison De Nina (2005)	[Wikipedia, Translated from Swedish] The film takes place during the Second World War in the Warsaw ghetto. It is about Nina and her [Jewish] family. Despite the war, she lives a fairly ordinary teenage life, except that everyone around her disappears, one by one.	12

Title	Summary	MPAA or Local Rating
<u>*1945 (2017)*</u>	While *The Shop on Main Street* (1965) concentrated on the brazenly systematic taking of Jewish property by individuals in a rural Czech community during the War, *1945* (2017) depicts the return of two despoiled Holocaust survivors just after the War to their rural Hungarian village. The question of communal culpability is overshadowed by greed. This excellent post-War slice of life makes its case with the pace of a Western showdown. [Wikipedia, translated from Hungarian] The film tells the story of a day in a village in eastern Hungary, at the end of World War II, in August 1945. The occupying German troops were replaced by the Soviets, and under their control they were preparing for the first post-war elections. They are preparing for another, closer event in the village: the wedding of the clerk, the son of István Szentes. The mood was quite tense as the bride's former fiancé had also just returned home from captivity. It is then that the news arrives that two orthodox Jewish men dressed in black got off the train at the village train station; the news quickly spread in the village: "they are back!"	Unrated (PG)
The Ninth Circle—Deveti krug (1960)	[Wikipedia] In the early 1940s, following the German invasion of Yugoslavia and creation of the Ustaše-run Croatian Nazi puppet state, citizens of Zagreb are facing many hardships. Things are especially difficult for the Jewish population that's marked for extermination. In order to save Ruth, a Jewish girl, from the Nazis and their collaborators, a Croatian Catholic family arranges for her to marry their young son, Ivo.	Unrated
Nippon no Shindorâ: Sugihara Chiune monogatari (TV 2005)	A dramatization of the heroic actions of the Japanese diplomat Sugihara Chiune, who saved thousands of Jews in Lithuania.	Unrated
Not All Were Murderers— Nicht alle waren Mörder (TV 2006)	[Wikipedia, translated from German] March 1943: When the SS picked up her neighbors for deportation, Anna Degen, a Jew, decided at the last minute to flee with her eleven-year-old son Michael in order to avoid being arrested by the Gestapo. Michael's father is already dead, having died sometime after his release from Sachsenhausen concentration camp. A good friend, Lona, arranges accommodation for the mother and son with Ludmilla Dimitrieff, a Russian émigrée.	Unrated
November Moon— Novembermond (1985)	[Wikipedia, translated from German] Shortly before the outbreak of the Second World War, the German Jew, November Messing, fled from Berlin to Paris. Working illegally in the bistro "La Cigale," which is owned by a former friend of her father's, ensures November's survival for the time being. In the bistro she meets the siblings Laurent and Férial. The two women fall in love.	Unrated (PG-13)

Title	Summary	MPAA or Local Rating
Nowhere in Africa—Nirgendwo in Afrika (2001)	[Wikipedia] In 1938, the Redlich family flees to Kenya from Leobschütz in Silesia, Nazi Germany, to escape the increasing persecution of the Jews. Walter, a former lawyer, finds work as a farm manager and sends for his family. His wife Jettel has trouble adjusting to life in Africa, although their daughter Regina quickly adapts to her new environment, easily learning the language of the country and showing interest in local culture. Regina soon forms a close friendship with the farm's cook, Owuor, who helped save Walter's life when he contracted malaria.	R for some sexual content.
Nuremberg (TV 2000)	[Wikipedia] At the close of World War II, Hermann Göring surrenders to the Americans and enjoys the hospitality of a U.S. Army Air Force base. Samuel Rosenman, acting on the orders of U.S. President Harry S. Truman, recruits U.S. Supreme Court Justice Robert H. Jackson to prepare a war crimes tribunal against Göring and the surviving Nazi leadership.	15
The Odessa File (1974)	The Odessa File (1974) is one of the few Perpetrator Holocaust films to include meaningful Holocaust flashbacks, which not only frame the motivation for killing the hidden Nazi, but also expose the underground of Nazis who are still plotting in West German society. [Wikipedia] …an elderly Jewish Holocaust survivor had committed suicide, leaving behind no family. The reporter obtains the diary of the man, which contains information on his life in the Riga Ghetto during World War II, including the name of the SS officer who ran the camp, Eduard Roschmann.	PG
Of a Thousand Delights—Sandra—Vaghe stelle dell'Orsa… (1965)	[Wikipedia, edited] A retelling of the Electra story, starting with Sandra returning to her ancestral home in Italy after the Holocaust. On the eve of an official ceremony commemorating the death of her Jewish father in a Nazi concentration camp, Sandra revives an intimate involvement with her brother, which troubles Sandra's naive husband.	X
Olga (2004)	[Wikipedia] A communist activist since her youth, Olga is persecuted by the police and flees to Moscow, where she undergoes military training. She is put in charge of escorting Luis Carlos Prestes to Brazil to lead the Communist Revolution of 1935, falling in love with him long the way. With the failure of the Revolution, Olga is arrested alongside Prestes. Seven-month pregnant Olga is deported by President Vargas' Government to Nazi Germany, where she gives birth to her daughter Anita Leocádia while incarcerated. Separated from her daughter, Olga is sent away to the Ravensbrück concentration camp, where she is executed in the gas chamber.	Unrated (PG)
One Day You'll Understand—Plus tard (2008)	[Wikipedia, translated from French] Victor discovers that part of his Jewish family was deported during the war. He tries to find out more about this buried past by questioning his mother.	Unrated (PG)

Title	Summary	MPAA or Local Rating
The Only Way (1970)	[Wikipedia] In October, 1943 in occupied Denmark, the Nazis decide to deport the Danish Jews to extermination camps. However, the Danish people decide to prevent this.	G
Operation Eichmann (1961)	[Wikipedia] It is a highly fictionalized account of the life of the war criminal Adolf Eichmann, from his career as a member of the SS and an architect of the Holocaust to his capture in Argentina by the Mossad.	TV-PG
Operation Finale (2018)	[Wikipedia] After World War II ends, Holocaust mastermind Adolf Eichmann disappears; other Nazi leaders commit suicide and none face trial for their crimes. Years later, Mossad agent Peter Malkin mistakenly kills the wrong person while hunting a Nazi war criminal in Austria, damaging his reputation. In Buenos Aires, Sylvia Hermann unknowingly begins courting the son of Adolf Eichmann, Klaus.	PG-13 for disturbing thematic content and related violent images, and for some language.
Operation Stadium—Akcija Stadion (1977)	Tells the story of Jews being separated at a stadium in Zagreb.	Unrated
~~*Our Father in Heaven—Otche nash—Pater Noster* (1989)~~	[Yad Vashem, edited] A young Jewish woman and her son in Eastern Europe are ordered to report for deportation. They avoid the round-up by wandering around the city. At night, they fall asleep on the bench and are frozen to death.	Unrated
Out of Evil—Mi Klalah L'Brahah (1950)	[Yad Vashem] In the 1920's a young couple give up their life on a pioneer kibbutz to move back to Germany. Their son returns to Israel after his parents are killed by the Nazis. The film shows the general development of Palestine and the kibbutz in particular during two decades. Interwoven with the story is a puppet opera dramatization of the biblical tale of "Bilam and the Ass." Based on book by Yehuda Yaari, *Brith*.	Unrated
Out of the Ashes (TV 2003)	[Wikipedia] It is a dramatization of the life of Holocaust concentration camp survivor Gisella Perl and is based on her book *I Was a Doctor in Auschwitz*.	R for violence—cruelty and some nudity.
The Painted Bird (2019)	[Wikipedia] In an unidentified area of war-torn Eastern Europe, a young boy is sent by his parents to live in safety with his aunt. She dies and he sets off on a journey to return home. His adventures are a series of horrific encounters with ignorance, exploitation, and depravity.	Unrated (R)
Passenger—Pasazerka (TV 1963)	[Wikipedia] *Passenger*, using the form of a documentary, relates the experiences of one female SS officer serving at the Auschwitz concentration camp during World War II, as well as her relationship with a Polish political inmate, Marta, whose life she manages to save on occasion.	Unrated
The Passerby—La passante du Sans-Souci (1982)	[Wikipedia] During an interview, Max Baumstein, respected chairman of a humanitarian organization, shoots the Paraguayan ambassador dead, in cold blood. Tried for first-degree murder, he explains himself: the ambassador was a former Nazi official, responsible for the extermination of his foster parents.	Unrated

Title	Summary	MPAA or Local Rating
Past Life (2016)	[Wikipedia] Two Israeli sisters, one a classical music composer and singer, and the other a budding journalist, try to find out what their father did during World War II in Poland, after a Polish woman runs up to one of them in a Berlin concert venue and calls her the daughter of a murderer.	Unrated
The Pawnbroker (1964)	*The Pawnbroker* (1964) is not the first Survivor film, but it was the first Holocaust film to depict an older Holocaust survivor twenty years after the War. The survivor in *The Pawnbroker* has disintegrated emotionally under the weight of his memories. There is nothing joyful or easy about the story, which implies that the pawnbroker can never recover. The allegorical style of memory suppression was innovative and extremely effective. [Wikipedia] With the rise of Adolf Hitler, Sol Nazerman, a German-Jewish university professor, is dragged to a concentration camp along with his family. He witnesses his two children die, one while riding the cattle car on the way to the camp, and his wife raped by Nazi officers. Twenty-five years later, Nazerman operates a pawnshop in East Harlem while living in an anonymous Long Island housing tract. Numbed by his experiences, he has worked hard not to show any emotions.	Sweden-15
The People vs. Fritz Bauer— Der Staat gegen Fritz Bauer (2015)	*The People vs. Fritz Bauer—Der Staat gegen Fritz Bauer* (2015), much like *Labyrinth of Lies* (2014) the previous year, is about the post-War West German bureaucracy hiding former Nazis. While *Labyrinth of Lies* is primarily about exposing a German Gentile to the actions of the previous generation, *The People vs. Fritz Bauer* concentrates on the perspective of a post-War Jewish German state prosecutor who is willing to violate West German laws to help Israel capture Adolf Eichmann. *The People vs. Fritz Bauer* thoroughly exposes racism and homophobia in post-War Germany. [Wikipedia] When Bauer discovers that the former Nazi Schneider at Daimler-Benz works in the human resources department for South America, he puts pressure on him to obtain Eichmann's code name in Argentina. He directs this to the Mossad to confirm the first lane. Eichmann is abducted in the sequence in Argentina by the Mossad and abducted to Israel. Bauer's application for extradition of Eichmann is rejected by the federal government under Konrad Adenauer, as there are extensive arms deals between the FRG and Israel and is feared by possible statements of Eichmann in front of a German court, a government crisis, as many former Nazis are represented in the state apparatus up to the Cabinet.	R for some sexual content.
Perlasca. The Courage of a Just Man—Perlasca. Un eroe italiano (TV 2002)	[Wikipedia] ...about the achievements of an Italian man in saving Jews in Hungary in 1944. During World War II, Perlasca worked at procuring supplies for the Italian army in the Balkans. In the autumn of 1943, he was appointed as an official delegate of the Italian government with diplomatic status and sent to eastern *(cont.)*	Unrated

Title	Summary	MPAA or Local Rating
	Europe with the mission of buying meat for the Italian army. On October 8, Italy surrendered unconditionally to the Allied forces. Italian citizens in Hungary were then considered the enemy of the Hungarian Government, which was allied with Germany, and were at risk of arrest and internment.	
Persian Lessons (2020)	[Wikipedia] A Jewish man in a German concentration camp pretends he is from Iran and is then forced to teach Persian, a language he does not speak, to a Nazi.	Unrated
Persona Non Grata—Sugihara Chiune (2015)	[Wikipedia] It depicts the life of Japanese diplomat Chiune Sugihara who was appointed a vice-consul and later a consul in Lithuania and served there from 1939 to 1940 and who saved lives of some 6,000 Jewish refugees by issuing transit visas to the Japanese Empire.	Unrated
Phoenix (2014)	*Phoenix* (2014) is a remake of the 1965 film *Return from the Ashes*, in which a disfigured Holocaust survivor returns after the War to reunite with her husband, who does not recognize her. She eventually discerns that he had betrayed her during the War. Like most films that depict just-post-War Europe, *Phoenix* is uplifting, with a protagonist who is eventually empowered and who can start anew. [Wikipedia] *Phoenix* is set in Germany in the aftermath of World War II, where Nelly, a Jew who managed to survive Auschwitz concentration camp, decides to go back to her husband Johnny in Berlin. She has had to have her face reconstructed owing to a bullet wound, and her husband does not recognize her.	PG-13 for some thematic elements and brief suggestive material.
The Pianist (2002)	*The Pianist* (2002) is one of the most beautifully made and highly decorated Holocaust films ever made. It does not create any heroes or embellish any villains, but paints the picture of a solitary man who survives Warsaw—from the creation of the Ghetto through its destruction, and to the end of the War—on little but dumb luck. *The Pianist*, which is based on a true story, is deserving of all its accolades. It is artistic, cinematically brilliant, and educational, without over sentimentalizing. [Wikipedia] In September 1939, Władysław Szpilman, a Polish-Jewish pianist, is playing live on the radio in Warsaw when the station is bombed during Nazi Germany's invasion of Poland. Hoping for a quick victory, Szpilman rejoices with his family at home when he learns that Britain and France have declared war on Germany, but the promised aid does not come. Fighting lasts for just over a month, with both the German and Soviet armies invading Poland at the same time on different fronts. Warsaw becomes part of the Nazi-controlled General Government. Jews are soon prevented from working or owning businesses, and are also made to wear blue Star of David armbands. By November 1940, Szpilman and his family are forced from their home into the isolated and overcrowded Warsaw Ghetto, where conditions only get worse.	R for violence and brief strong language.

Title	Summary	MPAA or Local Rating
Playing for Time (TV 1980)	[Wikipedia] Fania Fénelon, a French Jewish singer-pianist, is sent with other prisoners to the Auschwitz concentration camp in a crowded train during World War II. After having their belongings and clothes taken and their heads shaved, the prisoners are processed and enter the camp. Fénelon is recognized as being a famous musician and she finds that she will be able to avoid hard manual labor and survive longer by becoming a member of the prison's female orchestra, the Women's Orchestra of Auschwitz.	Unrated (PG)
The Poet—Hearts of War (2007)	[Wikipedia] In the early days of World War II in Poland, Rachel, a rabbi's daughter, is headed home when she runs into a snow storm and falls unconscious. She is rescued by Oscar Koenig, an officer in the German Army working undercover to search out resistance fighters. Over the next few days, Oscar nurses Rachel back to health and in the process the two fall in love, bonding over the poetry that Oscar writes.	R for some violence and sexual content.
Postcard from a Journey— Kartka z podrózy (1984)	[Wikipedia, translated from Polish] Jakub Rosenberg is a ghetto inhabitant who sweeps the streets. While waiting for a call for transport, he does not allow himself to be terrorized by fear, but prepares himself pragmatically and meticulously for the last journey. He gets the right clothes, gets beaten up in a provoked fight, sleeps on the floor, exercises with weights. He tries to keep his dignity until the very end. He tries to infuse little David, who is placed under his care, with his philosophy.	Unrated
The Pracht Inn (2014)	[Yad Vashem] It's the early sixties and a group of young Holocaust survivors reside at the Pracht hostel in Jerusalem. At night, they drink cognac and play cards as a way of escaping their post-war nightmares. During the day, they revolt against the owner of the hostel, Mrs. Pracht, a German-born intellectual who tries to discipline them and put their lives in order. In this atmosphere of chaos and revolt, Manfred lives his quiet life—that is, until one day he is inspired to do something great, something that will give meaning to his life.	Unrated
Prague (1992)	An American film director travels to Prague for work. While there, he learns about his family's plight during the Holocaust. He then falls in love with a woman who is already involved with another man.	Unrated (PG)
Prayer for Katerina Horovitzova— odlitba pro Katerinu Horovitzovou (TV 1965)	[Wikipedia] In 1943 a young Jewish woman, Kateřina Horovitzová, is placed in a group of wealthy Jewish men who bribe the Nazis in order to be exchanged to the USA for captured SS officers.	Unrated
Primo (TV 2005)	*Primo* (TV 2005) is a great starter film for the study of Auschwitz. One man stands on an empty stage and describes Auschwitz, exclusively relying on the words of Holocaust survivor Primo Levi. *Primo* reenacts nothing visually. Without any violence, *Primo* is an excellent primer before watching graphic Auschwitz films.	PG

Title	Summary	MPAA or Local Rating
Private Resistance—De ijssalon (1985)	[Wikipedia, translated from Dutch] Amsterdam, January 1941. The Netherlands has now been occupied by Nazi Germany for seven months. The occupation was generally quiet, especially in the first months, and the Germans tried to get the Dutch population on their side. But this policy seems to have failed and resistance, however primitive and amateurish it may be, is beginning to emerge. The freedom of the Jewish population, which is also the victim of harassment and violence on the part of the NSB, has already been curtailed. Jewish gangs oppose the violence tolerated by the occupying forces. The Jewish gangs soon receive support from other Amsterdammers. In the midst of all the violence, Otto Schneeweiss tries to keep going.	Unrated
Professor Mamlock (1961)	[Wikipedia] Professor Mamlock, a respected Jewish surgeon, is certain that the Weimar Republic would survive the political crisis of the early 1930s. He disapproves of his son, Rolf, a communist activist who openly opposes the Nazis. When Hitler rises to power, Mamlock loses his work and his dignity. Realizing the mistake he made by being politically apathetic, Mamlock commits suicide. The film ends with his dead face blending away from the screen, on which appears the inscription: "there is no greater crime than not wanting to fight when fight one must."	Unrated
Protector—Protektor (2009)	[Wikipedia] It is 1938 and the Nazis are just one step away from invading and occupying Czechoslovakia. Hana is a young Czech film actress who also happens to be Jewish. She has just appeared in her first feature with her leading man, an older Jewish actor, who warns her that her career is over. He furthermore tells her that their picture will "never see the light of day" due to the fact that the Nazis will never allow its release. He hands her a forged passport and papers to get out of the country but she throws them in the trash, not believing what he says about the imminent German invasion.	NR
Punch Me in the Stomach (1997)	The autobiography of a Holocaust survivor's daughter.	Unrated
The Quarrel (1991)	*The Quarrel* (1991) is the smallest of stories, about two Eastern European Holocaust survivors who meet just after the War in Montreal. These former best friends, who had been estranged before the War, both believed that the other had died in the Holocaust. The secular/observant theological questions concerning the Holocaust are argued between these two men, more organically than in *God on Trial*. There is nothing flashy about *The Quarrel*. As opposed to most other Survivor films, however, these survivors are functional, healthy members of society. [Wikipedia] Two estranged friends—one a rabbi and the other an agnostic writer—are compelled to resume an argument that caused a separation between the pair many years earlier, after a chance meeting pushes the duo together once more.	PG-13

Title	Summary	MPAA or Local Rating
~~Quezon's Game (2018)~~	[Wikipedia] In 1938, Philippine President Manuel L. Quezon, his military adviser Dwight Eisenhower along with other notable figures set out to rescue Jewish refugees fleeing Nazi Germany. Quezon also simultaneously deals with a relapse of tuberculosis.	Unrated (PG)
Raindrops—Regentropfen (1981)	[Yad Vashem] The story begins in the early 1930s as the Jewish-German Goldbach family, owners of a textile business, sees their customers thinning out, associates avoiding them and their little son Benny being ostracized at the playground. This new situation convinces them to apply for a visa at the American consulate in Stuttgart. They sell their business and move to Cologne, where they can study English. While in Cologne, they reside next to other Jewish families and wait for the visa. Benny spends his time at the movies, but then that pastime is cut off when Jews are no longer allowed inside the cinema. Once preparations are completed, they visit the American Consulate, where the visa application is refused time and time again till finally it is denied because of health reasons. The fate of the Goldbach family remains open.	Unrated
The Reader (2008)	[Wikipedia] The film tells the story of Michael Berg, a German lawyer who, as a 15-year-old in 1958, has a sexual relationship with an older woman, Hanna Schmitz. She disappears only to resurface years later as one of the defendants in a war crimes trial stemming from her actions as a guard at a Nazi concentration camp. Michael realizes that Hanna is keeping a personal secret she believes is worse than her Nazi past—a secret which, if revealed, could help her at the trial.	R for some scenes of sexuality and nudity.
Redemption Road—Landgericht (TV 2017)	A Jewish family splits up—some to England and Cube—to escape Nazi persecution. They reunite after the War.	Unrated
The Relief of Belsen (TV 2007)	*The Relief of Belsen* (TV 2007) is a historical reenactment of British efforts to save 60,000 dying Jews in the just liberated Bergen-Belsen Concentration Camp. No other Holocaust film comes close to depicting the challenges faced by the liberators of German camps. Although some of the side plots are superfluous, *The Relief of Belsen* is an absolute triumph in its difficult portrayal of the War's aftermath. [Wikipedia] It depicts events that unfolded at Bergen-Belsen concentration camp following the liberation of the camp by British troops in April 1945.	PG-13
Remember (2015)	[Wikipedia] In a New York City nursing home, Auschwitz concentration camp survivor Zev Guttman, an 89-year-old dementia patient, is sitting shiva for his wife, Ruth. Another elderly patient and fellow Auschwitz survivor, the incapacitated Max Rosenbaum, reminds Zev of what he promised to do when Ruth died. Max has continually reminded Zev that their families were murdered at the camp by the Blockführer Otto Wallisch, who was believed to have immigrated to North America under the false name Rudy Kurlander.	R for a sequence of violence and language.

Title	Summary	MPAA or Local Rating
Remember Your Name—Pomni imya svoye (1974)	[Wikipedia, translated from Russian] The events in the film unfold during the Great Patriotic War and after its end. The film is based on the real dramatic story of a Soviet prisoner of the Auschwitz concentration camp of Nazi Germany, who was separated from her son there and found him only twenty years later.	Unrated
Remembrance—Die verlorene Zeit (2011)	[Wikipedia] A German-Jewish young woman and Polish young man fall in love and escape a Nazi concentration camp. The film's story intercuts between a Nazi concentration camp in Poland in 1944 and New York City in 1976.	Unrated (R)
Remembrance of Love (TV 1982)	[Wikipedia] Television drama about a man separated from his lover and his unborn child during the Second World War who has no idea whether they survived the Holocaust. Beginning a new life in America he finds a wife and settles down. But he discovers that his old love is still alive following a reunion in Israel.	TV-14
The Resistance—The Invisibles—Die Unsichtbaren (2017)	[Wikipedia] The film recounts the struggle of Cioma Schönhaus, Hanni Lévy, Eugen Friede and Ruth Arndt-Gumpel to survive their persecution as Jews in Berlin from 1942 to 1945. Their individual situations are re-enacted, and, in interspersed interviews, they recollect and comment on their experience. Their survival is attributed to resilience, luck, and help from others. Their saviours come from different walks of life, including ordinary German citizens, communists, Christians, and people working within the Nazi hierarchy.	Unrated (PG)
Resistance (2020)	The wartime heroics of Jewish refuge Marcel Marceau, who ultimately became a famed pantomimist.	15
Return from the Ashes (1965)	[Wikipedia] Shortly before the Nazi invasion of France, Dr. Michele Wulf encounters the younger Stanislaus Pilgrin over a game of lightning chess, not being aware that Pilgrin is a chess master. She becomes intrigued with the fortune-hunting Pilgrin and the two begin a liaison. Upon the Nazi invasion, in order to protect Michele, who is Jewish, Stan marries her, to no avail it turns out when the Gestapo arrests her and sends her to a concentration camp. Sometime after the war, Michele returns under the identity of Mme. Robert and encounters her colleague, plastic surgeon Dr. Charles Bovard, who at first does not recognize her because of her disfigured state.	TV-PG
The Revolt of Job—Jób lázadása (1983)	[Wikipedia] Hungary, 1943. An elderly Jewish couple, Jób and Róza, adopt an unruly non-Jewish child (Lackó) to whom they intend to pass on their wealth and knowledge before Nazi oppression engulfs Hungary.	Unrated (PG)
Riphagen—Riphagen: The Untouchable (2016)	[Wikipedia] At the height of WWII in the Netherlands, Dries Riphagen and one of his associates find a Jewish woman in hiding; however, he informs the woman, Esther Schaap, that he wants to help her and other Jews in hiding, claiming because he was married to a Jewish girl who died. He treats Esther with *(cont.)*	Unrated

Title	Summary	MPAA or Local Rating
	hospitality and even has his photo taken with her, eventually gaining her trust. She tells all the other Jews she knows who are in hiding that they can trust Riphagen with their valuables.	
Romeo, Juliet and Darkness— Romeo, Julie a tma (1960)	[Wikipedia] Inspired by William Shakespeare's *Romeo and Juliet*, the film is about problems experienced by a young Jewish woman who is hidden from the Gestapo by a student lover.	Unrated
The Rose Garden— The Rosegarden (1989)	[Wikipedia] A Holocaust survivor, Aaron Reichenbach, returns to Germany and attacks ex-Nazi officer Arnold Krenn in a Frankfurt airport. When Arnold files assault charges, a public defender, Gabriele Schlüter-Freund, represents Aaron, expecting a straightforward case. But when Gabriele discovers that Aaron is one of many victims of cruel medical experiments in concentration camps, she resolves to seek justice. Aaron is reunited with his long lost sister who has also survived.	PG-13
~~A Rose in Winter (2018)~~	[Yad Vashem] It recounts the extraordinary life of Edith Stein. Born Jewish, she demonstrated uncompromising courage as an outspoken advocate for equity in the Woman's Right Movement at the onset of National Socialism in Germany, and though her actions, as a Carmelite Nun, challenging the very foundation of the Holy See to stand up against the Holocaust: a path which would lead to her martyrdom in Auschwitz.	Unrated
Rosenstrasse (2003)	[Wikipedia] In the present day, a widow mourns the death of her husband. She covers up the TV set and all the mirrors in the house. Her grown children are baffled by this behavior, asking why their mother has suddenly become Orthodox Jewish. The mother will not discuss her past, but her daughter wants to know what happened. Learning of a woman who "saved" her mother during the war, she goes to Germany to learn the whole story.	PG-13 for mature thematic material, some violence and brief drug content.
Rose's Songs—A Rózsa énekei (2003)	[Wikipedia] Autumn 1944. Yellow star, ghettos, Arrow Cross terror. The inhabitants of Hungary's capital, Budapest, await the tragic fulfilment of their fate with helpless resignation. However, above one of the city's villas, once a week in the evening the stars of hope sparkle, if only for a few minutes. This short time gives fresh heart to those hiding here and kindles hope in their tortured souls to live for another day.	Unrated (PG)
The Round Up—La rafle (2010)	[Wikipedia] Based on the true story of a young Jewish boy, the film depicts the Vel' d'Hiv Roundup, the mass arrest of Jews by French police who were accomplices of Nazi Germans in Paris in July 1942.	Unrated (PG)
Rua Alguem 5555: My Father (2003)	[Yad Vashem] A man who grew up an orphan finally gets to meet his father: The psychopath Dr. Josef Mengele, the Auschwitz surgeon who performed genetic experiments on concentration camp refugees during WWII.	Unrated

Title	Summary	MPAA or Local Rating
Run Boy Run—Lauf Junge lauf (2013)	*Run Boy Run—Lauf Junge lauf* (2013) is the most genuine of many films made about young Jewish boys hiding during the War. It is based on the autobiography of a Holocaust survivor who lost an arm while in hiding, but was able to persevere. The acting is compelling and the ending is perfect. *Run Boy Run* is based on a book that can also be used as a companion lesson with the film. [Wikipedia] …based on the life of Yoram Fridman, who as an eight-year-old Jewish boy in 1942, escaped the Warsaw Ghetto and survived, largely on his own, for the next three years in rural Nazi-occupied Poland.	Unrated (PG)
Salad Days—Zielone lata (1980)	[filmpolski.pl, translated from Polish] Sosnowiec [Poland], just before the outbreak of the War. Wojtek, the son of an unemployed person, is friends with a Jewish boy, Abramek, and the daughter of a German pharmacist, Erna. War breaks out when Germany invades. Abramek's family is displaced, his father is killed and he is seriously wounded. Wojtek and Erna take care of him. The Germans arrest Wojtek's mother and give his little sister to a German family for upbringing. Erna leaves for Hamburg. The boy is taken by a doctor he knows.	Unrated
Samson (1961)	[Wikipedia] A dark coming-of-age film, *Samson* follows its Jewish protagonist from an anti-Semitic private school to a prison, then into a Jewish ghetto, and finally over the ghetto wall to the outside world. Wajda uses this journey as a means to explore expressionist cinematography and the weighty issues facing the Jewish people.	Unrated
The Samuel Project (2018)	The grandson of a Holocaust survivor spends time with his grandfather and learns about his suffering during the War. The grandfather then becomes the subject of the grandson's school project.	PG-13
Sarah and the Squirrel—The Seventh Match (1982)	[Wikipedia] The story is about a little girl during the beginning of the Second World War. When the German soldiers invade, she and her family are forced to hide in the woods. When her grandmother gets sick, her father goes into town for medicine and disappears. Sarah goes out to pick berries and when she returns, the rest of her family is gone. Sarah is forced to survive alone in the woods with only the animals for company.	Unrated (PG)
Sarah's Key—Elle s'appelait Sarah (2010)	[Wikipedia] It tells the story of a young girl's experiences during and after the Vel' d'Hiv Roundup of Jews in German-occupied Paris in 1942 and the participation of bureaucracy in Vichy France and French citizens hiding and protecting Sarah from the French authorities.	PG-13 for thematic material including disturbing situations involving the Holocaust.
Saviors in the Night—Unter Bauern (2009)	[Wikipedia] Westphalia in 1943: The Jew Siegmund "Menne" Spiegel, formerly a horse dealer, does not want to lead his wife Marga and daughter Karin to their death and so he and his small family flee from the threatened deportation to the extermination camps in the east to their previous customers and war comrades from the First World War.	Unrated

Title	Summary	MPAA or Local Rating
The Scarlet and the Black (TV 1983)	[Wikipedia] In 1943, the German army occupies Rome. Pope Pius XII is approached by General Max Helm and SS Head of Police for Rome Lieutenant Colonel Herbert Kappler. The Colonel expresses concern that escaped Allied prisoners may attempt to seek refuge in the Vatican, and requests permission to paint a white line across St. Peter's Square in order to mark the extent of Vatican sovereignty.	Unrated (PG)
Schindler's List (1993)	[Wikipedia] The film follows Oskar Schindler, a German industrialist who together with his wife Emilie Schindler saved more than a thousand mostly Polish-Jewish refugees from the Holocaust by employing them in his factories during World War II.	R for language, some sexuality and actuality violence.
The Search (1948)	[Wikipedia] …a young Auschwitz survivor and his mother who search for each other across post–World War II Europe.	UK-Universal
A Secret—Un secret (2007)	[Wikipedia] The film follows Maxime Nathan and his family in France during in the years before and after World War II. François Grimbert grows up in Paris in the 1950s. He is the skinny, sickly son of two marvelously athletic parents, Tania and Maxime. For a while, he dreams of a stronger, fitter, more charismatic older brother to compensate for his own feelings of inadequacy.	Unrated (PG)
Sergeant Schmidt—Feldwebel Schmid (TV 1968)	[Yad Vashem] Docudrama produced by the German television network ZDF based on the true story of a Righteous Among the Nations Anton Schmid. Schmid, a sergeant in the German army, gave forged documents to Jews in the Vilna ghetto, for the purpose of aiding them to survive. He was tried and executed in 1942.	Unrated
Seven Journeys—In Those Days— In jenen Tagen (1947)	[Wikipedia] It was one of the cycle of Rubble films made in the wake of Germany's defeat during World War II. The film addresses issues of collective guilt during the Nazi era, using the device of a car built in 1933 and dismantled in 1947 narrating the various experiences of its owners in a series of seven separate episodes.	Unrated
The 17th Bride—Ha-Kala (1985)	[Yad Vashem] A gripping WWII drama featuring Lisa Hartman and Rosemary Leach, this powerful film, set in Czechoslovakia, is based on the book written by Ladislav Grossman, Oscar winning author of *The Shop on Main Street*. Set in a war-torn village in Czechoslovakia, the story centers on a strong Jewish woman who enters into marriage with a man she dislikes believing it will save her from deportation to a labor camp. Her decision is shared by the other women in her village but after she becomes The "17th Bride" in a single day to choose such a fate the Nazis declare the ceremonies invalid. The Jewish women are rounded up by the Germans and degraded, humiliated and manhandled as a prelude to being shipped off on the death trains.	Unrated
The Seventh Room— A hetedik szoba (1996)	[Wikipedia, translated from French] This film tells the story of Edith Stein, Sister Thérèse-Bénédicte de la Croix.	Unrated

Title	Summary	MPAA or Local Rating
~~*Shades of Truth* (2015)~~	[Wikipedia] …about the life of Pope Pius XII and his relation with Nazi Germany. Based on official documents and data, this film intends to show Pius XII as the Vatican's Schindler.	Unrated
~~*Shepherd: The Hero Dog* (2019)~~	A Jewish family's stray dog is used as a weapon against Jews in a concentration camp.	Unrated
Shine (1996)	[Wikipedia] …based on the life of David Helfgott, a pianist and the son of a Holocaust survivor, who suffered a mental breakdown and spent years in institutions.	Rated PG-13 for nudity—sensuality and intense thematic elements.
Ship of Fools (1965)	[Wikipedia] The action of the film takes place entirely on board a passenger ship in 1933, between Veracruz, Mexico, and Bremerhaven, Germany in 1933. Most of the scenes take place on the First Class deck, among the upper middle-class passengers there; but the ship is carrying 600 displaced workers, far more than the ship is certified to carry, in squalid conditions in steerage. They are being deported from Cuba back to Spain by the Cuban Machado dictatorship. Some passengers are happy to be bound for Nazi Germany, some are apprehensive, while others downplay the significance of fascist politics.	UK-14+
***The Shop on Main Street— Obchod na korze* (1965)**	*The Shop on Main Street—Obchod na korze* (1965) is an uncompromising depiction of Czech antisemitism and collaboration with the Germans. It portrays with great honesty the systematic, brazen "appropriation" of Jewish businesses by the local Czech community as the Jews are being deported. Given that depictions of Soviet suffering were the Communist party line until the fall of Communism, *The Shop on Main Street* is even more impressive considering that it was made behind the "Iron Curtain." [Wikipedia] During World War II, a mild-mannered Slovak carpenter, Anton "Tóno" Brtko, is offered ownership of the sewing notions (i.e. haberdasher) store of an old, near-deaf Jewish woman, Rozália Lautmannová, as an Aryanization regulation is enacted. As Brtko attempts to explain to Lautmannová, who is oblivious to the world outside and generally confused, that he is now her supervisor and the owner of the store, Imrich Kuchár, a Slovak opponent of Aryanization, informs Brtko that the business is unprofitable and Lautmannová relies on donations. The Jewish community then offers to pay Brtko a salary if he nevertheless stays in charge, to prevent it being given to a new, possibly ruthless Aryanizer. He accepts and lets Lautmannová believe he is her nephew who has come to help.	UK-14+
Simon Konianski (2009)	A farce about a 35-year-old man who takes his young son, his annoying relatives and his dead father on a road trip to Ukraine to discover their past.	NR

Title	Summary	MPAA or Local Rating
The Singing Forest (2003)	[Wikipedia] Christopher is a widower, his wife of 22 years Savannah having recently died, and he begins drinking and becomes obsessed with the theory of past lives. Before long, he is convinced he is actually the reincarnation of a German resistance fighter who was hanged by the Nazis for hiding Jews during the Holocaust. His situation becomes even more complex as his daughter Destiny's wedding approaches, and Christopher's sense of déjà vu around her fiancé, Ben, is enough to convince him that he and Ben were gay lovers during a past life.	Unrated (R)
Singing in the Dark (1956)	[Wikipedia] Leo, the main character, is a Holocaust survivor who suffers from total amnesia. When he immigrates to the U.S. he manages to find a job as a hotel desk clerk. When he accepts a drink in the hotel bar, he suddenly starts singing, amazing those around him—and himself—with his magnificent voice. Taking advantage of his gift, he begins singing in nightclubs. Eventually, with the help of a psychiatrist and partly as a result of a blow to the head during a mugging, his memories begin to return, and he realizes that he is the son of a great Jewish Hazzan (cantor) in Europe.	Unrated
Skipper Next to God— Maître après Dieu (1951)	[Wikipedia, translated from French] In 1938, in Hamburg, Captain Joris Knipper, a boorish buccaneer, arrived aboard his ship to unload food stolen from Africa. He negotiated the transport to Egypt of 150 Jewish passengers, but international law quickly prohibited him from disembarking them anywhere. His Christian faith resurfaces and he refuses to bring the unfortunate back to Germany, feeling himself invested with a divine mission. He will alert world opinion and will manage to save his passengers by sacrificing his ship.	Unrated
Skokie—Once They Marched Through a Thousand Towns (TV 1981)	[Wikipedia] The peace of Skokie, a comfortable suburban village located just north of Chicago, is threatened when Frank Collin, a politically astute neo-Nazi organizer, selects the place as the site of his next rally. Close to 40 percent of the village's population is Jewish, and many of them are survivors of the Holocaust. They see the march as a warning and reminder of their days as concentration camp prisoners. The Jewish community decides to stand against the rally at all costs to make sure that the Holocaust will never be forgotten or allowed to happen again.	Unrated
The Sky Is Falling—Il cielo cade (2000)	[Wikipedia, translated from Italian] 1943. In the middle years of the Second World War, Penny and Baby, two little Roman sisters, are orphaned by both parents. The two are thus taken into custody by the German uncles Katchen and Wilhelm Einstein, and they move to their villa in Tuscany. The two girls adapt with difficulty to the new reality: Penny, the older of the two, had an upbringing strongly influenced by the Catholic religion and fascist propaganda, while her uncle Wilhelm, a Jew by birth but an atheist and free thinker, cannot stand behaviors of the two girls.	Unrated (PG)

Title	Summary	MPAA or Local Rating
Sobibor (2018)	[Wikipedia] The film is based on the Sobibor revolt which occurred in 1943 in German-occupied Poland. The main character of the movie is the Jewish-Soviet soldier Alexander Pechersky, who was a lieutenant in the Red Army. In October 1943, he was deported to the Sobibor death camp, where Jews were being exterminated in gas chambers. In just three weeks, Pechersky planned an uprising with prisoners from Poland and other locations around Western Europe. This uprising was partly successful, allowing roughly 300 prisoners to escape, of whom roughly 60 survived the war.	Unrated (PG)
Son of Saul (2015)	*Son of Saul* (2015) is a Hungarian remake of *The Grey Zone* (2001). *Son of Saul*, however, only portrays one Sonderkommando, as opposed to the larger Sonder-kommando crew portrayed in *The Grey Zone*. The one Sonderkommando in *Son of Saul* finds a surviving child after a gassing. The Germans examine how the child survived the gas and then kill him. The Sonder-kommando then spends the rest of the film trying to ritually bury the child. The Birkenau revolt is barely portrayed. *Son of Saul* is recommended as a great rep-resentation of Auschwitz/Birkenau and of one Sonder-kommando. [Wikipedia] In October 1944, Saul Ausländer works as a Sonderkommando Jewish–Hungarian prisoner in Auschwitz. His job is to salvage valuables from the clothing of the dead, drag bodies from the gas chambers and scrub the chambers before the next group arrives to be gassed. He works stoically, seemingly having been numbed by the daily horrors. Among the dead after a gassing is a boy who is still barely alive, and Saul witnesses a Nazi physician suf-focate the boy and call for an autopsy. Saul steps forth and insists on carrying the body himself to the prison doctor, Miklós, a fellow Hungarian prisoner and a forced assistant to Josef Mengele. He asks Miklós to not cut up the boy, so he can give him a proper Jewish burial.	R for disturbing violent con-tent, and some graphic nudity.
The Song and the Silence (1968)	Life in a quiet Polish village is exterminated by the Germans.	Unrated
~~*The Song of Names* (2019)~~	[Wikipedia] Dovidl Rappaport, a 9-year-old from Poland who lost his parents and siblings in World War II, is also a prodigy at the violin. The Simmonds fam-ily adopt him and he is taken to England. Their son Martin starts bonding with his new adoptive brother as he likes Dovidl playing the violin. David [as he is now called] continues practicing the violin while still remembering his biological family. Years pass, and David and Martin are now 21 years old. There is just one day left for a concert featuring David, when he mysteriously disappears with his violin.	12

Title	Summary	MPAA or Local Rating
__Sophie's Choice (1982)__	*Sophie's Choice* (1982) is among the most famous of all Holocaust films, yet it tells the post-War story of a Gentile woman who survived Auschwitz. Although less than a fifth of the film is a depiction of Sophie's life in Auschwitz, *Sophie's Choice* was the first Western Holocaust film to represent the death camp with cinematic respect. *Sophie's Choice* is an essential link in the chain of must-see Holocaust films. [Wikipedia] The film stars Meryl Streep as Zofia "Sophie" Zawistowski, a Polish immigrant with a dark secret from her past who shares a boarding house in Brooklyn with her tempestuous lover, Nathan, and a young writer, Stingo.	15
Spring 1941 (2007)	[Shoreline Entertainment, edited] Artur Planck, his wife Clara and their two daughters seek shelter from Germans during the invasion of Poland. The family finds a safe house on the farm of war-widow Emilia. While they are in hiding from the Nazis, a love triangle ensues.	R for some disturbing violent content and brief sexuality.
Spring of Life—Pramen zivota (TV 2000)	[Wikipedia] The film depicts a little-known operation of the Nazi SS, started just before the outbreak of World War II. Grétka has been selected by the Nazis for the Lebensborn. She falls in love with the Jew Leo who has been hiding there.	Unrated (PG)
Springtime in Budapest— Budapesti tavasz (1955)	[Wikipedia, translated from Hungarian] During the Second World War, on Christmas Day 1944, two military fugitives fled to Budapest. Zoltán visits an apartment he thought was abandoned, but finds his relatives in it. The man then meets a young Jewish girl, Jutka, who is also trying to get through this period here. Young people will fall in love with each other. The man wants to survive the siege, and his fellow soldier Gozsó joins the partisans. Among the horrors of the Arrow Cross era, the protagonist tries to save his love.	Unrated
The Square of St. Elizabeth— Námestie svätej Alzbety (1966)	Slovakian friends suffer as Nazism takes hold in their village.	Unrated
Stars—Sterne (1959)	[Wikipedia, translated from German] A small town occupied by Germans in Bulgaria in 1943: The Wehrmacht sub-officer Walther supervises the civilian workers in a motor vehicle workshop, but the former painter prefers to draw the area and the people of the place. His superior mockingly calls him "Rembrandt," but his best friend Lieutenant Kurt proudly lets himself be portrayed by him. Walter in particular enjoys being apparently far from the war.	Unrated (PG)
The Statement (2003)	[Wikipedia] Pierre Brossard, a French Nazi collaborator, orders seven Jews executed during World War II. Some 40 years later, he is pursued by "David Manenbaum," a hitman who is under orders to kill Brossard and leave a printed "Statement" on his body proclaiming the assassination was vengeance for the Jews executed in 1944. Brossard kills "Manenbaum," hiding the dead body after finding the printed "Statement" and discovering that his pursuer was travelling on a Canadian passport.	R for violence.

Title	Summary	MPAA or Local Rating
Stielke, Heinz, Fifteen—Stielke, Heinz, fünfzehn... (1987)	[Wikipedia, translated from German] Heinz Stielke from Berlin is a fifteen-year-old fanatical Hitler Youth member who has just become a Rottenführer when it turns out that his father, who died as an officer and hero in the war, had Jewish ancestors. Because of his Jewish descent, Heinz is thrown out of the grammar school and his former friends avoid him. However, Heinz does not yet want to acknowledge that he has a non-Aryan past with his appearance and the next day he goes to school for a sporting competition.	Unrated
~~*A Story About a Bad Dream* (2000)~~	[Wikipedia] The Czech docudrama film was made to preserve Eva Erbenova's personal history for her children and grandchildren. While the film has an artistic appeal for adults, it maintains a tone that's gentle enough for a younger audience. Historic footage of the Nazis, drawings made by Jewish artists from inside the deportation camp, children's drawings of Nazi concentration camps that move and develop on screen, colorful reenacted scenes of her rescue, and Eva's family photographs are compiled to tell the story of a girl who survived the Holocaust. She lost both her parents for reasons she could not fully understand.	Unrated
~~*The Story of a Murder—Chronik eines Mordes* (1965)~~	[Wikipedia, translated from German] The focus of the action is the Jew Ruth Bodenheim, whose story is told in three time periods in the film, which are presented here chronologically: She lives in a town in southern Germany with her brother David, who is over ten years her junior, and her parents. The National Socialists have consolidated their power and Ruth and her parents have to wear the Star of David on their clothes.	Unrated (PG)
The Stranger (1946)	[Wikipedia] Wilson is an agent of the United Nations War Crimes Commission who is hunting for Nazi fugitive Franz Kindler, a war criminal who has erased all evidence which might identify him. He has left no clue to his identity except "a hobby that almost amounts to a mania—clocks." Wilson releases Kindler's former associate Meinike, hoping the man will lead him to Kindler. Wilson follows Meinike to a small town in Connecticut, but loses him before he meets with Kindler.	UK-PG
~~*Stream Line—La linea del fiume* (1976)~~	[Wikipedia, translated from Italian] Rome, October 16, 1943. The Germans deport the relatives and friends of little Giacomo Treves who fortunately escapes capture. The child is entrusted by a priest, Don Luigi, to the black marketeer Amedeo, then begins an adventurous journey to London where the father is a speaker at the BBC for the Italian broadcasts of Radio London.	Unrated
The Substance of Fire (1996)	[Wikipedia] Isaac Geldhart is a survivor of the Holocaust. He arrived in New York City an orphan, reinvented himself as a bon vivant, married well, and found fame and fortune as a champion of authors who are passionate about their work rather than its best-seller potential. He is faced with a family-business *(cont.)*	R

Title	Summary	MPAA or Local Rating
	conflict, the potential Japanese takeover of his increasingly insolvent firm. He must browbeat his three children, all principal stockholders whom he dismisses in varying degrees, into accepting his plan to publish a six-volume scholarly work on Nazi medical experiments, despite their belief that a highly successful commercial novel is the only thing that will keep them from going under.	
The Summer of Aviya—Aviya's Summer—Ha-Kayitz Shel Aviya (1988)	[Wikipedia] *Aviya's Summer* is set in the summer of 1951, in the newly established state of Israel. The film chronicles the life of ten-year-old Aviya, whose warm, loving, and fiercely independent mother, Henya, is tortured by periodic mental breakdowns. Henya's psychological and emotional scars stem from her horrid experience during the Holocaust, and from the loss of her husband during the war. Henya was once considered to be a beautiful and courageous partisan fighter, yet now she is constantly mocked by native Israelis for her erratic behavior.	Unrated (PG)
Sunshine (1999)	[Wikipedia] It follows five generations of a Hungarian Jewish family, originally named Sonnenschein, later changed to Sors, during changes in Hungary, focusing mostly on the three generations from the late 19th century through the mid-20th century. The family story traverses the creation of the Austro-Hungarian Empire through to the period after the 1956 Revolution, while the characters are forced to surrender much of their identity and endure family conflict.	R for strong sexuality, and for violence, language and nudity.
Surviving with Wolves—Survivre avec les loups (2007)	[Wikipedia] Misha, an 8-year-old Jewish girl, travels through Nazi Europe in search of her parents. Her father and mother have just been deported. She only knows one thing: they are in the east. Using a simple little compass, she leaves her native Belgium and walks to Ukraine, crossing Germany and Poland, in the hope of finding them. To survive, she steals food and clothing, avoids men and their violence, and joins a pack of wolves.	Unrated (PG)
Süskind (2012)	*Süskind* (2012) tells the true story of Jewish resistance in occupied Amsterdam where Walter Süskind saved more than 1,000 Jews. Slightly melodramatic, though not to the point of being offensive, *Süskind* gets its point across without humanizing the German officer who directs the deportation. *Süskind* also provides a rare glimpse of the Westerbork Concentration Camp. [Wikipedia] The film is set in Amsterdam during the German occupation of the Netherlands. A group of people, including Walter Süskind, try to help children escape the Holocaust.	Unrated (PG)
The Taras Family—The Unvanquished—Nepokoryonnye (1945)	[Wikipedia, translated from Russian] The film is set in Donbass during the Great Patriotic War. Taras Yatsenko is an old worker. He cannot evacuate due to the illness of his little granddaughter. His family is involved in an underground struggle. The Germans force Taras to restore the plant, but he sabotages the work. When the Germans decide to destroy the Jews *(cont.)*	Unrated

Title	Summary	MPAA or Local Rating
	of the city, the doctor hides his granddaughter with Taras. During the raid, she is discovered, but after leaving Taras, the policeman Vasilyok kills the SS man and hides her from the underground.	
~~A Tear in the Ocean— Une larme dans l'océan (1973)~~	[Wikipedia, translated from French] An artisanal film with a tiny budget inspired by the novel by Manès Sperber. In the Poland of the Warsaw ghetto in 1942, a Catholic aristocratic count sells part of his treasures to constitute a resistance against the Nazis and to protect a Jewish community divided into two movements: the first refuses to arm itself so as not to behave in the image of the tyrant and the second wants to take up arms and fight.	Unrated
~~Tel Aviv-Berlin (1987)~~	[Yad Vashem, translated from Hebrew] 1942. Benjamin is a Holocaust refugee who finds it difficult to acclimatize in Palestine.	Unrated
Temporary Paradise— Ideiglenes paradicsom (1981)	French POWs during the War try to escape towards Hungary.	Unrated
~~The Testament (2017)~~	[Yad Vashem] Feature film. Yoel, a senior Holocaust researcher, is in the midst of a widely covered legal battle with powerful forces in Austria, concerning a brutal massacre of Jews that took place toward the end of WWII in the village of Lensdorf. An influential family of industrialists on whose land the murder took place is planning to build a real estate project on the very same land. Yoel suspects that their aim is to bury the affair for good, but has trouble finding the conclusive evidence that would stop the project. While investigating the incident Yoel examines classified testimonies of Holocaust survivors, and to his shock and surprise he finds a testimony given by his mother, a testimony he didn't know existed. In her testimony she confesses to a substantial secret from her past. Yoel, who's conducting a double-investigation, personal and scientific, is trapped between walls of silence—on one side, denial of the Holocaust on the part of the villagers, and on the other, his mother's silence regarding her past. As a historian with an unshakeable commitment to the truth, he decides to continue his investigations even at the cost of ruining his personal and professional life.	Unrated
~~There Is Many Like Us (2015)~~	[Wikipedia] Set in Poland during the Second World War, this documentary film recounts the experiences of oppression and persecution under German military occupation in the city of Warsaw and the Pawiak Prison Camp. The story follows Max Fronenberg, who was put into forced labor at the prison camp, located in the center of the Warsaw ghetto, as a sheet metal worker in 1942. He later met a young woman named Rena Rosenbaum who was concealing her Jewish descent from the Germans and feared she would be discovered and killed.	Unrated

Title	Summary	MPAA or Local Rating
The Third Half—Treto poluvreme (2012)	[Wikipedia] The film is set in North Macedonia, then part of Yugoslavia, and follows the period shortly after the Nazi invasion of the region. In 1941, a young soccer player from Macedonia, Kosta, and a wealthy young Jewish woman, Rebecca, fall in love, despite her father's effort to keep them apart. With the war raging around their borders, the Macedonians remain cocooned in their world of patriotic pleasures, primarily concerned about getting the beleaguered Macedonia Football Club on a winning streak. Their manager hires the legendary German-Jewish coach Rudolph Spitz to turn them into champions.	Unrated (PG)
~~38 (1986)~~	[Yad Vashem] Vienna, Autumn 1937. Carola Hell, an actress at the Josefstadt Theater, is in love with a Jewish writer, Martin Hofmann. Hofmann's journalist friend, Drechsler, warns them that the Austrian Nazis will soon come into power and advises them to leave the country, but Martin and Carola are not very interested in politics. While on tour in Berlin, Carola gets to know the Nazis. Despite her success in *Emilia Galotti* she is detained by the police because she had dared to criticize the Nazis for their harassment of people. Carola obtains a film role and observes the increasing antisemitism. She intends to interpret her next role in the theatre from a political point of view. The situation becomes more critical. Schuschnigg has announced a referendum which will be held on March 13. Carola learns that she is pregnant but Martin's joy is tempered by the Germans marching into Austria. That very evening, Martin and Carola try to go by train to Prague but only Carola succeeds in getting there. Martin is stopped by the SA troops and beaten up and has to hide himself in Vienna. Some friends promise to help him but all of them are unable to do so. When Martin learns that Carola has arrived safely in Prague, he is arrested by an SS patrol. The fate of "unpolitical people" in Vienna, in March 1938.	Unrated
36 Hours (1964)	[Wikipedia] On June 2, 1944, a German army doctor tries to obtain vital information from an American military intelligence officer by convincing him that it is 1950 and World War II is long over.	UK-PG
This Boat Is Full— Das Boot ist voll (1981)	[Wikipedia] The title of the film derives from what was expressed by the Swiss during World War II, for as a nonbelligerent country many refugees desired entry there, with most being denied permission. They were frequently told, "Our boat is full," a reference to passengers of a lifeboat after a ship sinking frequently refusing to allow any further survivors to enter their craft after it had reached a level of occupancy felt to approach the limit of safety.	PG
This Must Be the Place (2011)	Like the Survivor film *Harold and Maude* (1971), 40 years later, *This Must Be the Place* (2011) is intensely quirky and beautifully made. *This Must Be the Place* features the estranged adult son of a just-deceased Auschwitz survivor. The son, a retired rock star, sets out to settle his father's score with a 90-year-old *(cont.)*	R for language, some sexual content and brief disturbing images.

Title	Summary	MPAA or Local Rating
	Auschwitz guard. While far more Holocaust-oriented than *Harold and Maude*, *This Must Be the Place* also is a celebration of life and growth. [Wikipedia] The film deals with a middle-aged wealthy rock star who becomes bored in his retirement and takes on the quest of finding his father's tormentor, a Nazi war criminal who is a refugee in the United States.	
Those Who Remained— Akik maradtak (2019)	[Wikipedia] A 16-year-old girl and a middle-aged doctor connect in Budapest after World War II, each mourning their families lost in concentration camps.	Unrated
Three Days in April— Drei Tage im April (TV 1995)	*Three Days in April—Drei Tage im April* (TV 1995) captures the moment just before German transition from supremacy to submission. It portrays the German despair near the end of the War when all is lost. Just then, cattle cars full of Jews in transit from one concentration camp to another are abandoned in a little German village. What, if anything, should the locals do with or for these dying Jews? If all is lost, what is gained by helping these people who, for more than a decade, have officially been deemed subhuman enemies of the German state? [Wikipedia] April 1945 in a Hohenlohe-Franconian village with the place name "Nesselbühl": Most of the residents are waiting for the American troops to march in and thus the end of the war. Gun thunder can be heard in the distance. In addition to retreating Wehrmacht troops, SS patrols are also present. They execute alleged deserters of the Wehrmacht who camped in the local inn without a marching order. After a locomotive is damaged one night shortly before the end of the war, the Reichsbahn had to uncouple three freight cars and one passenger car from an SS special train and simply leave them standing in the station.	Unrated (R)
~~*Toman* (2018)~~	[Wikipedia] The film follows the rise and fall of Zdeněk Toman, Head of Czechoslovak Intelligence from 1945 to 1948. The film starts in April 1948 when Toman is interrogated by Inspector Putna. The film then moves to March 1945 when Toman was a repatriation officer in Carpathian Ruthenia. He comes into conflict with NKVD officers who insist that nobody will be repatriated from Carpathian Ruthenia as it will become part of the Soviet Union. Toman bribes NKVD officers and later meets Imrich Rosenberg. Rosenberg asks Toman to help repatriate Jews from Carpathian Ruthenia.	Unrated
Tomorrow's a Wonderful Day— Adamah (1947)	[Wikipedia, edited] Benjamin, an adolescent Holocaust survivor, arrives with other boys to a village in British Palestine, just after the War. Benjamin suffers from trauma and begins to hoard bread. Teachers and staff realize that Benjamin is troubled. They help him adjust to his new life, turning him into a leader.	Unrated

Title	Summary	MPAA or Local Rating
Train of Life—Train de vie (1998)	[Wikipedia] The film starts off with a man, named Schlomo, running crazily through a forest, with his voice playing in the background, saying that he has seen the horror of the Nazis in a nearby town, and he must tell the others. Once he gets into town, he informs the rabbi, and together they run through the town and once they have got enough people together, they hold a town meeting. At first, many of the men do not believe the horrors they are being told, and many criticize Schlomo, for he is the town lunatic, and who could possibly believe him?	12
~~*Transit* (1980)~~	[Wikipedia] A Jew who escaped from Nazi Germany and immigrated to Israel decides to return to his homeland, Germany. But, before his journey, he must undergo a process of self-purity which takes him through Israel's underworld.	Unrated
Treason—Prodosia (1964)	[Yad Vashem, translated from Hebrew] Full-length feature film. A love story between Lisa, a young Greek Jew hiding in a professor's house in Athens, and Carl von Stein, an SS officer. Lisa first identifies as the professor's sister. In the midst of an affair between her and the German, she reveals to him her true identity.	Unrated
Triumph of the Spirit (1989)	[Wikipedia] A stevedore in Thessaloniki, Greece, Salamo Arouch's passion is boxing. Captured along with his family and fiancé Allegra in 1943 and interned in Auschwitz, Arouch is used by his SS captors as entertainment, forced to box against fellow prisoners. He knows that if he refuses, his family will be punished; if he wins, he will be given extra rations which he can share with them; if he loses, he will be sent to the gas chamber.	15
The Truce—La tregua (1997)	[Wikipedia] Although liberated on January 27, 1945, Primo Levi did not reach Turin until October 19 of that year. After spending some time in a Soviet camp for former concentration camp inmates, he embarked on an arduous journey home in the company of Italian former prisoners of war from the Italian Army in Russia. His long railway journey home to Turin took him on a circuitous route from Poland, through Russia, Romania, Hungary, Austria and Germany.	R for some language and sexual content.
The 25th Hour— La vingt-cinquième heure (1967)	[Wikipedia] In a small Transylvanian village in Romania, a local police constable frames Johann Moritz on charges of being Jewish, because Moritz' wife, Suzanna, has refused his advances. Moritz is sent to a Romanian concentration camp as a Jew, Jacob Moritz. He escapes to Hungary with some Jewish prisoners, where the Hungarians imprison them for being citizens of an enemy country. The Hungarian authorities eventually send them to Germany to fill German "requests" for foreign labourers.	Unrated (PG)

Title	Summary	MPAA or Local Rating
25 Firemen's Street—Tüzoltó utca 25. (1973)	[Play.Google] In Hungary, residents of a building slated to be demolished gather to ruminate on the past four decades of their lives. Recalling their personal sagas in the context of Hungary's turbulent political history, the residents—including a woman jailed for her political beliefs, a soldier fearful of war and a woman whose husband is about to die—create a haunted tapestry of lives permanently scarred by war and political repression.	Unrated
Twist of Fate—Pursuit (TV 1989)	[Yad Vashem] A two-part miniseries about an SS-Lieutenant Colonel Helmut Von Schreader who, in the waning days of the Third Reich, undergoes plastic surgery and becomes a concentration-camp prisoner to avoid prosecution as a war criminal. In an ironic twist of fate, he is shipped to the wrong camp and forced to live with those he has victimized, where he learns to respect them. After the war, he becomes involved in the founding of Israel, marries and fathers a son, who eventually stumbles across his identity 20 years later.	Unrated
Two Men (TV 1988)	[Yad Vashem] In this TV drama, a Toronto Hungarian immigrant believes that a respected businessman killed his family at Auschwitz during WWII.	Unrated
The Two of Us—Le vieil homme et l'enfant (1967)	*The Two of Us—Le vieil homme et l'enfant* (1967) is an early, small story about a Jewish boy who is hidden in Vichy France by elderly antisemites who do not know that he is Jewish. The film humanizes both the boy and his caregivers, while offering a view of occupied France. *The Two of Us* subtly exposes the Vichy French mentality in the simplest terms. Although no one dies (except for the family dog), the anxiety of being a hidden Jewish child is masterfully recreated. [Wikipedia] Claude is an 8-year-old Jewish boy living in France during the Nazi occupation. To reduce the chance that he would be sent to Auschwitz or a similar fate, his parents send him to live with a farm family, the elderly parents of Catholic friends of his parents. The elderly couple honestly think that the boy has been sent to live with them because Paris is dangerous; it never crosses their mind that Claude is a Jew.	Sweden-15
The Unborn (2009)	[Wikipedia, edited] A young woman is tormented by a dybbuk [a malicious possessing spirit]. She seeks the help of a rabbi. Two generations earlier in Auschwitz, Josef Mengele had experimented on the girl's grandmother and the grandmother's twin brother, who is connected to the dybbuk. The dybbuk must be exorcised.	PG-13 for intense sequences of violence and terror, disturbing images, thematic material and language including some sexual references.

Title	Summary	MPAA or Local Rating
Under the Domim Tree— Etz Hadomim Tafus (1994)	*Under the Domim Tree—Etz Hadomim Tafus* (1994) is a vivid window into the lives of adolescent Holocaust survivors and of Israel in the early 1950s. The young survivors struggle with normal issues of teenage life while grappling with memories of the War and trying to remember their former lives in eastern Europe. While some of the story concerns a custody battle, *Under the Domim Tree* is mostly a testament to those adults and Israeli institutions which cared for child survivors and orphans from the Holocaust. [Wikipedia] Both the book and the film are sequels to Almagor's 1985 autobiographical book, *Summer of Aviya*, about the protagonist's childhood in the 1950s in Israel. *Under the Domim Tree* tells of Aviya's years in the Oudim boarding school and about the relations that are formed between the Israeli-born students and the students who survived the Holocaust.	Unrated (PG)
Unfair Competition Concorrenza sleale (2001)	[Wikipedia] Rome 1938. Umberto and Leone have got a men's costume shop, on the same street. Umberto is Catholic, Leone is Jewish. Racial laws are approved in Italy in 1938 after Hitler's visit to Rome.	11
Uprising (TV 2001)	[Wikipedia] On 1 September 1939, Germany invades Poland and after which the regulation was promulgated that all Polish Jews should move to the newly created Warsaw Ghetto. As in all the ghettos, a Judenrat was appointed and was responsible for the administration of the ghetto. The film tells the moral dilemmas faced by Adam Czerniaków, head of the Judenrat in the Warsaw Ghetto, who had to carry out orders of the German authorities, including sending Jews to the Treblinka Concentration Camp. A group of Polish Jews decide to rebel against the Germans and not to lend a hand to the murder of their brethren.	12
Valentina's Mother— Ima shel Valentina (2008)	[Wikipedia, translated from Hebrew] The film tells the story of Paula, a Holocaust survivor from Poland who enlists the help of Valentina, a young foreign worker. Coincidentally, the name of the foreign worker is also the name of Paula's close friend from childhood. The relationship between the two is tightening, and the old woman is flooded with repressed memories from the war period. Paula, who sees Valentina as a tragic reflection of her life, becomes dependent on her; despite the opposition of her son and acquaintances she longs to adopt her as a daughter.	Unrated
Varian's War: The Forgotten Hero (TV 2001)	[Wikipedia] …based on the life and wartime exploits of Varian Fry who saved more than 2,000 Jewish artists from Vichy France, the conquered ally of Nazi Germany.	12
Victor Young Perez (2013)	[Wikipedia] Victor "Young" Perez tells the astonishing, harrowing and poignant story of a Tunisian Jewish boxer, who became the World Flyweight Champion in 1931 and 1932. Perez got arrested in Paris on September 21, 1943, and was detained in the Drancy internment camp in France, before being transported to the German extermination camp in Auschwitz where he *(cont.)*	Unrated

Title	Summary	MPAA or Local Rating
	was assigned to the Monowitz subcamp to serve as a slave laborer. Victor Perez arrived at Auschwitz on October 10, 1943, as part of "Transport 60," a group of 1,000.	
Voyage of the Damned (1976)	[Wikipedia] The story was inspired by actual events concerning the fate of the ocean liner *St. Louis* carrying Jewish refugees from Germany to Cuba in 1939.	PG
~~*Voyages* (1999)~~	[Yad Vashem] Three remarkable tales that come together in a short instant at the film's end. A woman on a bus tour of Poland is left behind at a Jewish cemetery. A Parisian widow receives a call from a man claiming to be her long-lost father. And a newly arrived 85-year-old Russian immigrant wanders the streets of Tel Aviv looking for a distant cousin. Slow-paced and breathtaking. Winner of numerous awards and rave reviews.	Unrated (PG)
Walk on Water (2004)	[Wikipedia] Eyal is an agent in Mossad, the Israeli security service. He is a hitman who targets enemies of Israel. His wife has recently committed suicide, and the agency decides that he needs to take on a less challenging assignment: to find an aging Nazi war criminal and get him "before God does." In order to track down the old man, Eyal poses as a tour guide and befriends the Nazi's adult grandchildren, Axel and Pia. Pia lives on a kibbutz, an Israeli commune. Her brother Axel visits her in order to convince Pia to return to Germany for their father's seventieth birthday.	R for some language including sexual references, and for brief nudity.
Walking with the Enemy (2013)	[Wikipedia] Set in Budapest and nearby villages, it depicts the German occupation of Hungary during the final months of the Second World War. The story is about a young Hungarian-Jewish man, Elek Cohen, who dons an SS uniform to pose as an officer to find out the fate of his family and to rescue fellow Jews from the Holocaust.	PG-13
The Wall (TV 1982)	[Yad Vashem] Adapted by Millard Lampell from his own 1960 Broadway play, which was inspired by John Hersey's 1950 novel, *The Wall* tells of the Warsaw Ghetto Uprising of April 1943. The story is told through the eyes of Warsaw Jew Dolek Benson, who is a passive observer of the atrocities all around him until he learns the truth about the Nazis' "resettlement" program. Rachel Roberts, cast as Regina Kowalski, a former schoolteacher, made her final appearance in this film. Filmed on location in Sosnowiec, Poland, and first telecast February 16, 1982, *The Wall* earned a Peabody Award the following year.	Unrated
Wallenberg—A Hero's Story (TV 1985)	[Wikipedia] …about Raoul Wallenberg, a Swedish diplomat who was instrumental in saving thousands of Hungarian Jews from the Holocaust.	PG
The Wandering Jew— L'ebreo errante (1948)	[Wikipedia, translated from Italian] Adapted from the novel of the same name by Eugène Sue, it narrates the vicissitudes of a Jew, Mathieu Blumenthal, condemned to wander the streets of the world, both in space and in time. In the Second World War he lives in Paris *(cont.)*	Unrated

Title	Summary	MPAA or Local Rating
	with Elena. With the arrival of the Germans, Mathieu takes refuge in the synagogue, where he meets other members of the community, including Esther. The group arrested by the Germans will be deported to a concentration camp, where Mathieu, falling in love with Esther, organizes an escape taking the girl with him.	
War and Love (1985)	[Yad Vashem] This drama is based on the autobiography of its producer, Jack P. Eisner. Jacek and Halina are two adolescent Polish Jews whose romance comes to an abrupt end when Halina flees Warsaw with her parents as the Nazis invade their homeland. Jacek remains in what soon becomes the Jewish ghetto and helps the underground movement smuggle in food. When the Nazis ship ghetto residents to the death camps, Jacek manages to escape and once again meets Halina. The reunited lovers join in the resistance movement, but they are eventually captured by the Nazis. Though separated from Halina, Jacek survives the inhumane life of the concentration camp and is liberated by American troops after two hellish years. Jacek begins a new search for Halina and eventually returns to Warsaw. There the two survivors are finally reunited in the small cottage where they first made love, though their happiness is all too brief. Halina's health has been destroyed by her experiences; having traveled great distances in hopes of finding Jacek, she dies as her lover holds her close. The film was to be made at Auschwitz, an event generating media attention.	PG-13
Warsaw: Year 5703— Warszawa. Année 5703 (1992)	[Yad Vashem] Feature film taking place in the winter of 1943. Two young Jews, Alek and Fryda, escape via sewer tunnels from the atrocities underway in the Warsaw ghetto. Alek, entrusted with undeveloped photos of the horrors within, makes his way to a supposedly safe apartment only to find it occupied by Germans. Another tenant, a Pole, Stefania, abruptly offers to shelter him in her spacious apartment. She comforts him and they make love that very night. Stefania is uncommonly generous and willing to jeopardize her own safety by hiding a Jew. She even goes to a nearby church and rescues Fryda. But Fryda is ungrateful and proceeds to sabotage the trio's safety in insidious ways.	Unrated (R)
The Wave (TV 1981)	[Wikipedia] High school social studies teacher Ben Ross shows his class a film about the Holocaust. When the students question how the German people could have allowed such a thing to occur, Ross finds himself unable to answer their questions. Instead he begins a classroom experiment to demonstrate the dangers of fascism. The experiment begins simply, with Ross demonstrating how proper posture and simple classroom rules create greater efficiency. The students follow the new rules so enthusiastically that Ross carries on the experiment the following day by introducing "the Wave," which he claims is a youth movement.	G

Title	Summary	MPAA or Local Rating
~~Welcome in Vienna—Wohin und zurück (1986)~~	[Yad Vashem] Freddy, a Viennese Jew who emigrated to New York after Hitler's invasion, and Adler, a left-wing intellectual originally from Berlin, return to Austria in 1944 as soldiers in the U.S. Army. Freddy falls in love with the daughter of a Nazi, and Adler attempts to go over to the Communist Zone. But with the advent of the Cold War and continuing anti-Semitism, the idealism of both characters is shattered as they find themselves surrounded by cynicism, opportunism, and universal self-deception. This acclaimed work is part three of a trilogy, following *God Does Not Believe in Us Anymore* and *Santa Fe*.	Unrated
~~We'll Go to the City—Andremo in città (1966)~~	[Wikipedia] In rural Yugoslavia, Lenka lives with her blind brother, Miscia. They were orphaned of their Greek Orthodox mother and their Jewish father, Rasco, is believed to have been killed in the war. As the Second World War continues to rage and fascist activity blights Europe, Lenka and her brother become increasingly vulnerable targets to anti-semitic sentiment. She finds support in Ivan, a partisan in love with her. Meanwhile, Rasco returns alive, despite reports of his death. Rasco ultimately sacrifices himself to save the life of Ivan, who lies injured in the family's attic. The SS return to collect Lenka and Miscia, who do not reveal the whereabouts of Ivan.	Unrated
When Day Breaks—Kad svane dan (2012)	[Wikipedia, translated from Serbian] The film is the story of a retired music professor, Misha Brankov, who discovers his true origins under unusual circumstances. At the place where there used to be a Nazi camp for Jews in the Second World War, workers accidentally find a tin box with documents that was buried back in 1941 by camp inmate Isaac Weiss. The professor finds out that his real parents are the Weisses, who gave him to his friends, the Brankov family, for safekeeping before they were taken to the camp. The box also contains an unfinished musical score called "Kad svane dan," composed by Isaac Weiss.	Unrated (PG)
~~When Hitler Stole Pink Rabbit—Als Hitler das rosa Kaninchen stahl (2019)~~	[Wikipedia, translated from German] In 1933 in Berlin, Anna is only nine years old when her life changes radically. To escape the Nazis, her father Arthur Kemper, a well-known Jewish journalist, has to flee to Zurich. His family—Anna, her twelve-year-old brother Max and her mother Dorothea—follow him a short time later. Anna has to leave everything behind, including her beloved pink stuffed rabbit, and face a new life full of challenges and hardships abroad. The film ends with the exiled family moving from Paris to London in autumn 1935.	Unrated
~~Where to and Back—Part 1: God Doesn't Believe in Us—Ferry or How It Was—Wohin und zurück—Teil 1: An uns glaubt Gott nicht mehr—Ferry oder Wie es war (TV 1982)~~	[Yad Vashem] Freddy, a Viennese Jew who emigrated to New York after Hitler's invasion, and Adler, a left-wing intellectual originally from Berlin, return to Austria in 1944 as soldiers in the U.S. Army. Freddy falls in love with the daughter of a Nazi, and Adler attempts to go over to the Communist Zone. But with the advent of the Cold War and continuing anti-Semitism, the idealism of both characters is shattered as *(cont.)*	Unrated

Title	Summary	MPAA or Local Rating
	they find themselves surrounded by cynicism, opportunism, and universal self-deception. This acclaimed, work is part three of a trilogy, following *God Does Not Believe in Us Anymore* and *Santa Fe*.	
Who Will Write Our History (2018)	[Yad Vashem, edited] *Who Will Write Our History* tells the untold story of a resistance group in the Warsaw Ghetto who risked their lives so that the truth would survive even if they did not. Led by historian Emanuel Ringelblum, this clandestine organization established the Oneg Shabbat Archives and on the eve of the Warsaw Ghetto Uprising, buried hundreds of thousands of eye-witness accounts and recordings that would "let the world read and know." *Who Will Write Our History* is based entirely on the letters and diaries of the secret archive, read by Adrien Brody and Joan Allan and brought to life in on-screen performances from leading Polish actors.	Unrated
Witness Out of Hell— Zeugin aus der Hölle (1966)	[Wikipedia, translated from Germany] Public Prosecutor Dr. Hoffmann from the Central Office of the State Judicial Administrations to Solve National Socialist Crimes in Ludwigsburg is an extremely resolute representative of the federal republican state power when it comes to tracking down Nazi criminals. Ever since he read a book by the Yugoslav author Bora Petrovic that had just been translated into German and was written about twenty years ago, an older, cultivated gentleman has come under Hoffmann's sights: a doctor by the name of Dr. Berger. This man is said to have carried out criminal experiments on prisoners as a camp doctor in a concentration camp.	Unrated (R)
~~*Witnesses—Svideteli* (2018)~~	[Wikipedia] …consisting of three novellas, "Shoes," "Brutus" and "Violin," united by a common concept and dedicated to the memory of Holocaust victims.	Unrated
Woman in Gold (2015)	[Wikipedia] The film is based on the true story of Maria Altmann, an elderly Jewish refugee living in Los Angeles, who, together with her young lawyer, Randy Schoenberg, fought the government of Austria for almost a decade to reclaim Gustav Klimt's iconic painting of her aunt, *Portrait of Adele Bloch-Bauer I*, which was stolen from her relatives by the Nazis in Vienna just prior to World War II.	PG-13 for some thematic elements and brief strong language.
A Woman's Pale Blue Handwriting— Eine blaßblaue Frauenschrift (TV 1984)	[Wikipedia, translated from German] In Austria in 1936, 50-year-old Leonidas Tachezy proudly looks back on his life so far. The son of a poor high school teacher has risen to the highest circles in society by marrying the beautiful heiress Amélie Paradini. As section head in the Ministry of Education, he belongs to the country's political elite. On his birthday he received a letter in pale blue women's handwriting. It is a letter from the Jewess Vera Wormser, the love of his life.	Unrated

Title	Summary	MPAA or Local Rating
The Wooden Gun—Roveh Huliot (1979)	[Wikipedia, translated from Hebrew] …a violent struggle between two groups of youths, studying in the same class as the background of exhausted parents, some of whom are Holocaust survivors. The boys are sure that the war between them for control is as just as the war of the adults. One group is equipped with dangerous weapons, which they produce themselves. It was a wooden board polished to the shape of a rifle, and to its front was attached a thick rubber band held in the trigger. Metal bullets were used as a projectile to support the mattresses of agency beds. Such a bullet was capable of seriously injuring or dislocating an eye.	Unrated
Wunderkinder (2011)	[Wikipedia, translated from German] The narrated story is embedded as a flashback in a short framework story that takes place in the present: the celebrated violin virtuoso Hanna Reich gives her last concert. During the rehearsal, an old man appears at the door of the hall, pretending to be acquainted with Hanna. He is turned away, but leaves the old manuscript of a piece of music and a personal message for Hanna. When Hanna sees both, she is shocked. Her granddaughter Nina, who recently appeared at the rehearsal, wants to know what this is all about. Hanna begins to tell.	Unrated (PG)
X-Men (2000)	[Wikipedia] In Nazi-occupied Poland, in 1944, young Erik Lehnsherr is separated from his parents upon entrance into the Auschwitz concentration camp. While he attempts to reach them, he causes a set of metal gates to bend toward him. This is the result of a mutant ability to create magnetic fields and control metal manifesting, but he is knocked out by the guards. In the not too distant future, U.S. Senator Robert Kelly attempts to pass a "Mutant Registration Act" in Congress, which would force mutants to reveal their identities and abilities.	PG-13 for sci-fi action violence.
X-Men: First Class (2011)	[Wikipedia] In 1944, in the Auschwitz Concentration Camp, Nazi officer Klaus Schmidt witnesses young prisoner Erik Lehnsherr bend a metal gate with his mind upon being separated from his mother. In his office, Schmidt orders Erik to move a coin on his desk, and kills the boy's mother when Erik cannot. In grief and anger, Erik's magnetic power manifests, killing two guards and destroying the room. Meanwhile, at a mansion in Westchester County, New York, child telepath Charles Xavier meets young shapeshifter Raven, whose natural form is blue-skinned and scaly. Overjoyed to meet someone "different," like himself, he invites her to live with his family as his foster sister.	PG-13 for intense sequences of action and violence, some sexual content including brief partial nudity and language.
The Zookeeper's Wife (2017)	[Wikipedia] The film tells the true story of how Jan and Antonina Żabiński rescued hundreds of Polish Jews from the Germans by hiding them in their Warsaw Zoo during World War II.	PG-13 for thematic elements, disturbing images, violence, brief sexuality, nudity and smoking.

Appendix II

Non-Holocaust Films Often
Miscategorized as Holocaust Films

A minimal amount of Holocaust content is required for a motion picture to qualify as a Holocaust film. The 130 titles below have either been incorrectly listed by other sources as Holocaust films or are not full-length films or are miniseries. The reason for their disqualification as Holocaust films is listed for each film. This list is certainly incomplete.

Title	Reason DQ	Summary (or Excerpt)
Alone in Berlin (2016)	World War II	[Wikipedia] In 1940, a working-class couple in World War II-era Berlin, Otto and Anna Quangel, decide to resist Adolf Hitler and the Nazis after receiving news of the death of their only son. Their growing resistance to the regime is also strengthened by the fate of an old Jewish woman living in their building. Although the official deportation of Jews to death camps had not yet started, Jews have no recourse to any legal protection. Ruthless Nazis—and "non-ideological" common criminals—use the opportunity to loot the old woman's apartment with impunity. Despite the efforts of the Quangels and other kind neighbors to help her, the persecution ends with the old woman jumping to her death from a high window.
And Many Happy Returns (1995)	World War II	[Director's website: owenjshapiro.com] An experimental drama/documentary about old age. Filmed on site at two summer camps for senior citizens. The film incorporates reenactments, jokes told by seniors, and interview materials, all presented in a good-natured, often humorous manner constructed, in part, by the seniors themselves.
And the Violins Stopped Playing— I skrzypce przestaly grac (1988)	World War II	[Wikipedia] And the Violins Stopped Playing (Polish: I Skrzypce Przestały Grać) (1988) is a Polish/American historical drama film written produced and directed by Alexander Ramati and based upon his biographical novel about an actual group of Romani people who were forced to flee from persecution by the Nazi regime at the height of the Porajmos (Romani holocaust), during World War II.

The Army of Crime—L'armée du crime (2009)	World War II	[Wikipedia] The film deals with the development of the Manouchian Group, a 23-member resistance unit led by an Armenian exile. They were captured in 1944, tried by a German military court, and executed. The title of the film was taken from a propaganda poster known as L'Affiche Rouge (red poster), in which the Nazis sought to present these French Resistance fighters as foreign criminals. The caption read "Liberators? Liberation by the army of crime."
Army of Shadows—L'armée des ombres (1969)	World War II	[Wikipedia] *Army of Shadows* follows a small group of Resistance fighters as they move between safe houses, work with the Allied militaries, kill informers and attempt to evade the capture and execution that they know is their most likely fate. While portraying its characters as heroic, the film presents a bleak, unromantic view of the Resistance.
Assassination in Davos—Konfrontation (1974)	Not Primarily Holocaust Depiction	[Wikipedia] *Assassination in Davos* (German: *Konfrontation*) is a 1974 Swiss thriller film directed by Rolf Lyssy and starring Peter Bollag, Gert Haucke and Marianne Kehlau. It is based on the assassination of the Swiss Nazi Wilhelm Gustloff by a student in 1936.
At the Fountainhead (of German Strength) (1980)	Not Primarily Holocaust Depiction	Based on the experiences of a German Jew who lived in Berlin in the thirties and eventually settled in England in order to escape from Nazi Germany. Covers specific events in his life from 1933 until the present day. Uses dramatic devices and encompasses many elements of documentary as well as archive footage in order to illustrate, clarify or question the main points raised.
Band of Brothers (Miniseries 2001)	Miniseries	[Wikipedia] The series dramatizes the history of "Easy" Company, 2nd Battalion, 506th Parachute Infantry Regiment, of the 101st Airborne Division, from jump training in the United States through its participation in major actions in Europe, up until Japan's capitulation and the end of World War II.
Banjica (TV 1984)	TV Episode	[Wikipedia, Translated from Croatian] The series was filmed on the occasion of the fortieth anniversary of the liberation of Belgrade, in October 1944. The series follows the life of the camp inmates in the last year of the infamous Banjica camp.
Beast in Heat—Horrifying Experiments of the S.S. Last Days— La bestia in calore (1977)	Nazisploitation	[Wikipedia] A beautiful yet nefarious female SS officer/doctor Ellen Kratsch (Magall) creates a genetic, incubus-like mutant human beast (Baccaro) in a castle in occupied Europe. The beast is a rapacious, squat sex fiend which she uses to torture and molest female prisoners as part of a new medical experiment. The dwarfish beast is kept on a diet of mega-aphrodisiacs. In addition to the beast, as the Nazis battle a local insurgency, male and female captives are stripped naked and forced to endure various torture and interrogation including electric shocks, systematic rape by the beast, finger-nail pulling, castration and beatings. During the film's climax, the partisans attack the castle, and Kratsch is given to the beast in revenge.

Berlin-Jerusalem—Berlin-Yerushalaim (1989)	Israel Oriented	[Wikipedia] The film tells the story of two women in the 1930s. The first, Else Lasker-Schüler (Lisa Kreuzer), a German expressionist poet, observes the rise of Nazism in Berlin before leaving for Jerusalem. The second, the Russian Manya Shochat (Rivka Neumann), called Tania in the film, settles in a community in Israel.
Between Yesterday and Tomorrow— Zwischen gestern und morgen (1947)	World War II	[Wikipedia] In post-war Germany a group of former guests return to a luxurious Munich hotel where they are haunted by memories of their past interaction with Nelly Dreifuss, a Jewish woman who had died during the Nazi era. It was part of both the cycle of rubble films and subgenre of hotel films. As with many other German rubble films, it examines issues of collective guilt and future rebuilding.
Blind Man's Bluff—Dummy in a Circle— Golem Ba'Maagal (1993)	Israel Oriented	Coming of age story about an Israeli girl whose parents are Holocaust survivors.
The Book Thief (2013)	Not Primarily Holocaust Depiction	[Wikipedia] The film is about a young girl living with her adoptive German family during the Nazi era. Taught to read by her kind-hearted foster father, the girl begins "borrowing" books and sharing them with the Jewish refugee being sheltered by her foster parents in their home.
The Bridge—Die Brücke (1959)	World War II	[Wikipedia] The story was based on an actual event, upon the personal report of a surviving veteran who in his own youth experienced a similar situation in World War II.
Broken Glass (TV 1996)	World War II	After reading about Kristallnacht, a Jewish woman becomes paralyzed.
The Bunker (TV 1981)	World War II	[Wikipedia] The film opens in 1945, with O'Donnell (James Naughton) gaining entry to the Führerbunker by bribing a Soviet sentry with a packet of cigarettes. It is followed by the film's moving to flashbacks to the months between January and May 1945 as Hitler and those in the bunker faced their last days and nights.
The Children from Number 67— Die Kinder aus Nr. 67 (1980)	Not Primarily Holocaust Depiction	The lives of a group of children living in a tenement house in Berlin during the early years of the Third Reich.
The Cold Room (TV 1984)	World War II	[Wikipedia] Carla Martin is leaving an English parochial boarding school for the summer to live with her estranged father at an inn in East Berlin. The headmistress, a nun, gives her a 1936 guide to Berlin, telling Carla that she may find it useful, even though Berlin has surely changed as much as she has. Her best friend, Sophie, gives her a bag of marijuana.
Come and See—Idi i smotri (1985)	World War II	[Wikipedia] In 1943, two Belarusian boys dig in a sand-filled trench looking for abandoned rifles in order to join the Soviet partisan forces. Their village elder warns them not to dig up the weapons as it will arouse the suspicions of the Germans. One of the boys, Flyora, finds an SVT-40 rifle, though both of them are seen by an Fw 189 flying overhead.
Commando Mengele—Angel of Death (1987)	Nazisploitation	Nazisploitation film about Josef Mengele in hiding after World War II.

The Commissar—Komissar (1967)	Not Primarily Holocaust Depiction	[Wikipedia] During the Russian Civil War (1918–1922), a female commissar of the Red Army cavalry, Klavdia Vavilova (Nonna Mordyukova), finds herself pregnant. Until her child is born, she is forced to stay with the family of a poor Jewish blacksmith, Yefim Magazannik (Rolan Bykov), his wife, mother-in-law, and six children. At first, both the Magazannik family and "Madame Vavilova," as they call her, are not enthusiastic about living under one roof, but soon they share their rationed food, make her civilian clothes, and help her with the delivery of her newborn son. Vavilova seemingly embraces motherhood, civilian life, and new friends.
The Cremator—Spalovac mrtvol (1969)	World War II	[Wikipedia] The story is set in 1930s Prague, where the cremator Karel Kopfrkingl lives and works. Kopfrkingl slowly devolves from an odd but relatively well-meaning cremator of the dead into a murderer of his family and mass murderer who runs the ovens at the extermination camps due to the influence of the Nazi party and Tibetan Buddhism, under which he believes his murders are "liberating" the souls of the diseased into a better life.
The Custard Boys (1979)	Not Primarily Holocaust Depiction	[British Film Institute] The setting is a village where evacuated teenagers are sent during the last world war, and the film shows how boys in wartime reflect on and interpret what is going on in the adult world.
The Damned—La caduta degli dei (1969)	World War II	[Wikipedia] The plot centers on the Essenbecks, a wealthy industrialist family who have begun doing business with the Nazi Party, a thinly-veiled reference to the Essen-based Krupp family of steel industrialists. Helmut Berger, in his breakthrough role, plays Martin von Essenbeck, the family's amoral and unstable heir who is embroiled in his family's machinations.
The Dancing Dogs of Dombrova (2018)	Not Primarily Holocaust Depiction	[Official website: www.ezeqialproductions.com/production/the-dancing-dogs-of-dombrova] On a cold winter night, estranged siblings Sarah and Aaron Cotler arrive at an empty train station in Dombrova, Poland. With their only available ride being a silent Driver, they embark on a quest to fulfill their dying grandmother's wish—find, dig up, and bring home the bones of her favourite childhood dog, Peter.
David Proshker (2000)	Short	A child becomes interested in his father's wartime experiences because of a photograph.
The Dead and the Living—Die Lebenden (2012)	World War II	[Wikipedia, Translated from German] Sita is a 25-year-old Romanian-Austrian student who earns her living at a television station in Berlin. Her private life is chaotic—after a work colleague ends his affair with her, she meets the photo artist Jocquin in a club, with whom she spends the night. After the 95th birthday of her grandfather, who comes from Transylvania, Sita finds a photo of him in SS uniform. Frightened and curious, she goes looking for the background against her father's will.

Diary of an Italian— *Diario di un italiano* (1973)	Not Primarily Holocaust Depiction	[Wikipedia, Translated from Italian] The love between the typographer Valerio and the Jewish Wanda in Florence in 1938, when the racial laws were recently in force. Although the son of a socialist who died in prison when he was still a child, Valerio does not get involved in politics and would just like to live his dream of love with the girl. Wanda hides her semitic origins from him, afraid that the young man might get scared and leave her. At one point, however, the girl is forced to flee, which throws Valerio into despair. Searching for Wanda around the city, he runs into the girl's father who is taken to jail by the police. Despite learning the truth about Wanda, Valerio longs to see his beloved again, but by now it is too late to save her life.
Downfall—Der Untergang (2004)	World War II	A drama about Hitler's last days, from the point of view of his secretary, Traudl Junge.
The Empty Mirror (1996)	World War II	[Wikipedia] *The Empty Mirror* is an experimental dramatic feature-length film using historical images and speculative fiction to study the life and mind of Adolf Hitler. The film is a psychological journey that examines the nature of evil and the dark strands of human nature.
Eva.Stories (2019)	Streaming Miniseries	Eva Heyman was a Jewish girl in occupied Hungary who journaled about her life and her deportation to Auschwitz. Her story is told through a series of Instagram reenactments.
Facing Windows—La Finestra di fronte (2003)	Not Primarily Holocaust Depiction	A young Italian couple helps an old man who has amnesia. The woman has an affair with a neighbor while trying to help the old man.
The Fascist Jew—L'ebreo fascista (1980)	Not Primarily Holocaust Depiction	[Wikipedia, Translated from Italian] Oberdan, the son of a Jewish fanatic of fascism, marries Rosa in a civil ceremony, belonging to the Emilian upper middle class, but he has to leave for the war in Ethiopia, in which he wants to participate as a volunteer despite the contrary opinion of his wife. On his return, the man moves alone to Bologna where he works as a journalist; his distance from his family and the lack of interest in his seriously ill son push his wife to leave Oberdan.
Fire Birds (2015)	Not Primarily Holocaust Depiction	A detective unravels the murder of a tattooed Holocaust survivor.
The Fires Are Still Alive— *Ognie sa jeszcze zywe* (1976)	World War II	[Wikipedia, Translated from Polish] A young man dies of radiation sickness in Hiroshima. His parents were killed in the atomic bomb blast at Hiroshima. His younger brother Takao does not feel the effects of the disease. It was the same with Nobito, who graduated in medicine and traveled the world. Doctors have no doubts: Nobito has several hours to live. He remembers a time when he was on a scholarship in Paris.

Führer Ex (2002)	World War II	[Wikipedia] Friends Heiko and Tommy dream of escaping from communist Berlin that has become disgusting to them. Attempting to cross the border leads them to jail. In contrast to the sluggish and closed Heiko, the experienced and courageous Tommy is already familiar with the harsh orders of the model prisons of the GDR, where neo-Nazi groups are in charge. Caught in this hell, where only the snitches and mad beasts survive, Heiko escapes, enlisting the friendship of a local fascist leader, and Tommy decides to desperately escape.
The Gestapo's Last Orgy—L' Ultima orgia del III Reich (1977)	Nazisploitation	[Wikipedia] The film begins with a man named Conrad von Starke driving down a road, listening to a war crimes trial on the radio. He stops the car and exits at the ruins of an old death camp. There he meets Lise Cohen. It is revealed that Lise is a former prisoner of the camp and that the man, Conrad, is the former Commandant who has arranged to meet her several years after World War II, to thank her for testimony she provided which saved him from certain death and helped him integrate into the new West Germany. After touring the camp, Lise and the Commandant make love.
The Great Dictator (1940)	Too Early	In Charlie Chaplin's first "talkie," he plays a Jewish barber and Adolf Hitler. [Wikipedia] In his 1964 autobiography, Chaplin stated that he could not have made the film if he had known about the true extent of the horrors of the Nazi concentration camps at that time.
The Green Bird—Der grüne Vogel (1980)	World War II	The story of a recurring affair between a German doctor and a Polish peer.
Guernica (1978)	Short	[Wikipedia, Translated from Spanish] *Guernica* is a half-hour film about a boy, a Jew, who one afternoon in 1939 remembers at home when he saw Picasso's *Guernica* with his father. In Paris there was much talk then about Jews. He asks his father what it means to be Jewish, to which he replies: "Look, it's having your nose a little longer than your neighbor. Today that's important, tomorrow it won't be." The child feels that something sinister is passing through his family and begins to surround the noses, heads and members of the photos of his family with lipstick.
Habermann (2010)	World War II	[Wikipedia] In the story, the lives of a German mill owner and his family in the Sudetenland are changed dramatically as Europe heats up in 1938.
Hanussen—Hitler's Astrologer (1988)	World War II	Dr Emil Bettelheim rehabilitates World War I veteran Klaus Schneider who recreates himself as Eric Jan Hanussen, a performer and hypnotist during the rise of Nazism.
Hill 24 Doesn't Answer—Giv'a 24 Eina Ona (1955)	Not Primarily Holocaust Depiction	[Wikipedia] The plot revolves around the personal stories of a number of soldiers who are on their way to defend a strategic hill overlooking the road to Jerusalem.
Hitler: A Film from Germany (1977)	World War II	[Wikipedia] *Hitler: A Film from Germany* has no clear plot or chronology. Instead, each part explores one particular topic.

Hitler: The Rise of Evil (TV 2003)	World War II	[Wikipedia] It stars Robert Carlyle in the lead role and explores Adolf Hitler's rise and his early consolidation of power during the years after the First World War and focuses on how the embittered, politically fragmented and economically buffeted state of German society following the war made that ascent possible. The film also focuses on Ernst Hanfstaengl's influence on Hitler's rise to power.
Hitler's S.S.: Portrait in Evil (1985)	World War II	[Wikipedia] Helmut and Karl Hoffman are two brothers who grow up in the Great Depression of the Weimar Republic, witness the coming to power of the Nazi Party and the establishment of the Third Reich. Karl, an unemployed mechanic, is enthusiastic about the Nazis and joins the Sturmabteilung (SA), the Nazi Party militia, after hearing its commander, Ernst Röhm, speak at a Nazi Party rally. Helmut is reluctant and thinks the Nazis are simply another political party.
Holocaust (Miniseries 1978)	Miniseries	[Wikipedia] American four-part television miniseries which explores the Holocaust from the perspectives of the fictional Weiss family of German Jews and that of a rising member of the SS, who gradually becomes a war criminal. Holocaust highlights numerous events which occurred up to and during World War II, such as Kristallnacht, the creation of Jewish ghettos, and later, the use of gas chambers.
Hospital of the Transfiguration— Szpital Przemienienia (1979)	Not Primarily Holocaust Depiction	The film depicts Nazi medical experiments at a mental hospital.
Ilsa: She Wolf of the SS (1975)	Nazisploitation	[Wikipedia] 1975 Canadian exploitation film about a sadistic and sexually-voracious Nazi prison camp commandant.
The Inspector—Lisa (1962)	Not Primarily Holocaust Depiction	[Wikipedia] In 1946 Holland, Lisa Held (Dolores Hart), a survivor of Auschwitz concentration camp during World War II, has fallen prey to ex-Nazi Thorens (Marius Goring), who has promised to smuggle her into Palestine. In reality, Thorens plans to send her to South America for sex work.
An Irrepressible Woman— Je ne rêve que de vous (2019)	World War II	[Wikipedia, Translated from French] The story of the film takes place before the war and then during the Occupation, between 1940 and 1945. It traces the passionate relationship that Léon Blum continues to maintain despite the vicissitudes of war with a wealthy Jewish woman, Jeanne Reichenbach, who refuses to emigrate with her husband to the United States. His lover, whose son engages in the fight against the German enemy, will follow Mr. Blum in his various places of detention in France and to the Buchenwald concentration camp in Germany, where she gets to know Renée, the beautiful daughter of Blum and her trusted person.
The Jewish Wife (1978)	Short	A Jewish refuge and her non-Jewish husband struggle during the War.
Kanal (1957)	World War II	[Wikipedia] It was the first film made about the 1944 Warsaw Uprising, telling the story of a company of Home Army resistance fighters escaping the Nazi onslaught through the city's sewers.

Katyń (2007)	World War II	[Wikipedia] Polish film about the 1940 Katyn massacre
The Last Illusion—Der Ruf (1949)	Not Primarily Holocaust Depiction	[Wikipedia] A Jewish university professor returns from exile following the end of the Second World War. His hopes of rebuilding a new Germany are undermined by the continuing antisemitism of his colleagues and students.
Liability Crisis (1995)	World War II	The love story of a young Jewish man whose obsession with the Holocaust and Hitler threatens to destroy his romance.
The Long Days of Summer (1980)	Not Primarily Holocaust Depiction	[Wikipedia] … the story follows now 13-year-old Danny (Ronnie Scribner, taking over the role played Chris Peterson in the 1978 film) and the Cooper family in 1938, as they begin to experience the effects of growing antisemitism in their small New England town, parallelling what is happening overseas in Hitler's Germany.
Magic Men (2014)	Not Primarily Holocaust Depiction	[Jewish Film Institute] … this road trip comedy explores challenges of faith across generations. In modern-day Israel, an aging father and his middle-aged son have grown bitterly estranged over their beliefs.
Man and Beast—Mensch und Bestie (1963)	World War II	[Wikipedia, Translated from German] The film is set in 1944. Franz Köhler is imprisoned in the Mauthausen concentration camp. The camp is a labor camp where the detainees are tortured by hard labor. Franz's half-brother works here as a security guard. As an SS man, Willy is the exact opposite of his brother Franz. When the Red Army moves closer to the camp on its advance on the Eastern Front, the camp commandant decides that all inmates should be murdered. They are to be enclosed in a mine tunnel and the tunnel then blown up.
The Man with the Iron Heart—HHhH (2017)	World War II	[Wikipedia] English-language French-Belgian biographical action-thriller … based on French writer Laurent Binet's 2010 novel *HHhH*, and focuses on Operation Anthropoid, the assassination of Nazi leader Reinhard Heydrich in Prague during World War II.
Massacre at Noon—Crvena zemlja (1975)	World War II	[Wikipedia, Translated from Croatian] It shows the events in Serbia in the fall of 1941, that is, the uprising against the German occupier, which will cause brutal and bloody revenge and a great massacre in Kraljevo.
The Matchmaker—Once I Was (2010)	Israel Oriented	[Wikipedia, Translated from Hebrew] The plot of the film, with the exception of the opening and closing scenes, takes place in Haifa during one month in the summer of 1968. A special bond is forged between Arik, a 16-year-old boy, and Yaakov Braid, a scarred, Holocaust survivor matchmaker. Braid and Eric's father, Yuji, were childhood friends in Romania, and Braid offers Eric, a lover of detective literature, a job for the summer: to track down matchmakers and recruit clients. Braid's office is located in the lower city of Haifa, in the aisle of a movie theater belonging to seven dwarfs from one family of Romanian descent, who survived Auschwitz because Josef Mengele conducted experiments on them.

Mephisto (1981)	World War II	[Wikipedia] *Mephisto* follows a German stage actor who finds unexpected success and mixed blessings in the popularity of his performance in a Faustian play as the Nazis take power in pre-WWII Germany.
Metallic Blues (2004)	Not Primarily Holocaust Depiction	[Wikipedia] … two Israeli car salesmen who initially think the world is their oyster after a rare 1985 Lincoln Continental limousine falls into their laps at their used-car dealership in Tel Aviv.
Moloch—Molokh (1999)	World War II	[Wikipedia] It portrays Adolf Hitler living life in an unassuming manner during an abrupt journey to the Bavarian Alps.
The Monuments Men (2014)	World War II	[Wikipedia] It follows an Allied group from the Monuments, Fine Arts, and Archives program that is given the task of finding and saving pieces of art and other culturally important items before Nazis destroy or steal them, during World War II.
Mother Night (1996)	World War II	[Wikipedia] … an American who moves with his family to Germany after World War I and goes on to become a successful German language playwright. As World War II looms, Campbell meets a man who claims to be from the United States Department of War, and is recruited to spy for the U.S., transmitting Nazi propaganda containing hidden messages that can only be decoded by Allied intelligence. After the war, Campbell relocates to New York City, where he attempts to live in obscurity.
The Ninth Day—Der neunte Tag (2004)	World War II	[Wikipedia] The film is about a Catholic priest from Luxembourg who is imprisoned in Dachau concentration camp, but released for nine days.
None Shall Escape (1944)	Too Early	[Wikipedia] Even though the film was made during World War II, the setting is a post-war Nuremberg-style war crimes trial.
Notorious (1946)	World War II	[Wikipedia] … three people whose lives become intimately entangled during an espionage operation.
Numbers of Life—Jai vida (2005)	Short	The granddaughter of Auschwitz survivors writes the grandmother's tattoo number on her own arm.
Obsession (1968)	Not Primarily Holocaust Depiction	A man remembers a Jewish refugee whom he raped.
Occupation in 26 Pictures—Okupacija u 26 slika (1978)	World War II	[Wikipedia] It shows three friends just before World War II in Dubrovnik—Miho (a Jew), Niko (a Croat) and Toni (an Italian)—who during the war undergo different fates.
Operation Valkyrie—Stauffenberg (TV 2004)	World War II	[Wikipedia] Claus Schenk Graf von Stauffenberg becomes an enemy of Hitler's policy, because Generalmajor Henning von Tresckow informs him about German war crimes behind the Russian front. On 20 July 1944 he goes with a time bomb in his briefcase to a conference room at Hitler's headquarter Wolfsschanze near Rastenburg in East Prussia. Four people were killed immediately, but Hitler survived.
Partizan—Hell River—Partizani (1974)	Not Primarily Holocaust Depiction	[Wikipedia] Yugoslav raised in America who returns home to fight the Germans as a Partisan in World War II.

The Photographer of Mauthausen— El fotógrafo de Mauthausen (2018)	World War II	[Wikipedia] The film tells the history of the photographer Francisco Boix during his life in the Mauthausen-Gusen concentration camp complex.
Pilecki (2015)	World War II	A fictional Polish documentary about a young man who survives World War II but then dies a few years later.
Porcelain Unicorn (2010)	Short	A Hitler Youth boy who finds a Jewish girl hiding in a storage closet during the Holocaust.
Prague Duet—Lies and Whispers (1998)	World War II	A psychiatrist discovers that her grandfather was a Nazi.
QB VII (Miniseries 1974)	Miniseries	[Wikipedia] Dr. Adam Kelno, a Pole, escapes from a Nazi concentration camp. During his recovery, he romances his nurse, Angela, and eventually marries her and settles in England. After the end of World War II, the communists try to extradite Dr. Kelno for war crimes as a doctor working for the Nazis, performing medical experiments on Jewish prisoners. They fail to prove their case and Kelno is vindicated, but he takes his wife to the Middle East to escape the notoriety afterward.
Reinhard Heydrich— Manager des Terrors (TV 1977)	World War II	About the assassination of Reinhard Heydrich.
The Resistance Banker (2018)	Not Primarily Holocaust Depiction	[Wikipedia] It is based on the life of banker Walraven van Hall who financed the Dutch resistance during the war.
The Ring (TV 1996)	World War II	[Wikipedia] During World War II, a young aristocratic German woman, Ariana von Gotthardt, is separated from her family and imprisoned. After being freed she falls in love with military officer Manfredd von Tripp, of a similar aristocratic background, and they get married. When Berlin falls to the Soviets and her husband is killed, she flees to the United States carrying his unborn child, not giving up hope that she will find her family, which is tied together by her mother's ring.
Rotation (1949)	World War II	[Wikipedia] The film opens to scenes of Berlin during World War II, with the ongoing war depicted by bombs and explosions, both onscreen and in the background soundtrack. The film then jumps back twenty years in time, and, through a series of vignettes about worker Hans Behnke, traces the way in which a typical worker who opposes Nazi party ideology could be drawn into complying and cooperating with the Nazi regime.
School of Fear—Sieben Tage Frist (1969)	World War II	The murder/mystery of a student in a German boarding school.
Schtonk! (1992)	World War II	[Wikipedia] Fritz Knobel (the film's alter-ego of real-life forger Konrad Kujau) supports himself by faking and selling Nazi memorabilia. He sells a portrait of Eva Braun and one volume of Hitler's alleged diaries to factory owner Karl Lenz. Lenz presents this to his guests during a "birthday party for the Führer," among whom is sleazy journalist Hermann Willié. Willié works for the magazine *HH press,* which links to Hamburg (as a license plate abbreviation), where the Stern magazine is located and also to the common abbreviation for "Heil Hitler" among neo-Nazis.

Sealed Verdict (1948)	Not Primarily Holocaust Depiction	[Wikipedia] Maj. Robert Lawson (Ray Milland), a lawyer working in Germany as part of the American Army's tribunal for prosecuting Nazi war criminals, successfully convicts Gen. Otto Steigmann (John Hoyt) of war crimes. Defense witness Themis DeLisle (Florence Marly), whose French Resistance father's life was saved by Steigmann, insists the German officer is innocent. Despite pressure from his superiors, Lawson decides to reopen his investigation, uncovering evidence that may clear Steigmann.
The Second Front (2005)	World War II	A thriller about a Jewish scientist during World War II who has invented the ultimate weapon and is hunted down by many governments for it.
A Self Made Hero—Un héros très discret (1996)	World War II	[Wikipedia] Albert Dehousse has grown up on heroic novels; unfortunately his life isn't quite so exciting. Albert lives in a village in Northern France with his mother, who lives in memory of her husband, who she claims died a hero in the First World War. World War Two passes the pair by, as Albert is not called up as he is the only child of a war widow, denying him his chance to become a hero. Having married the daughter of a member of the resistance, he leaves his family and his marriage for Paris where heroes are truly celebrated.
Seven Beauties— Pasqualino Settebellezze (1975)	World War II	[Wikipedia] The picaresque story follows its protagonist, Pasqualino (Giannini), a dandy and small-time hood in Naples in Fascist and World War II Italy. To save the family honour, Pasqualino kills a pimp who had turned his sister into a prostitute. To dispose of the victim's body, he dismembers it and places the parts in suitcases. Caught by the police, he is convicted and sent to prison. Pasqualino succeeds in getting himself transferred to a psychiatric ward but, desperate to get out, he volunteers for the Italian Army, which is allied with the German army. With an Italian comrade, he eventually deserts the army, but they are captured and sent to a German concentration camp.
Seven Minutes (TV 1989)	World War II	The true story of Johann Georg Elser who tried in 1939 to assassinate Adolf Hitler.
Seventeen Moments of Spring— Semnadtsat mgnoveniy vesny (TV 1973)	World War II	[Wikipedia, edited] A Twelve-part Soviet television series that portrays the exploits of a Soviet spy in Nazi Germany.
The Seventh Cross (1944)	Too Early	[Wikipedia] … a prisoner who escaped from a concentration camp. The story chronicles how he interacts with ordinary Germans, and gradually sheds his cynical view of humanity.
Shadows (2000)	Short	A young man in a concentration camp becomes a Kapo.

Shining Through (1992)	World War II	[Wikipedia] In the present (1992), elderly Linda Voss (Melanie Griffith) is interviewed by a BBC documentary team about her experiences before and during World War II. She explains that, growing up in New York City as a young woman of Irish/German Jewish parentage, she always dreamed of visiting Berlin and finding her family members there. In 1940, Linda applies for a job as a secretary with a major law firm, but is rejected because she did not graduate from a prestigious women's college.
Sky Without Stars—Himmel ohne Sterne (1955)	Not Primarily Holocaust Depiction	About a family struggling between East and West Germany.
So We Said Goodbye—Nifradnu Kach (1991)	Short	An old man remembers his last goodbye to his parents in 1937.
Soldier of Orange—Soldaat van Oranje (1977)	Not Primarily Holocaust Depiction	[Wikipedia] The film is set around the German occupation of the Netherlands during World War II, and shows how individual students have different roles in the war.
Soldiers Without Arms— Soldaten zonder geweren (1985)	Not Primarily Holocaust Depiction	[Wikipedia, translated from Dutch, edited] The February Strike of 1941 was the first large-scale Dutch resistance against their German occupier, starting in Amsterdam and spreading across the Netherlands. The strike organizer is arrested and executed. His wife is devastated and struggles without him.
Soleil (1997)	Not Primarily Holocaust Depiction	[Wikipedia, Translated from French] A cardiologist, victim of a heart attack, reviews his childhood life.
Sophie Scholl—Die letzten Tage (2005)	World War II	[Wikipedia] It is about the last days in the life of Sophie Scholl, a 21-year-old member of the anti-Nazi non violent student resistance group the White Rose, part of the German Resistance movement. She was found guilty of high treason by the People's Court and executed the same day, 22 February 1943.
The Sound of Music (1965)	World War II	[Wikipedia] Maria is a free-spirited young Austrian woman studying to become a nun at Nonnberg Abbey in Salzburg in 1938. Her youthful enthusiasm and lack of discipline cause some concern. The Mother Abbess sends Maria to the villa of retired naval officer Captain Georg von Trapp to be governess to his seven children—Liesl, Friedrich, Louisa, Kurt, Brigitta, Marta, and Gretl. The Captain has been raising his children alone using strict military discipline following the death of his wife. Although the children misbehave at first, Maria responds with kindness and patience, and soon the children come to trust and respect her.
A Square of Sky—Ein Stück Himmel (Miniseries 1982)	Miniseries	[Wikipedia] German television series based on Janina David's autobiography *A Square of Sky: A Jewish Childhood in Wartime Poland.*
SS Experiment Love Camp—Lager SSadis Kastrat Kommandantur (1976)	Nazisploitation	[Wikipedia] The plot concerns consensual sexual experimenting with female prisoners of a concentration camp run by Colonel von Kleiben (Giorgio Cerioni), a Nazi officer who needs a testicle transplant after being castrated by a Russian girl.

Swing Kids (1993)	World War II	[Wikipedia] In pre-World War II Germany, two high school students, Peter Müller and Thomas Berger, attempt to be swing kids by night and Hitler Youth by day, a decision that acutely impacts their friends and families.
Take a Deep Breath (1962)	Short	Short student film about a Kapo who falls in love with a Jewish woman.
Taking Sides (2001)	World War II	[Wikipedia] The story is set during the period of denazification investigations conducted in post-war Germany after the Second World War, and it is based on the real interrogations that took place between a U.S. Army investigator and the musical conductor Wilhelm Furtwängler, who had been charged with serving the Nazi regime.
Tent City—Ir Ha'ohalim (1951)	Not Primarily Holocaust Depiction	About immigration to Israel by Holocaust survivors.
The Tin Drum—Die Blechtrommel (1979)	World War II	[Wikipedia] In 1899, Joseph Kolaizcek, the grandfather of Oskar Matzerath, the main character, is being pursued by the police through rural Kashubia (located in modern-day Poland). He hides underneath the skirts of a young woman named Anna Bronski. He has sex with her and she tries to hide her emotions, as the troops pass close by. She later gives birth to their daughter, who is Oskar's mother. Joseph evades the authorities for a year, but when they find him again, he either drowns or escapes to America and becomes a millionaire.
To Be or Not to Be (1942)	Too Early	[Wikipedia] The plot concerns a troupe of actors in Nazi-occupied Warsaw who use their abilities at disguise and acting to fool the occupying troops.
To Be or Not to Be (1983)	World War II	[Wikipedia] The film is a remake of the 1942 film of the same name.
Torte Bluma (2005)	Short	The story of the commandant of Treblinka and his cook.
Toyland—Spielzeugland (2007)	Short	[Wikipedia] The film is set in Nazi Germany in 1942. An Aryan family, the Meißners, and a Jewish family, the Silbersteins, are neighbors and friends. The respective sons in each family, Heinrich Meißner and David Silberstein, discreetly take piano lessons together. The deportation of the Silbersteins to a concentration camp is imminent, and when Heinrich asks why they may have to go soon, Frau Meißner does not tell Heinrich the truth. She instead invents a story that the Silbersteins will go to a new place called "Toyland." Heinrich says that when the Silbersteins go, he wants to go with them, so that he can still be with his friend David, which terrifies Frau Meißner.
A Trip to the Unknown— Wycieczka w nieznane (1968)	World War II	[Wikipedia, Translated from Polish] A young and talented writer treats his life lightly, which changes when he meets and loves Jolka. During a trip to Oświęcim, where a film is filmed according to a screenplay by his friend, his approach to life will also change.
Twilight Zone: The Movie (1983)	Not Primarily Holocaust Depiction	[Wikipedia] "Time Out" is an original story, loosely based on the episodes "Deaths-Head Revisited" and "A Quality of Mercy."

Verboten! (1959)	Not Primarily Holocaust Depiction	[Wikipedia] Near the end of World War II in Europe, American soldier Sergeant David Brent (James Best) loses two men and is himself wounded while hunting down and killing a sniper in a German city. He falls unconscious in front of a young German woman, Helga Schiller (Susan Cummings). When he awakes, he finds that she has tended his wound rather than killing him. She also protects him from her bitter younger brother, Franz (Harold Daye). When the SS set up an artillery observation post in Helga's building, she hides David to prove she is not a Nazi. Later, the Americans capture the city, and David is sent to a hospital.
Visas and Virtue (1997)	Short	[Wikipedia] It was inspired by the true story of Holocaust rescuer Chiune "Sempo" Sugihara, who is known as "The Japanese Schindler." Sugihara issued over 2,000 transit visas to Polish and Lithuanian Jews from his consulate in Kaunas, Lithuania, in August 1940, in defiance of his own government (Japan), thereby allowing an estimated 6,000 individuals to escape the impending Holocaust.
Wait for the Dawn—Escape by Night—Era notte a Roma (1960)	World War II	Three Allied soldiers hide in an Italian village during World War II.
Walerjan Wrobel's Homesickness (1991)	World War II	A young boy struggles to hide and survive during World War II.
War and Remembrance (TV Miniseries)	Miniseries	[Wikipedia] … covers the period of World War II from the American entry into World War II immediately after Pearl Harbor in December 1941 to the day after the bombing of the Japanese city of Hiroshima.
Warsaw '44—Miasto 44 (2014)	World War II	[Wikipedia] In the summer of 1944, the Red Army advances from the east in the direction of Warsaw. For that reason, the Polish underground Home Army launches a revolt against the German occupying force. Underground fighter Stefan joins the armed uprising. He loves nurse Ala, but also has feelings for an underground fighter named Kama. As the uprising is crushed, with heavy casualties and most of the city destroyed, both women are killed. Stefan saves himself by retreating to an island in the Vistula River, where he had taught Ala how to swim. As he arrives, he ostensibly sees her there, but in the end, sits alone.
Warsaw Story (1996)	Short	The true story of one family trying to survive while retaining their child's innocence.
The Way Out—Der Auftritt (2015)	Short	[Wikipedia] The story takes place in Eastern Europe in late 1941. Edith (Elina Amromina) is a Jewish opera diva that has been hidden away from the Nazis by Gustav (Alexander Alexeyev), who puts her in the theater's cellar during the occupation. Despite his reassurances that she will not be found, Edith knows that Gustav's help puts his own life at risk and decides that she must leave the theater to avoid this. Gustav tries to convince her that there must be a different option, but Edith is too terrified to listen and tries to escape. She's brought back by Gustav but is unfortunately seen by Nazis in the process.

Wergili (TV 1977)	World War II	[Wikipedia, translated from Polish, edited] At Auschwitz-Birkenau, many years after the War, a French widow whose estranged ex-husband died in the camp tours the Auschwitz camp/memorial. She meets an American businessman and they share an emotional experience.
The Witness (TV 1993)	Short	With no dialogue, every day a Jewish boy at a death camp watches a guard lead prisoners to the gas chamber.
The Young Lions (1958)	World War II	[Wikipedia] German ski instructor Christian Diestl is hopeful that Adolf Hitler will bring new prosperity and social mobility to Germany, so when war breaks out he joins the army, becoming a lieutenant. Dissatisfied with police duty in Paris, he requests to be transferred and is assigned to the North African campaign front. While there, he sees what the war has done to his captain and the captain's wife, and he is sickened by their behavior.

Chapter Notes

Preface and Introduction

1. Wiesel, Elie (June 11, 1989). "Art and the Holocaust: Trivializing Memory." *New York Times.* https://www.nytimes.com/1989/06/11/movies/art-and-the-holocaust-trivializing-memory.html.

2. Boerner, Heather. "Schindler's List." *Common Sense Media.* https://www.commonsensemedia.org/movie-reviews/schindlers-list.

3. Rosenthal, Donna (January 22, 1994). "Did Cultures Clash Over 'Schindler's'?: Movies: Some say Oakland high schoolers evicted from theater for laughing were ignorant of Holocaust, others say kids are too used to violence." *Los Angeles Times.* http://articles.latimes.com/1994–01–22/entertainment/ca-14266_1_oakland-high-school.

4. Carr, Steven Alan (Volume 40, Issue 3, 2016). "Son of Saul and the Crisis of Holocaust Film." *Film Criticism.* https://quod.lib.umich.edu/f/fc/13761232.0040.310/--son-of-saul-and-the-crisis-of-holocaust-film?rgn=main;view=fulltext.

5. "Minions." *Box Office Mojo.* https://www.boxofficemojo.com/release/rl2271380993/.

6. Garber, Zev. "The Slaughter of Six Million Jews: A Holocaust or a Shoah?." *The Torah.com.* https://www.thetorah.com/article/the-slaughter-of-six-million-jews-a-holocaust-or-a-shoah.

7. Berenbaum, Michael (September 1981). "The Uniqueness And Universality Of The Holocaust." *American Journal of Theology & Philosophy.* https://www.jstor.org/stable/27943596?read-now=1&seq=4#page_scan_tab_contents.

8. "Introduction to The Holocaust." *United States Holocaust Memorial Museum.* https://encyclopedia.ushmm.org/content/en/article/introduction-to-the-holocaust.

9. "Antisemitism." *Yad Vashem.* https://www.yadvashem.org/education/educational-videos/video-toolbox/hevt-antisemitism.html.

Chapter 1

1. Staff (March 13, 2013). "Motions—Human Rights, Fiji—Treatment of Detainees, Iran Hostage Crisis, 1979—Fictional Representation of Role of New Zealand Diplomats, Black Sox—2013 Men's World Softball Championships Victory". New Zealand Parliament. https://www.parliament.nz/en/pb/hansard-debates/rhr/document/50HansD_20130312_00000008/motions-human-rights-fiji-treatment-of-detainees-iran.

2. Bradley, Bill (March 8, 2016). "The Coen Brothers Reveal 'Fargo' Is Based On A True Story After All." *The HuffPost.* https://www.huffingtonpost.com/entry/coen-brothers-fargo-true-story_us_56de2c53e4b0ffe6f8ea78c4.

3. Kovalchik, Kara (April 22, 2014). "Who Originally Said 'I'm Not A Doctor, But I Play One on TV'?" *Mentalfloss.com.* http://mentalfloss.com/article/56279/who-originally-said-im-not-doctor-i-play-one-tv.

4. McLuhan, Marshall (1964). *Understanding Media: The Extensions Of* Man. Signet Books, The New American Library.

5. June 7, 2016, "Testimony of Dame Helen Mirren Before the Subcommittee on the Constitution & Subcommittee on Oversight, Agency Action, Federal Rights and Federal Courts Committee on the Judiciary." *United States Senate.* https://www.judiciary.senate.gov/imo/media/doc/06–07–16%20Mirren%20Testimony.pdf.

6. Claudet, Joseph G. (September 2016). "Deconstructing the Breakthrough Leadership Thinking of Visionary Social Change Agents–Insights and Strategies for Leading Transformative Change from Four Case Studies." *Advances in Applied Sociology.* https://www.scirp.org/journal/PaperInformation.aspx?paperID=70691.

7. "All Holocaust Movies | List of Every Holocaust Film." *Ranker.Com.* https://www.Ranker.Com/list/all-holocaust-movies-or-list-of-every-holocaust-film/all-genre-movies-lists.

8. https://www.imdb.com/search/keyword?keywords=holocaust.

9. *Love and Sacrifice* (1936). *IMDb.* https://www.imdb.com/title/tt0027911/?ref_=kw_li_tt.

10. "List of Holocaust films." *Wikipedia.com.* https://en.wikipedia.org/wiki/List_of_Holocaust_films#Narrative_films.

11. "The Visual Center—Online Film Database." *Yad Vashem.* http://db.yadvashem.org/films/search.html?language=en.

12. "The Visual Center—Online Film Database—Useful Information." *Yad Vashem.* https://www.yadvashem.org/visual-center/finding-film.html.

13. "Charlie Grant's War (1984)." *IMDb*. https://www.*IMDb*.com/title/tt0173722/.

14. Zeltserman, Lea (June 12, 2013). "Ghosts Of Soviet Holocaust Cinema Finally Escape From The Censors' Files: Long-Lost And Suppressed Classics With Complicated Depictions Of The Shoah Have Found A Revivalist Champion." *Tablet Magazine*. https://www.tabletmag.com/jewish-arts-and-culture/134722/soviet-holocaust-cinema.

15. The history of Soviet Holocaust films is an ongoing academic discipline, championed by Olga Gershenson, Professor of Judaic and Near Eastern Studies at the University of Massachusetts-Amherst. See Gershenson, Olga (2013). *The Phantom Holocaust: Soviet Cinema and Jewish Catastrophe*. New Brunswick, NJ: Rutgers University Press.

16. Porton, Richard (September 9, 2019). "The Child-Rape Holocaust Movie That's Causing Festival Walkouts." *The Daily Beast*. https://www.thedailybeast.com/the-painted-bird-the-child-rape-holocaust-movie-thats-causing-festival-walkouts.

17. Schneider, David (January 3, 2016). "The Story Of The Day The Clown Cried." *BBC Radio Solent Special*. https://www.bbc.co.uk/programmes/p03dj9kr.

18. Bierman, Noah (August 5, 2015). "Great Read: Silent-movie buffs search the screen for clues to origins of 'Mostly Lost' films." *Los Angeles Times*. https://www.latimes.com/nation/great-reads/la-na-c1-lost-films-20150805-story.html.

19. "Nazisploitation! The Nazi Image in Low-Brow Cinema and Culture." *Bloomsbury Publishing Plc*. https://www.bloomsbury.com/us/nazisploitation-9781441183590/.

20. "Ilsa, She Wolf of the SS." *Wikipedia.com*. https://en.wikipedia.org/wiki/Ilsa,_She_Wolf_of_the_SS.

21. "All Holocaust Movies | List of Every Holocaust Film." *Ranker.Com*. https://www.*Ranker*.Com/list/all-holocaust-movies-or-list-of-every-holocaust-film/all-genre-movies-lists.

22. "Helga, la louve de Stilberg (1978)." *IMDb*.com. https://www.*IMDb*.com/title/tt0215837/plotsummary?ref_=tt_ov_pl.

23 Commando Mengele (1987), *IMDb*.com. https://www.*IMDb*.com/title/tt0090642/plotsummary?ref_=ttls_pl.

24. Hilberg, Raul (1993). Perpetrators, Victims, Bystanders. The Jewish Catastrophe 1933–1945. Harper Perennial, New York.

25. *Yad Vashem*. "The Righteous Among the Nations." https://www.yadvashem.org/righteous/faq.html.

26. "Names of Righteous by Country: Names and Numbers of Righteous Among the Nations—per Country & Ethnic Origin, as of January 1, 2018." *Yad Vashem*. https://www.yadvashem.org/righteous/statistics.html.

27. Mueller, Lucy (February 23, 2005). "20 things more likely to happen to you than winning the lottery." *Review Journal*. https://www.reviewjournal.com/business/20-things-more-likely-to-happen-to-you-than-winning-the-lottery/.

28. Brown, Hannah (July 30, 2010). "The Good, The Bad And The Cute. 'La Rafle' continues the cinematic trend of feel-good Holocaust films." *The Jerusalem Post*. https://www.jpost.com/Arts-and-Culture/Entertainment/The-good-the-bad-and-the-cute.

29. Pogrebin, Abigail (November 16, 2006). "Dustin Hoffman: Finally, I can say I'm Jewish." *The Jewish Chronicle*. https://www.thejc.com/culture/interviews/dustin-hoffman-finally-i-can-say-i-m-jewish-1.1818.

30. Smith, Stephen D. (March 12, 2020). "Shoah Foundation Director: Amazon Must Cancel 'Hunters.'" *Jewish Journal*. https://jewishjournal.com/commentary/columnist/312011/shoah-foundation-director-amazon-must-cancel-hunters/.

31. For more about this topic, see Daniel Jonah Goldhagen's remarkable book from 1996, *Hitler's Willing Executioners: Ordinary Germans And The Holocaust*. New York: Knopf.

32. For more about made-for-television Holocaust programming, see Jeffrey Shandler's *While America Watches: Televising the Holocaust* (New York: Oxford University Press, 1999).

33. *Imaginary Witness: Hollywood and the Holocaust*. Directed by Daniel Anker, Anker Productions, 2004.

34. *Ibid.*

35. April 23, 1978, "In Defence of 'Holocaust,'" *New York Times*. https://www.nytimes.com/1978/04/23/archives/tv-view-in-defense-of-holocaust-defending-holocaust.html?url=http%3A%2F%2Ftimesmachine.nytimes.com%2Ftimesmachine%2F1978%2F04%2F23%2F110839935.html%3Faction%3Dclick&region=ArchiveBody&module=LedeAsset&pgtype=article&contentCollection=Archives.

36. June 22, 2013, "35 Years after the Miniseries 'Holocaust,' 35 Years after 'The Deer Hunter': How Meryl Streep Spurred the Memory Boom." *Find Your Glasses*. https://fyg.hypotheses.org/74.

37. Stefan, Hedmar (January 16, 2016). "War And Remembrance: The Last Of The Elephants." *ThrillMeSoftly.com*. http://www.thrillmesoftly.com/2016/01/war-and-remembrance-the-last-of-the-elephants/.

Chapter 2

1. Andrzej Wajda. *IMDb*. https://www.*IMDb*.com/name/nm0906667/awards?ref_=nm_awd.

2. "Movie Eras—History of Cinema and the First Film." *HistoryOfFilm.net*. http://www.historyoffilm.net/movie-eras/history-of-cinema/.

3. Carr, Steven Alan (Volume 40, Issue 3, 2016). "Son of Saul and the Crisis of Holocaust Film." *Film Criticism*. https://quod.lib.umich.edu/f/fc/13761232.0040.310/--son-of-saul-and-the-crisis-of-holocaust-film?rgn=main;view=fulltext.

4. Carr, Steven Alan (Volume 40, Issue 3, 2016). "Son of Saul and the Crisis of Holocaust Film." *Film Criticism*. https://quod.lib.umich.edu/f/fc/13761232.0040.310/--son-of-saul-and-the-crisis-of-holocaust-film?rgn=main;view=fulltext.

Chapter 3

1. *Shmoop.com.* https://www.shmoop.com/life-is-beautiful/setting.html.
2. Atkinson, Michael (August 14, 2008). "Revisiting the Early Days of the Nazi Comedy." *The Forward.* https://forward.com/culture/13978/revisiting-the-early-days-of-the-nazi-comedy-02350/.
3. Eremenko, S.B. "On Question of war Losses (in Russian)." *MOD Russian Federation.* http://encyclopedia.mil.ru/encyclopedia/history/more.htm?id=11359251@cmsArticle.
4. Wenzeler, Barbara M. (July 2003). "The Presentation of the Holocaust in German and English School History Textbooks—A Comparative Study." *Global Citizenship Education.* https://www.gcedclearinghouse.org/resources/presentation-holocaust-german-and-english-school-history-textbooks-comparative-study.
5. *Baseball Almanac.* https://www.baseball-almanac.com/recbooks/walks_by_pitchers_records.shtml.
6. *Basketball-Reference.* https://www.basketball-reference.com/leaders/fgx_career.html.
7. Verhoef, Reinier. "Uprising." *myfilmreview.nl.* http://www.myfilmreview.nl/u/uprising.htm.
8. Maltz, Judy (December 6, 2018). "25 Years On, Would Spielberg's 'Schindler's List' Still Be a Hit if It Were Made Today?." *Haaretz.* https://www.haaretz.com/us-news/.premium-25-years-on-would-spielberg-s-schindler-s-list-still-be-a-hit-if-it-were-made-tod-1.6723522.
9. Maslin, Janet (May 9, 1982). "Bringing 'Sophie's Choice' To The Screen." *New York Times.* https://www.nytimes.com/1982/05/09/movies/bringing-sophie-s-choice-to-the-screen.html.
10. Oshinsky, David (April 5, 2013). ". . . Congress Disposes." *New York Times.* https://www.nytimes.com/2013/04/07/books/review/fdr-and-the-jews-by-richard-breitman-and-allan-j-lichtman.html.
11. "Gassing Operations." *United States Holocaust Memorial Museum.* https://encyclopedia.ushmm.org/content/en/article/gassing-operations.
12. Lichtblau, Eric (March 1, 2013). "The Holocaust Just Got More Shocking." *New York Times.* https://www.nytimes.com/2013/03/03/sunday-review/the-holocaust-just-got-more-shocking.html.
13. Rubinstein, William D. (1997). The Myth of Rescue: Why the Democracies Could Not Have Saved More Jews from the Nazis. Routledge Press, London.
14. United States Government (September 30, 1945). "The United States Strategic Bombing Survey." *Anesi.com.* https://www.anesi.com/ussbs02.htm.
15. "Einsatzgruppen: An Overview." United States Holocaust Memorial Museum. https://encyclopedia.ushmm.org/content/en/article/einsatzgruppen.
16. Fredrickson, George M. (2003). "The Historical Origins and Development of Racism." *PBS.* https://www.pbs.org/race/000_About/002_04-background-02-01.htm.

17. Berenbaum, Michael. "Why wasn't Auschwitz bombed?" *Encyclopædia Britannica.* https://www.britannica.com/topic/Why-wasnt-Auschwitz-bombed-717594.
18. Margolick, David (January, 31, 1999). "Television and the Holocaust: An Odd Couple." *New York Times.* https://www.nytimes.com/1999/01/31/arts/television-radio-television-and-the-holocaust-an-odd-couple.html.
19. "The Holocaust: Definition and Preliminary Discussion." *Yad Vashem.* https://www.yadvashem.org/yv/en/holocaust/resource_center/the_holocaust.asp.
20. Religion (January 27, 2015). "The Holocaust's Forgotten Victims: The 5 Million Non-Jewish People Killed By The Nazis." *The HuffPost.* https://www.huffingtonpost.com/2015/01/27/holocaust-non-jewish-victims_n_6555604.html.
21. The Archive Collection (February 8, 2017). "3 millionth copy of The Hiding Place." *Billy Graham Evangelistic Association.* https://billygrahamlibrary.org/3-millionth-copy-of-the-hiding-place/.
22. Nicholls, William (1993). *Christian Antisemitism: A History of Hate.* Jason Aronson, Inc.

Chapter 4

1. Wiesel, Elie (April 16, 1978). "Trivializing the Holocaust: Semi-Fact and Semi-Fiction." *New York Times.* https://www.nytimes.com/1978/04/16/archives/tv-view-trivializing-the-holocaust-semifact-and-semifiction-tv-view.html.
2. *Imaginary Witness: Hollywood and the Holocaust* (2004). Directed by Daniel Anker. Anker Productions, Inc.
3. Wiesel, Elie (June 11, 1989). "Art and the Holocaust: Trivializing Memory." *New York Times.* https://www.nytimes.com/1989/06/11/movies/art-and-the-holocaust-trivializing-memory.html.
4. *Ibid.*
5. *Ibid.*
6. April 23, 1978, "In Defence of 'Holocaust,'" *New York Times.* https://www.nytimes.com/1978/04/23/archives/tv-view-in-defense-of-holocaust-defending-holocaust.html?url=http%3A%2F%2Ftimesmachine.nytimes.com%2Ftimesmachine%2F1978%2F04%2F23%2F110839935.html%3Faction%3Dclick&region=ArchiveBody&module=LedeAsset&pgtype=article&contentCollection=Archives.
7. *Imaginary Witness: Hollywood and the Holocaust* (2004). Directed by Daniel Anker. Anker Productions, Inc.
8. Broszat, Martin (1987). Nach Hitler: Der schwierige Umgang mit unsere Geschichte. Oldenbourg, Munich.
9. Staff (May 31, 2005). "Holocaust Education in Germany: An Interview." *PBS: Frontline.* https://www.pbs.org/wgbh/pages/frontline/shows/germans/germans/education.html.
10. Eizenstat, Stuart (July 25, 2011). Video Interview. *Rich Brownstein.*
11. "Press Kit." *United States Holocaust Memorial Museum.* https://www.ushmm.org/information/

press/press-kits/united-states-holocaust-memorial-museum-press-kit/.

12. Wiesel, Elie (June 11, 1989). "Art and the Holocaust: Trivializing Memory." *New York Times*. https://www.nytimes.com/1989/06/11/movies/art-and-the-holocaust-trivializing-memory.html.

13. Moss, Mark (2009). *Toward the Visualization of History: The Past as Image*. Lexington Books. Lanham, Maryland.

14. 2013. "Algemeiner 'Jewish 100' Gala: Harvey Weinstein presents Elie Wiesel with Warrior for Truth Award." https://www.youtube.com/watch?v=WQ_pHJ7ODi4.

15. Reilly, Katie (October 16, 2017). "Retailers Remove Anne Frank Halloween Costume After Backlash." *Time Magazine*. https://time.com/4985058/anne-frank-halloween-costume-holocaust/.

16. Ankel, Sophia (September 20, 2020,). "A makeup brand received a backlash for naming a liquid blush 'Dream Like Anne' after the Holocaust's Anne Frank." *Insider*. https://www.insider.com/makeup-brand-gets-backlash-naming-liquid-blush-after-anne-frank-2020-9.

17. Siegal, Nina (May 15, 2018). "Researchers Uncover Two Hidden Pages in Anne Frank's Diary." *New York Times*. https://www.nytimes.com/2018/05/15/books/anne-frank-diary-new-pages.html?smid=fb-nytimes&smtyp=cur.

18. "The Different Versions of Anne's Diary." *Anne Frank House*. http://web.annefrank.org/en/Anne-Frank/Publication-of-the-diary/The-different-versions-of-Annes-diary/.

19. "The Impact of the Diary." *Anne Frank House*. http://diary.annefrank.org/the-impact-of-the-diary/.

20. Moore, Jeff. "The Best Selling Books of All Time." *Ranker.Com*. https://www.Ranker.Com/list/best-selling-books-of-all-time/jeff419.

21. Marks, Kathy (August 27, 1998). "Anne Frank's lost pages published." *Independent*. https://www.independent.co.uk/news/anne-franks-lost-pages-published-1174313.html.

22. Frank, Anne, 1929–1945 author. (1995). *The Diary of a Young Girl: The Definitive Edition*. New York: Doubleday.

23. Marks, Kathy (August 27, 1998). "Anne Frank's lost pages published." *Independent*. https://www.independent.co.uk/news/anne-franks-lost-pages-published-1174313.html.

24. Nussbaum, Laureen. "A Diary as a Best Friend." *Anne Frank House*. http://web.annefrank.org/en/Anne-Frank/A-diary-as-a-best-friend/At-last-seriously-taken-as-a-writer/.

25. "The Diary of Anne Frank: The Critical Edition." *Amazon*. https://www.amazon.com/Diary-Anne-Frank-Critical/dp/0385240236.

26. "The Diary of a Young Girl: The Definitive Edition." *Amazon*. https://www.Amazon.com/Diary-Young-Girl-Definitive/dp/0385473788.

27. "The Diary of Anne Frank: The Revised Critical Edition." *Amazon*. https://www.Amazon.com/Diary-Anne-Frank-Revised-Critical/dp/0385508476.

28. Siegal, Nina (May 15, 2018). "Researchers Uncover Two Hidden Pages in Anne Frank's Diary." *New York Times*. https://www.nytimes.com/2018/05/15/books/anne-frank-diary-new-pages.html?smid=fb-nytimes&smtyp=cur.

29. Landfried, Jessica (June 2002). "Anne Frank, the Holocaust Victim: The Controversy about Her Diary in School Education, and the Controversy about Her Image." http://www.history.ucsb.edu/projects/holocaust/Research/AnneFrank/AnneF20pFinalHM.htm.

30. "Teaching the Lessons of the Holocaust." *Education World*. https://www.educationworld.com/a_curr/profdev066.shtml.

31. Rosenbaum, Ron (September 29, 2017). "Elie Wiesel's Secret." *Tablet Magazine*. https://www.tabletmag.com/jewish-arts-and-culture/245896/elie-wiesels-secret.

32. Nelson, Tim Blake (2003). The Grey Zone: the Directors Notes and Screenplay. Newmarket.

33. *Imaginary Witness: Hollywood and the Holocaust* (2004). Directed by Daniel Anker. Anker Productions, Inc.

34. https://www.*IMDb*.com/search/title?title=anne%20frank&view=simple.

35. "List of films about Anne Frank." *Wikipedia.com*. https://en.wikipedia.org/wiki/List_of_films_about_Anne_Frank.

36. *Ibid.*

37. "List of films about Anne Frank." *Wikipedia*. https://en.*Wikipedia*.org/wiki/List_of_films_about_Anne_Frank.

38. Rosenbaum, Ron (September 29, 2017). "Elie Wiesel's Secret." *Tablet Magazine*. https://www.tabletmag.com/jewish-arts-and-culture/245896/elie-wiesels-secret.

39. Weinraub, Bernard (April 10, 2001). "TV Film Rekindles Dispute Over Anne Frank's Legacy." *New York Times*. https://www.nytimes.com/2001/04/10/arts/tv-film-rekindles-dispute-over-anne-frank-s-legacy.html.

40. Crowther, Bosley (March 19, 1959). "An Eloquent 'Diary of Anne Frank'; Stevens Is Director of Film at Palace." *New York Times*. https://www.nytimes.com/1959/03/19/archives/an-eloquent-diary-of-anne-frank-stevens-is-director-of-film-at.html.

41. Staff (January 26, 2006). "The Diary of Anne Frank." *Time Out*. https://www.timeout.com/london/film/the-diary-of-anne-frank.

42. Webb, Andy. "The Diary of Anne Frank (1980)." *The Movie Scene*. https://www.themoviescene.co.uk/reviews/the-diary-of-anne-frank-1980/the-diary-of-anne-frank-1980.html.

43. Rosenberg, Howard (April 16, 1988). "'The Attic' Looks at Those Who Helped Anne Frank." *Los Angeles Times*. http://articles.latimes.com/1988-04-16/entertainment/ca-1241_1_anne-frank.

44. "Forget Me Not: The Anne Frank Story (1996)." *IMDb*. https://www.*IMDb*.com/title/tt1196629/.

45. "Anne Frank: The Whole Story (TV 2001)." *Anne Frank Wiki*.

46. Roxborough, Scott (January 22, 2014). "Rival

Anne Frank Film, TV Projects Spark Furor." *The Hollywood Reporter.* https://www.hollywoodreporter.com/news/rival-anne-frank-projects-spark-673004.

47. *IMDb.* "Where Is Anne Frank." https://imdb.com/title/tt3454424/plotsummary?ref_=tt_ov_pl.

48. Guść, Iwona (2019). "P. Seibert u.a. (Hrsg.): Anne Frank: Mediengeschichte." *H-Soz-Kult.* https://www.hsozkult.de/publicationreview/id/rezbuecher-23303

49. *Ricky Gervais Out Of England—The Stand-Up Special* (TV 2008). Directed by John Moffitt. Moffitt-Lee Productions.

50. Brink, Tom (April 10, 2020). Audio Interview. *Rich Brownstein.*

51. *Ibid.*

52. Lynch, John (October 30, 2017). "The 50 best movies of all time, according to critics on Metacritic." *The Independent.* https://www.independent.co.uk/arts-entertainment/films/best-movies-films-of-all-time-ever-according-critics-metacritic-a8027856.html.

53. Tennison, Patricia (July 18, 1995). "Mom Unhappy School Ran 'Schindler's List.'" *Chicago Tribune.* https://www.chicagotribune.com/news/ct-xpm-1995-07-18-9507180249-story.html.

54. Parker, Ryan (December 5, 2018). "Steven Spielberg on 'Schindler's List' Rerelease: 'This Is Maybe the Most Important Time.'" *The Hollywood Reporter.* https://www.hollywoodreporter.com/news/steven-spielberg-now-maybe-important-time-schindlers-list-1166775.

55. Hooton, Christopher (April 16, 2018). "Steven Spielberg becomes first director to have total box office gross of over $10 billion." *The Independent.* https://www.independent.co.uk/arts-entertainment/films/news/steven-spielberg-highest-box-office-gross-director-et-jaws-indiana-jones-a8306586.html.

56. "Names of Righteous by Country: Names and Numbers of Righteous Among the Nations—per Country & Ethnic Origin, as of January 1, 2018." *Yad Vashem.* https://www.yadvashem.org/righteous/statistics.html.

57. "Raoul Wallenberg." *Yad Vashem.* https://www.yadvashem.org/righteous/stories/wallenberg.html.

58. *Ibid.*

59. Lanzmann, Claude (March 3, 1994). "Schindler's List is an impossible story." *NRC Handelsblad.* http://www.phil.uu.nl/~rob/2007/hum291/lanzmannschindler.shtml.

60. Burr, Ty (February 25, 2019). "Did 'Green Book' win the Oscar just because it makes white people feel good?." *The Boston Globe.* https://bostonglobe.com/arts/movies/2019/02/25/did-green-book-win-oscar-just-because-makes-white-people-feel-good/Z56N6H1cLThbYn2jqaGVDK/story.html

61. Lebovic, Matt (August 30, 2019). "80 years ago, how a very different Schindler's 'list' helped ignite WWII." *The Times of Israel.* https://www.timesofisrael.com/80-years-ago-how-a-very-different-schindlers-list-helped-ignite-wwii/.

62. Klein, Uri (Apr 30, 2019). "With 'Schindler's List,' Steven Spielberg Turned the Holocaust Into 'Jurassic Park.'" *HaAretz.* https://www.haaretz.com/jewish/holocaust-remembrance-day/.premium-with-schindler-s-list-steven-spielberg-turned-the-holocaust-into-jurassic-park-1.7109242.

63. Weinraub, Bernard (December 12, 1993). "'Schindler's List' Steven Spielberg Faces the Holocaust." *New York Times.* https://archive.nytimes.com/www.nytimes.com/packages/html/movies/bestpictures/schindler-ar1.html.

64. Heilman, Jeremy (May 27, 2004). "Schindler's List." *MovieMartyr,com.* http://www.moviemartyr.com/1993/schindlerslist.htm.

65. Leibovitz, Liel (December 13, 2011). "Listless." *Tablet Magazine.* https://www.tabletmag.com/jewish-arts-and-culture/85945/listless.

66. Lanzmann, Claude (March 3, 1994). "Schindler's List is an impossible story." *NRC Handelsblad.* http://www.phil.uu.nl/~rob/2007/hum291/lanzmannschindler.shtml.

67. Rothstein, Edward (April 29, 2011). "Making the Holocaust the Lesson on All Evils." *New York Times.* https://www.nytimes.com/2011/04/30/arts/design/museums-make-the-holocaust-a-homily.html.

68. Klein, Uri (April 30, 2019). "With 'Schindler's List,' Steven Spielberg Turned the Holocaust Into 'Jurassic Park.'" *HaAretz.* https://www.haaretz.com/jewish/holocaust-remembrance-day/.premium-with-schindler-s-list-steven-spielberg-turned-the-holocaust-into-jurassic-park-1.7109242.

69. "Wilhelm (Wilm) Hosenfeld." *Yad Vashem.* https://www.yadvashem.org/righteous/stories/hosenfeld.html.

70. *Ibid.*

71. Calhoun, Dave (2009). "Michael Haneke discusses 'The White Ribbon.'" *Time Out.* https://www.timeout.com/london/film/michael-haneke-discusses-the-white-ribbon-1.

72. Lobet, Ernest S. (Feb. 15, 1994). "'Schindler's List' Errs on Gas Chambers." *New York Times.* https://www.nytimes.com/1994/02/25/opinion/l-schindler-s-list-errs-on-gas-chambers-299499.html.

73. Brown, Hannah (July 30, 2010). "The Good, The Bad And The Cute. 'La Rafle' continues the cinematic trend of feel-good Holocaust films." *The Jerusalem Post.* https://www.jpost.com/Arts-and-Culture/Entertainment/The-good-the-bad-and-the-cute.

74. Ebert, Roger (October 30, 1998). "Life Is Beautiful." *RogerEbert.Com.* https://www.RogerEbert.Com/reviews/life-is-beautiful-1998.

75. Schickel, Richard (November 9, 1998). "Cinema: Fascist Fable. A farce trivializes the horror of the Holocaust." *Time Magazine.* http://content.time.com/time/subscriber/article/0,33009,989504,00.html.

76. Patterson, John (October 16, 2002). "Atrocity Exhibitions." *LA Weekly.* http://www.laweekly.com/film/atrocity-exhibitions-2135459.

77. https://www.IMDb.com/title/tt0914798/goofs?ref_=tt_ql_trv_2.

78. Jones, J.R. "The Boy in the Striped Pajamas." *Chicago Reader.* https://www.chicagoreader.

com/chicago/the-boy-in-the-striped-pajamas/Film?oid=1054736.

79. Dargis, Manohla (November 6, 2008). "Horror Through a Child's Eyes." *New York Times*. https://www.nytimes.com/2008/11/07/movies/07paja.html.

80. Thompson, Anne (September 30, 2016). "Why Movies Keep Going Back to the Holocaust." *IndieWire*. https://www.indiewire.com/2016/09/holocaust-movies-oscars-denial-defying-the-nazis-the-sharps-war-ken-burns-1201732059/.

81. Mueller, Lucy (February 23, 2015). "20 things more likely to happen to you than winning the lottery." *Review Journal*. https://www.reviewjournal.com/business/20-things-more-likely-to-happen-to-you-than-winning-the-lottery/.

82. Ebert, Roger (March 21, 1986). "Angry Harvest." *RogerEbert.Com*. https://www.RogerEbert.Com/reviews/angry-harvest-1986.

83. Ebert, Roger (August 29, 2014). "The Notebook." *RogerEbert.Com*. https://www.RogerEbert.Com/reviews/the-notebook-2014.

84. "Top Lifetime Grosses." *BoxOfficeMojo.com*. https://www.boxofficemojo.com/chart/top_lifetime_gross/?area=XWW.

85. Uhlich, Keith (September 9, 2019). "Review: Jojo Rabbit Is Taika Waititi's Marvel Presents Mein Kampf." *Slant Magazine*. https://www.slantmagazine.com/film/review-jojo-rabbit-is-taika-waititis-marvel-presents-mein-kampf/.

86. *Ibid*.

87. Spiro, Amy (August 29, 2018). "Vanessa Redgrave doesn't regret 'Zionist hoodlums' speech." *Jerusalem Post*. https://www.jpost.com/diaspora/vanessa-redgrave-doesnt-regret-zionist-hoodlums-speech-566066.

88. Fretts, Bruce (Jan. 11, 2019). "Oscars Rewind: The Most Political Ceremony in Academy History." *New York Times*. https://www.nytimes.com/2019/01/11/movies/oscars-1978-politics-vanessa-redgrave.html.

89. "Paddy Chayefsky and Politics at the Oscars AWESOME!" *YouTube.com*. https://www.youtube.com/watch?v=VeV3GpUY1B4.

90. JTA Staff (August 31, 2018). "Vanessa Redgrave Backs 'Zionist Hoodlums' Comment Made During 1978 Oscar Speech." *Haaretz*. https://www.haaretz.com/jewish/vanessa-redgrave-backs-zionist-hoodlums-comment-during-oscar-speech-1.6433807.

91. Mann, William J. (December 15, 2019). "How Marlon Brando Made Hollywood Face Its Racism—at the Oscars." *The Daily Beast*. https://www.thedailybeast.com/how-marlon-brando-made-hollywood-face-its-racism-at-the-oscars.

Chapter 5

1. Ho, Jean (February 5, 2015). "'You Get the Rep Sweats': Why 'Fresh Off.'" *Flavorwire.com*. http://flavorwire.com/503143/you-get-the-rep-sweats-why-fresh-off-the-boat-matters-to-asian-americans.

2. Zelinsky, Mark (September 1, 2015). "The Philadelphia Phenomenon." *The Gay & Lesbian Review*. https://glreview.org/article/the-philadelphia-phenomenon/.

3. Rossen, Jake (April 12, 2017). "When the Mob Protested The Godfather." *Mental Floss*. http://mentalfloss.com/article/558580/hotel-breakfast-bandit-dalton-georgia-police.

4. Lenker, Maureen Lee (December 14, 2017). "Mel Brooks calls The Producers the 'miracle of my life.'" *Entertainment Weekly*. https://ew.com/movies/2017/12/14/mel-brooks-the-producers-50th-anniversary/.

5. mauludSADIQ (December 6, 2015). "Was Arsenio Ended Over Farrakhan? Lies and Misconceptions Used to Distract You From the Real Issues." *A Medium Corporation*. https://medium.com/the-brothers/was-arsenio-ended-over-farrakhan-b463b76b24f2.

6. Gabler, Neal (1988). "An Empire of Their Own." Publisher: *Crown*. ISBN 13: 9780517568088.

7. Rosenberg, Howard (February 28, 1994). "Arsenio Hall vs. Louis Farrakhan: It's a Rout: Television: The talk-show host's soft-interviewing style proves no match for the smooth Nation of Islam leader." *Los Angeles Times*. http://articles.latimes.com/1994-02-28/entertainment/ca-28353_1_arsenio-hall.

8. October 24, 1972, "Jewish Groups Score New TV Show for Intermarriage Theme." *Jewish Telegraphic Agency*. https://www.jta.org/1972/10/24/archive/jewish-groups-score-new-tv-show-for-intermarriage-theme.

9. "The Definitive Article? Representing the Holocaust in Schindler's List." *Real Cruelty in Imaginary Gardens*. https://realcruelty.wordpress.com/representing-the-holocaust/.

10. McBride, Joseph (1997). *Steven Spielberg: A Biography*. New York: Simon & Schuster.

11. Margulies, Abby (March 28, 2013). "Kubrick's Lost Holocaust Film." *Tablet Magazine*. https://www.tabletmag.com/jewish-arts-and-culture/128033/kubricks-lost-holocaust-film.

12. Gourevitch, Philip (February 1, 1994). "A Dissent on "Schindler's List&rdquo." *Commentary Magazine*. https://www.commentarymagazine.com/articles/a-dissent-on-schindlers-listrdquo/.

13. Scott, Henry E. (2004, 2010). Shocking True Story, The Rise and Fall of "Confidential," America's Most Scandalous Magazine. Pantheon.

14. Lewis, Jon (2000). Hollywood v. Hard Core: How the Struggle Over Censorship Saved the Modern Film Industry. New York University Press.

15. Faraci, Devin (November 20, 2014). "How Mike Nichols Humped The Hostess And Helped End The Production Code." *Birth Movies Death*. https://birthmoviesdeath.com/2014/11/20/how-mike-nichols-humped-the-hostess-and-helped-end-the-production-code.

16. Leff, Leonard J. (1996). "Hollywood and the Holocaust: Remembering The Pawnbroker." *American Jewish History*. 84 (4): 353–376.

17. Coggan, Devan (February 22, 2018). "Inside the complicated legacy of Hattie McDaniel, the first

black Oscar winner." *Entertainment Weekly*. https://ew.com/oscars/2018/02/22/hattie-mcdaniel-first-black-oscar-winner-legacy/.

18. Garnersept, Dwight (September 30, 2010). "A Grotesque Artifact Starts a Journey From Garage Sale to Buchenwald." *New York Times*. https://www.nytimes.com/2010/10/01/books/01book.html?mtrref=www.google.co.il&gwh=0CB802A77F7BBBA4A99D4879B093FC6D&gwt=pay.

19. "Jewish Victims of the Holocaust: The Soap Myth." *Jewish Virtual Library*. https://www.jewishvirtuallibrary.org/the-soap-myth.

20. Cesarini, David (2005). *Eichmann: His Life and Crimes*. Vintage Books, New York.

21. Gutman, Israel (1998). "Goldhagen—His Critics and His Contribution." Yad-Vashem Studies, Vol. 26. https://www.yadvashem.org/articles/academic/goldhagen%E2%80%94his-critics-and-his-contribution.html.

22. Browning, Christopher (1985). "The Revised Hilberg." *Museum of Tolerance*. http://www.museumoftolerance.com/education/archives-and-reference-library/online-resources/simon-wiesenthal-center-annual-volume-3/annual-3-chapter-13.html.

23. Friess, Steve (May 18, 2015). "When 'Holocaust' Became 'The Holocaust.'" *The New Republic*. https://newrepublic.com/article/121807/when-holocaust-became-holocaust.

24. "Tattoos And Numbers: The System Of Identifying Prisoners At Auschwitz." *The United States Holocaust Memorial Museum*. https://encyclopedia.ushmm.org/content/en/article/tattoos-and-numbers-the-system-of-identifying-prisoners-at-auschwitz.

25. Rosenberg, Jennifer (April 04, 2018). "A History of Mengele's Gruesome Experiments on Twins." *ThoughtCo*. https://www.thoughtco.com/mengeles-children-twins-of-auschwitz-1779486.

26. "Tattoos And Numbers: The System Of Identifying Prisoners At Auschwitz." *The United States Holocaust Memorial Museum*. https://encyclopedia.ushmm.org/content/en/article/tattoos-and-numbers-the-system-of-identifying-prisoners-at-auschwitz.

27. *Ibid*.

28. "Deaths-Head Revisited." *Revolvy*. https://www.revolvy.com/page/Deaths%252DHead-Revisited?cr=1.

29. *Ibid*.

30. Rohter, Larry (December 6, 2010). "Maker of 'Shoah' Stresses Its Lasting Value." *New York Times*. https://www.nytimes.com/2010/12/07/movies/07shoah.html.

31. *Imaginary Witness: Hollywood and the Holocaust* (2004). Directed by Daniel Anker. Anker Productions, Inc.

32. Broszat, Martin (1987). Nach Hitler: Der schwierige Umgang mit unsere Geschichte. Oldenbourg, Munich.

33. Handy, Bruce (August 21, 2017). "The French Film Critic Who Saw Jerry Lewis's Infamous Holocaust Movie—and Loved It." *Vanity Fair*. https://www.vanityfair.com/hollywood/2017/08/jerry-lewis-day-the-clown-cried-holocaust-movie-review.

34. Alice Agneskirchner. How the Holocaust came on TV—Wie Holocaust ins Fernsehen kam (2019).

35. "War and Love aka The Children's War." *The Visual Center—Online Film Database*. http://db.yadvashem.org/films/item.html?language=en&itemId=6853100.

36. Travers, Peter (December 8, 1989). "Triumph of the Spirit." *Rolling Stone*. https://www.rollingstone.com/movies/movie-reviews/triumph-of-the-spirit-252966/.

37. Ebert, Roger (February 2, 1990). "Triumph of the Spirit." *RogerEbert.Com*. https://www.RogerEbert.Com/reviews/triumph-of-the-spirit-1990.

38. John, Tara (February 1, 2018). "Poland Just Passed a Holocaust Bill That Is Causing Outrage. Here's What You Need to Know." *Time Magazine*. http://time.com/5128341/poland-holocaust-law/.

39. Haithman, Diane (November 10, 1988). "The Long March of 'War and Remembrance.'" *Los Angeles Times*. http://articles.latimes.com/1988–11–10/entertainment/ca-21_1_war-and-remembrance.

40. *Imaginary Witness: Hollywood and the Holocaust* (2004). Directed by Daniel Anker. Anker Productions, Inc.

Chapter 6

1. "The Grey Zone." *Box Office Mojo*. https://www.boxofficemojo.com/movies/?page=main&id=greyzone.htm.

2. "List of synagogues in Oklahoma." https://en.*Wikipedia*.org/wiki/List_of_synagogues_in_Oklahoma.

3. Gleiberman, Owen (November 01, 2002). "The Grey Zone." *Entertainment Weekly*. http://ew.com/article/2002/11/01/grey-zone-2/.

4. Patterson, John (October 16, 2002). "Atrocity Exhibitions." *LA Weekly*. http://www.laweekly.com/film/atrocity-exhibitions-2135459.

5. Nyiszli, M., Kremer, T., Seaver, R. & Bettelheim, B. (2011). *Auschwitz: A doctors eyewitness account*. New York: Arcade Publishing, which was based on *I was Dr. Mengele's autopsy at the Auschwitz Crematorium*. Oradea. 1946.

6. "The Grey Zone: Production Information." *Cinema.com*. http://cinema.com/articles/1633/grey-zone-the-production-information.phtml.

7. *Ibid*.

8. Gourevitch, Philip (February 1, 1994). "A Dissent on "Schindler's List&rdquo." *Commentary Magazine*. https://www.commentarymagazine.com/articles/a-dissent-on-schindlers-listrdquo/.

9. *The Forward's* A.J. Goldmann wrote: "Tim Blake Nelson's 'The Grey Zone' from 2001, was a failure, partially because everyone spoke English with silly foreign accents. https://forward.com/culture/321477/capturing-the-brutal-nightmare-of-auschwitz/.

10. "The Grey Zone: Production Information." *Cinema.com*. http://cinema.com/

articles/1633/grey-zone-the-production-information.phtml.

11. Hornaday, Ann (October 20, 2002). "'The Grey Zone's' Stark Divide." *The Washington Post*. https://www.washingtonpost.com/archive/lifestyle/style/2002/10/20/the-grey-zones-stark-divide/3ffb0299–5a76–4aaf-81d4–6f4b669d9fac/?utm_term=.0c36f9e5a525; McCarthy, Todd (September 27, 2001). "The Grey Zone." *Variety*. https://*Variety*.com/2001/film/reviews/the-grey-zone-3–1200469741/; Kobrynskyy, Oleksandr, and Bayer, Gerd (2015). *Holocaust Cinema in the Twenty-First Century: Memory, Images, and the Ethics of Representation*. Wallflower Press.

12. Blake, Leslie (Hoban) (October 22, 2002). "Shades of Grey." *Theater Mania*. https://www.theatermania.com/new-york-city-theater/news/shades-of-grey_2674.html.

13. Reed, Rex (October 21, 2002). "Not Swept Away By Madonna." *Observer*. http://observer.com/2002/10/not-swept-away-by-madonna/.

14. Carr, Steven Alan (Volume 40, Issue 3, 2016). "Son of Saul and the Crisis of Holocaust Film." *Film Criticism*. https://quod.lib.umich.edu/f/fc/13761232.0040.310/--son-of-saul-and-the-crisis-of-holocaust-film?rgn=main;view=fulltext.

15. Mengoni, Martina (2012). "The Gray Zone: Power And Privilege In Primo Levi." https://www.auschwitz.be/images/_inedits/mengoni.pdf.

16. Blake, Leslie (Hoban) (October 22, 2002). "Shades of Grey." *Theater Mania*. https://www.theatermania.com/new-york-city-theater/news/shades-of-grey_2674.html.

17. Kirsch, Adam (September 21, 2015). "Primo Levi's Unlikely Suicide Haunts His Lasting Work." *Tablet Magazine*. https://www.tabletmag.com/jewish-arts-and-culture/books/193650/primo-levis-complete-works.

18. Baron, Lawrence (2012). "The Grey Zone: The Cinema of Choiceless Choices." In Petropoulos J. & Roth J. (Eds.), *Gray Zones: Ambiguity and Compromise in the Holocaust and its Aftermath* (pp. 286–292). Berghahn Books.

19. Blake, Leslie (Hoban) (October 22, 2002). "Shades of Grey." *Theater Mania*. https://www.theatermania.com/new-york-city-theater/news/shades-of-grey_2674.html.

20. Walsh, David (October 29, 2002). "An essentially unprincipled approach." *World Socialist Web Site*. https://www.wsws.org/en/articles/2002/10/heav-o29.html.

21. Axmaker, Sean (October 24, 2002). "Strong acting colors the banal evil of 'The Grey Zone.'" *Seattle Post-Intelligencer*. https://www.seattlepi.com/ae/movies/article/Strong-acting-colors-the-banal-evil-of-The-Grey-1099221.php.

22. Hevesi, Dennis (May 3, 2009). "Salamo Arouch, Who Boxed for His Life in Auschwitz, Is Dead at 86." *New York Times*. https://www.nytimes.com/2009/05/04/world/europe/04arouch.html?_r=0.

23. Reed, Rex (October 21, 2002). "Not Swept Away By Madonna." *Observer*. http://observer.com/2002/10/not-swept-away-by-madonna/.

24. Ebert, Roger (October 25, 2002). "The Grey Zone." *RogerEbert.Com*. https://www.*RogerEbert.Com*/reviews/the-grey-zone-2002.

25. Ebert, Roger (September 23, 2009). "Great Movie: The Grey Zone." *RogerEbert.Com*. https://www.*RogerEbert.Com*/reviews/great-movie-the-grey-zone-2001.

26. Ebert, Roger (December 31, 2002). "The Best 10 Movies of 2002." *RogerEbert.Com*. https://www.*RogerEbert.Com*/rogers-journal/the-best-10-movies-of-2002.

27. Ebert, Roger (January 3, 2003). "The Pianist." *RogerEbert.Com*. https://www.*RogerEbert.Com*/reviews/the-pianist-2003.

28. Denerstein, Robert (November 8, 2002). "The Grey Zone." *Rocky Mountain News*. http://www.rockymountainnews.com/drmn/movies/.

29. Wilmington, Michael (October 25, 2002). "Holocaust horror enters noir 'Zone.'" *Chicago Tribune*. https://www.chicagotribune.com/news/ct-xpm-2002–10–25–0210250283-story.html.

30. "Belzec." Holocaust Music. https://holocaustmusic.ort.org/fr/places/camps/death-camps/belzec/.

31. Badt, Karin (December 6, 2017). "Cannes Grand Prix Winner "Son of Saul": A Critical Review." *HuffPost*. https://www.huffingtonpost.com/karin-badt/cannes-grand-prix-winner_b_7549248.html.

32. https://www.boxofficemojo.com/movies/?id=schindlerslist.htm.

33. http://www.boxofficemojo.com/movies/?id=greyzone.htm.

34. https://www.*IMDb*.com/title/tt0252480/.

35. https://www.*IMDb*.com/title/tt0253474/?ref_=nv_sr_1.

36. https://www.*IMDb*.com/title/tt3808342/?ref_=nv_sr_1.

37. "The Grey Zone—Trailer. *YouTube*. https://www.youtube.com/watch?v=cz0Cbi7-evg.

38. Baron, Lawrence (2012). "The Grey Zone: The Cinema of Choiceless Choices." In Petropoulos J. & Roth J. (Eds.), *Gray Zones: Ambiguity and Compromise in the Holocaust and its Aftermath* (pp. 286–292). Berghahn Books.

39. https://hk.answers.yahoo.com/question/index?qid=20070311181922AAS0d07.

Chapter 7

1. Barber, Nicholas (November 10, 2016). "Can Mel Gibson ever be rehabilitated?." *The Guardian*. https://www.theguardian.com/film/2016/nov/10/can-mel-gibson-ever-be-rehabilitated-hacksaw-ridge.

2. Orth, Maureen (March 1, 2019). "10 Undeniable Facts About the Michael Jackson Sexual-Abuse Allegations." *Vanity Fair*. https://www.vanityfair.com/hollywood/2019/03/10-undeniable-facts-about-the-michael-jackson-sexual-abuse-allegations.

3. Dillow, Gordon (1994). "O.J. Is Edited Out Of Firm's 'Morality' Video." *The Seattle Times*. http://community.seattletimes.nwsource.com/archive/?date=19940626&slug=1917342.

4. Fisher, Luchina and Murphy, Eileen (June 13, 2012). "Henry Hill: 7 Things to Know About Infamous 'Goodfella.'" *ABC News.* https://abcnews.go.com/Entertainment/things-goodfellas-henry-hill/story?id=16557945.

5. Ebert, Roger (January 3, 2003). "The Pianist." *RogerEbert.Com.* https://www.RogerEbert.Com/reviews/the-pianist-2003.

6. Ebert, Roger (September 21, 1976). "Diary of Forbidden Dreams." *RogerEbert.Com.* https://www.RogerEbert.Com/reviews/diary-of-forbidden-dreams-1976.

7. Nikolic, Isabella (August 5, 2019). "Director Roman Polanski will take part in the Venice Film Festival via Skype because he faces extradition to the U.S. over 1978 statutory rape conviction if he steps foot in Italy." *The Daily Mail.* https://www.dailymail.co.uk/news/article-7319919/Director-Roman-Polanski-Venice-Film-Festival-Skype-faces-extradition.html.

8. Ng, David (April 3, 2017). "Roman Polanski is denied latest bid to resolve 40-year-old statutory rape case." *Los Angeles Times.* https://www.latimes.com/business/hollywood/la-fi-ct-roman-polanski-decision-20170403-story.html.

9. Stern, Itay (November 25, 2018). "Judge Rejects Roman Polanski's Libel Suit Against Israeli Journalist." *Haaretz.* https://www.haaretz.com/israel-news/.premium-polanski-ordered-to-pay-court-costs-to-israeli-journalist-after-pulling-libel-suit-1.6682184; Grady, Constance (October 23, 2017,). "Roman Polanski is now facing a 5th accusation of sexual assault against a child." *Vox.com.* https://www.vox.com/culture/2017/8/17/16156902/roman-polanski-child-rape-charges-explained-samantha-geimer-robin-m.

10. JTA Staff (October 24, 2017). "Roman Polanski Accused of Sexually Molesting 10-year-old Girl in 1975." *Haaretz.* https://www.haaretz.com/world-news/roman-polanski-accused-of-sexually-molesting-10-year-old-girl-in-1975–1.5459990.

11. Knegt, Peter (September 29, 2009). "Over 100 In Film Community Sign Polanski Petition." *IndieWire.* https://www.indiewire.com/2009/09/over-100-in-film-community-sign-polanski-petition-55821/.

12. Sperling, Nicole (May 24, 2019). "'Who Would Want to Spend Their Time on That?': Hollywood Weighs New Releases from Woody Allen and Roman Polanski." *Vanity Fair.* https://www.vanityfair.com/hollywood/2019/05/woody-allen-roman-polanski-new-movies-distribution-hollywood-cannes.

13. Farrow, Ronan (October 10, 2017). "From Aggressive Overtures to Sexual Assault: Harvey Weinstein's Accusers Tell Their Stories. Multiple women share harrowing accounts of sexual assault and harassment by the film executive." *The New Yorker.* https://www.newyorker.com/news/news-desk/from-aggressive-overtures-to-sexual-assault-harvey-weinsteins-accusers-tell-their-stories.

14. Cieply, Michael (May 5, 2018). "As Cosby And Polanski Exit the Film Academy, Memories of A Past Oscar Linger." *Deadline Hollywood.* https://deadline.com/2018/05/bill-cosby-roman-polanski-academy-of-motion-picture-arts-and-sciences-exit-harassment-1202383419/.

15. Wiseman, Andreas (August 26, 2019). "Should Film Festivals and Distributors Steer Clear of Controversial Directors in the #MeToo Era?." *Deadline.com.* https://deadline.com/2019/08/metoo-venice-roman-polanski-film-festivals-distributors-steer-clear-controversial-directors-1202702746/.

16. JTA Staff (August 24, 2019). "Woody Allen's Latest Film Doesn't Have A U.S. Release." *The Jerusalem Post.* https://www.jpost.com/International/Woody-Allens-latest-film-doesnt-have-a-U.S.-release-599532.

17. Deb, Sopan (February 7, 2019). "Woody Allen Sues *Amazon* Over Canceled $68 Million Deal." *New York Times.* https://www.nytimes.com/2019/02/07/movies/woody-allen-*Amazon*-lawsuit.html.

18. Ruiz, Michelle (January 16, 2018). "Timothée Chalamet Is the Latest Star to Donate His Salary From a Woody Allen Movie to Charity." *Vogue.* https://www.vogue.com/article/timothee-chalamet-donates-woody-allen-salary-times-up-rebecca-hall.

19. Wiseman, Andreas (August 26, 2019). "Should Film Festivals and Distributors Steer Clear of Controversial Directors in the #MeToo Era?." *Deadline.com.* https://deadline.com/2019/08/metoo-venice-roman-polanski-film-festivals-distributors-steer-clear-controversial-directors-1202702746/.

20. Bradley, Laura (August 29, 2019). "Roman Polanski Compares His Rape Case to the Dreyfus Affair in New Interview." *Vanity Fair.* https://www.vanityfair.com/hollywood/2019/08/roman-polanski-an-officer-and-a-spy-rape-allegations-interview.

21. Gleiberman, Owen (August 30, 2019). " Venice Film Review: Roman Polanski's 'J'Accuse (An Officer and a Spy)': Roman Polanski's dramatization of the Dreyfus affair is a grandly mounted film that still feels lacking, maybe because Polanski thinks it's about him." *Variety.* https://*Variety*.com/2019/film/reviews/jaccuse-an-office-and-a-spy-review-roman-polanski-1203319146/.

22. Donnelly, Matt and Lang, Brent (April 19, 2019). "Academy Responds to Roman Polanski: 'Procedures Were Fair and Reasonable.'" *Variety.* https://*Variety*.com/2019/film/news/roman-polanski-sues-film-academy-1203193579/.

23. JTA Staff (August 24, 2019). "Woody Allen's Latest Film Doesn't Have A U.S. Release." *The Jerusalem Post.* https://www.jpost.com/International/Woody-Allens-latest-film-doesnt-have-a-U.S.-release-599532.

24. Balle, Catherine (November 8, 2019). "The new Polanski case: a French woman accuses him of rape." *Le Parisien.* http://www.leparisien.fr/faits-divers/une-francaise-accuse-le-realisateur-roman-polanski-de-viol-08–11–2019–8189568.php.

25. Gardner, Eriq (November 9, 2019). "Woody Allen Ends Lawsuit Against *Amazon*." *The Hollywood Reporter.* https://www.hollywoodreporter.com/thr-esq/woody-allen-ends-lawsuit-

Amazon-1253646?utm_source=Sailthru&utm_medium=email&utm_campaign=THR%20Breaking%20News_now_2019–11–09%2007:02:35_tberesford&utm_term=hollywoodreporter_breakingnews.

26. Kaye, Ben (November 11, 2019). "Woody Allen and *Amazon* resolve lawsuit out of court." *Consequence Of Sound.* https://consequenceofsound.net/2019/11/woody-allen-*Amazon*-resolve-lawsuit/

27. Haney, Tyler (October 30, 2009). "Roman Polanski and Manhattan." *GuysGuideToFeminism.* http://guysguidetofeminism.blogspot.com/2009/10/roman-polanski-and-manhattan.html.

28. Orth, Maureen (November 1992). "Mia's Story." *Vanity Fair.* https://www.vanityfair.com/magazine/1992/11/farrow199211.

29. Goodfellow, Melanie (July 9, 2018). "Roman Polanski's wife Emmanuelle Seigner turns down Academy invite." *ScreenDaily.com.* https://www.screendaily.com/news/roman-polanskis-wife-emmanuelle-seigner-turns-down-academy-invite/5130747.article.

30. Cieply, Michael (October. 10, 2009). "In Polanski Case, '70s Culture Collides With Today." *New York Times.* https://www.nytimes.com/2009/10/11/movies/11polanski.html?_r=1&sq=Woody%20Allen%20Polanski&st=cse&scp=6&pagewanted=all.

31. McGrath, Charles (June 21, 2012). "Good Art, Bad People." *New York Times.* https://www.nytimes.com/2012/06/22/opinion/global-agenda-magazine-good-art-bad-people.html.

32. Li, David K. (April 13, 2009). "Phil Spector Faces The Music." *New York Post.* https://nypost.com/2009/04/13/phil-spector-faces-the-music/.

33. Sheff, David (January 1981). "Playboy Interview with John Lennon and Yoko Ono." *BeatlesInterviews.org.* http://www.beatlesinterviews.org/dbjypb.int3.html.

Chapter 8

1. Staff (August 11, 2013). "Holocaust Facts: Where Does the Figure of 6 Million Victims Come From?" *Haaretz.* https://www.haaretz.com/jewish/holocaust-remembrance-day/.premium-6-million-where-is-the-figure-from-1.5319546.

2. Salmons, Paul (July 1, 2010). "Teaching or Preaching? The Holocaust and intercultural education in the U.K." *Journal Intercultural Education.* https://www.tandfonline.com/doi/abs/10.1080/14675980304568.

3. "Teaching the Lessons of the Holocaust." *Education World.* https://www.educationworld.com/a_curr/profdev066.shtml

4. Imber, Shulamit. "The Pedagogical Approach to Teaching the Holocaust." International School for Holocaust Studies—*Yad Vashem.* https://www.yadvashem.org/yv/en/education/international_projects/australian_educators/pdf/index1.pdf.

5. "Guidelines for Teaching about the Holocaust." *United States Holocaust Memorial Museum.* https://www.ushmm.org/educators/teaching-about-the-holocaust/general-teaching-guidelines.

6. Staff (February 1, 2018). "Education Ministry vows it will 'tell the truth' to youth trips visiting Poland." *The Times of Israel.* https://www.timesofisrael.com/education-ministry-vows-it-will-tell-the-truth-to-youth-trips-visiting-poland/.

7. Pfeffer, Anshel (January 27, 2015). "Nobody Wanted to Hear Our Stories: Israeli Auschwitz Survivors Look Back." *Haaretz.* https://www.haaretz.com/jewish/.premium-israeli-holocaust-survivors-remember-1.5365754.

8. Wikler, Meir (April 15, 2012). "*Yad Vashem* Only Honors Holocaust's Secular Victims." *Haaretz.* https://www.haaretz.com/opinion/1.5214051.

9. Lazareva, Inna (April 11, 2016). "Leading Israeli Principal Warns Annual Trip to Concentration Camps Fuel Extreme Nationalism." *Time Magazine.* http://time.com/4285002/herzilya-gymnasium-cancels-camp-trips/.

10. Rothstein, Edward (February 1, 2016). "The Problem With Jewish Museums." *Mosaic Magazine.* https://mosaicmagazine.com/essay/history-ideas/2016/02/the-problem-with-jewish-museums/.

11. Oster, Marcy (January 9, 2020). "Auschwitz-Birkenau visited by a record 2.32 million people in 2019." *The Jerusalem Post.* https://www.jpost.com/Diaspora/Auschwitz-visited-by-record-number-of-232-million-people-in-2019–613566.

12. "Lesson Plan." *United States Holocaust Memorial Museum.* https://www.ushmm.org/educators/lesson-plans/organizing-the-history.

13. "Lesson Plan for Elementary School: I Wanted to Fly Like a Butterfly." *Yad Vashem.* https://www.yadvashem.org/education/educational-materials/learning-environment/butterfly.html.

14. Wilmoth, Josh (December 27, 2016). "How the MPAA Movie Rating Scale Fails Our Children." *ReelRundown.* https://reelrundown.com/film-industry/Is-the-MPAA-Rating-Scale-Enough.

15. "The Unborn (2009." https://www.*IMDb*.com/title/tt1139668/parentalguide?ref_=tt_ql_stry_5.

16. Nolen, Jeannette L. "Bobo doll experiment." *Britannica.* https://www.britannica.com/event/Bobo-doll-experiment.

17. January 4, 1988. "Tipper Gore Widens War on Rock." *New York Times.* https://www.nytimes.com/1988/01/04/arts/tipper-gore-widens-war-on-rock.html.

18. "Holocaust Books for Middle Grade Readers." *Jewish Book Council.* https://www.jewishbookcouncil.org/subject-reading-list/holocaust-books-for-middle-grade-readers.

19. "Holocaust Books for Children." *Jewish Book Council.* https://www.jewishbookcouncil.org/subject-reading-list/holocaust-books-for-children.

20. Ebert, Roger (January 3, 2003). "The Pianist." *RogerEbert.Com.* https://www.*RogerEbert.Com*/reviews/the-pianist-2003.

21. Sink, Mindy (January 28, 1998). "Colorado Board Limits Films in Classrooms to PG and PG-13, and Discontent Arises." *New York Times.* https://www.nytimes.com/1998/01/28/

us/colorado-board-limits-films-in-classrooms-to-pg-and-pg-13-and-discontent-arises.html.

Chapter 9

1. "The Best Movies About the Holocaust." https://www.*Ranker.Com*/list/best-movies-about-the-holocaust/ranker-film.

2. Adler, Renata and Thompson, Howard (March 15, 1968). "Screen: Focusing on the Outer Edge of Existence." *New York Times*. https://www.nytimes.com/1968/03/15/archives/screen-focusing-on-the-outer-edge-of-existence.html.

3. Hynes, Eric (November 5, 2013). "Diamonds of the Night: movie review." *Time Out*. https://www.timeout.com/us/film/diamonds-of-the-night-movie-review.

4. Scherstuhl, Alan (December 19, 2017). "Claude Berri's *The Two of Us* Remains Greatest Film About a Boy Dealing With His Grampa's Noxious Views." *The Village Voice*. https://www.villagevoice.com/2017/12/19/claude-berris-the-two-of-us-remains-greatest-film-about-a-boy-dealing-with-his-grampas-noxious-views/.

5. Ebert, Roger (August 25, 2005). "The Two of Us." *RogerEbert.Com*. https://www.*RogerEbert.Com*/reviews/the-two-of-us-2005.

6. Ebert, Roger (September 3, 1968). "The Two of Us." *RogerEbert.Com*. https://www.*RogerEbert.Com*/reviews/the-two-of-us-1968.

7. Kauffman, Jeffrey (May 27, 2018). "The Two of Us Blu-ray Review; Archie Bunker's Place, WWII style." *Blu-ray.com*. https://www.blu-ray.com/movies/The-Two-of-Us-Blu-ray/194691/#Review.

8. Gutman, Israel (1998). "Goldhagen—His Critics and His Contribution." Yad-Vashem Studies, Vol. 26. https://www.yadvashem.org/articles/academic/goldhagen%E2%80%94his-critics-and-his-contribution.html.

9. Ebert, Roger (January 1, 1971). "The Garden of the Finzi-Continis." *RogerEbert.Com*. https://www.*RogerEbert.Com*/reviews/the-garden-of-the-finzi-continis-1971.

10. Wiesel, Elie (June 11, 1989). "Art and the Holocaust: Trivializing Memory." *New York Times*. https://www.nytimes.com/1989/06/11/movies/art-and-the-holocaust-trivializing-memory.html.

11. Robey, Tim (November 21, 2012). "Tim Robey recommends ... The Garden of the Finzi-Continis (1970)." *The Telegraph*. https://www.telegraph.co.uk/culture/film/recommendations/9691610/Tim-Robey-recommends...-The-Garden-of-the-Finzi-Continis-1970.html.

12. Schickel, Richard (February 18, 1972). "The Garden of the Finzi-Continis." *Life Magazine*. https://scrapsfromtheloft.com/2017/08/11/garden-finzi-continis-review-richard-schickel/.

13. Canby, Vincent (April 12, 1991). "Review/Film; Of a Saintly Jewish Doctor in Poland Who Died at Treblinka." *New York Times*. https://www.nytimes.com/1991/04/12/movies/review-film-of-a-saintly-jewish-doctor-in-poland-who-died-at-treblinka.html.

14. Kempley, Rita (August 16, 1991). "'Korczak' (NR)." *Washington Post*. http://www.washingtonpost.com/wp-srv/style/longterm/movies/videos/korczaknrkempley_a0a171.htm.

15. Berger, Daphna (October 23, 1997). "The Island on Bird Street (1997)." *Cinemagazine*. https://cinemagazine.nl/the-island-on-bird-street-1997-recensie/.

16. Beitiks, Edvins (December 18, 1998). "WWII drama leaves unanswered questions." *San Francisco Examiner*. https://www.sfgate.com/news/article/WWII-drama-leaves-unanswered-questions-3053841.php.

17. Reuters (October 26, 2000). "'Diary of Anne Frank' to be subject of new film." *CNN.com*. http://edition.cnn.com/2000/books/news/10/26/film.dish.anne.frank.reut/.

18. Weinraub, Bernard (April 10, 2001). "TV Film Rekindles Dispute Over Anne Frank's Legacy." *New York Times*. https://www.nytimes.com/2001/04/10/arts/tv-film-rekindles-dispute-over-anne-frank-s-legacy.html.

19. Christian, John St. "Anne Frank: The Whole Story." *Christian Spotlight on Entertainment*. https://christiananswers.net/spotlight/movies/2002/annefrank.html.

20. P.R. (January 6, 2006). "Movie Guide." *The Christian Science Monitor*. https://www.csmonitor.com/2006/0106/p15s01-almo.html.

21. Cockrell, Eddie (February 8, 2005). "Fateless." *Variety*. https://*Variety*.com/2005/film/awards/fateless-1200528134/.

22. Scott, A. O. (January 6, 2006). "Finding the Beauty in a Boy's Days of Horror." *New York Times*. http://movies2.nytimes.com/2006/01/06/movies/06fate.html?mtrref=undefined&gwh=C85AC8F2D32762D197F5BD4E79EC2072&gwt=pay.

23. Bradshaw, Peter (February 16, 2005). "Fateless." *The Guardian*. https://www.theguardian.com/film/2005/feb/16/festivals.berlinfilmfestival2005.

24. Hepple, Peter (October 4, 2004). "Primo review at Cottesloe London." *The Stage*. https://www.thestage.co.uk/reviews/2004/primo-review-at-cottesloe-london/?login_to=https%3A%2F%2Fwww.thestage.co.uk%2Faccounts%2Fusers%2Fsign_up.popup.

25. Smagge, Patricia. "The Last Train (2006)." *Cinemagazine*. https://cinemagazine.nl/der-letzte-zug-the-last-train-2006-recensie/.

26. Small, Marcus (November 9, 2006). "The Last Train—Martyrdom Without Return." *Marcus Little Movie Page*. http://marcus-filmseite.blogspot.com/2006/11/der-letzte-zug-martyrium-ohne.html.

27. Levin, Robert (August 14, 2009). "Show Time for Hitler and Germany." *Critic's Notebook*. https://www.criticsnotebook.com/2009/08/my-fuhrer.html.

28. Holden, Stephen (August, 13, 2009). "Some Unexpected Behavior Therapy for the Not-So-Great Dictator." *New York Times*. https://www.nytimes.com/2009/08/14/movies/14fuhrer.html.

29. Bernstein, Adam (March 21, 2008). "Fake Money, Real Horror." *Washington Post*. http://

www.washingtonpost.com/wp-dyn/content/article/2008/03/20/AR2008032003201.html.

30. Howell, Peter (February 29, 2008). "'The Counterfeiters': On the money." *The Toronto Star*. https://www.thestar.com/entertainment/movies/2008/02/29/the_counterfeiters_on_the_money.html.

31. Ebert, Roger (January 14, 2009). "Defiance." *RogerEbert.Com*. https://www.*RogerEbert.Com*/reviews/defiance-2009.

32. Scott, A.O. (December 30, 2008). "A Society in the Forest, Banding Together to Escape Persecution." *New York Times*. https://www.nytimes.com/2008/12/31/movies/31defi.html.

33. Ebert, Roger (January 14, 2009). "Defiance." *RogerEbert.Com*. https://www.*RogerEbert.Com*/reviews/defiance-2009.

34. McNamara, Mary (November 07, 2008). "Suffering in plain sight of God 'God on Trial' asks the theological question: Does the Holocaust prove he broke covenant with Israel?" *Los Angeles Times*. https://www.latimes.com/archives/la-xpm-2008-nov-07-et-godontrial7-story.html.

35. Gotlieb, Meshulam. "Whose God is on Trial in Frank Cottrell Boyce's God on Trial?." *Lookstein Center for Jewish Education*. http://listserv.biu.ac.il/cgi-bin/wa?A3=ind1312&L=LOOKJED&E=-quoted-printable&P=105218&B=------%3D_NextPart_000_04E6_01CEF412.0702DD60&T=text%2Fhtml;%20charset=us-ascii.

36. Scheepers, Martijn (January 19, 2012). "Süskind (2012)." *Cinemagazine*. https://*Cinemagazine*.nl/Süskind-2012-recensie/.

37. Boyd Hoeij, Van (February 8, 2012). "Sueskind." *Variety*. https://*Variety*.com/2012/film/markets-festivals/sueskind-1117947030/.

38. Hartwich, Dorota (January 17, 2014). "Run Boy Run: a race for life." *Cineuropa*. https://cineuropa.org/en/newsdetail/250914/.

39. Dege, Stefan (February 19, 2015). "German film tells Anne Frank's story through her father's eyes." *DW.com*. https://www.dw.com/en/german-film-tells-anne-franks-story-through-her-fathers-eyes/a-18268340.

40. Staff (2014). "Meine Tochter Anne Frank." *Fernsehserien*. https://www.fernsehserien.de/filme/meine-tochter-anne-frank.

41. Brown, Hannah (August 19, 2019). "Sam Spiegel named one of top film schools by Hollywood: *The Hollywood Reporter* named the Jerusalem Sam Spiegel Film School as one of the top 15 international film schools in the world." *The Jerusalem Post*. https://www.jpost.com/Israel-News/Sam-Spiegel-named-one-of-top-film-schools-by-Hollywood-599062.

42. https://www.the-numbers.com/movie/Saul-fia#tab=summary.

43. https://www.rottentomatoes.com/m/son_of_saul/.

44. Gill, Joshua (April 28, 2016). "Second Opinion—Son of Saul (2015)." *Flickering Myth*. https://www.flickeringmyth.com/2016/04/second-opinion-son-of-saul-2015/.

45. Chang, Justin (May 14, 2015). "Film Review: 'Son of Saul.'" *Variety*. https://*Variety*.com/2015/film/festivals/son-of-saul-review-cannes-laszlo-nemes-1201495470/.

46. Gil, Joshua (April 28, 2016). "Second Opinion—Son of Saul (2015)." *Flickering Myth*. https://www.flickeringmyth.com/2016/04/second-opinion-son-of-saul-2015/.

47. Carr, Steven Alan (Volume 40, Issue 3, 2016). "Son of Saul and the Crisis of Holocaust Film." *Film Criticism*. https://quod.lib.umich.edu/f/fc/13761232.0040.310/--son-of-saul-and-the-crisis-of-holocaust-film?rgn=main;view=fulltext.

48. Edelstein, David (January 8, 2016). "Son of Saul Is a Harrowing First-Person Look at the Holocaust—With a Big Cheat of an Ending." *New York Magazine/Vulture*. http://www.vulture.com/2016/01/movie-review-son-of-saul.html.

49. Santos, Pau Bosch (November 2016). "Soft Porn for Refined People: Son of Saul within the History of Holocaust Representation." *East European Film Bulletin*. https://eefb.org/perspectives/son-of-saul-within-the-history-of-holocaust-representation/.

50. *Ibid*.

51. Boy, Christian (March 3, 2016). "Trembling before the Nazis." *NZZ Media Group*. https://www.nzz.ch/nzzas/nzz-am-sonntag/frame-filmtipp-zittern-vor-den-nazis-ld.6109.

52. Staben, Andreas. "The Diary of Anne Frank." *Filmstarts*. http://www.filmstarts.de/kritiken/216290/kritik.html.

53. Tooze, Gary. "'The Shop on Main Street.'" *DVDBeaver*. http://www.dvdbeaver.com/film5/bluray_reviews_73/the_shop_on_main_street_bluray_.htm.

54. Schwartz, Dennis (February 9, 2007). "One of the more memorable films about the Holocaust." *Ozus' World Movie Reviews*. http://homepages.sover.net/~ozus/shoponmainstreet.htm.

55. Schwartz, Dennis (October 10, 2008). "Great acting by Delon, a great premise and great atmosphere, make this nearly a great film." *Ozus' World Movie Reviews*. http://homepages.sover.net/~ozus/mrklein.htm.

56. Smagge, Patricia (2009). "Mr. Klein (1976)." *Cinemagazine*. https://*Cinemagazine*.nl/mr-klein-1976-recensie/.

57. Canby, Vincent (February 12, 1988). "Film: 'Au Revoir les Enfants,' From Louis Malle." *New York Times*. https://www.nytimes.com/1988/02/12/movies/film-au-revoir-les-enfants-from-louis-malle.html.

58. Ebert, Roger (May 7, 2006). "Au Revoir les Enfants." *RogerEbert.Com*. https://www.*RogerEbert.Com*/reviews/great-movie-au-revoir-les-enfants-1987.

59. "Raoul Wallenberg." *Yad Vashem*. https://www.yadvashem.org/righteous/stories/wallenberg.html.

60. Harris, Haley (June 20, 2010). "365 days ... 300 movies." *MovieReviewsByHaley.com*. http://moviereviewsbyhaley.blogspot.com/2010/06/good-evening-mr-wallenberg-1990.html?m=0.

61. Holden, Stephen (April 23, 1993). "Review/Film; A Quiet Hero Lost at End Of the War." *New*

York Times. https://www.nytimes.com/1993/04/23/movies/review-film-a-quiet-hero-lost-at-end-of-the-war.html.

62. *TittelBach.* http://www.tittelbach.tv/programm/fernsehfilm/artikel-4613.html.

63. Schickel, Richard (July 15, 2001). "Three Buried Gems." *Time Magazine.* http://content.time.com/time/magazine/article/0,9171,1101010723-167596,00.html.

64. Scott, A.O. (June 8, 2001). "Film In Review; 'Divided We Fall.'" *New York Times.* https://www.nytimes.com/2001/06/08/movies/film-in-review-divided-we-fall.html.

65. Fries, Laura (May 15, 2001). "Conspiracy." *Variety.* https://Variety.com/2001/tv/reviews/conspiracy-1200468305/.

66. Tatum, Charles (August 27, 2004). "Conspiracy." *Efilmcritic.* http://www.efilmcritic.com/review.php?movie=10536&reviewer=325.

67. Backman, Melvin (August 22, 2018). "*Conspiracy*, a Withering Study of the Bureaucracy of the Holocaust." *The New Yorker.* https://www.newyorker.com/recommends/watch/conspiracy-a-withering-study-of-nazis-in-a-room.

68. Mani, Mohan (January 29, 2014). "Akte Grüninger—Schindler's List Made in Switzerland (Review)." *Newly Swissed.* https://www.newlyswissed.com/akte-grueninger-movie-review/.

69. Lori, Ellinor. "Cinema Review: File Grüninger." *Rockstar.ch.* https://www.rockstar.ch/keine_kategorie/kino-review-akte-grueninger-start-30-januar-tickets-zu-gewinnen/.

70. Boyd Ilocij, Van (September 11, 2014) "'Labyrinth of Lies' ('Im Labyrinth des Schweigens'): Toronto Review." *The Hollywood Reporter.* https://www.hollywoodreporter.com/review/labyrinth-lies-im-labyrinth-des-732388.

71. Ivanov, Oleg (September 23, 2015). "Film Review: Labyrinth of Lies." *Slant.* https://www.slantmagazine.com/film/labyrinth-of-lies/.

72. Kenigsberg, Ben (October 31, 2017). "Villagers Are Forced to Revisit Wartime Sins." *New York Times.* https://www.nytimes.com/2017/10/31/movies/1945-review-ferenc-torok.html.

73. Turan, Kenneth (November 22, 2017). "'1945' is a lean, unadorned parable about guilt and the nature and consequences of evil." *Los Angeles Times.* https://www.latimes.com/entertainment/movies/la-et-mn-1945-review-20171122-story.html.

74. Rainer, Peter (December 8, 2017). "'1945' is a compact study of wartime guilt." *Christian Science Monitor.* https://www.csmonitor.com/The-Culture/Movies/2017/1208/1945-is-a-compact-study-of-wartime-guilt.

75. Simon, Alissa (February 11, 2017). "Berlin Film Review: '1945.'" *Variety.* https://Variety.com/2017/film/reviews/1945-review-1201985200/.

76. Tooze, Gary W. "*DVDBeaver Blu-ray.*" http://www.dvdbeaver.com/film4/blu-ray_reviews_61/the_pawnbroker_blu-ray.htm.

77. Levy, Emanuel (June 30, 2007). "Pawnbroker, The (1965): Lumet's Post-Holocaust Tale, Starring Rod Steiger in Oscar-Nominated Role." *EmanuelLevy.com.* http://emanuellevy.com/review/pawnbroker-the-1965-5/.

78. *Imaginary Witness: Hollywood and the Holocaust.* Directed by Daniel Anker, Anker Productions, 2004.

79. Blakeslee, David (May 19, 2014). "David Reviews Sidney Lumet's The Pawnbroker." *Criterioncast.* https://criterioncast.com/reviews/blu-ray-reviews/sidney-lumet-pawnbroker.

80. Patterson, Troy (May 20, 2003). "Why 'Harold and Maude' is one of the top 10 cult movies." *Entertainment Weekly.* https://ew.com/article/2003/05/20/why-harold-and-maude-one-top-10-cult-movies/; Rolling Stone Staff (May 7, 2014). "Readers' Poll: The 25 Best Cult Movies of All Time." *Rolling Stone Magazine.* https://www.rollingstone.com/movies/movie-lists/readers-poll-the-25-best-cult-movies-of-all-time-18696/25-army-of-darkness-44502/; Ricard, Gabriel (May 14, 2019). "15 Best Cult Movies of All-time." *CulturedVultures.com.* https://culturedvultures.com/best-cult-movies-all-time/.

81. Ebert, Roger (January 1, 1972). "Harold And Maude." *RogerEbert.Com.* https://www.RogerEbert.Com/reviews/harold-and-maude-1972.

82. Jewniverse (January 27, 2011). "The Number on Maude's Arm." *Jewish Telegraphic Agency.* https://www.jta.org/jewniverse/2011/the-number-on-maudes-arm.

83. *Moviepooper.* http://www.moviepooper.com/1/109.html.

84. Tobias, Scott (April 17, 2008). "Harold And Maude." *AV Club.* https://film.avclub.com/harold-and-maude-1798213751.

85. Doneson, Judith E. (2002). *The Holocaust in American Film.* Syracuse, NY: Syracuse University Press. Page 120.

86. Megahey, Noel (2003). "The Man In The Glass Booth Review." *The Digital Fix.* https://www.thedigitalfix.com/film/content/12231/page/.

87. "The Man In The Glass Booth." AFI Catalog Of Feature Films: The First 100 Years 1893–1993. https://catalog.afi.com/Catalog/MovieDetails/55476.

88. DVD release (2003). "The Man In The Glass Booth." Transcription of interview with Arthur Hiller. *Kino Video.*

89. Hinson, Hal (December 25, 1992). "'The Quarrel' (NR)." *Washington Post.* http://www.washingtonpost.com/wp-srv/style/longterm/movies/videos/thequarrelnrhinson_a0a7d7.htm?noredirect=on.

90. Holden, Stephen (November 4, 1992). "Review/Film; On Faith, Reason and the Holocaust." *New York Times.* https://www.nytimes.com/1992/11/04/movies/review-film-on-faith-reason-and-the-holocaust.html?mtrref=www.google.com&gwh=A9829D641DA771ADAA665DFECB3BB47D&gwt=pay.

91. Brown, Hannah (August 5, 2019). "Gila Almagor Renews Wedding Vows To Mark Her 80th Birthday." *The Jerusalem Post.* https://www.jpost.com/J-Spot/Gila-Almagor-renews-wedding-vows-to-mark-her-80th-birthday-597623.

92. Holden, Stephen (May 10, 1996). "Under the Domim Tree." *New York Times*. https://archive.nytimes.com/www.nytimes.com/library/filmarchive/under_the_donim_tree.html.

93. Weems, Mary (June 19, 1996). "Under the Domim Tree." *Movie Magazine International*. http://www.shoestring.org/mmi_revs/domitree.html.

94. Stratton, David (February 24, 2003). "The Birch-tree Meadow." *Variety*. https://Variety.com/2003/film/reviews/the-birch-tree-meadow-1200543161/.

95. McCarthy, Todd (September 4, 2005). "Everything Is Illuminated." *Variety*. https://Variety.com/2005/film/markets-festivals/everything-is-illuminated-1200523512/.

96. Ebert, Roger (September 22, 2005). "Everything Is Illuminated." *RogerEbert.Com*. https://www.RogerEbert.Com/reviews/everything-is-illuminated-2005.

97. Miller, Prairie (March 23, 2008). "Dear Mr. Waldman DVD Review." *NewsBlaze*. https://newsblaze.com/entertainment/movie-reviews/dear-mr-waldman-dvd-review_4304/.

98. Propes, Richard. ""Dear Mr. Waldman" Review." *The Independent Critic*. https://theindependentcritic.com/dear_mr__waldman.

99. http://cannes.juryoecumenique.org/IMG/pdf/2012/dossier_jury_oecumenique2012_web_en.pdf.

100. Bailey, Jason (January 21, 2012). "This Must Be the Place." *DVDtalk*. http://www.dvdtalk.com/reviews/54272/this-must-be-the-place/.

101. Whitfield, Ed (October 26t2011). "LFF Film Review: This Must Be The Place." *Theoohtray*. http://theoohtray.com/2011/10/lff-film-review-this-must-be-the-place/.

102. Weissberg, Jay (May 20, 2011). "This Must Be the Place." *Variety*. https://Variety.com/2011/film/markets-festivals/this-must-be-the-place-1117945279/.

103. Lattimer, James (July 19, 2015). "FILM Review: Phoenix." *Slant*. https://www.slantmagazine.com/film/phoenix-2/.

104. Mintzer, Jordan (September 6, 2014). ""Phoenix": Toronto Review." *Hollywood Reporter*. https://www.hollywoodreporter.com/review/phoenix-toronto-review-730679.

105. Kohn, Eric (September 6, 2014). "Review: Nina Hoss is Extraordinary in Holocaust Drama 'Phoenix.'" *IndieWire*. https://www.indiewire.com/2014/09/review-nina-hoss-is-extraordinary-in-holocaust-drama-phoenix-22504/.

106. Walters, Guy (2009). *Hunting Evil: The Nazi War Criminals Who Escaped and the Hunt to Bring Them to Justice*. Broadway Books.

107. Lipstadt, Deborah E.(Winter 2011). "Simon Wiesenthal and the Ethics of History." *Jewish Review of Books*. https://jewishreviewofbooks.com/articles/217/simon-wiesenthal-and-the-ethics-of-history/.

108. Brown, Helen (May 21, 2011). "Forty years since 'The Day of the Jackal' transformed the thriller, its author Frederick Forsyth talks to Helen Brown about the curious allure of his cold-blooded assassin." *The Telegraph*. https://www.telegraph.co.uk/culture/books/authorinterviews/8524091/Frederick-Forsyth-I-had-expected-women-to-hate-him.-But-no....html.

109. Martin, Peter (July 9 2011). "70s Rewind: Ronald Neame's The Odessa File." *Screen Anarchy*. https://screenanarchy.com/2011/07/70s-rewind-ronald-neames-the-odessa-file.html.

110. Druker, Don (1974). "The Odessa File." *Chicago Reader*. https://www.chicagoreader.com/chicago/the-odessa-file/Film?oid=1075022.

111. Jameson, Richard T. (October 7, 2015). "Review: The Odessa File." *Parallax View*. http://parallax-view.org/2015/10/07/review-the-odessa-file/.

112. Sayre, Nora (October 19, 1974). "The Screen: Neame's 'Odessa File': Thriller About Secret SS Society Opens." *New York Times*. https://www.nytimes.com/1974/10/19/archives/the-screen-neames-odessa-filethriller-about-secret-ss-society-opens.html.

113. Reuben, Michael (April 30, 2012). "The Odessa File Blu-ray Review: Imperious Bastards." *Blu-Ray*. https://www.blu-ray.com/movies/The-Odessa-File-Blu-ray/37801/#Review.

114. Mcguigan, Colin (August 23, 2018). "The Odessa File." *Riding the High Country*. https://livius1.wordpress.com/2018/08/23/the-odessa-file/.

115. Ebert, Roger (October 18, 1976). "Marathon Man." *RogerEbert.Com*. https://www.RogerEbert.Com/reviews/marathon-man-1976.

116. *Variety* Staff (December 31, 1975). "Marathon Man." *Variety*. https://Variety.com/1975/film/reviews/marathon-man-2-1200423690/.

117. Simkins, Michael (March 31, 2016). "Method acting can go too far—just ask Dustin Hoffman." *The Guardian*. https://www.theguardian.com/commentisfree/2016/mar/31/method-acting-dustin-hoffman-meryl-streep.

118. Williams, Robin (2002). "Robin Williams 'Germans not funny because they killed the funny people'" *You Tube*. https://www.youtube.com/watch?v=VF2P_LuEF80.

119. Tucker, Ken (November 4, 1994). "TV Show Review: 'Genghis Cohn.'" *Entertainment Weekly*. https://ew.com/article/1994/11/04/tv-show-review-genghis-cohn/.

120. Elley, Derek (November 21, 1993). "Genghis Cohn." *Variety*. https://Variety.com/1993/film/reviews/genghis-cohn-1200434279/.

121. Pinto, Goel (July 15, 2002). "Seven Dwarfs and One Snow White. A look back at Israeli films of the last year." *Haaretz*. https://www.haaretz.com/israel-news/culture/1.5211349.

122. Jaworowski, Ken (Aug. 18, 2016). "The People vs. Fritz Bauer." *New York Times*. https://www.nytimes.com/2016/08/19/movies/the-peoplevs.fritz-bauer-review.html.

123. Turan, Kenneth (August 18, 2016). "'The People vs. Fritz Bauer' brings a largely unknown Nazi hunter to light." *Los Angeles Times*. https://www.latimes.com/entertainment/movies/la-et-mn-people-fritz-bauer-review-20160815-snap-story.html.

124. Kozak, Oktay Ege (August 18, 2016). "'The

People vs Fritz Bauer' Is A Terrific, Emotionally Engaging Post-Holocaust Thriller." *ThePlayList.* https://theplaylist.net/peoplevs.fritz-bauer-terrific-emotionally-engaging-post-holocaust-thriller-review-20160818/.

125. Filmsite.org Staff. "Cabaret (1972)." *Filmsite. org.* https://www.filmsite.org/caba.html.

126. Glatzer, Robert. "Can We Ever Forget 'The Sound Of Music?' Let's Try." *Movies 101.* http://www.movies101.com/thesoundofmusic.html.

127. Lanzendorfer, Joy (December 18, 2016). "14 Facts About The Sound of Music." *MentalFloss.com.* https://www.mentalfloss.com/article/61706/14-things-you-might-not-know-about-sound-music.

128. Wood, Jennifer M (August 1, 2018). "15 Actors Who Hated Their Own Films." *Mental Floss.* http://mentalfloss.com/article/29791/actors-who-hated-their-own-films.

129. Glatzer, Robert. "Can We Ever Forget 'The Sound Of Music?' Let's Try." *Movies 101.* http://www.movies101.com/THESOUNDOFMUSIC.HTML.

130. Ebert, Roger (June 26, 2008). "Triumph Of The Will." *RogerEbert.Com.* https://www.*RogerEbert.Com*/reviews/great-movie-triumph-of-the-will-1935.

131. Ruud, Jay (April 27, 2015). "Movie Review: The Sound of Music by Robert Wise." *JayRuud.com.* http://jayruud.com/movie-review-the-sound-of-music-by-robert-wise/.

132. Ebert, Roger (January 1, 1972). "Cabaret." *RogerEbert.Com.* https://www.*RogerEbert.Com*/reviews/cabaret-1972.

133. Ebert, Roger (January 1, 1982). "Sophie's Choice." *RogerEbert.Com.* https://www.*RogerEbert. Com*/reviews/sophies-choice-1982.

134. Maslin, Janet (December, 10, 1982). "Styron's 'Sophie's Choice.'" *New York Times.* https://www.nytimes.com/1982/12/10/movies/styron-s-sophie-s-choice.html.

135. Holden, Stephen (August, 20, 1993). "Review/Film; A Holocaust Witness, Eloquent in His Silence." *New York Times.* https://www.nytimes.com/1993/08/20/movies/review-film-a-holocaust-witness-eloquent-in-his-silence.html.

136. Lasalle, Mick (August 20, 2009). "Inglourious Basterds." *Houston Chronicle.* https://www.chron.com/entertainment/movies/article/Inglourious-Basterds-1749688.php.

137. Ebert, Roger (August 19, 2009). "Inglourious Basterds." *Roger Ebert.com.* https://www.*RogerEbert. Com*/reviews/inglourious-basterds-2009.

138. Tugend, Tom (September 23, 2009). "Real-Life Avengers." *The Jewish Journal.* https://jewishjournal.com/culture/arts/72784/.

Epilogue

1. Zapruder, Alexandra (2002). "The Diary of Eva Heyman: Child of the Holocaust (Yomanah Shel Evah Hayman)." *Encyclopedia.com.* https://www.encyclopedia.com/arts/encyclopedias-almanacs-transcripts-and-maps/diary-eva-heyman-child-holocaust-yomanah-shel-evah-hayman.

2. Holmes, Oliver (May 8, 2019). "Instagram Holocaust diary Eva.Stories sparks debate in Israel: Jewish girl's life is documented on social media to teach young people about WWII genocide." https://www.theguardian.com/world/2019/may/08/instagram-holocaust-diary-evastories-sparks-debate-in-israel.

3. Miller, Jordana (May 1, 2019). "What if you could Instagram the Holocaust? A question sparks controversy." https://abcnews.go.com/International/instagrammed-version-holocaust-stirs-controversy/story?id=62725980.

4. Kershner, Isabel (April 30, 2019). "A Holocaust Story for the Social Media Generation." *New York Times.* https://www.nytimes.com/2019/04/30/world/middleeast/eva-heyman-instagram-holocaust.html.

5. Staff. (February 04, 2019). "Super Bowl Liii Draws 98.2 Million TV Viewers, 32.3 Million Social Media Interactions." *Nielsen Media Research.* https://web.archive.org/web/20190205000209/https://www.nielsen.com/us/en/insights/news/2019/super-bowl-liii-draws-98-2-million-tv-viewers-32-3-million-social-media-interactions.html.

6. Gourevitch, Philip (February 1, 1994). "A Dissent on "Schindler's List&rdquo." *Commentary Magazine.* https://www.commentarymagazine.com/articles/a-dissent-on-schindlers-listrdquo/.

7. Kahn, Gabe (May 22, 2019). "Eva.stories: Believe the hype, ignore the indignation." *The New Jersey Jewish News.* https://njjewishnews.timesofisrael.com/eva-stories-believe-the-hype-ignore-the-indignation/.

Bibliography

Arendt, Hannah. *Eichmann in Jerusalem: A Report on the Banality of Evil.* New York, NY: Viking Press, 1969.

Avisar, Ilan. *Screening the Holocaust: Cinema's Images of the Unimaginable.* Bloomington: Indiana University Press, 1988.

Baron, Lawrence. *Projecting the Holocaust into the Present: The Changing Focus of Contemporary Holocaust Cinema.* Lanham, MD: Rowman & Littlefield, 2005.

_____. *The Modern Jewish Experience in World Cinema.* Waltham, Massachusetts: Brandeis University Press, 2011.

Bartov, Omer. *The "Jew" in Cinema: From The Golem to Don't Touch My Holocaust.* Bloomington: Indiana University Press, 2005.

Bathrick, David, Brad Prager, and Michael D. Richardson, eds. *Visualizing the Holocaust: Documents, Aesthetics, Memory.* Rochester, NY: Camden House, 2008.

Bauer, Yehuda, and Nili Keren. *A History of the Holocaust.* New York, NY: Franklin Watts, 2002.

Berenbaum, Michael, and Arnold Kramer. *The World Must Know: The History of the Holocaust as Told in the United States Holocaust Memorial Museum.* Baltimore: Johns Hopkins University Press, 2005.

Black, Edwin. *IBM and the Holocaust: The Strategic Alliance Between Nazi Germany and America's Most Powerful Corporation.* New York, NY: Three Rivers Press, 2002.

Breitman, Richard, and Allan J. Lichtman. *FDR and the Jews.* Cambridge, Massachusetts: Belknap Press of Harvard University Press, 2014.

Browning, Christopher R. *Ordinary Men: Reserve Police Battalion 101 and the Final Solution in Poland.* New York, NY: Harper Perennial, 1998.

Colombat, André Pierre. *The Holocaust in French Film.* Metuchen, NJ: Scarecrow, 1993.

Dawidowicz, Lucy S. *The War Against the Jews 1933–45: Tenth Anniversary Edition.* London: Penguin Books, 1987.

Doherty, Thomas Patrick. *Hollywood and Hitler, 1933-1939 (Film and Culture Series).* New York, NY: Columbia University Press, 2013.

Doneson, Judith E. *The Holocaust in American Film.* Syracuse University Press, 2002.

Elsaesser, Thomas. *German Cinema: Terror and Trauma: Cultural Memory Since 1945.* New York, NY: Routledge, 2014.

Frodon, Jean-Michel, Anna Harrison, and Tom Mes. *Cinema and the Shoah: an Art Confronts the Tragedy of the Twentieth Century.* Albany: State University of New York Press, 2010.

Gabler, Neal. *An Empire of Their Own: How the Jews Invented Hollywood.* New York, NY: Anchor Books, 1989.

Gershenson, Olga. "Holocaust Cinema." New York, NY: Oxford Bibliographies, 2017.

_____. *Phantom Holocaust: Soviet Cinema and Jewish Catastrophe.* New Brunswick, NJ: Rutgers University Press, 2013.

Gertz, Nurith. *Holocaust Survivors, Aliens, and Others in Israeli Cinema and Literature.* Tel Aviv: Am Oved, 2004.

Gilbert, Martin. *The Holocaust: A History of the Jews of Europe During the Second World War.* New York, NY: Henry Holt and Company, 1985.

Goldhagen, Daniel Jonah. *Hitler's Willing Executioners: Ordinary Germans and the Holocaust.* New York, NY: Knopf, 1996.

Gonshak, Henry. *Hollywood and the Holocaust.* Lanham, Maryland: Rowman & Littlefield, 2015.

Gutman, Israel, and Michael Berenbaum. *Anatomy of the Auschwitz Death Camp.* Bloomington: Indiana University Press, 1994.

Haggith, Toby, and Joanna Newman. *Holocaust and the Moving Image: Representations in Film and Television Since 1933.* London: Wallflower, 2005.

Haltof, Marek. *Polish Film and the Holocaust: Politics and Memory.* New York, NY: Berghahn Books, 2011.

Hilberg, Raul. *Perpetrators, Victims, Bystanders The Jewish Catastrophe 1933-1945.* London: Secker and Warburg, 1995

_____. *The Destruction of the European Jews.* New York, NY: Harper & Row, 1961.

Hirsch, Marianne, and Irene Kacandes. *Teaching the Representation of the Holocaust.* New York, NY: Modern Language Association of America, 2004.

Hornstein, Shelley, and Florence Jacobowitz. *Image and Remembrance: Representation and the Holocaust.* Bloomington: Indiana University Press, 2003.

Imre, Anikó. *A Companion to Eastern European*

Cinemas. Chichester, West Sussex: Wiley-Blackwell, 2012.

Insdorf, Annette. *Indelible Shadows: Film and the Holocaust*, 3rd Edition. New York, NY: Vintage Books, 2003.

Kerner, Aaron. *Film and the Holocaust: New Perspectives on Dramas, Documentaries, and Experimental Films*. London: Continuum, 2011.

Kobrynskyy, Oleksandr, and Gerd Bayer. *Holocaust Cinema in the Twenty-First Century: Memory, Images, and the Ethics of Representation*. New York, NY: Wallflower Press, 2015.

Kwiet, Konrad, and Jürgen Matthäus. *Contemporary Responses to the Holocaust*. Westport, Connecticut: Praeger, 2004.

Langer, Lawrence L. *Using and Abusing the Holocaust*. Bloomington: Indiana University Press, 2006.

Levi, Neil, and Michael Rothberg. *The Holocaust: Theoretical Readings*. New Brunswick, NJ: Rutgers University Press, 2003.

Loshitzky, Yosefa. *Spielberg's Holocaust: Critical perspectives on "Schindler's List."* Bloomington: Indiana University Press, 1997.

Marcus, Millicent Joy. *Italian Film in the Shadow of Auschwitz*. Toronto: University of Toronto Press, 2007.

Mintz, Alan. *Popular Culture and the Shaping of Holocaust Memory in America*. Seattle: University of Washington Press, 2015.

Picart, Caroline Joan. *The Holocaust Film Sourcebook, Two Volume Set*. Westport, Connecticut: Praeger, 2004.

Picart, Caroline Joan, and David Frank. A. *Frames of Evil: The Holocaust as Horror in American Film*. Carbondale: Southern Illinois University Press, 2006.

Poliakov, Léon. *Harvest of Hate: The Nazi Program for the Destruction of the Jews of Europe*. New York: Syracuse University Press, 1954.

Reimer, Robert Charles, Carol J. Reimer, and Jon Woronoff. *Historical Dictionary of Holocaust Cinema*. Lanham, Maryland: Scarecrow Press, 2012.

Seibert, Peter, Jana Piper, and Alfonso Meoli, eds. *Anne Frank: Mediengeschichten*. Berlin: Metropol-Verlag, 2014.

Shandler, Jeffrey. *While America Watches: Televising the Holocaust*. New York, NY: Oxford University Press, 1999.

Taylor, Jennifer. *National Responses to the Holocaust: National Identity and Public Memory*. University of Delaware Press, 2014.

Wiesel, Elie (April 16, 1978). "The Trivializing the Holocaust: Semi-Fact and Semi-Fiction." *New York Times*, page 75.

Wiesel, Elie (June 11, 1989). "Art and the Holocaust: Trivializing Memory." *New York Times,* section 2, page 1.

Zapruder, Alexandra. *Salvaged Pages: Young Writers' Diaries of the Holocaust*. New Haven, Connecticut: Yale University Press, 2002.

Index

447